CHAPTER 43

Belldandy's Tempestuous Heart

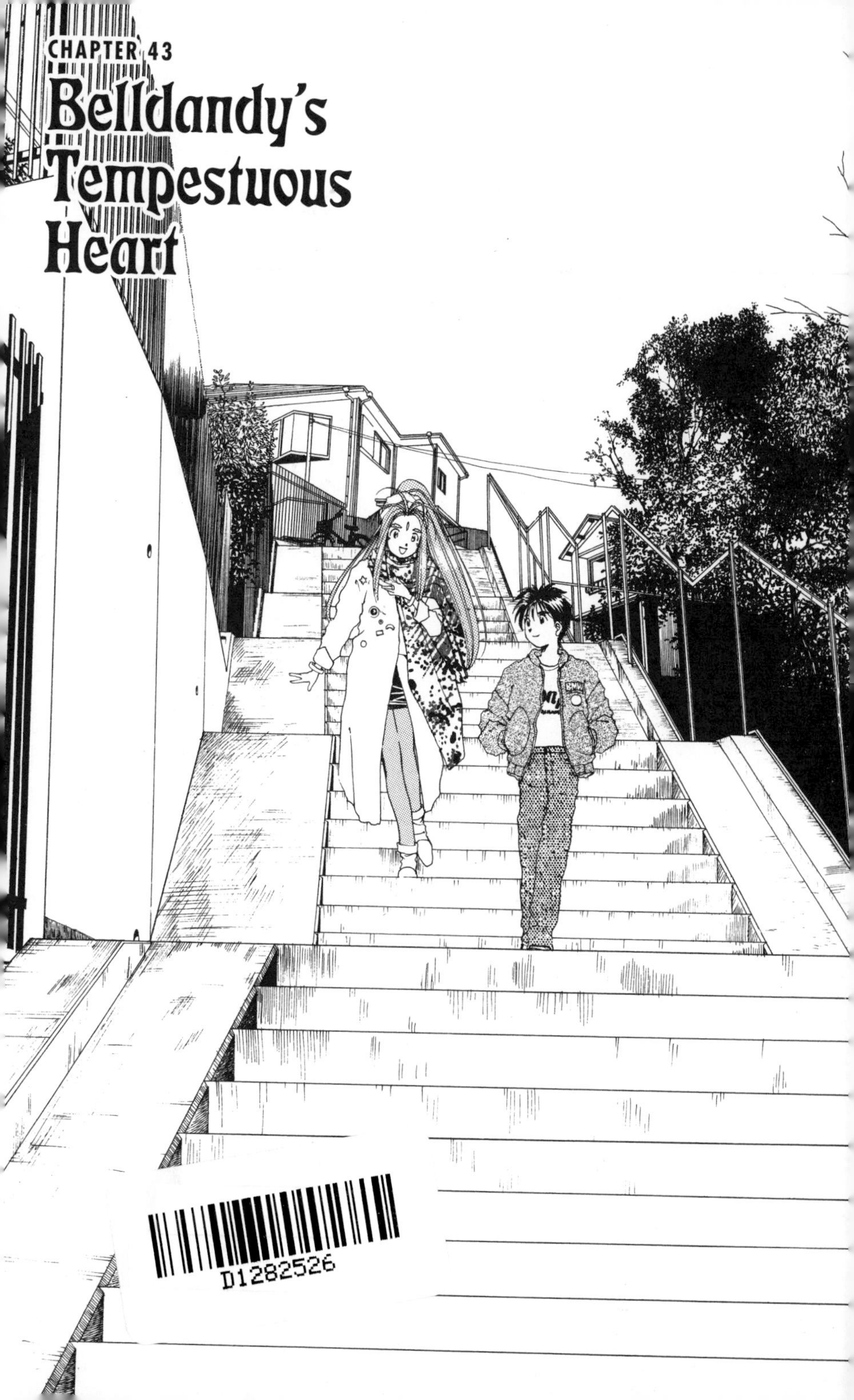

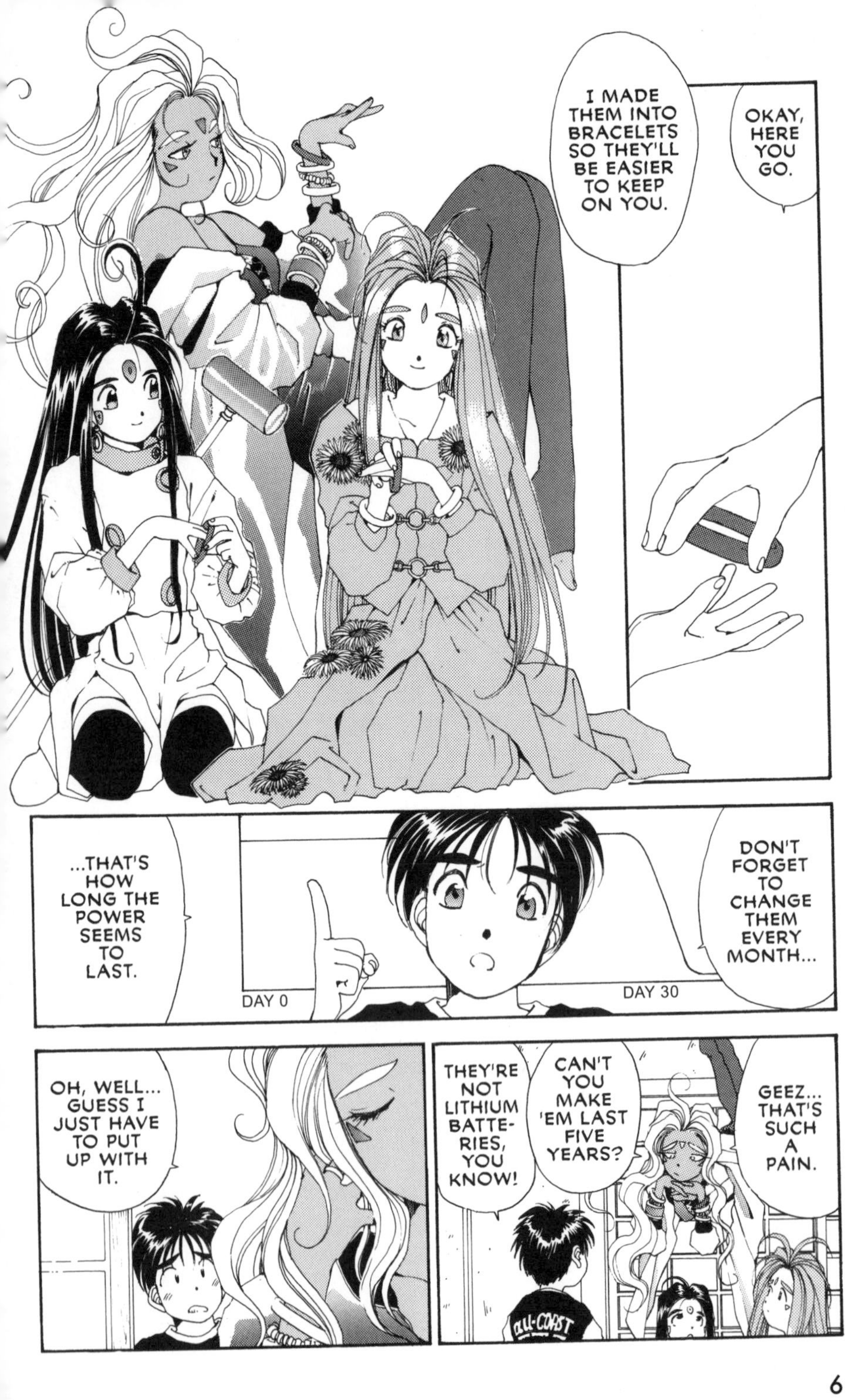
OKAY, HERE YOU GO.
I MADE THEM INTO BRACELETS SO THEY'LL BE EASIER TO KEEP ON YOU.
DON'T FORGET TO CHANGE THEM EVERY MONTH...
DAY 30
DAY 0
...THAT'S HOW LONG THE POWER SEEMS TO LAST.
GEEZ... THAT'S SUCH A PAIN.
CAN'T YOU MAKE 'EM LAST FIVE YEARS?
THEY'RE NOT LITHIUM BATTE-RIES, YOU KNOW!
OH, WELL... GUESS I JUST HAVE TO PUT UP WITH IT.

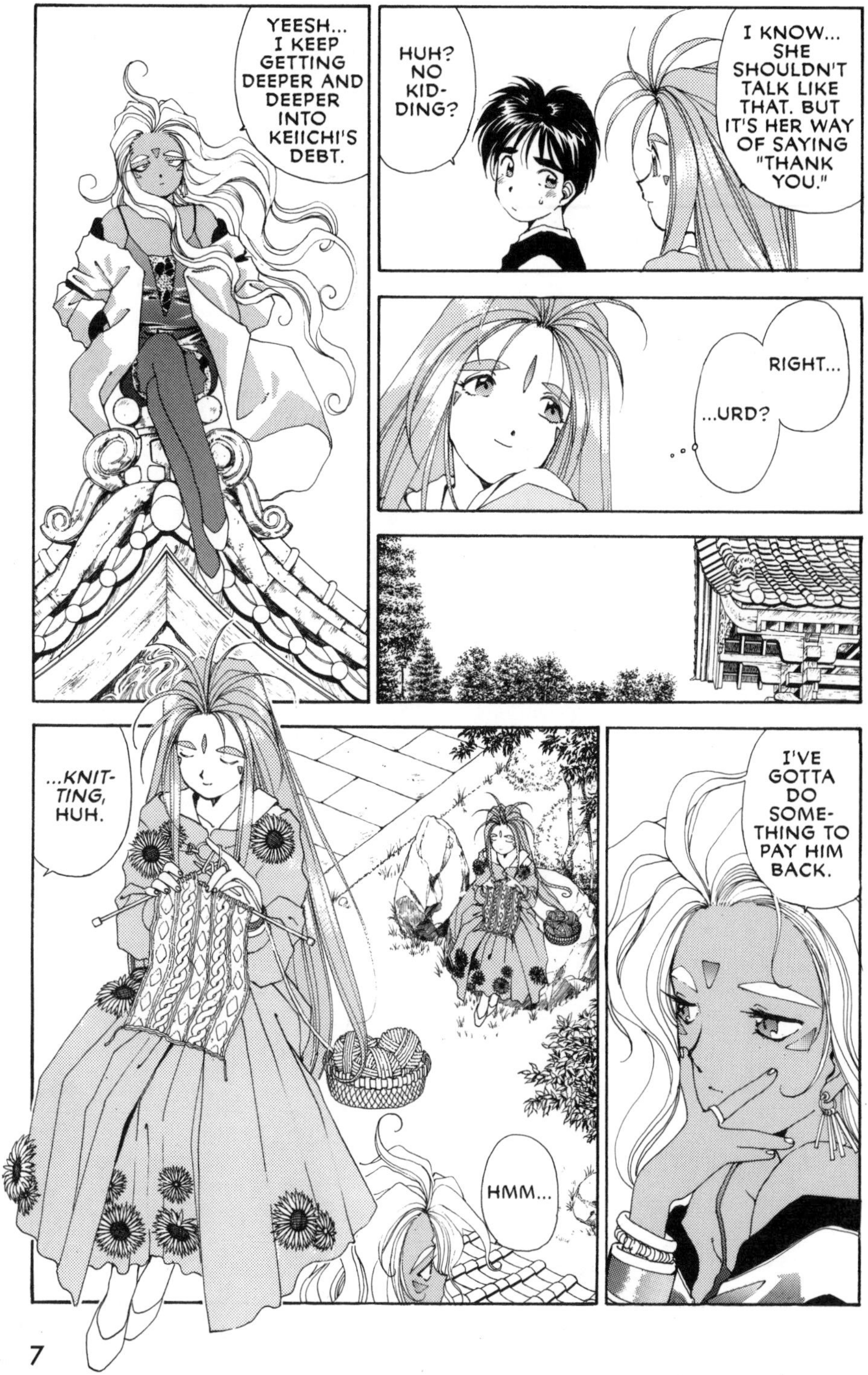
I KNOW... SHE SHOULDN'T TALK LIKE THAT. BUT IT'S HER WAY OF SAYING "THANK YOU."
HUH? NO KID-DING?
RIGHT...
...URD?
YEESH... I KEEP GETTING DEEPER AND DEEPER INTO KEIICHI'S DEBT.
I'VE GOTTA DO SOME-THING TO PAY HIM BACK.
...*KNIT-TING,* HUH.
HMM...

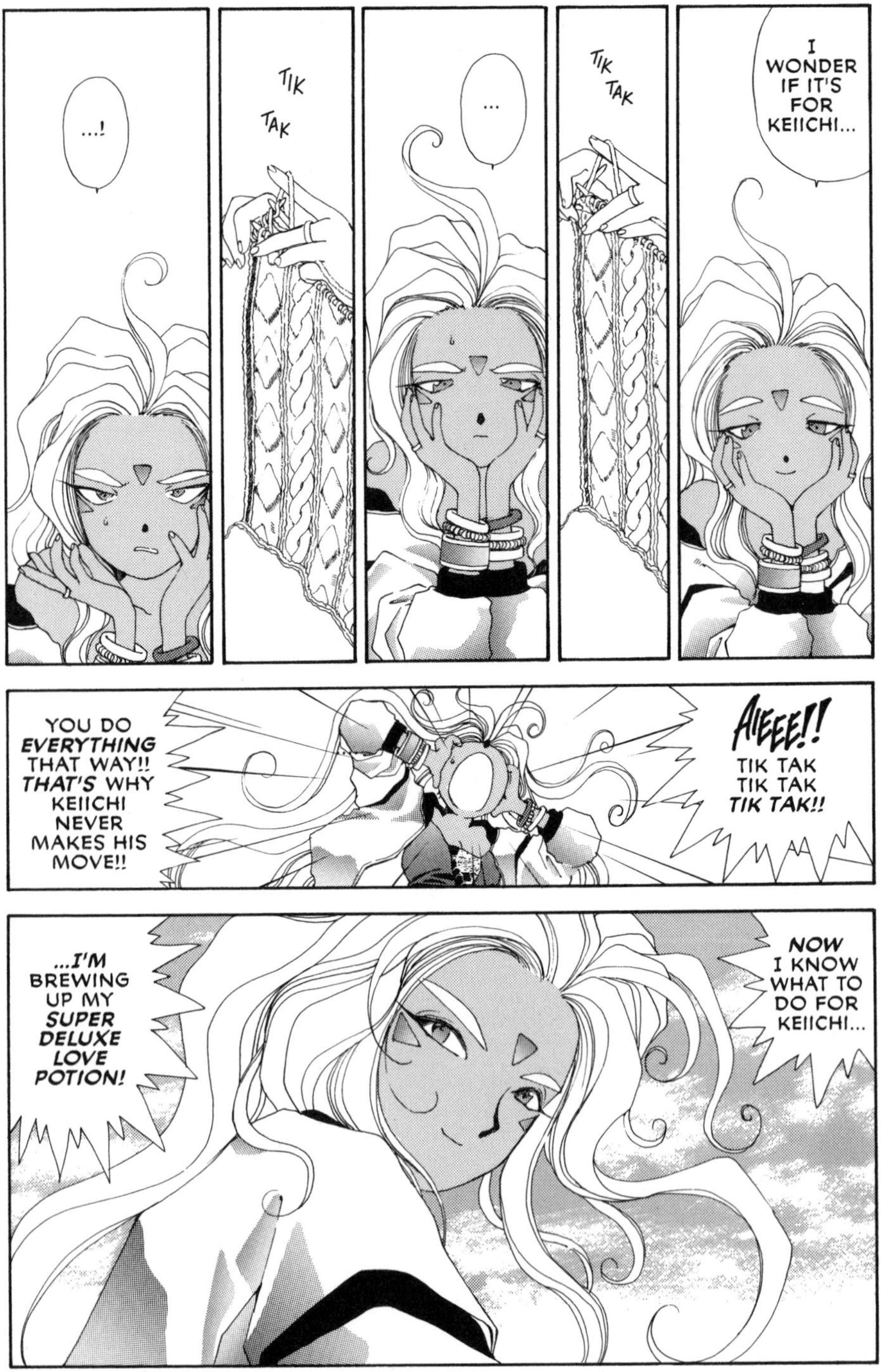
I WONDER IF IT'S FOR KEIICHI...
TIK TAK
...
TIK TAK
...!
AIEEE!!
TIK TAK TIK TAK TIK TAK!!
YOU DO EVERYTHING THAT WAY!! THAT'S WHY KEIICHI NEVER MAKES HIS MOVE!!
NOW I KNOW WHAT TO DO FOR KEIICHI...
...I'M BREWING UP MY SUPER DELUXE LOVE POTION!

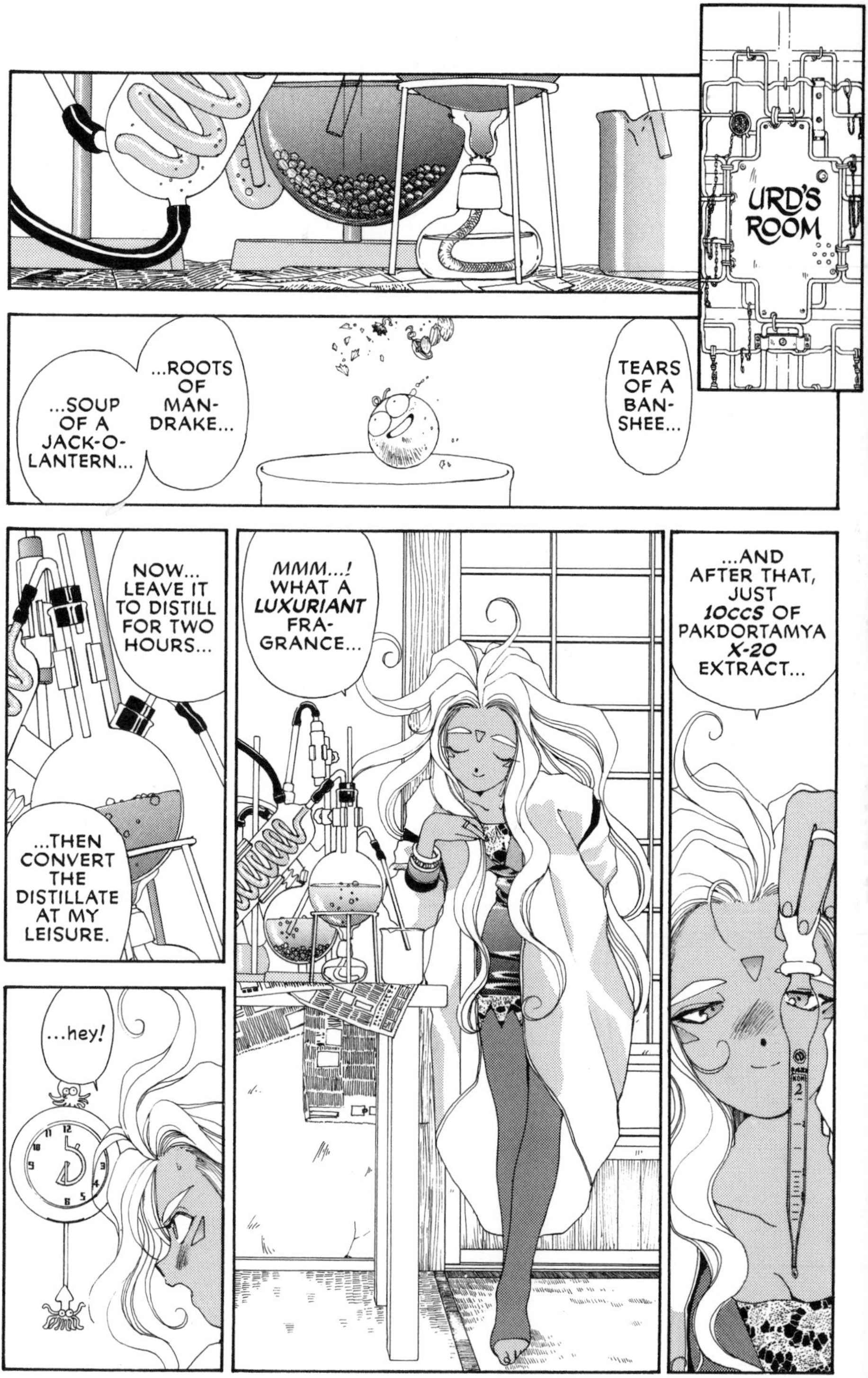
URD'S ROOM
TEARS OF A BANSHEE...
...ROOTS OF MANDRAKE...
...SOUP OF A JACK-O-LANTERN...
...AND AFTER THAT, JUST 10CCS OF PAKDORTAMYA X-20 EXTRACT...
MMM...! WHAT A LUXURIANT FRAGRANCE...
NOW... LEAVE IT TO DISTILL FOR TWO HOURS...
...THEN CONVERT THE DISTILLATE AT MY LEISURE.
...hey!

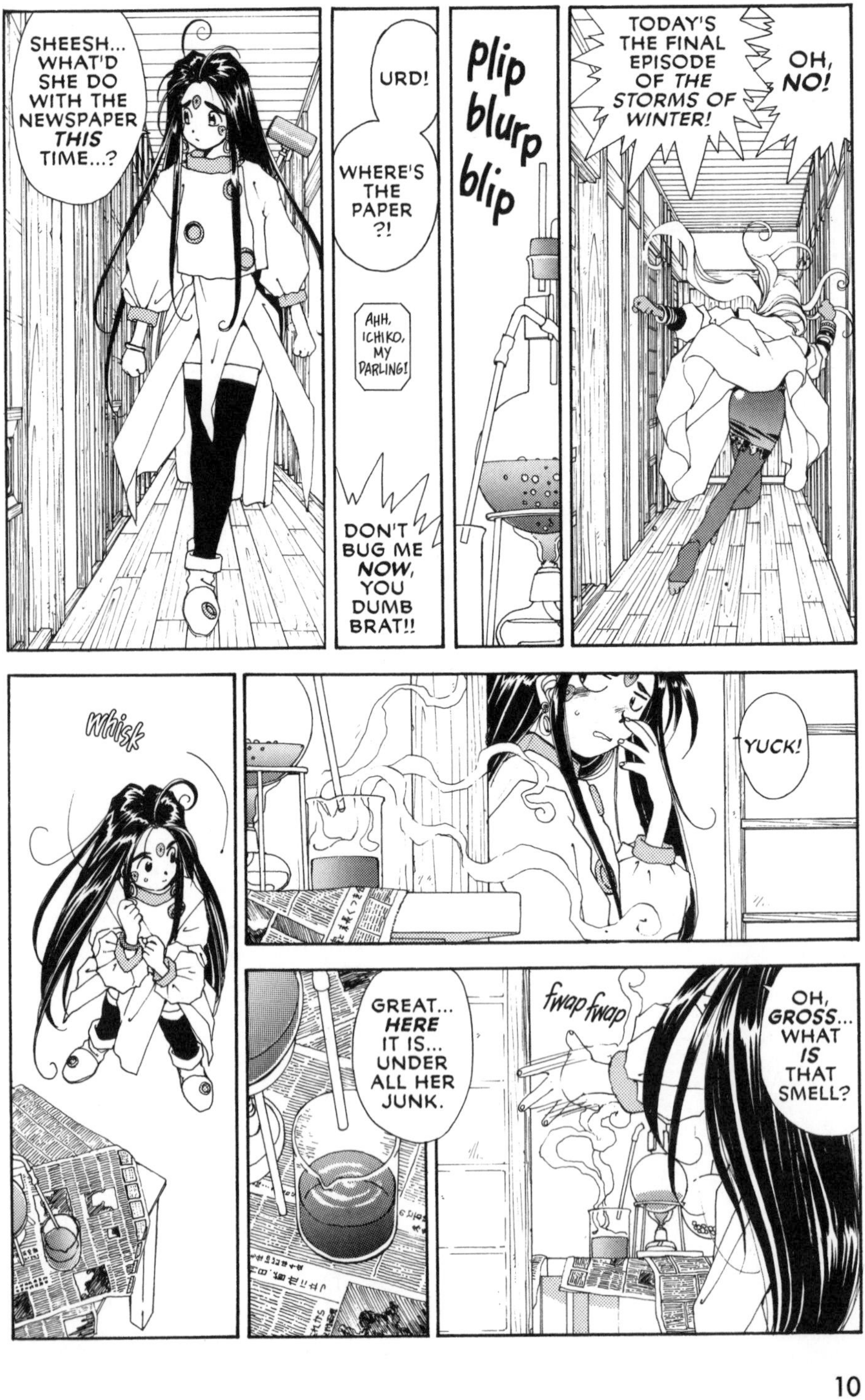
OH, NO!
TODAY'S THE FINAL EPISODE OF THE STORMS OF WINTER!
plip blurp blip
URD!
WHERE'S THE PAPER ?!
AHH, ICHIKO, MY DARLING!
DON'T BUG ME NOW, YOU DUMB BRAT!!
SHEESH... WHAT'D SHE DO WITH THE NEWSPAPER THIS TIME...?
YUCK!
OH, GROSS... WHAT IS THAT SMELL?
fwap fwap
GREAT... HERE IT IS... UNDER ALL HER JUNK.
whisk

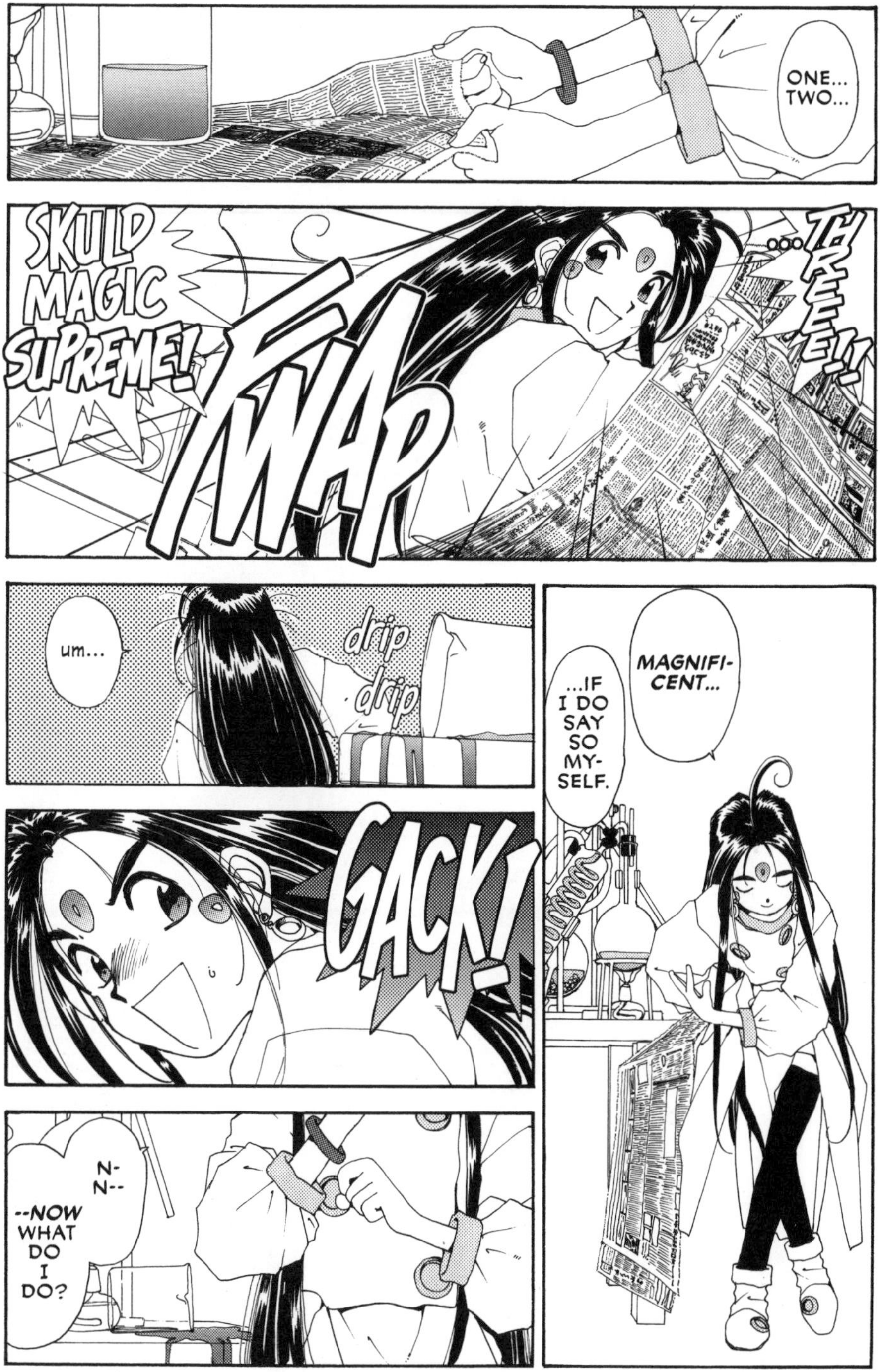
ONE... TWO...
...THREE!!
FWAP
SKULD MAGIC SUPREME!
MAGNIFI-CENT...
...IF I DO SAY SO MY-SELF.
um...
drip drip
GACK!
N- N--
--NOW WHAT DO I DO?

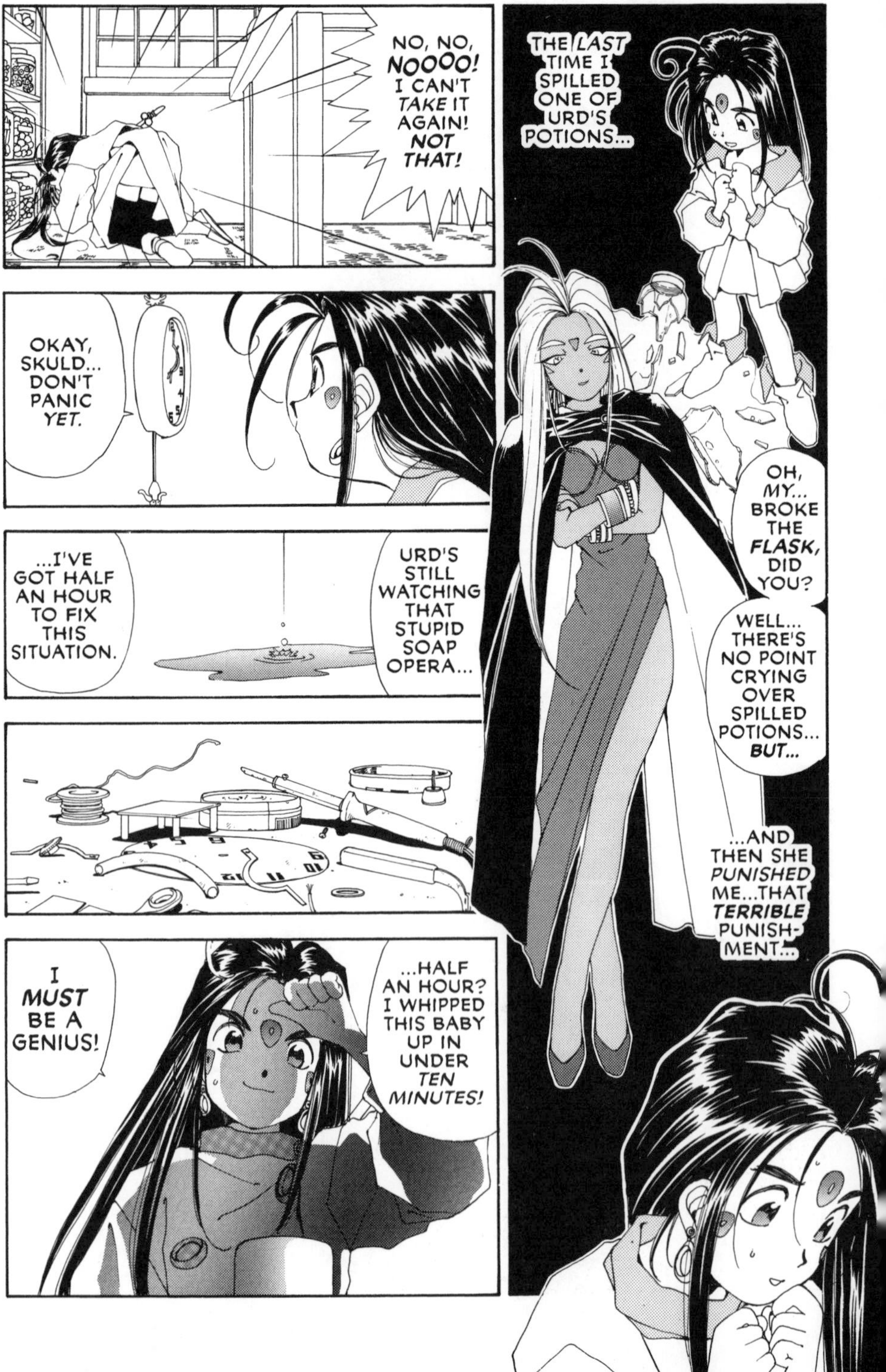
THE *LAST* TIME I SPILLED ONE OF URD'S POTIONS...
OH, *MY*... BROKE THE ***FLASK,*** DID YOU?
WELL... THERE'S NO POINT CRYING OVER SPILLED POTIONS... ***BUT...***
...AND THEN SHE *PUNISHED* ME...THAT ***TERRIBLE*** PUNISHMENT...
NO, NO, ***NOOOO!*** I CAN'T *TAKE* IT AGAIN! ***NOT THAT!***
OKAY, SKULD... DON'T PANIC *YET.*
URD'S STILL WATCHING THAT STUPID SOAP OPERA...
...I'VE GOT HALF AN HOUR TO FIX THIS SITUATION.
...HALF AN HOUR? I WHIPPED THIS BABY UP IN UNDER *TEN MINUTES!*
I ***MUST*** BE A GENIUS!

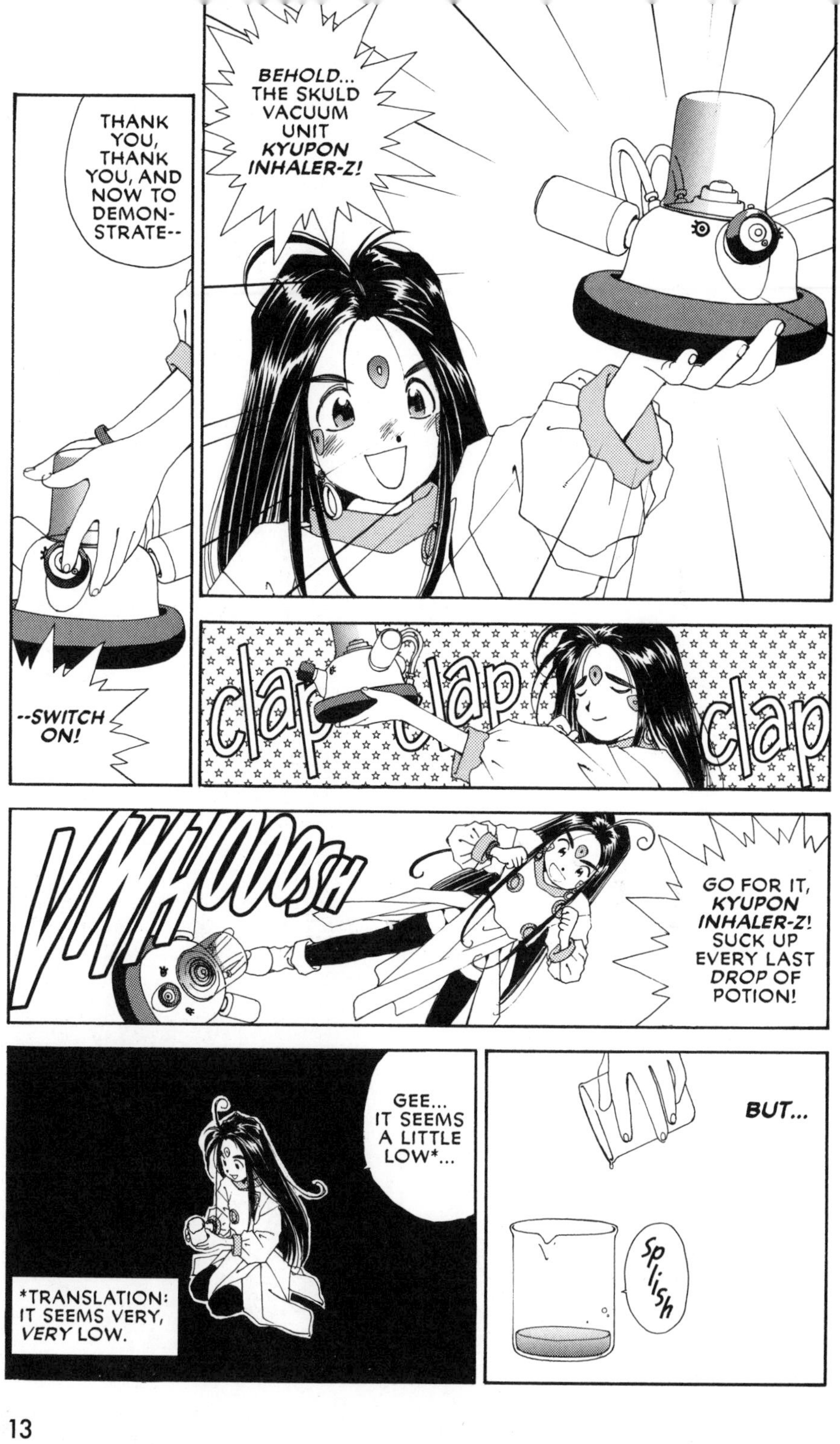
BEHOLD... THE SKULD VACUUM UNIT KYUPON INHALER-Z!
clap clap clap
THANK YOU, THANK YOU, AND NOW TO DEMON-STRATE--
--SWITCH ON!
GO FOR IT, KYUPON INHALER-Z! SUCK UP EVERY LAST DROP OF POTION!
VWHOOOSH
BUT...
splish
GEE... IT SEEMS A LITTLE LOW*...
*TRANSLATION: IT SEEMS VERY, VERY LOW.

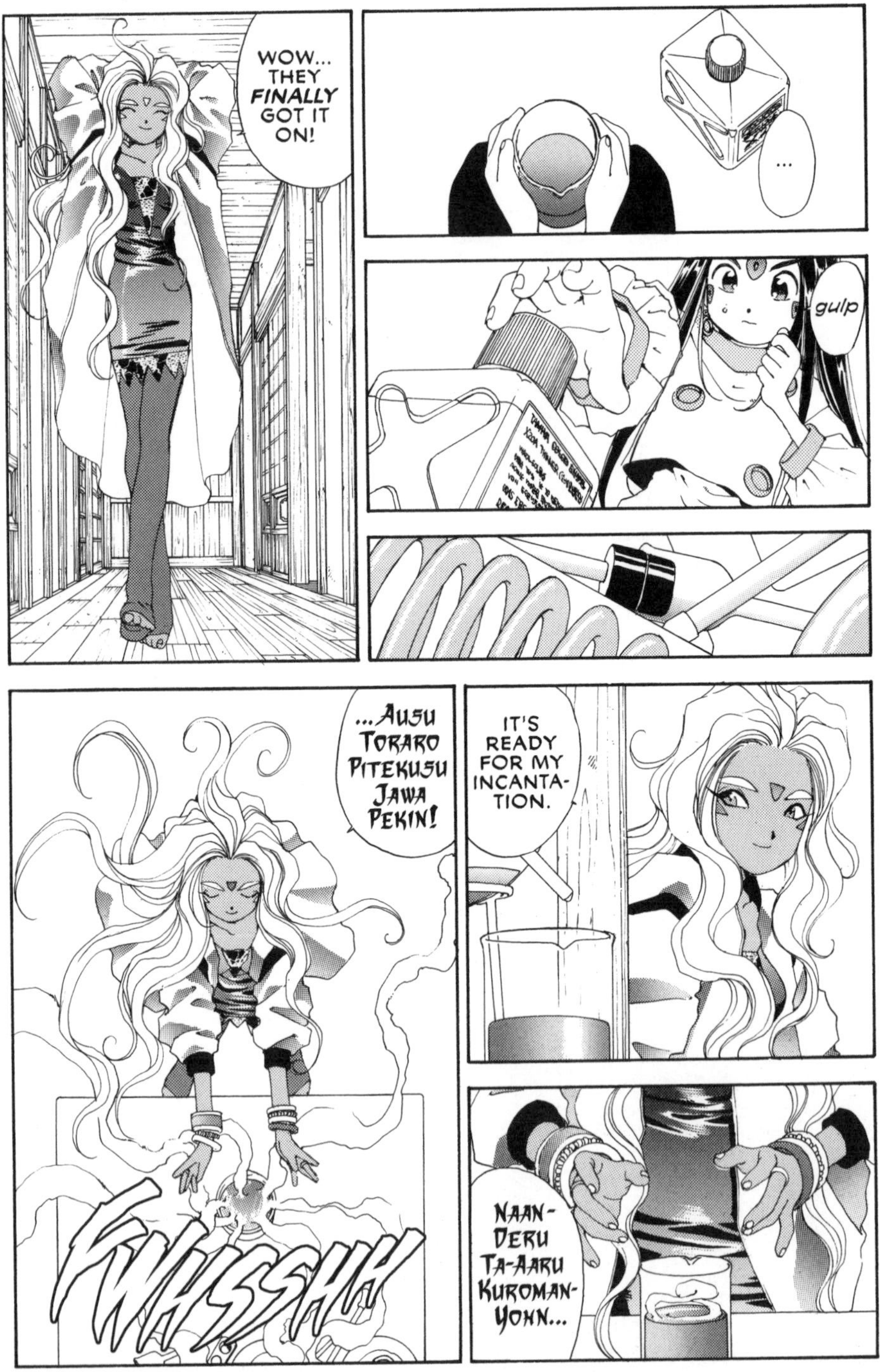
...
gulp
WOW... THEY FINALLY GOT IT ON!
IT'S READY FOR MY INCANTATION.
NAAN-DERU TA-AARU KUROMAN-YOHN...
...AUSU TORARO PITEKUSU JAWA PEKIN!
FWHSSHH

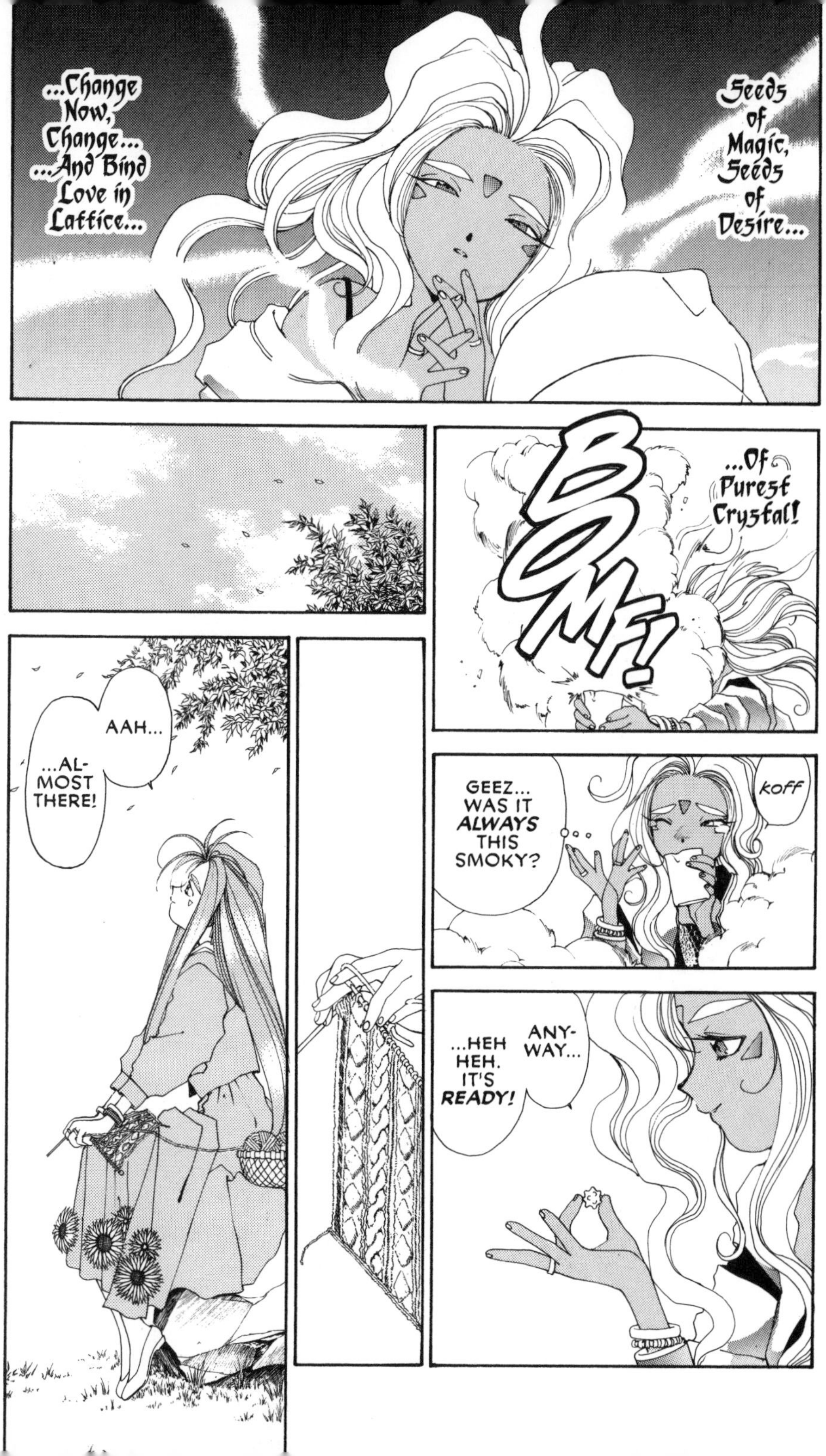

Seeds of Magic, Seeds of Desire...
...Change Now, Change... ...And Bind Love in Lattice...
BOMF!
...Of Purest Crystal!
GEEZ... WAS IT *ALWAYS* THIS SMOKY?
koff
ANY-WAY...
...HEH HEH. IT'S *READY!*
AAH...
...AL-MOST THERE!

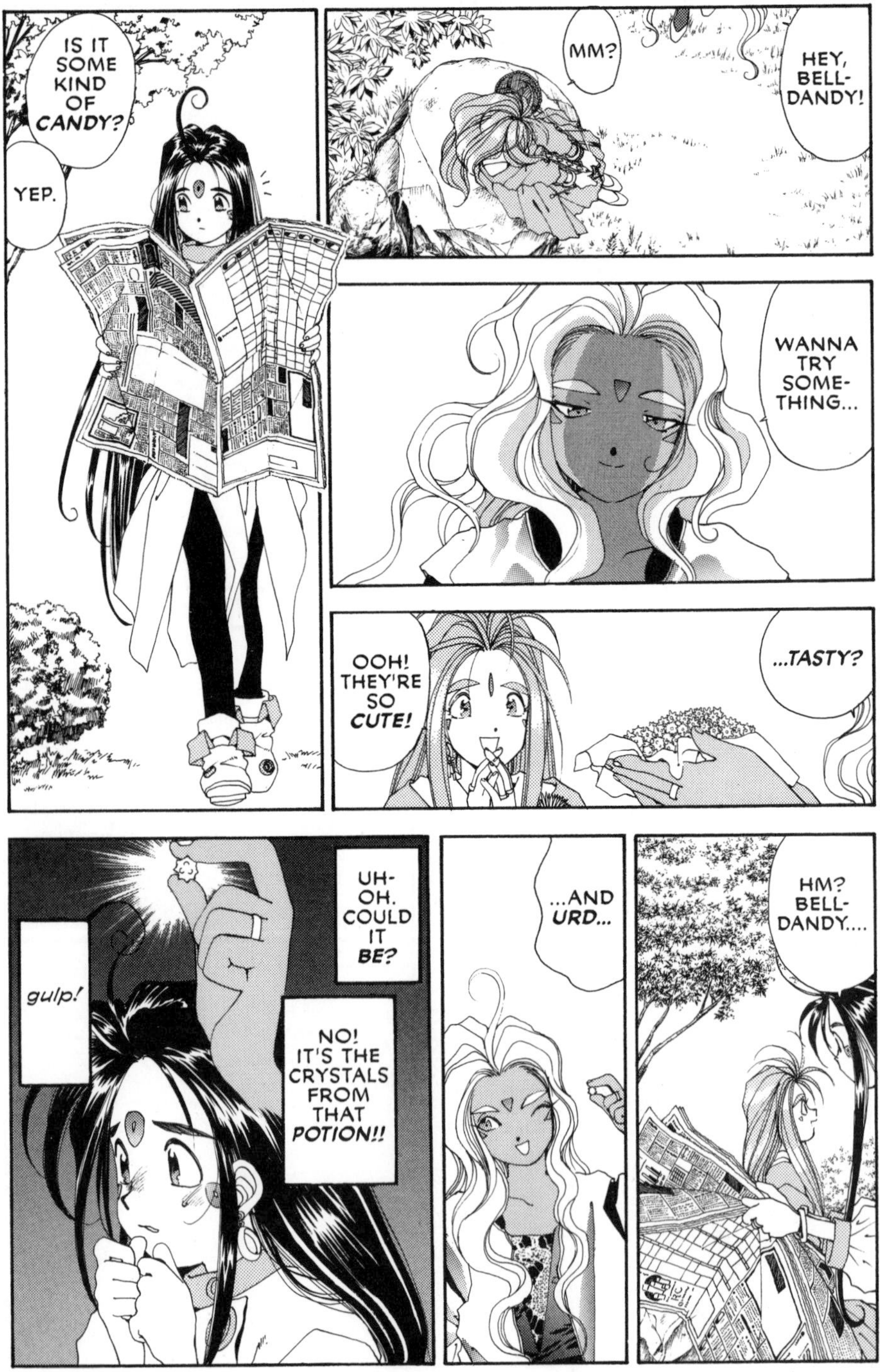
HEY, BELL-DANDY!
MM?
WANNA TRY SOME-THING...
...TASTY?
OOH! THEY'RE SO CUTE!
IS IT SOME KIND OF CANDY?
YEP.
HM? BELL-DANDY....
...AND URD...
UH-OH. COULD IT BE?
NO! IT'S THE CRYSTALS FROM THAT POTION!!
gulp!

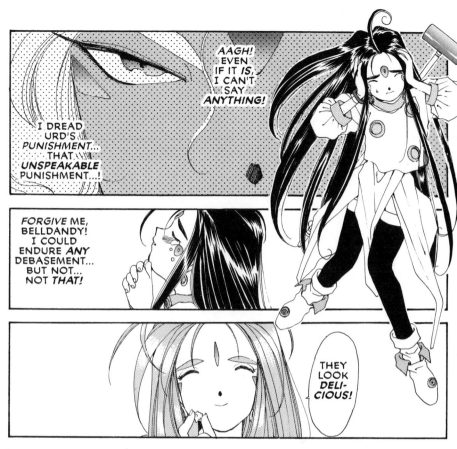

AAGH! EVEN IF IT *IS*, I CAN'T SAY *ANYTHING*!

I DREAD URD'S *PUNISHMENT*... THAT *UNSPEAKABLE* PUNISHMENT...!

FORGIVE ME, BELLDANDY! I COULD ENDURE *ANY* DEBASEMENT... BUT NOT... NOT *THAT*!

THEY LOOK *DELICIOUS*!

mmm...

do it! *do* it!

NO! NO!

...

COME ON ...!

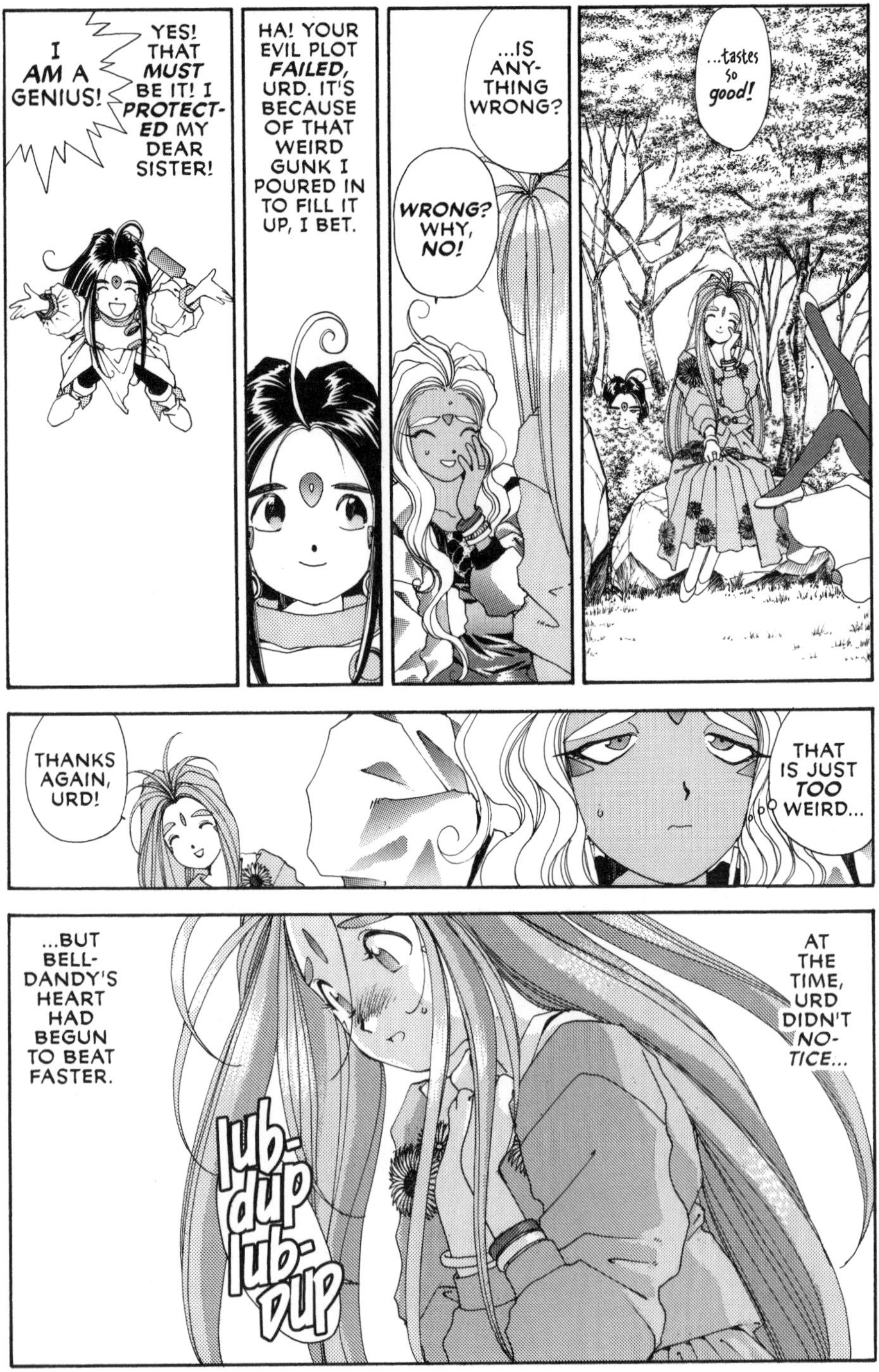
...tastes so good!
...IS ANYTHING WRONG?
WRONG? WHY, NO!
HA! YOUR EVIL PLOT FAILED, URD. IT'S BECAUSE OF THAT WEIRD GUNK I POURED IN TO FILL IT UP, I BET.
YES! THAT MUST BE IT! I PROTECTED MY DEAR SISTER!
I AM A GENIUS!
THAT IS JUST TOO WEIRD...
THANKS AGAIN, URD!
AT THE TIME, URD DIDN'T NOTICE...
...BUT BELL-DANDY'S HEART HAD BEGUN TO BEAT FASTER.
lub-dup lub-DUP

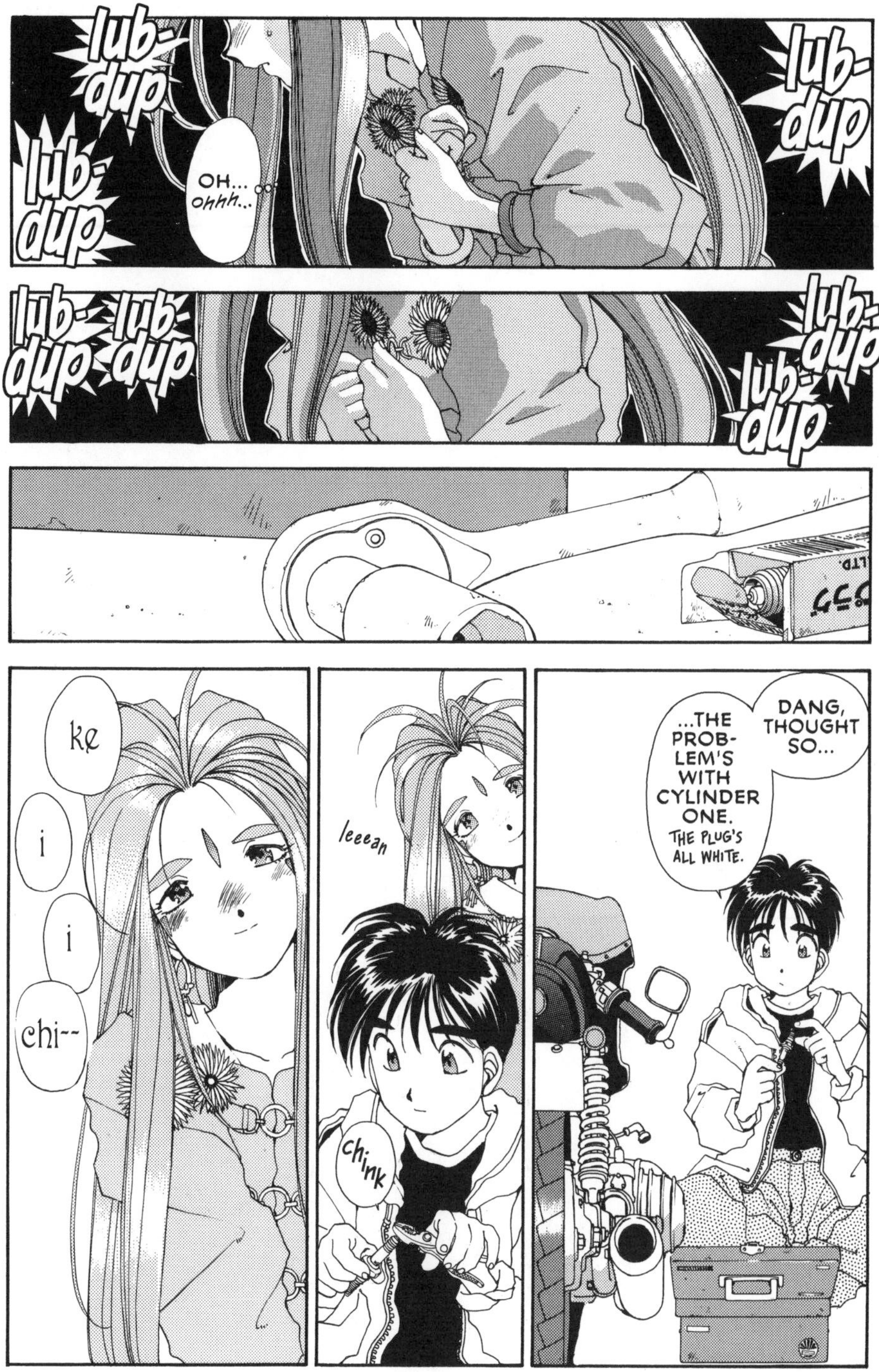
lub-dup
lub-dup
OH... ohhh...
lub-dup
lub-dup
lub-dup
lub-dup
lub-dup
DANG, THOUGHT SO...
...THE PROB-LEM'S WITH CYLINDER ONE. THE PLUG'S ALL WHITE.
leeean
chink
ke
i
i
chi--

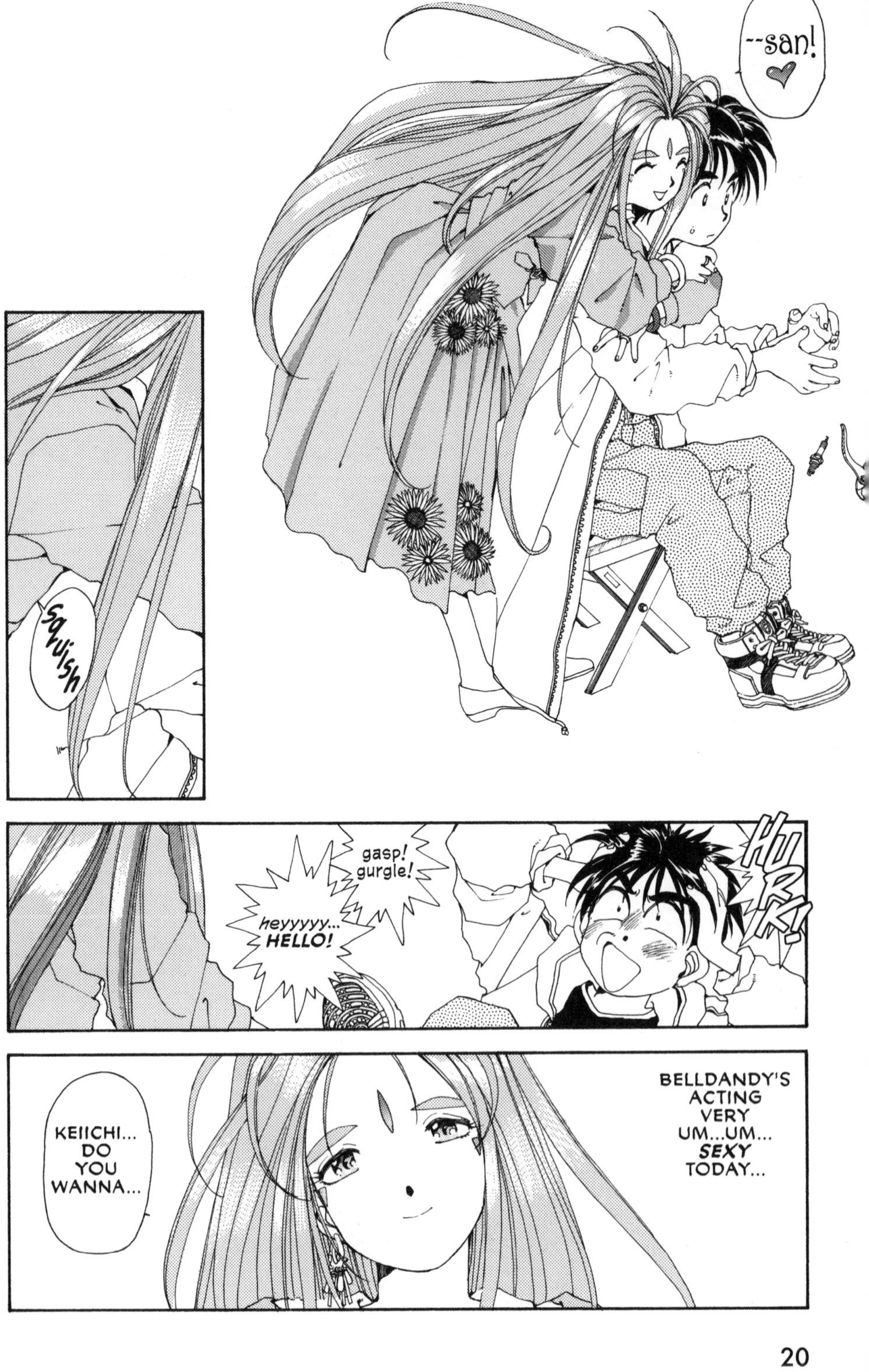
--san! ♥
squish
HURK!
gasp! gurgle!
heyyyyy... HELLO!
BELLDANDY'S ACTING VERY UM...UM... SEXY TODAY...
KEIICHI... DO YOU WANNA...

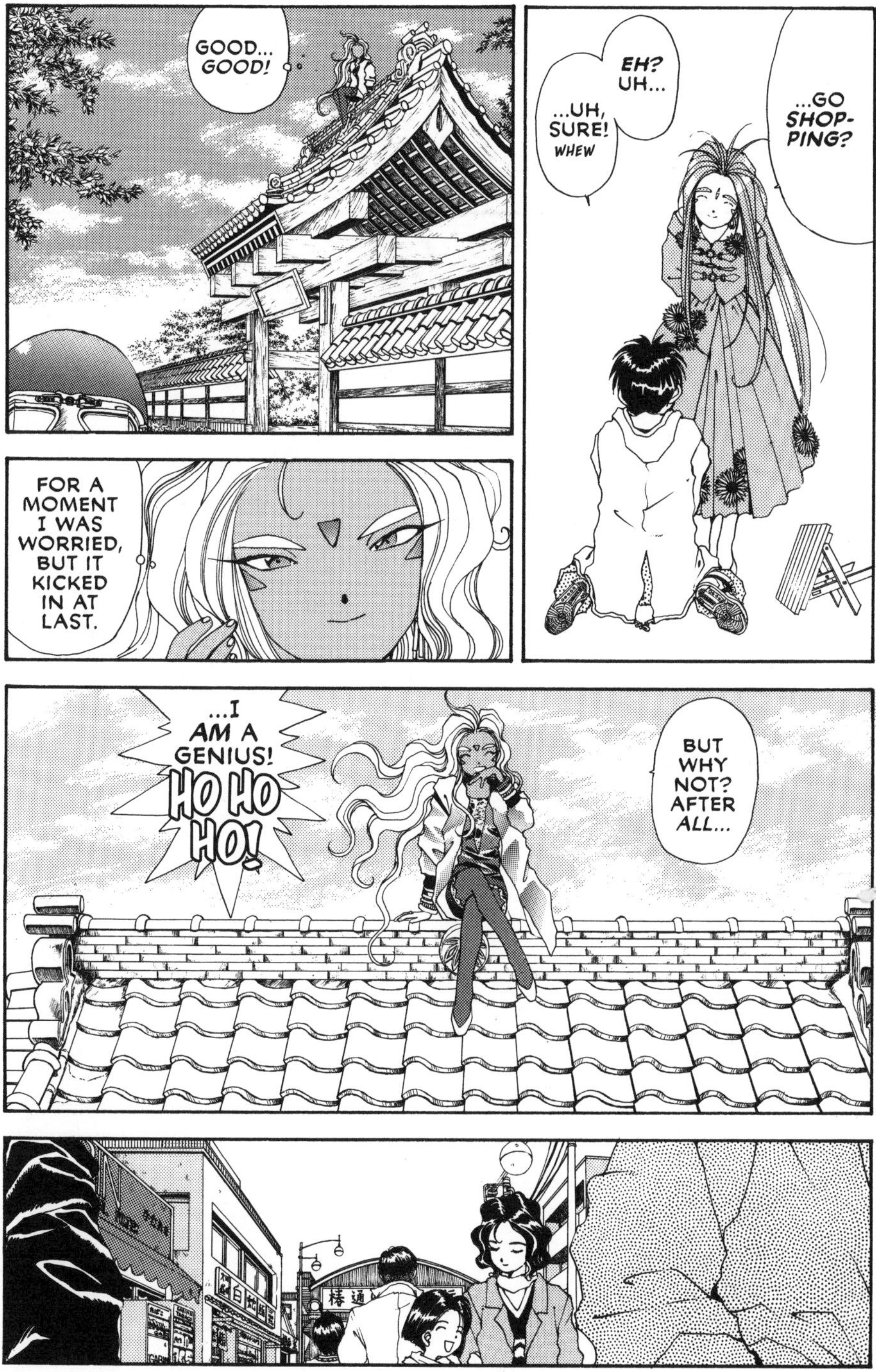
...GO SHOPPING?
EH? UH...
...UH, SURE! WHEW
GOOD... GOOD!
FOR A MOMENT I WAS WORRIED, BUT IT KICKED IN AT LAST.
BUT WHY NOT? AFTER ALL...
...I AM A GENIUS!
HO HO HO!

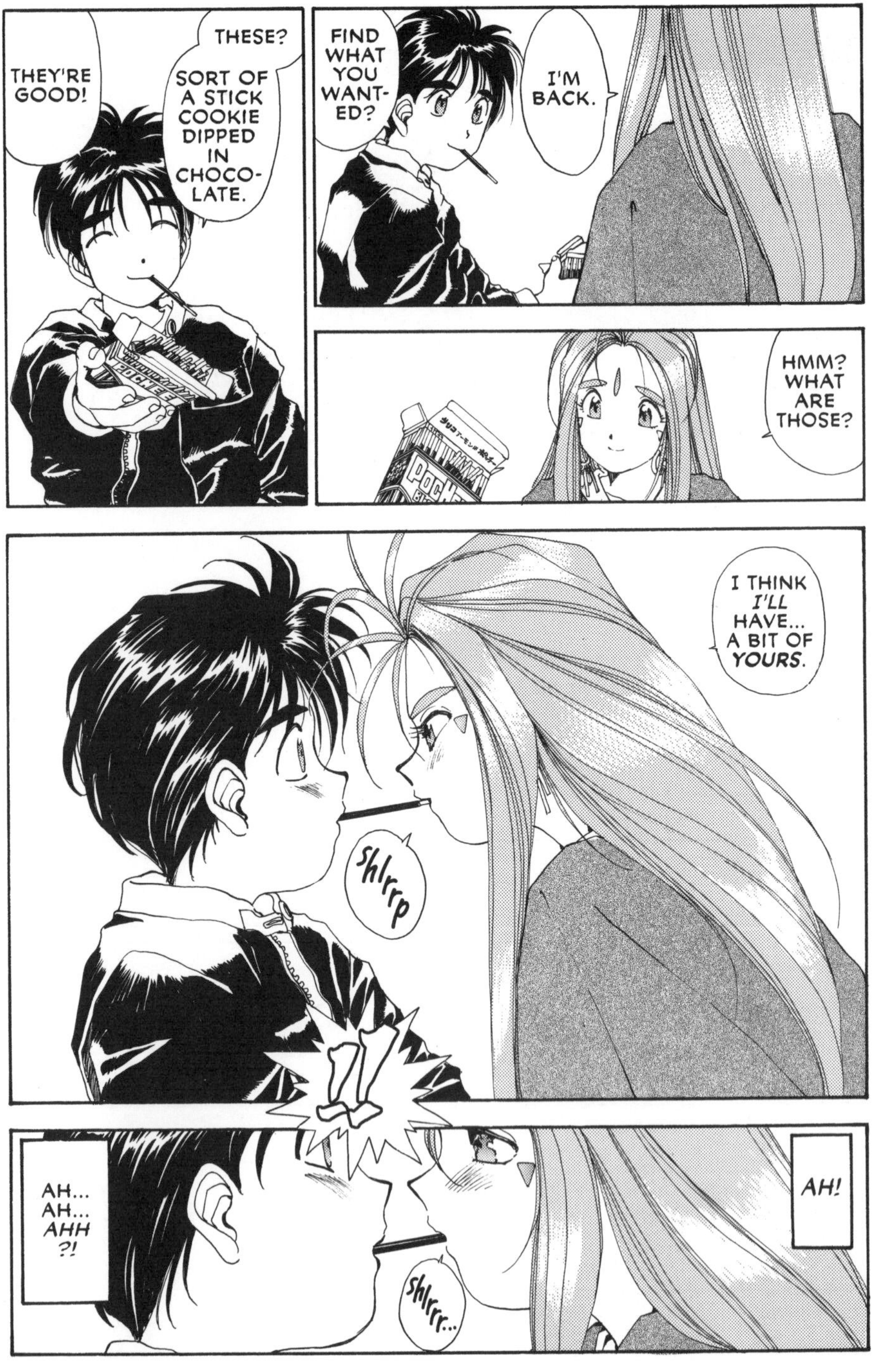
I'M BACK.
FIND WHAT YOU WANT-ED?
HMM? WHAT ARE THOSE?
THESE?
SORT OF A STICK COOKIE DIPPED IN CHOCO-LATE.
THEY'RE GOOD!
I THINK *I'LL* HAVE... A BIT OF ***YOURS***.
shlrrp
!!
AH!
AH... AH... *AHH* ?!
shlrrr...

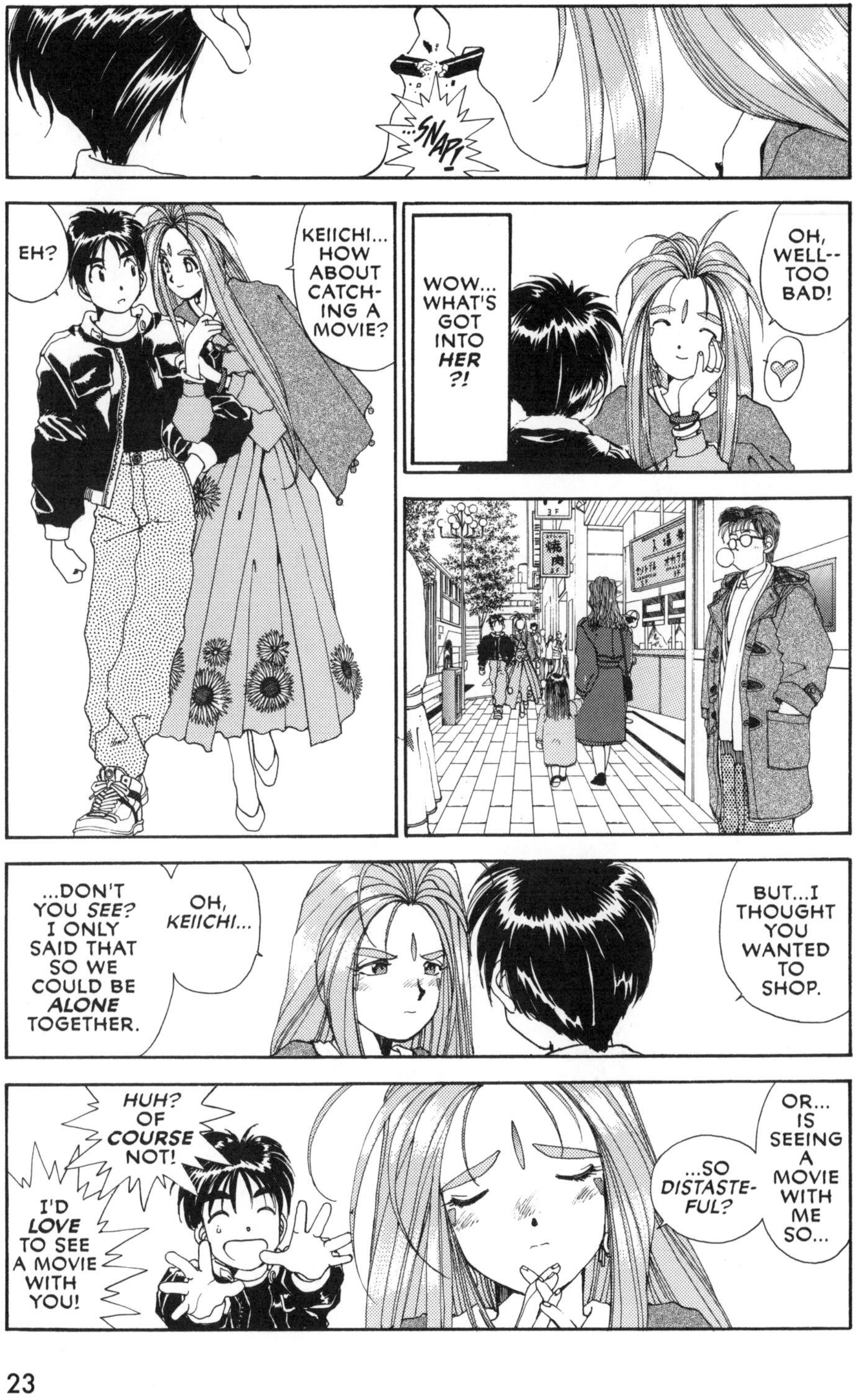

...SNAP!
OH, WELL-- TOO BAD!
WOW... WHAT'S GOT INTO HER?!
KEIICHI... HOW ABOUT CATCHING A MOVIE?
EH?
BUT...I THOUGHT YOU WANTED TO SHOP.
OH, KEIICHI...
...DON'T YOU SEE? I ONLY SAID THAT SO WE COULD BE ALONE TOGETHER.
OR... IS SEEING A MOVIE WITH ME SO...
...SO DISTASTEFUL?
HUH? OF COURSE NOT!
I'D LOVE TO SEE A MOVIE WITH YOU!

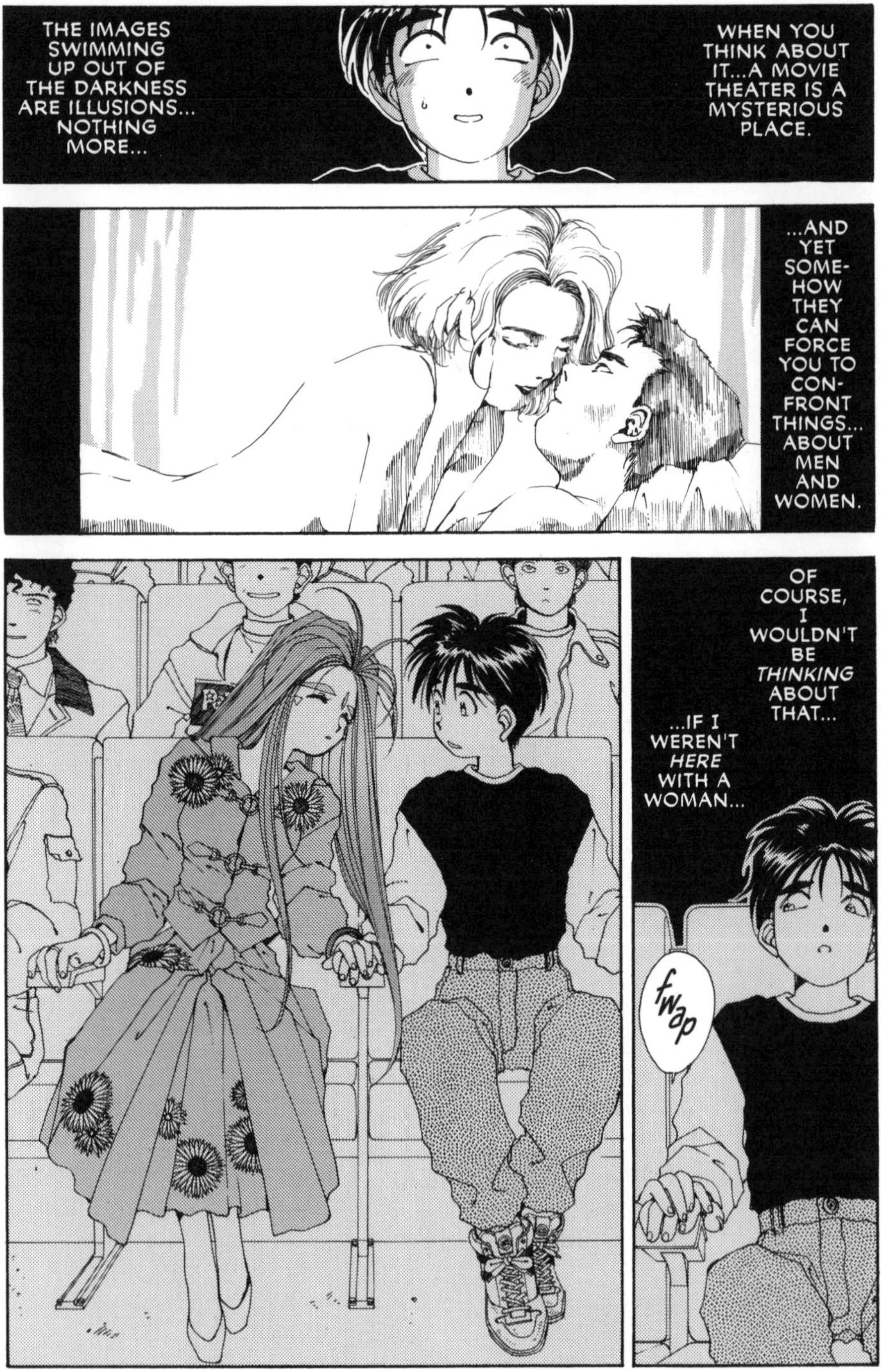
WHEN YOU THINK ABOUT IT...A MOVIE THEATER IS A MYSTERIOUS PLACE.
THE IMAGES SWIMMING UP OUT OF THE DARKNESS ARE ILLUSIONS... NOTHING MORE...
...AND YET SOME-HOW THEY CAN FORCE YOU TO CON-FRONT THINGS... ABOUT MEN AND WOMEN.
OF COURSE, I WOULDN'T BE *THINKING* ABOUT THAT...
...IF I WEREN'T *HERE* WITH A WOMAN...
fwap

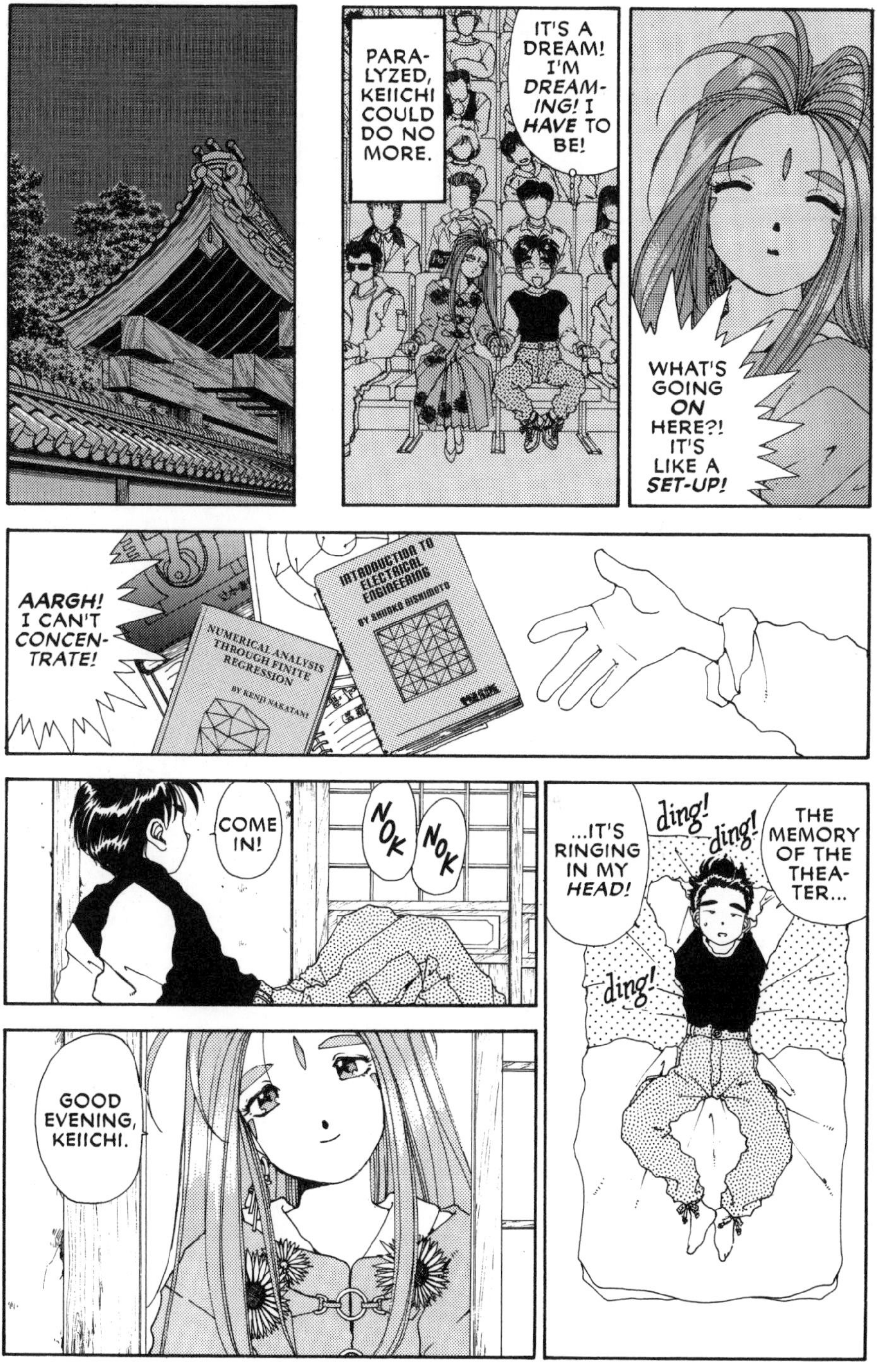
WHAT'S GOING ON HERE?! IT'S LIKE A SET-UP!
IT'S A DREAM! I'M DREAMING! I HAVE TO BE!
PARALYZED, KEIICHI COULD DO NO MORE.
INTRODUCTION TO ELECTRICAL ENGINEERING
NUMERICAL ANALYSIS THROUGH FINITE REGRESSION
BY KENJI NAKATANI
AARGH! I CAN'T CONCENTRATE!
THE MEMORY OF THE THEATER...
ding!
ding!
...IT'S RINGING IN MY HEAD!
ding!
NOK
NOK
COME IN!
GOOD EVENING, KEIICHI.

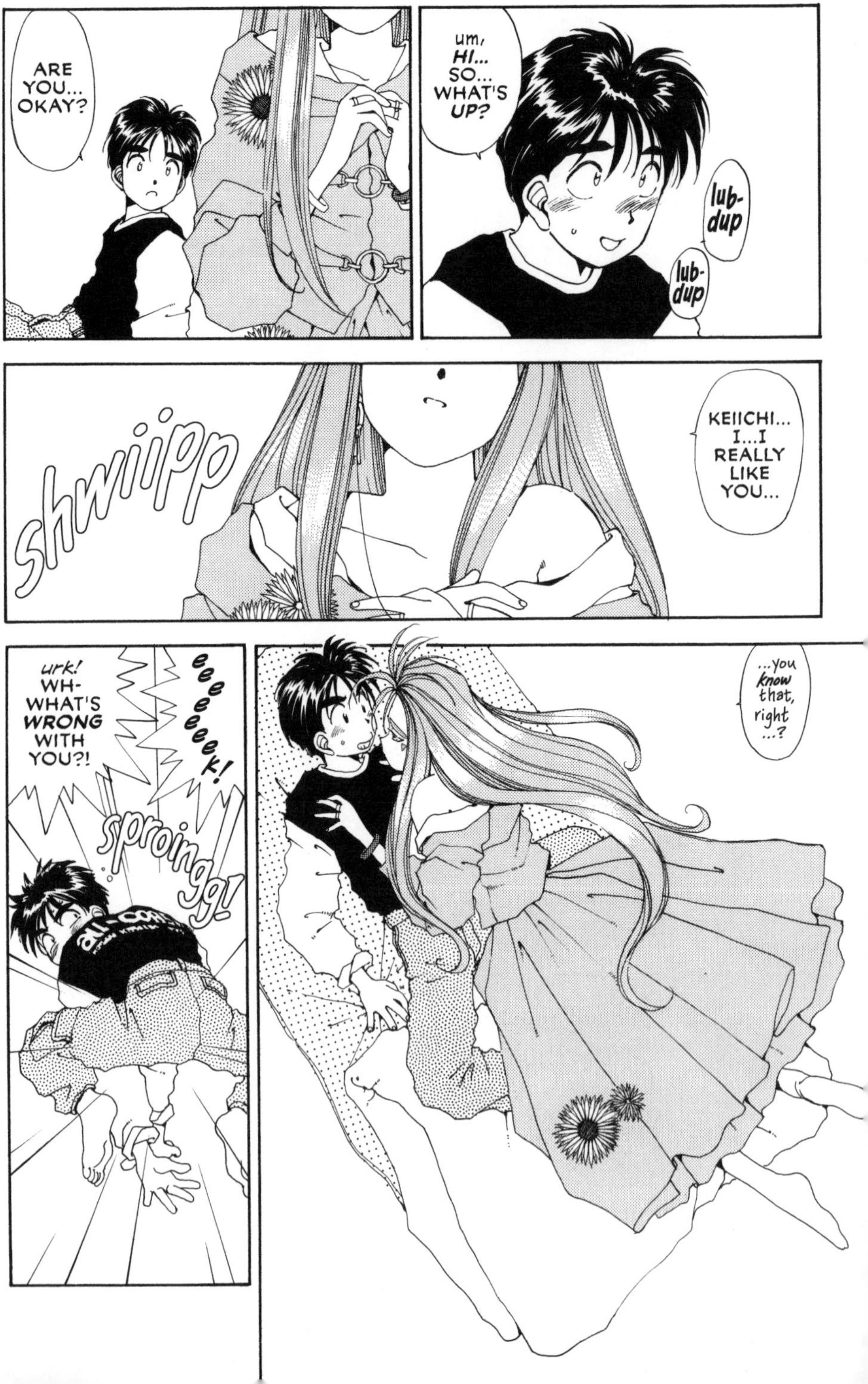
um, HI... SO... WHAT'S UP?
lub-dup
lub-dup
ARE YOU... OKAY?
KEIICHI... I...I REALLY LIKE YOU...
shwiipp
...you know that, right...?
eeeeeeeek!
urk! WH-WHAT'S WRONG WITH YOU?!
sproingg!

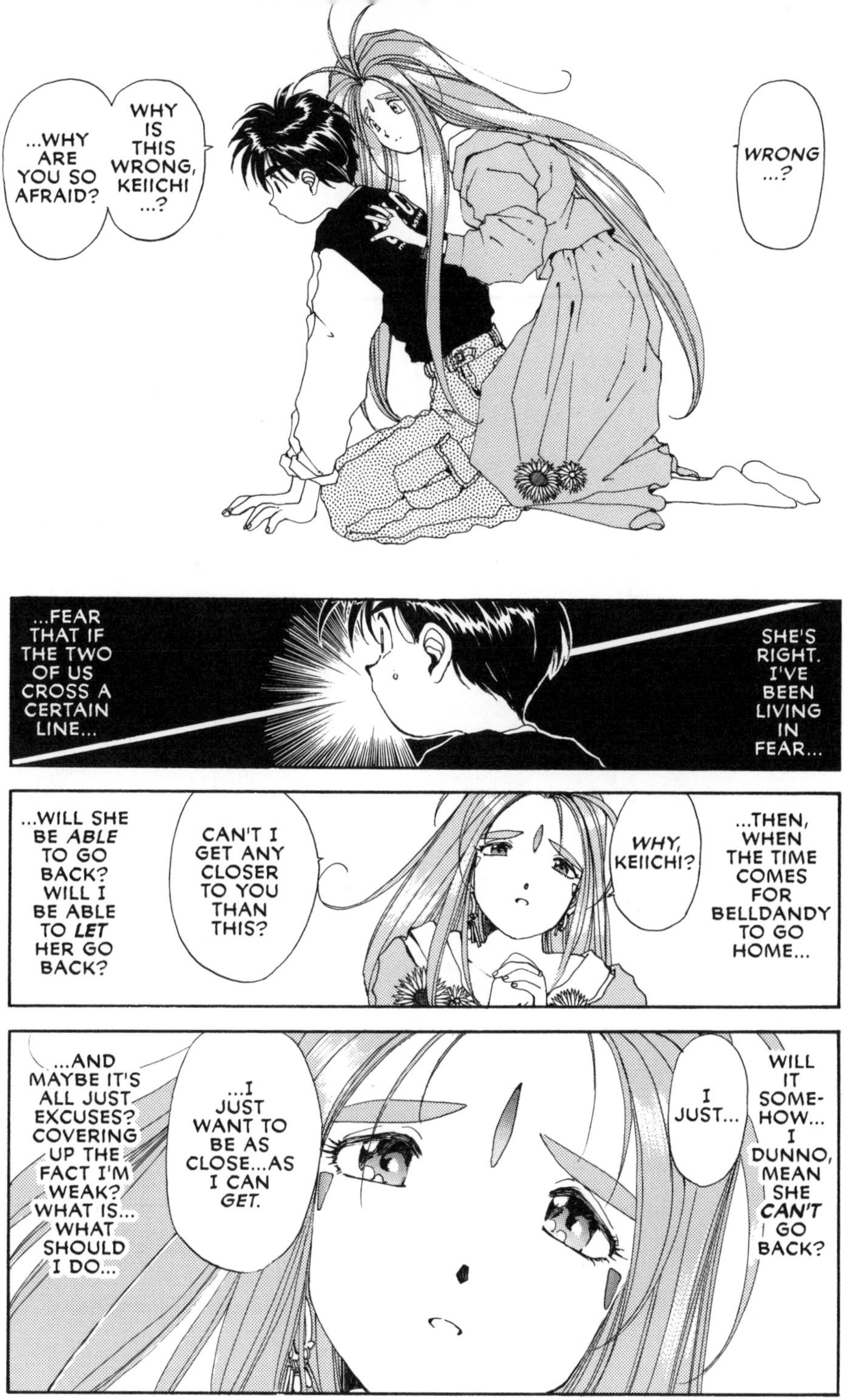
WRONG ...?
WHY IS THIS WRONG, KEIICHI ...?
...WHY ARE YOU SO AFRAID?
SHE'S RIGHT. I'VE BEEN LIVING IN FEAR...
...FEAR THAT IF THE TWO OF US CROSS A CERTAIN LINE...
...THEN, WHEN THE TIME COMES FOR BELLDANDY TO GO HOME...
WHY, KEIICHI?
CAN'T I GET ANY CLOSER TO YOU THAN THIS?
...WILL SHE BE *ABLE* TO GO BACK? WILL I BE ABLE TO *LET* HER GO BACK?
WILL IT SOME-HOW... I DUNNO, MEAN SHE ***CAN'T*** GO BACK?
I JUST...
...I JUST WANT TO BE AS CLOSE...AS I CAN *GET*.
...AND MAYBE IT'S ALL JUST EXCUSES? COVERING UP THE FACT I'M WEAK? WHAT IS... WHAT SHOULD I DO...

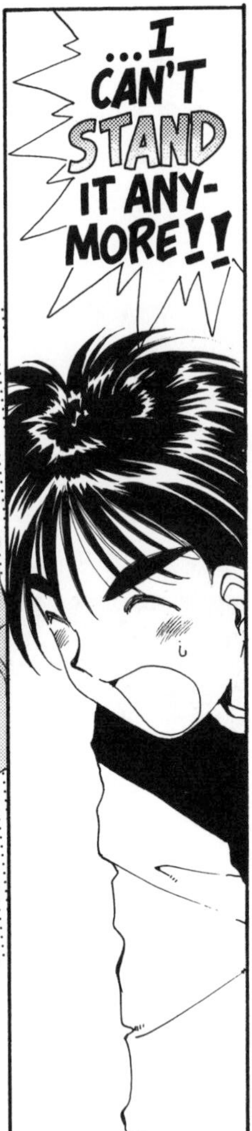
...I CAN'T STAND IT ANY-MORE!!
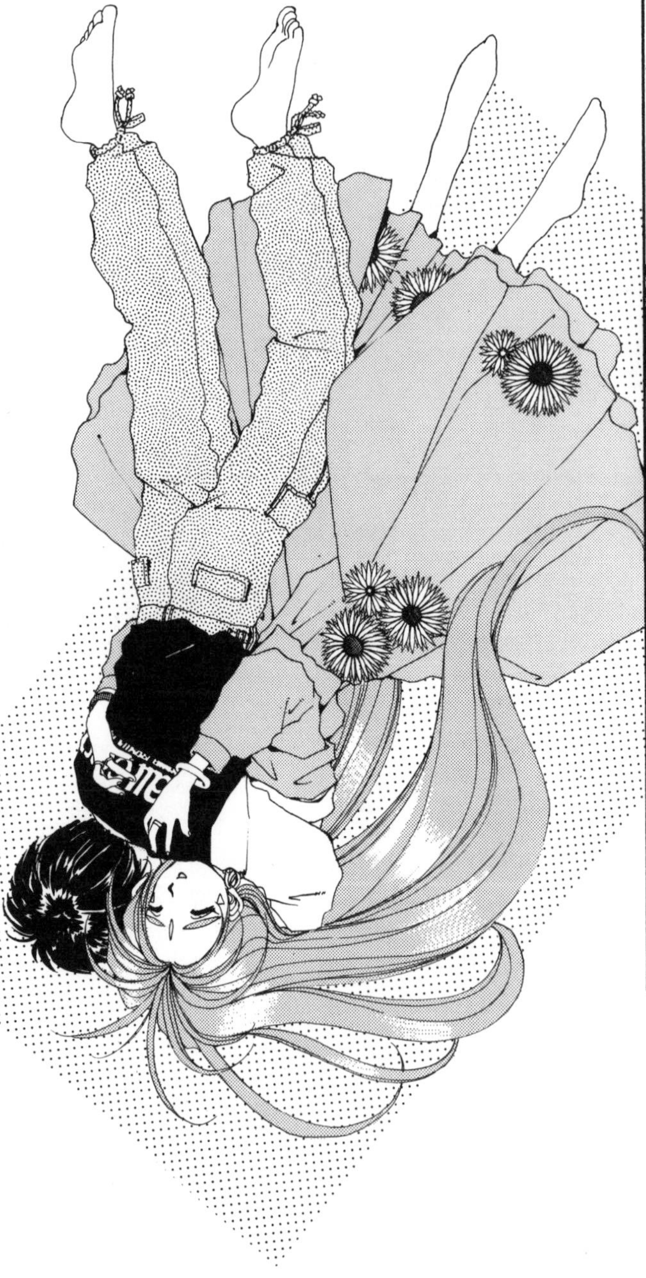

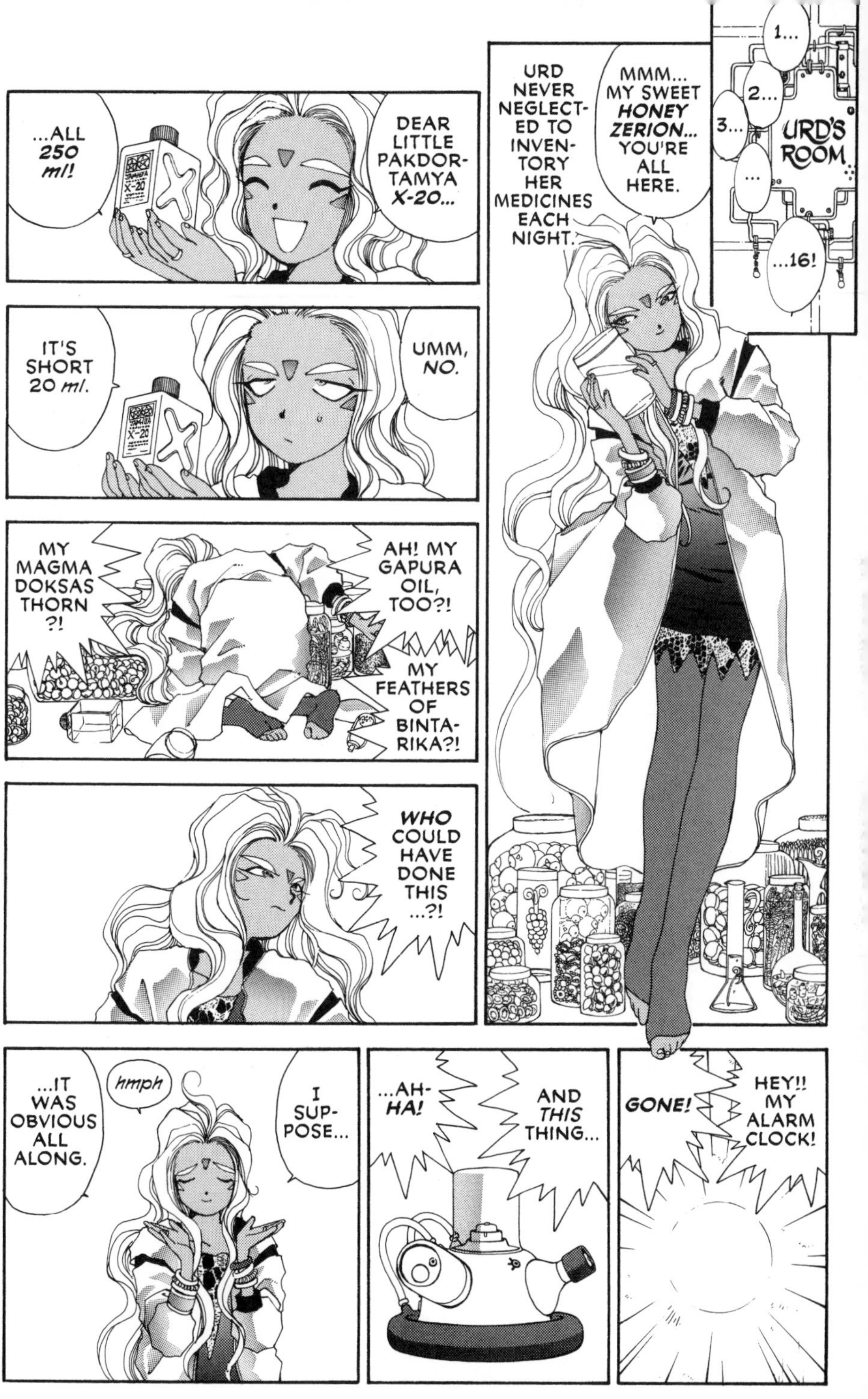
URD'S ROOM
1...
2...
3...
...
...16!
MMM... MY SWEET HONEY ZERION... YOU'RE ALL HERE.
URD NEVER NEGLECTED TO INVENTORY HER MEDICINES EACH NIGHT.
DEAR LITTLE PAKDOR-TAMYA X-20...
...ALL 250 ml!
UMM, NO.
IT'S SHORT 20 ml.
AH! MY GAPURA OIL, TOO?!
MY MAGMA DOKSAS THORN ?!
MY FEATHERS OF BINTARIKA?!
WHO COULD HAVE DONE THIS ...?!
HEY!! MY ALARM CLOCK!
GONE!
AND THIS THING...
...AH-HA!
I SUPPOSE...
hmph
...IT WAS OBVIOUS ALL ALONG.

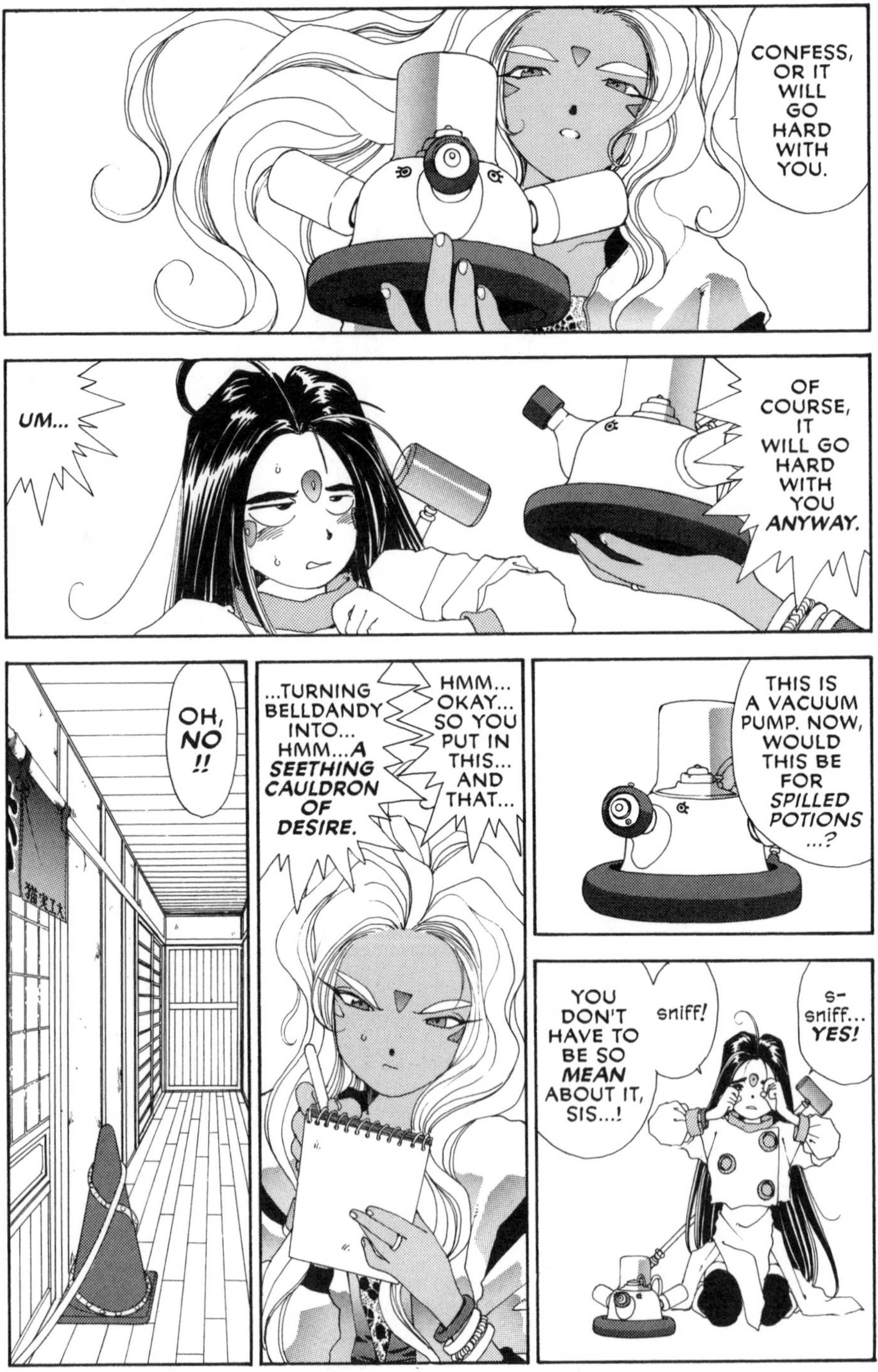
CONFESS, OR IT WILL GO HARD WITH YOU.
OF COURSE, IT WILL GO HARD WITH YOU *ANYWAY.*
UM...
THIS IS A VACUUM PUMP. NOW, WOULD THIS BE FOR *SPILLED POTIONS* ...?
S- SNIFF... *YES!*
SNIFF!
YOU DON'T HAVE TO BE SO *MEAN* ABOUT IT, SIS...!
HMM... OKAY... SO YOU PUT IN THIS... AND THAT...
...TURNING BELLDANDY INTO... HMM... *A SEETHING CAULDRON OF DESIRE.*
OH, *NO !!*

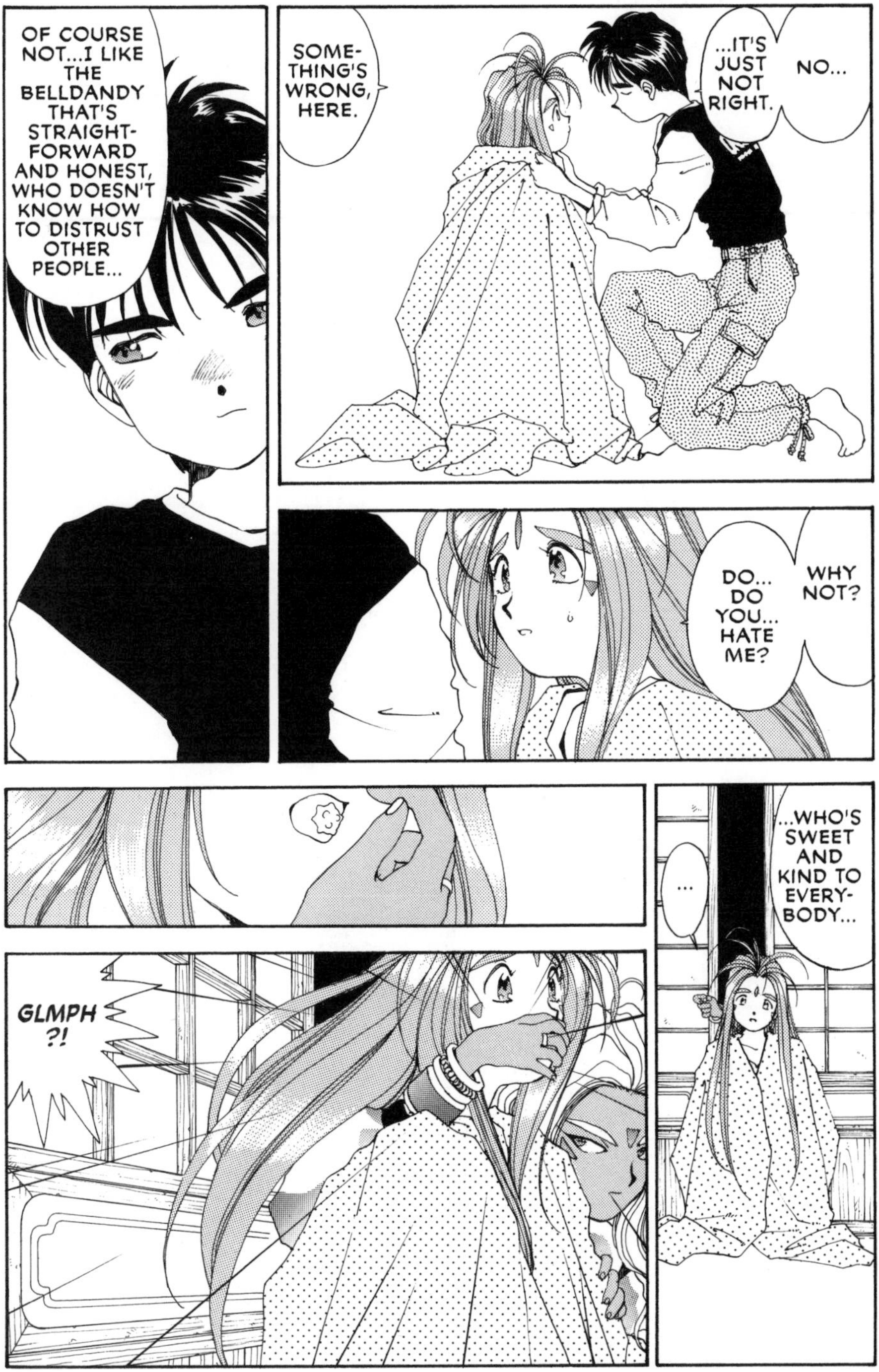
NO...
...IT'S JUST NOT RIGHT.
SOME-THING'S WRONG, HERE.
WHY NOT?
DO... DO YOU... HATE ME?
OF COURSE NOT...I LIKE THE BELLDANDY THAT'S STRAIGHT-FORWARD AND HONEST, WHO DOESN'T KNOW HOW TO DISTRUST OTHER PEOPLE...
...WHO'S SWEET AND KIND TO EVERY-BODY...
...
GLMPH ?!

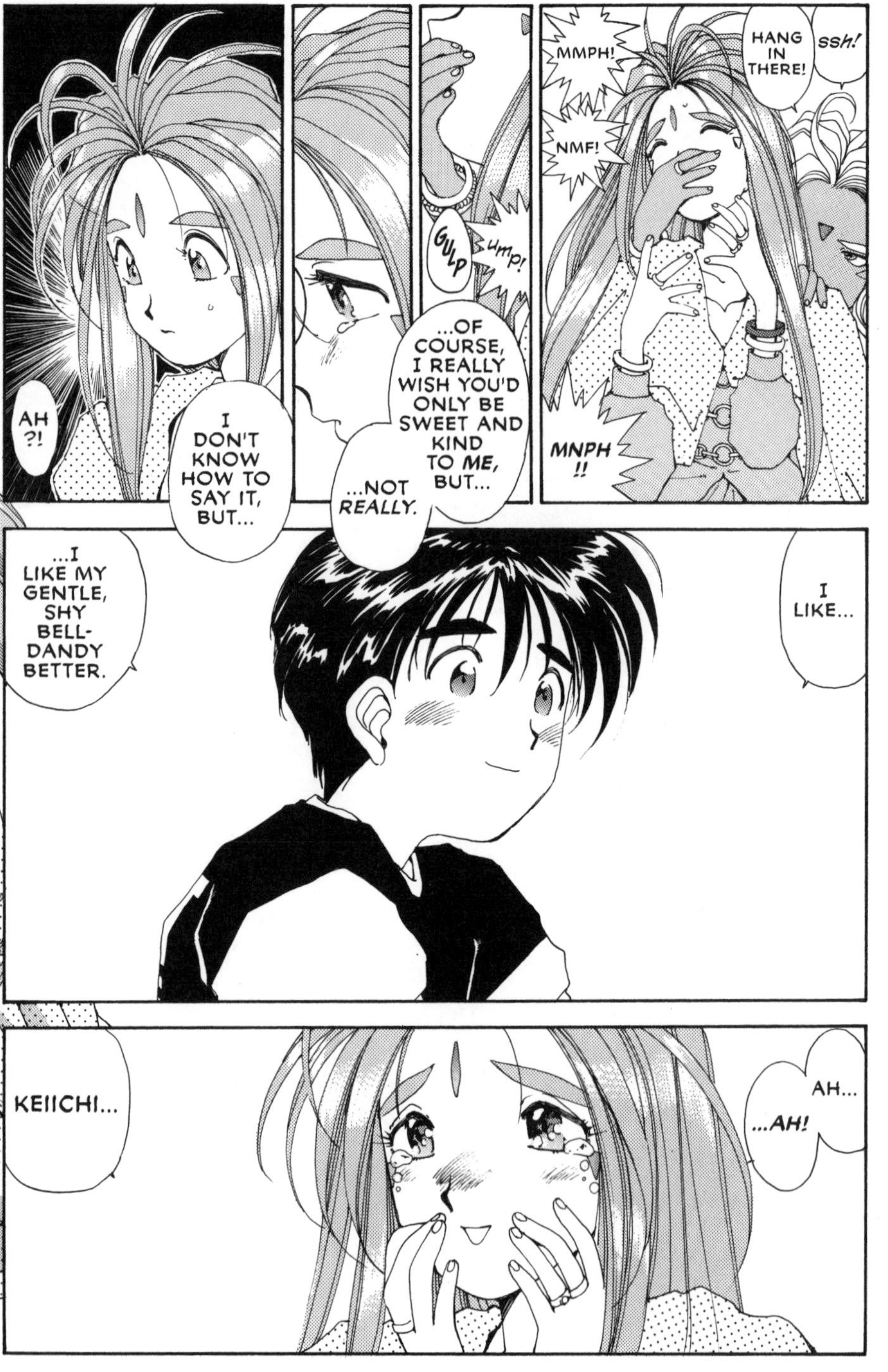
ssh!
HANG IN THERE!
MMPH!
NMF!
MNPH !!
GULP
ump!
...OF COURSE, I REALLY WISH YOU'D ONLY BE SWEET AND KIND TO *ME,* BUT...
...NOT *REALLY.*
I DON'T KNOW HOW TO SAY IT, BUT...
AH ?!
I LIKE...
...I LIKE MY GENTLE, SHY BELL-DANDY BETTER.
AH...
...*AH!*
KEIICHI...

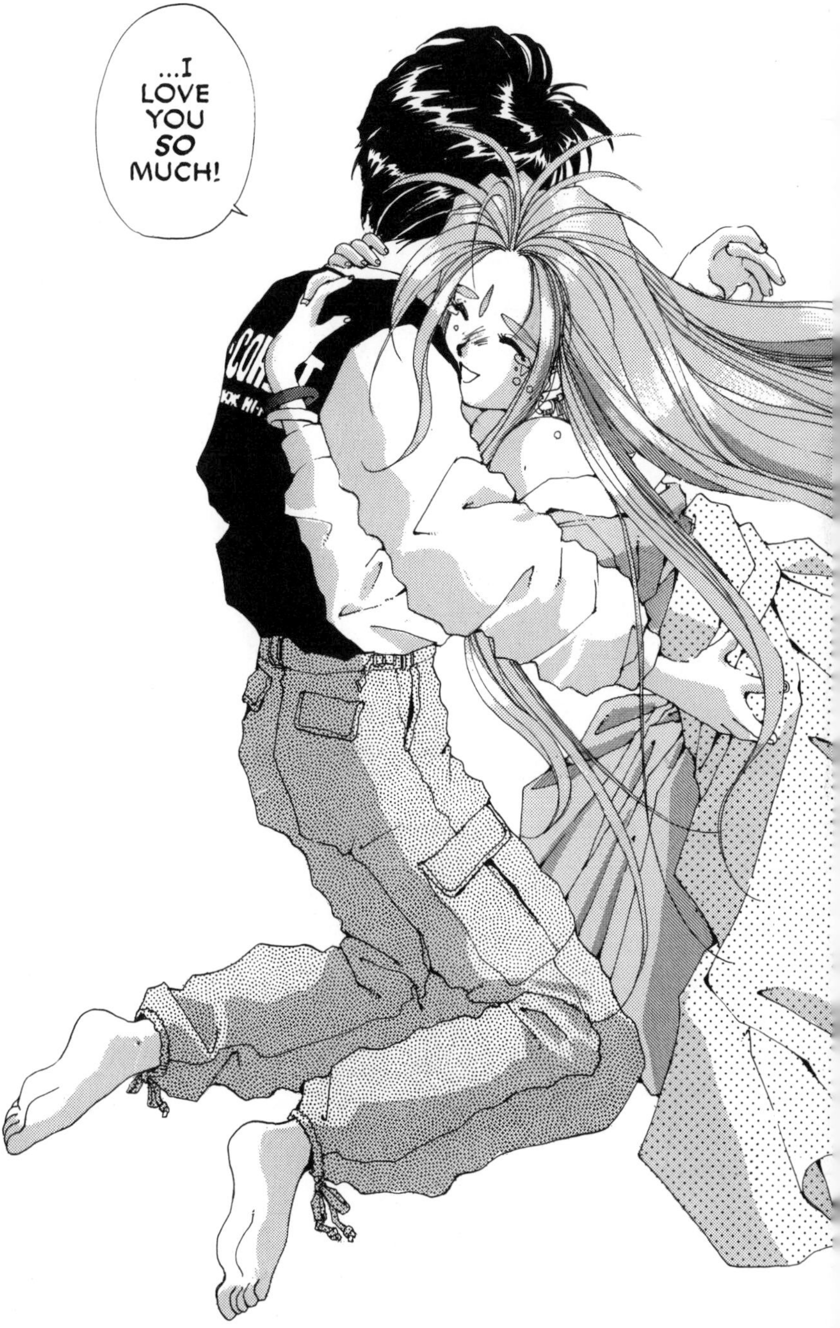
...I LOVE YOU SO MUCH!

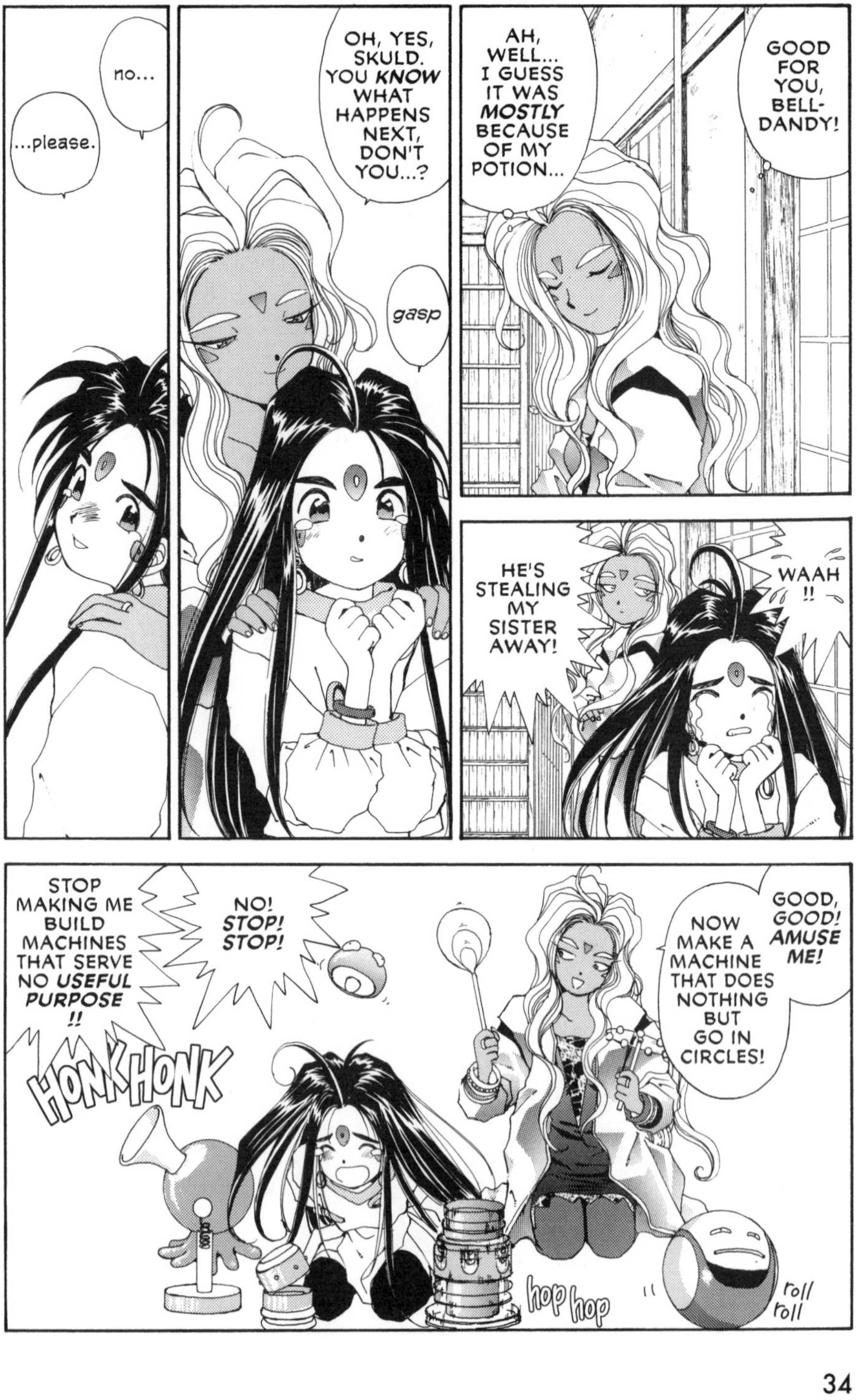
GOOD FOR YOU, BELL-DANDY!
AH, WELL... I GUESS IT WAS MOSTLY BECAUSE OF MY POTION...
WAAH !!
HE'S STEALING MY SISTER AWAY!
OH, YES, SKULD. YOU KNOW WHAT HAPPENS NEXT, DON'T YOU...?
gasp
no...
...please.
GOOD, GOOD! AMUSE ME!
NOW MAKE A MACHINE THAT DOES NOTHING BUT GO IN CIRCLES!
NO! STOP! STOP!
STOP MAKING ME BUILD MACHINES THAT SERVE NO USEFUL PURPOSE !!
HONK HONK
roll roll
hop hop

THE ADVENTURES OF MINI-URD

In the handy PETITE SIZE!

◆ CATCHING RAYS ◆

ssshhhhsssshhh
WHEW... AM I *HOT!*
fwap
I'M HOT ENOUGH TO MELT...
OOOGH... IT FEELS LIKE I REALLY *AM* MELTING...
GLRSSHH
AH?! *AAA!!*
URD! DON'T YOU KNOW IT'S NOT NICE TO MELT PEOPLE?!
ssshhhss
I THOUGHT YOU *WANTED* TO MELT...

◆ A COOL BREEZE IN SUMMER ◆

OH, ALL RIGHT.
I'LL TAKE YOU SOME PLACE NICE AND COOL.
REAL-LY?! YOU *MEAN* IT?!
OOOH... IT'S *TRUE!*
IT'S SO *COOL* IN HERE!
TOLD YA SO!
PARTY ICE
THIRTY MIN-UTES LATER...
Big
AIEEE!!
NOW I'M *FROZEN!!*
THERE'S NO PLEAS-ING SOME PEOPLE.

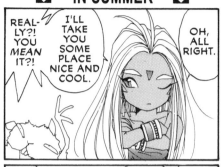

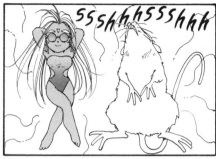

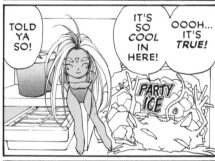

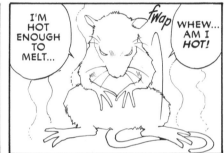

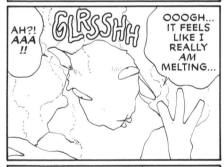

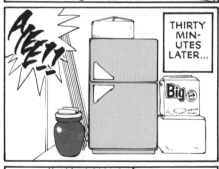

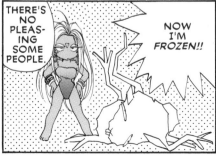

GOLDEN GOURMAND

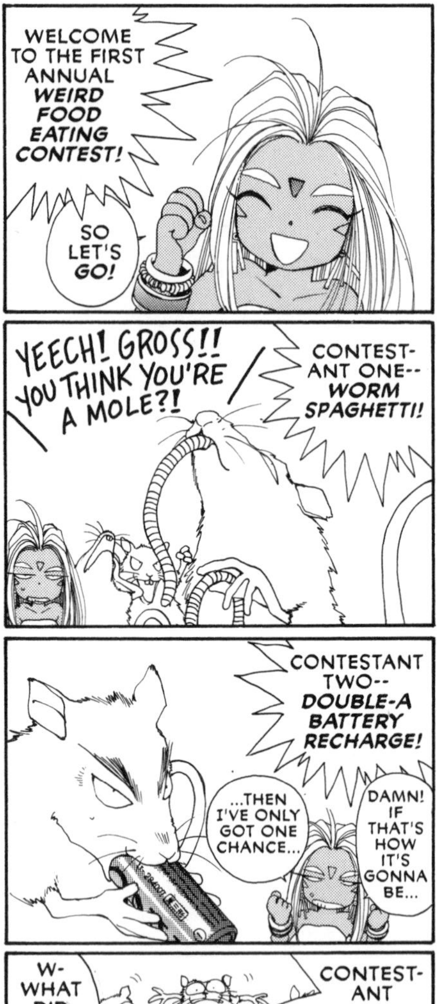
WELCOME TO THE FIRST ANNUAL WEIRD FOOD EATING CONTEST!
SO LET'S GO!
CONTESTANT ONE-- WORM SPAGHETTI!
YEECH! GROSS!! YOU THINK YOU'RE A MOLE?!
CONTESTANT TWO-- DOUBLE-A BATTERY RECHARGE!
DAMN! IF THAT'S HOW IT'S GONNA BE...
...THEN I'VE ONLY GOT ONE CHANCE...
CONTESTANT THREE-- BBQ RAT ON A STICK!
W-WHAT DID YOU SAY ...?!

AMAZING! THE ALL-YOU-CAN-EAT CONTEST!

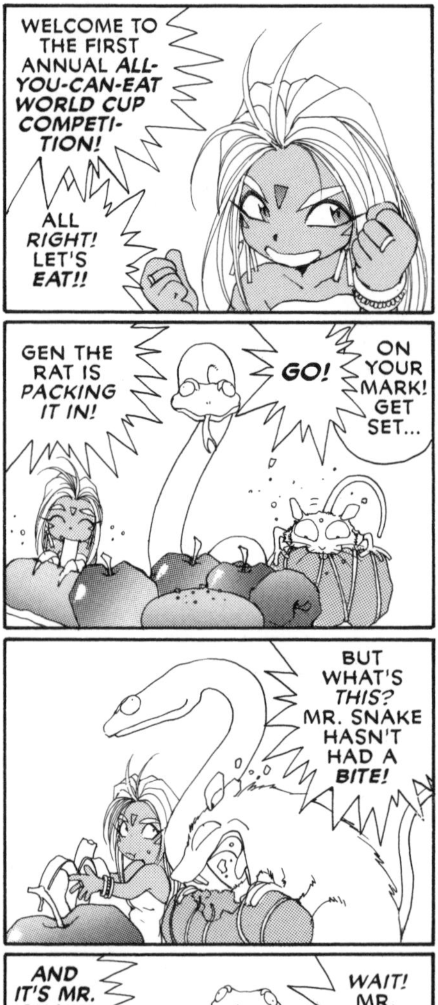
WELCOME TO THE FIRST ANNUAL ALL-YOU-CAN-EAT WORLD CUP COMPETITION!
ALL RIGHT! LET'S EAT!!
ON YOUR MARK! GET SET...
GO!
GEN THE RAT IS PACKING IT IN!
BUT WHAT'S THIS? MR. SNAKE HASN'T HAD A BITE!
WAIT! MR. SNAKE JUST ATE GEN THE RAT!!
AND IT'S MR. SNAKE BY A MILE!!
GEEZ, IT WAS JUST ANOTHER "WEIRD FOOD EATING CONTEST" AFTER ALL...

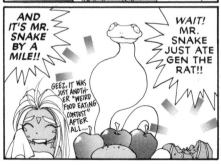

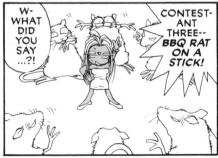

CHAPTER 44

The Queen of Vengeance

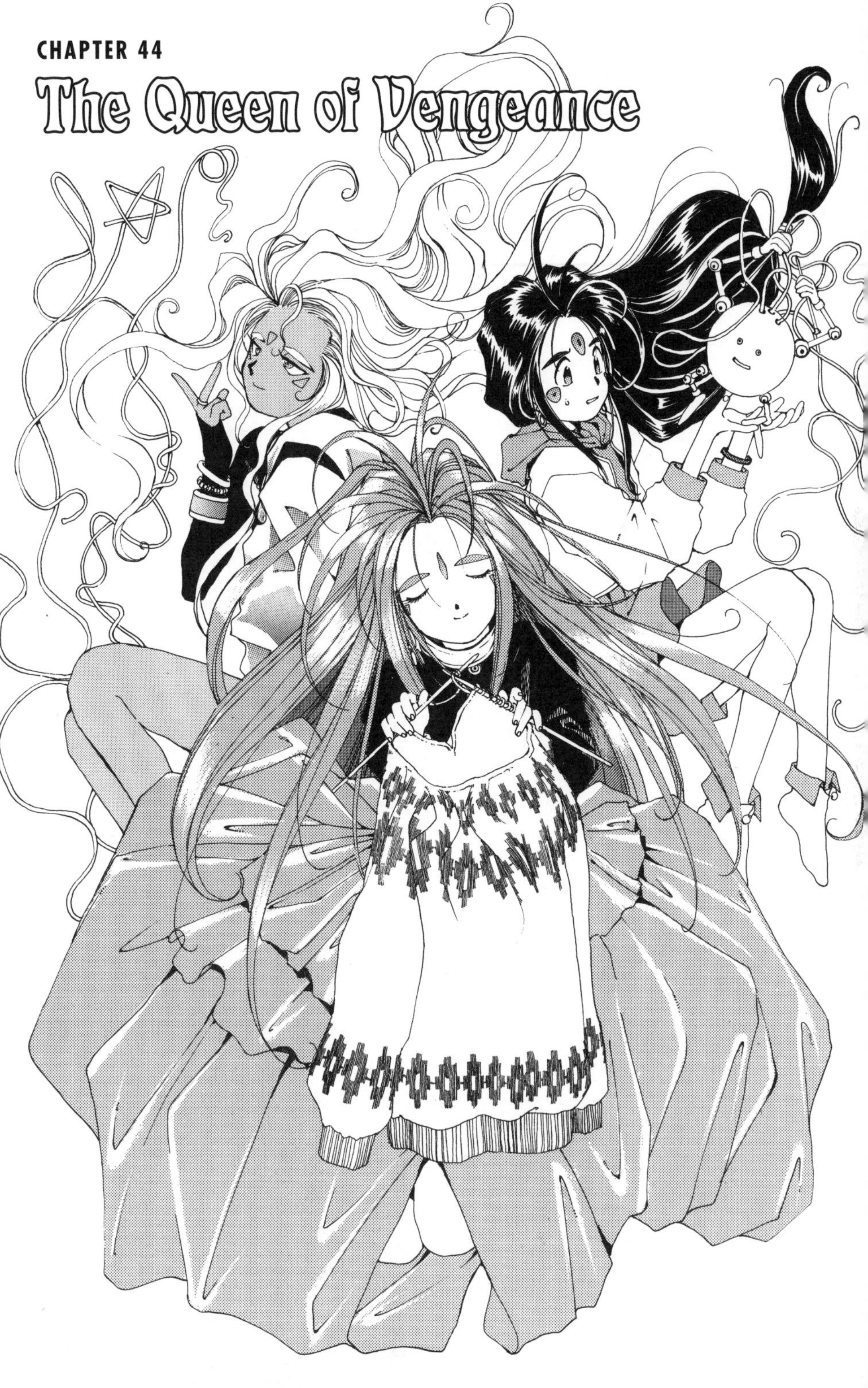

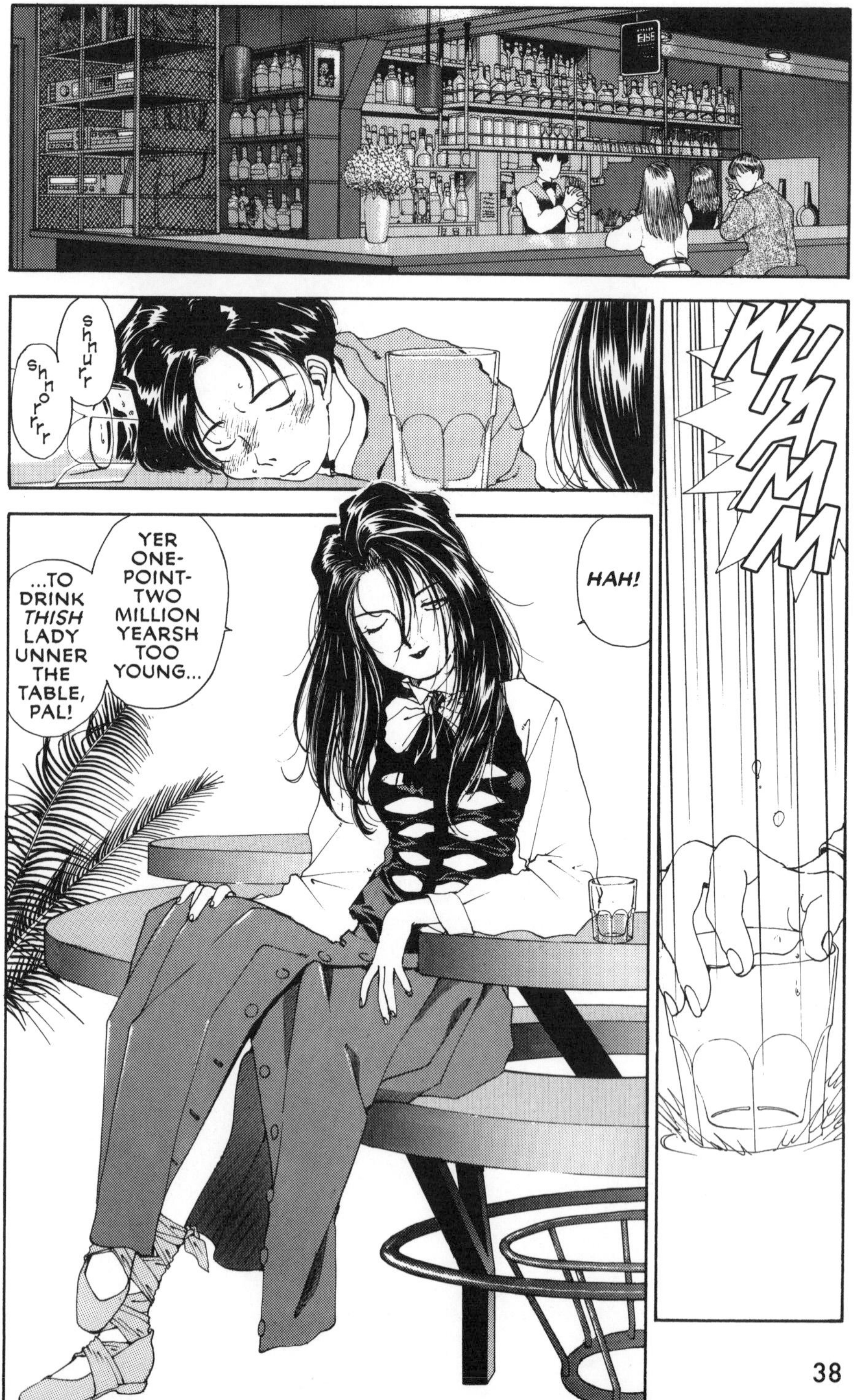
WHAMM
shnurr
shnorrrr
HAH!
YER ONE-POINT-TWO MILLION YEARSH TOO YOUNG...
...TO DRINK *THISH* LADY UNNER THE TABLE, PAL!

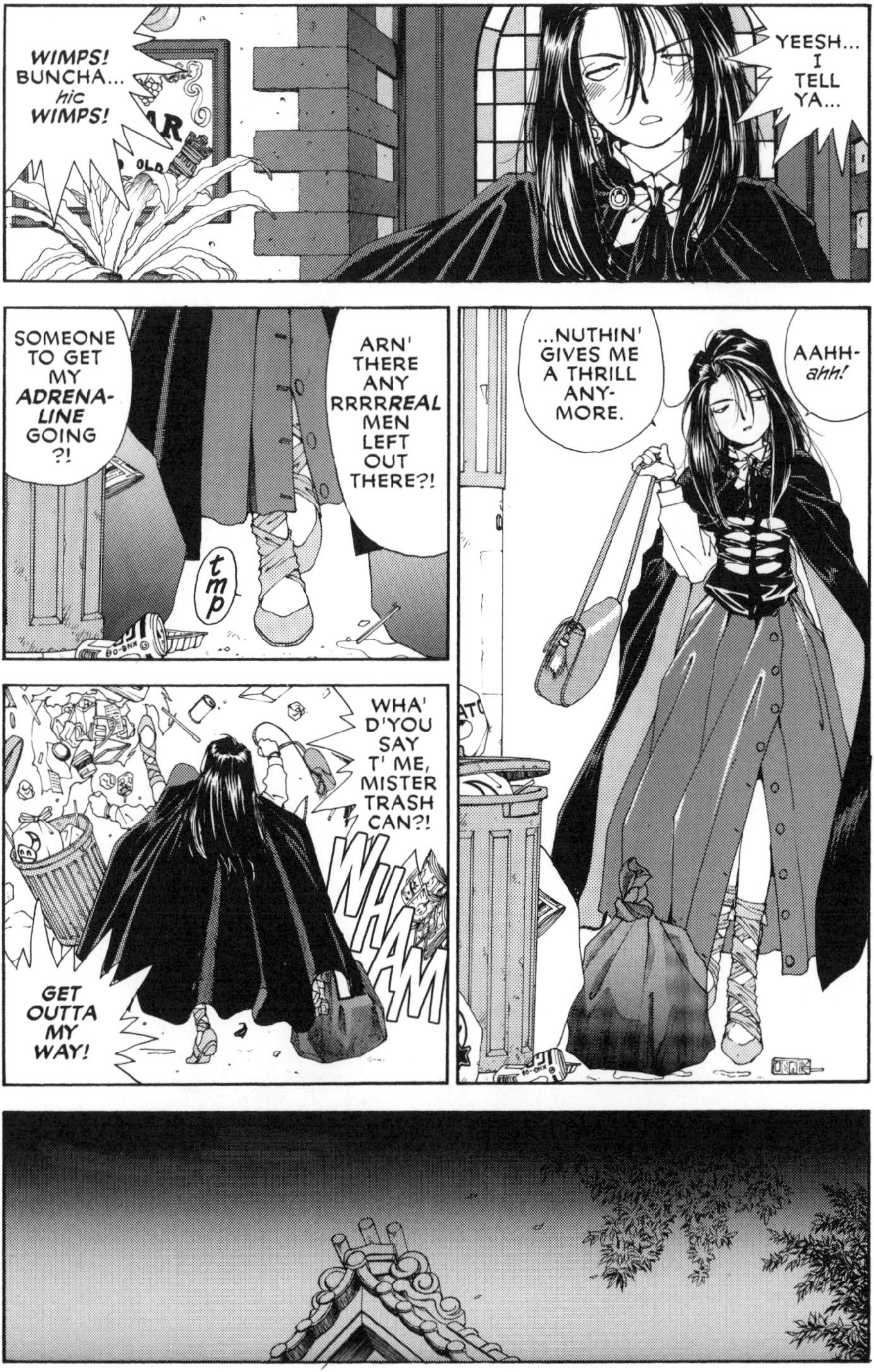
YEESH... I TELL YA...
WIMPS! BUNCHA... hic WIMPS!
AAHH-ahh!
...NUTHIN' GIVES ME A THRILL ANY-MORE.
ARN' THERE ANY RRRRREAL MEN LEFT OUT THERE?!
SOMEONE TO GET MY ADRENA-LINE GOING ?!
tmp
WHA' D'YOU SAY T' ME, MISTER TRASH CAN?!
WHAM
GET OUTTA MY WAY!

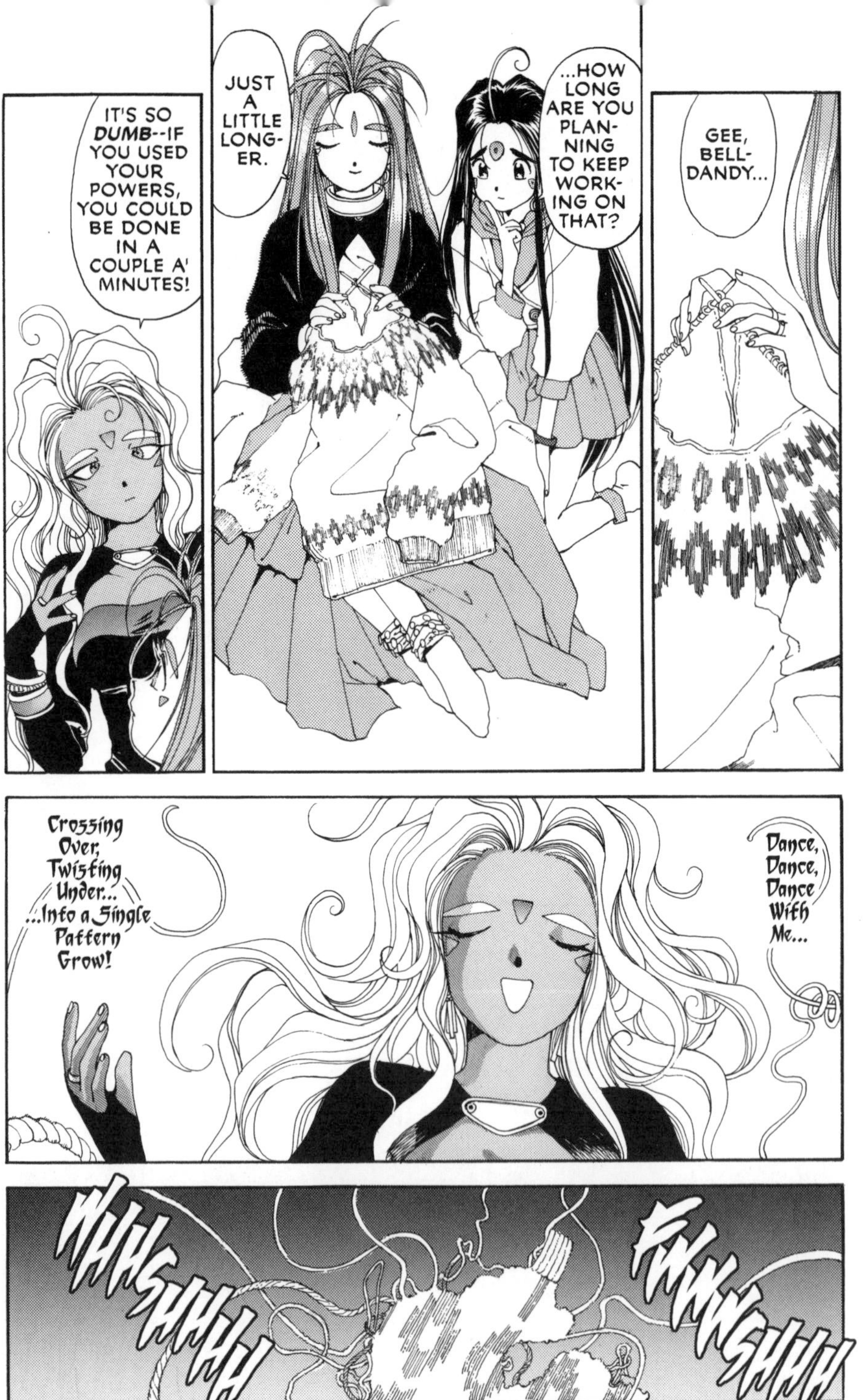
GEE, BELL-DANDY...
...HOW LONG ARE YOU PLAN-NING TO KEEP WORK-ING ON THAT?
JUST A LITTLE LONG-ER.
IT'S SO DUMB--IF YOU USED YOUR POWERS, YOU COULD BE DONE IN A COUPLE A' MINUTES!
Dance, Dance, Dance With Me...
Crossing Over, Twisting Under... ...Into a Single Pattern Grow!
FWWWSHHHH
WHHSHHHHH

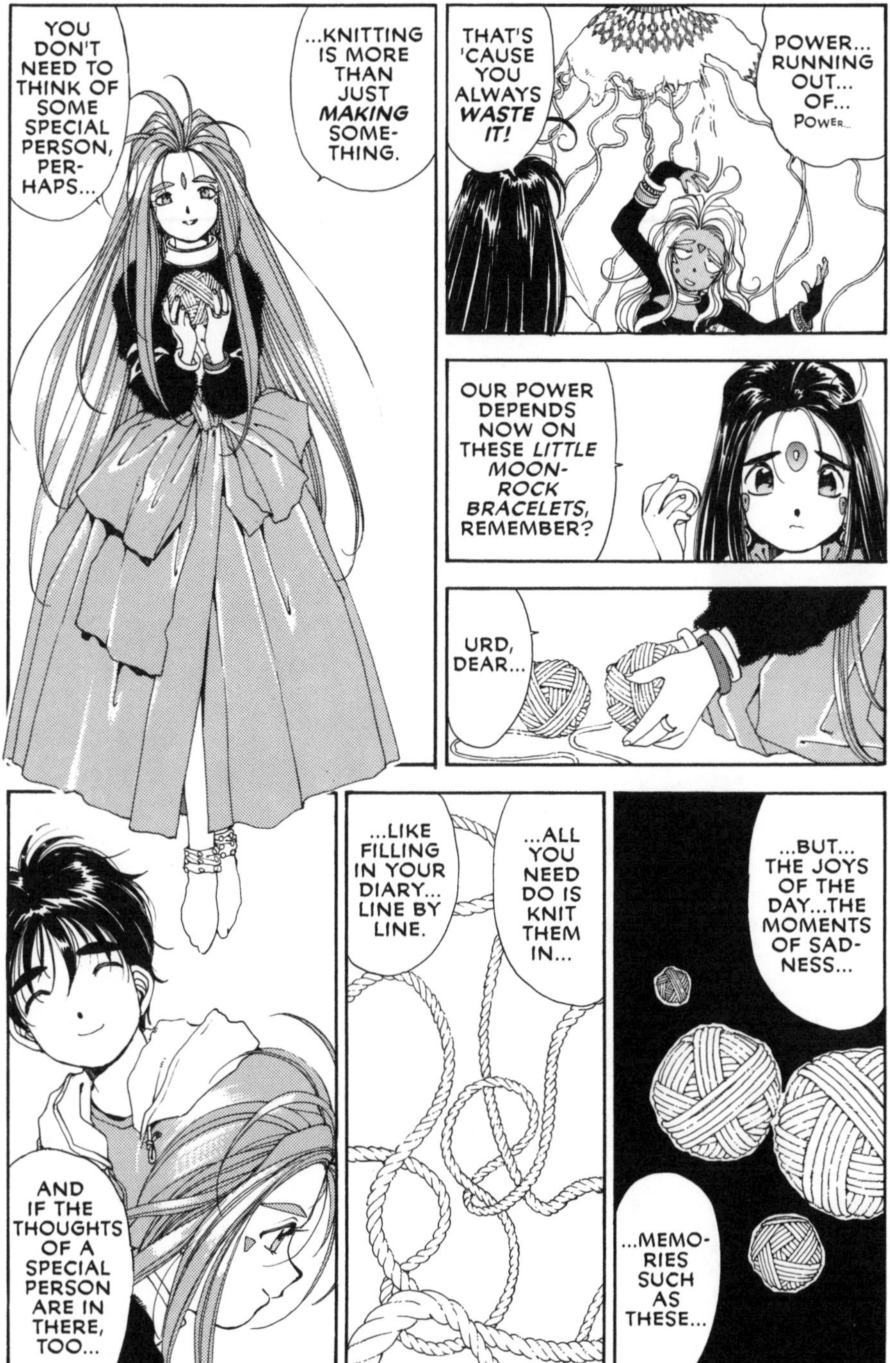
POWER... RUNNING OUT... OF... POWER...
THAT'S 'CAUSE YOU ALWAYS *WASTE IT!*
OUR POWER DEPENDS NOW ON THESE *LITTLE MOON-ROCK BRACELETS*, REMEMBER?
URD, DEAR...
...KNITTING IS MORE THAN JUST *MAKING* SOME-THING.
YOU DON'T NEED TO THINK OF SOME SPECIAL PERSON, PER-HAPS...
...BUT... THE JOYS OF THE DAY...THE MOMENTS OF SAD-NESS...
...MEMO-RIES SUCH AS THESE...
...ALL YOU NEED DO IS KNIT THEM IN...
...LIKE FILLING IN YOUR DIARY... LINE BY LINE.
AND IF THE THOUGHTS OF A SPECIAL PERSON ARE IN THERE, TOO...

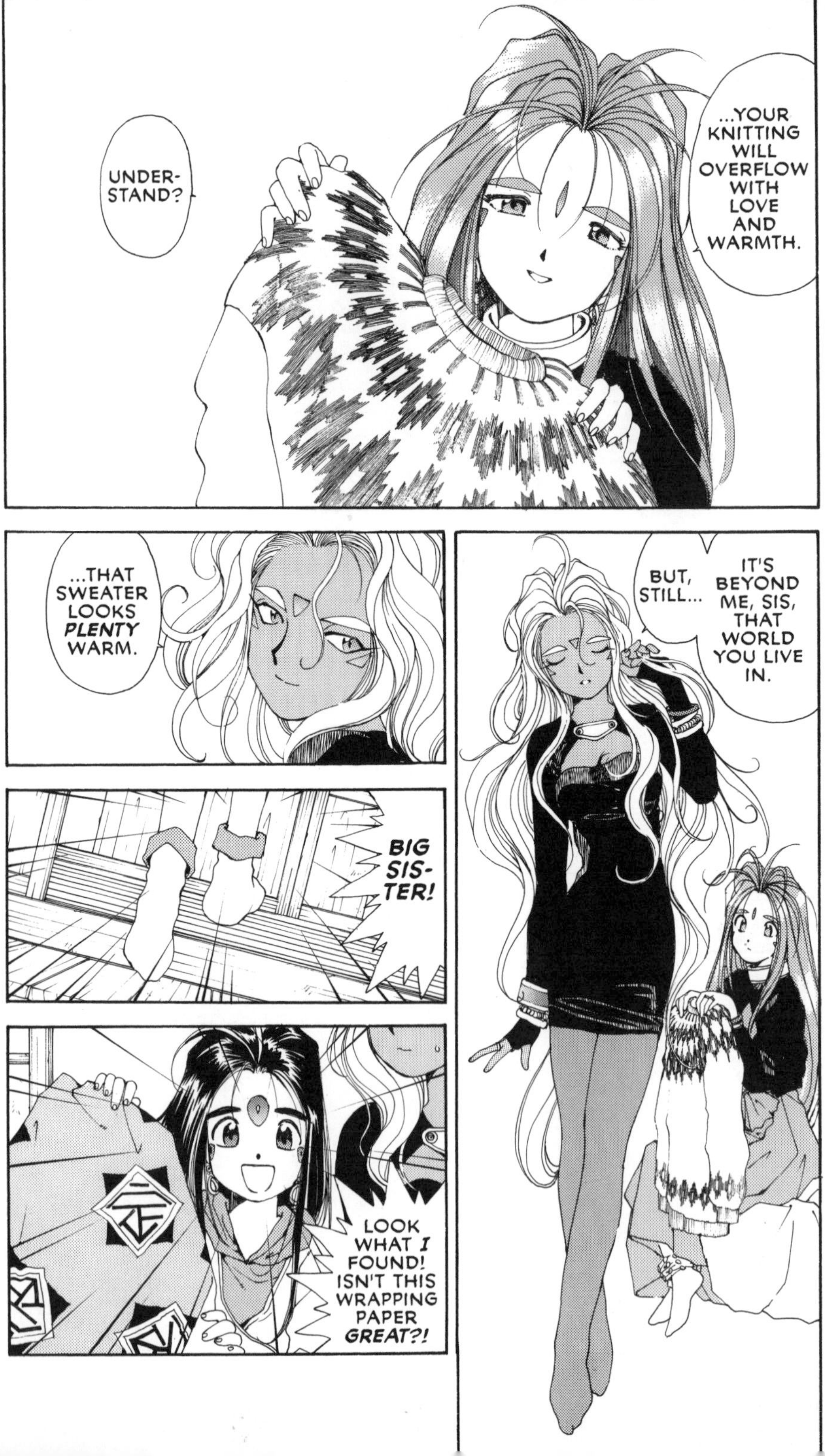
...YOUR KNITTING WILL OVERFLOW WITH LOVE AND WARMTH.
UNDER-STAND?
IT'S BEYOND ME, SIS, THAT WORLD YOU LIVE IN.
BUT, STILL...
...THAT SWEATER LOOKS *PLENTY* WARM.
BIG SIS-TER!
LOOK WHAT *I* FOUND! ISN'T THIS WRAPPING PAPER *GREAT?!*

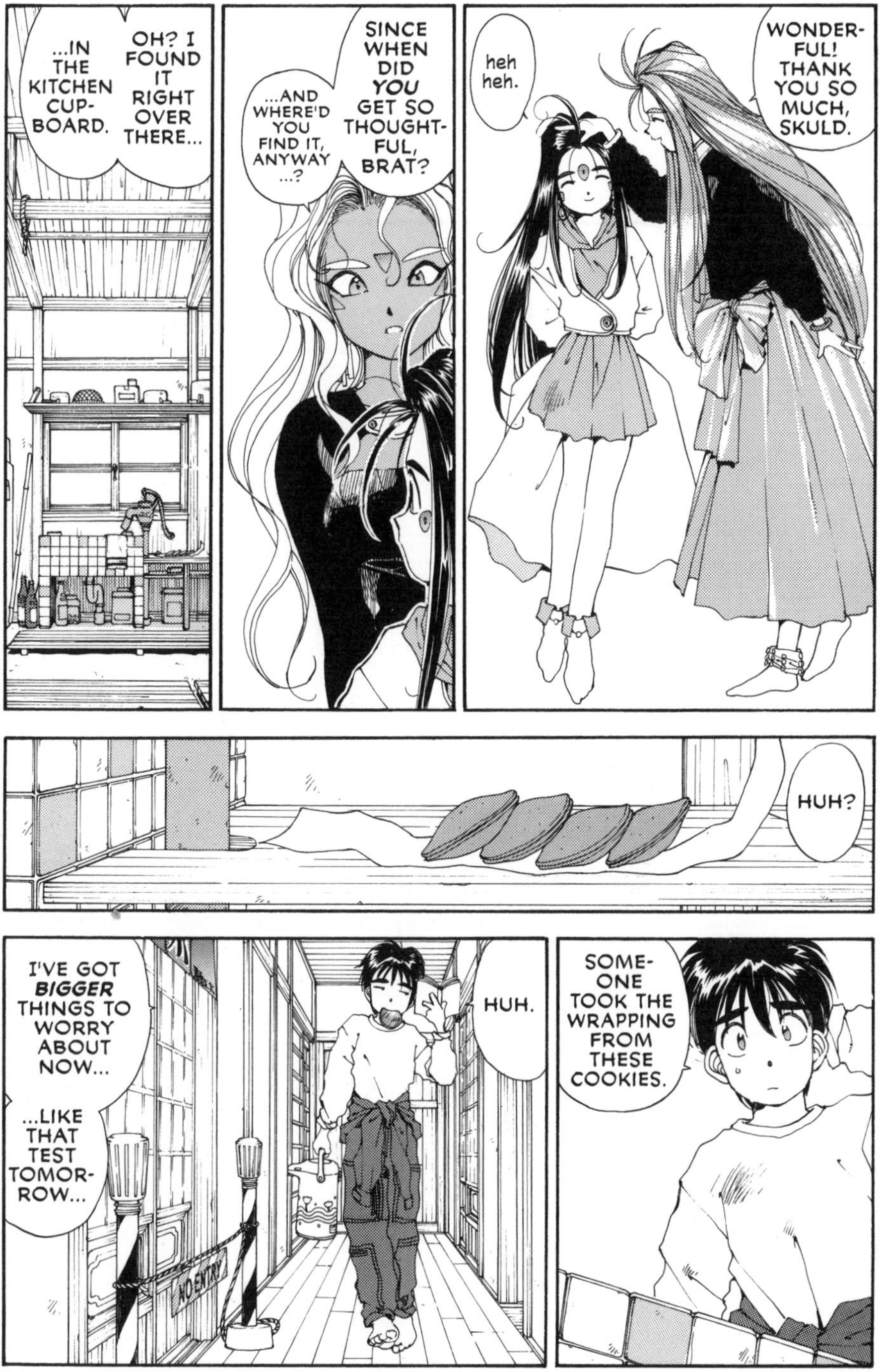
WONDERFUL! THANK YOU SO MUCH, SKULD.
heh heh.
SINCE WHEN DID *YOU* GET SO THOUGHTFUL, BRAT?
...AND WHERE'D YOU FIND IT, ANYWAY...?
OH? I FOUND IT RIGHT OVER THERE...
...IN THE KITCHEN CUPBOARD.
HUH?
SOMEONE TOOK THE WRAPPING FROM THESE COOKIES.
HUH.
I'VE GOT **BIGGER** THINGS TO WORRY ABOUT NOW...
...LIKE THAT TEST TOMORROW...
NO ENTRY

BONGGG
THIS ISN'T GOING TO HELP ME STUDY.
BONGG
WIMPS! WIMPS!!
HA HA HA (HIC) HA!!
BONNGGG

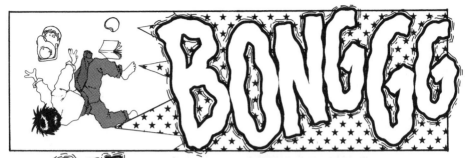

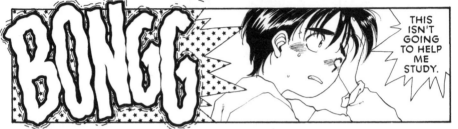

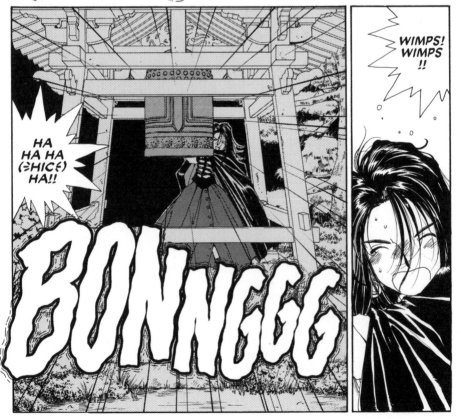

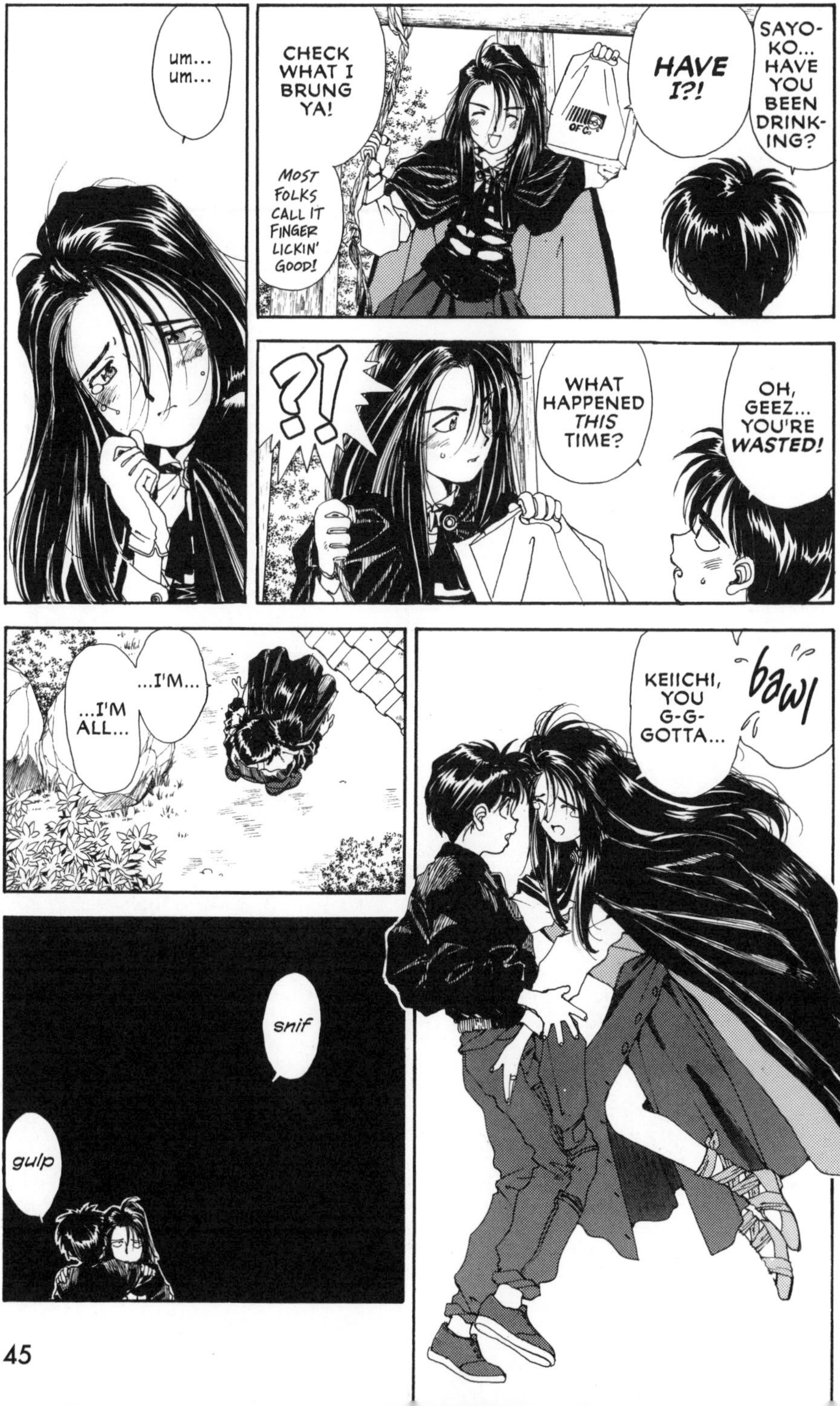
SAYO-KO... HAVE YOU BEEN DRINK-ING?
HAVE I?!
CHECK WHAT I BRUNG YA!
MOST FOLKS CALL IT FINGER LICKIN' GOOD!
OH, GEEZ... YOU'RE WASTED!
WHAT HAPPENED THIS TIME?
?!
um... um...
KEIICHI, YOU G-G-GOTTA...
bawl
...I'M...
...I'M ALL...
snif
gulp

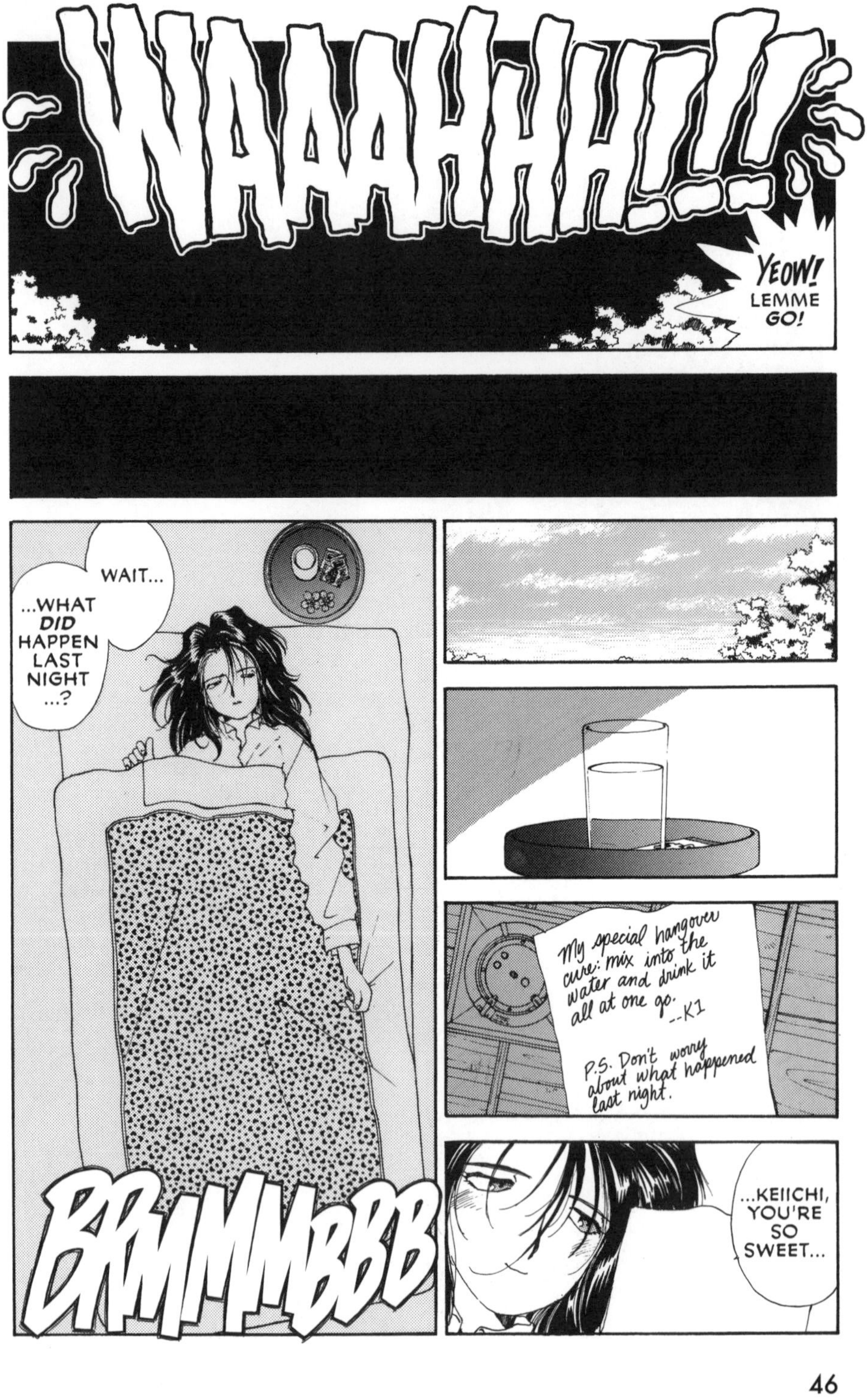
WAAAHHH!!!
YEOW! LEMME GO!
My special hangover cure: mix into the water and drink it all at one go.
--K1
P.S. Don't worry about what happened last night.
...KEIICHI, YOU'RE SO SWEET...
WAIT...
...WHAT DID HAPPEN LAST NIGHT ...?
BRMMMBBB

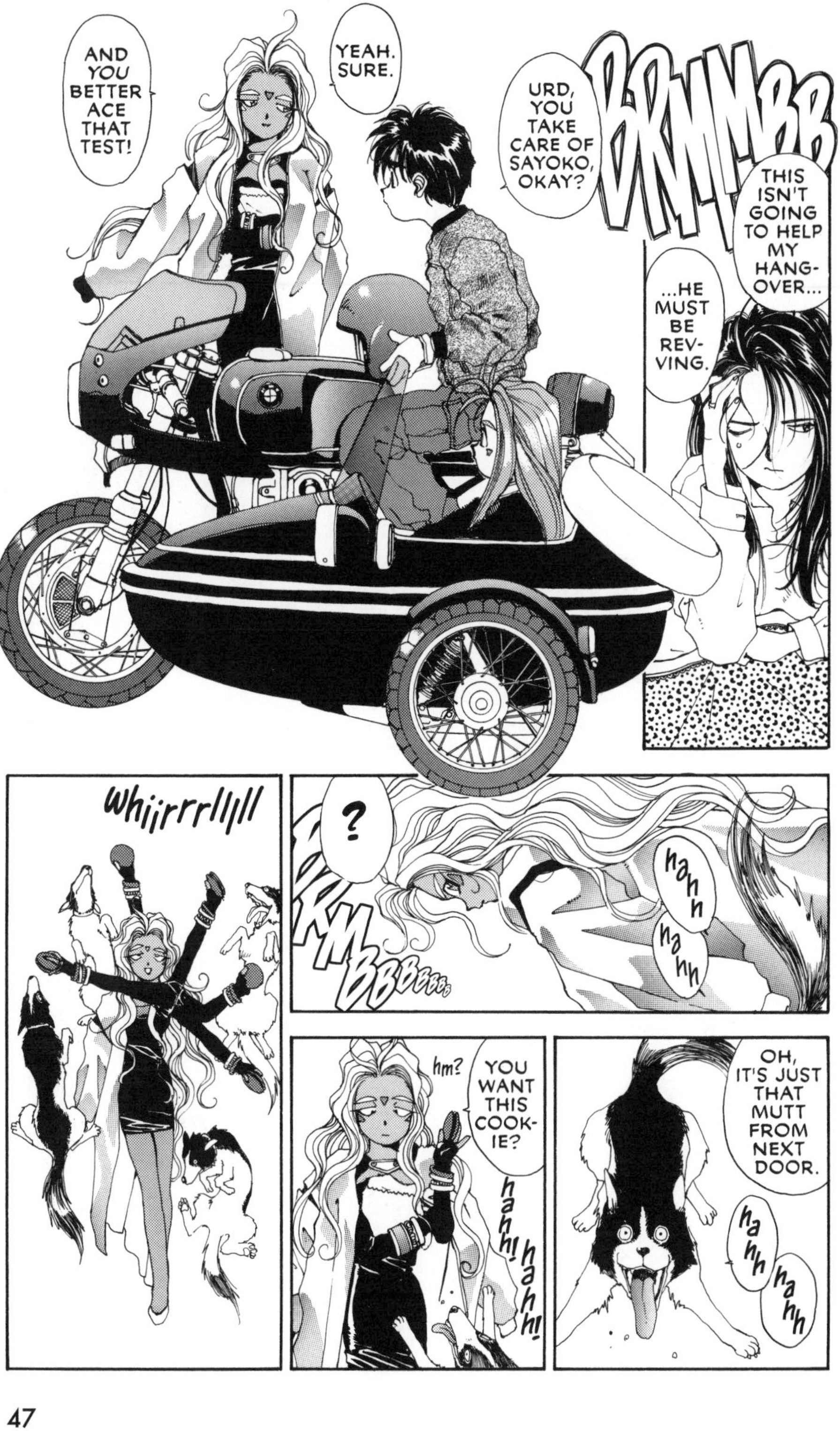
URD, YOU TAKE CARE OF SAYOKO, OKAY?
YEAH. SURE.
AND YOU BETTER ACE THAT TEST!
BRMMBB
THIS ISN'T GOING TO HELP MY HANG-OVER...
...HE MUST BE REV-VING.
?
hanh
hanh
OH, IT'S JUST THAT MUTT FROM NEXT DOOR.
hanh
hanh
hm?
YOU WANT THIS COOK-IE?
hanh!
hanh!
whiirrrlllll

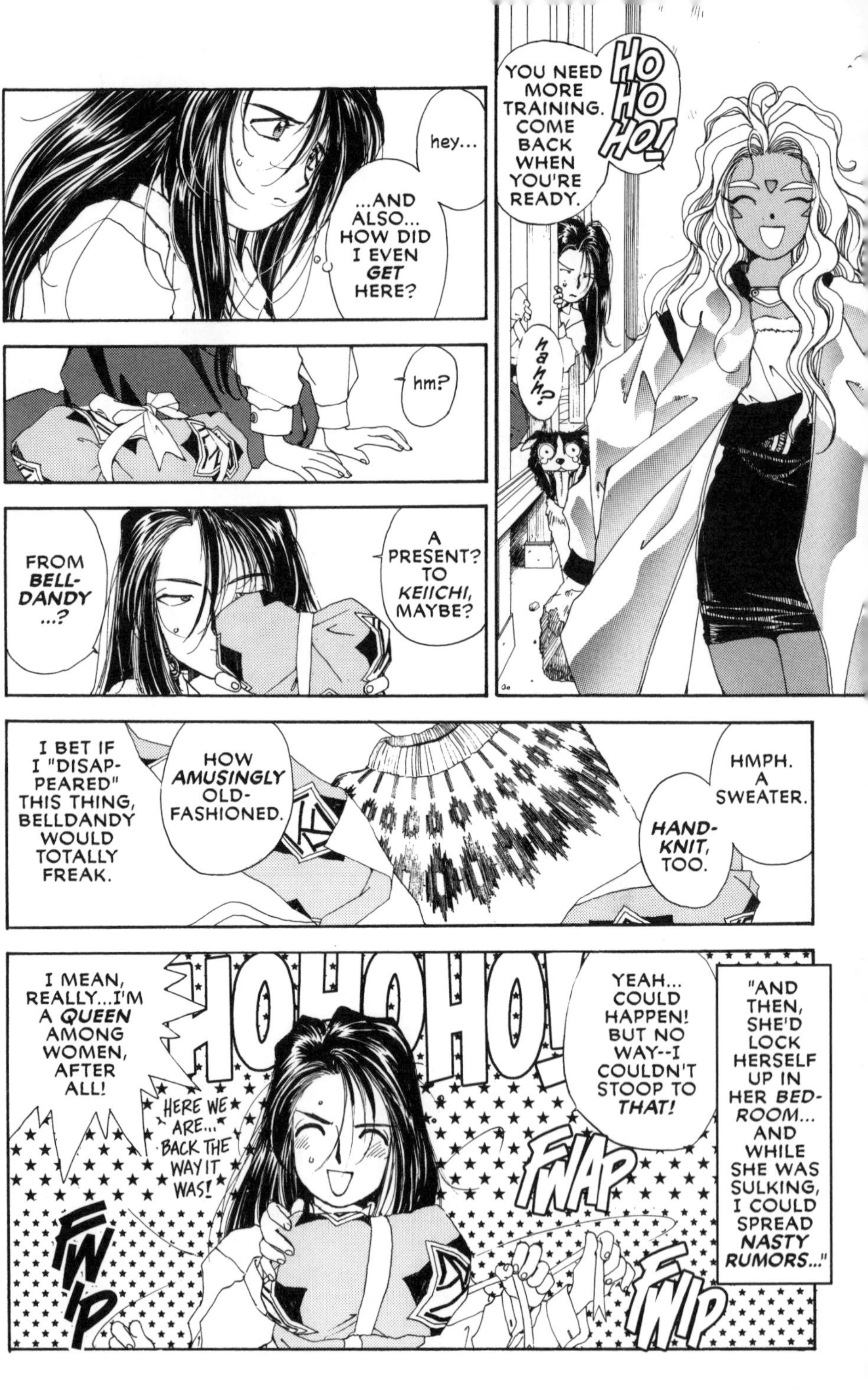
HO HO HO!
YOU NEED MORE TRAINING. COME BACK WHEN YOU'RE READY.
hahh?
hey...
...AND ALSO... HOW DID I EVEN *GET* HERE?
hm?
A PRESENT? TO *KEIICHI*, MAYBE?
FROM *BELL-DANDY* ...?
HMPH. A SWEATER.
HAND-KNIT, TOO.
HOW *AMUSINGLY* OLD-FASHIONED.
I BET IF I "DISAP-PEARED" THIS THING, BELLDANDY WOULD TOTALLY FREAK.
"AND THEN, SHE'D LOCK HERSELF UP IN HER *BED-ROOM*... AND WHILE SHE WAS SULKING, I COULD SPREAD *NASTY RUMORS*..."
YEAH... COULD HAPPEN! BUT NO WAY--I COULDN'T STOOP TO *THAT!*
HOHOHO
I MEAN, REALLY...I'M A *QUEEN* AMONG WOMEN, AFTER ALL!
HERE WE ARE... BACK THE WAY IT WAS!
FWAP
FWIP
FWIP

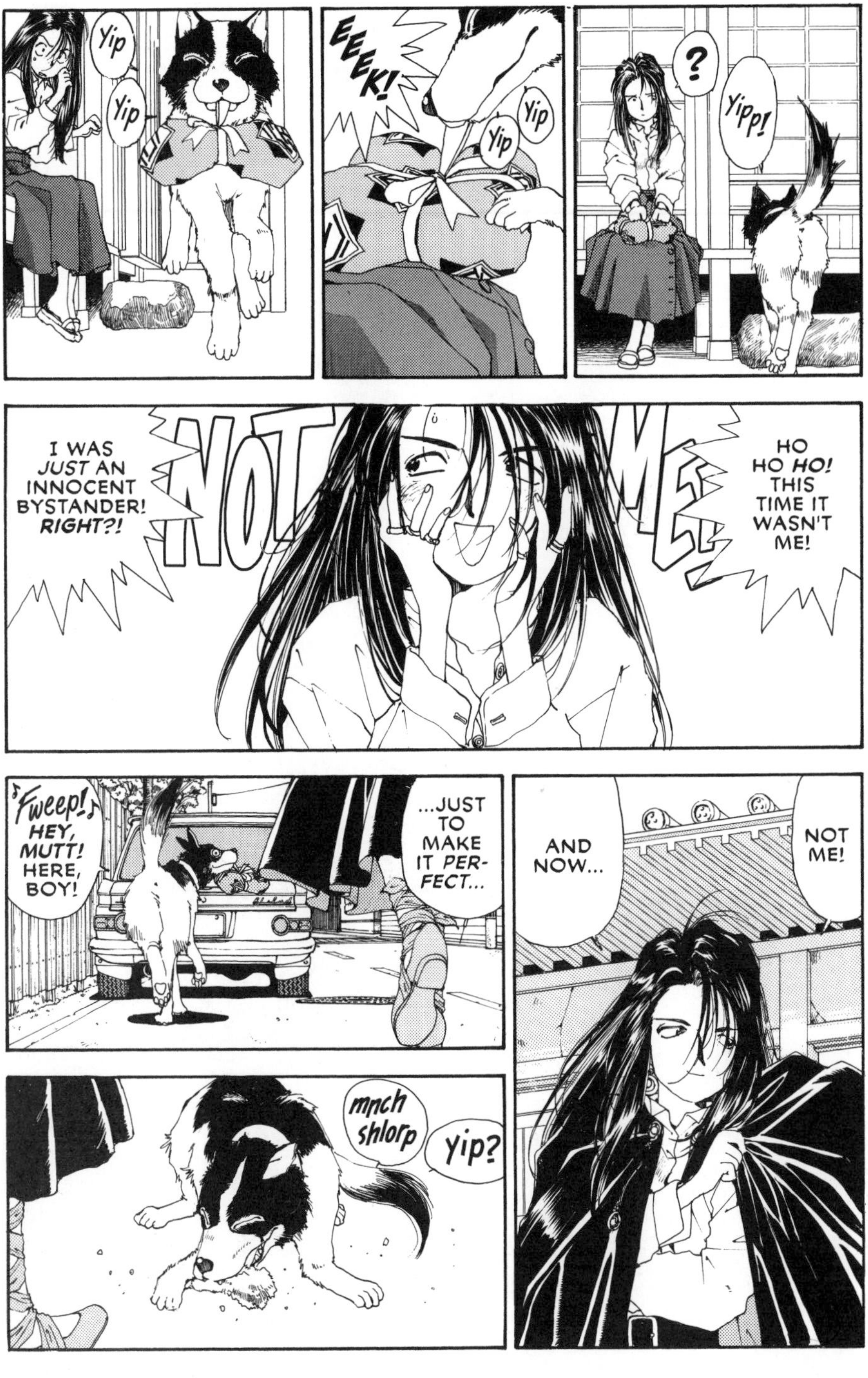
?
Yipp!
EEEK!
Yip
Yip
Yip
Yip
HO HO HO! THIS TIME IT WASN'T ME!
NOT
ME
I WAS JUST AN INNOCENT BYSTANDER! RIGHT?!
NOT ME!
AND NOW...
...JUST TO MAKE IT PERFECT...
Fweep!
HEY, MUTT! HERE, BOY!
mnch shlorp
yip?

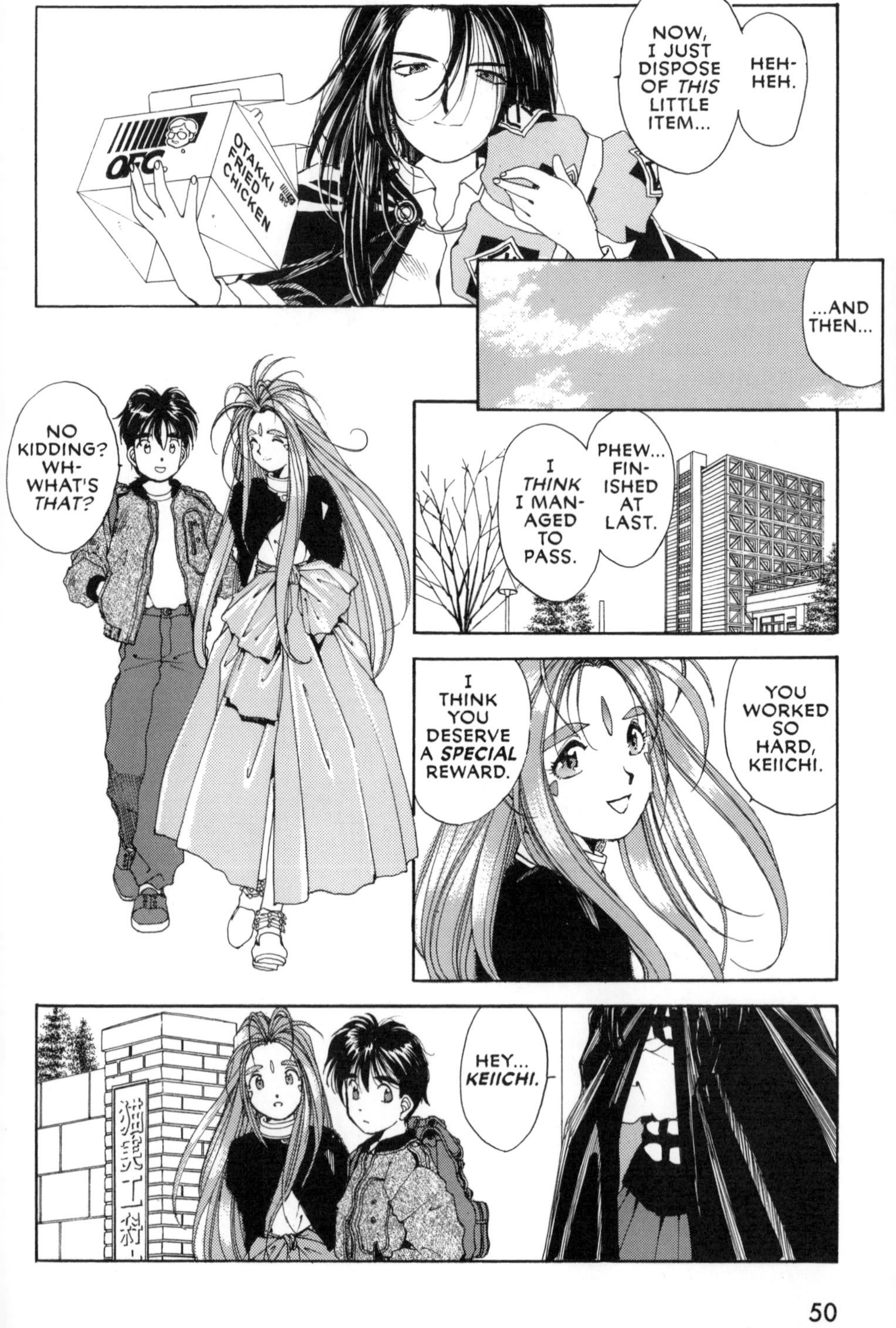
OTAKKI FRIED CHICKEN
OFC
HEH-HEH.
NOW, I JUST DISPOSE OF *THIS* LITTLE ITEM...
...AND THEN...
PHEW... FINISHED AT LAST.
I *THINK* I MANAGED TO PASS.
YOU WORKED SO HARD, KEIICHI.
I THINK YOU DESERVE A *SPECIAL* REWARD.
NO KIDDING? WH-WHAT'S *THAT?*
HEY... ***KEIICHI.***

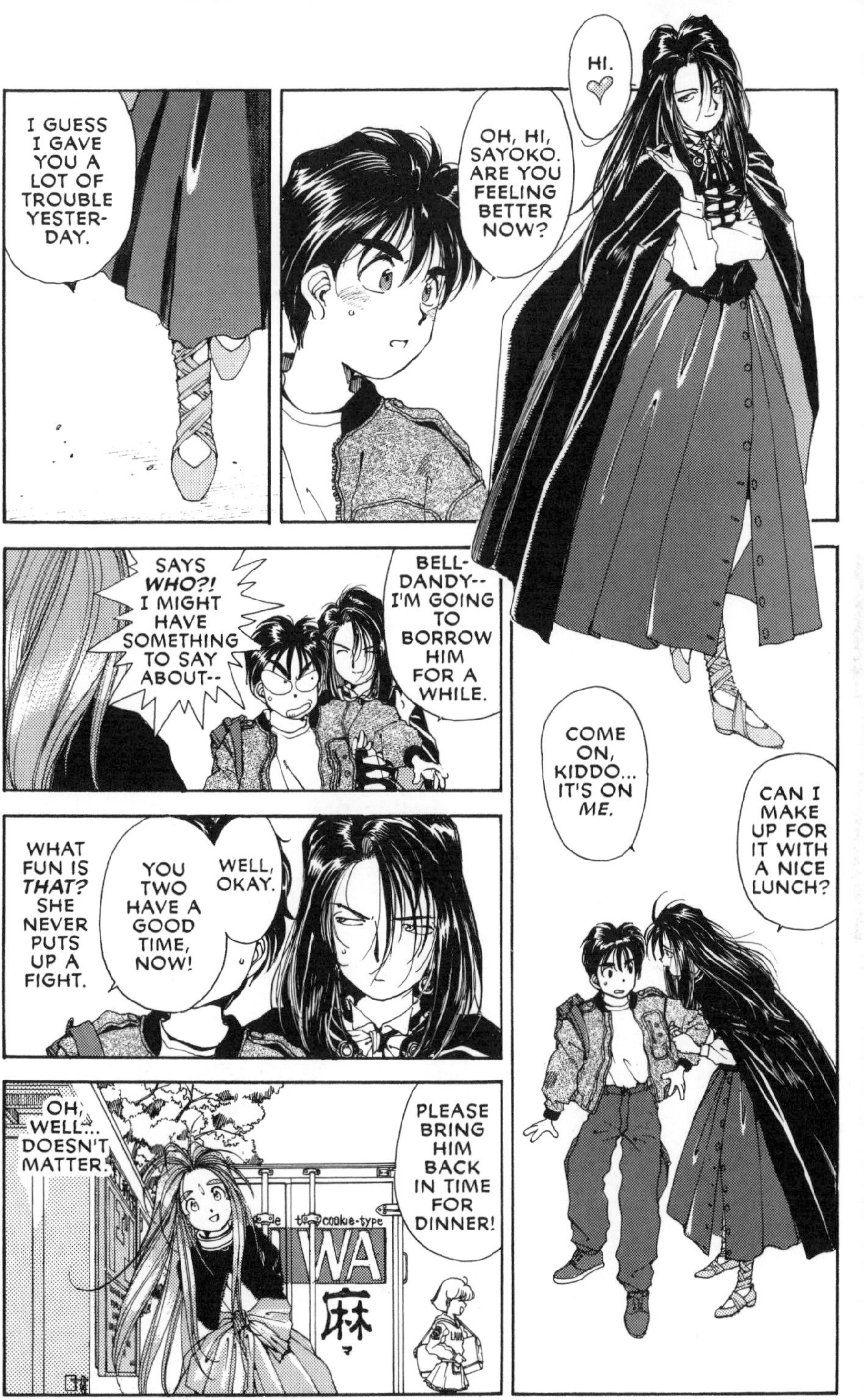
HI. ♥
OH, HI, SAYOKO. ARE YOU FEELING BETTER NOW?
I GUESS I GAVE YOU A LOT OF TROUBLE YESTER-DAY.
CAN I MAKE UP FOR IT WITH A NICE LUNCH?
COME ON, KIDDO... IT'S ON *ME.*
BELL-DANDY-- I'M GOING TO BORROW HIM FOR A WHILE.
SAYS ***WHO?!*** I MIGHT HAVE SOMETHING TO SAY ABOUT--
WELL, OKAY.
YOU TWO HAVE A GOOD TIME, NOW!
WHAT FUN IS ***THAT?*** SHE NEVER PUTS UP A FIGHT.
PLEASE BRING HIM BACK IN TIME FOR DINNER!
cookie-type
WA
麻
OH, WELL... DOESN'T MATTER.

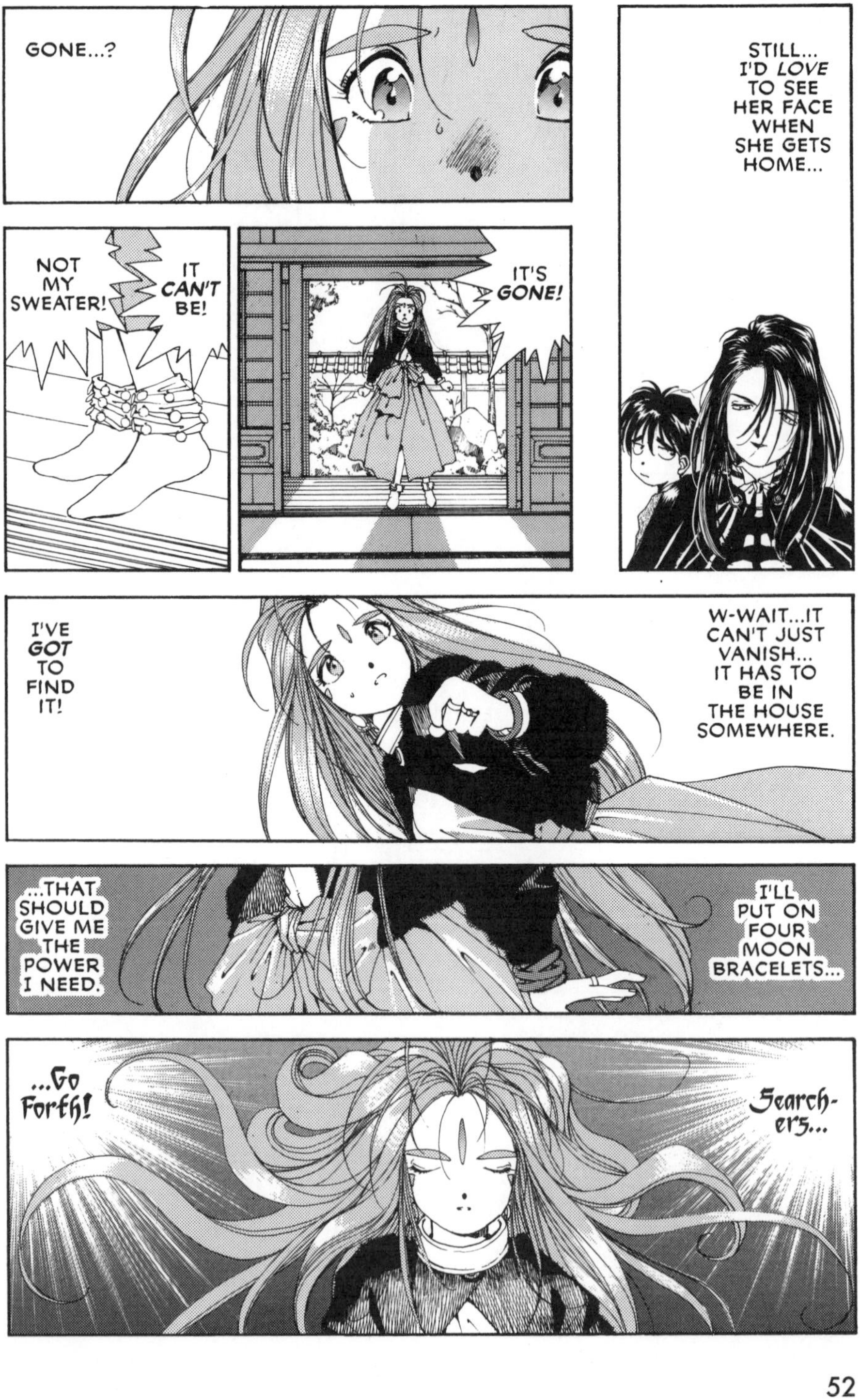
STILL... I'D LOVE TO SEE HER FACE WHEN SHE GETS HOME...
GONE...?
IT'S GONE!
IT CAN'T BE!
NOT MY SWEATER!
W-WAIT...IT CAN'T JUST VANISH... IT HAS TO BE IN THE HOUSE SOMEWHERE.
I'VE GOT TO FIND IT!
I'LL PUT ON FOUR MOON BRACELETS...
...THAT SHOULD GIVE ME THE POWER I NEED.
Searchers...
...Go Forth!

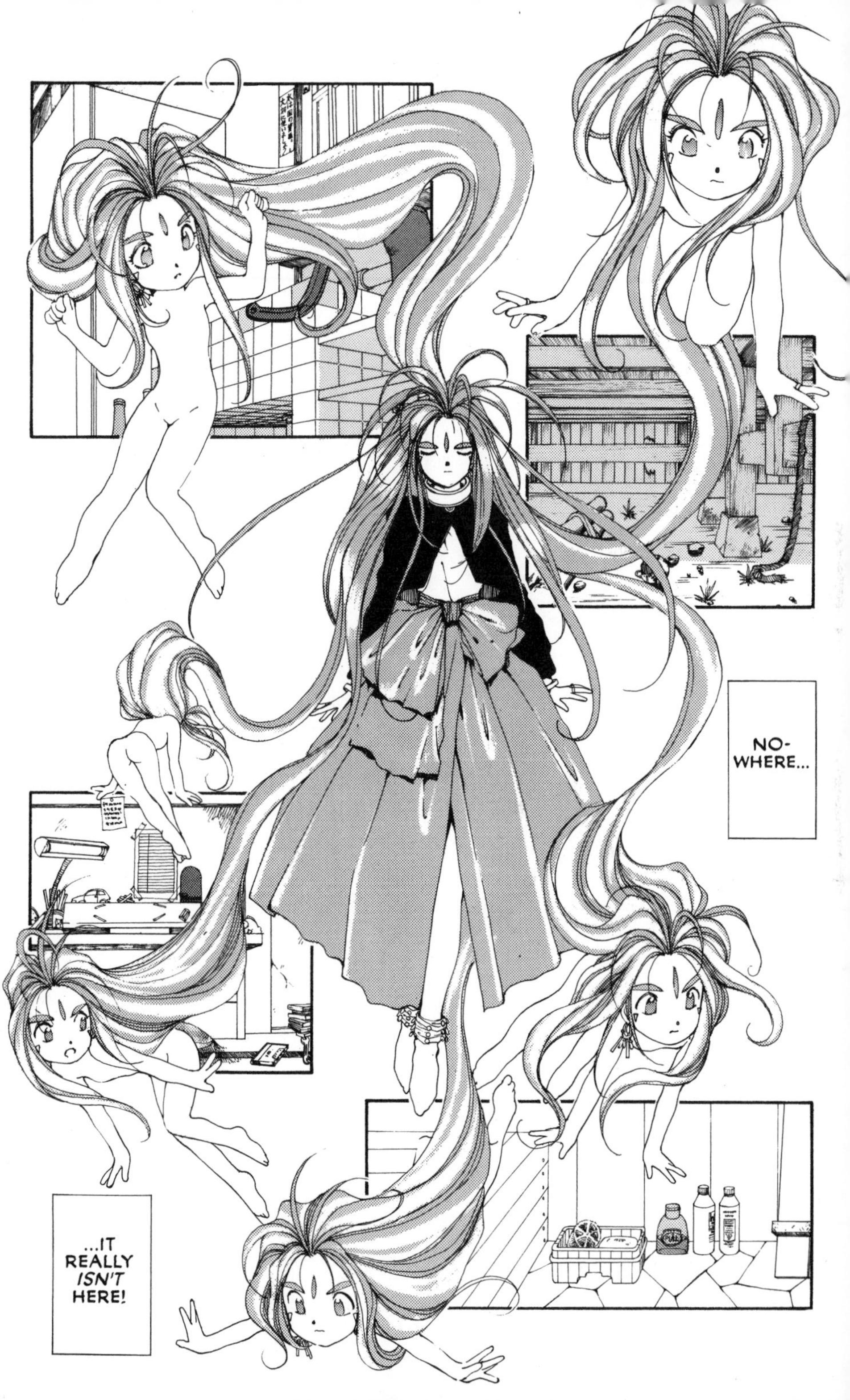
NO-WHERE...
...IT REALLY *ISN'T* HERE!

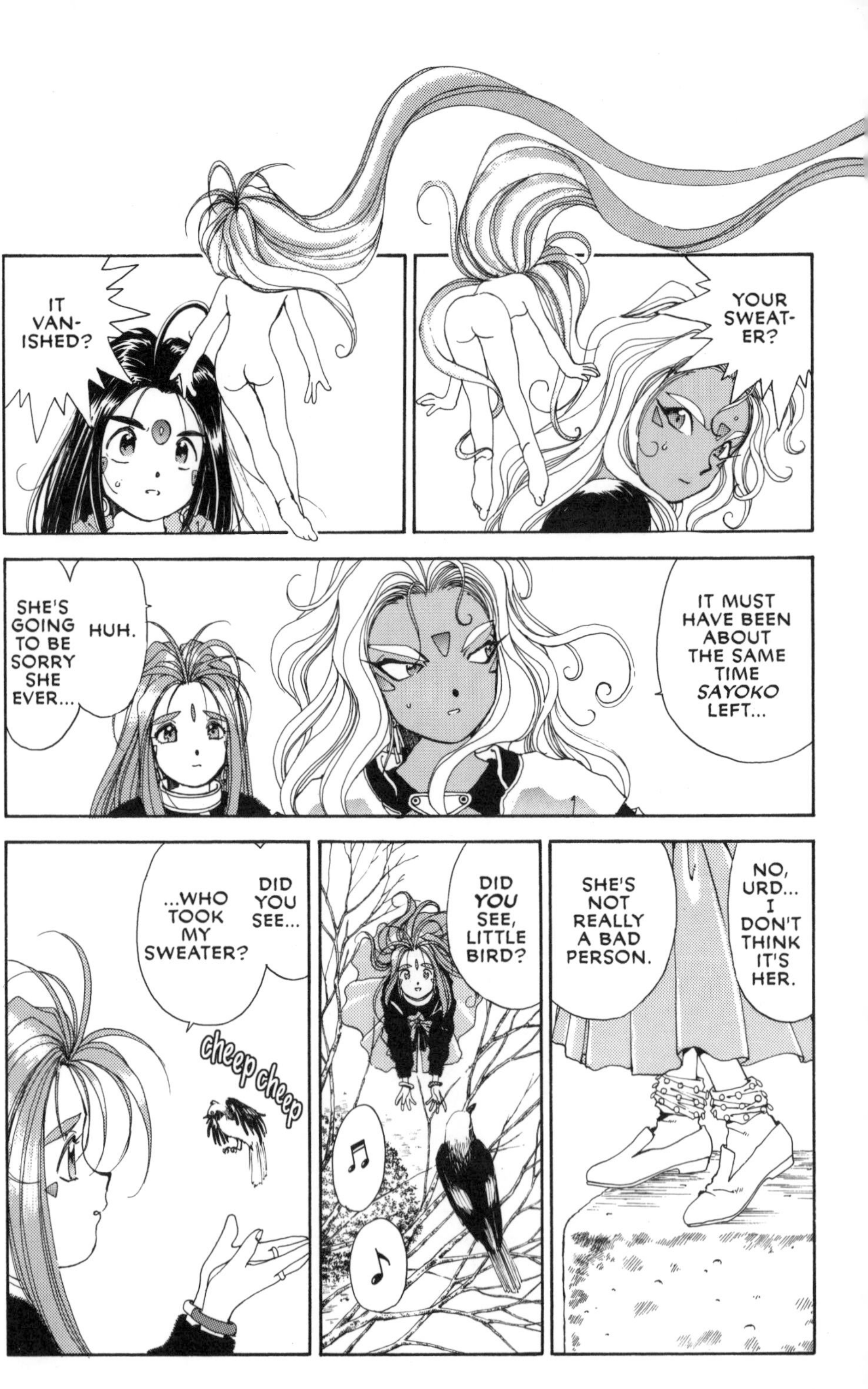
YOUR SWEATER?
IT VANISHED?
IT MUST HAVE BEEN ABOUT THE SAME TIME SAYOKO LEFT...
HUH.
SHE'S GOING TO BE SORRY SHE EVER...
NO, URD... I DON'T THINK IT'S HER.
SHE'S NOT REALLY A BAD PERSON.
DID YOU SEE, LITTLE BIRD?
DID YOU SEE...
...WHO TOOK MY SWEATER?
cheep cheep

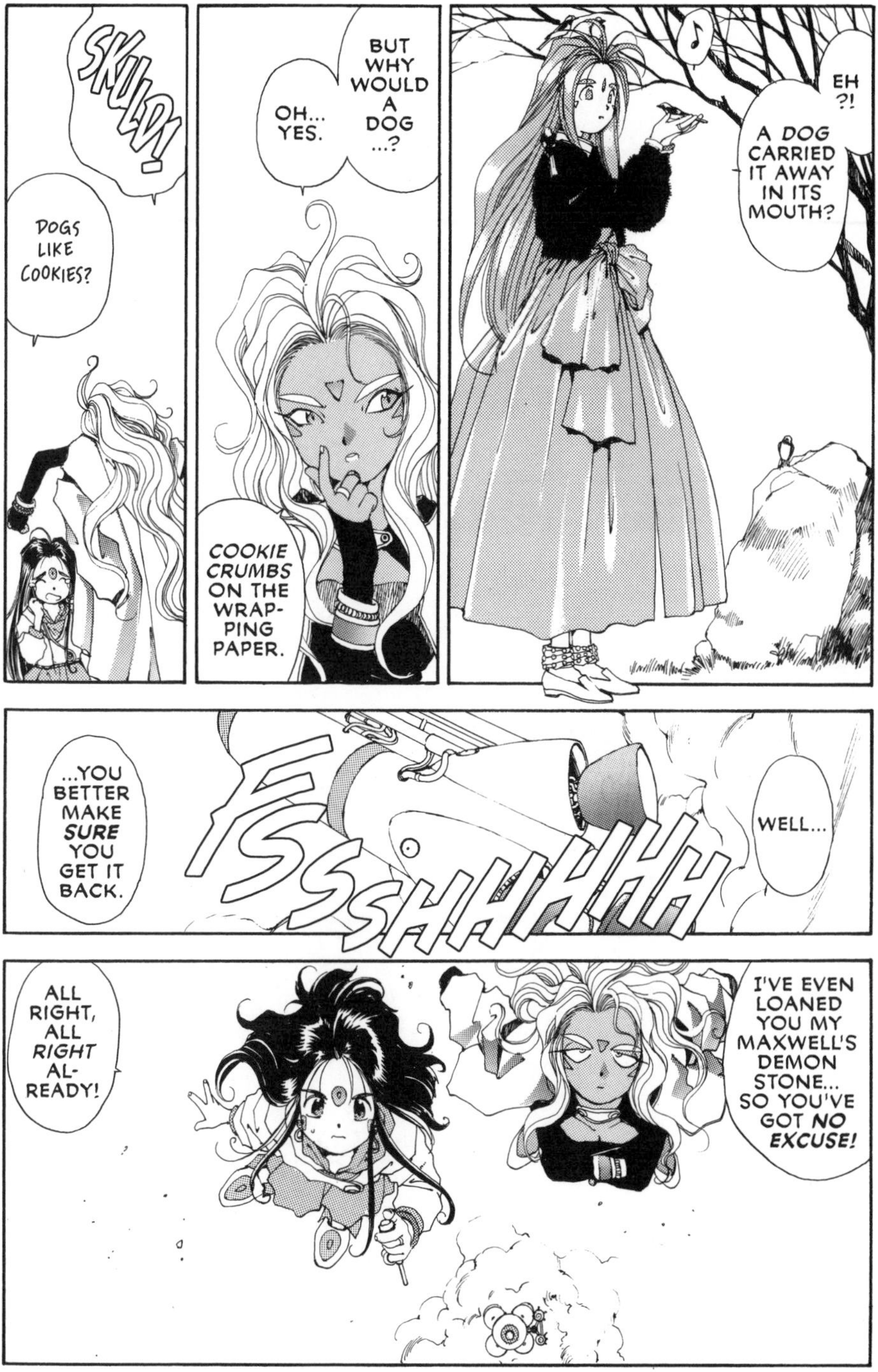
♪
EH ?!
A *DOG* CARRIED IT AWAY IN ITS MOUTH?
BUT WHY WOULD A DOG ...?
OH... YES.
COOKIE CRUMBS ON THE WRAP-PING PAPER.
SKULD!
DOGS LIKE COOKIES?
WELL...
FSSSHHHHHH
...YOU BETTER MAKE *SURE* YOU GET IT BACK.
I'VE EVEN LOANED YOU MY MAXWELL'S DEMON STONE... SO YOU'VE GOT *NO EXCUSE!*
ALL RIGHT, ALL *RIGHT* AL-READY!

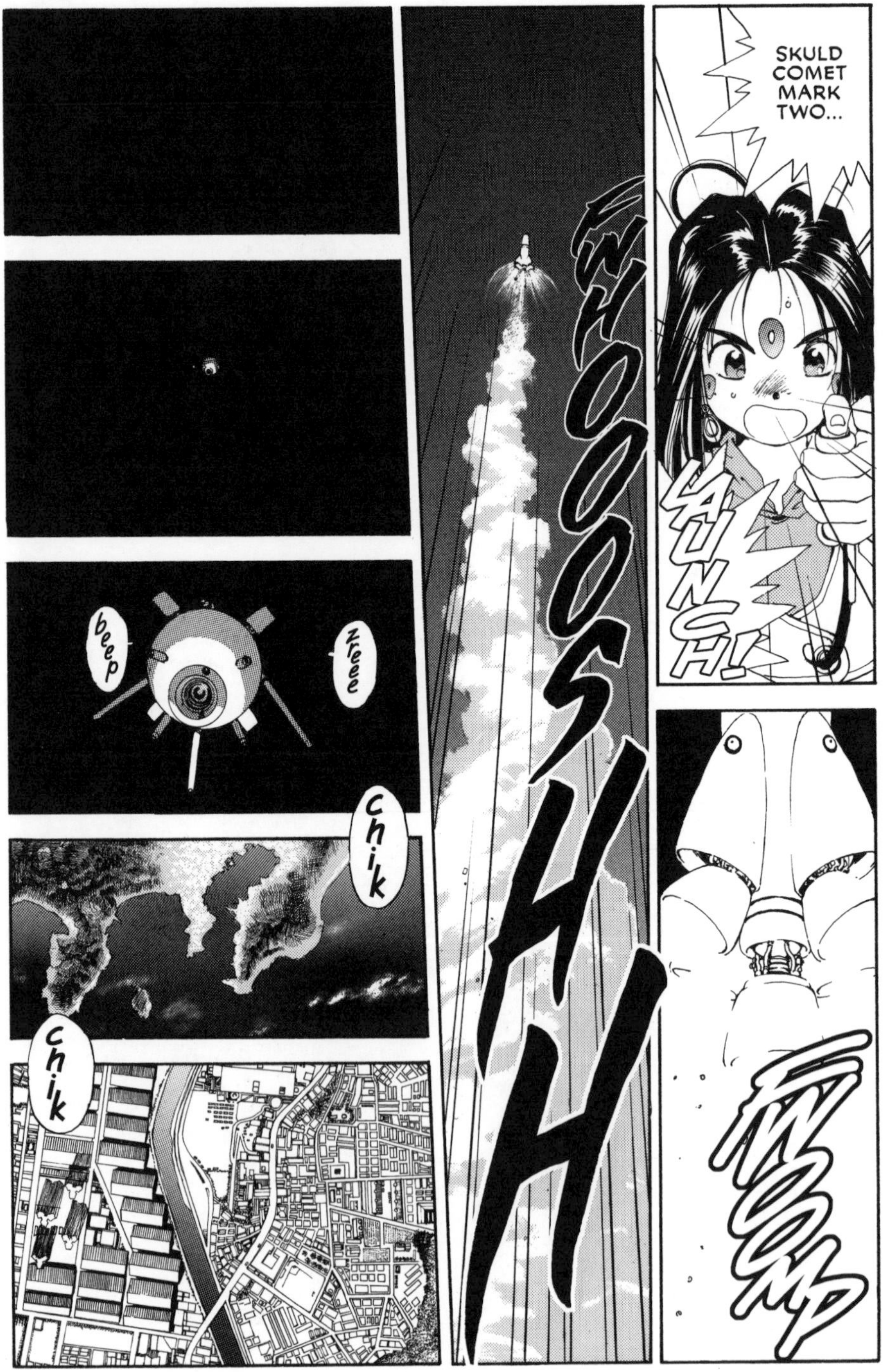
SKULD COMET MARK TWO...
LAUNCH!
FWOOOMP
FWHOOOOSHHHH
beep
zreee
chik
chik

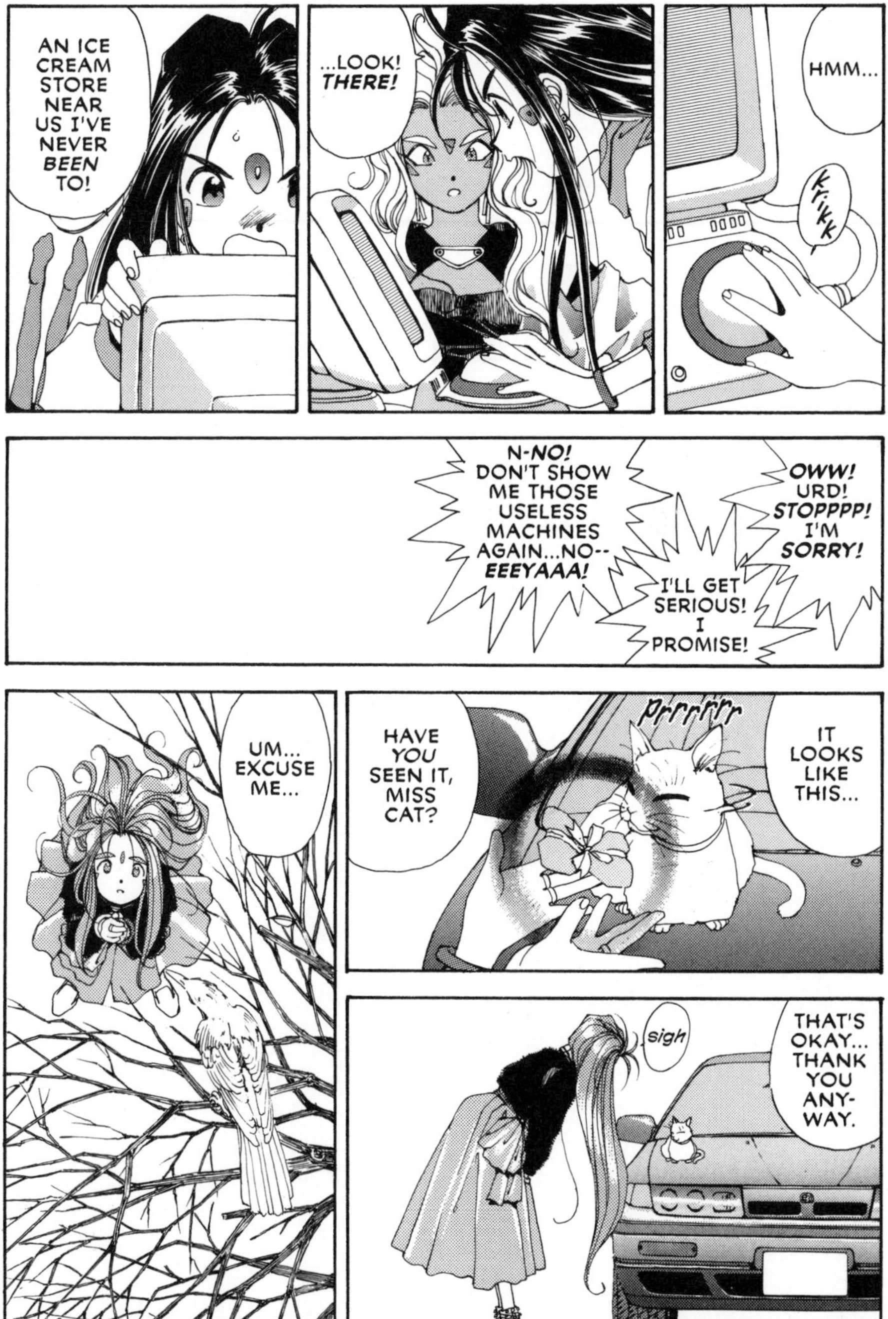
AN ICE CREAM STORE NEAR US I'VE NEVER *BEEN* TO!
...LOOK! *THERE!*
HMM...
krikk
N-*NO!* DON'T SHOW ME THOSE USELESS MACHINES AGAIN...NO-- *EEEYAAA!*
OWW! URD! *STOPPPP!* I'M *SORRY!*
I'LL GET SERIOUS! I PROMISE!
UM... EXCUSE ME...
HAVE *YOU* SEEN IT, MISS CAT?
Prrrrrr
IT LOOKS LIKE THIS...
sigh
THAT'S OKAY... THANK YOU ANY-WAY.

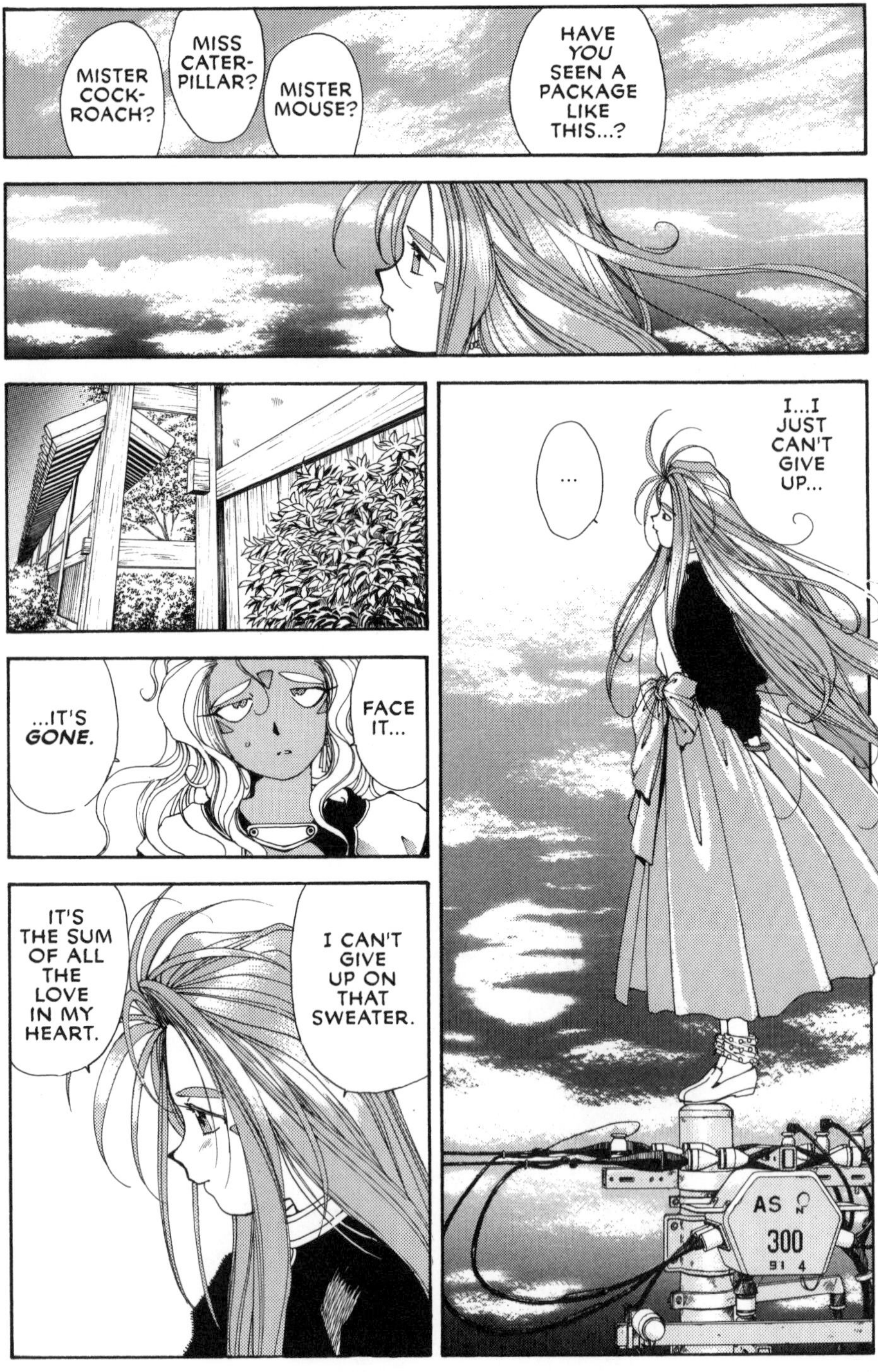
HAVE *YOU* SEEN A PACKAGE LIKE THIS...?
MISTER MOUSE?
MISS CATER-PILLAR?
MISTER COCK-ROACH?
I...I JUST CAN'T GIVE UP...
...
FACE IT...
...IT'S ***GONE.***
I CAN'T GIVE UP ON THAT SWEATER.
IT'S THE SUM OF ALL THE LOVE IN MY HEART.

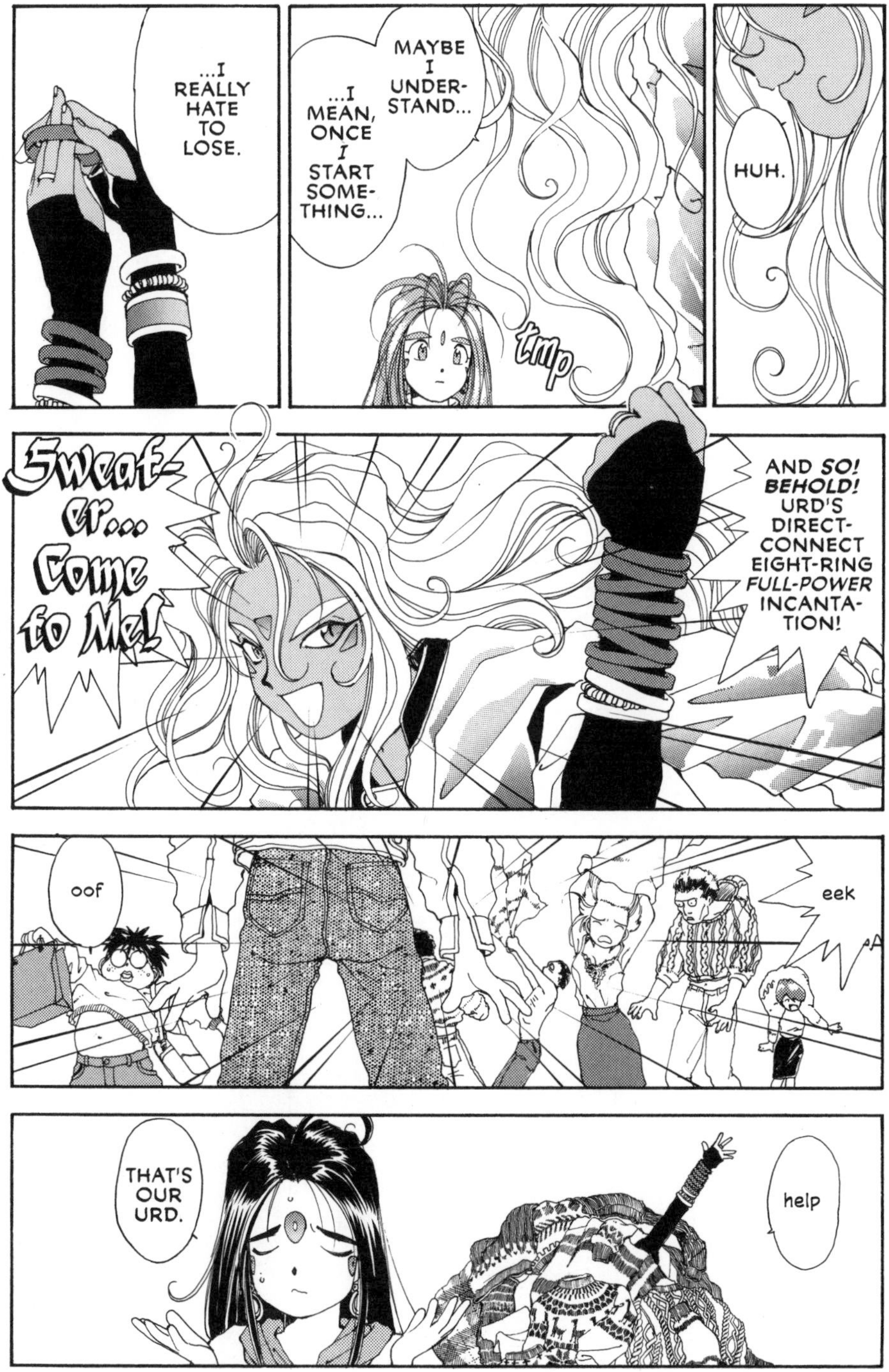
HUH.
MAYBE I UNDERSTAND...
...I MEAN, ONCE *I* START SOMETHING...
tmp
...I REALLY HATE TO LOSE.
AND *SO! BEHOLD!* URD'S DIRECT-CONNECT EIGHT-RING *FULL-POWER* INCANTATION!
Sweat-er... Come to Me!
eek
oof
help
THAT'S OUR URD.

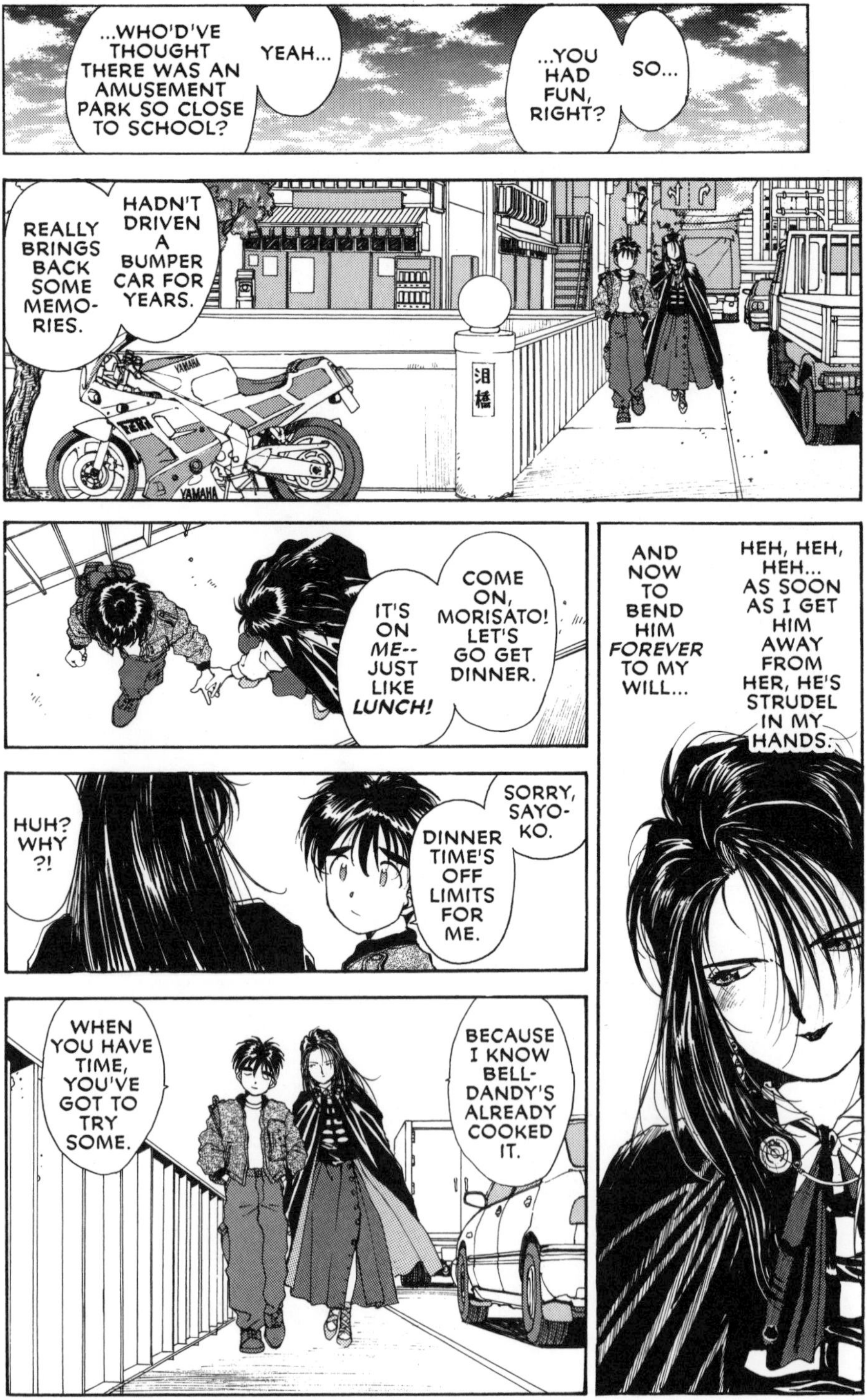
SO...
...YOU HAD FUN, RIGHT?
YEAH...
...WHO'D'VE THOUGHT THERE WAS AN AMUSEMENT PARK SO CLOSE TO SCHOOL?
HADN'T DRIVEN A BUMPER CAR FOR YEARS.
REALLY BRINGS BACK SOME MEMO-RIES.
HEH, HEH, HEH... AS SOON AS I GET HIM AWAY FROM HER, HE'S STRUDEL IN MY HANDS.
AND NOW TO BEND HIM *FOREVER* TO MY WILL...
COME ON, MORISATO! LET'S GO GET DINNER.
IT'S ON *ME*-- JUST LIKE *LUNCH!*
SORRY, SAYO-KO.
DINNER TIME'S OFF LIMITS FOR ME.
HUH? WHY ?!
BECAUSE I KNOW BELL-DANDY'S ALREADY COOKED IT.
WHEN YOU HAVE TIME, YOU'VE GOT TO TRY SOME.

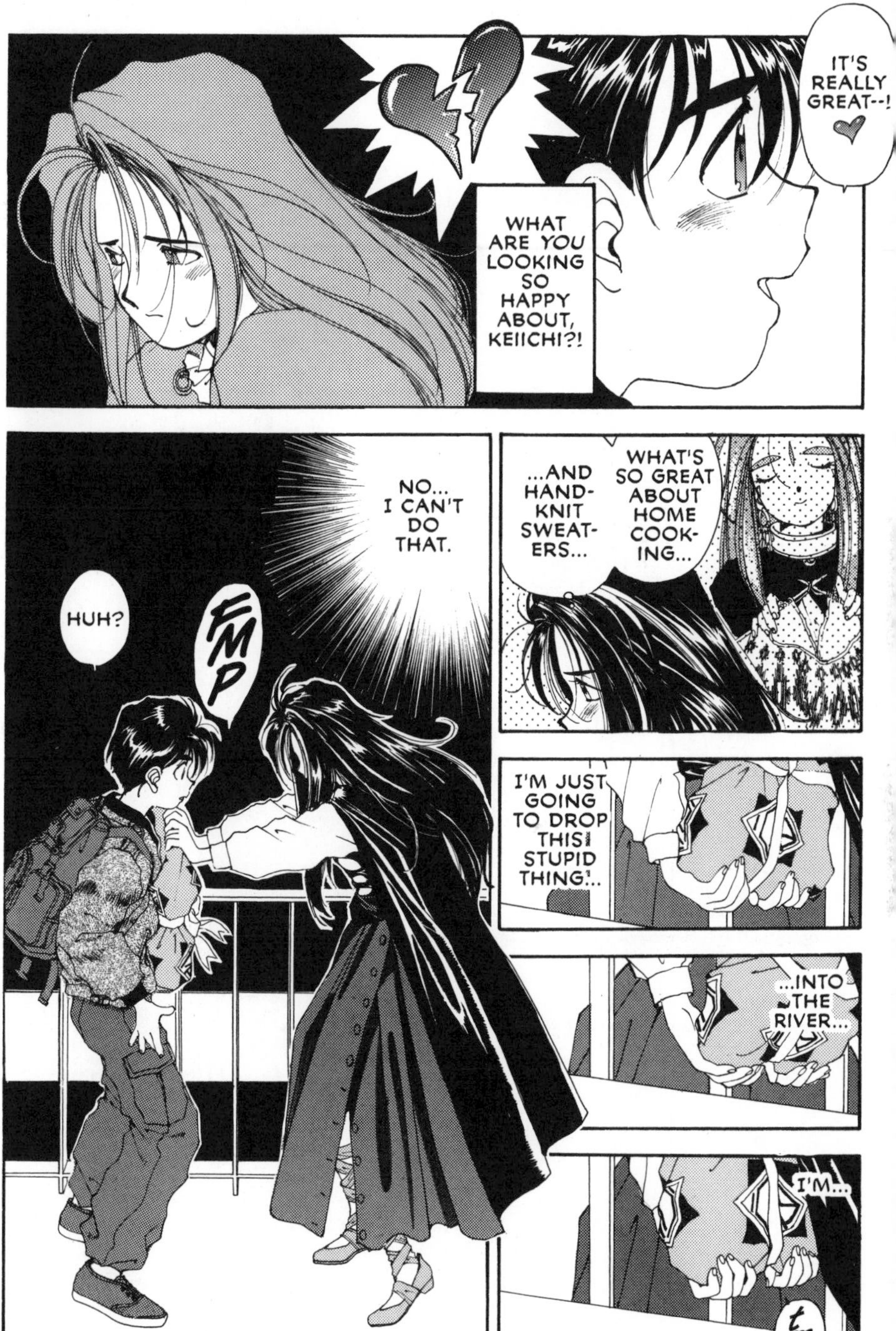

IT'S REALLY GREAT--! ♥
WHAT ARE YOU LOOKING SO HAPPY ABOUT, KEIICHI?!
WHAT'S SO GREAT ABOUT HOME COOKING...
...AND HAND-KNIT SWEATERS...
I'M JUST GOING TO DROP THIS STUPID THING...
...INTO THE RIVER...
I'M...
tmp
NO... I CAN'T DO THAT.
EMP
HUH?

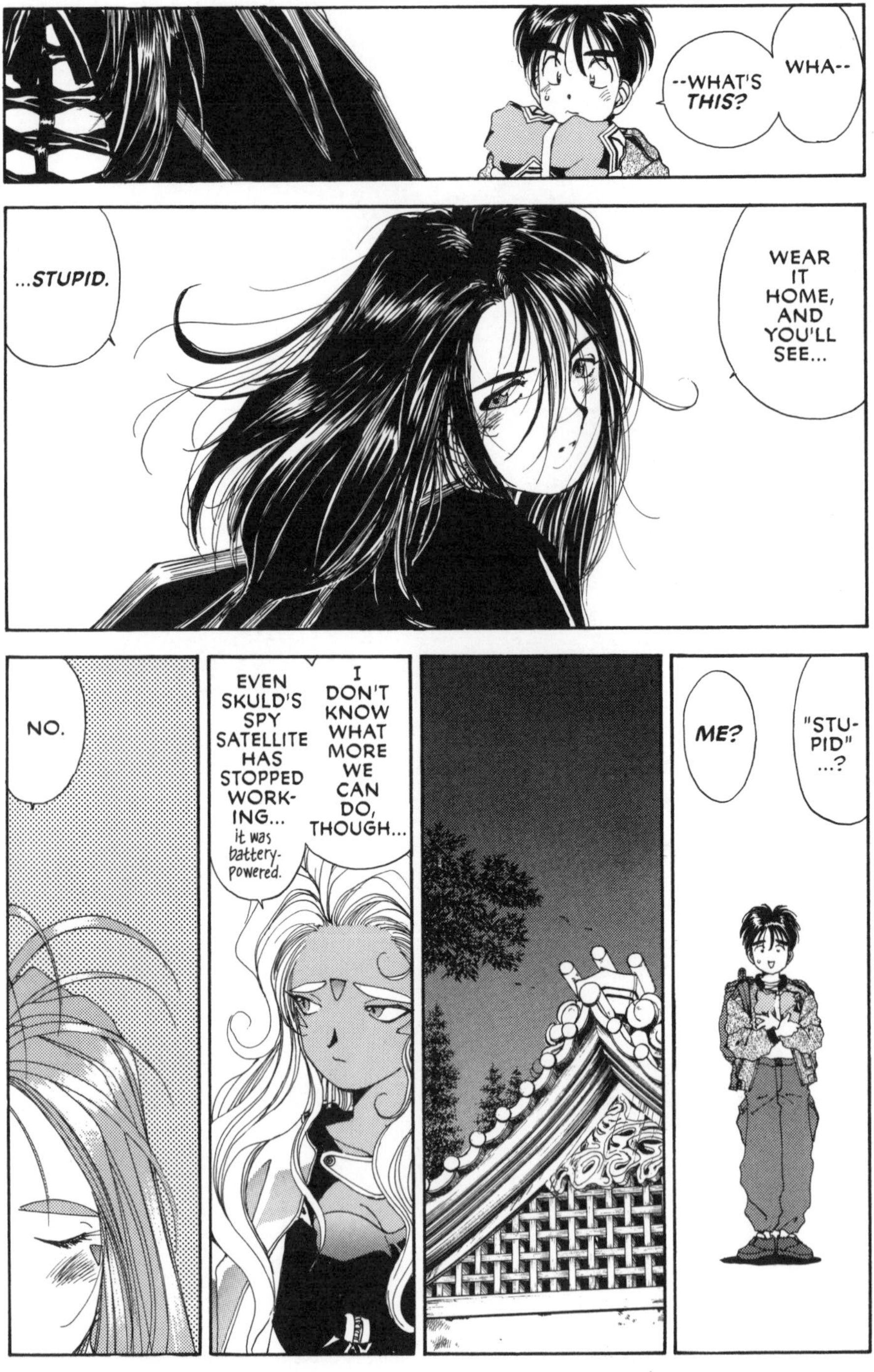
WHA--
--WHAT'S THIS?
WEAR IT HOME, AND YOU'LL SEE...
...STUPID.
"STU-PID" ...?
ME?
I DON'T KNOW WHAT MORE WE CAN DO, THOUGH...
EVEN SKULD'S SPY SATELLITE HAS STOPPED WORKING... it was battery-powered.
NO.

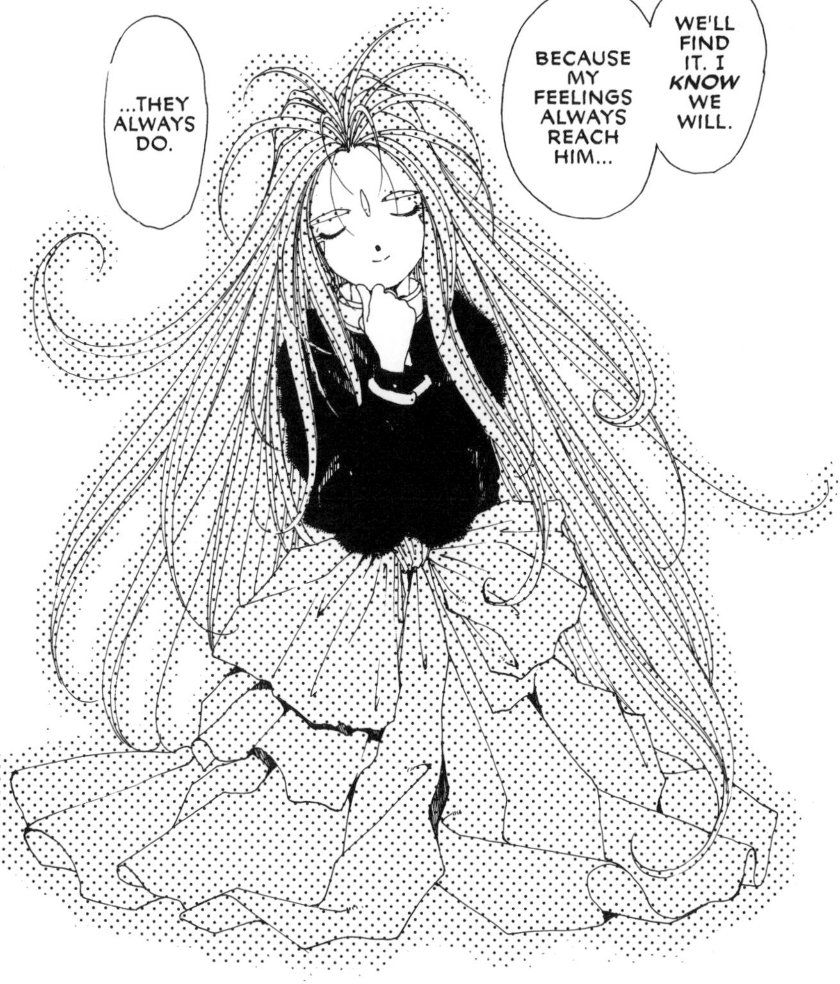
WE'LL FIND IT. I *KNOW* WE WILL.
BECAUSE MY FEELINGS ALWAYS REACH HIM...
...THEY ALWAYS DO.
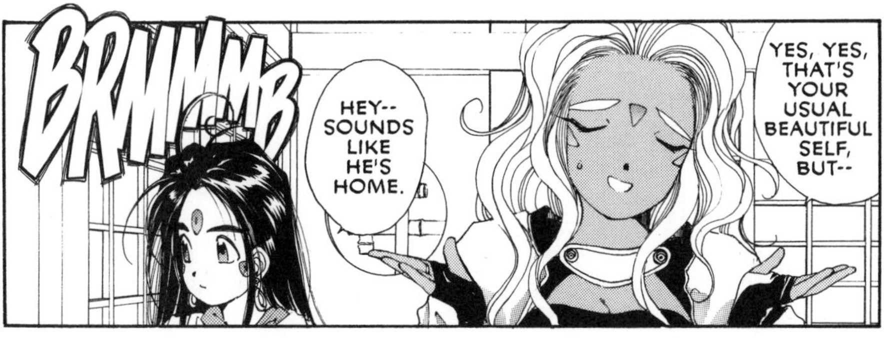
YES, YES, THAT'S YOUR USUAL BEAUTIFUL SELF, BUT--
BRMMMB
HEY-- SOUNDS LIKE HE'S HOME.

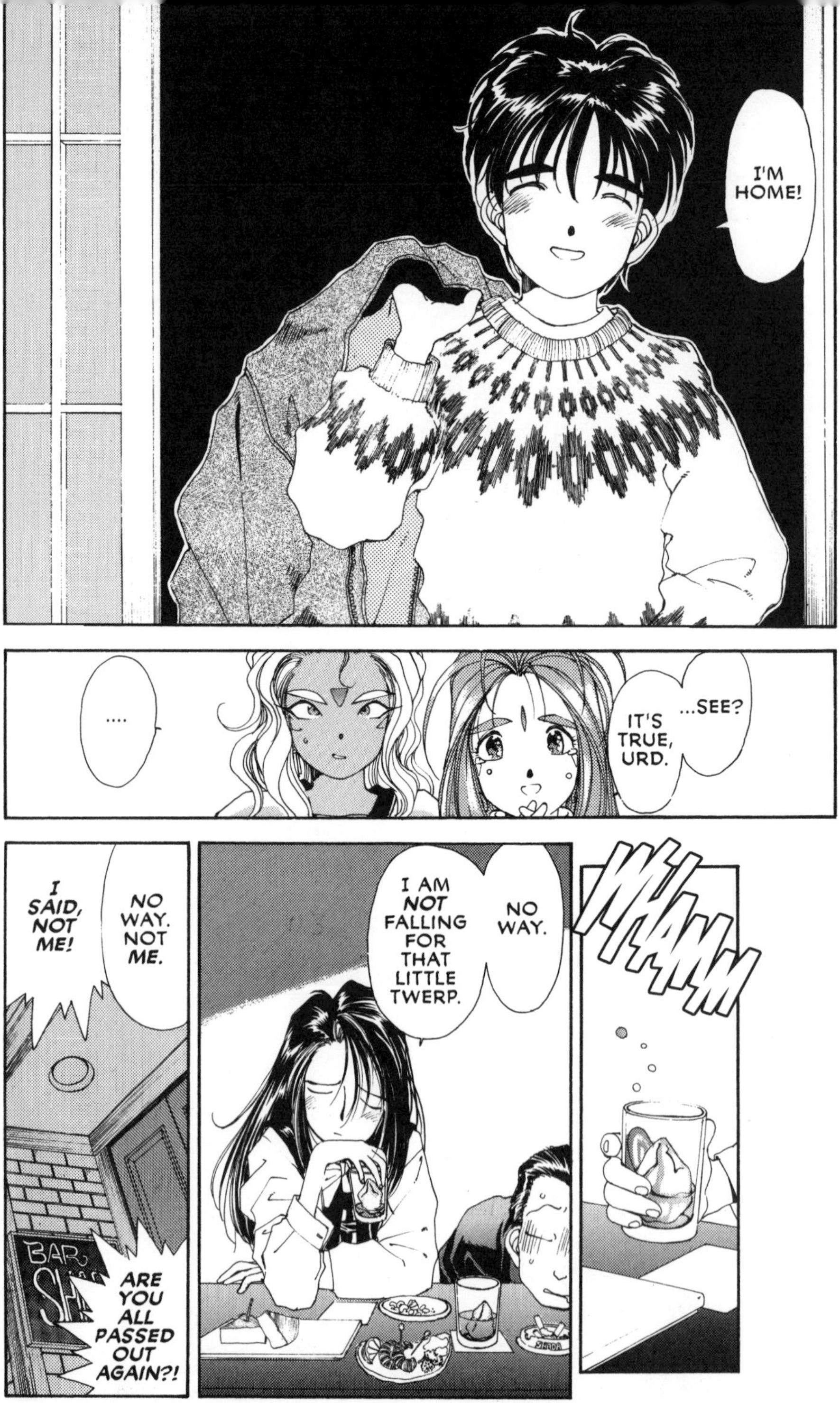
I'M HOME!
...SEE? IT'S TRUE, URD.
....
NO WAY.
I AM NOT FALLING FOR THAT LITTLE TWERP.
NO WAY. NOT ME.
I SAID, NOT ME!
ARE YOU ALL PASSED OUT AGAIN?!

THE ADVENTURES OF MINI-URD

Now with added MINI-SKULD!

◆ STORMWRACK--A TALE OF BASEBALL ◆

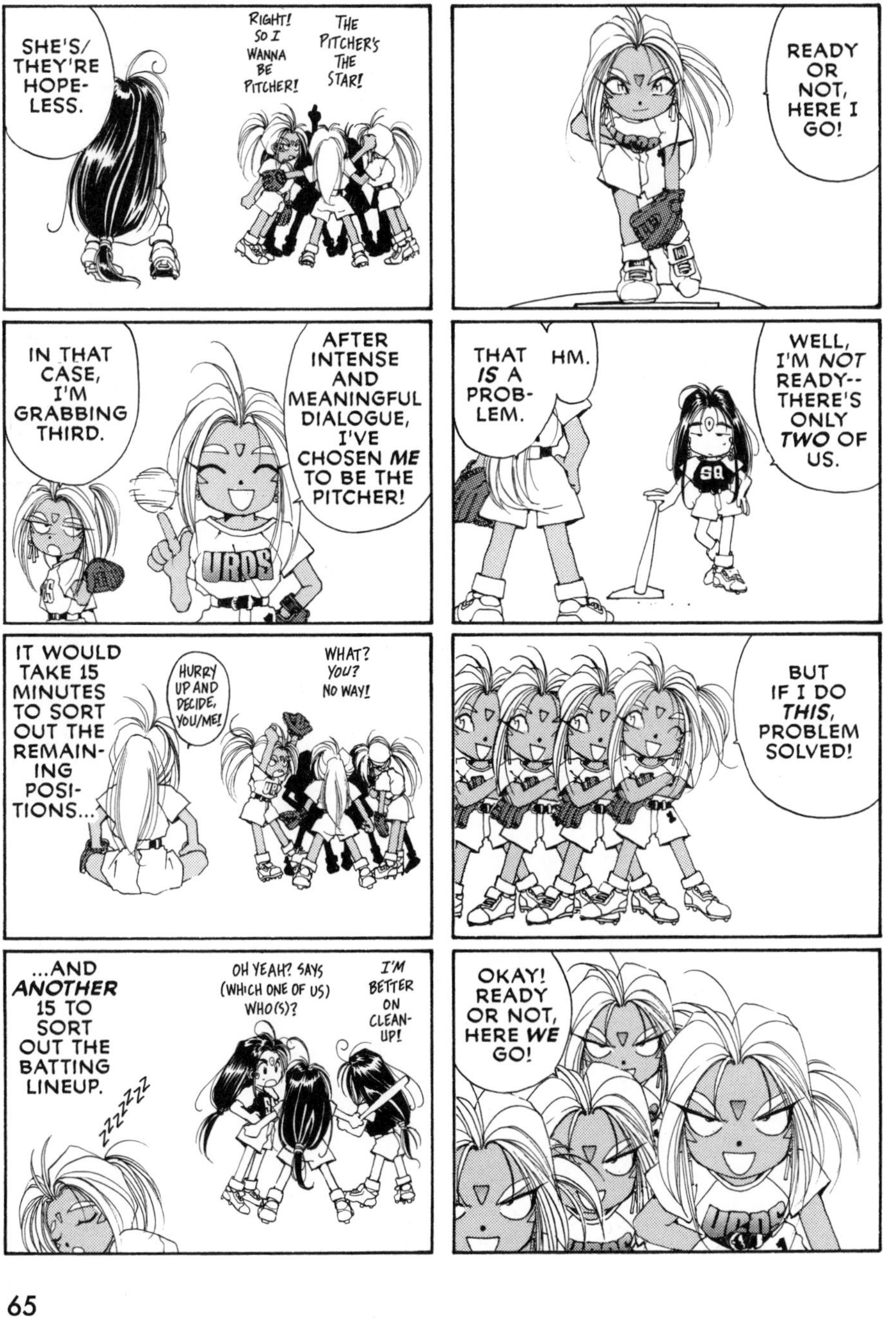
READY OR NOT, HERE I GO!
THE PITCHER'S THE STAR!
RIGHT! SO I WANNA BE PITCHER!
SHE'S/THEY'RE HOPE-LESS.
WELL, I'M *NOT* READY-- THERE'S ONLY *TWO* OF US.
HM.
THAT *IS* A PROB-LEM.
AFTER INTENSE AND MEANINGFUL DIALOGUE, I'VE CHOSEN *ME* TO BE THE PITCHER!
IN THAT CASE, I'M GRABBING THIRD.
BUT IF I DO *THIS*, PROBLEM SOLVED!
WHAT? *YOU?* NO WAY!
HURRY UP AND DECIDE, YOU/ME!
IT WOULD TAKE 15 MINUTES TO SORT OUT THE REMAIN-ING POSI-TIONS...
OKAY! READY OR NOT, HERE *WE* GO!
I'M BETTER ON CLEAN-UP!
OH YEAH? SAYS (WHICH ONE OF US) WHO(S)?
...AND ***ANOTHER*** 15 TO SORT OUT THE BATTING LINEUP.

◆ STORMWRACK--A TALE OF BASEBALL (PART DEUX) ◆

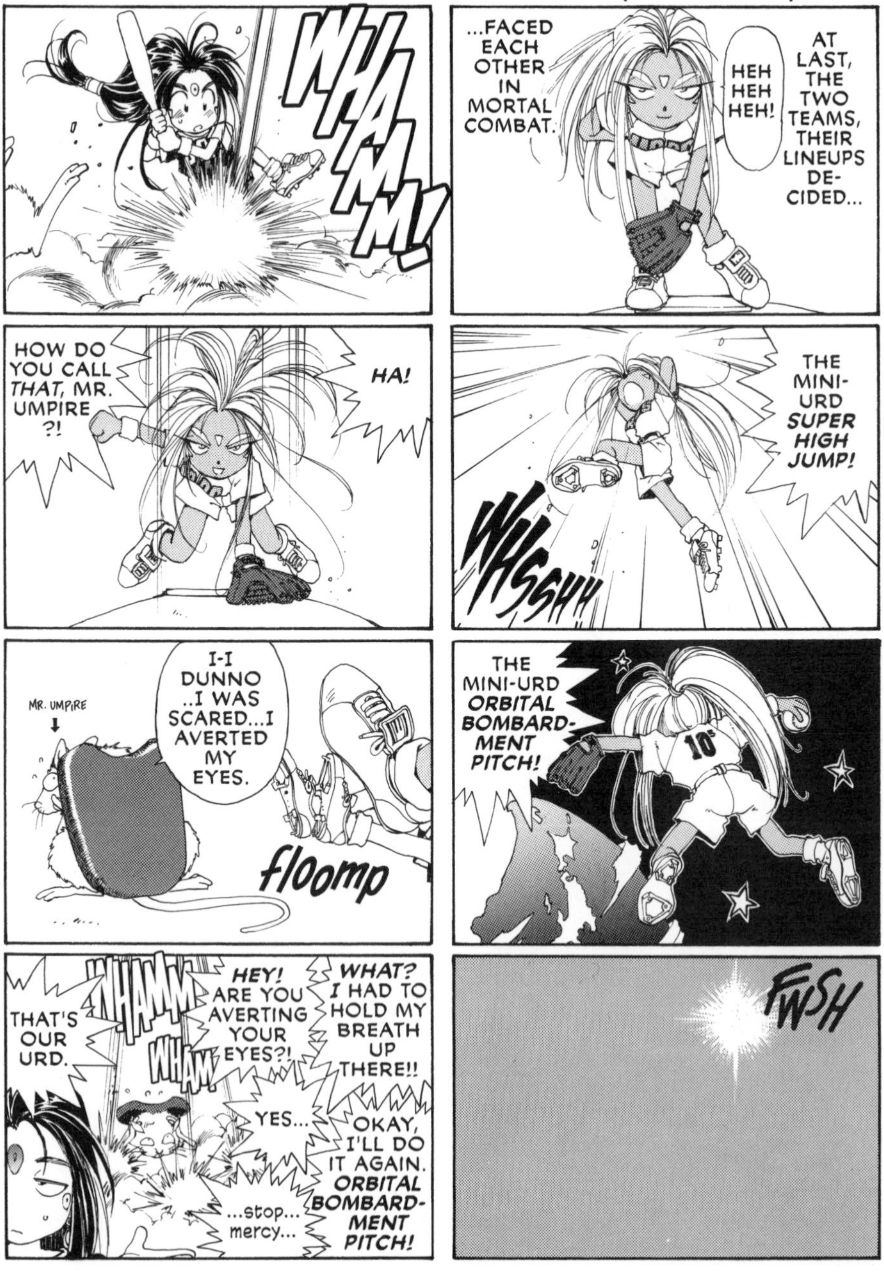
AT LAST, THE TWO TEAMS, THEIR LINEUPS DE-CIDED...
HEH HEH HEH!
...FACED EACH OTHER IN MORTAL COMBAT.
THE MINI-URD SUPER HIGH JUMP!
WHSSHH
THE MINI-URD ORBITAL BOMBARD-MENT PITCH!
10
FWSH
WHAMM!
HA!
HOW DO YOU CALL THAT, MR. UMPIRE ?!
I-I DUNNO ..I WAS SCARED...I AVERTED MY EYES.
MR. UMPIRE
floomp
WHAT? I HAD TO HOLD MY BREATH UP THERE!!
HEY! ARE YOU AVERTING YOUR EYES?!
WHAMM
THAT'S OUR URD.
WHAM
OKAY, I'LL DO IT AGAIN. ORBITAL BOMBARD-MENT PITCH!
YES...
...stop... mercy...

◆STORMWRACK--A TALE OF BASEBALL (PART DER DRITTE)◆

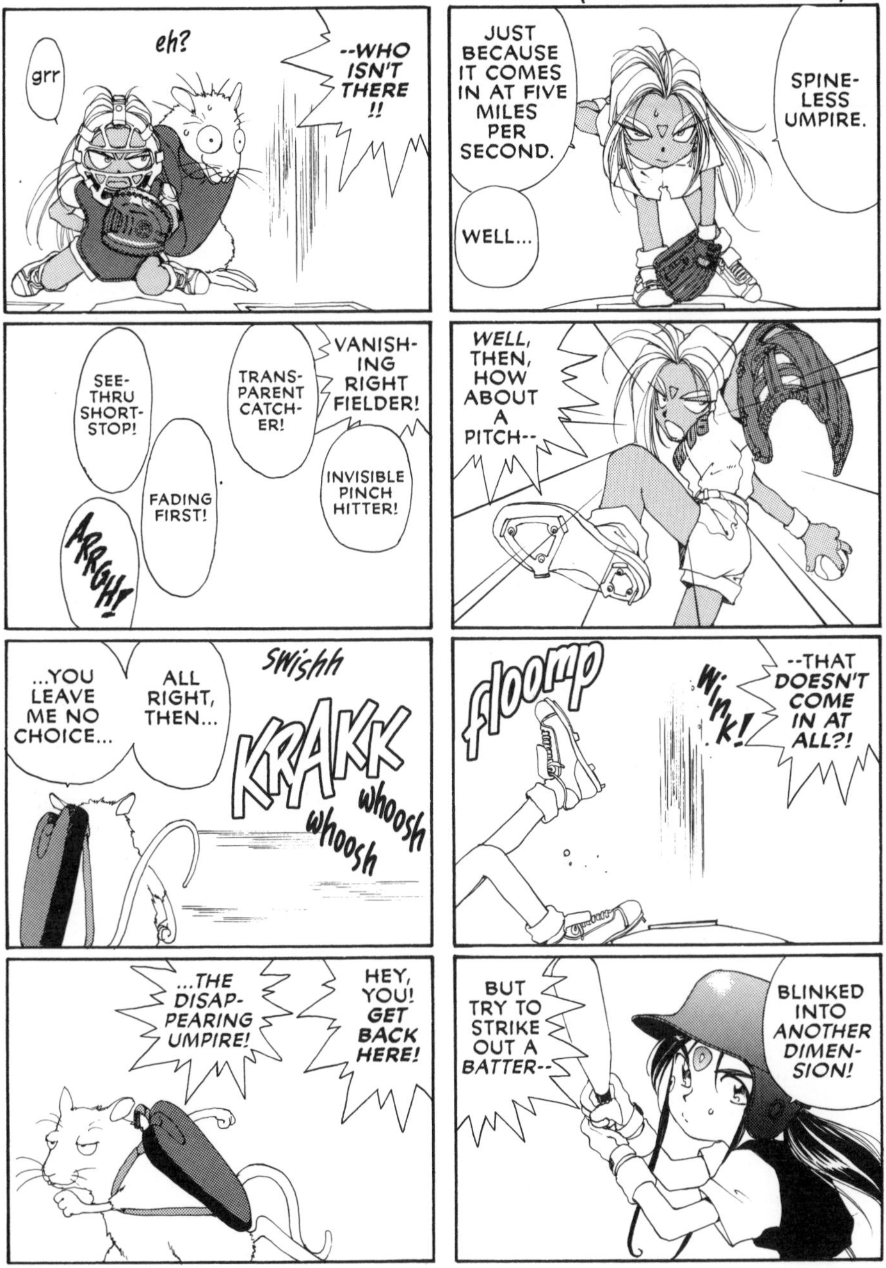
SPINELESS UMPIRE.
JUST BECAUSE IT COMES IN AT FIVE MILES PER SECOND.
WELL...
WELL, THEN, HOW ABOUT A PITCH--
--THAT DOESN'T COME IN AT ALL?!
wink!
floomp
BLINKED INTO ANOTHER DIMENSION!
BUT TRY TO STRIKE OUT A BATTER--
--WHO ISN'T THERE !!
eh?
grr
VANISHING RIGHT FIELDER!
TRANSPARENT CATCHER!
INVISIBLE PINCH HITTER!
SEE-THRU SHORTSTOP!
FADING FIRST!
ARRGH!
ALL RIGHT, THEN...
...YOU LEAVE ME NO CHOICE...
swishh
KRAKK
whoosh
whoosh
HEY, YOU! GET BACK HERE!
...THE DISAPPEARING UMPIRE!

STORMWRACK--A TALE OF BASEBALL
(WHATEVER COMES AFTER THAT)

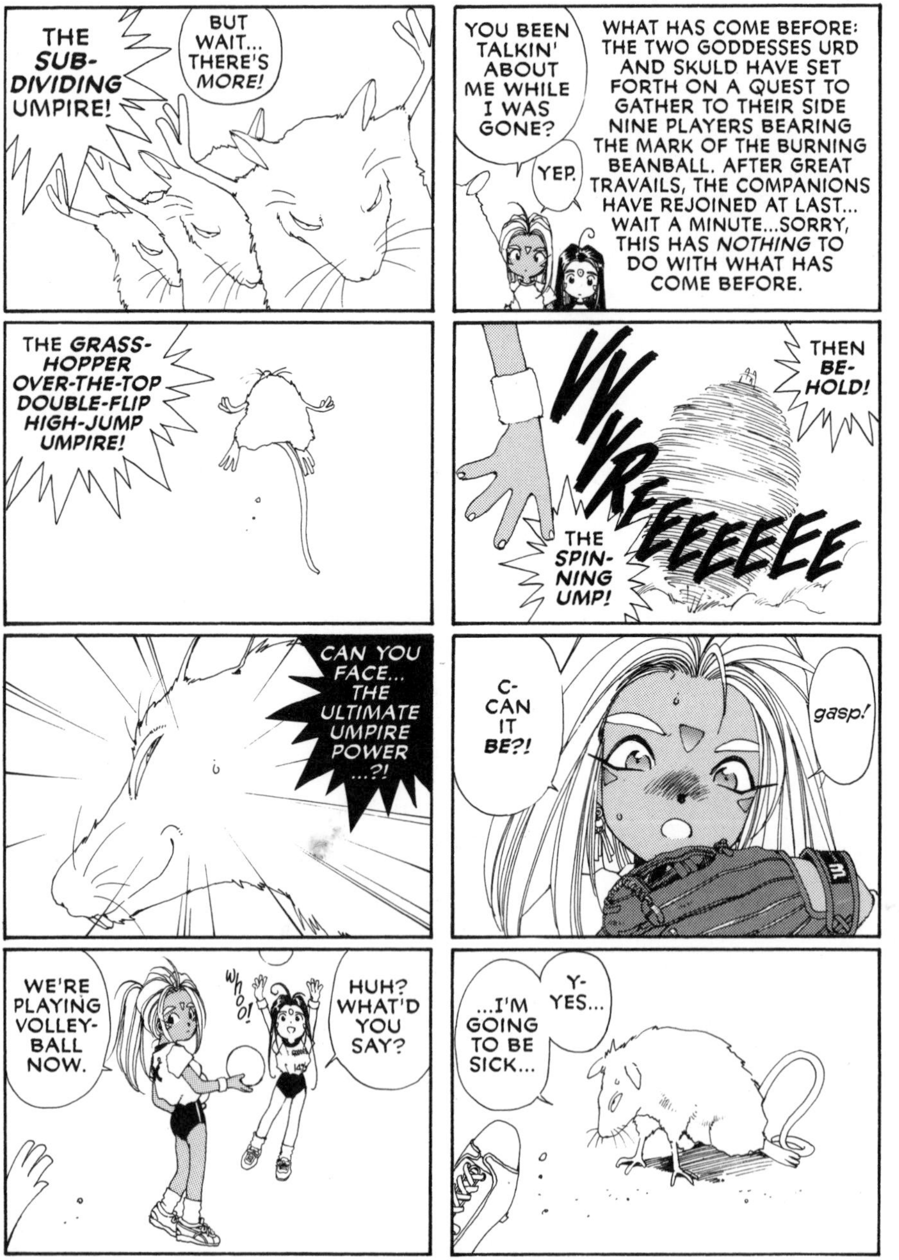

YOU BEEN TALKIN' ABOUT ME WHILE I WAS GONE?
WHAT HAS COME BEFORE: THE TWO GODDESSES URD AND SKULD HAVE SET FORTH ON A QUEST TO GATHER TO THEIR SIDE NINE PLAYERS BEARING THE MARK OF THE BURNING BEANBALL. AFTER GREAT TRAVAILS, THE COMPANIONS HAVE REJOINED AT LAST... WAIT A MINUTE...SORRY, THIS HAS *NOTHING* TO DO WITH WHAT HAS COME BEFORE.
YEP.
THEN *BE-HOLD!*
VVVREEEEEEE
THE *SPIN-NING UMP!*
C-CAN IT *BE?!*
gasp!
Y-YES...
...I'M GOING TO BE SICK...
BUT WAIT... THERE'S *MORE!*
THE *SUB-DIVIDING* UMPIRE!
THE *GRASS-HOPPER OVER-THE-TOP DOUBLE-FLIP HIGH-JUMP UMPIRE!*
CAN YOU FACE... THE ULTIMATE UMPIRE POWER ...?!
HUH? WHAT'D YOU SAY?
Whoo!
WE'RE PLAYING VOLLEY-BALL NOW.

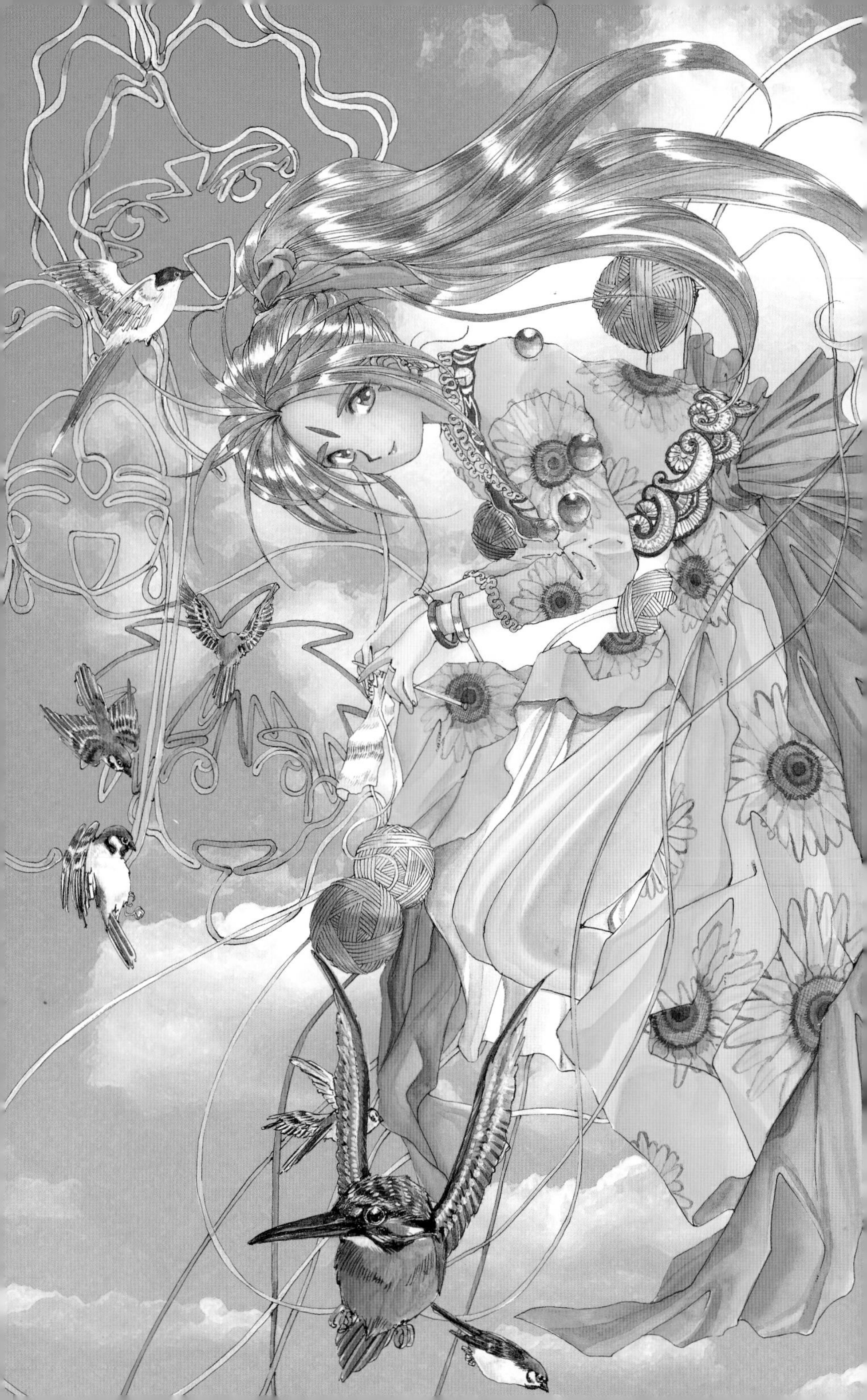

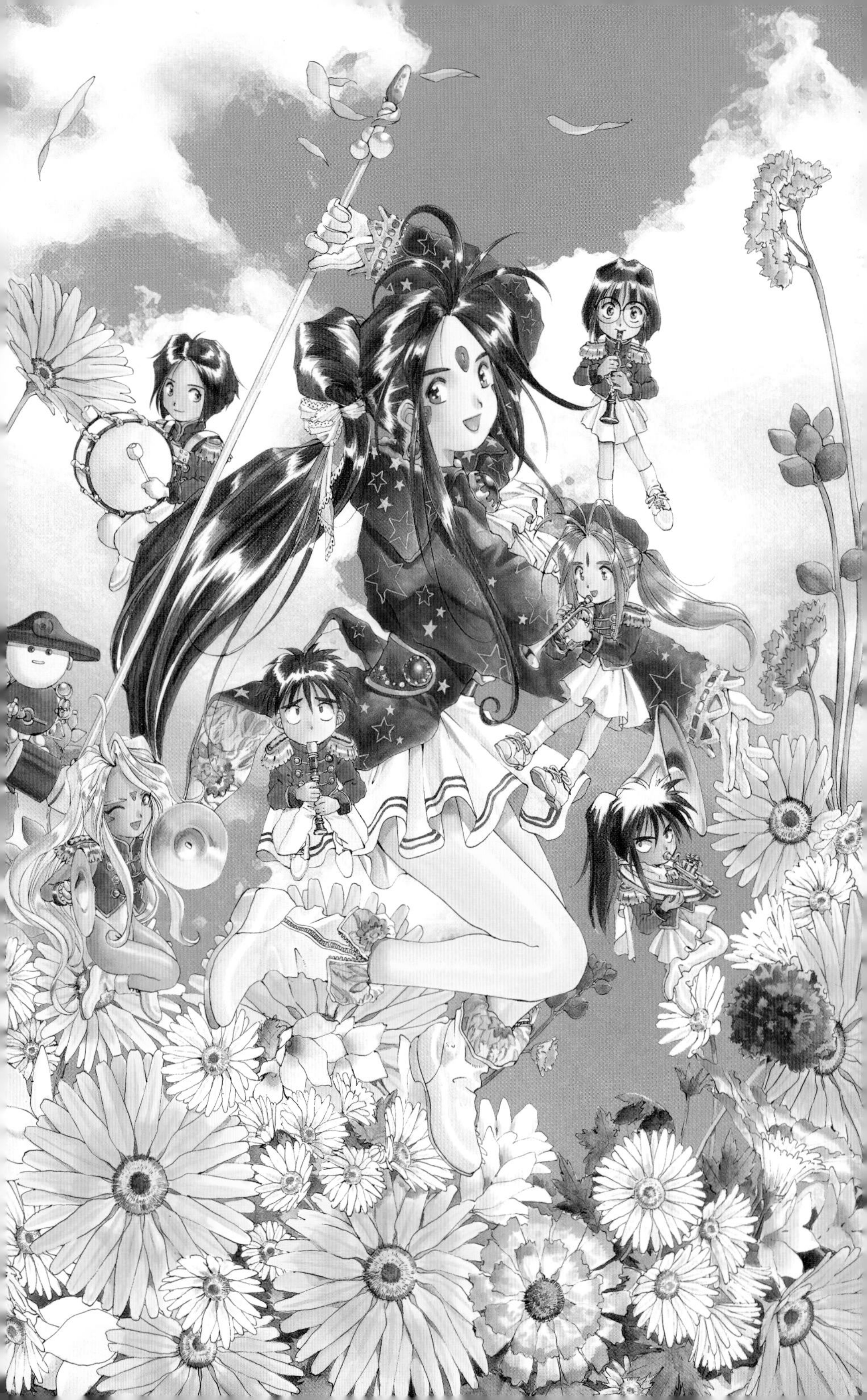

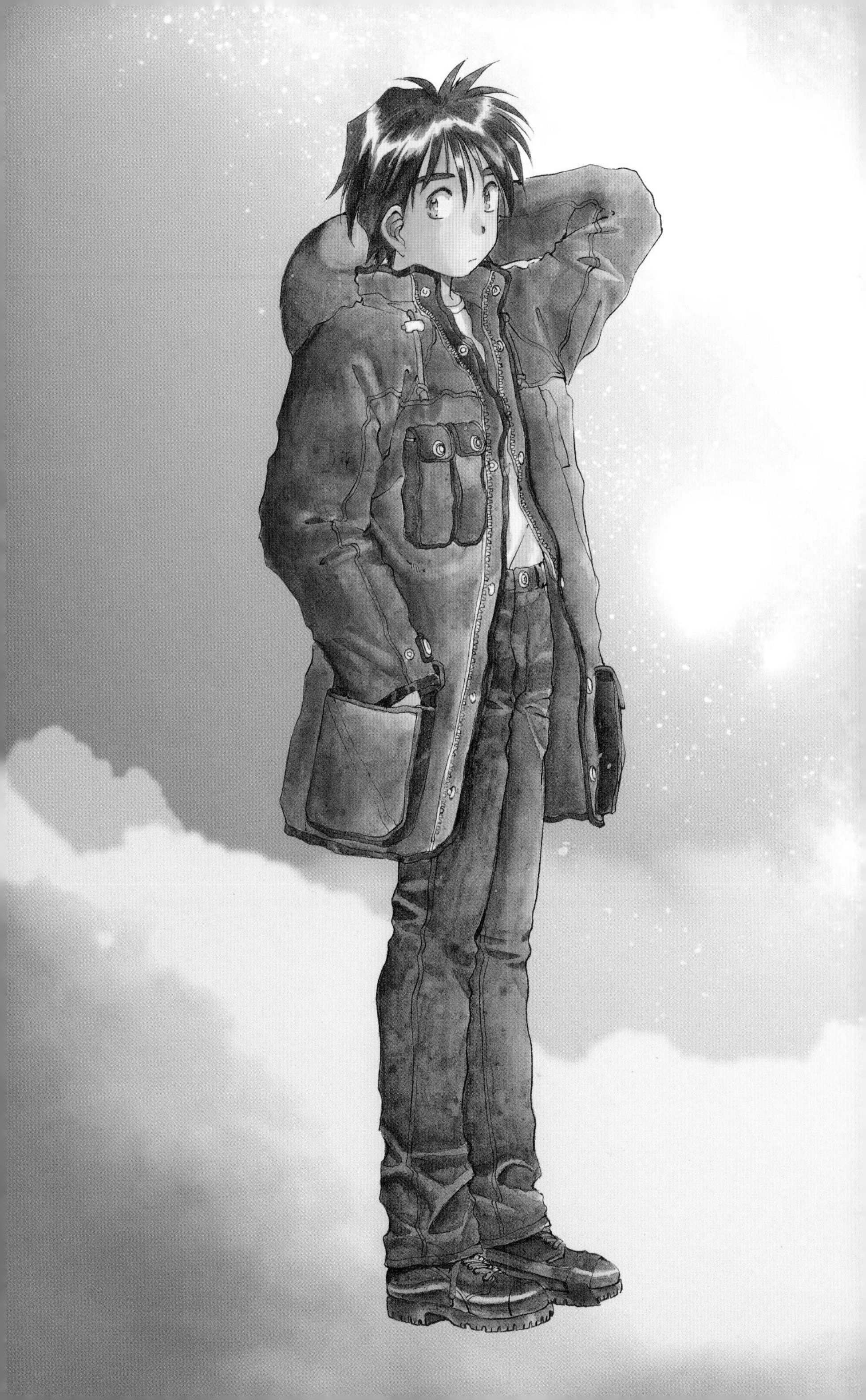

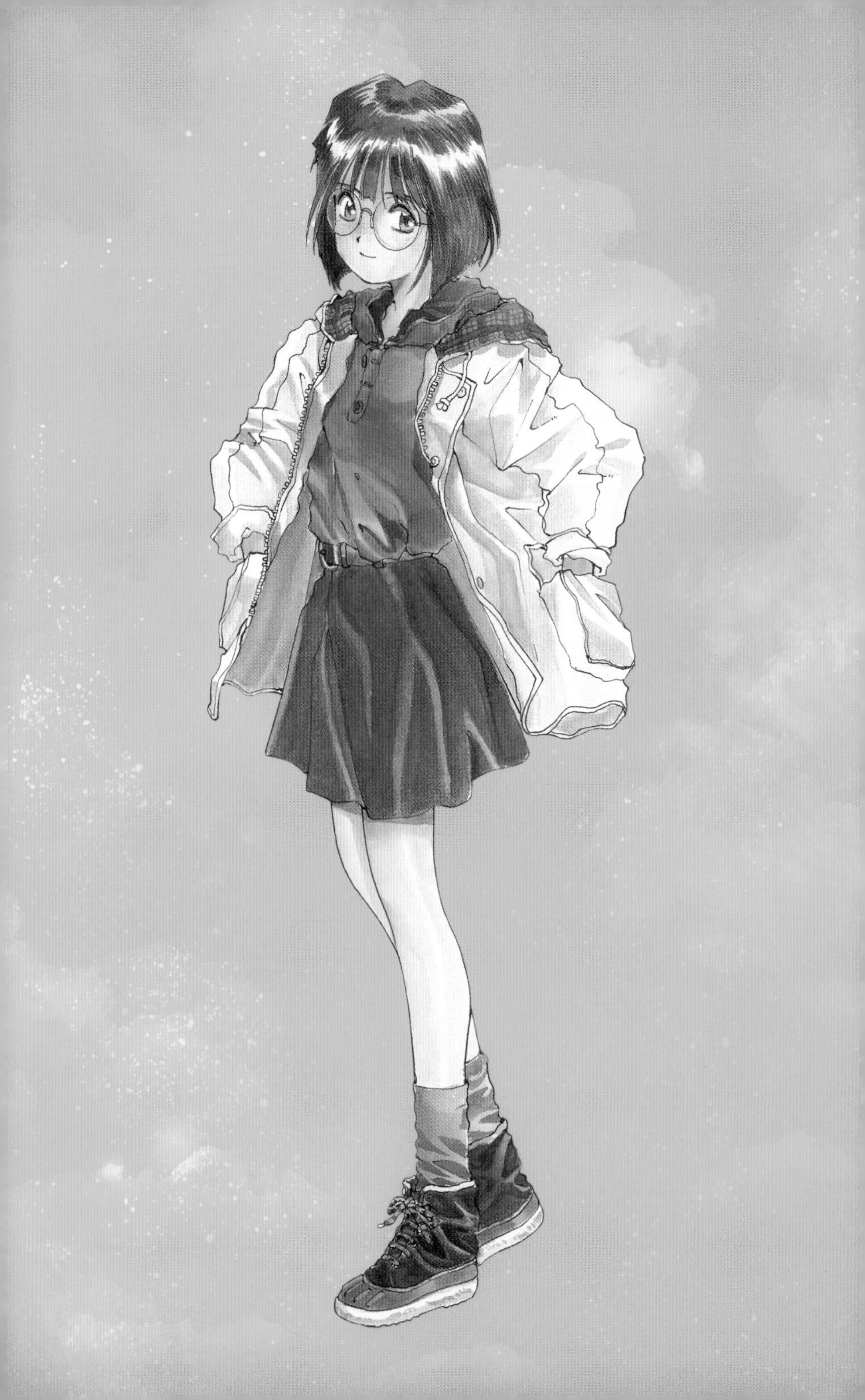

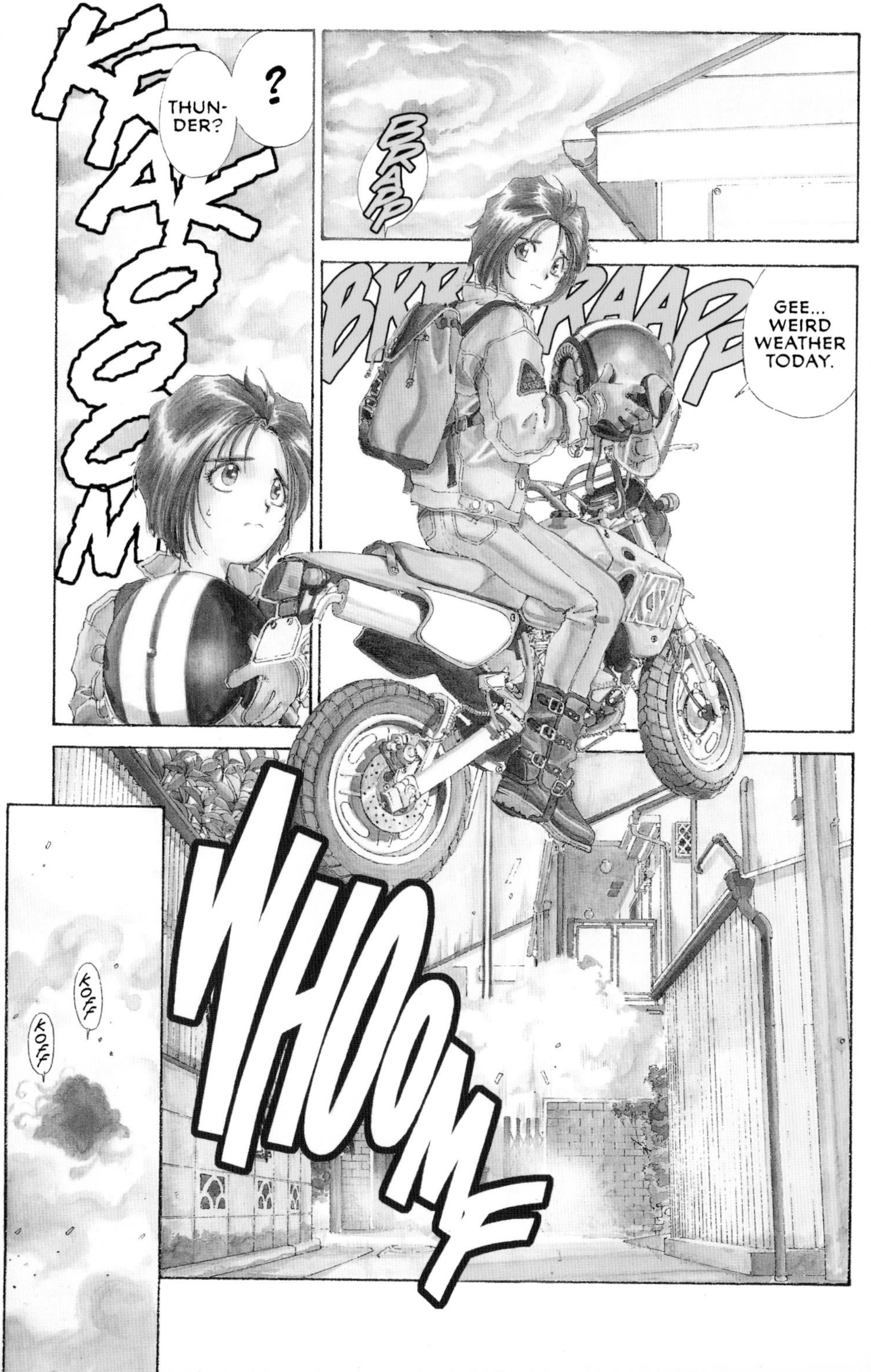
BRAAP
GEE... WEIRD WEATHER TODAY.
?
THUN-DER?
WHOOMF
KOFF
KOFF

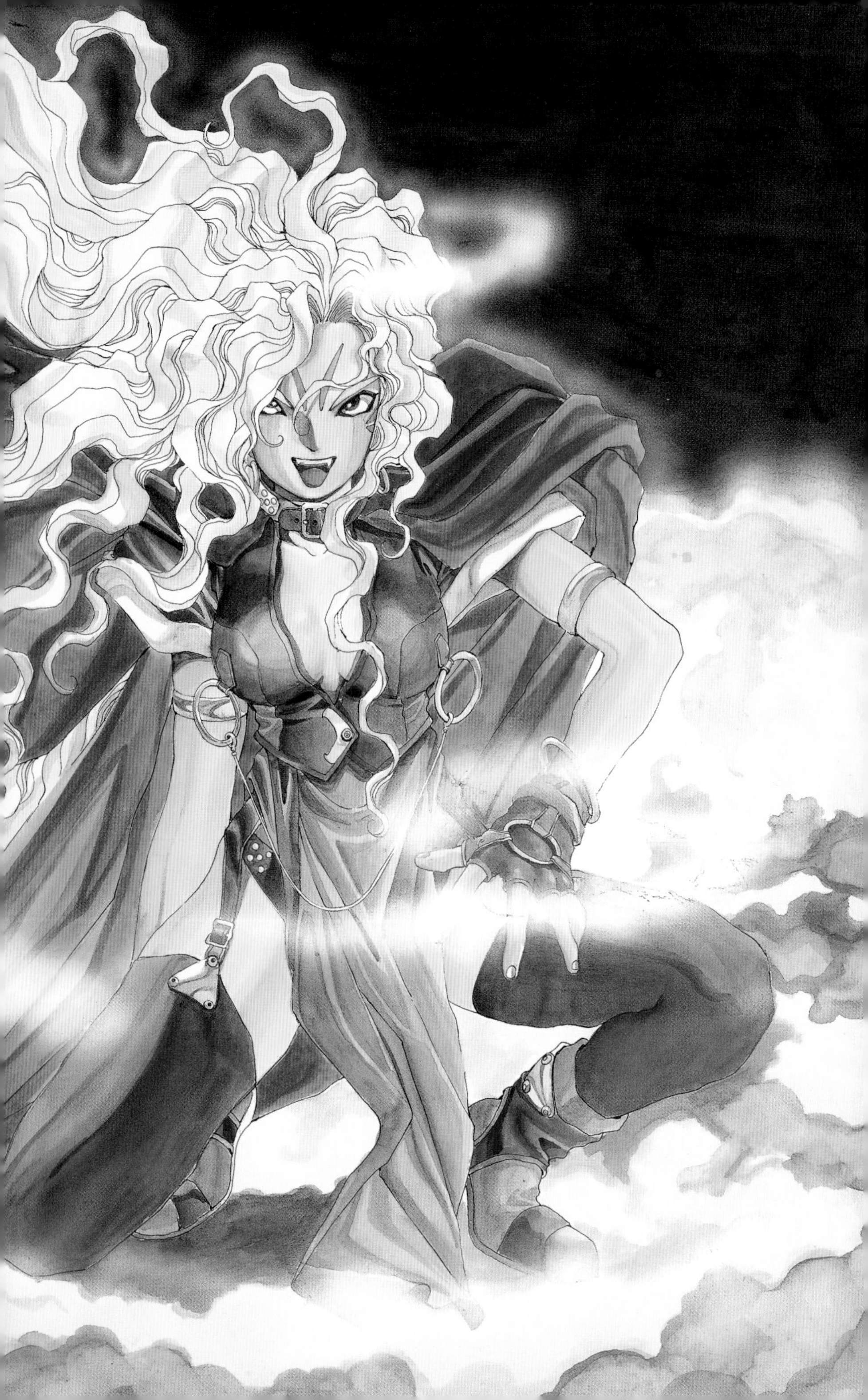

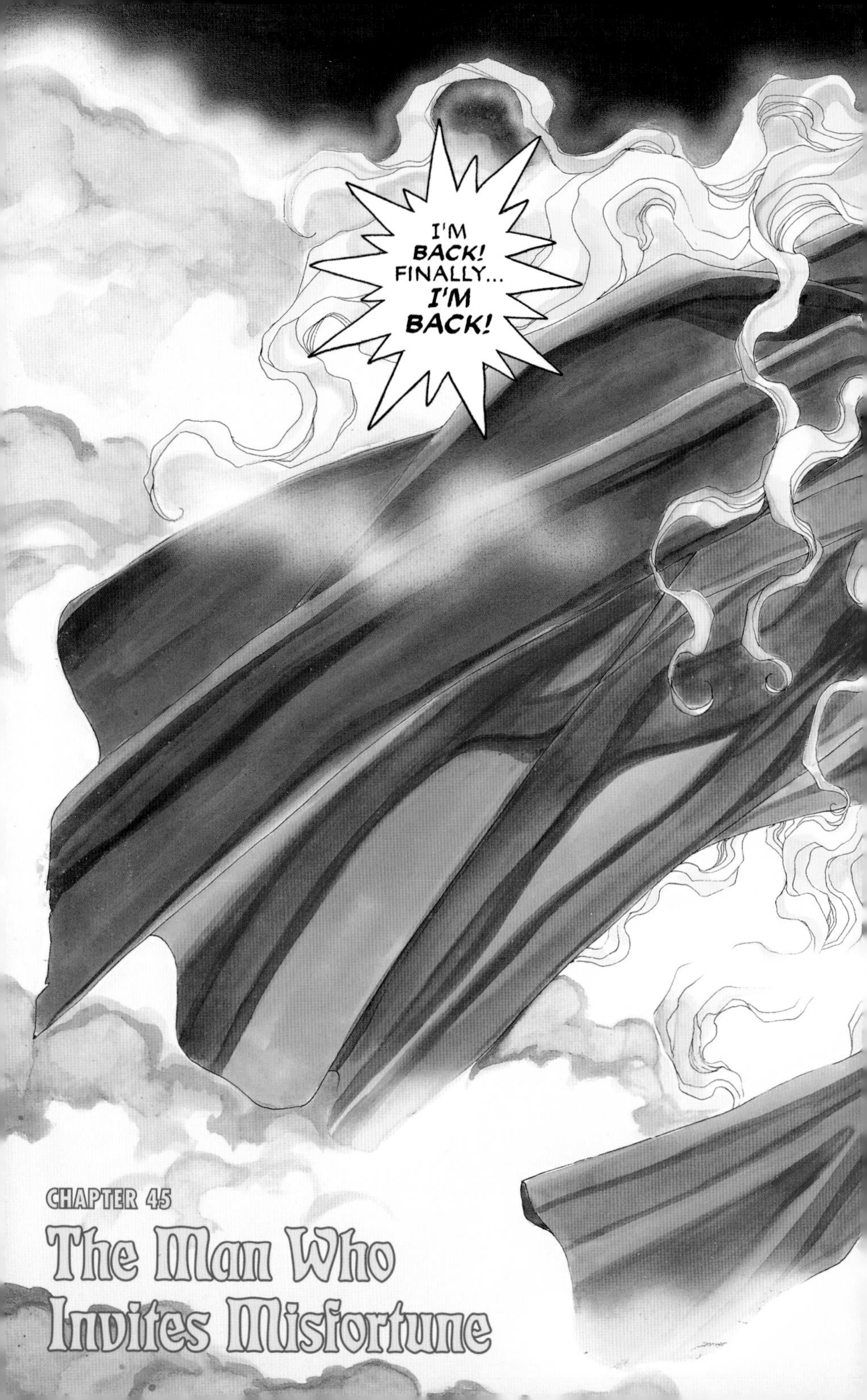
I'M BACK! FINALLY... I'M BACK!
CHAPTER 45
The Man Who Invites Misfortune

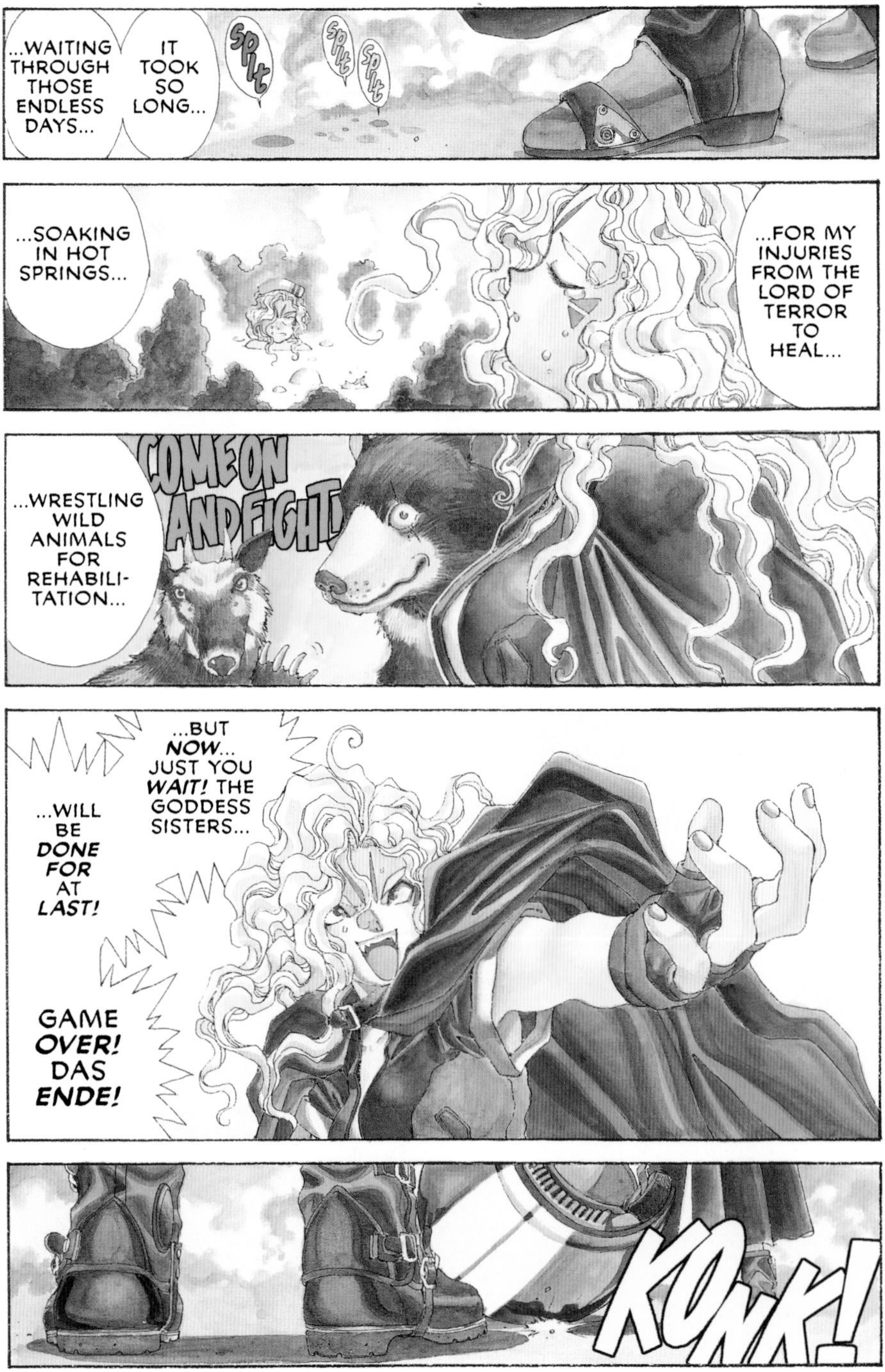
spit
spit
spit
IT TOOK SO LONG...
...WAITING THROUGH THOSE ENDLESS DAYS...
...FOR MY INJURIES FROM THE LORD OF TERROR TO HEAL...
...SOAKING IN HOT SPRINGS...
COME ON AND FIGHT!
...WRESTLING WILD ANIMALS FOR REHABILI-TATION...
...BUT *NOW*... JUST YOU *WAIT!* THE GODDESS SISTERS...
...WILL BE *DONE FOR* AT *LAST!*
GAME *OVER!* DAS *ENDE!*
KONK!

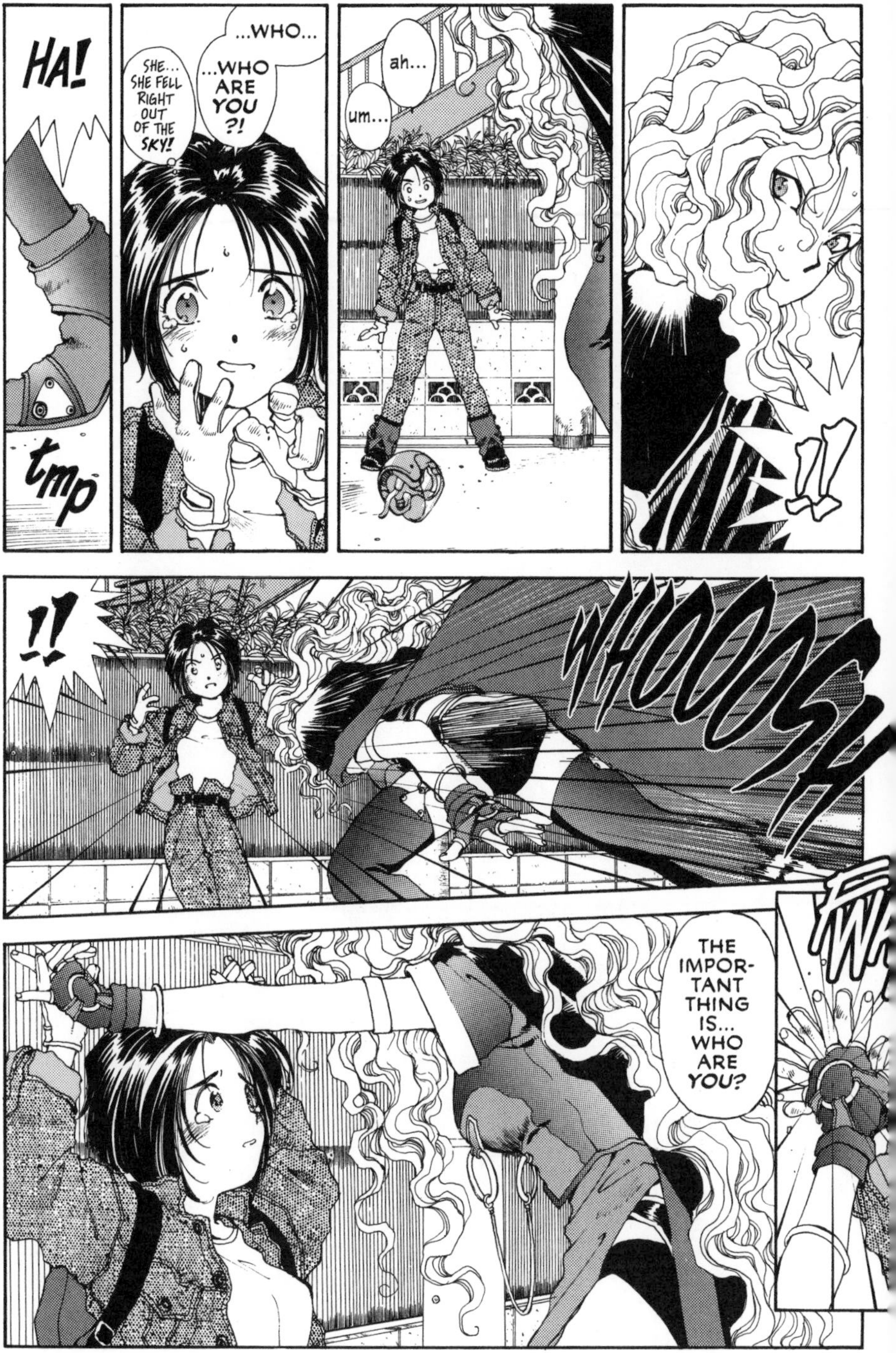
!!
ah...
um...
...WHO...
...WHO ARE YOU?!
SHE... SHE FELL RIGHT OUT OF THE SKY!
HA!
tmp
WHOOOSH
!!
THE IMPOR-TANT THING IS... WHO ARE YOU?

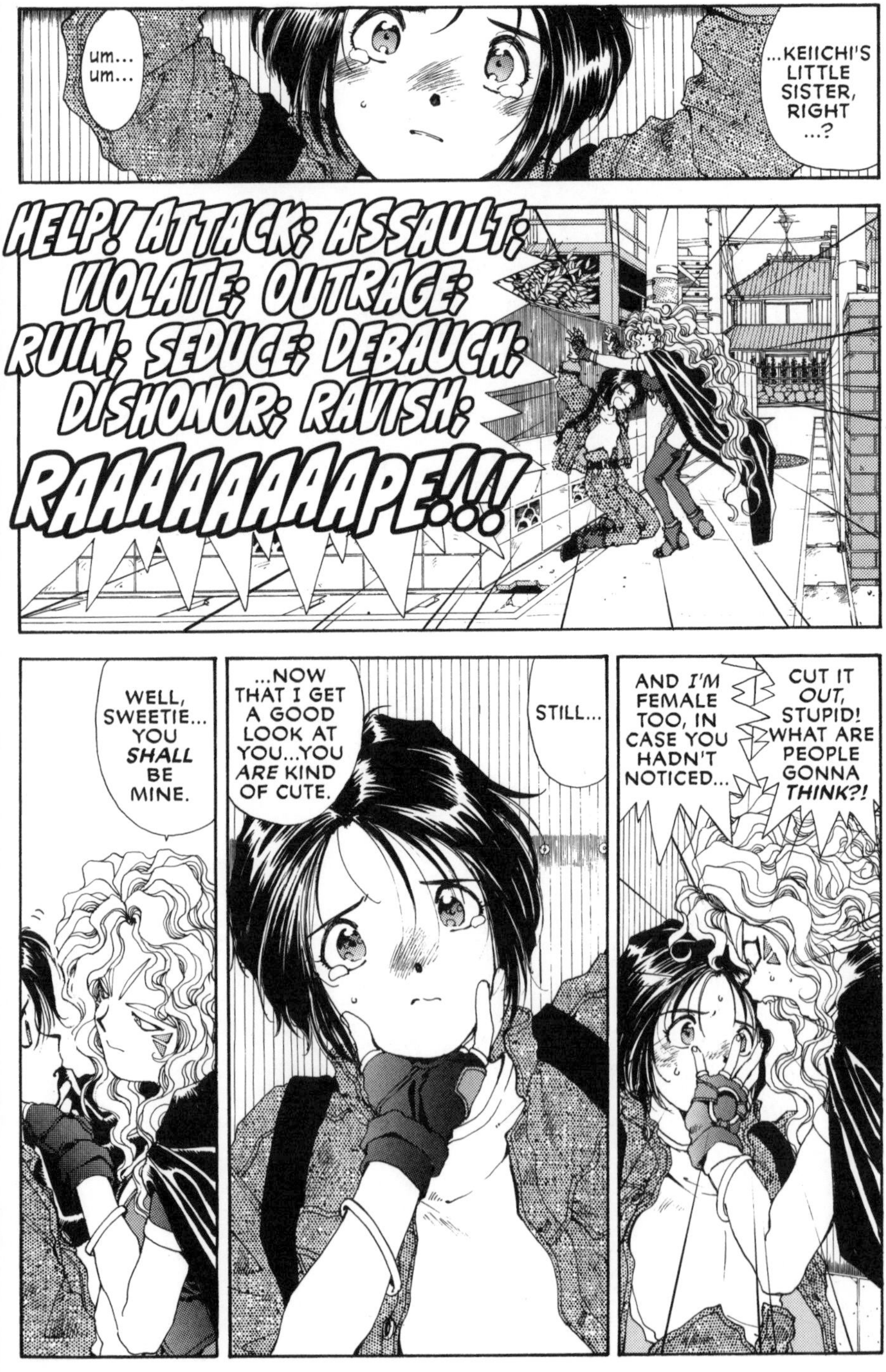
...KEIICHI'S LITTLE SISTER, RIGHT ...?
um... um...
HELP! ATTACK; ASSAULT; VIOLATE; OUTRAGE; RUIN; SEDUCE; DEBAUCH; DISHONOR; RAVISH;
RAAAAAAAAAPE!!!
CUT IT *OUT*, STUPID! WHAT ARE PEOPLE GONNA *THINK?!*
AND *I'M* FEMALE TOO, IN CASE YOU HADN'T NOTICED...
STILL...
...NOW THAT I GET A GOOD LOOK AT YOU...YOU *ARE* KIND OF CUTE.
WELL, SWEETIE... YOU *SHALL* BE MINE.

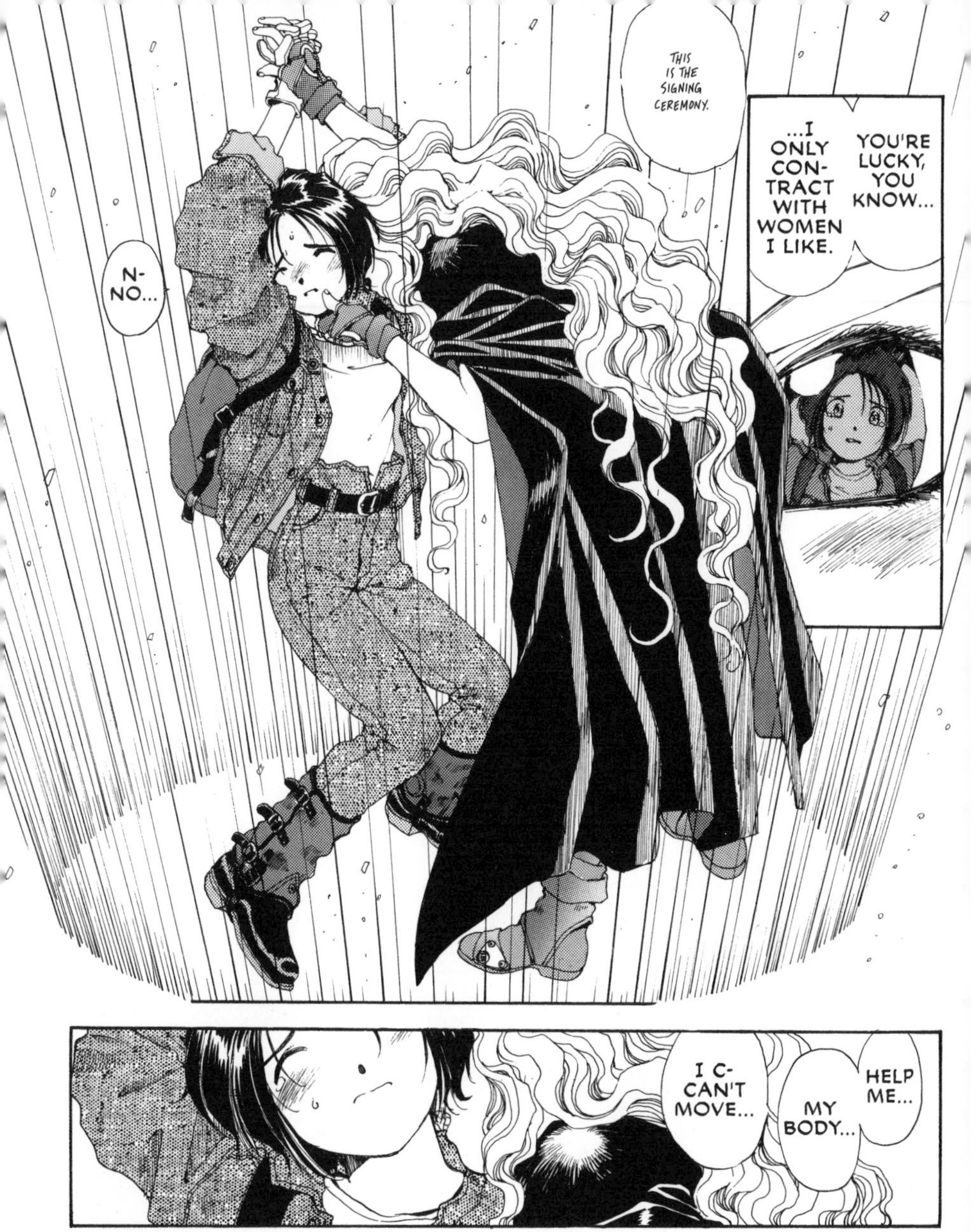
YOU'RE LUCKY, YOU KNOW...
...I ONLY CON-TRACT WITH WOMEN I LIKE.
THIS IS THE SIGNING CEREMONY.
N-NO...
HELP ME...
MY BODY...
I C-CAN'T MOVE...
...help me...
...Kei-chan...
KTHMP

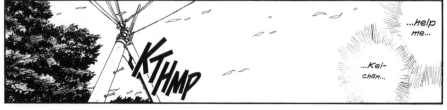

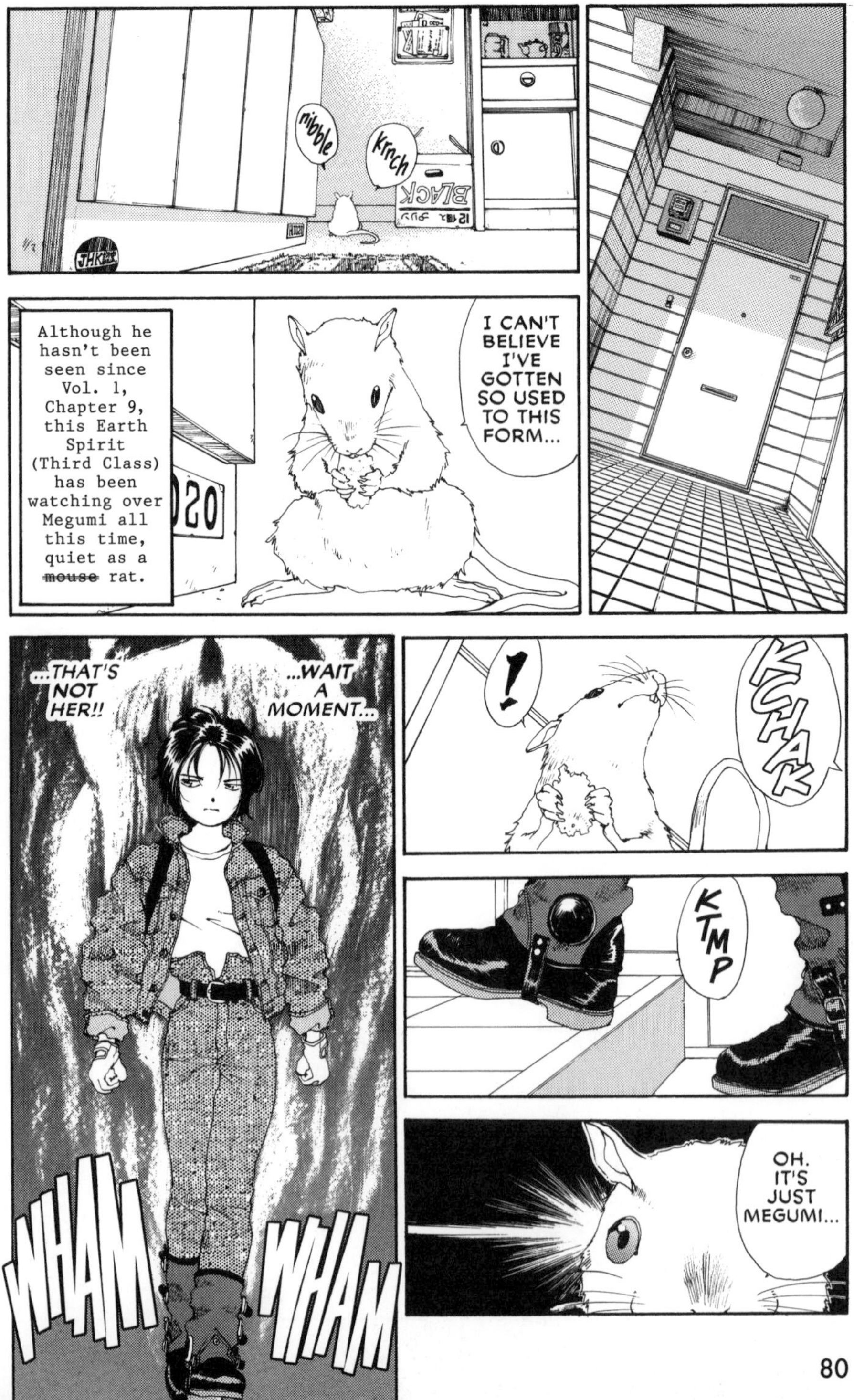
krrch
nibble
I CAN'T BELIEVE I'VE GOTTEN SO USED TO THIS FORM...
Although he hasn't been seen since Vol. 1, Chapter 9, this Earth Spirit (Third Class) has been watching over Megumi all this time, quiet as a ~~mouse~~ rat.
KCHAK
!
KTMP
OH. IT'S JUST MEGUMI...
...WAIT A MOMENT...
...THAT'S NOT HER!!
WHAM
WHAM

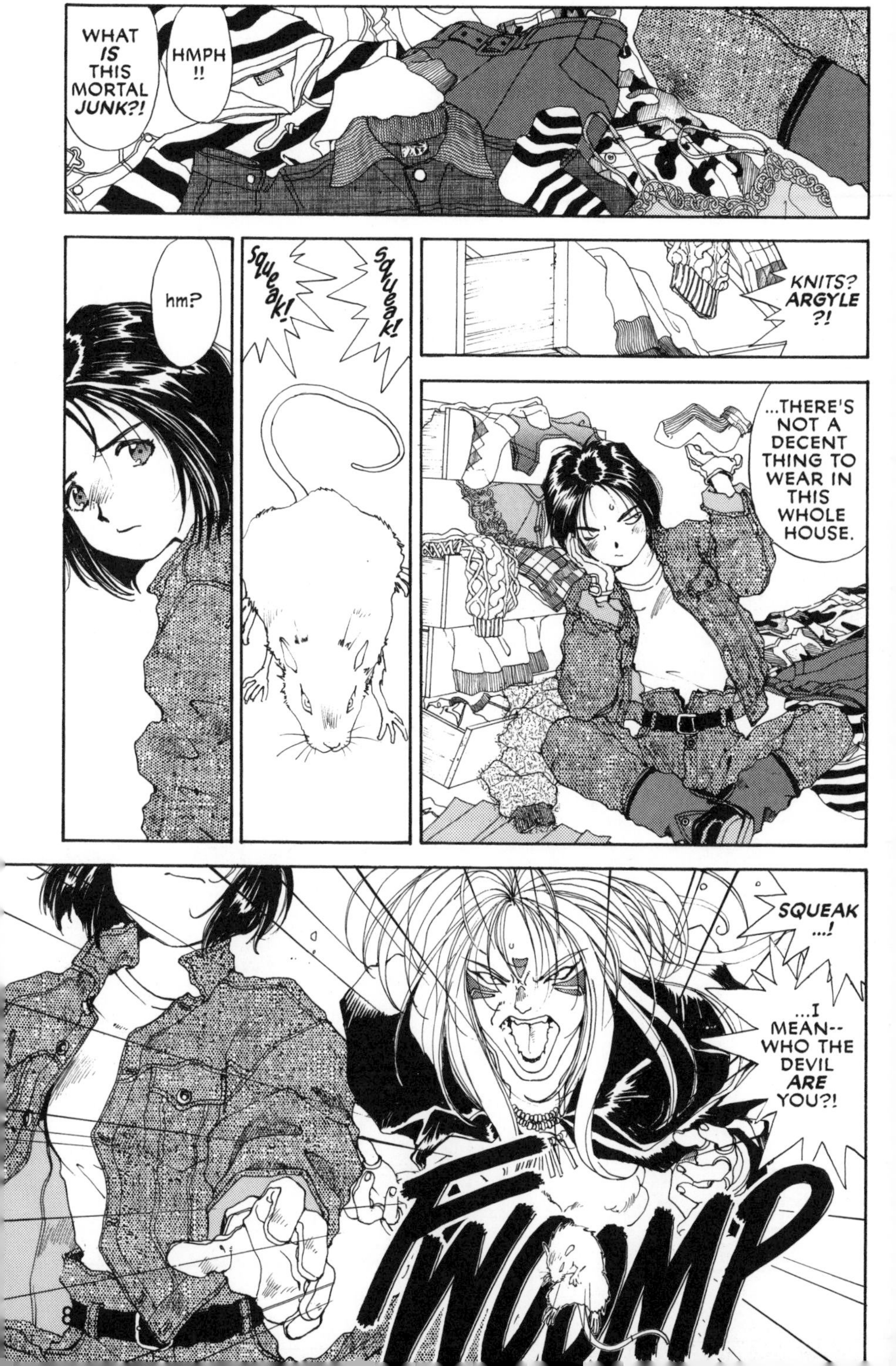
HMPH!!
WHAT IS THIS MORTAL JUNK?!
KNITS? ARGYLE?!
...THERE'S NOT A DECENT THING TO WEAR IN THIS WHOLE HOUSE.
squeak!
squeak!
hm?
SQUEAK...!
...I MEAN--WHO THE DEVIL ARE YOU?!
THOMP

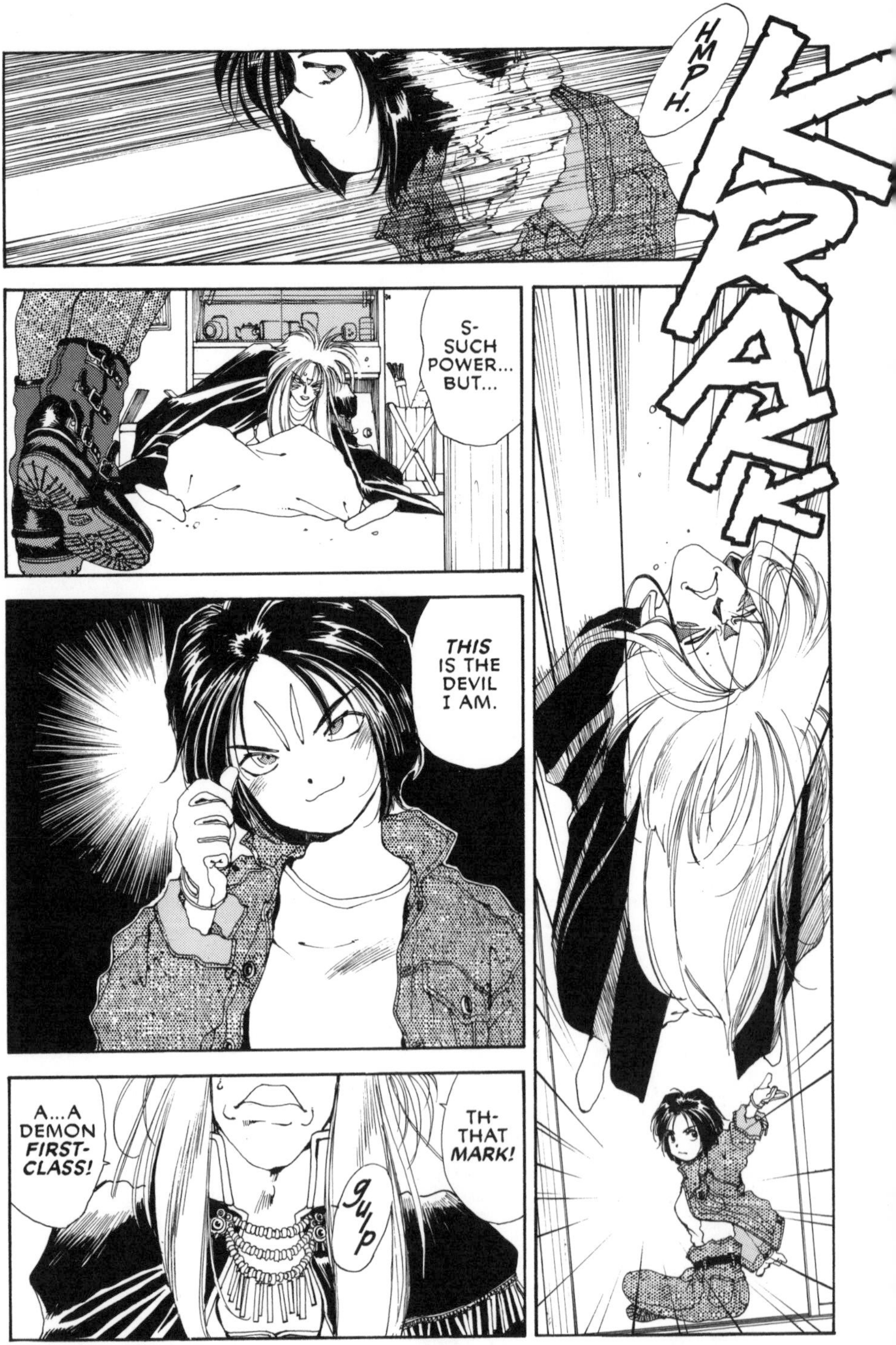
HMPH.
KRAKK
S-SUCH POWER... BUT...
THIS IS THE DEVIL I AM.
TH-THAT MARK!
gulp
A...A DEMON FIRST-CLASS!

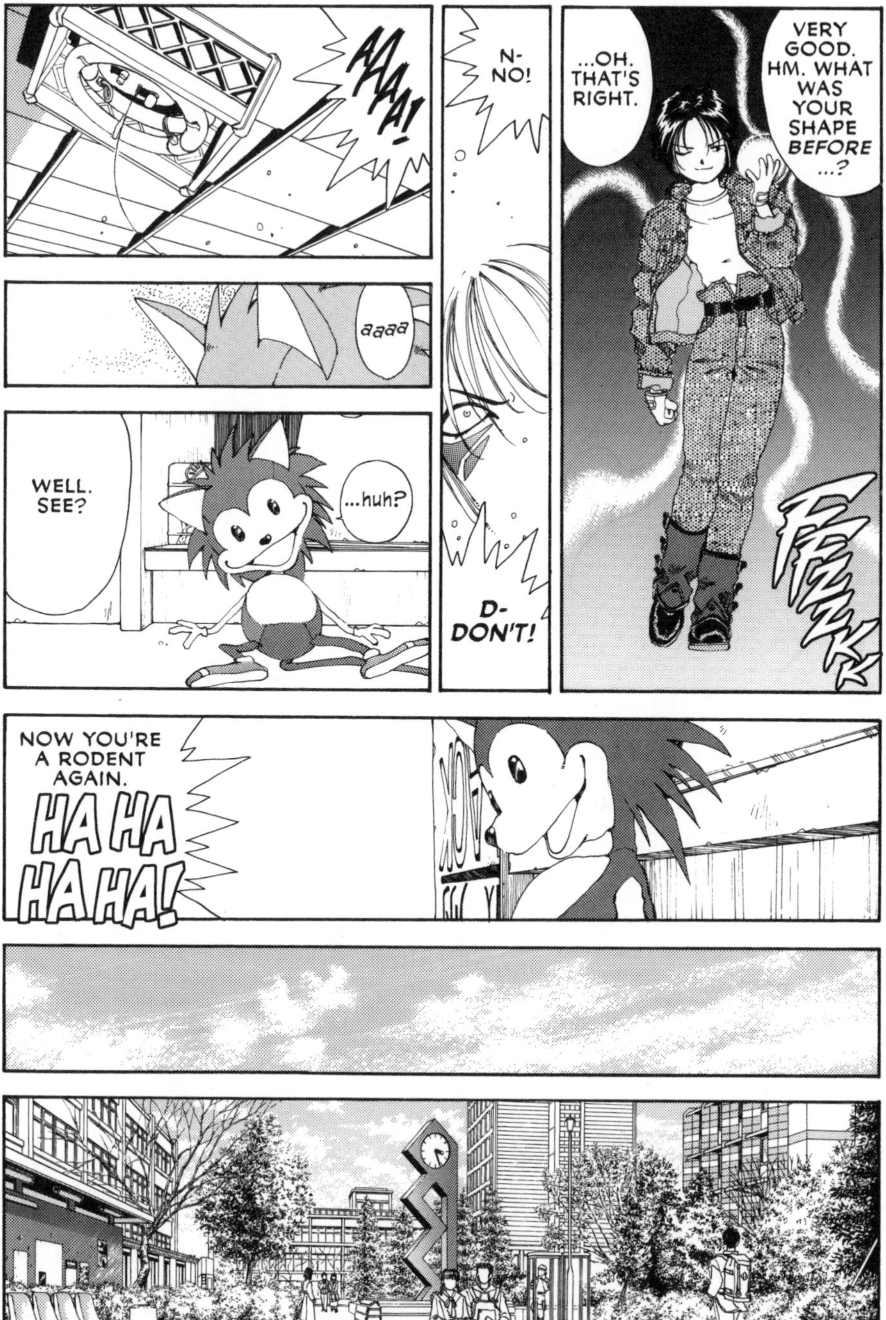

VERY GOOD. HM. WHAT WAS YOUR SHAPE *BEFORE* ...?
...OH. THAT'S RIGHT.
FZZNK
N- NO!
D- DON'T!
AAAAA!
aaaa
...huh?
WELL. SEE?
NOW YOU'RE A RODENT AGAIN.
HA HA HA HA!

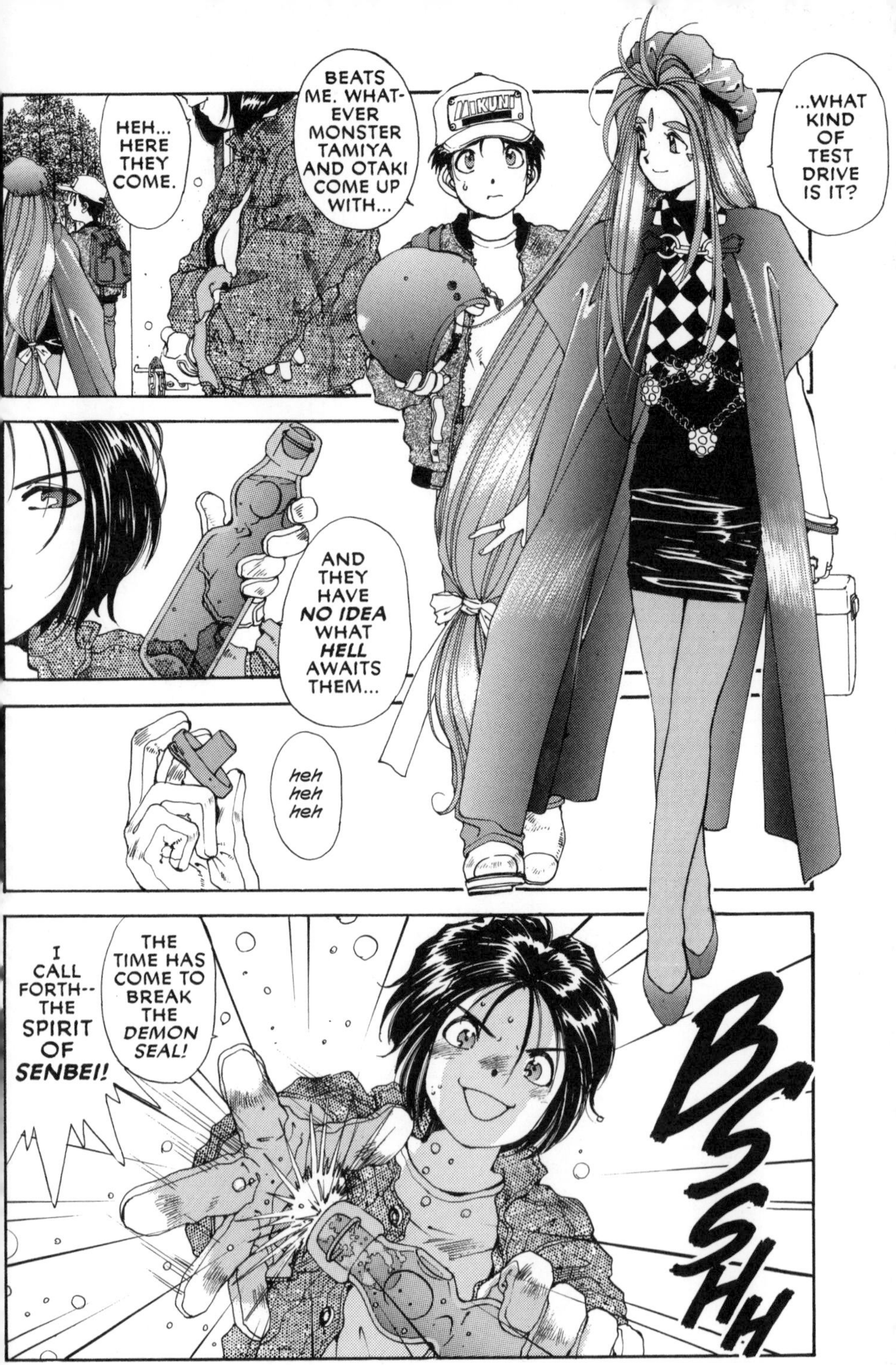
...WHAT KIND OF TEST DRIVE IS IT?
BEATS ME. WHAT-EVER MONSTER TAMIYA AND OTAKI COME UP WITH...
HEH... HERE THEY COME.
AND THEY HAVE *NO IDEA* WHAT *HELL* AWAITS THEM...
heh heh heh
THE TIME HAS COME TO BREAK THE *DEMON SEAL!*
I CALL FORTH-- THE SPIRIT OF *SENBEI!*
BSSHH

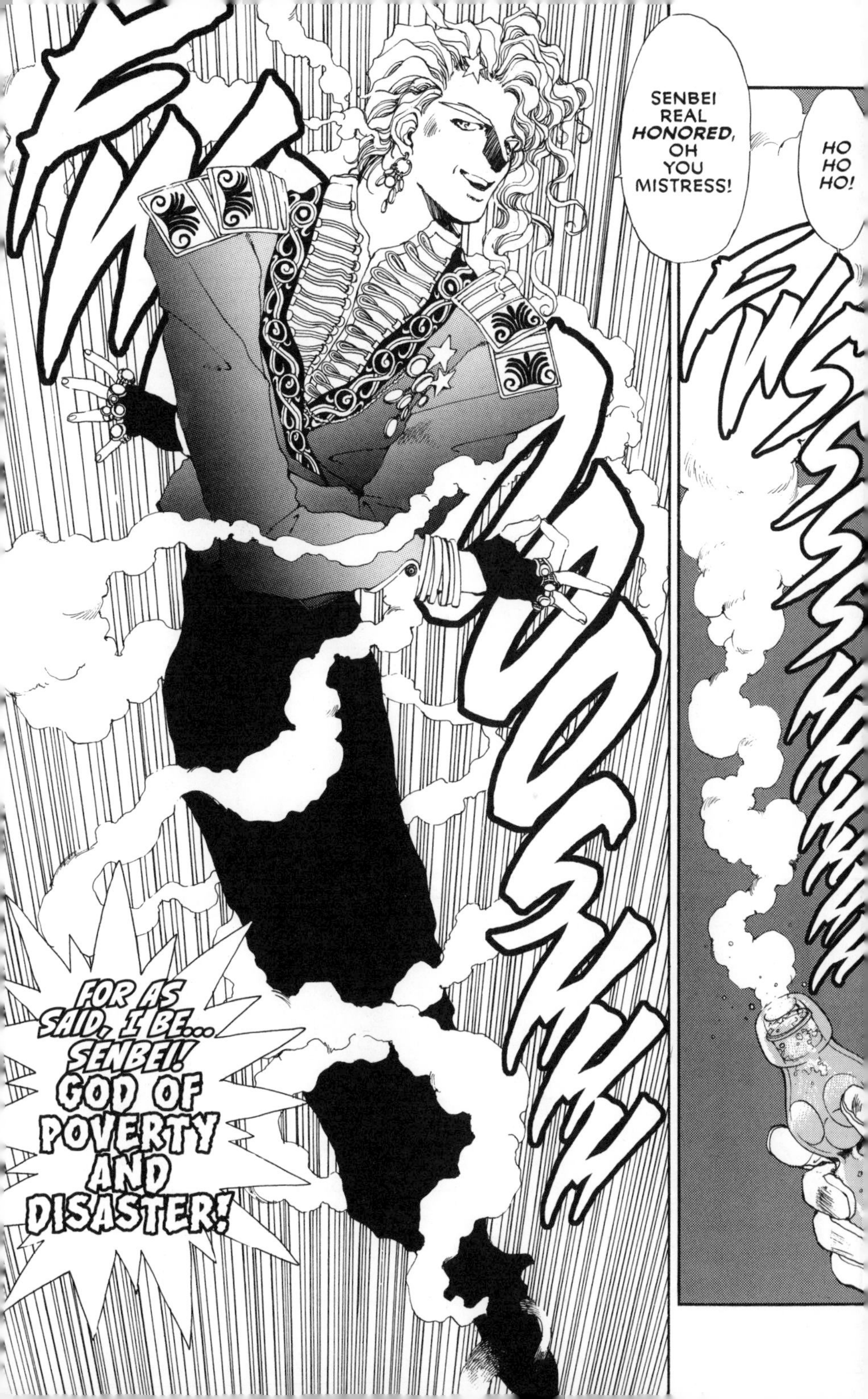
HO HO HO!
SENBEI REAL *HONORED,* OH YOU MISTRESS!
FOR AS SAID, I BE... SENBEI! GOD OF POVERTY AND DISASTER!

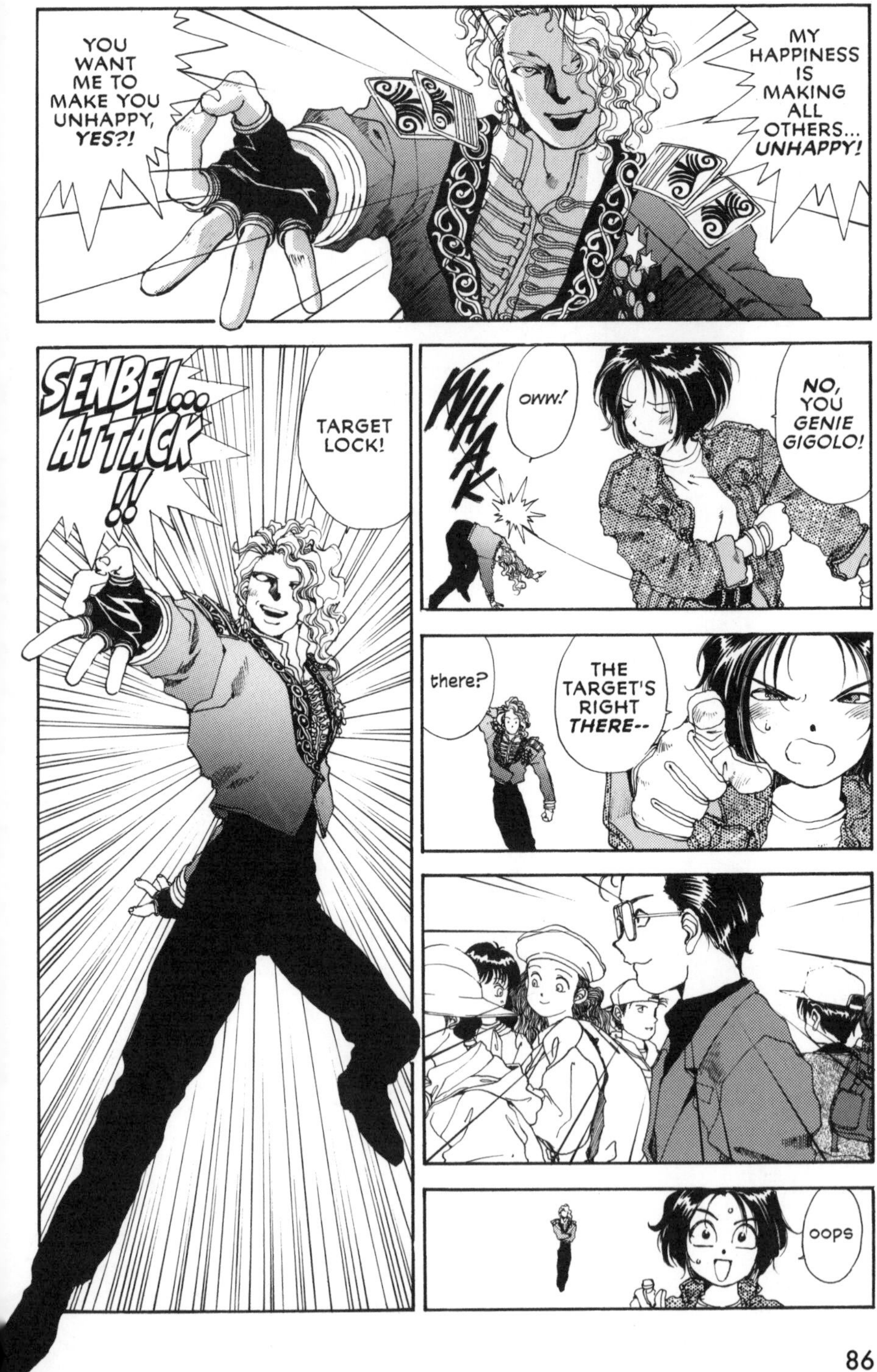
MY HAPPINESS IS MAKING ALL OTHERS... UNHAPPY!
YOU WANT ME TO MAKE YOU UNHAPPY, YES?!
NO, YOU GENIE GIGOLO!
oww!
WHAK
THE TARGET'S RIGHT THERE--
there?
oops
TARGET LOCK!
SENBEI... ATTACK!!

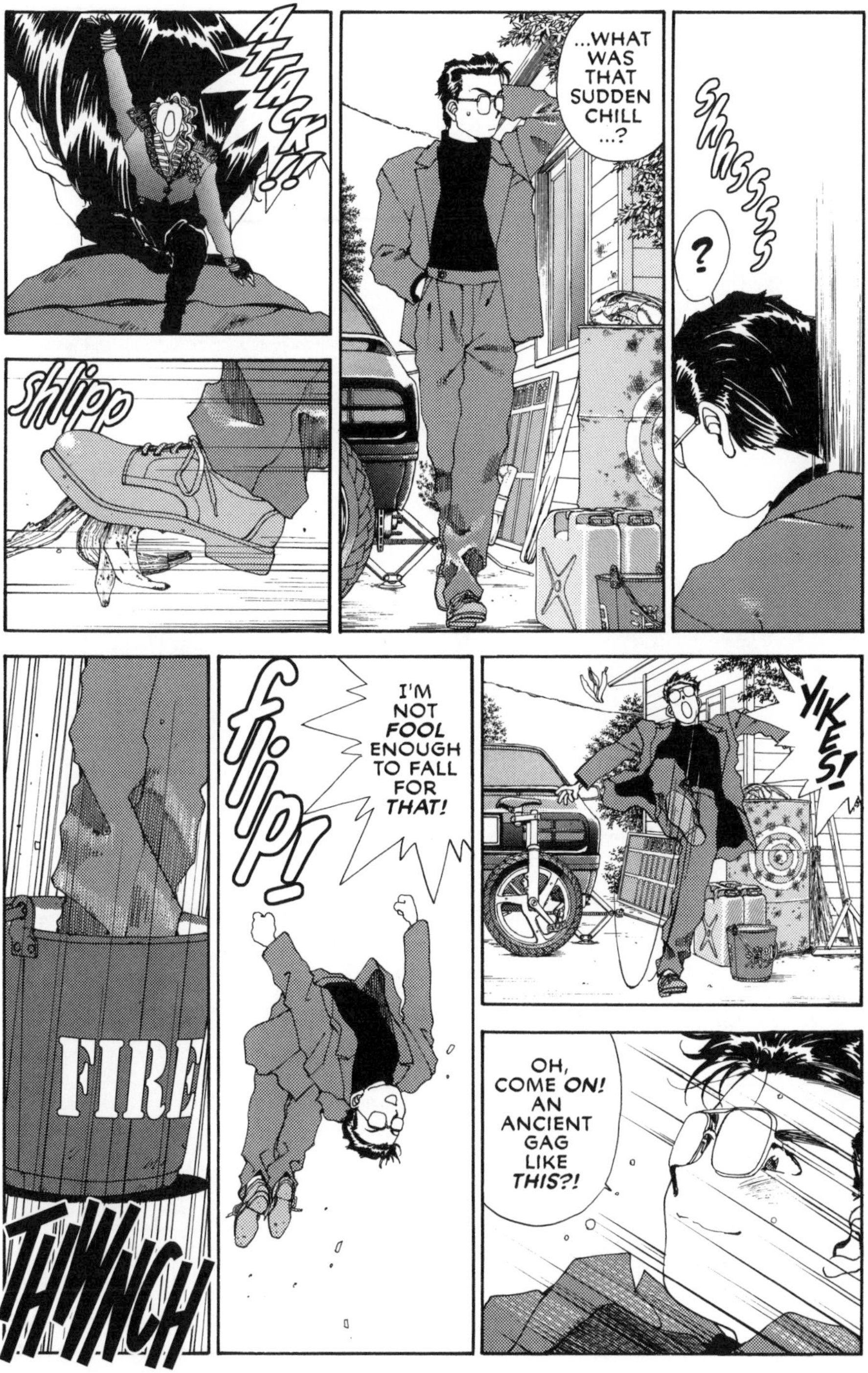
SHHSSSS
?
...WHAT WAS THAT SUDDEN CHILL ...?
ATTACK!!
shlipp
YIKES!
OH, COME ON! AN ANCIENT GAG LIKE THIS?!
flip!
I'M NOT FOOL ENOUGH TO FALL FOR THAT!
FIRE
THWNCH

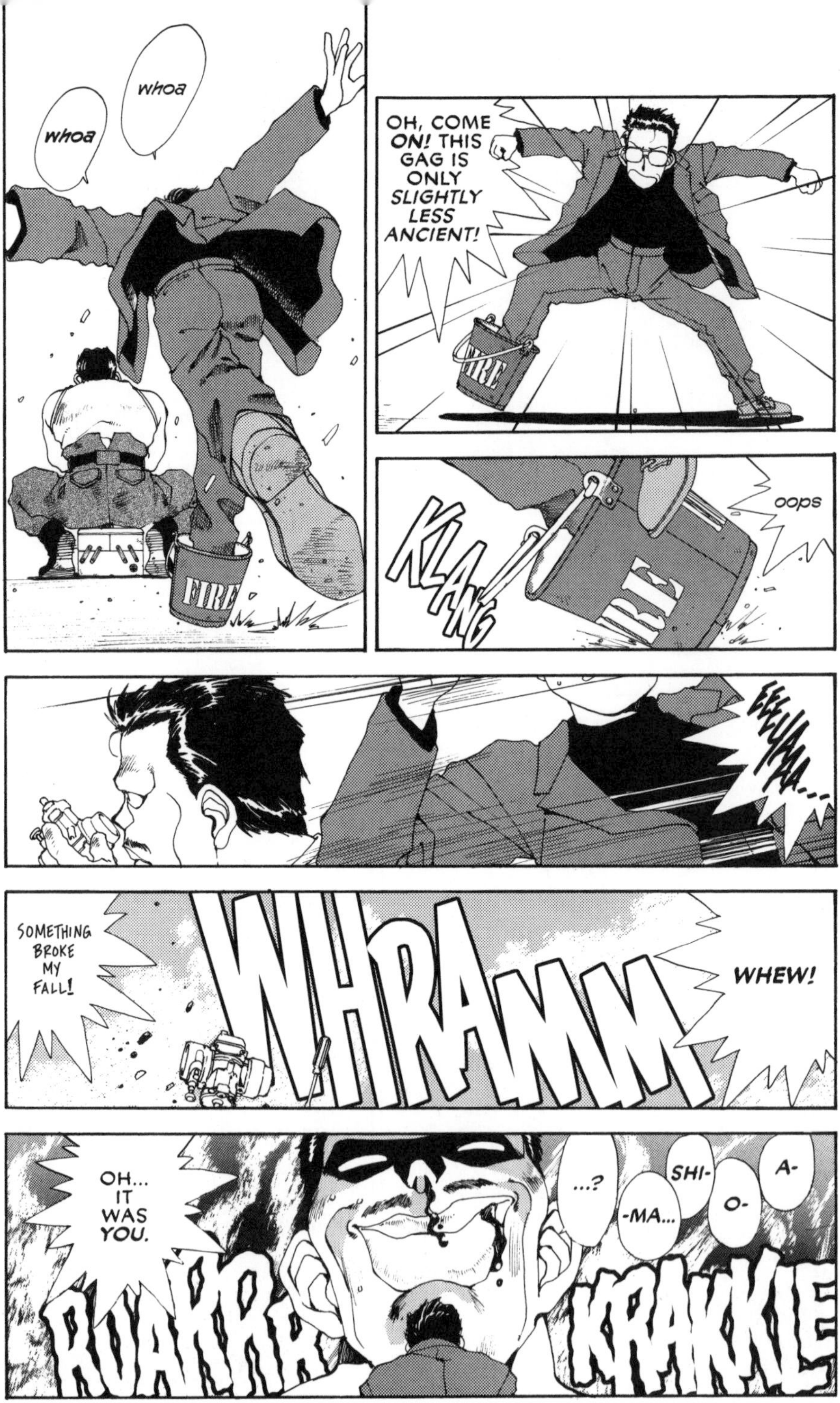
OH, COME ON! THIS GAG IS ONLY SLIGHTLY LESS ANCIENT!
oops
KLANG
whoa
whoa
FIRE
EEEYAAA...
WHEW!
WHRAMM
SOMETHING BROKE MY FALL!
A-
O-
SHI-
-MA...
...?
KRAKKLE
OH... IT WAS YOU.
RUAKRR

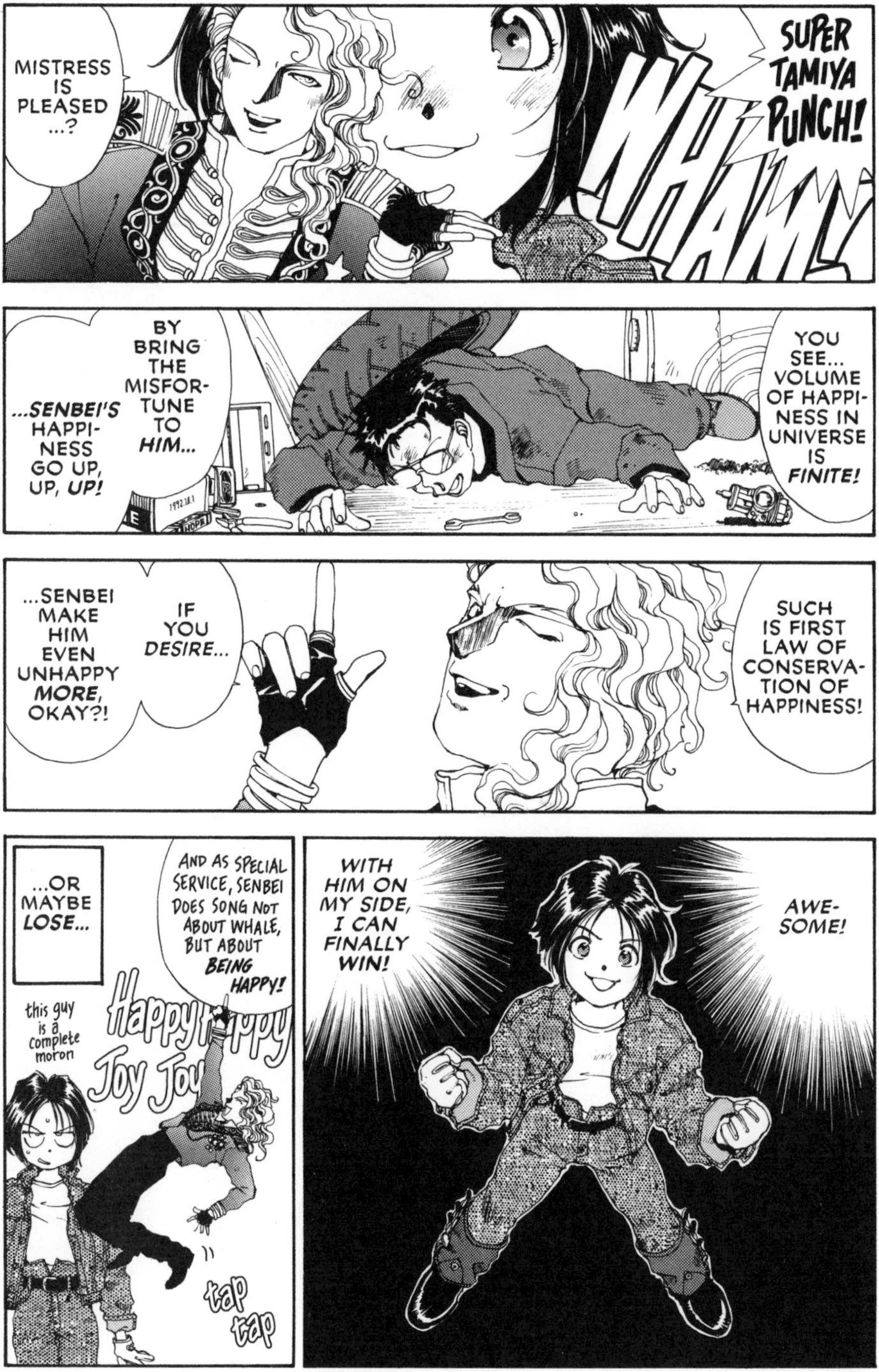
SUPER TAMIYA PUNCH!
WHAM!
MISTRESS IS PLEASED...?
YOU SEE... VOLUME OF HAPPINESS IN UNIVERSE IS *FINITE!*
BY BRING THE MISFORTUNE TO *HIM...*
...SENBEI'S HAPPINESS GO UP, UP, *UP!*
SUCH IS FIRST LAW OF CONSERVATION OF HAPPINESS!
IF YOU *DESIRE...*
...SENBEI MAKE HIM EVEN UNHAPPY *MORE*, OKAY?!
AWESOME!
WITH HIM ON MY SIDE, I CAN FINALLY WIN!
AND AS SPECIAL SERVICE, SENBEI DOES SONG NOT ABOUT WHALE, BUT ABOUT *BEING HAPPY!*
...OR MAYBE *LOSE...*
Happy Happy Joy Joy
this guy is a complete moron
tap tap

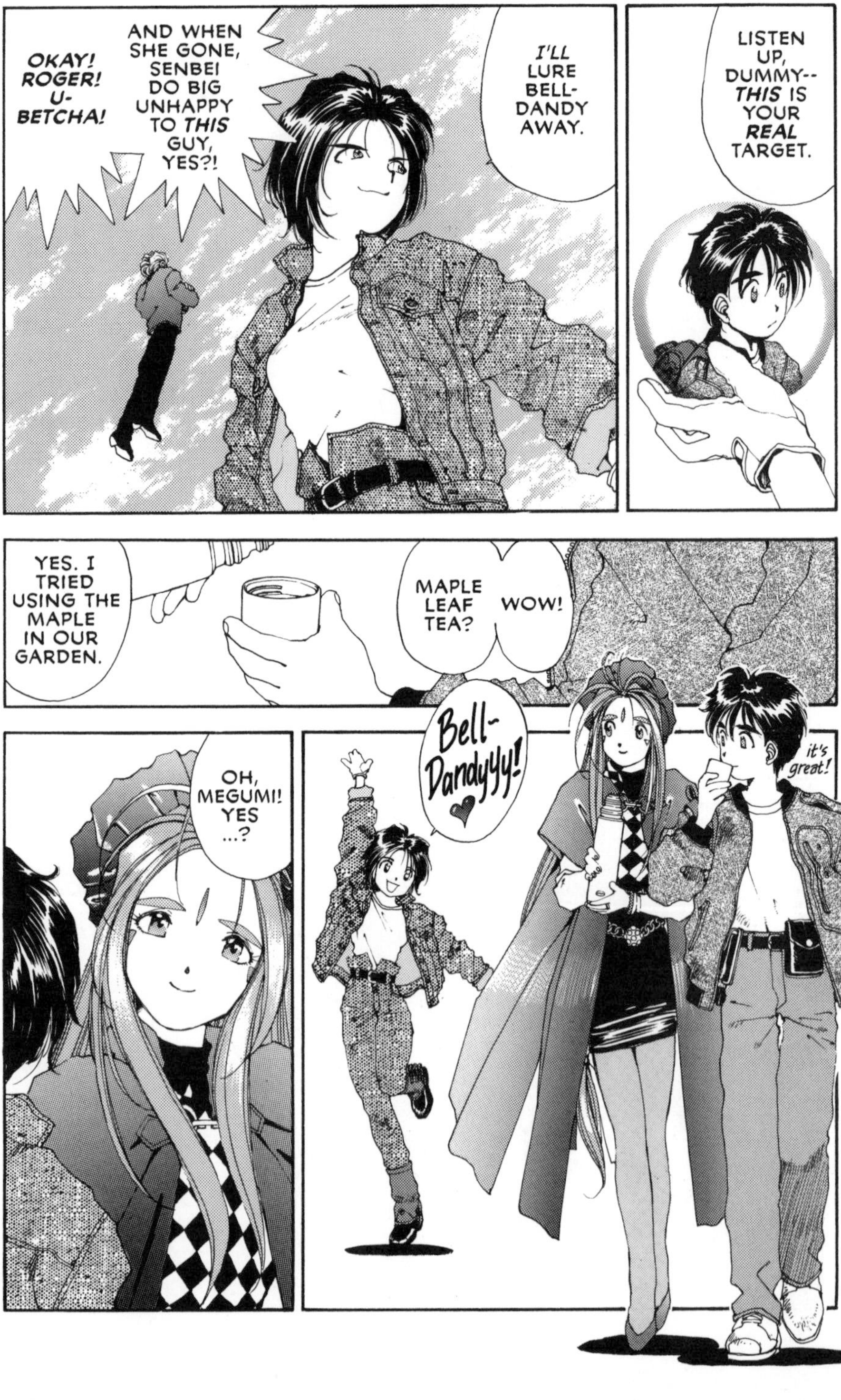
LISTEN UP, DUMMY-- *THIS* IS YOUR *REAL* TARGET.
I'LL LURE BELL-DANDY AWAY.
AND WHEN SHE GONE, SENBEI DO BIG UNHAPPY TO *THIS* GUY, YES?!
OKAY! ROGER! U-BETCHA!
WOW!
MAPLE LEAF TEA?
YES. I TRIED USING THE MAPLE IN OUR GARDEN.
it's great!
Bell-Dandyyy!
OH, MEGUMI! YES ...?

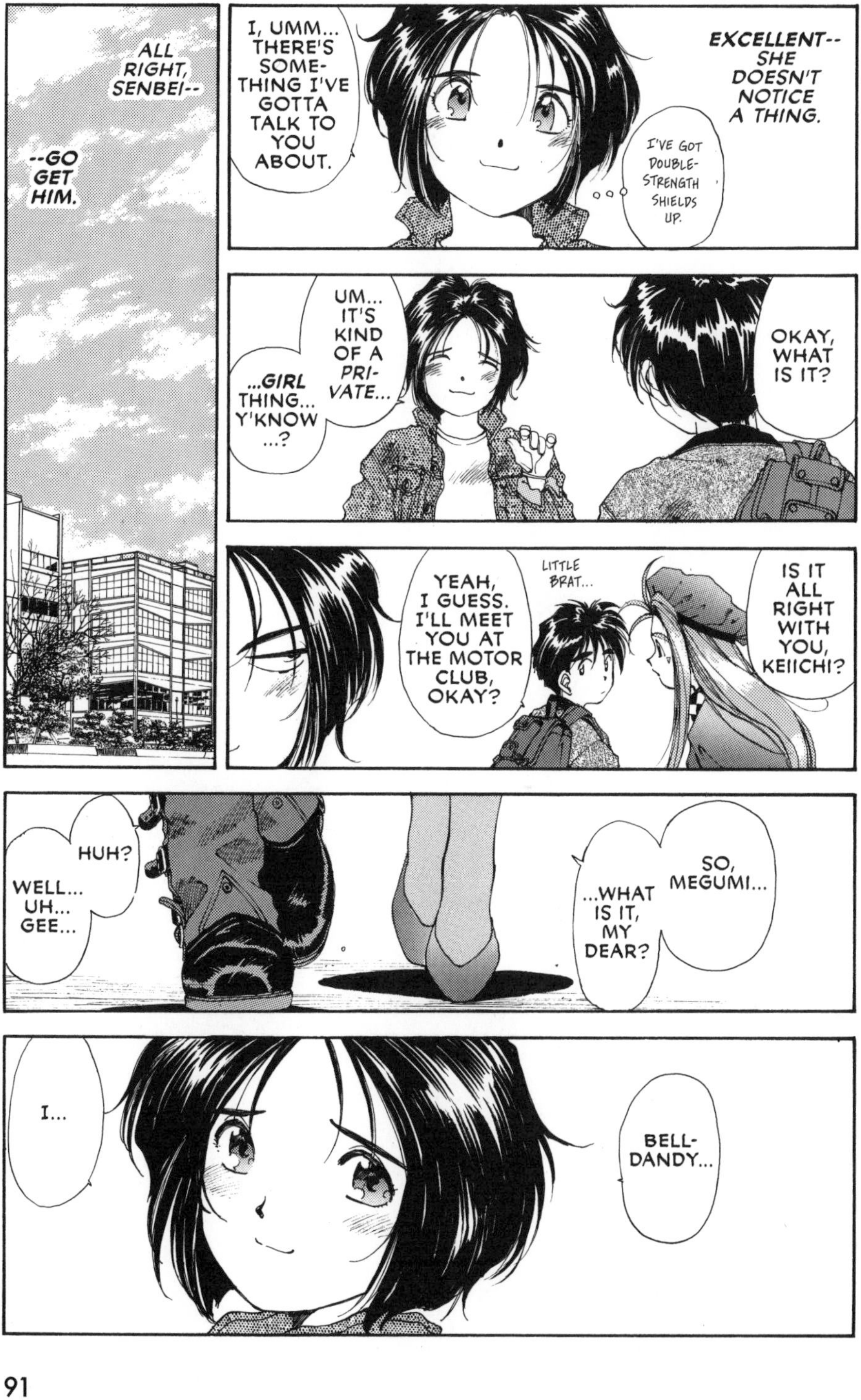
EXCELLENT-- SHE DOESN'T NOTICE A THING.
I'VE GOT DOUBLE-STRENGTH SHIELDS UP.
I, UMM... THERE'S SOME-THING I'VE GOTTA TALK TO YOU ABOUT.
OKAY, WHAT IS IT?
UM... IT'S KIND OF A PRI-VATE...
...GIRL THING... Y'KNOW ...?
IS IT ALL RIGHT WITH YOU, KEIICHI?
LITTLE BRAT...
YEAH, I GUESS. I'LL MEET YOU AT THE MOTOR CLUB, OKAY?
ALL RIGHT, SENBEI--
--GO GET HIM.
SO, MEGUMI...
...WHAT IS IT, MY DEAR?
HUH?
WELL... UH... GEE...
BELL-DANDY...
I...

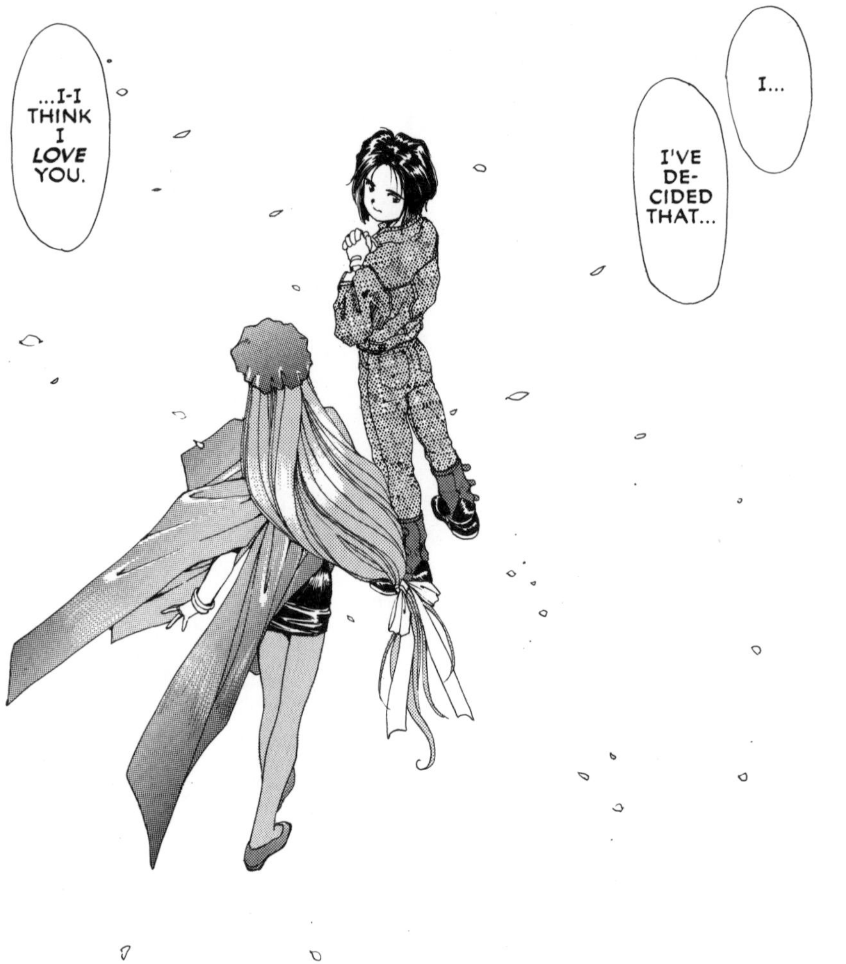
I...
I'VE DE-CIDED THAT...
...I-I THINK I *LOVE* YOU.

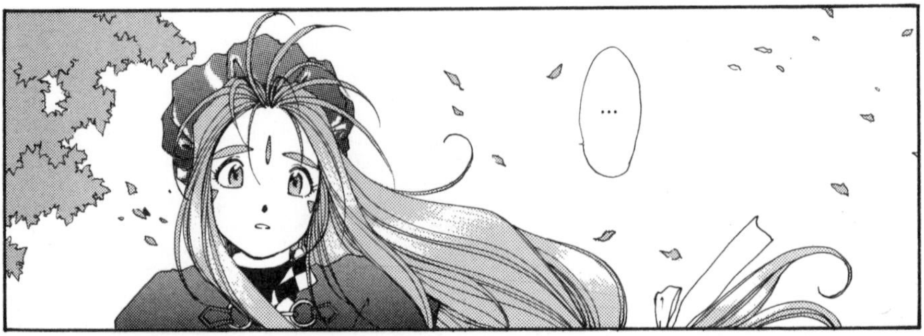
...

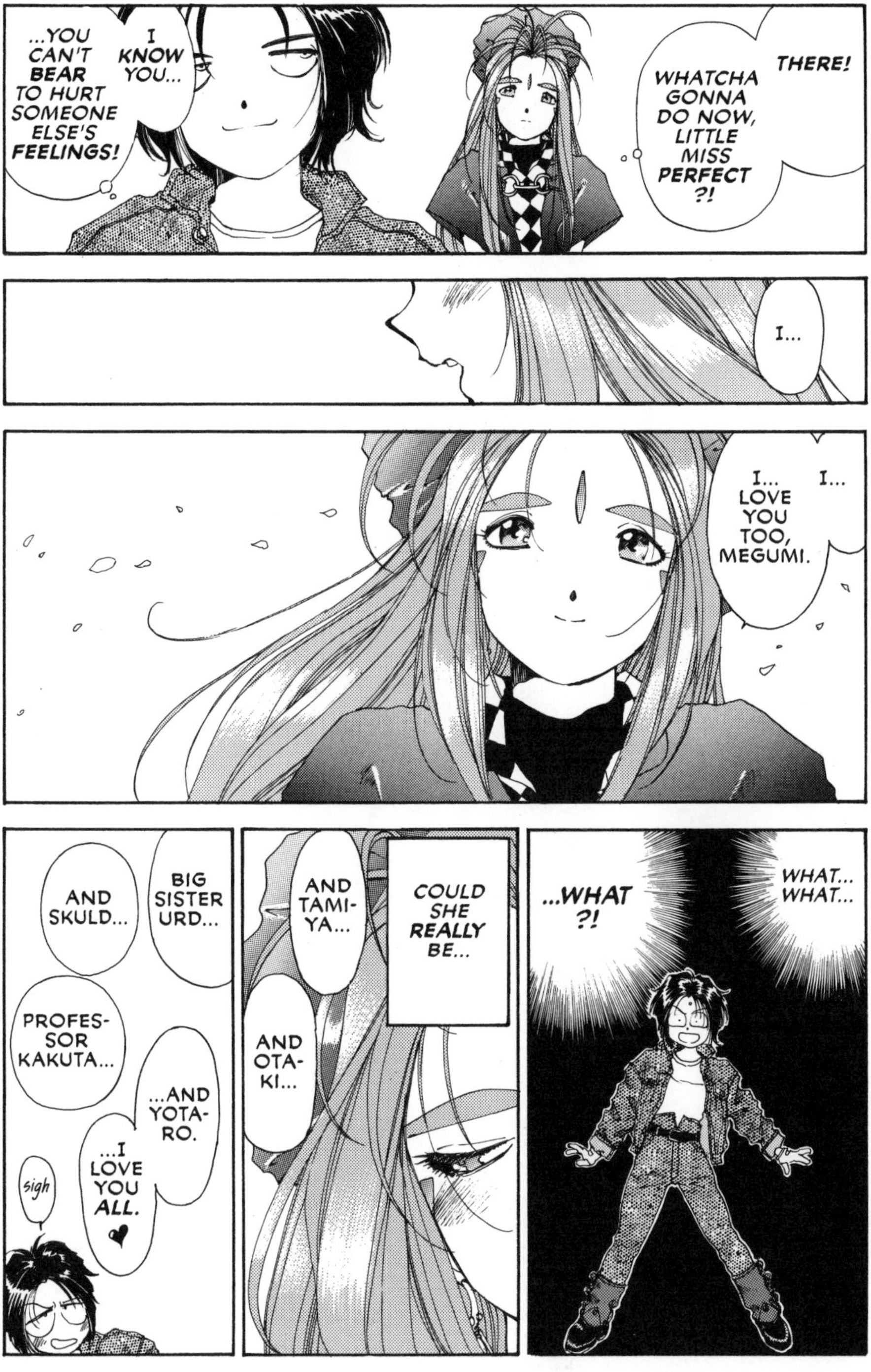
THERE!
WHATCHA GONNA DO NOW, LITTLE MISS PERFECT?!
I KNOW YOU...
...YOU CAN'T BEAR TO HURT SOMEONE ELSE'S FEELINGS!
I...
I...
I... LOVE YOU TOO, MEGUMI.
WHAT... WHAT...
...WHAT?!
COULD SHE REALLY BE...
AND TAMIYA...
AND OTAKI...
BIG SISTER URD...
AND SKULD...
PROFESSOR KAKUTA...
...AND YOTARO.
...I LOVE YOU ALL. ♥
sigh

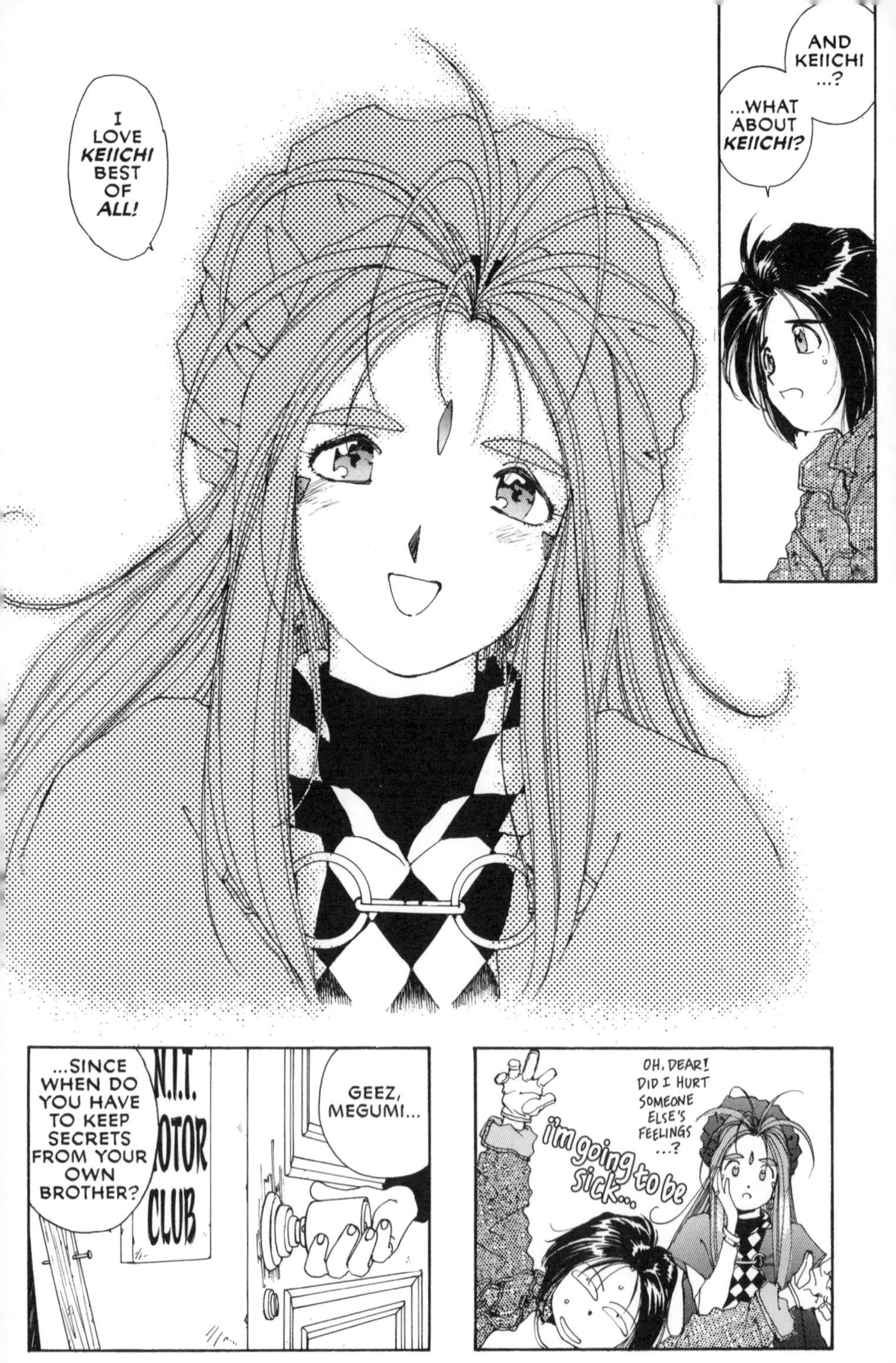
AND KEIICHI ...?
...WHAT ABOUT KEIICHI?
I LOVE KEIICHI BEST OF ALL!
OH, DEAR! DID I HURT SOMEONE ELSE'S FEELINGS ...?
i'm going to be sick...
GEEZ, MEGUMI...
...SINCE WHEN DO YOU HAVE TO KEEP SECRETS FROM YOUR OWN BROTHER?
N.I.T.
CLUB

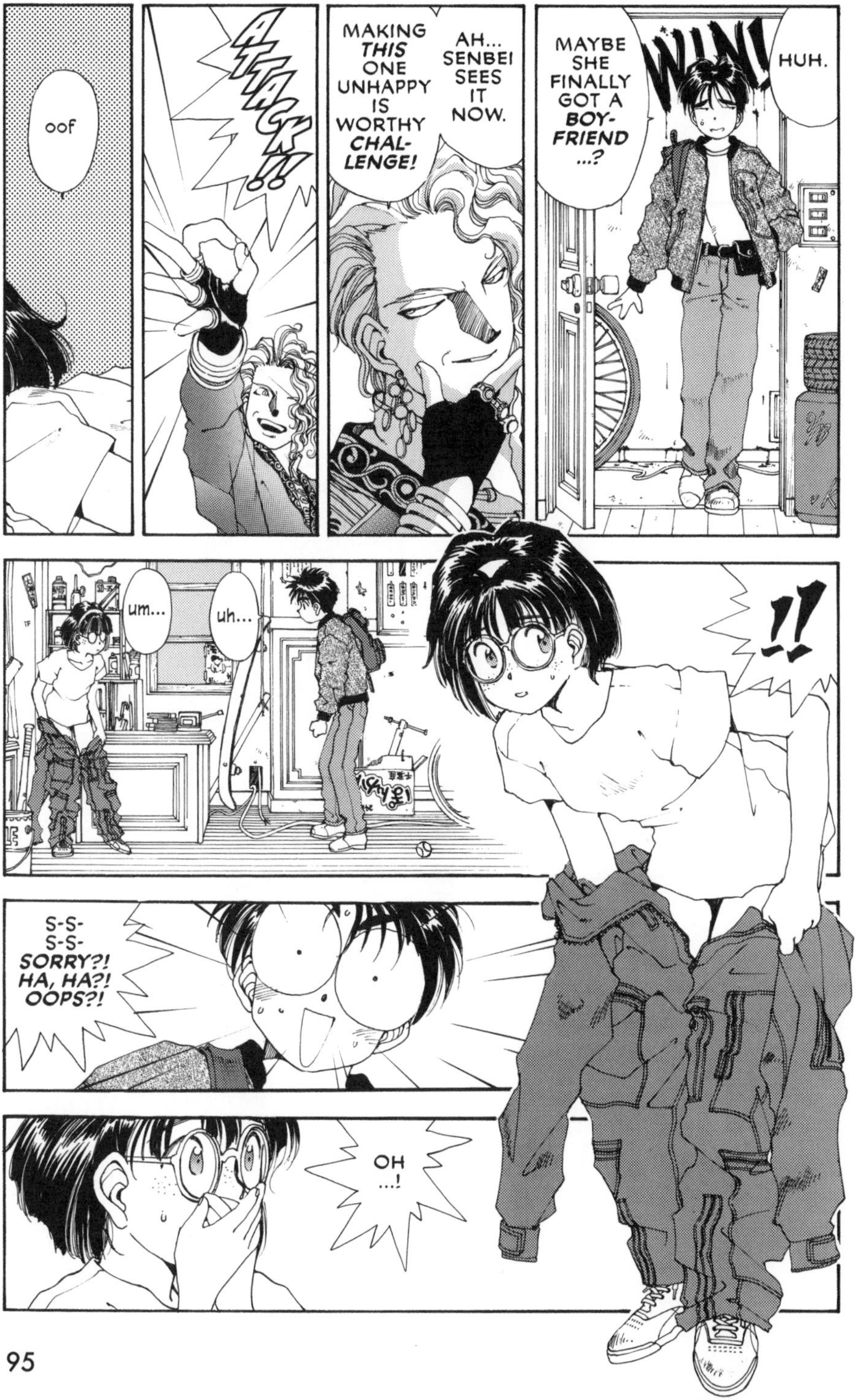
HUH.
WIN!
MAYBE SHE FINALLY GOT A *BOY-FRIEND* ...?
AH... SENBEI SEES IT NOW.
MAKING *THIS* ONE UNHAPPY IS WORTHY *CHAL-LENGE!*
ATTACK!!
oof
!!
uh...
um...
S-S-S-S- *SORRY?! HA, HA?! OOPS?!*
OH ...!
←CLUB MEMBER SORA HASEGAWA

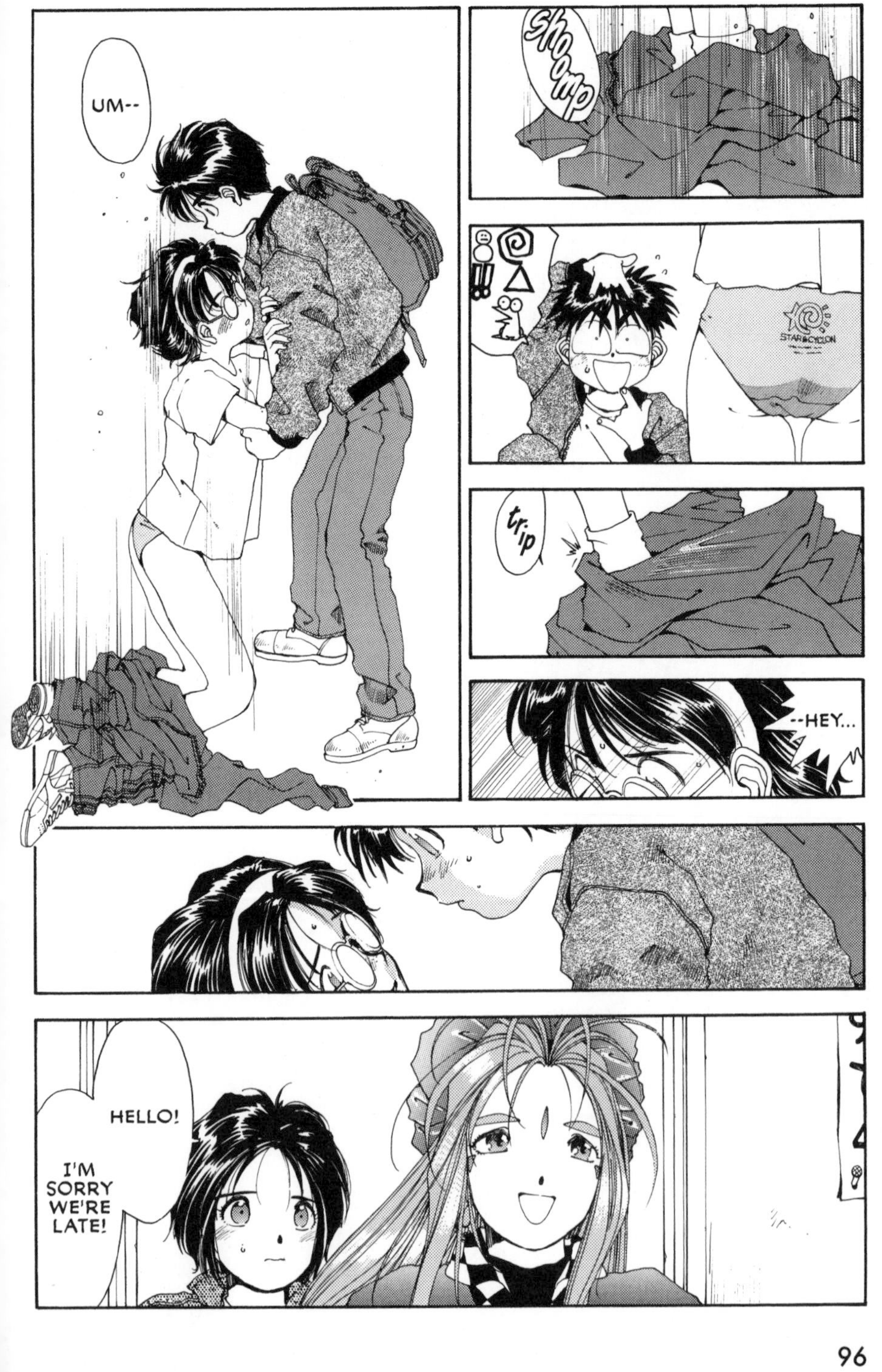
shoomp
STAR&CYCLON
trip
--HEY...
UM--
HELLO!
I'M SORRY WE'RE LATE!

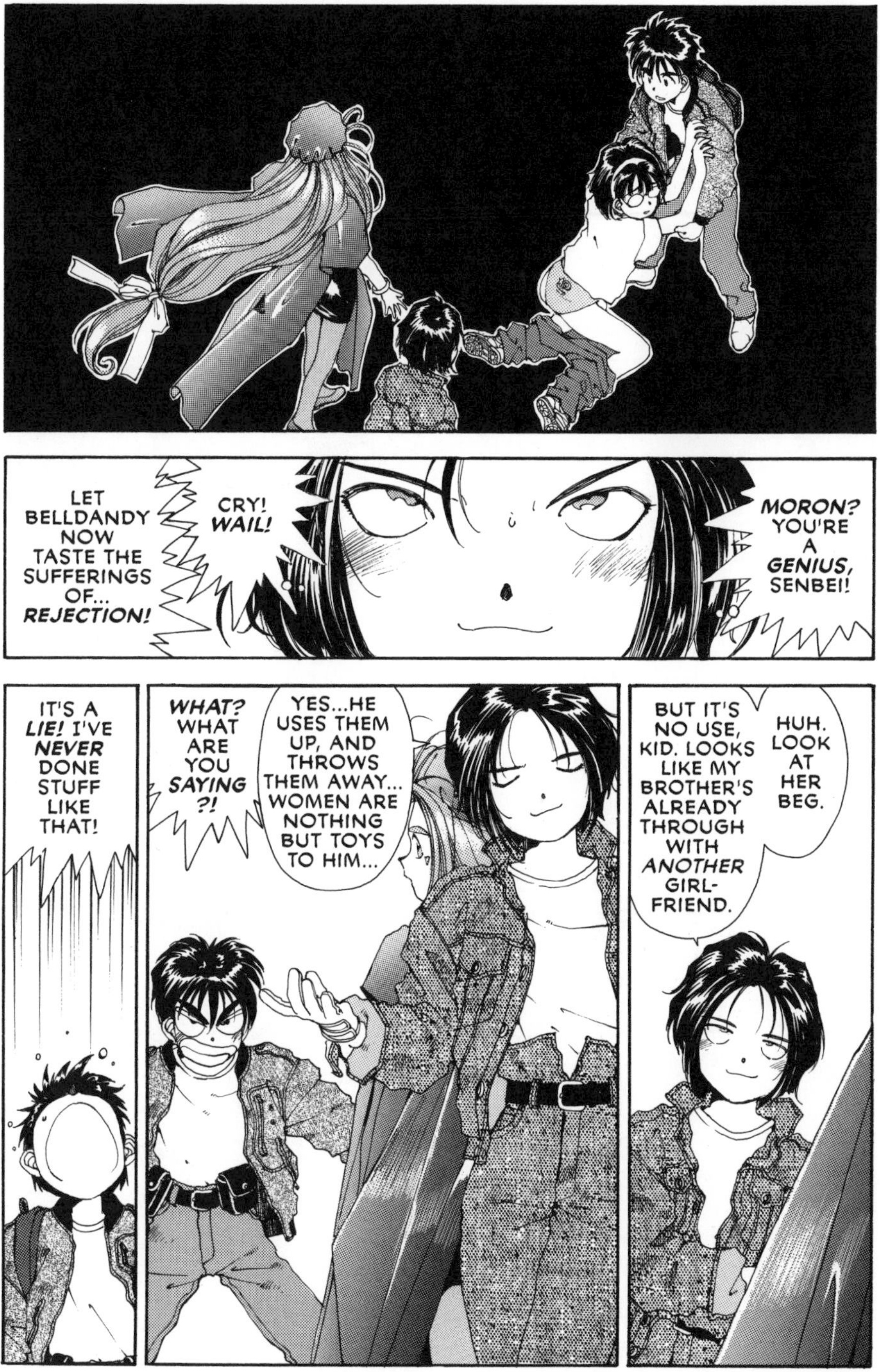
MORON? YOU'RE A GENIUS, SENBEI!
CRY! WAIL!
LET BELLDANDY NOW TASTE THE SUFFERINGS OF... REJECTION!
HUH. LOOK AT HER BEG.
BUT IT'S NO USE, KID. LOOKS LIKE MY BROTHER'S ALREADY THROUGH WITH ANOTHER GIRL-FRIEND.
YES...HE USES THEM UP, AND THROWS THEM AWAY... WOMEN ARE NOTHING BUT TOYS TO HIM...
WHAT? WHAT ARE YOU SAYING?!
IT'S A LIE! I'VE NEVER DONE STUFF LIKE THAT!

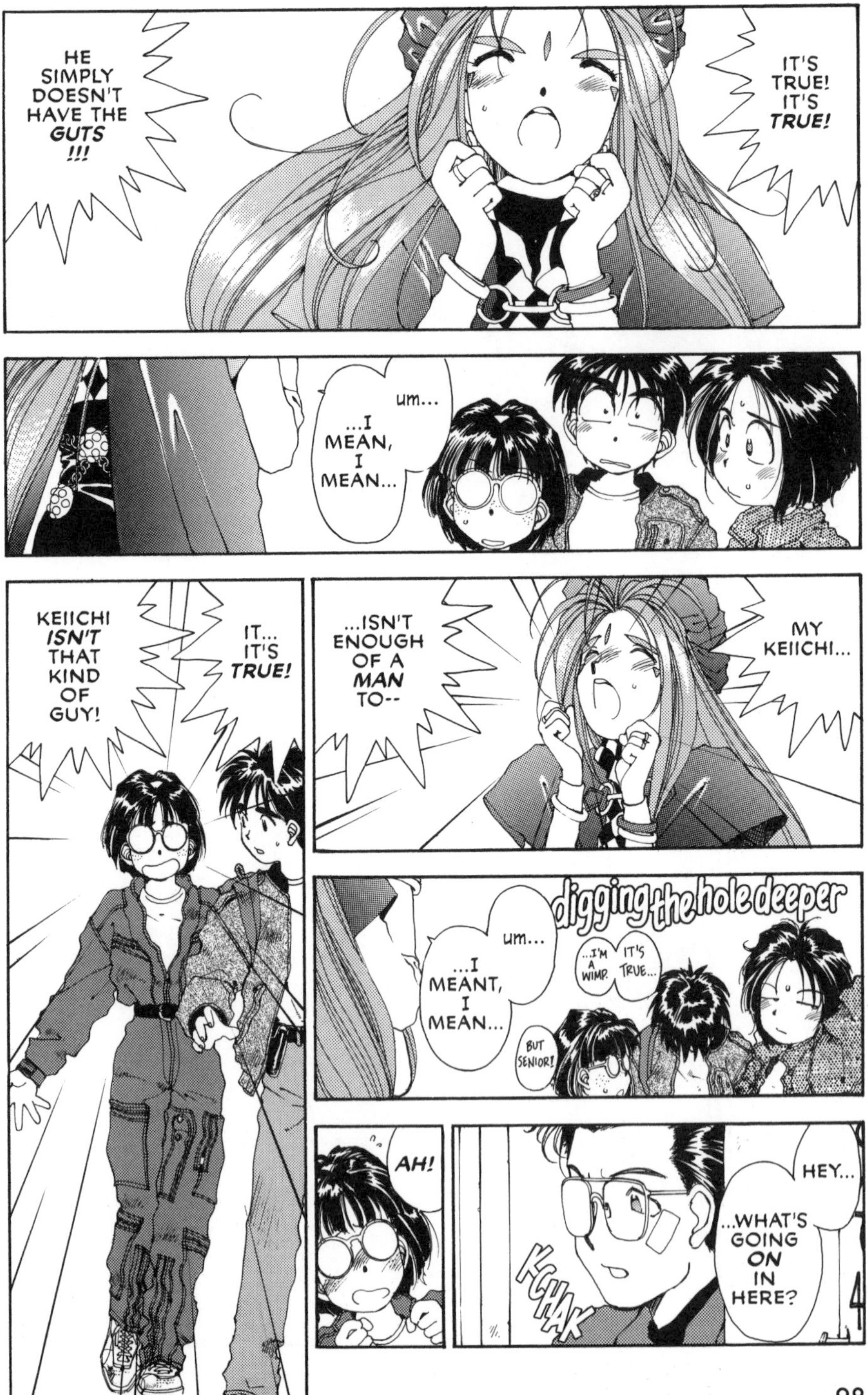
IT'S TRUE! IT'S TRUE!
HE SIMPLY DOESN'T HAVE THE GUTS!!!
um... ...I MEAN, I MEAN...
MY KEIICHI...
...ISN'T ENOUGH OF A MAN TO--
digging the hole deeper
IT'S TRUE...
...I'M A WIMP.
um... ...I MEANT, I MEAN...
BUT SENIOR!
HEY... ...WHAT'S GOING ON IN HERE?
K'CHAK
AH!
IT... IT'S TRUE!
KEIICHI ISN'T THAT KIND OF GUY!

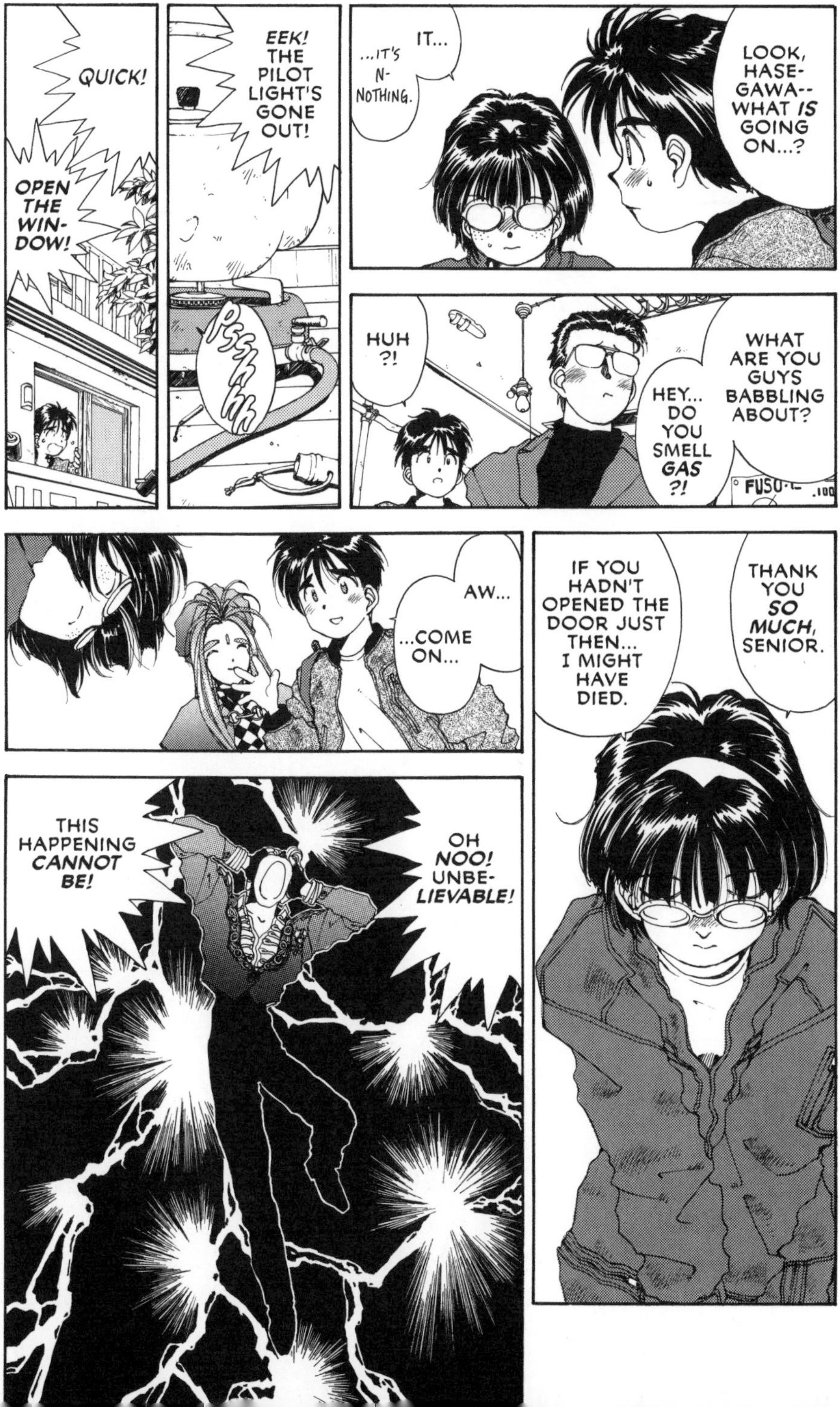
LOOK, HASEGAWA-- WHAT IS GOING ON...?
IT...
...IT'S N-NOTHING.
WHAT ARE YOU GUYS BABBLING ABOUT?
HEY... DO YOU SMELL GAS?!
HUH?!
EEK! THE PILOT LIGHT'S GONE OUT!
PSSHHH
QUICK!
OPEN THE WINDOW!
THANK YOU SO MUCH, SENIOR.
IF YOU HADN'T OPENED THE DOOR JUST THEN... I MIGHT HAVE DIED.
AW...
...COME ON...
OH NOO! UNBELIEVABLE!
THIS HAPPENING CANNOT BE!

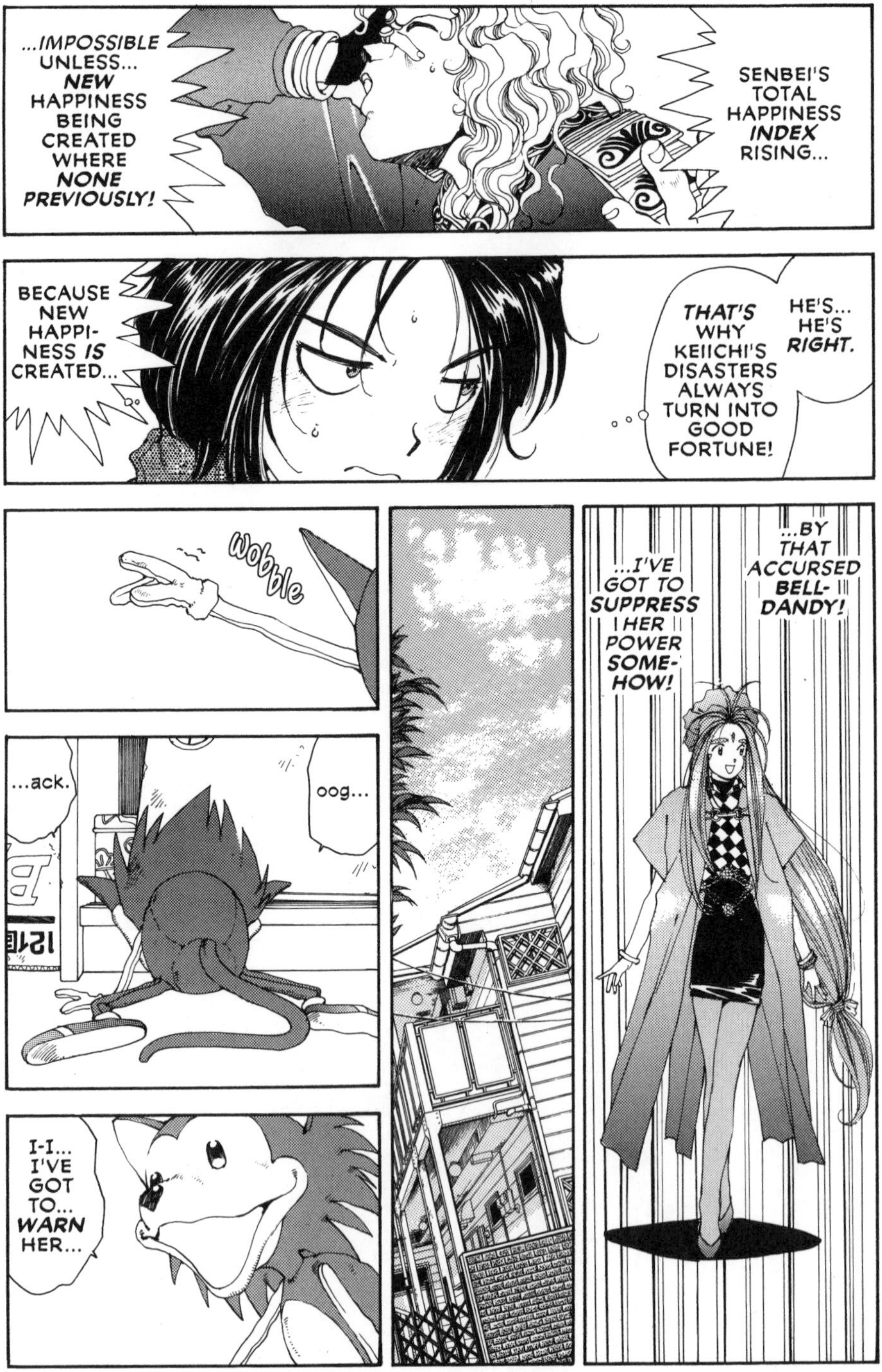
SENBEI'S TOTAL HAPPINESS INDEX RISING...
...IMPOSSIBLE UNLESS... NEW HAPPINESS BEING CREATED WHERE NONE PREVIOUSLY!
HE'S... HE'S RIGHT.
THAT'S WHY KEIICHI'S DISASTERS ALWAYS TURN INTO GOOD FORTUNE!
BECAUSE NEW HAPPINESS IS CREATED...
...BY THAT ACCURSED BELL-DANDY!
...I'VE GOT TO SUPPRESS HER POWER SOME-HOW!
wobble
oog...
...ack.
I-I... I'VE GOT TO... WARN HER...

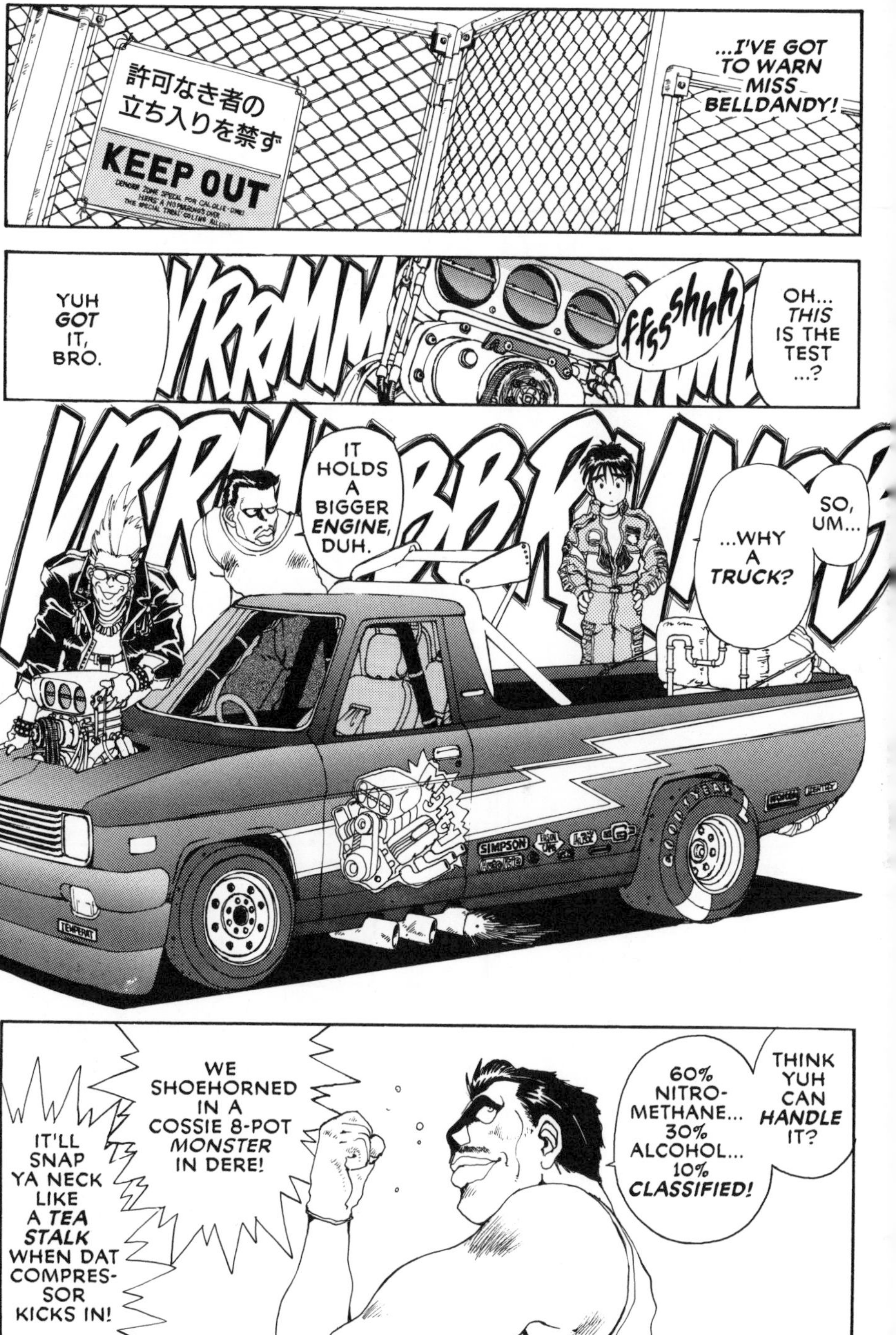

許可なき者の立ち入りを禁ず
KEEP OUT
...I'VE GOT TO WARN MISS BELLDANDY!
OH... THIS IS THE TEST ...?
ffssshhh
VRRMM
YUH GOT IT, BRO.
SO, UM...
...WHY A TRUCK?
IT HOLDS A BIGGER ENGINE, DUH.
SIMPSON
THINK YUH CAN HANDLE IT?
60% NITRO-METHANE... 30% ALCOHOL... 10% CLASSIFIED!
WE SHOEHORNED IN A COSSIE 8-POT MONSTER IN DERE!
IT'LL SNAP YA NECK LIKE A TEA STALK WHEN DAT COMPRES-SOR KICKS IN!

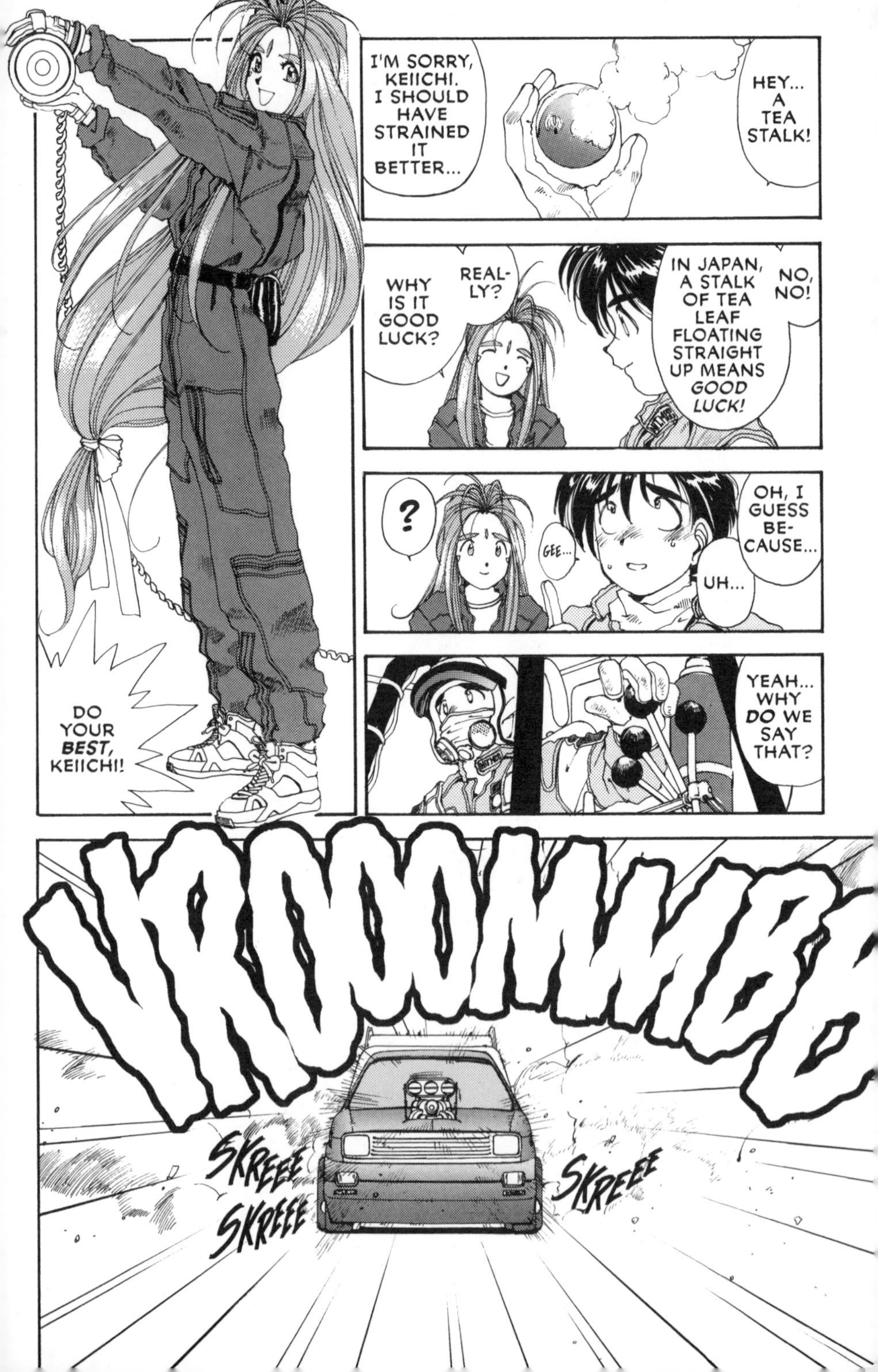
HEY... A TEA STALK!
I'M SORRY, KEIICHI. I SHOULD HAVE STRAINED IT BETTER...
NO, NO!
IN JAPAN, A STALK OF TEA LEAF FLOATING STRAIGHT UP MEANS *GOOD LUCK!*
REAL-LY?
WHY IS IT GOOD LUCK?
OH, I GUESS BE-CAUSE...
UH...
GEE...
?
YEAH... WHY *DO* WE SAY THAT?
DO YOUR *BEST,* KEIICHI!
VROOMMB
SKREEEE
SKREEEE
SKREEE

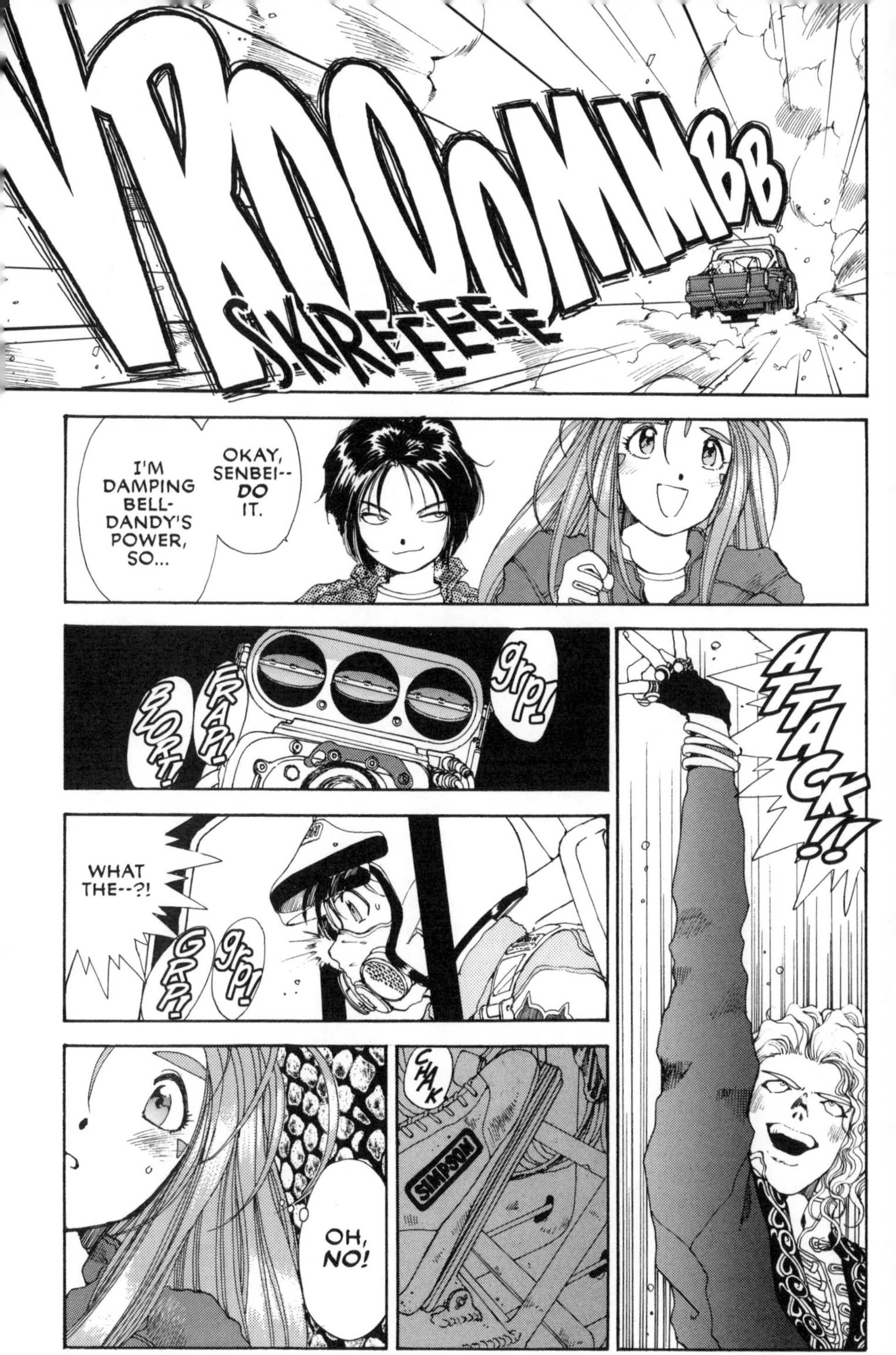
VROOOMMBB
SKREEEEE
OKAY, SENBEI-- DO IT.
I'M DAMPING BELL-DANDY'S POWER, SO...
ATTACK!!
grp!
FRAP!
BLORT!
WHAT THE--?!
grp!
GRP!
CHAK
SIMPSON
OH, NO!

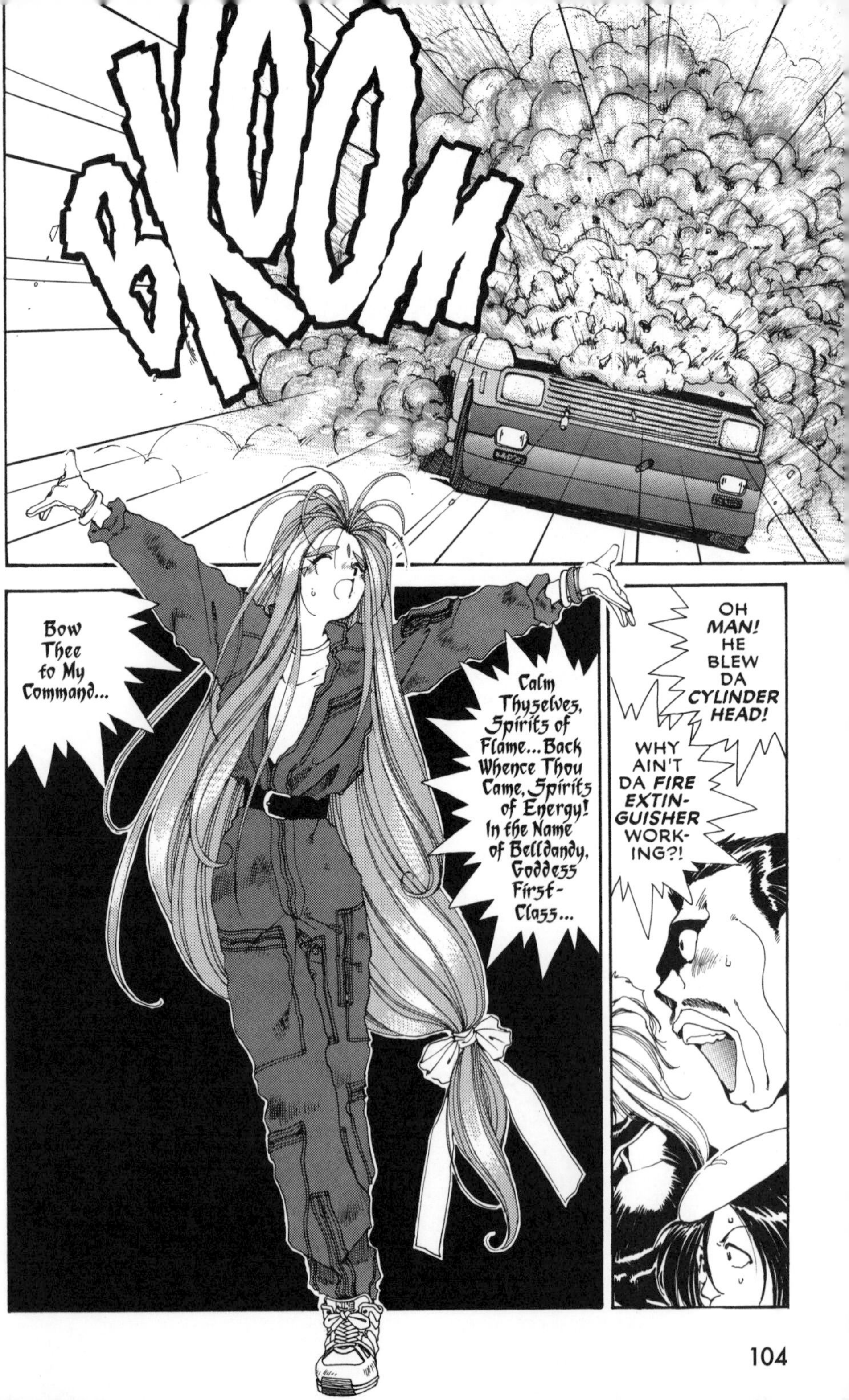
BKOOM
OH MAN! HE BLEW DA CYLINDER HEAD!
WHY AIN'T DA FIRE EXTINGUISHER WORKING?!
Calm Thyselves, Spirits of Flame... Back Whence Thou Came, Spirits of Energy! In the Name of Belldandy, Goddess First-Class...
Bow Thee to My Command...

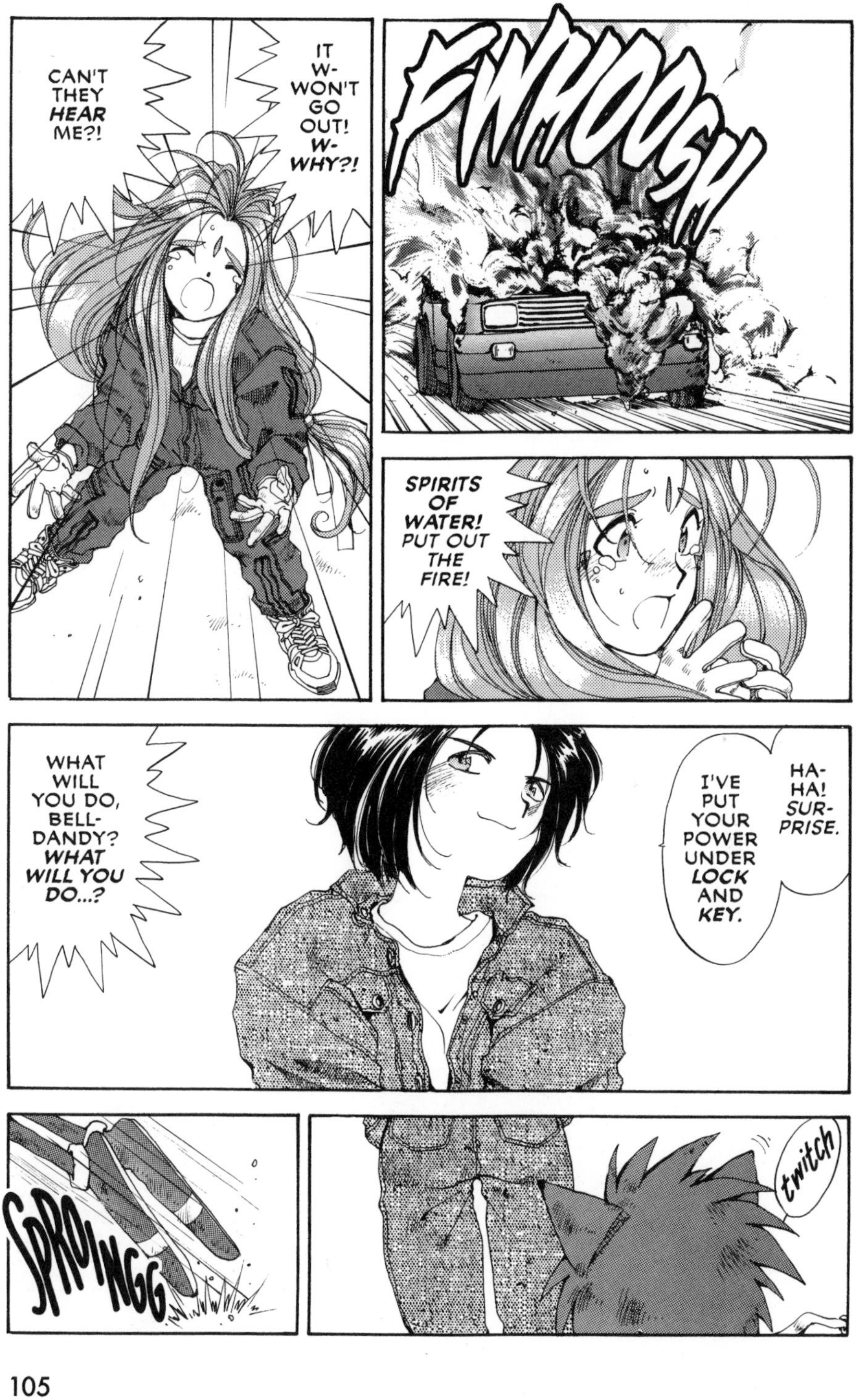
FWHOOSH
SPIRITS OF WATER! PUT OUT THE FIRE!
IT W-WON'T GO OUT! W-WHY?!
CAN'T THEY HEAR ME?!
HA-HA! SURPRISE.
I'VE PUT YOUR POWER UNDER LOCK AND KEY.
WHAT WILL YOU DO, BELL-DANDY? WHAT WILL YOU DO...?
twitch
SPROINGG

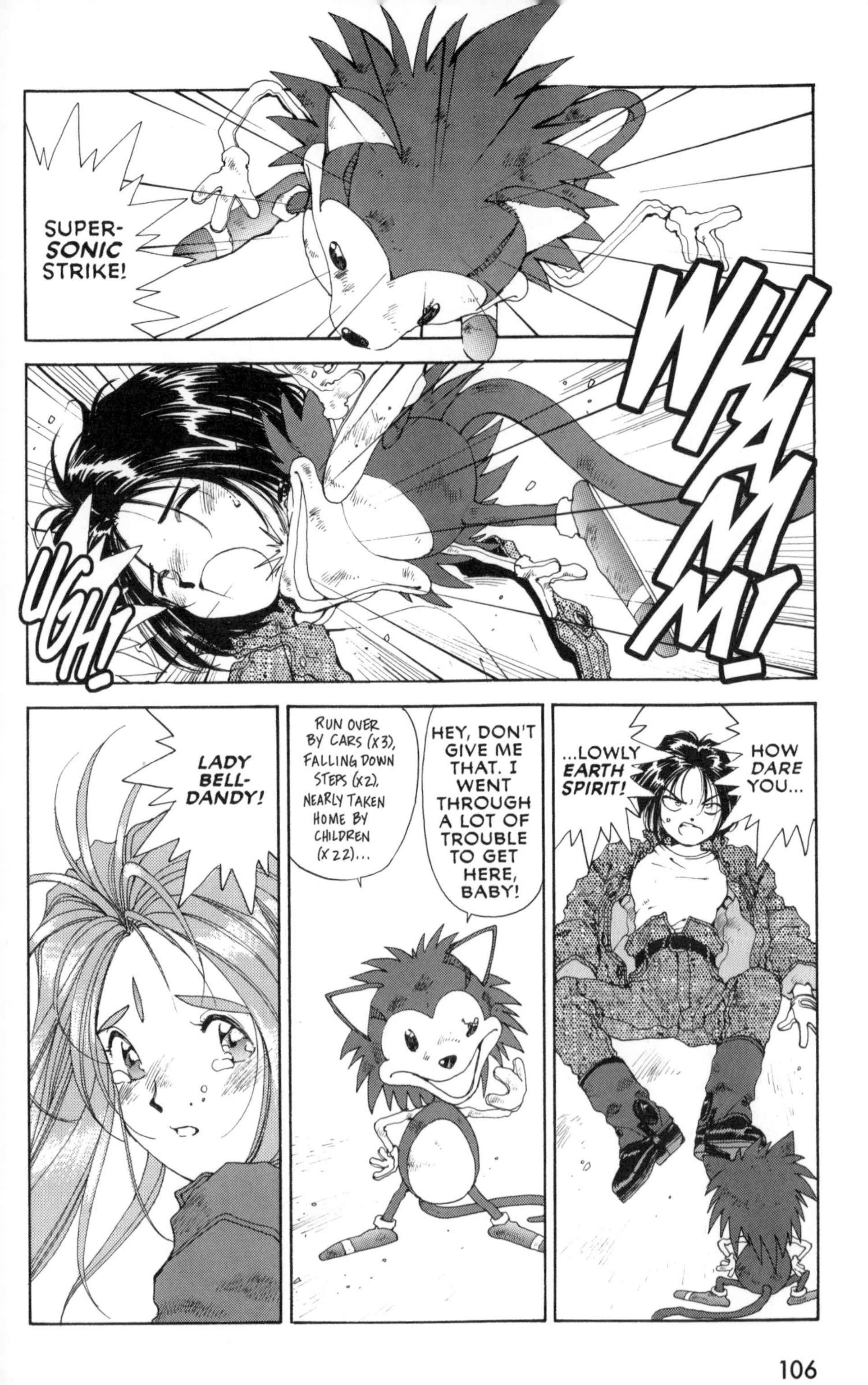
SUPER-SONIC STRIKE!
WHAMMM!
UGH!
HOW DARE YOU...
...LOWLY EARTH SPIRIT!
HEY, DON'T GIVE ME THAT. I WENT THROUGH A LOT OF TROUBLE TO GET HERE, BABY!
RUN OVER BY CARS (X3), FALLING DOWN STEPS (X2), NEARLY TAKEN HOME BY CHILDREN (X22)...
LADY BELL-DANDY!

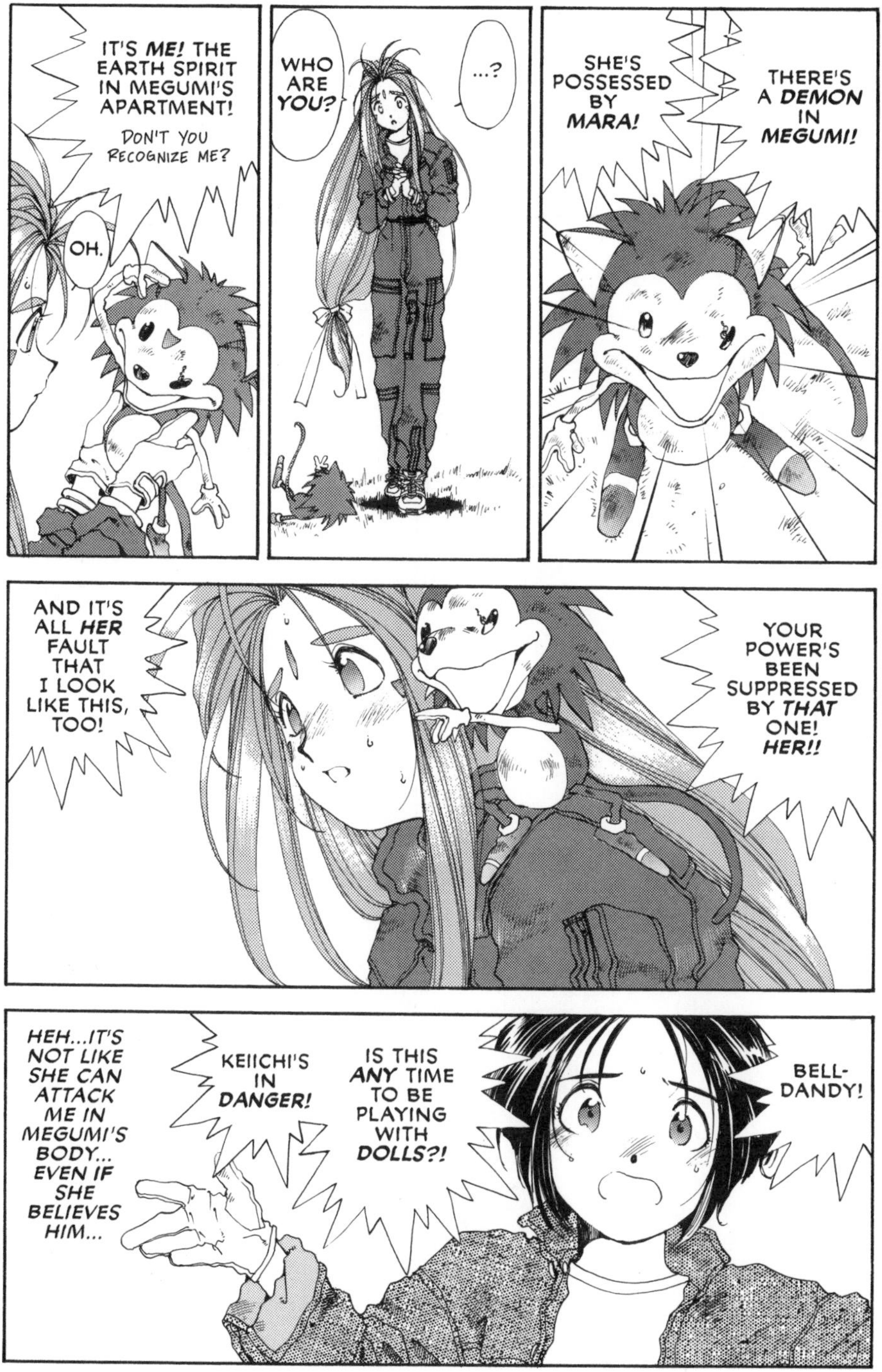
THERE'S A DEMON IN MEGUMI!
SHE'S POSSESSED BY MARA!
...?
WHO ARE YOU?
IT'S ME! THE EARTH SPIRIT IN MEGUMI'S APARTMENT!
DON'T YOU RECOGNIZE ME?
OH.
YOUR POWER'S BEEN SUPPRESSED BY THAT ONE! HER!!
AND IT'S ALL HER FAULT THAT I LOOK LIKE THIS, TOO!
BELL-DANDY!
IS THIS ANY TIME TO BE PLAYING WITH DOLLS?!
KEIICHI'S IN DANGER!
HEH...IT'S NOT LIKE SHE CAN ATTACK ME IN MEGUMI'S BODY... EVEN IF SHE BELIEVES HIM...

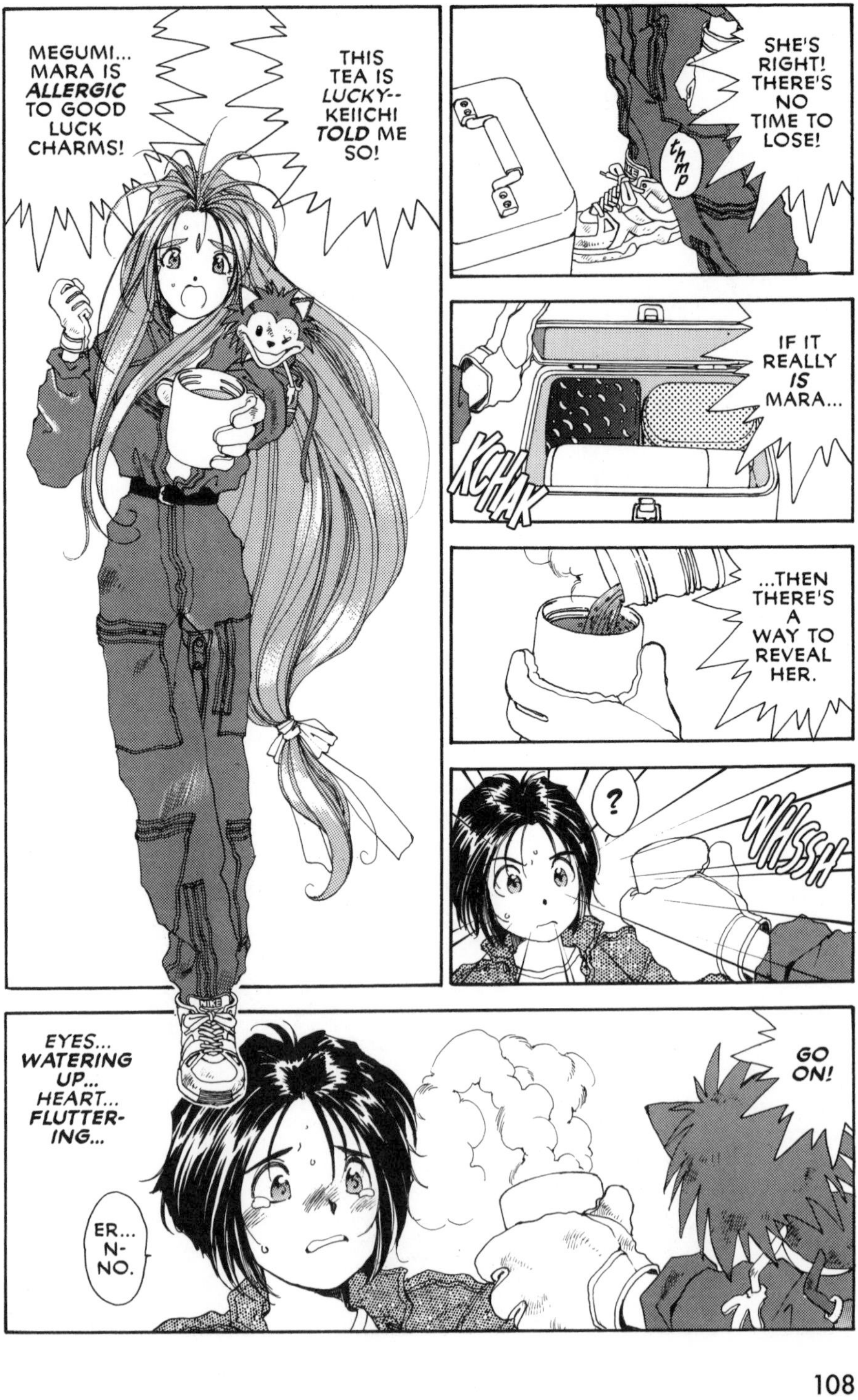
SHE'S RIGHT! THERE'S NO TIME TO LOSE!
thmp
IF IT REALLY IS MARA...
KCHAK
...THEN THERE'S A WAY TO REVEAL HER.
?
WHSSH
THIS TEA IS LUCKY-- KEIICHI TOLD ME SO!
MEGUMI... MARA IS ALLERGIC TO GOOD LUCK CHARMS!
GO ON!
EYES... WATERING UP... HEART... FLUTTERING...
ER... N-NO.

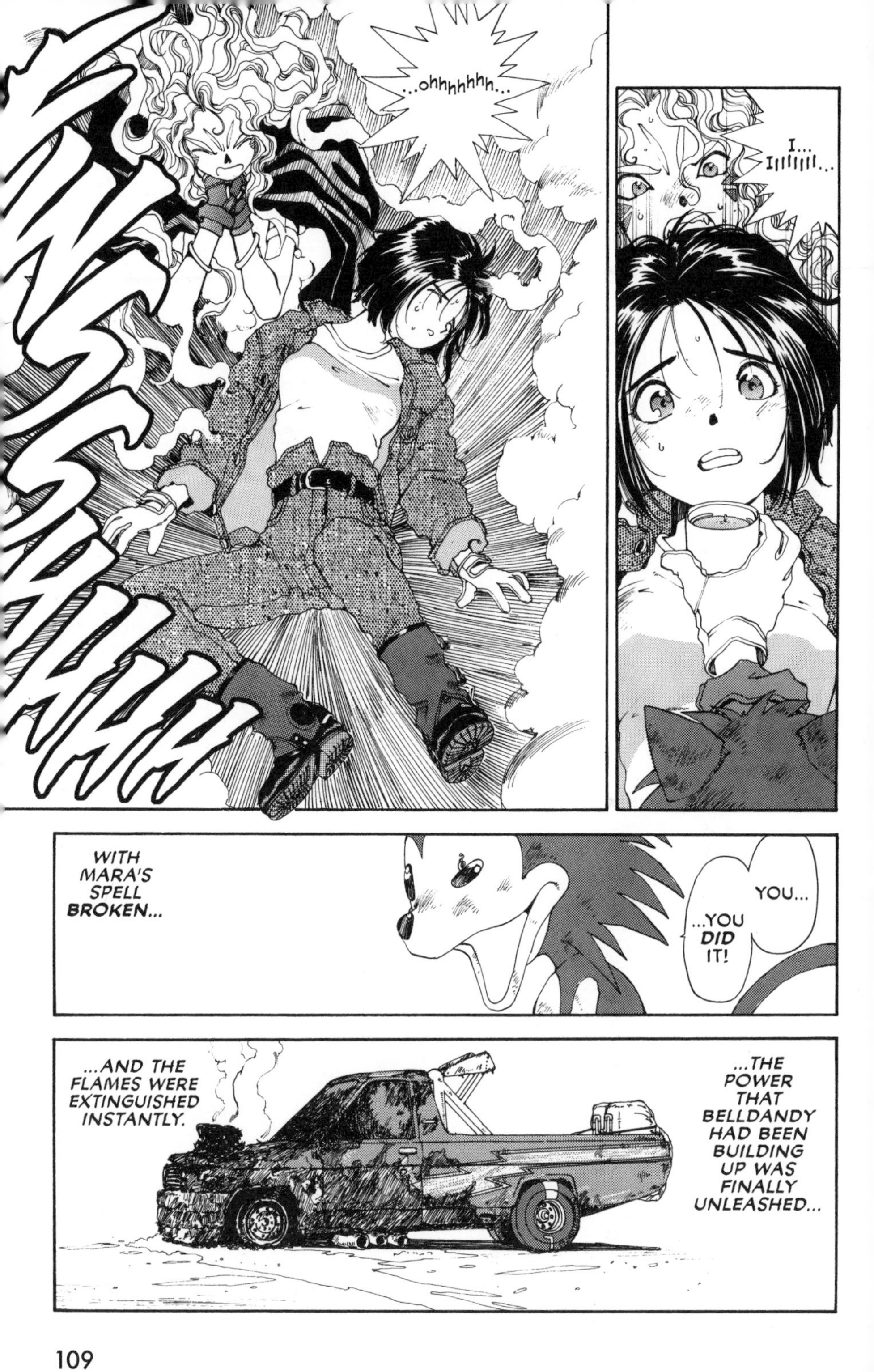
I... Illllll...
...ohhhhhhh...
YOU... ...YOU DID IT!
WITH MARA'S SPELL BROKEN...
...THE POWER THAT BELLDANDY HAD BEEN BUILDING UP WAS FINALLY UNLEASHED...
...AND THE FLAMES WERE EXTINGUISHED INSTANTLY.

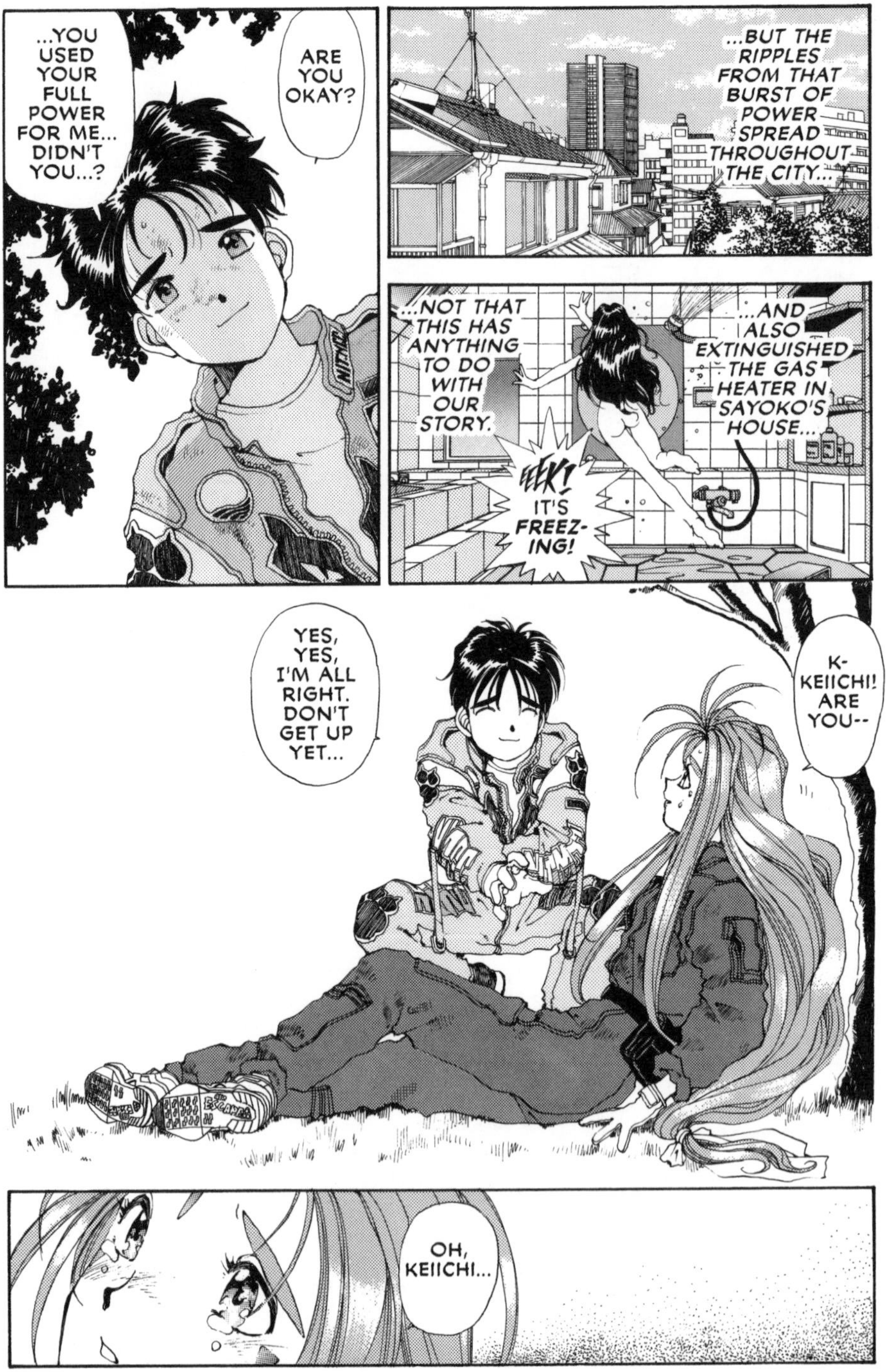

...BUT THE RIPPLES FROM THAT BURST OF POWER SPREAD THROUGHOUT THE CITY...
...AND ALSO EXTINGUISHED THE GAS HEATER IN SAYOKO'S HOUSE...
...NOT THAT THIS HAS ANYTHING TO DO WITH OUR STORY.
EEEK! IT'S FREEZ-ING!
ARE YOU OKAY?
...YOU USED YOUR FULL POWER FOR ME... DIDN'T YOU...?
K-KEIICHI! ARE YOU--
YES, YES, I'M ALL RIGHT. DON'T GET UP YET...
OH, KEIICHI...

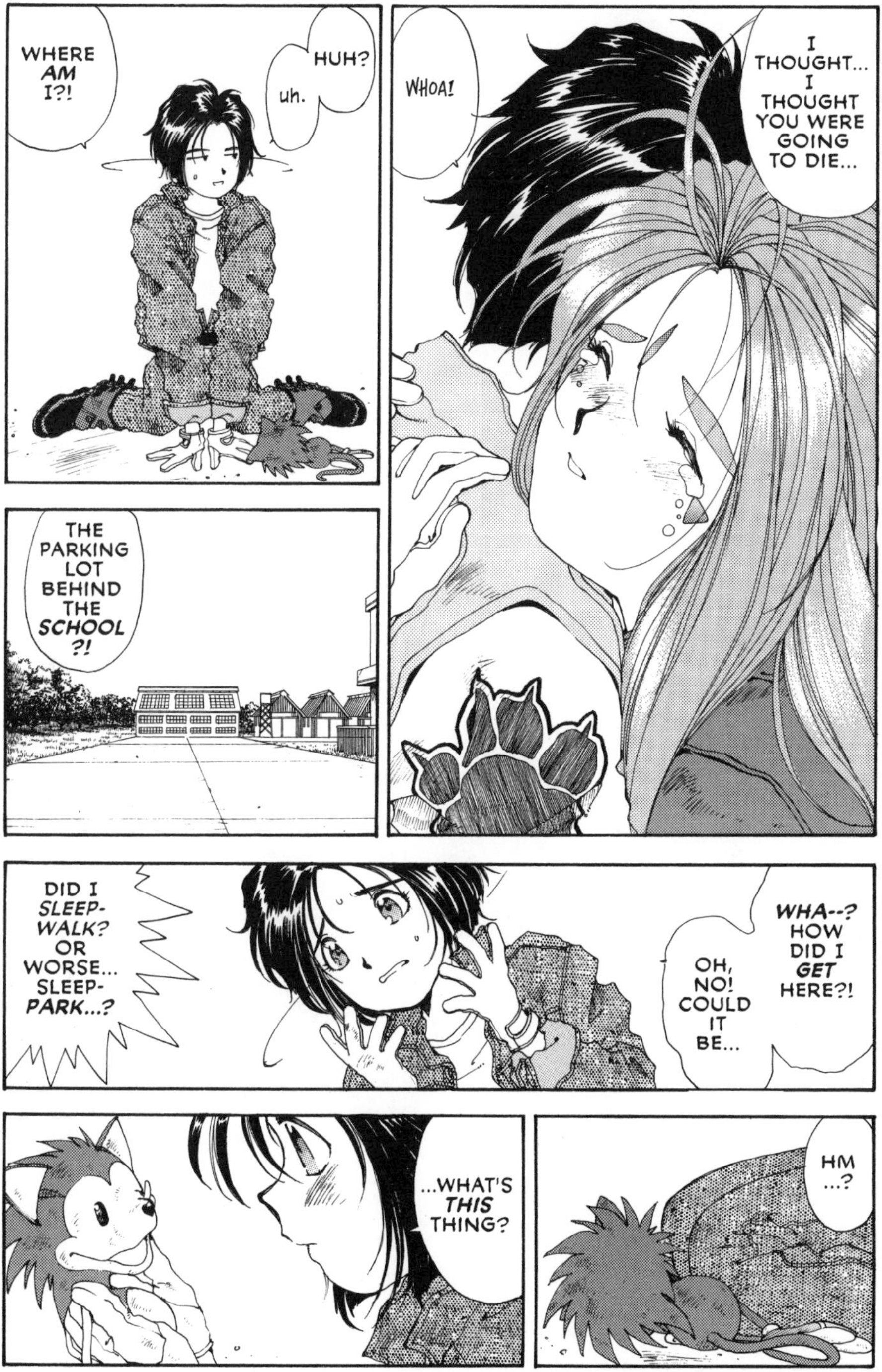

I THOUGHT... I THOUGHT YOU WERE GOING TO DIE...
WHOA!
HUH?
uh.
WHERE AM I?!
THE PARKING LOT BEHIND THE SCHOOL?!
WHA--? HOW DID I GET HERE?!
OH, NO! COULD IT BE...
DID I SLEEP-WALK? OR WORSE... SLEEP-PARK...?
HM ...?
...WHAT'S THIS THING?

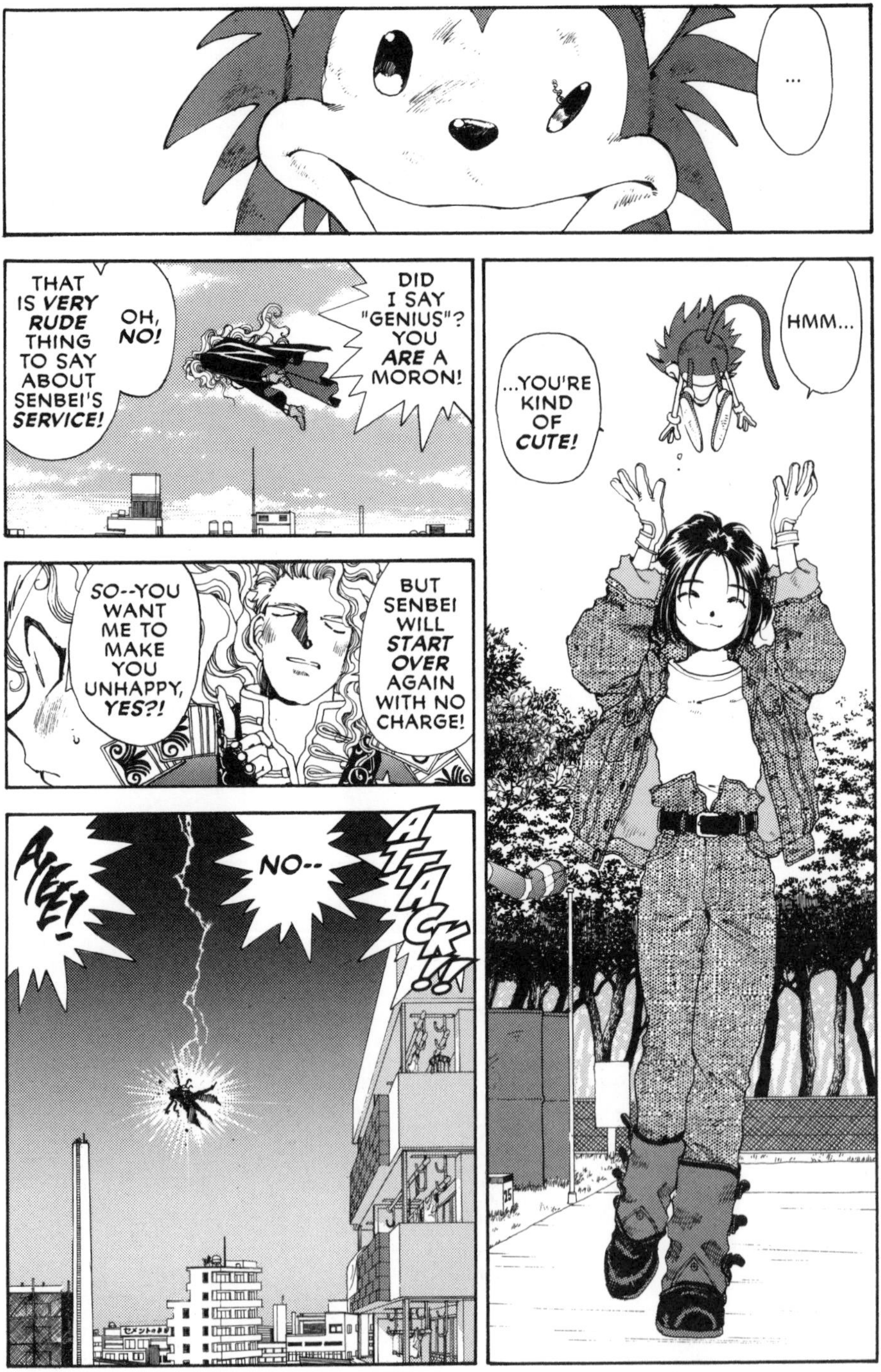
...
HMM...
...YOU'RE KIND OF CUTE!
DID I SAY "GENIUS"? YOU ARE A MORON!
OH, NO!
THAT IS VERY RUDE THING TO SAY ABOUT SENBEI'S SERVICE!
BUT SENBEI WILL START OVER AGAIN WITH NO CHARGE!
SO--YOU WANT ME TO MAKE YOU UNHAPPY, YES?!
ATTACK!!
NO--
AIEE!

CHAPTER 46

Thank You

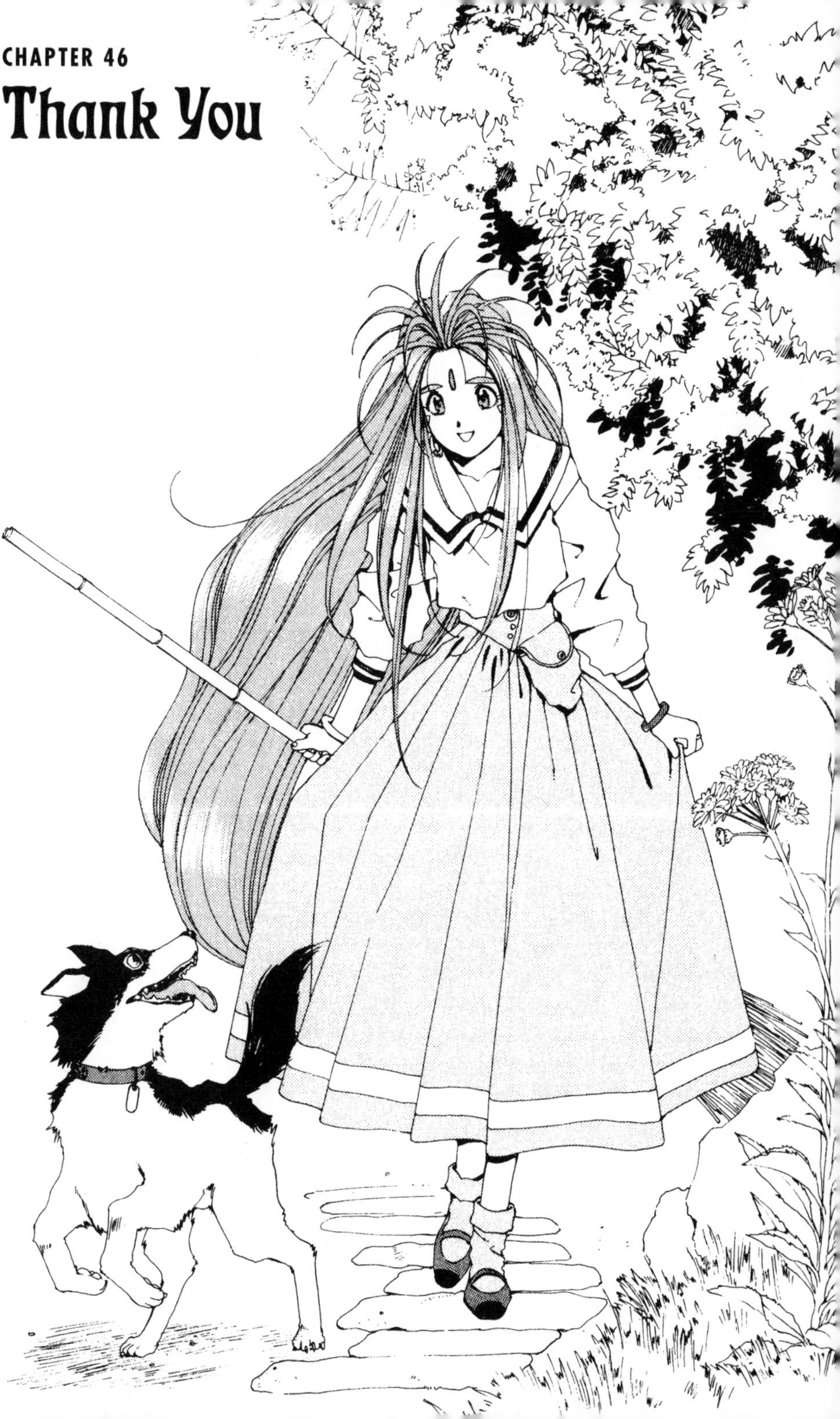

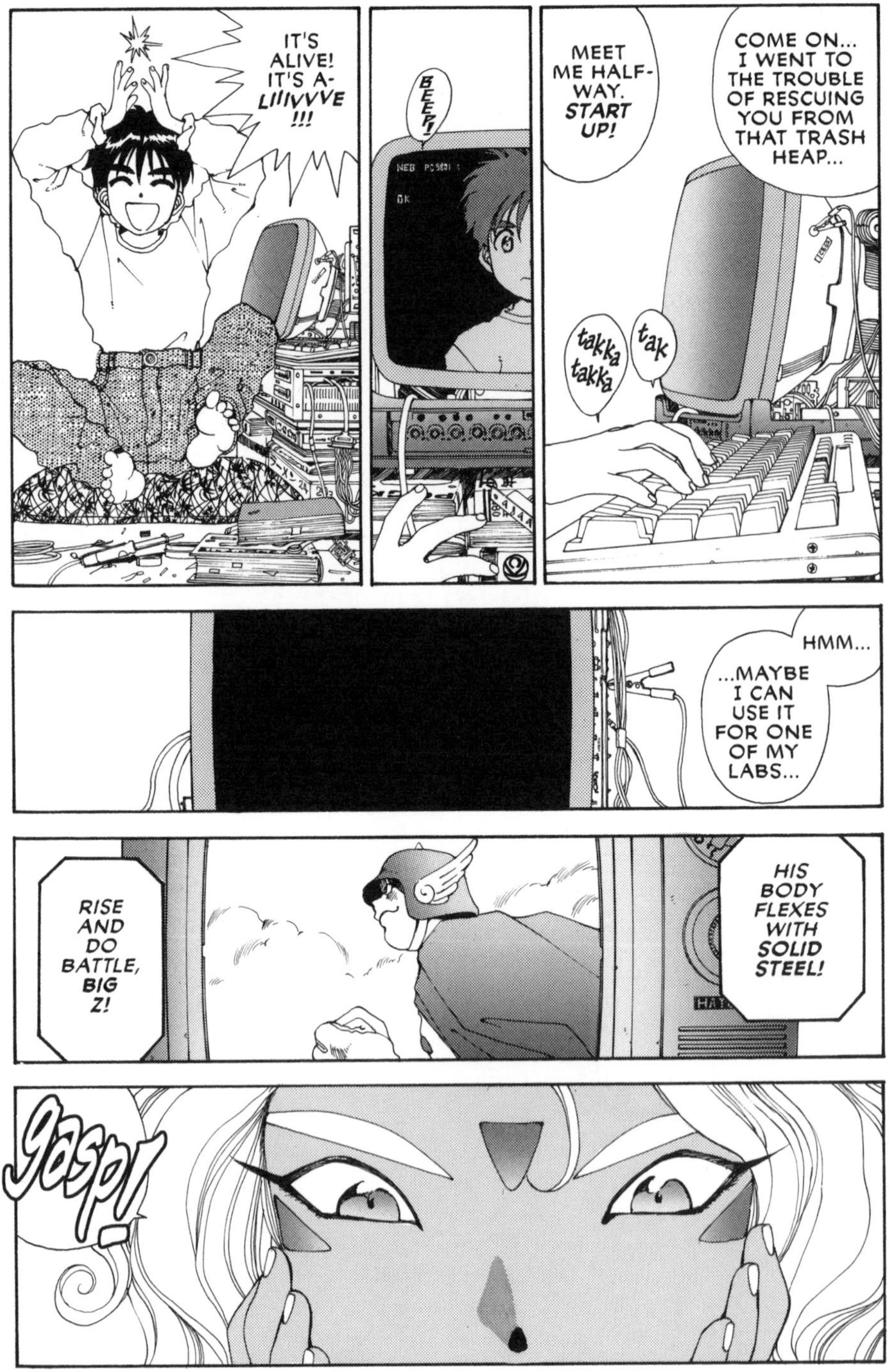
COME ON... I WENT TO THE TROUBLE OF RESCUING YOU FROM THAT TRASH HEAP...
MEET ME HALF-WAY. START UP!
tak
takka takka
BEEP!
IT'S ALIVE! IT'S A-LIIIVVVE!!!
HMM...
...MAYBE I CAN USE IT FOR ONE OF MY LABS...
HIS BODY FLEXES WITH SOLID STEEL!
RISE AND DO BATTLE, BIG Z!
gasp!

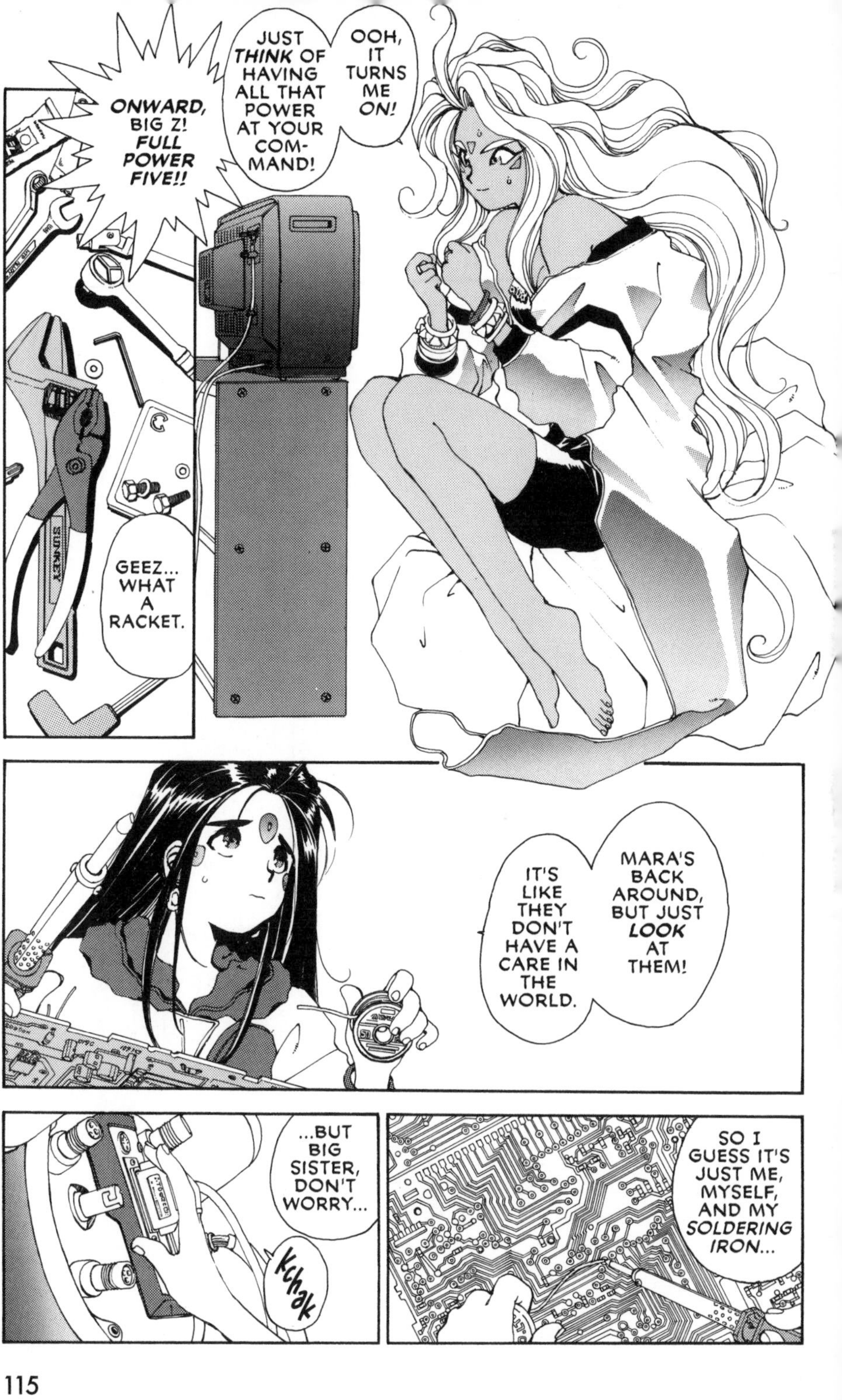
OOH, IT TURNS ME *ON!*
JUST *THINK* OF HAVING ALL THAT POWER AT YOUR COM-MAND!
ONWARD, BIG Z! ***FULL POWER FIVE!!***
GEEZ... WHAT A RACKET.
MARA'S BACK AROUND, BUT JUST ***LOOK*** AT THEM!
IT'S LIKE THEY DON'T HAVE A CARE IN THE WORLD.
SO I GUESS IT'S JUST ME, MYSELF, AND MY ***SOLDERING IRON...***
...BUT BIG SISTER, DON'T WORRY...
Kchak

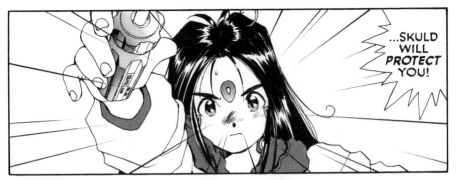

...SKULD WILL PROTECT YOU!
AAH... NOW, WITH MY LITTLE INVENTION STANDING GUARD...
...BELL-DANDY IS SAFE.
BACK-UP POWER ON!
VOLTAGE NOMINAL!
INITIATE DATA TRANSFER!
GYRO POWER ON!
RELEASING FINAL SAFETY!
CUT POWER TO THE REST OF THE HOUSE--
--AND ACTI-VATE!

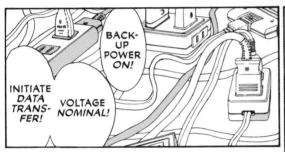

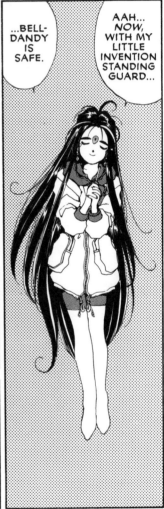

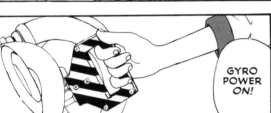

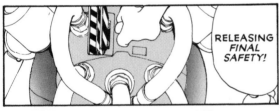

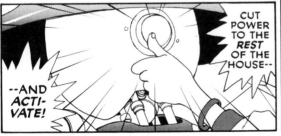

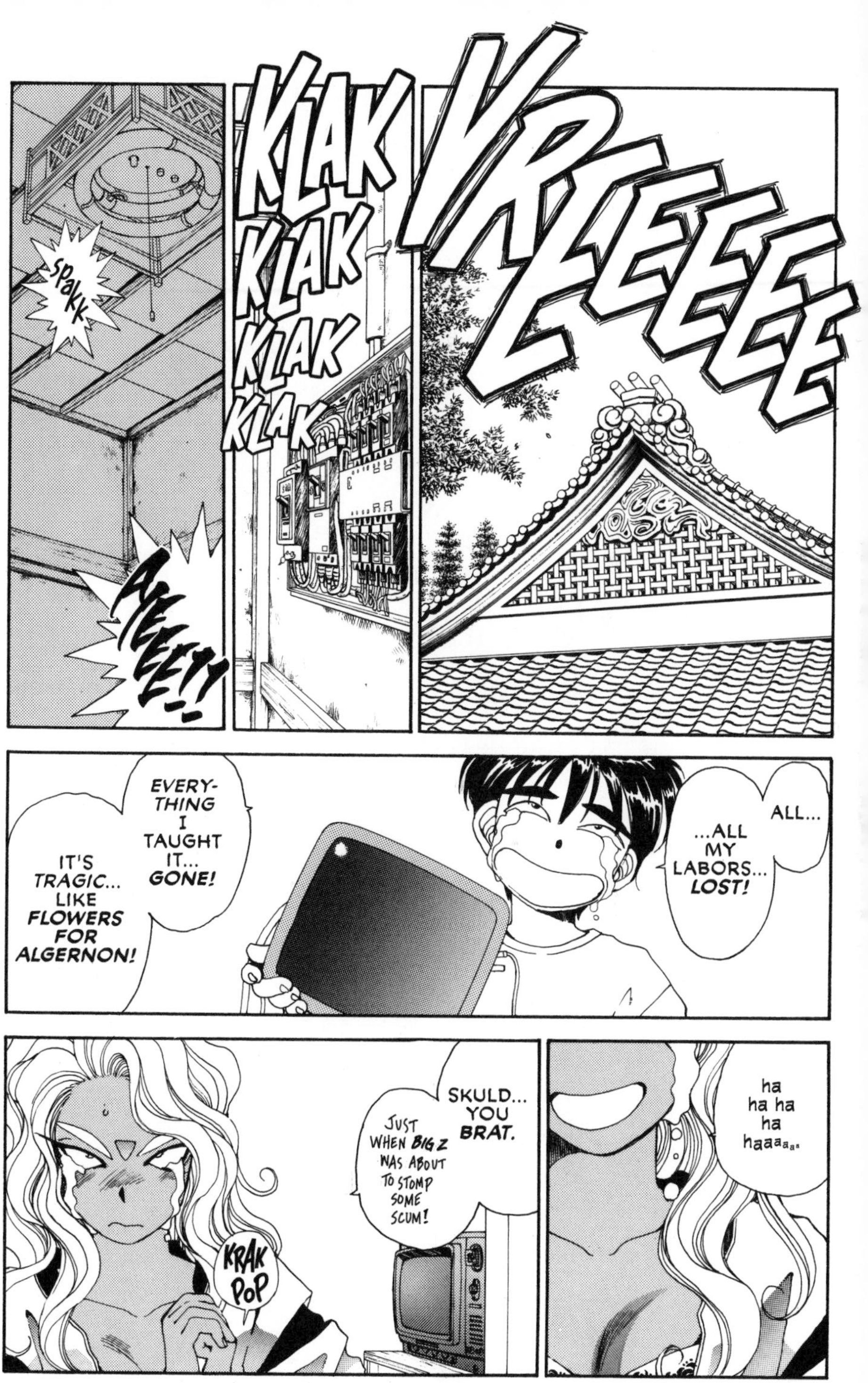
VRIEEEEEE
KLAK KLAK KLAK KLAK
spakk
ALL...
...ALL MY LABORS... LOST!
EVERY-THING I TAUGHT IT... GONE!
IT'S TRAGIC... LIKE FLOWERS FOR ALGERNON!
ha ha ha ha haaaaaa
SKULD... YOU BRAT.
JUST WHEN BIG Z WAS ABOUT TO STOMP SOME SCUM!
KRAK POP

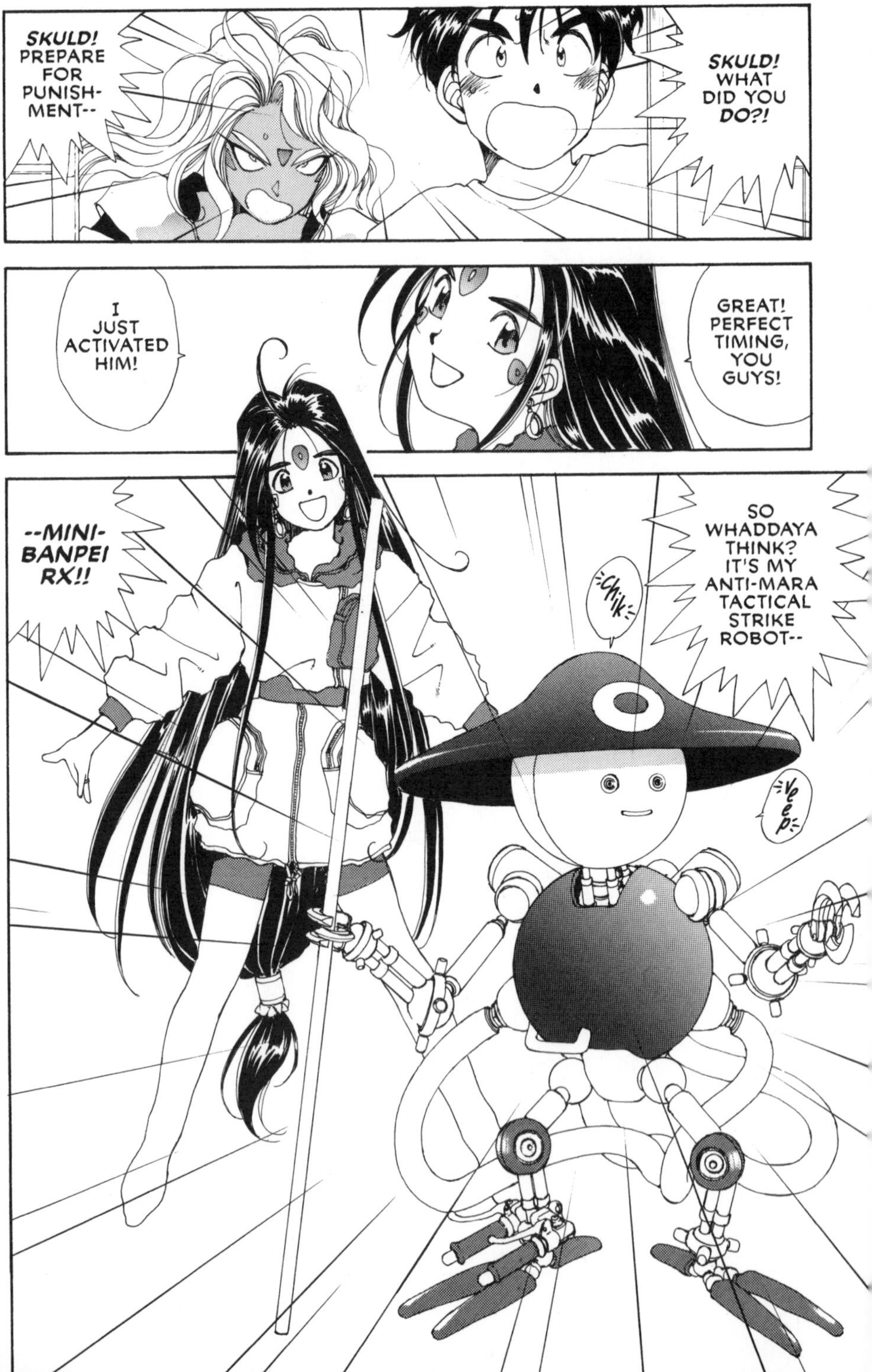

SKULD! WHAT DID YOU DO?!
SKULD! PREPARE FOR PUNISHMENT--
GREAT! PERFECT TIMING, YOU GUYS!
I JUST ACTIVATED HIM!
SO WHADDAYA THINK? IT'S MY ANTI-MARA TACTICAL STRIKE ROBOT--
Chik
Veep
--MINI-BANPEI RX!!

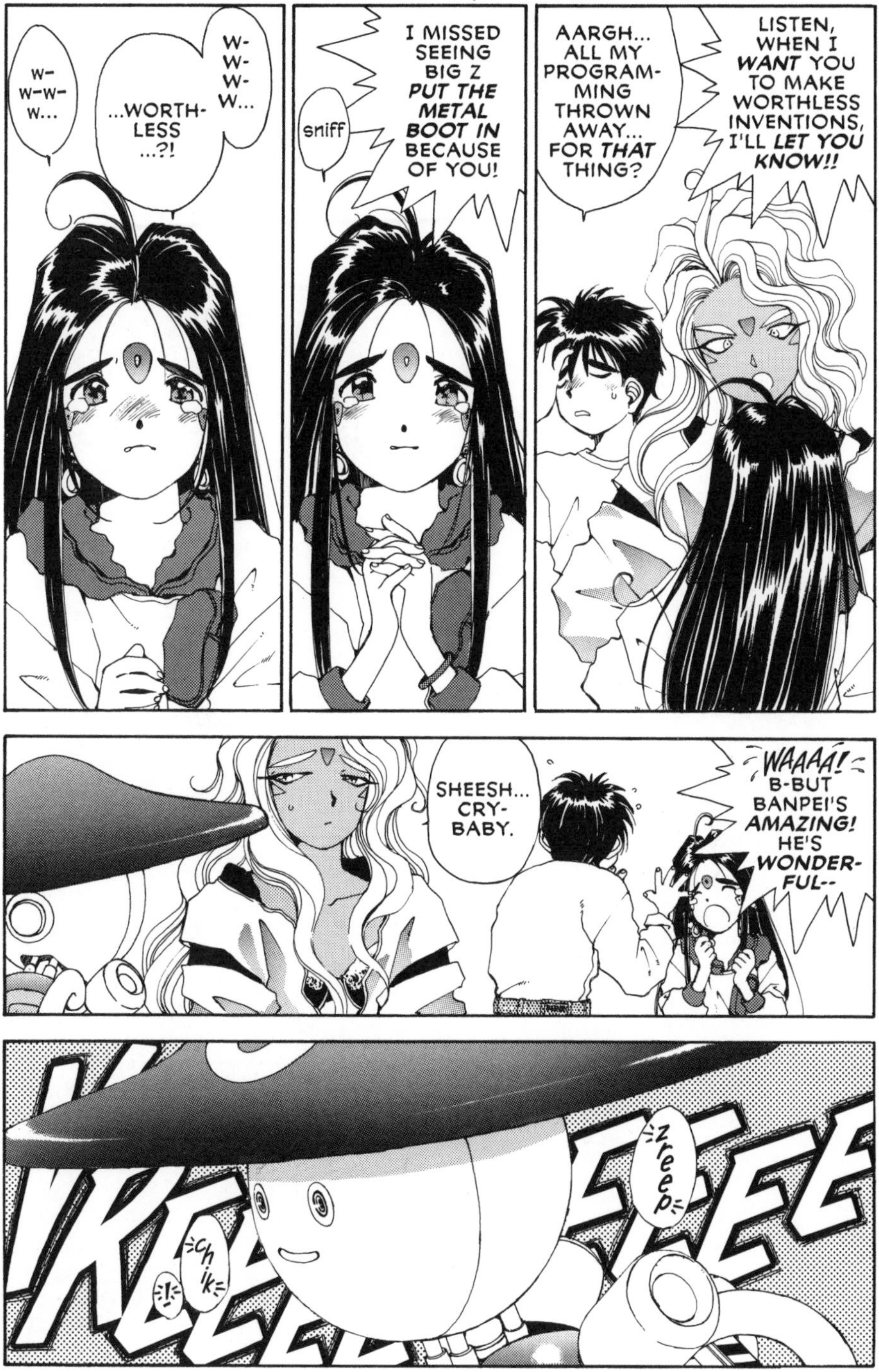
LISTEN, WHEN I WANT YOU TO MAKE WORTHLESS INVENTIONS, I'LL LET YOU KNOW!!
AARGH... ALL MY PROGRAM-MING THROWN AWAY... FOR THAT THING?
I MISSED SEEING BIG Z PUT THE METAL BOOT IN BECAUSE OF YOU!
sniff
W-W-W-W...
...WORTH-LESS ...?!
W-W-W-W...
WAAAA! B-BUT BANPEI'S AMAZING! HE'S WONDER-FUL--
SHEESH... CRY-BABY.
zreep
chik
!

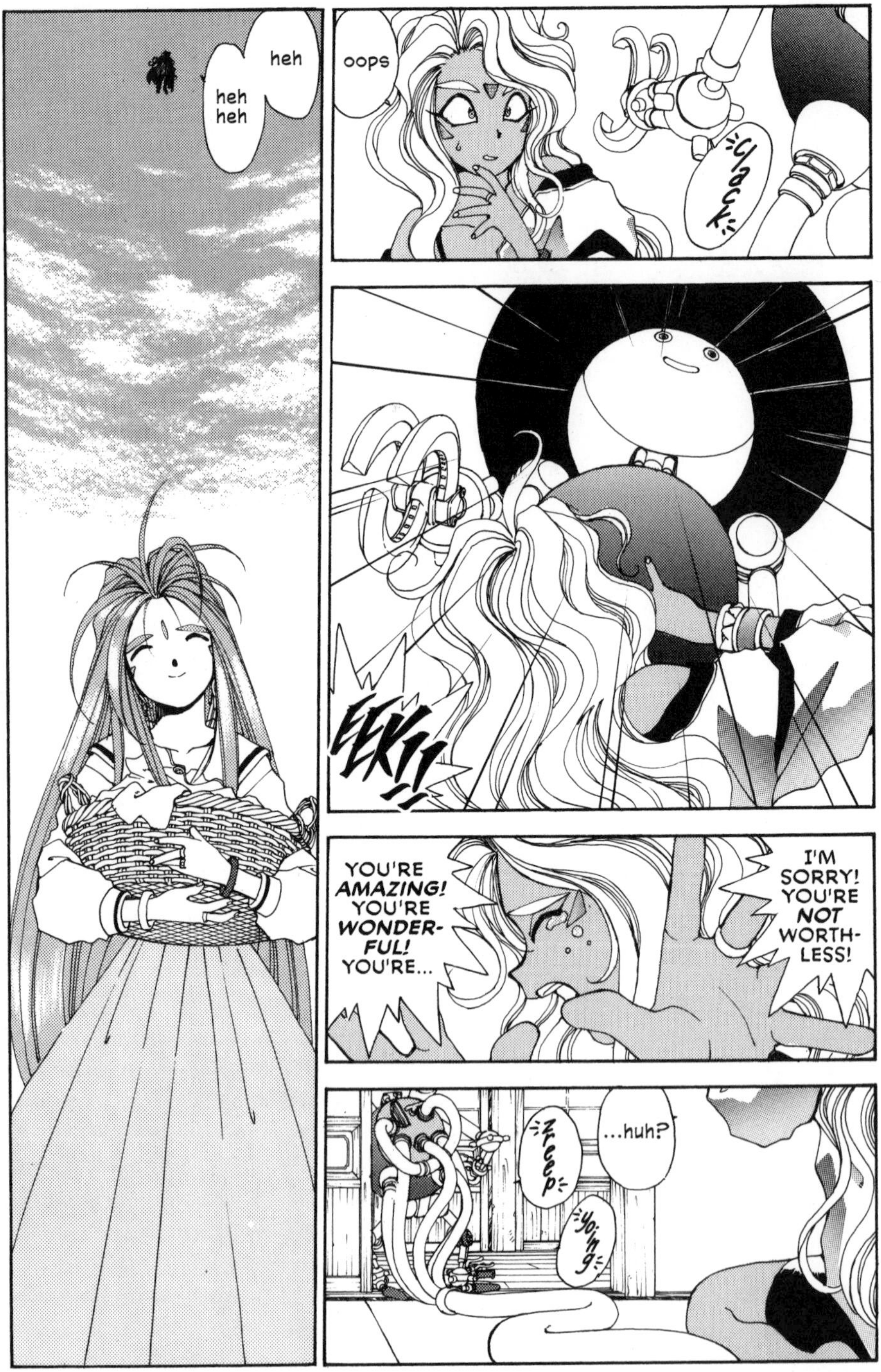
oops
CLACK
EEK!!
I'M SORRY! YOU'RE NOT WORTHLESS!
YOU'RE AMAZING! YOU'RE WONDERFUL! YOU'RE...
...huh?
zreep
yoing
heh
heh heh

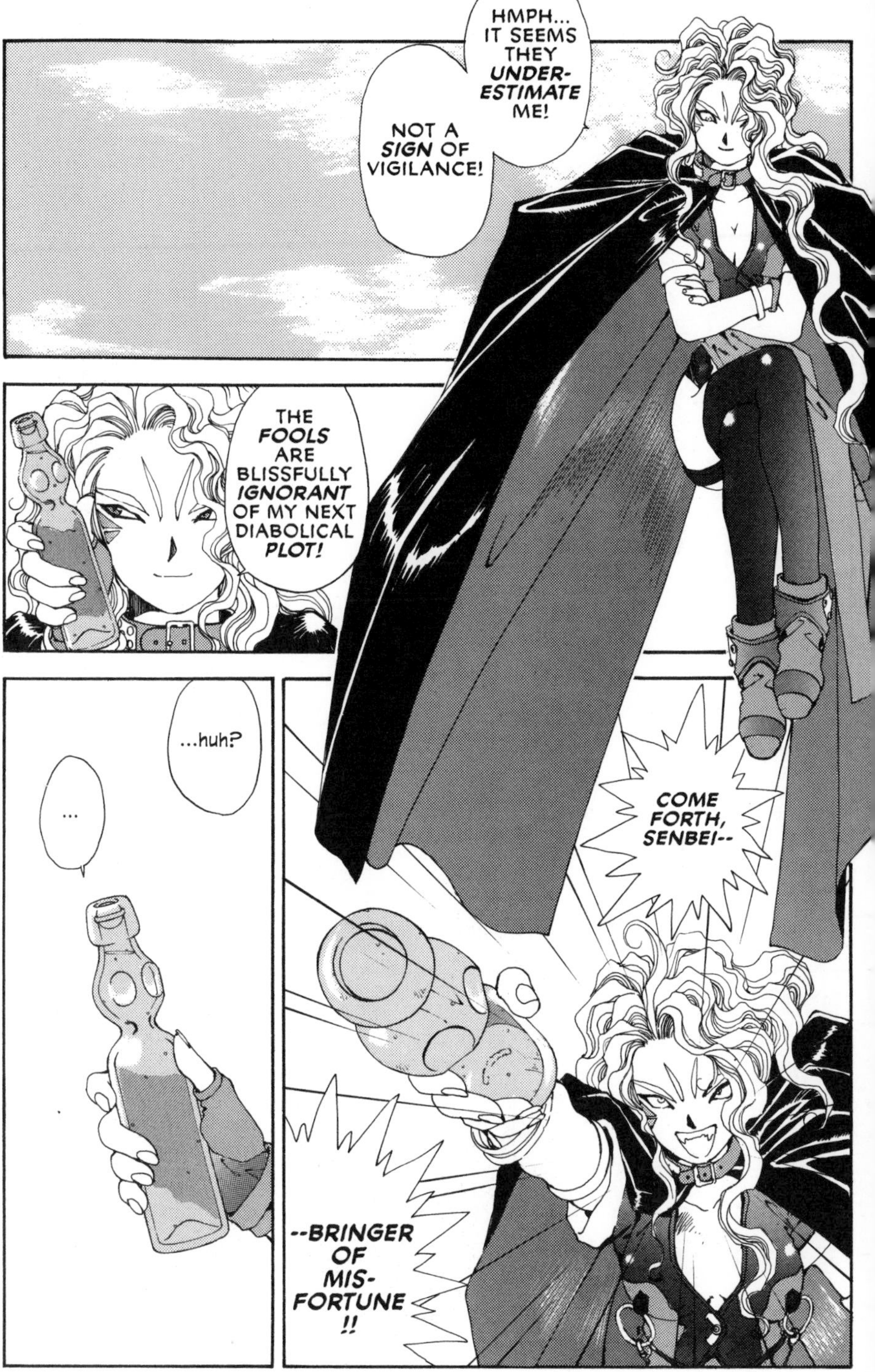
HMPH... IT SEEMS THEY UNDER-ESTIMATE ME!
NOT A SIGN OF VIGILANCE!
THE FOOLS ARE BLISSFULLY IGNORANT OF MY NEXT DIABOLICAL PLOT!
COME FORTH, SENBEI--
--BRINGER OF MIS-FORTUNE !!
...huh?
...

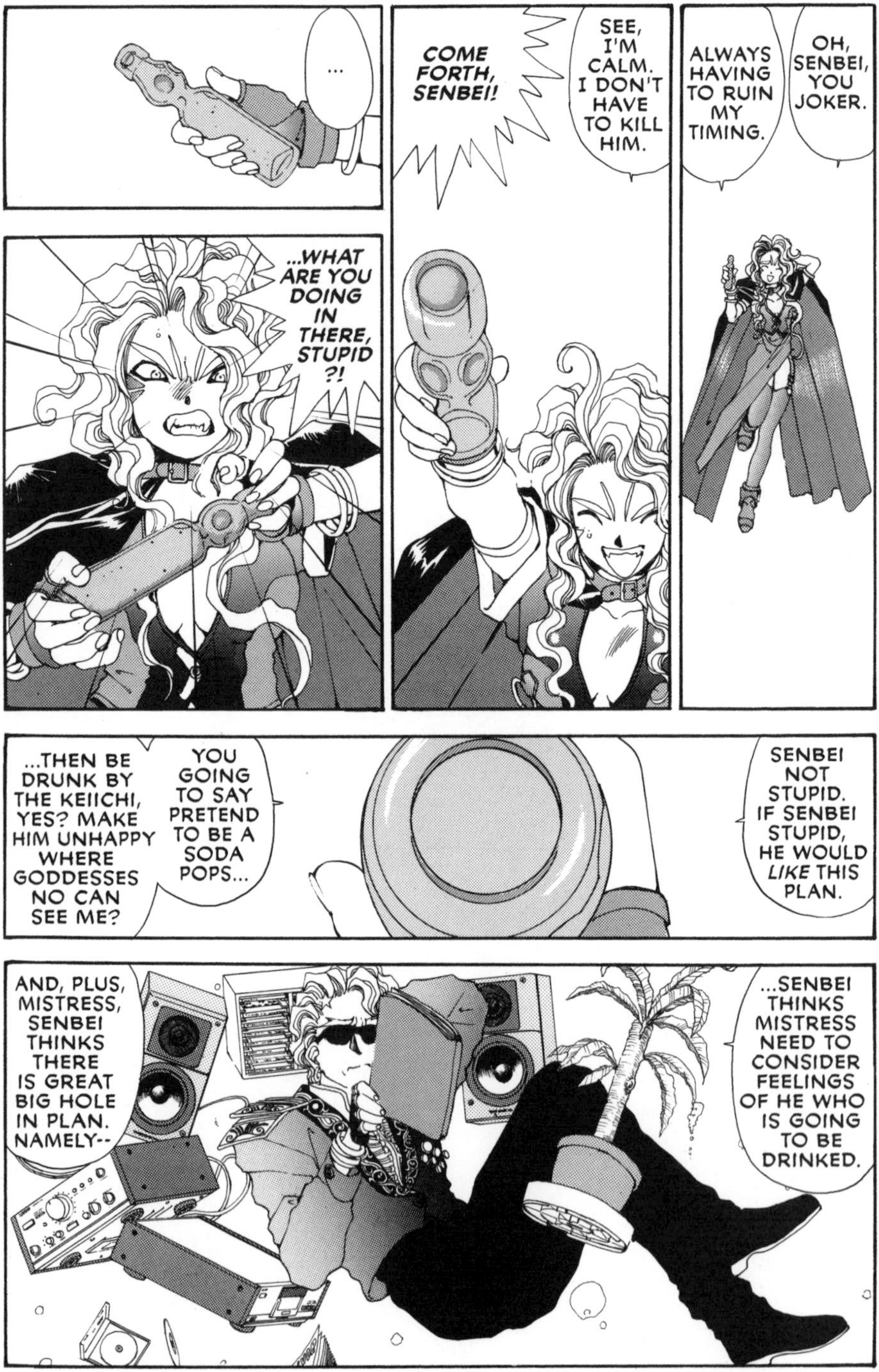
OH, SENBEI, YOU JOKER.
ALWAYS HAVING TO RUIN MY TIMING.
SEE, I'M CALM. I DON'T HAVE TO KILL HIM.
COME FORTH, SENBEI!
...
...WHAT ARE YOU DOING IN THERE, STUPID?!
SENBEI NOT STUPID. IF SENBEI STUPID, HE WOULD *LIKE* THIS PLAN.
YOU GOING TO SAY PRETEND TO BE A SODA POPS...
...THEN BE DRUNK BY THE KEIICHI, YES? MAKE HIM UNHAPPY WHERE GODDESSES NO CAN SEE ME?
...SENBEI THINKS MISTRESS NEED TO CONSIDER FEELINGS OF HE WHO IS GOING TO BE DRINKED.
AND, PLUS, MISTRESS, SENBEI THINKS THERE IS GREAT BIG HOLE IN PLAN. NAMELY--

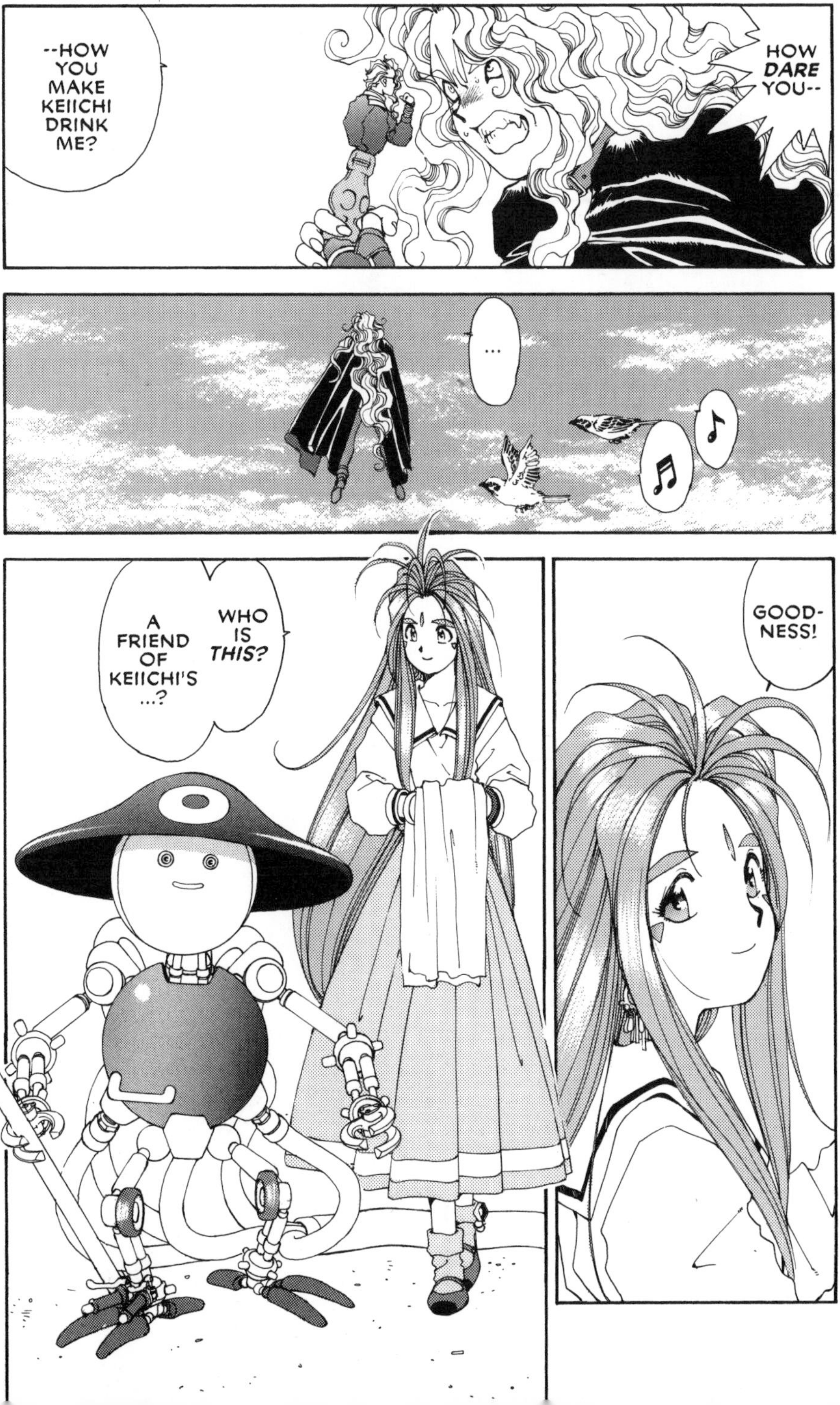

HOW DARE YOU--
--HOW YOU MAKE KEIICHI DRINK ME?
...
♫
♪
GOOD-NESS!
WHO IS THIS?
A FRIEND OF KEIICHI'S ...?

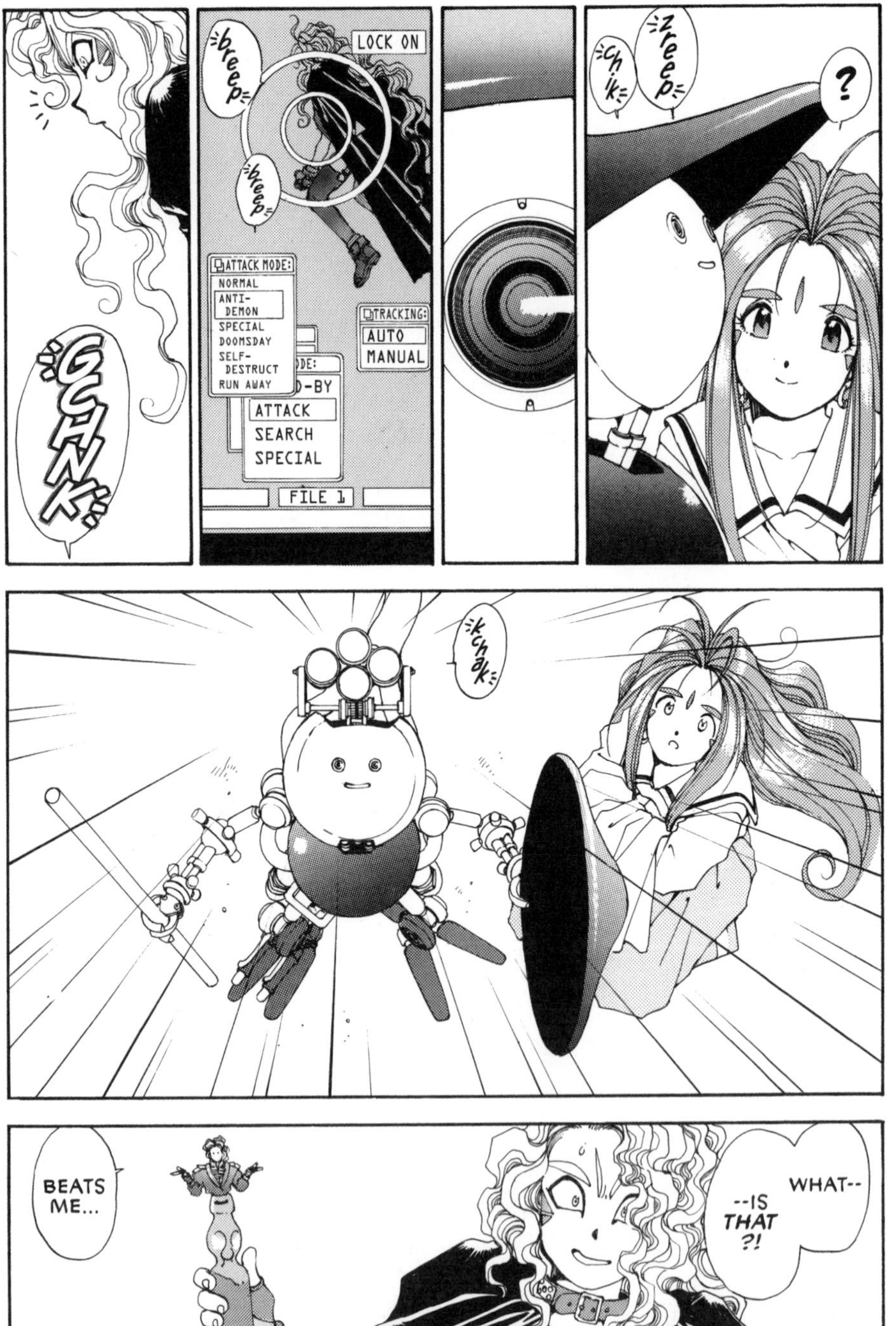
?
zreeep
chik
LOCK ON
breep
breep
TRACKING:
AUTO
MANUAL
ATTACK MODE:
NORMAL
ANTI-DEMON
SPECIAL
DOOMSDAY
SELF-DESTRUCT
RUN AWAY
ATTACK
SEARCH
SPECIAL
FILE 1
GCHNK
kchak
WHAT--
--IS THAT?!
BEATS ME...

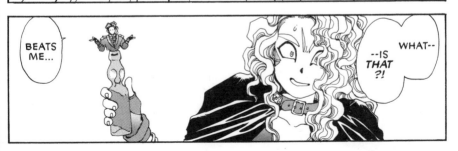

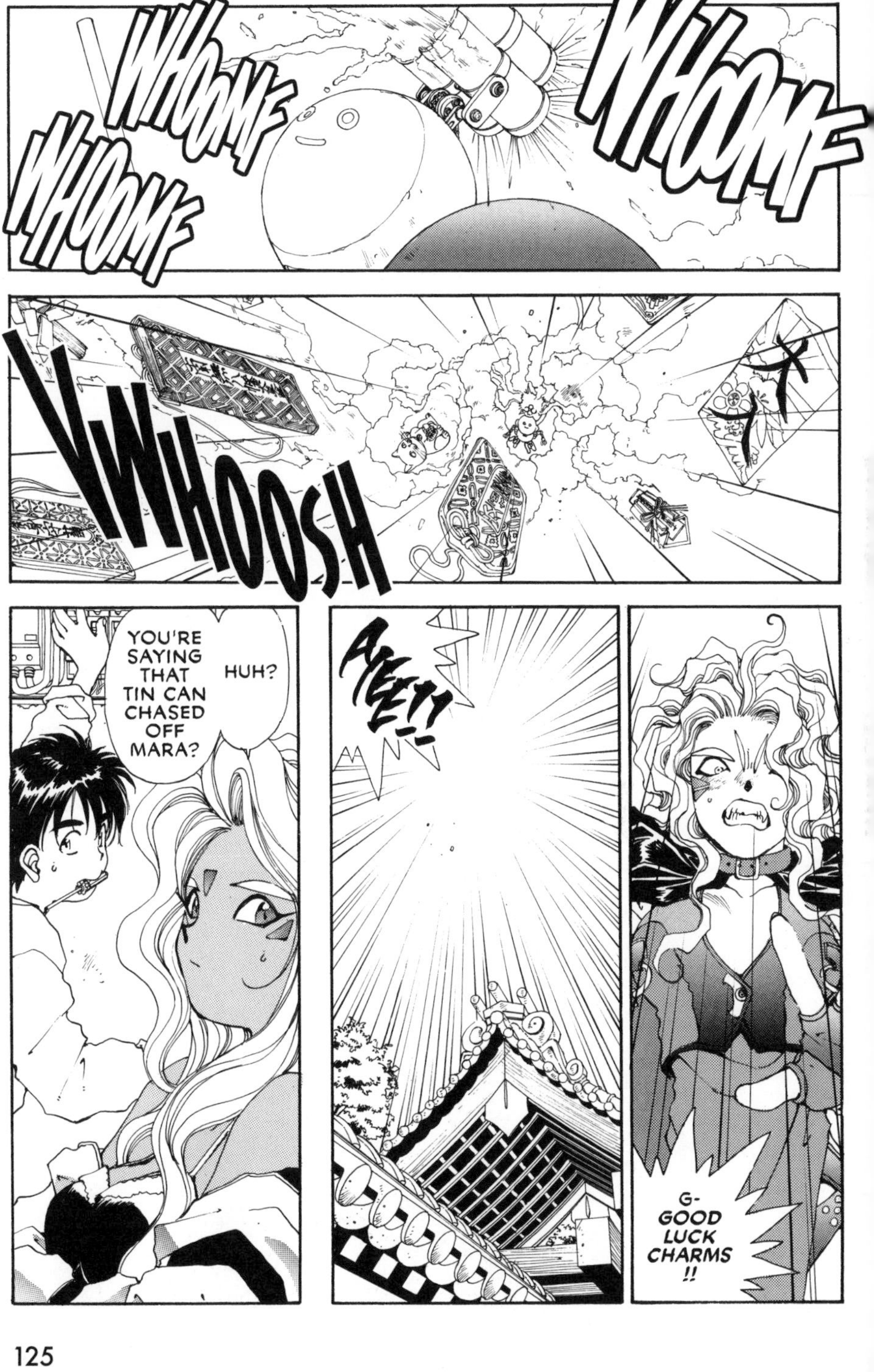
WHOOMF
WHOOMF
WHOOMF
VWHOOSH
G-GOOD LUCK CHARMS!!
AIEE!!
YOU'RE SAYING THAT TIN CAN CHASED OFF MARA?
HUH?

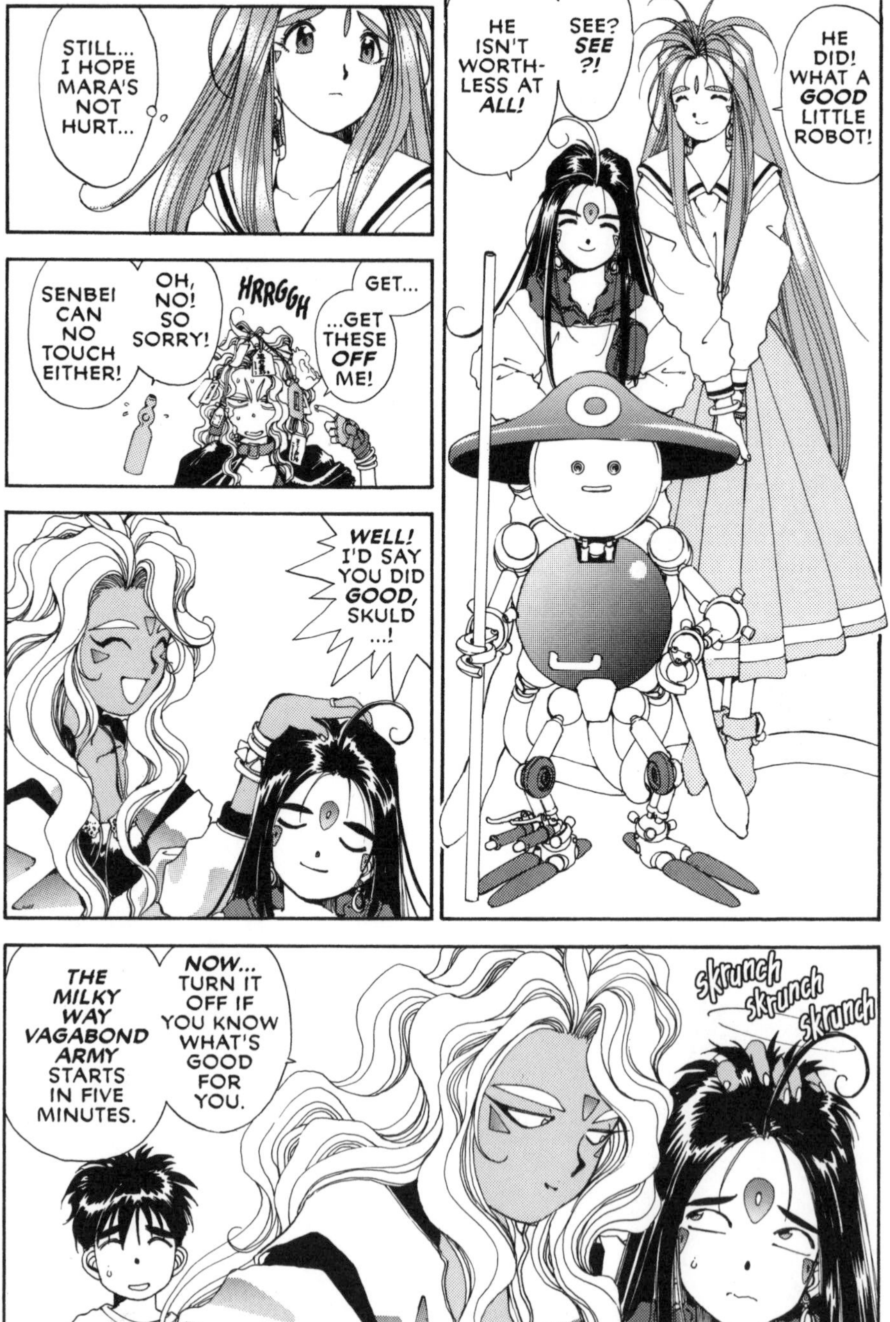
HE DID! WHAT A GOOD LITTLE ROBOT!
SEE? SEE?!
HE ISN'T WORTHLESS AT ALL!
STILL... I HOPE MARA'S NOT HURT...
GET...
...GET THESE OFF ME!
HRRGGH
OH, NO! SO SORRY!
SENBEI CAN NO TOUCH EITHER!
WELL! I'D SAY YOU DID GOOD, SKULD ...!
SKRUNCH SKRUNCH SKRUNCH
NOW... TURN IT OFF IF YOU KNOW WHAT'S GOOD FOR YOU.
THE MILKY WAY VAGABOND ARMY STARTS IN FIVE MINUTES.

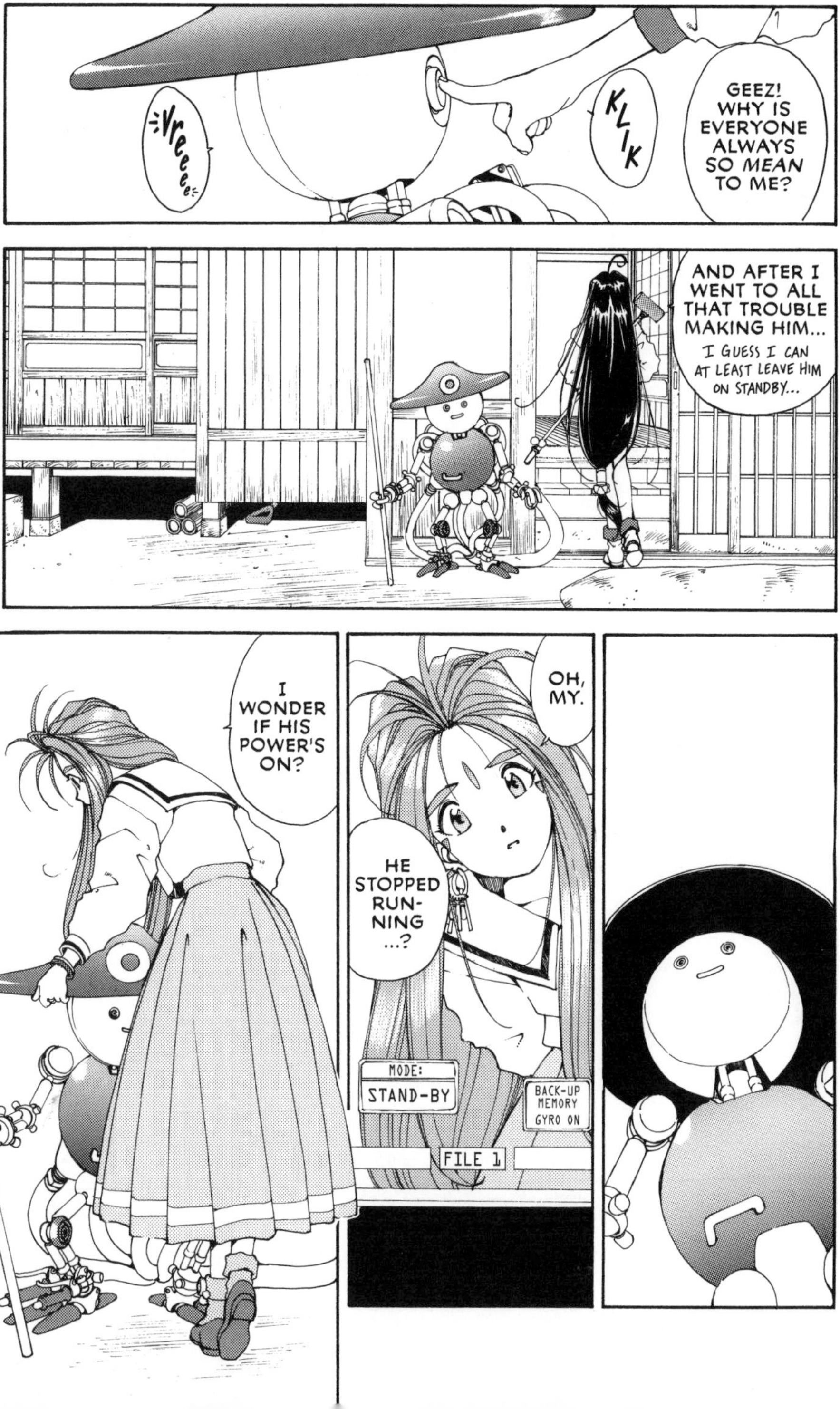
GEEZ! WHY IS EVERYONE ALWAYS SO *MEAN* TO ME?
KLIK
Vreeee
AND AFTER I WENT TO ALL THAT TROUBLE MAKING HIM...
I GUESS I CAN AT LEAST LEAVE HIM ON STANDBY...
OH, MY.
HE STOPPED RUN-NING ...?
MODE:
STAND-BY
BACK-UP MEMORY GYRO ON
FILE 1
I WONDER IF HIS POWER'S ON?

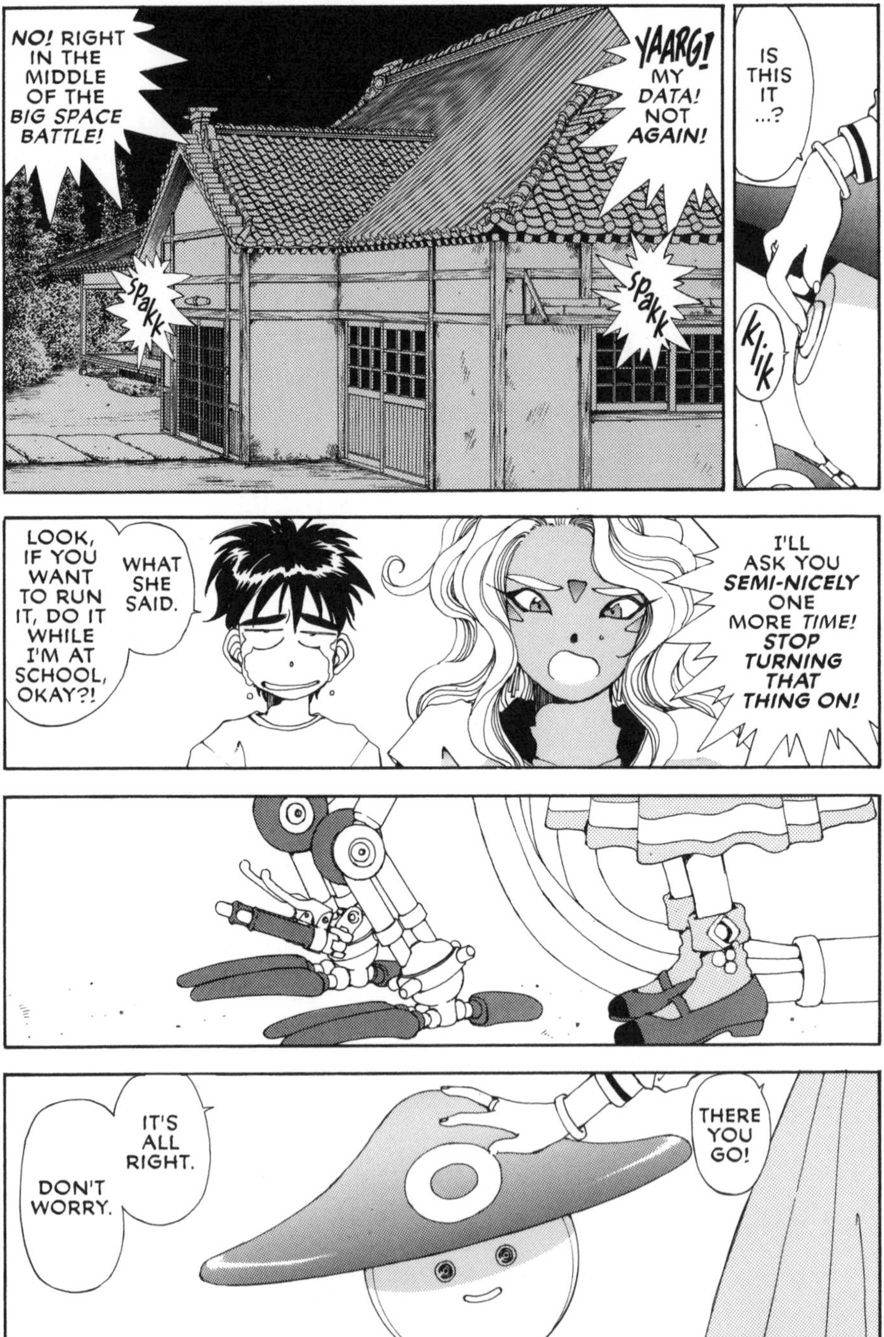
IS THIS IT ...?
Klik
YAARG! MY DATA! NOT AGAIN!
NO! RIGHT IN THE MIDDLE OF THE BIG SPACE BATTLE!
spakk
spakk
I'LL ASK YOU SEMI-NICELY ONE MORE TIME! STOP TURNING THAT THING ON!
WHAT SHE SAID.
LOOK, IF YOU WANT TO RUN IT, DO IT WHILE I'M AT SCHOOL, OKAY?!
THERE YOU GO!
IT'S ALL RIGHT.
DON'T WORRY.

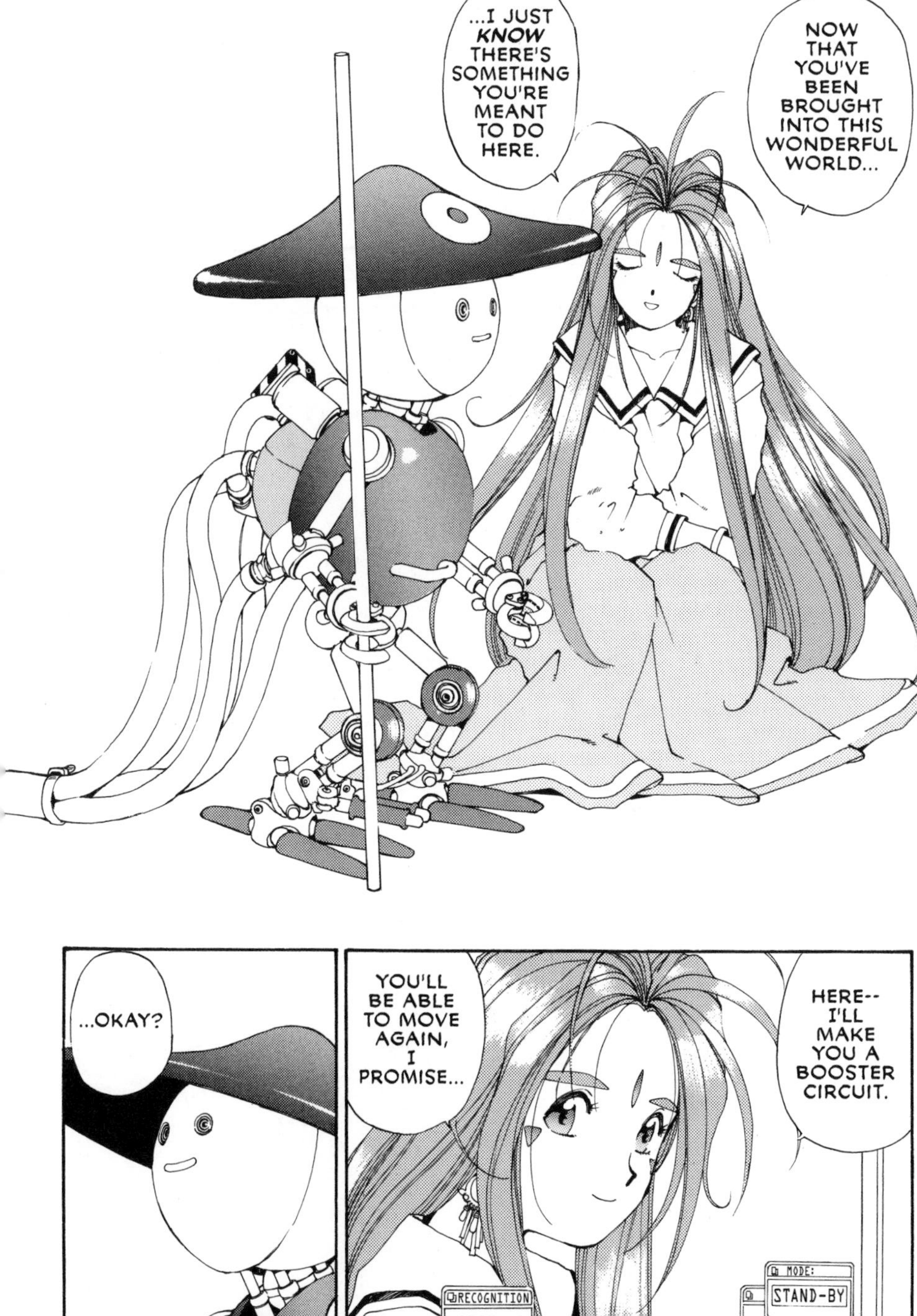
NOW THAT YOU'VE BEEN BROUGHT INTO THIS WONDERFUL WORLD...
...I JUST *KNOW* THERE'S SOMETHING YOU'RE MEANT TO DO HERE.
HERE-- I'LL MAKE YOU A BOOSTER CIRCUIT.
YOU'LL BE ABLE TO MOVE AGAIN, I PROMISE...
MODE:
STAND-BY
RECOGNITION
VOICE ON
...OKAY?

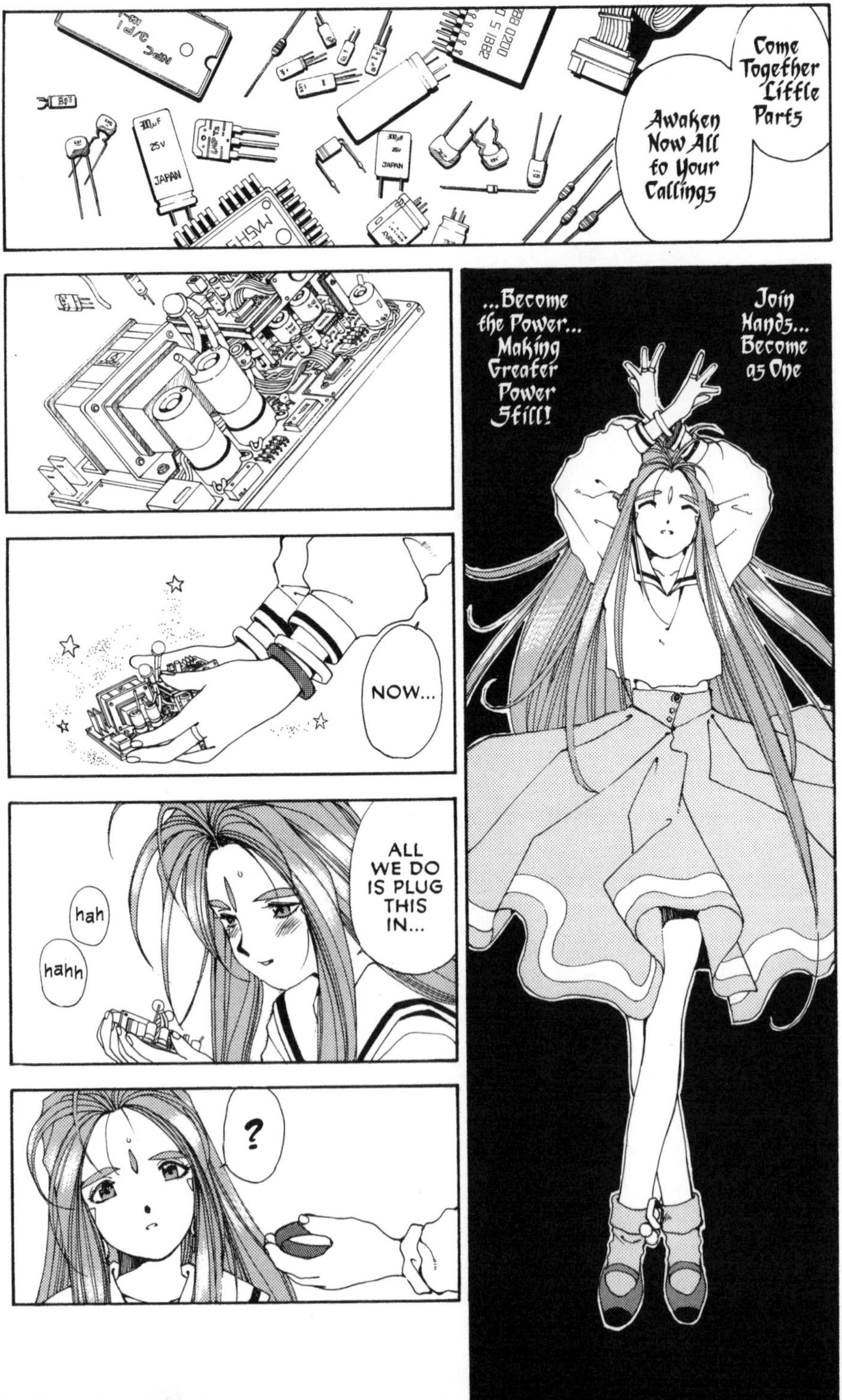
Come Together Little Parts
Awaken Now All to Your Callings
Join Hands... Become as One
...Become the Power... Making Greater Power Still!
NOW...
ALL WE DO IS PLUG THIS IN...
hah
hahh
?

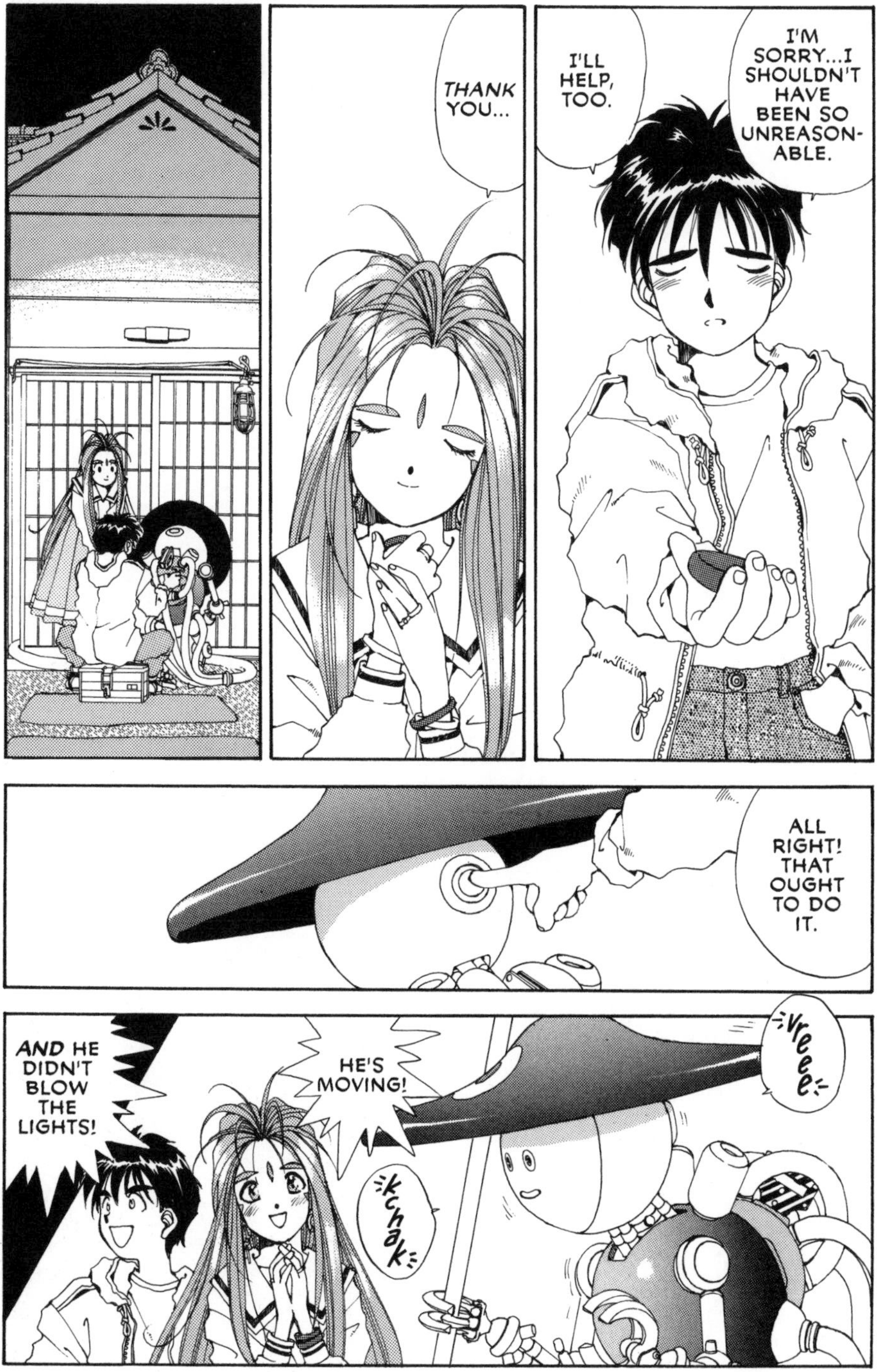
I'M SORRY...I SHOULDN'T HAVE BEEN SO UNREASON-ABLE.
I'LL HELP, TOO.
THANK YOU...
ALL RIGHT! THAT OUGHT TO DO IT.
vreeee
HE'S MOVING!
kchak
AND HE DIDN'T BLOW THE LIGHTS!

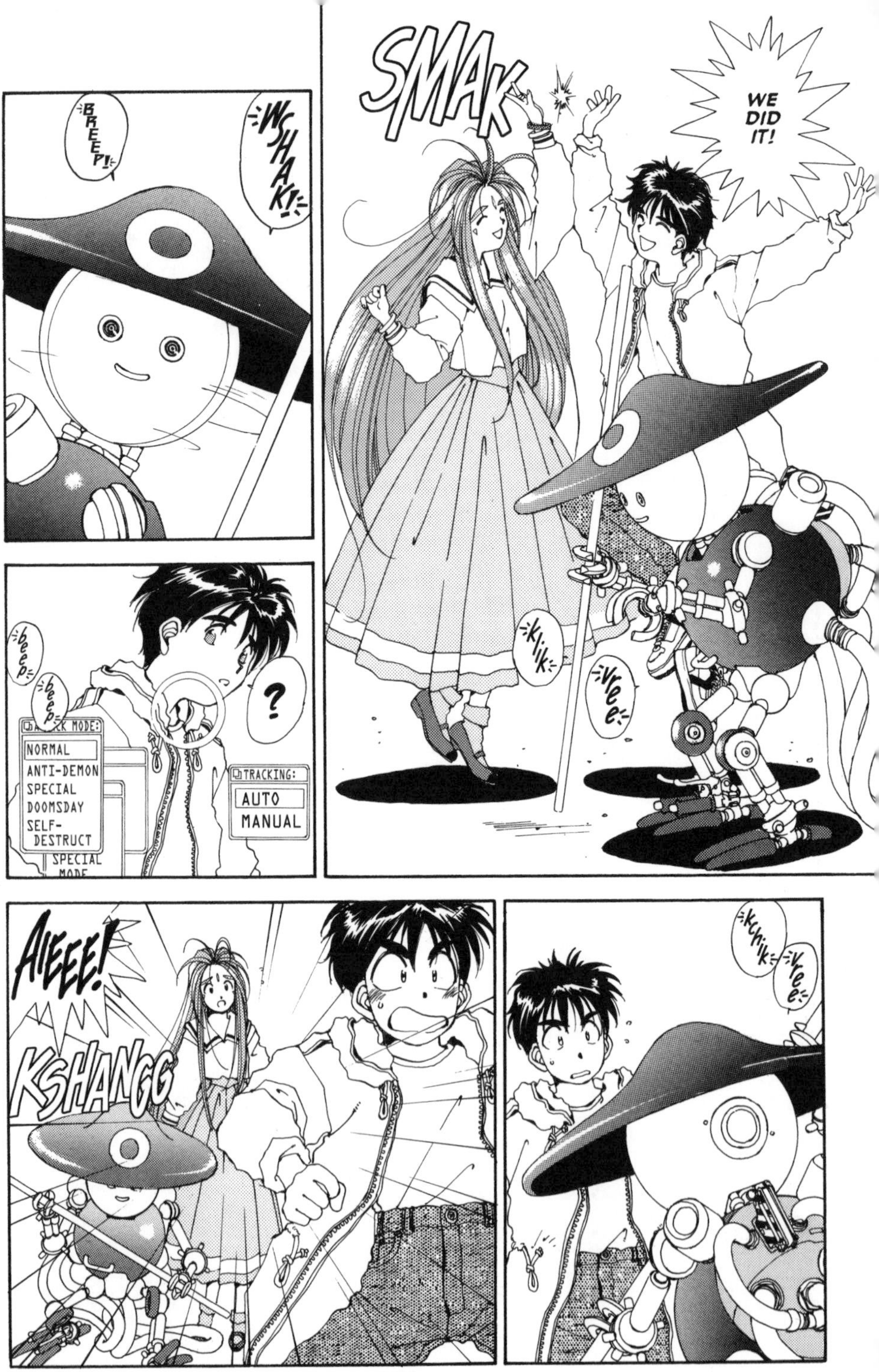
SMAK
WE DID IT!
klik
vree
WSHAK!
BREEP!
beep
beep
?
CK MODE:
NORMAL
ANTI-DEMON
SPECIAL
DOOMSDAY
SELF-DESTRUCT
SPECIAL MODE
TRACKING:
AUTO
MANUAL
kchik
vree
AIEEE!
KSHANGG

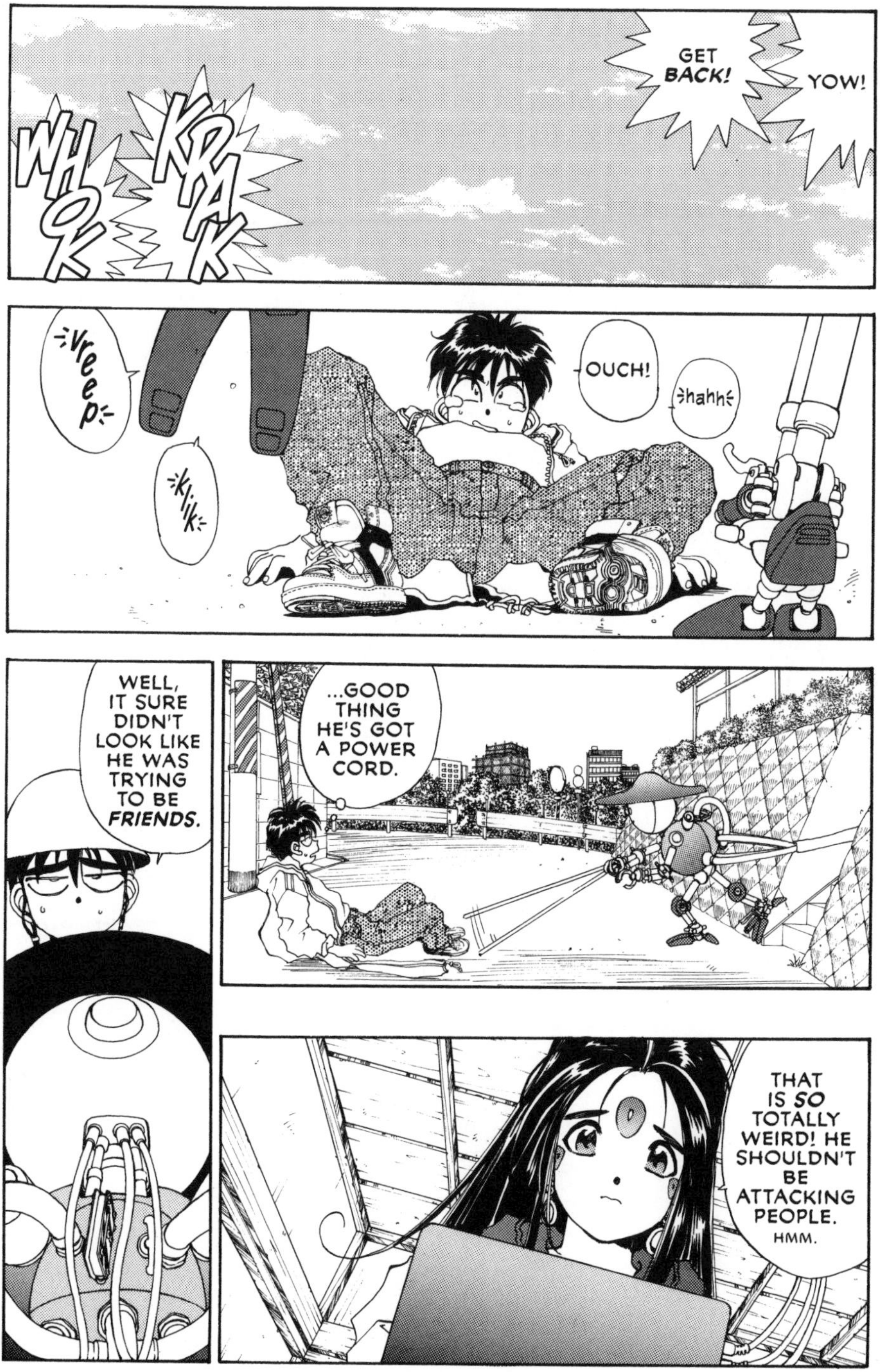
YOW!
GET BACK!
KRAK
WHOK
hahh
OUCH!
vreep
klik
...GOOD THING HE'S GOT A POWER CORD.
THAT IS SO TOTALLY WEIRD! HE SHOULDN'T BE ATTACKING PEOPLE.
HMM.
WELL, IT SURE DIDN'T LOOK LIKE HE WAS TRYING TO BE FRIENDS.

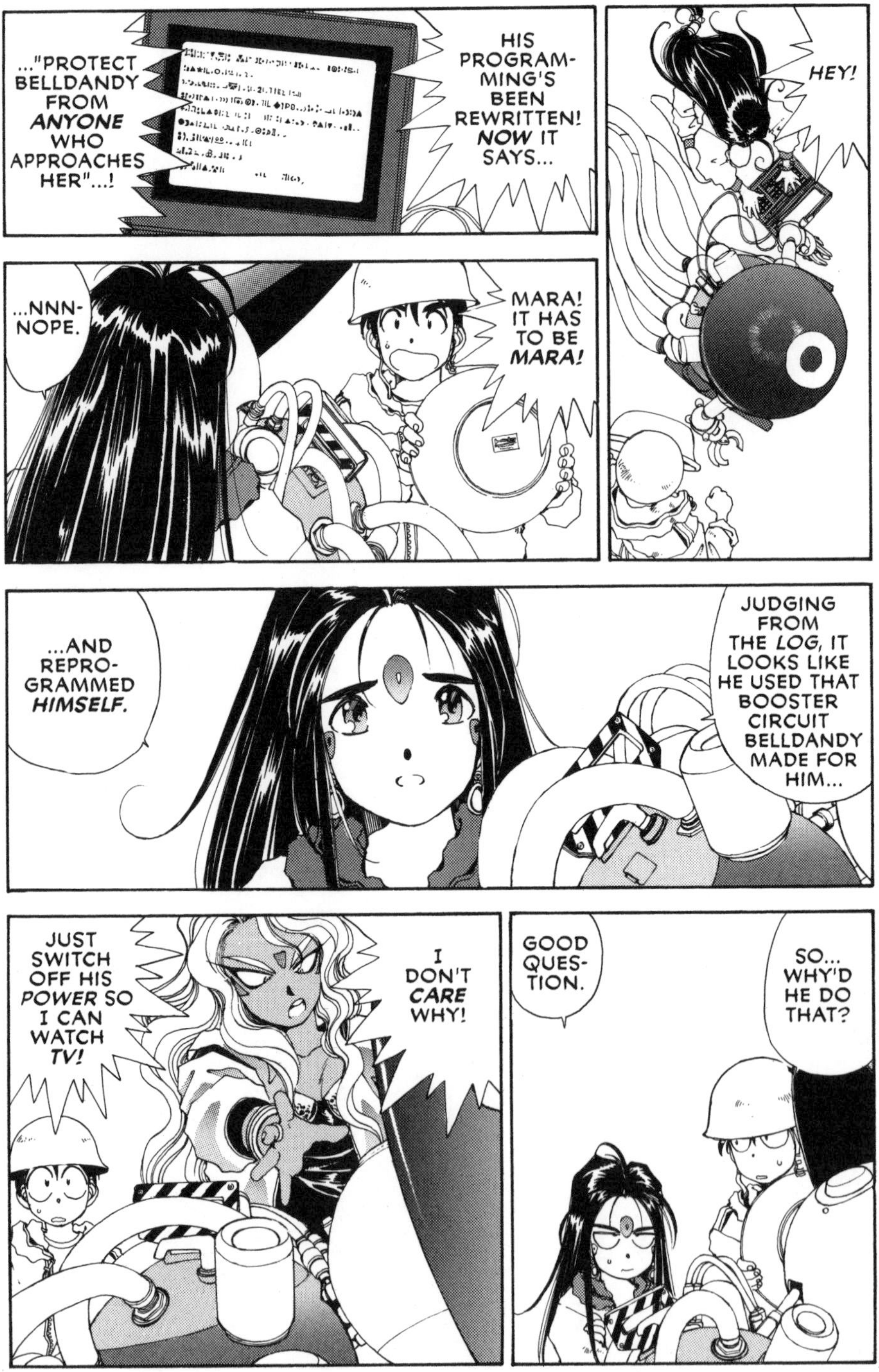
HEY!
HIS PROGRAMMING'S BEEN REWRITTEN! NOW IT SAYS...
..."PROTECT BELLDANDY FROM ANYONE WHO APPROACHES HER"...!
MARA! IT HAS TO BE MARA!
...NNN-NOPE.
JUDGING FROM THE LOG, IT LOOKS LIKE HE USED THAT BOOSTER CIRCUIT BELLDANDY MADE FOR HIM...
...AND REPROGRAMMED HIMSELF.
SO... WHY'D HE DO THAT?
GOOD QUESTION.
I DON'T CARE WHY!
JUST SWITCH OFF HIS POWER SO I CAN WATCH TV!

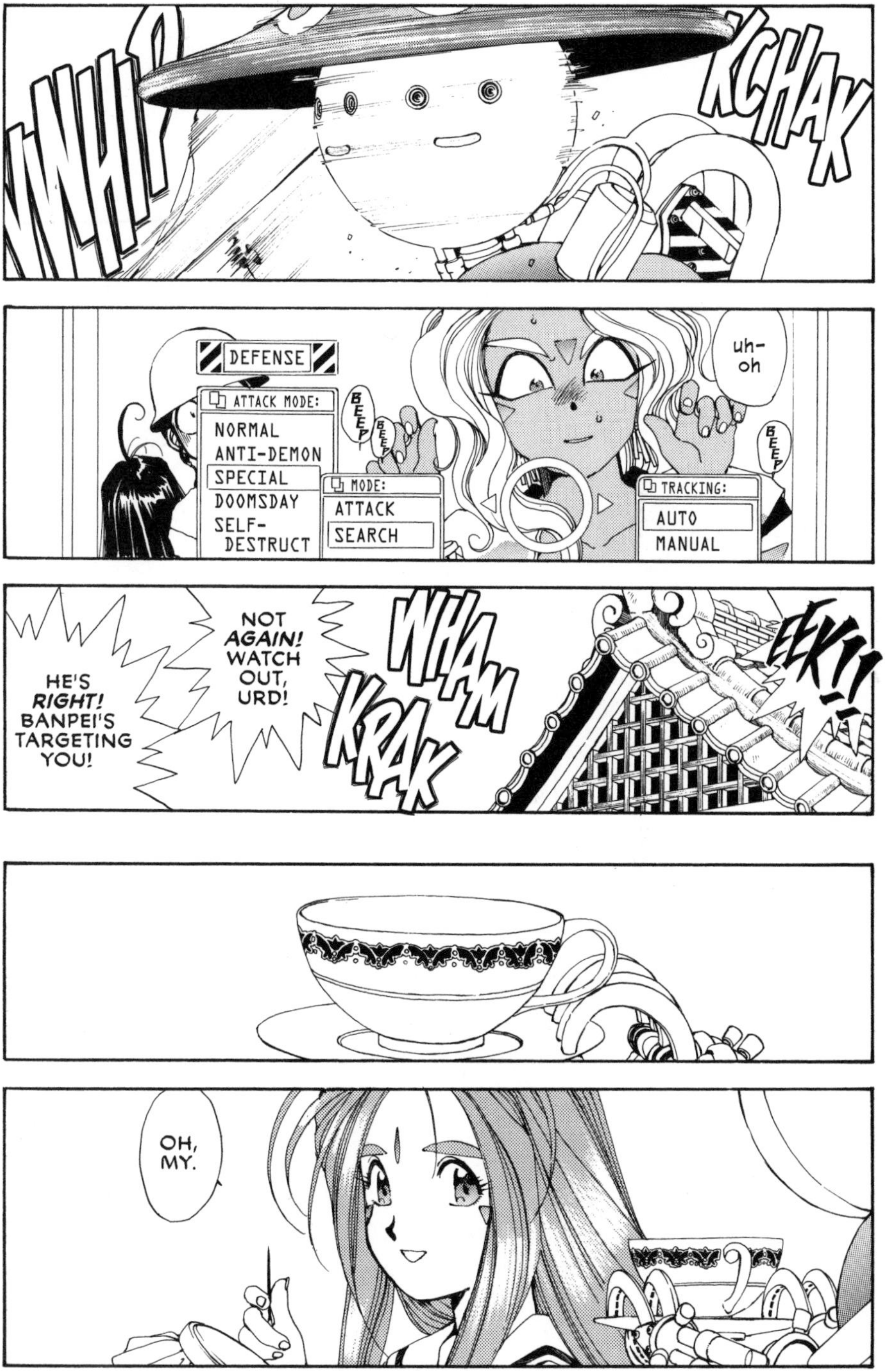
KCHAK
WHIP
uh-oh
BEEP
TRACKING:
AUTO
MANUAL
BEEP
BEEP
MODE:
ATTACK
SEARCH
DEFENSE
ATTACK MODE:
NORMAL
ANTI-DEMON
SPECIAL
DOOMSDAY
SELF-DESTRUCT
EEK!!
WHAM
KRAK
NOT *AGAIN!* WATCH OUT, URD!
HE'S *RIGHT!* BANPEI'S TARGETING YOU!
OH, MY.

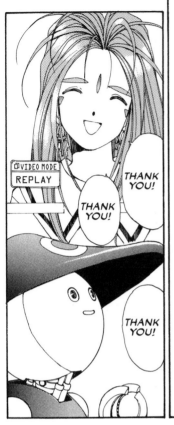

VIDEO MODE
REPLAY

THANK YOU!

THANK YOU!

THANK YOU!

THANK YOU!

YOU MADE *TEA* FOR ME...?

I... I'M NOT...

...SURE.

...WHAT DO YOU THINK?

SO...

LOVE AT FIRST SIGHT.

136

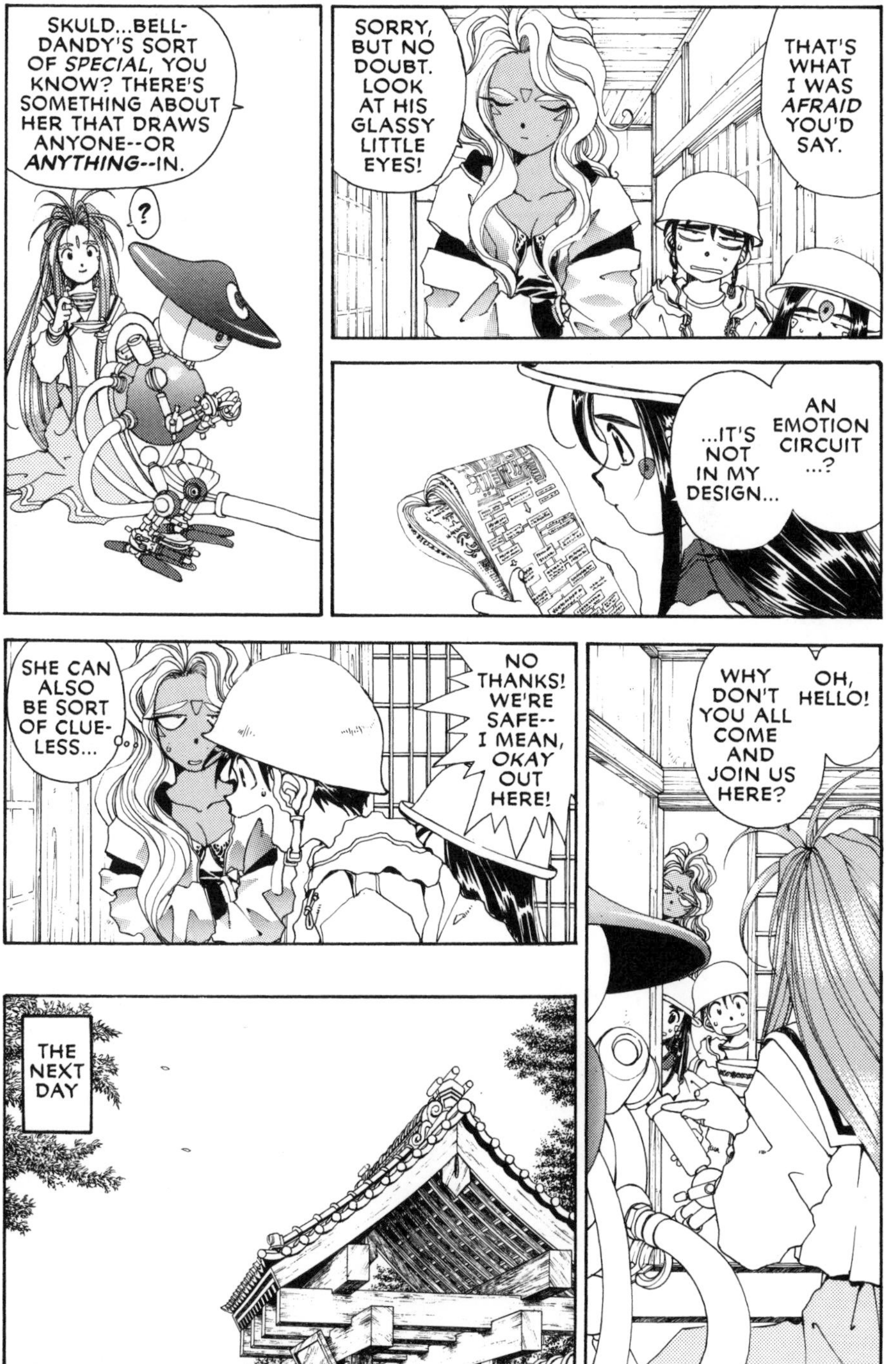
SORRY, BUT NO DOUBT. LOOK AT HIS GLASSY LITTLE EYES!
THAT'S WHAT I WAS *AFRAID* YOU'D SAY.
AN EMOTION CIRCUIT ...?
...IT'S NOT IN MY DESIGN...
SKULD...BELL-DANDY'S SORT OF *SPECIAL*, YOU KNOW? THERE'S SOMETHING ABOUT HER THAT DRAWS ANYONE--OR ***ANYTHING***--IN.
?
OH, HELLO!
WHY DON'T YOU ALL COME AND JOIN US HERE?
NO THANKS! WE'RE SAFE-- I MEAN, *OKAY* OUT HERE!
SHE CAN ALSO BE SORT OF CLUE-LESS...
THE NEXT DAY

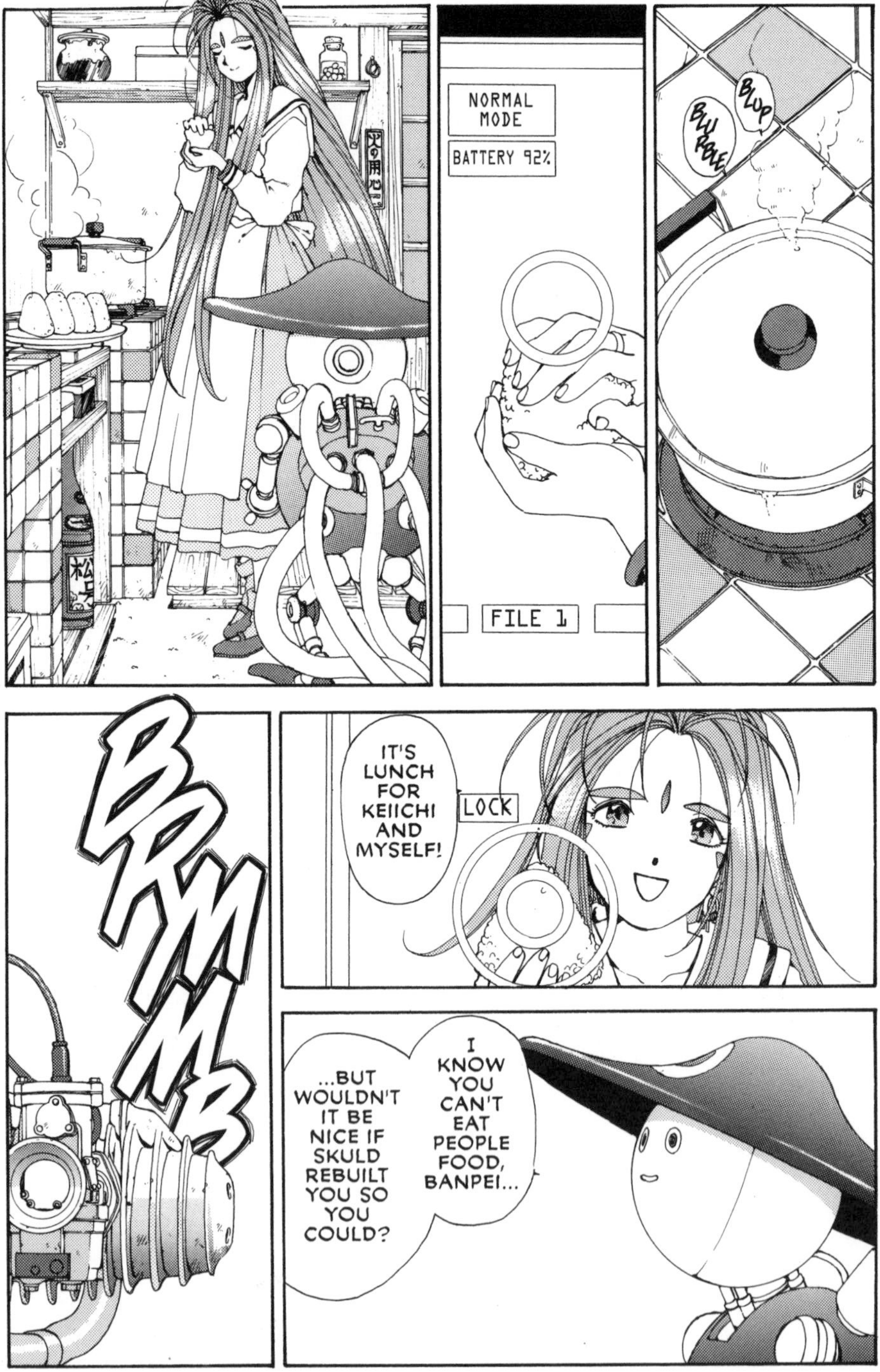
BLUP
BLUBBLE
NORMAL MODE
BATTERY 92%
FILE 1
LOCK
IT'S LUNCH FOR KEIICHI AND MYSELF!
I KNOW YOU CAN'T EAT PEOPLE FOOD, BANPEI...
...BUT WOULDN'T IT BE NICE IF SKULD REBUILT YOU SO YOU COULD?
BRMMB

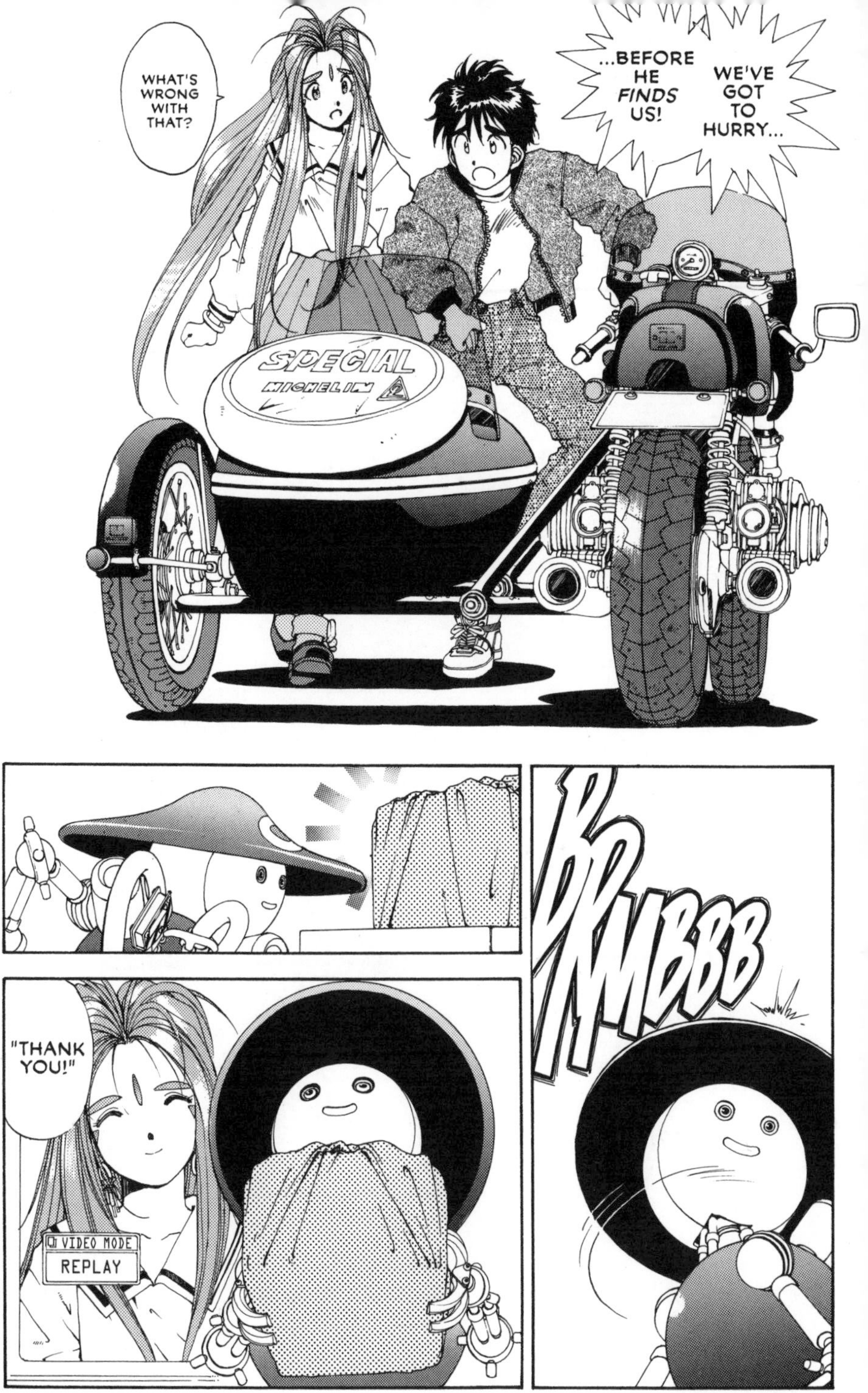
WE'VE GOT TO HURRY...
...BEFORE HE *FINDS* US!
WHAT'S WRONG WITH THAT?
BRMBBB
"THANK YOU!"
VIDEO MODE
REPLAY

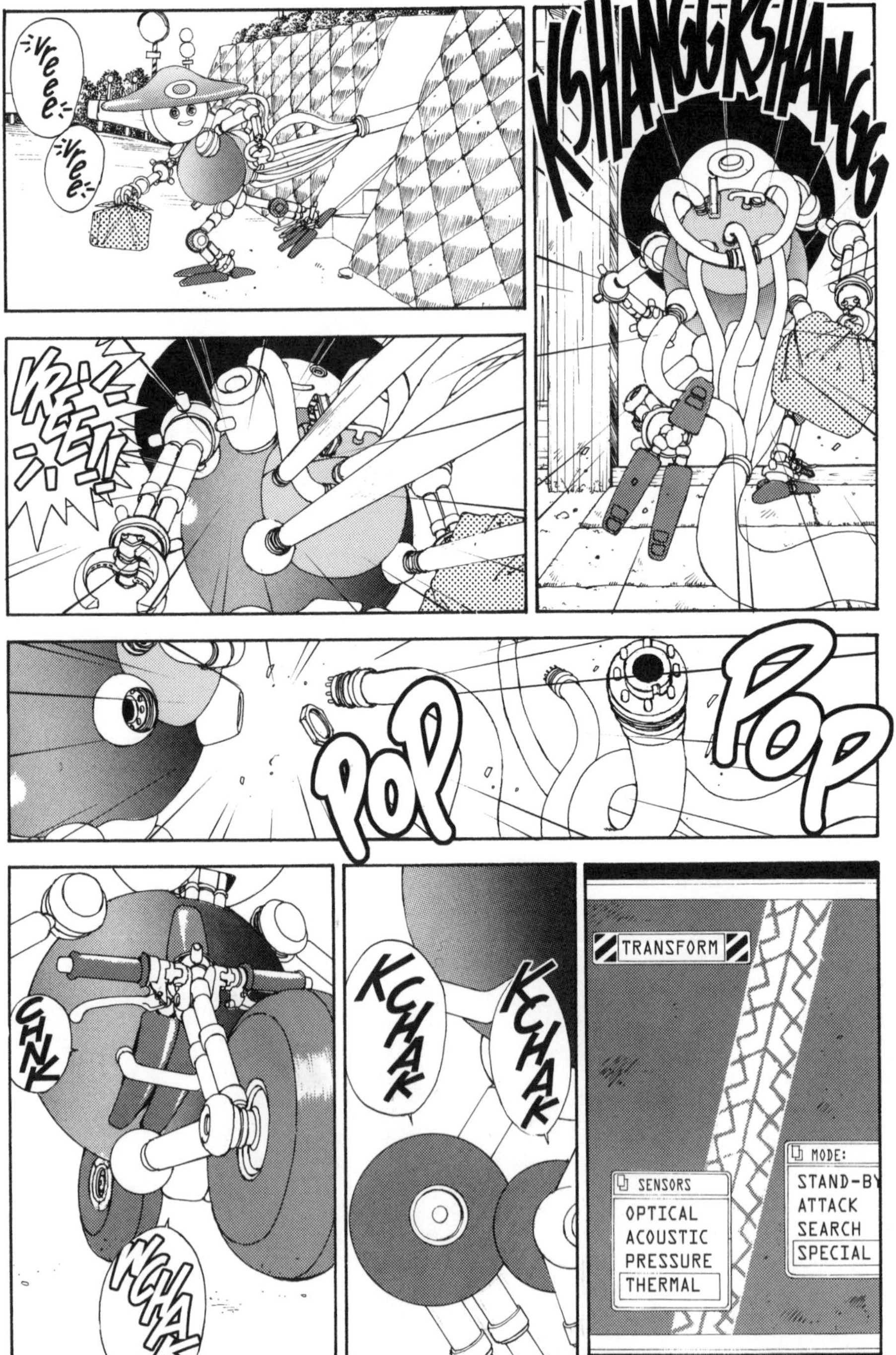
KSHANGG KSHANGG
vreee
vree
VREEE!!
POP
POP
TRANSFORM
MODE:
STAND-BY
ATTACK
SEARCH
SPECIAL
SENSORS
OPTICAL
ACOUSTIC
PRESSURE
THERMAL
KCHAK
KCHAK
CHNK
WCHAK

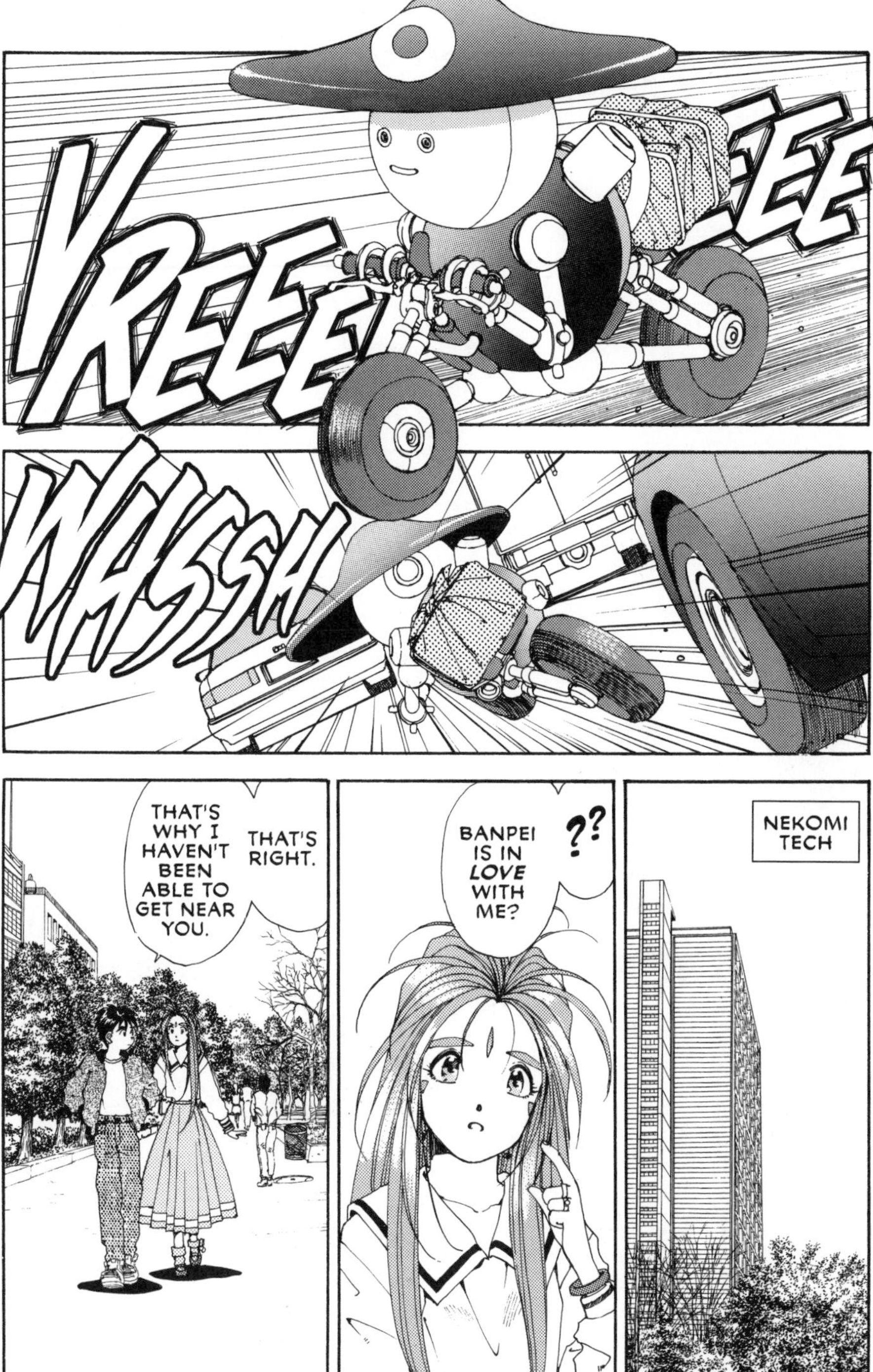
VREEEEEEE
WHSSH
NEKOMI TECH
??
BANPEI IS IN *LOVE* WITH ME?
THAT'S RIGHT.
THAT'S WHY I HAVEN'T BEEN ABLE TO GET NEAR YOU.

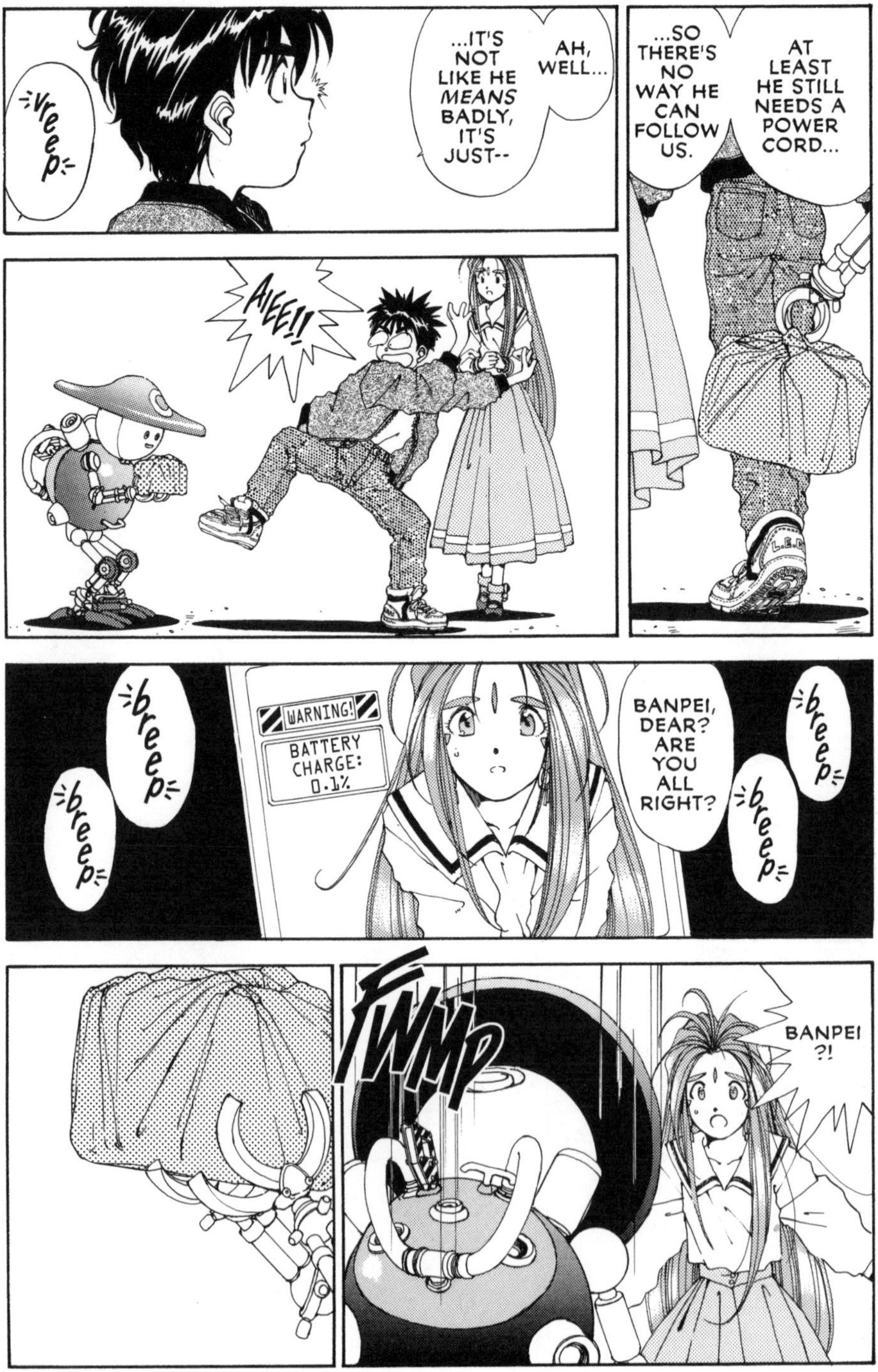
AT LEAST HE STILL NEEDS A POWER CORD...
...SO THERE'S NO WAY HE CAN FOLLOW US.
AH, WELL...
...IT'S NOT LIKE HE *MEANS* BADLY, IT'S JUST--
vreep
AIEE!!
breep
BANPEI, DEAR? ARE YOU ALL RIGHT?
breep
WARNING!
BATTERY CHARGE: 0.1%
breep
breep
FWMP
BANPEI ?!

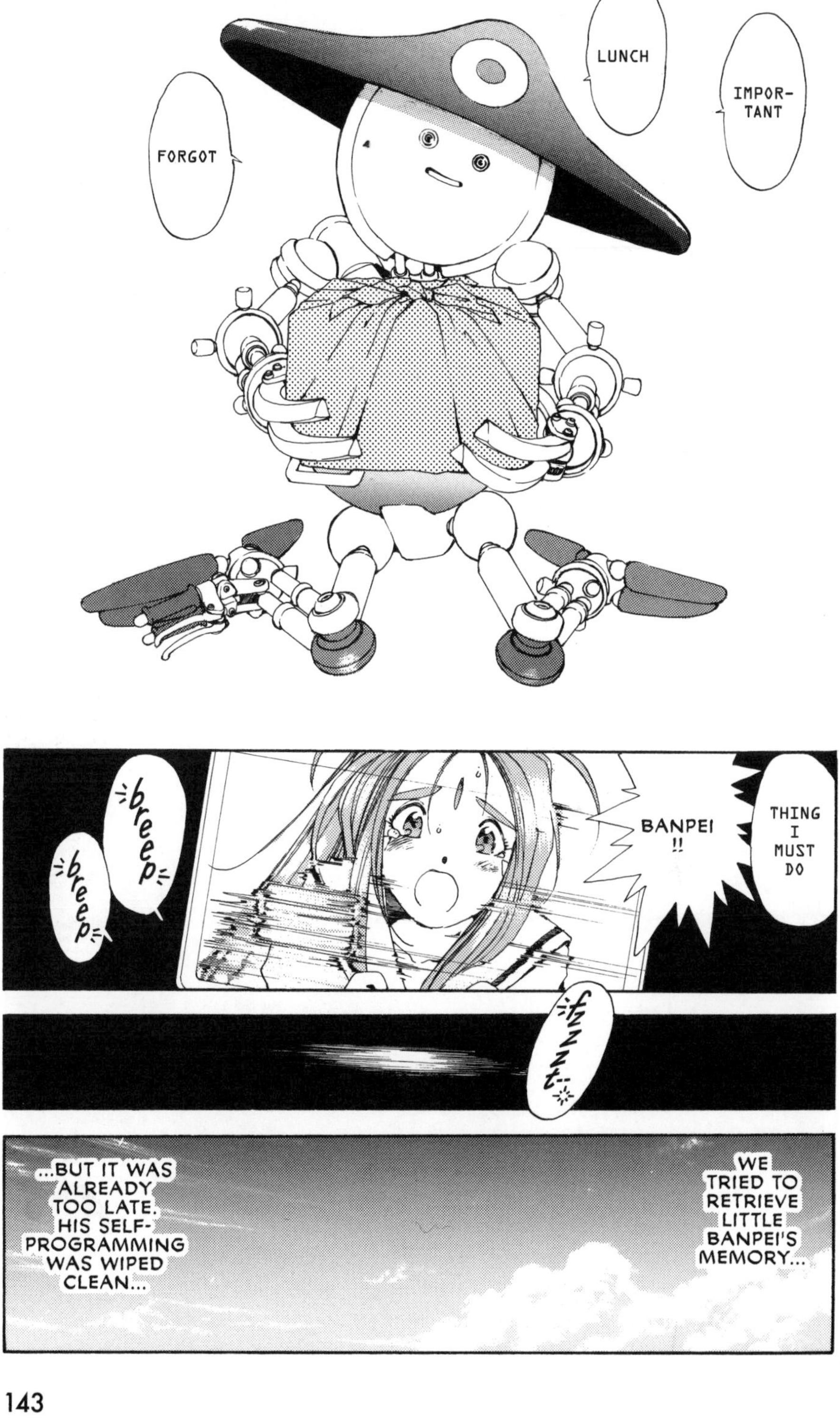
IMPORTANT
LUNCH
FORGOT
THING I MUST DO
BANPEI !!
breep
breep
fnzzt
WE TRIED TO RETRIEVE LITTLE BANPEI'S MEMORY...
...BUT IT WAS ALREADY TOO LATE. HIS SELF-PROGRAMMING WAS WIPED CLEAN...

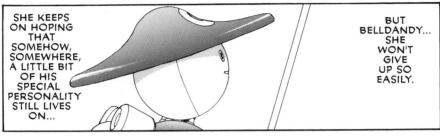

BUT BELLDANDY... SHE WON'T GIVE UP SO EASILY.
SHE KEEPS ON HOPING THAT SOMEHOW, SOMEWHERE, A LITTLE BIT OF HIS SPECIAL PERSONALITY STILL LIVES ON...
SEE YOU LATER, BANPEI!
Vreeee
COME BACK SOON.

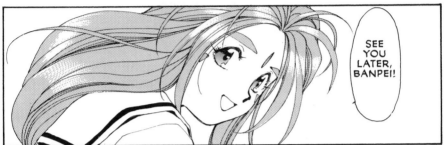

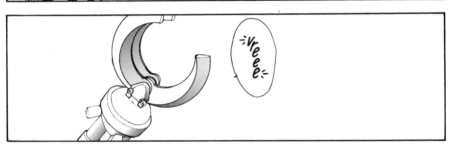

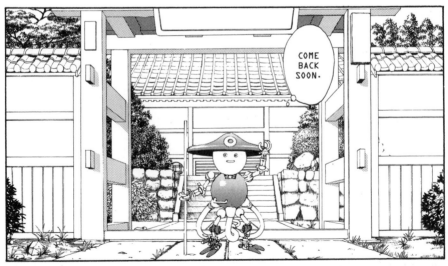

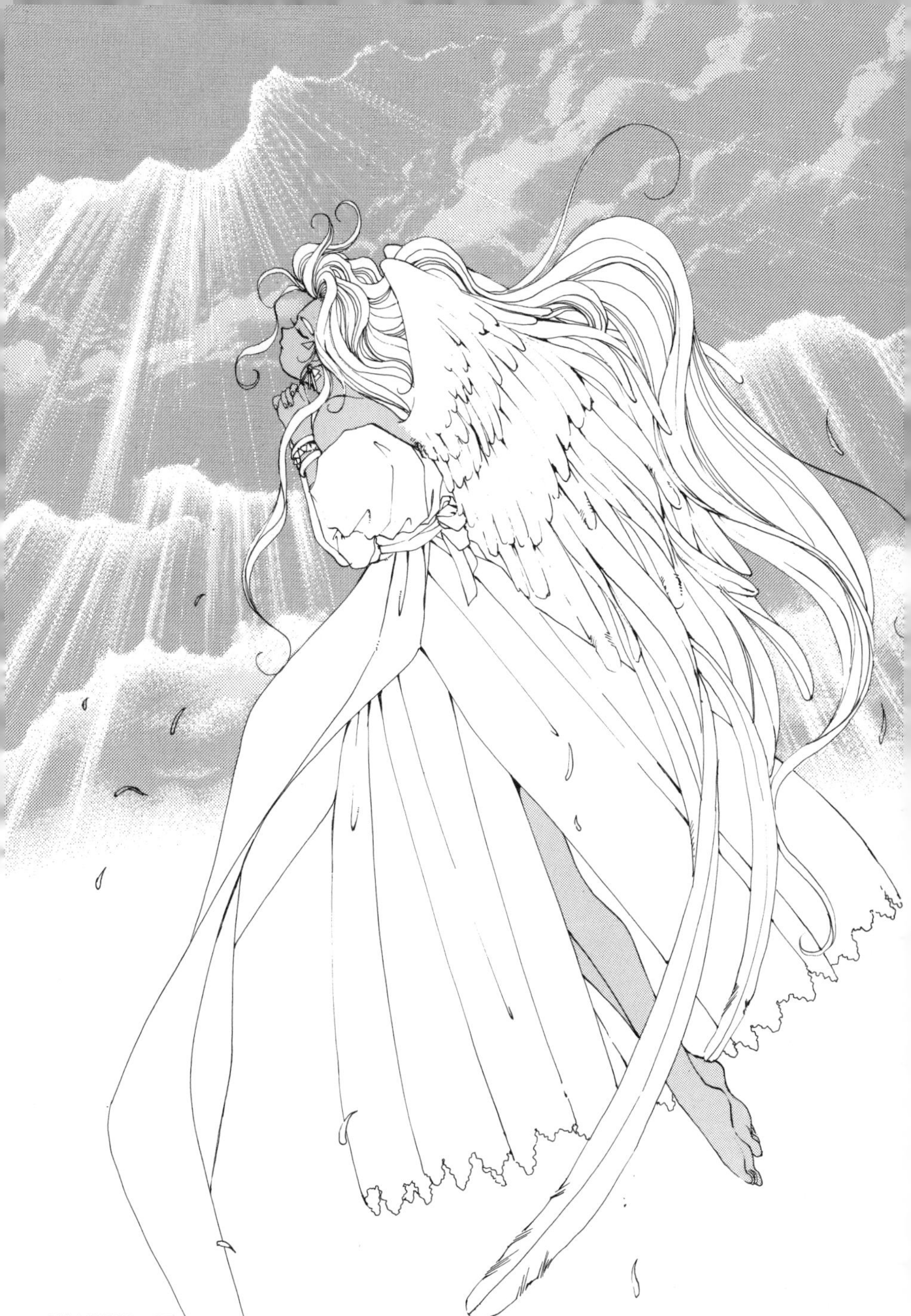

CHAPTER 47

Goodbye and Hello

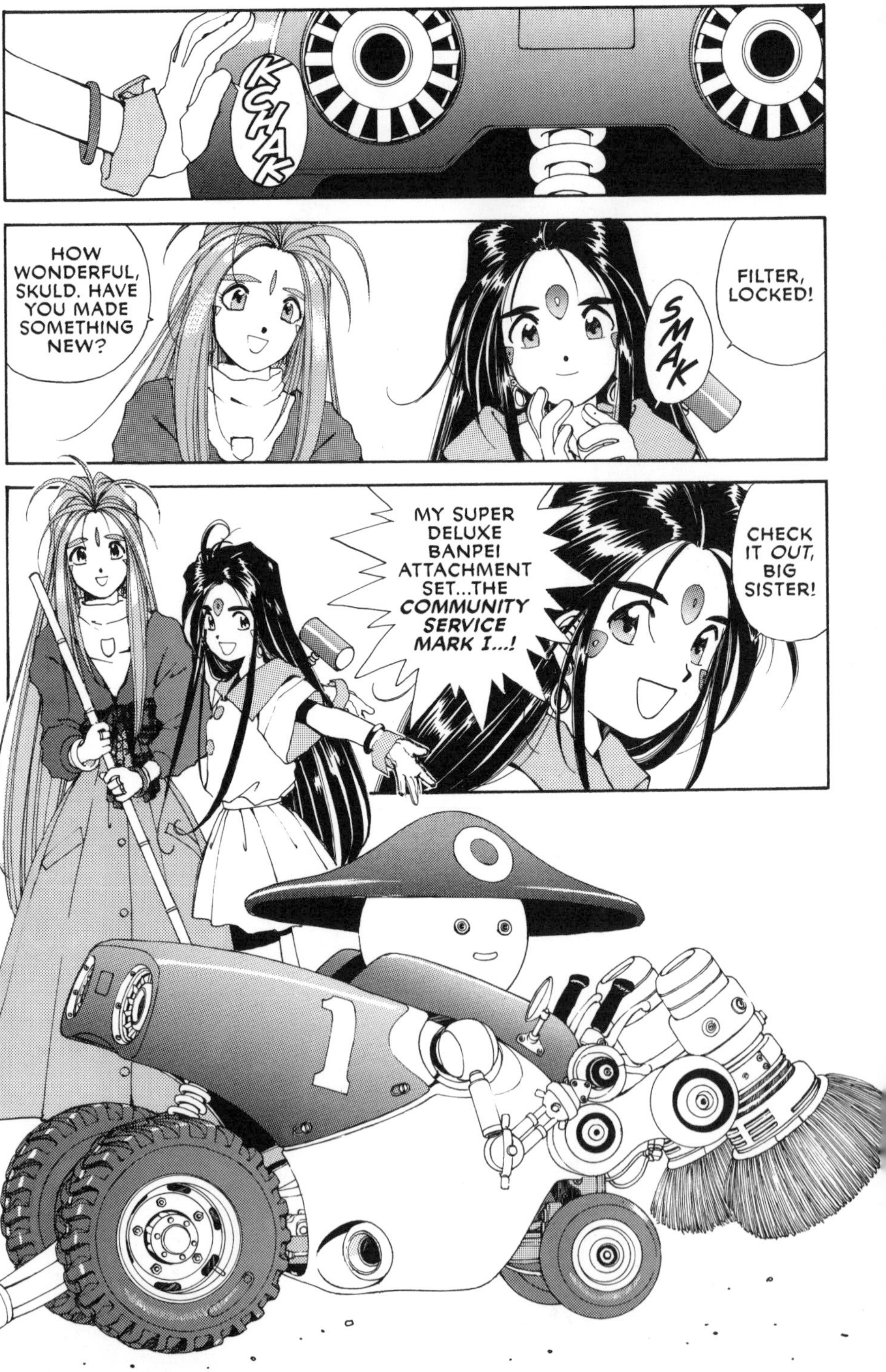
KCHAK
FILTER, LOCKED!
SMAK
HOW WONDERFUL, SKULD. HAVE YOU MADE SOMETHING NEW?
CHECK IT *OUT*, BIG SISTER!
MY SUPER DELUXE BANPEI ATTACHMENT SET...THE ***COMMUNITY SERVICE MARK I...!***

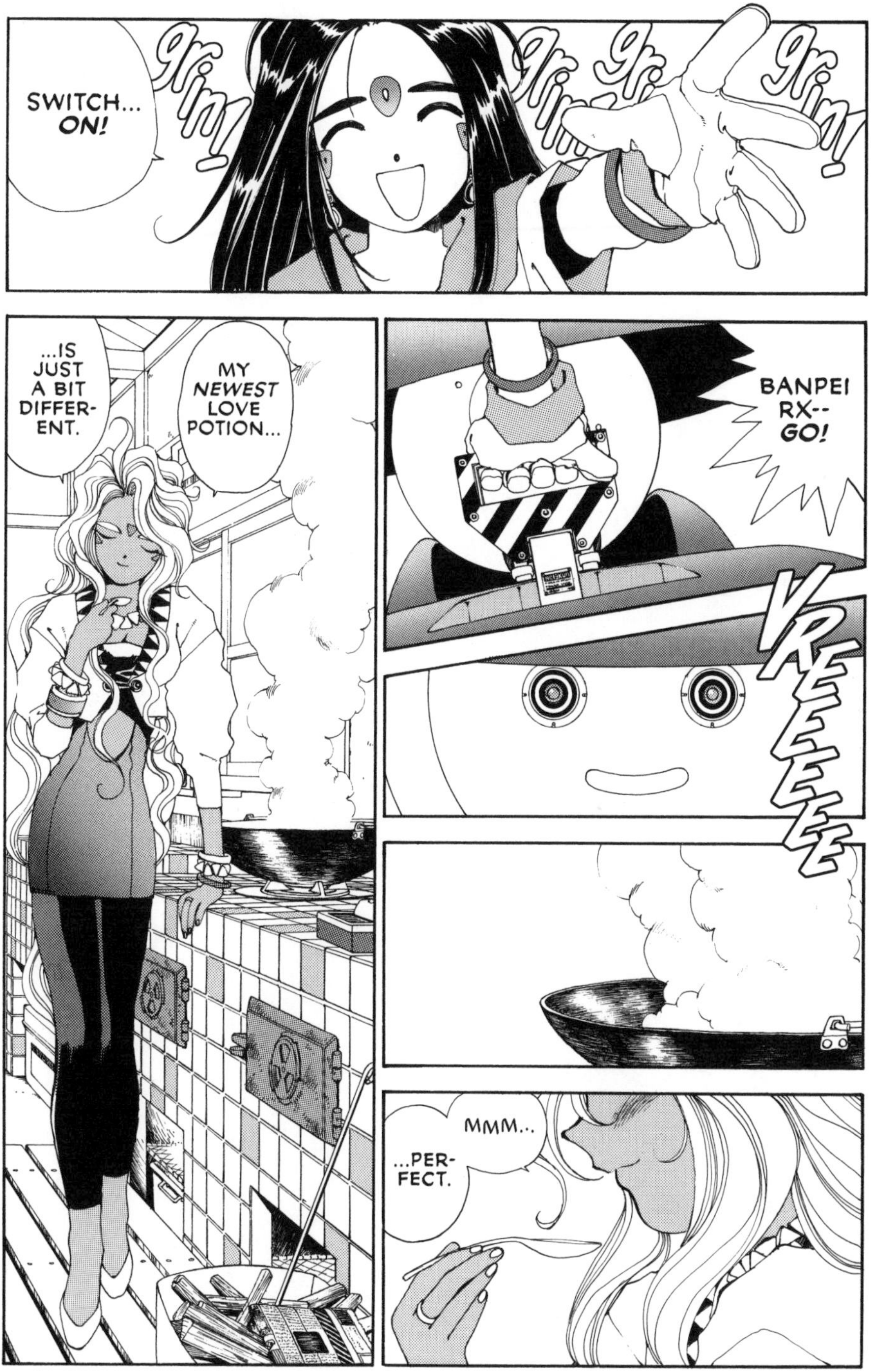
grin!
grin!
grin!
grin!
SWITCH... ON!
BANPEI RX-- GO!
VREEEEEE
MMM...
...PER- FECT.
MY NEWEST LOVE POTION...
...IS JUST A BIT DIFFER- ENT.

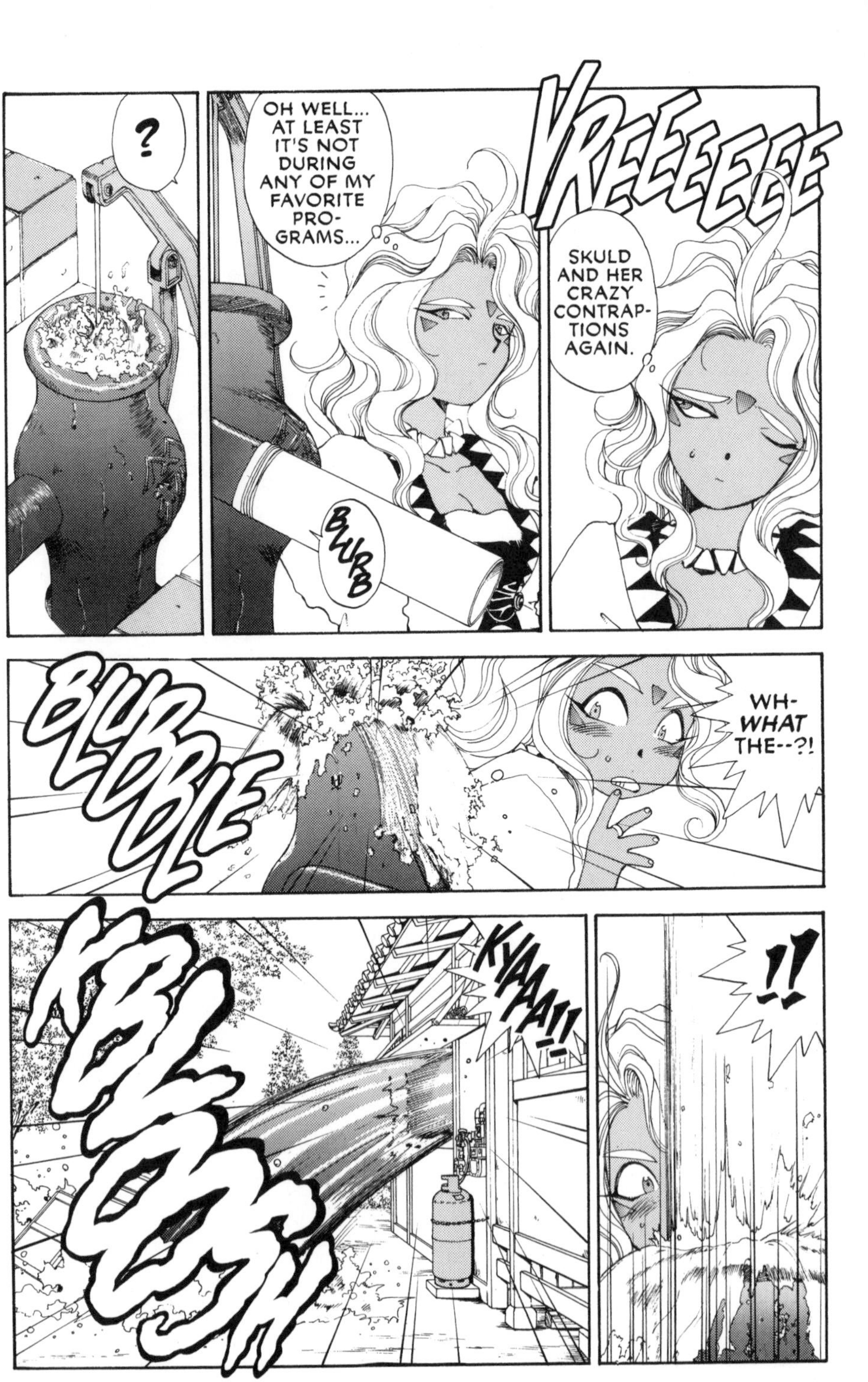
VREEEEEE
SKULD AND HER CRAZY CONTRAPTIONS AGAIN.
OH WELL... AT LEAST IT'S NOT DURING ANY OF MY FAVORITE PRO-GRAMS...
BLURB
?
WH- WHAT THE--?!
BLUBBLE
!!
KYAAA!!
KBLOOSH

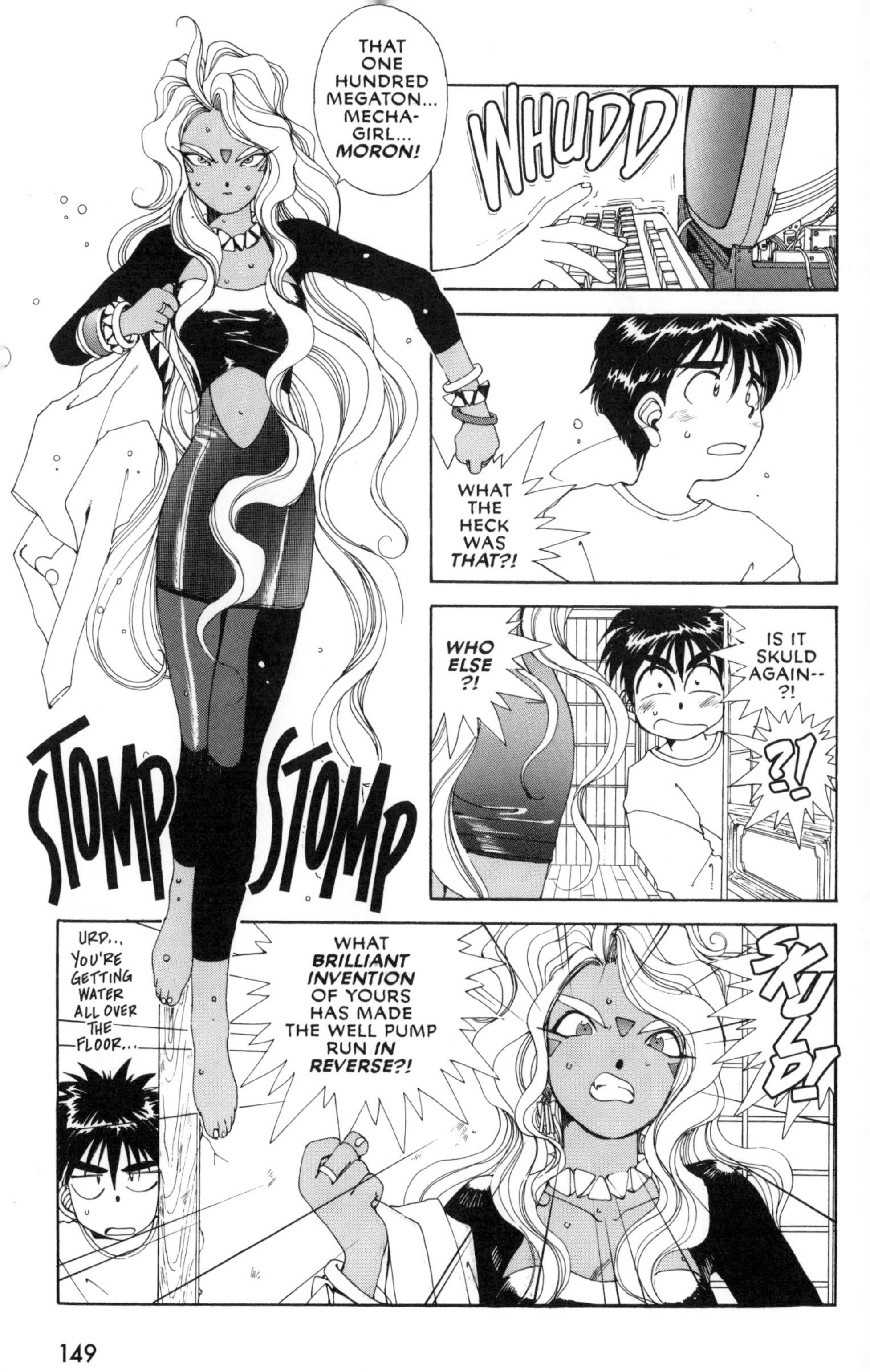
WHUDD
WHAT THE HECK WAS *THAT?!*
IS IT SKULD AGAIN--?!
?!
WHO ELSE?!
THAT ONE HUNDRED MEGATON... MECHA-GIRL... *MORON!*
STOMP STOMP
SKULD!
WHAT ***BRILLIANT INVENTION*** OF YOURS HAS MADE THE WELL PUMP RUN ***IN REVERSE?!***
URD... YOU'RE GETTING WATER ALL OVER THE FLOOR...

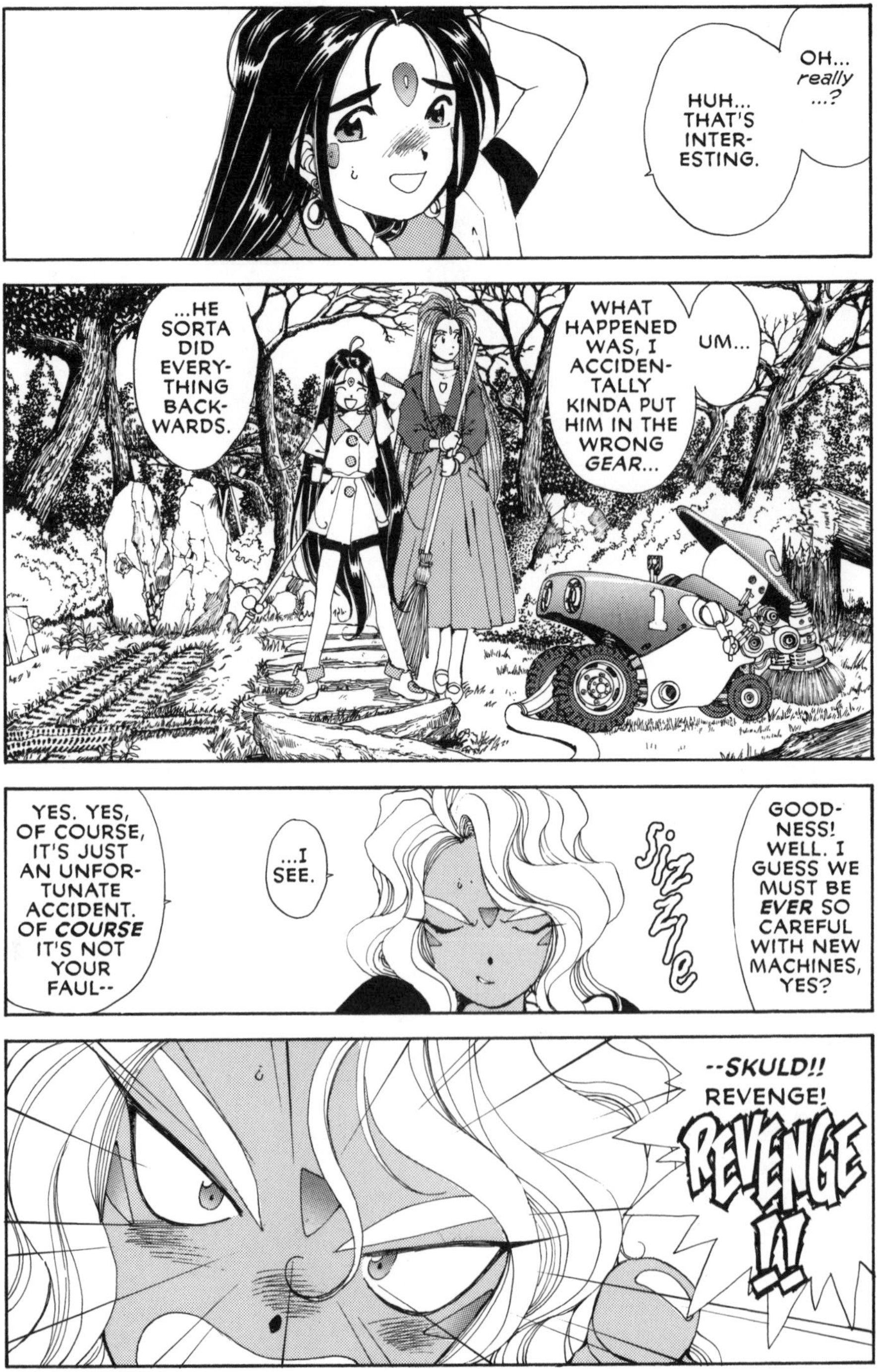
OH... *really* ...?
HUH... THAT'S INTERESTING.
UM...
WHAT HAPPENED WAS, I ACCIDENTALLY KINDA PUT HIM IN THE WRONG *GEAR*...
...HE SORTA DID EVERYTHING BACKWARDS.
GOODNESS! WELL. I GUESS WE MUST BE ***EVER*** SO CAREFUL WITH NEW MACHINES, YES?
Sizzle
...I SEE.
YES. YES, OF COURSE, IT'S JUST AN UNFORTUNATE ACCIDENT. OF ***COURSE*** IT'S NOT YOUR FAUL--
--SKULD!!
REVENGE!
REVENGE!!

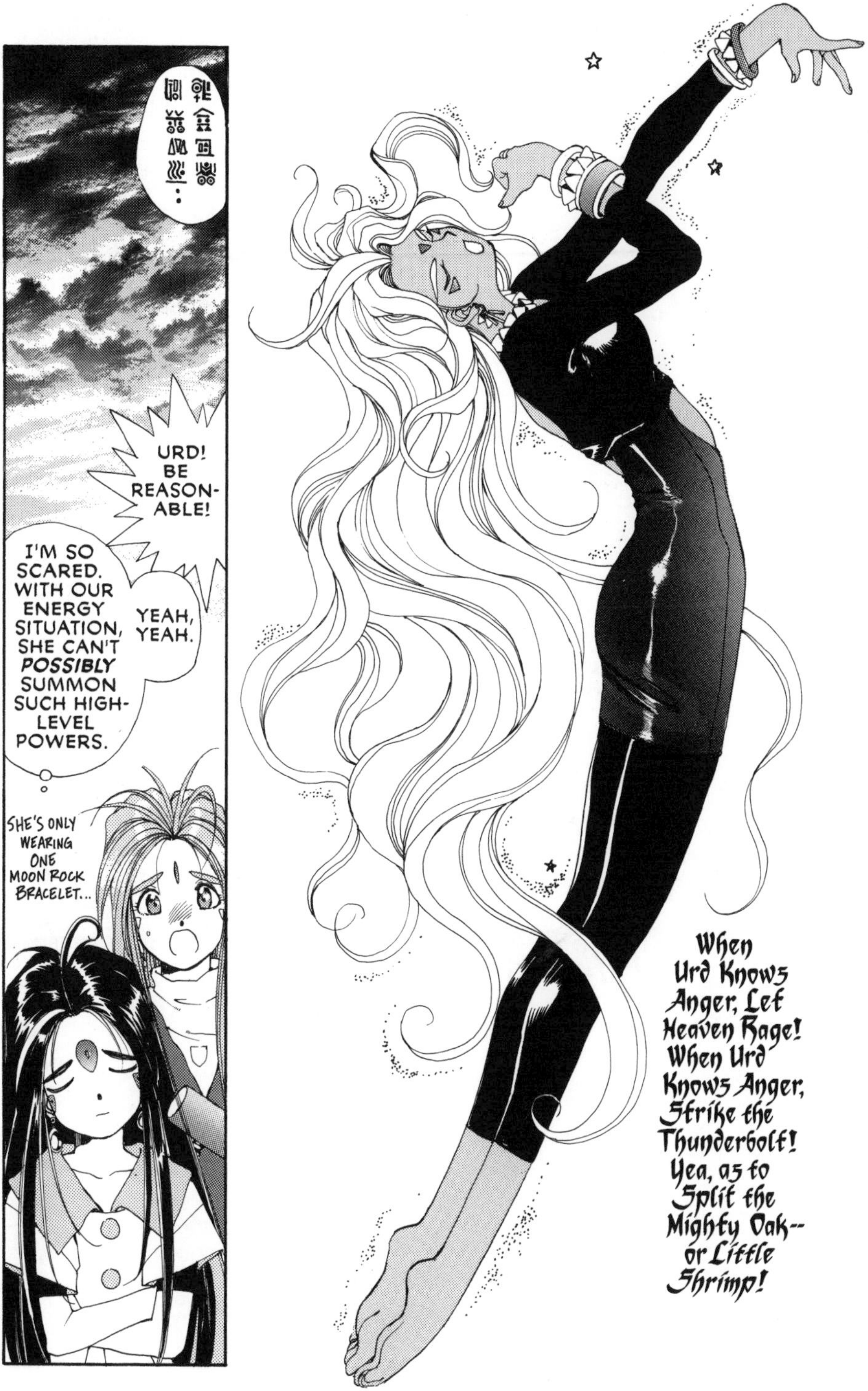
When Urd Knows Anger, Let Heaven Rage! When Urd Knows Anger, Strike the Thunderbolt! Yea, as to Split the Mighty Oak-- or Little Shrimp!
URD! BE REASON-ABLE!
YEAH, YEAH.
I'M SO SCARED. WITH OUR ENERGY SITUATION, SHE CAN'T *POSSIBLY* SUMMON SUCH HIGH-LEVEL POWERS.
SHE'S ONLY WEARING ONE MOON ROCK BRACELET...

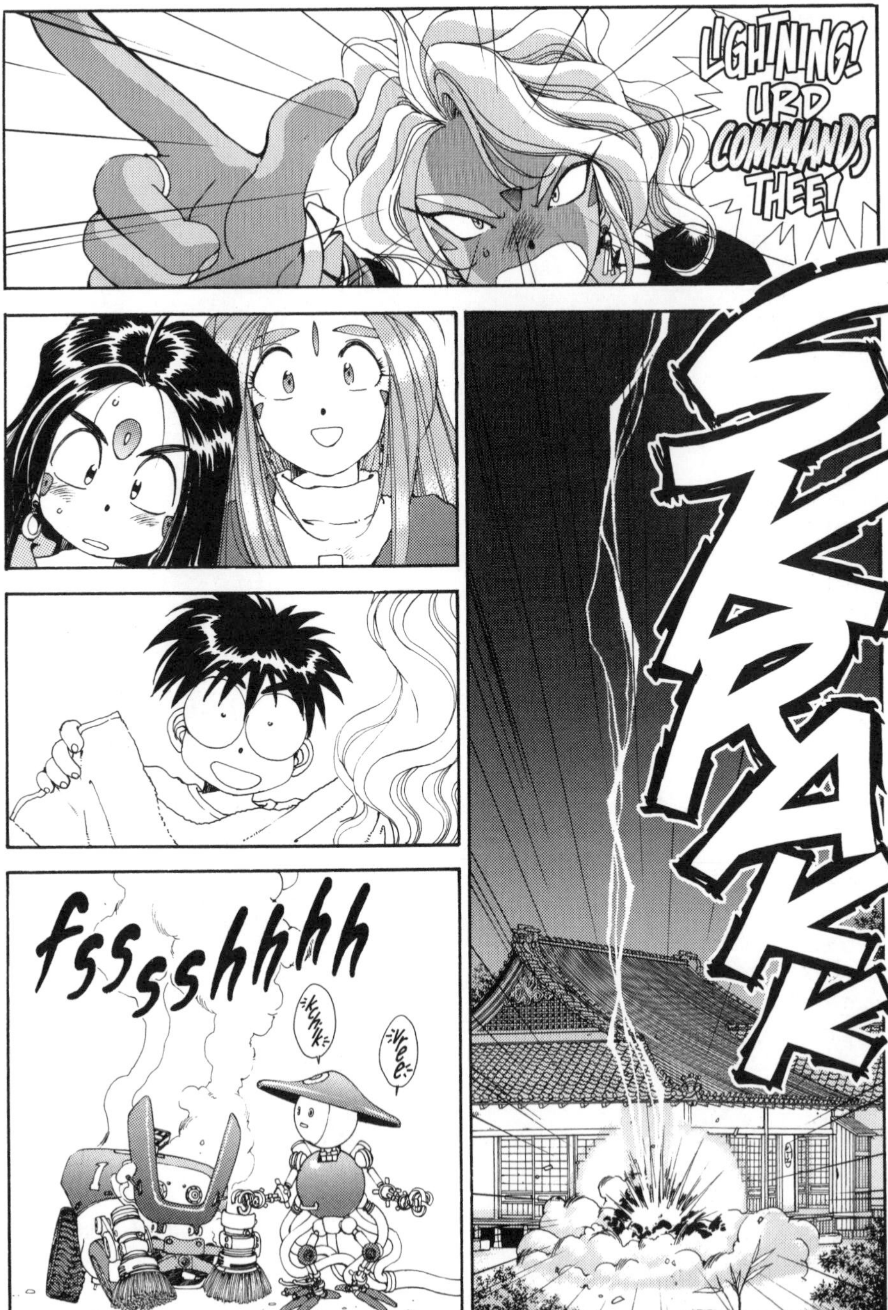
LIGHTNING! URD COMMANDS THEE!
fssssshhhhh
vree
kchik

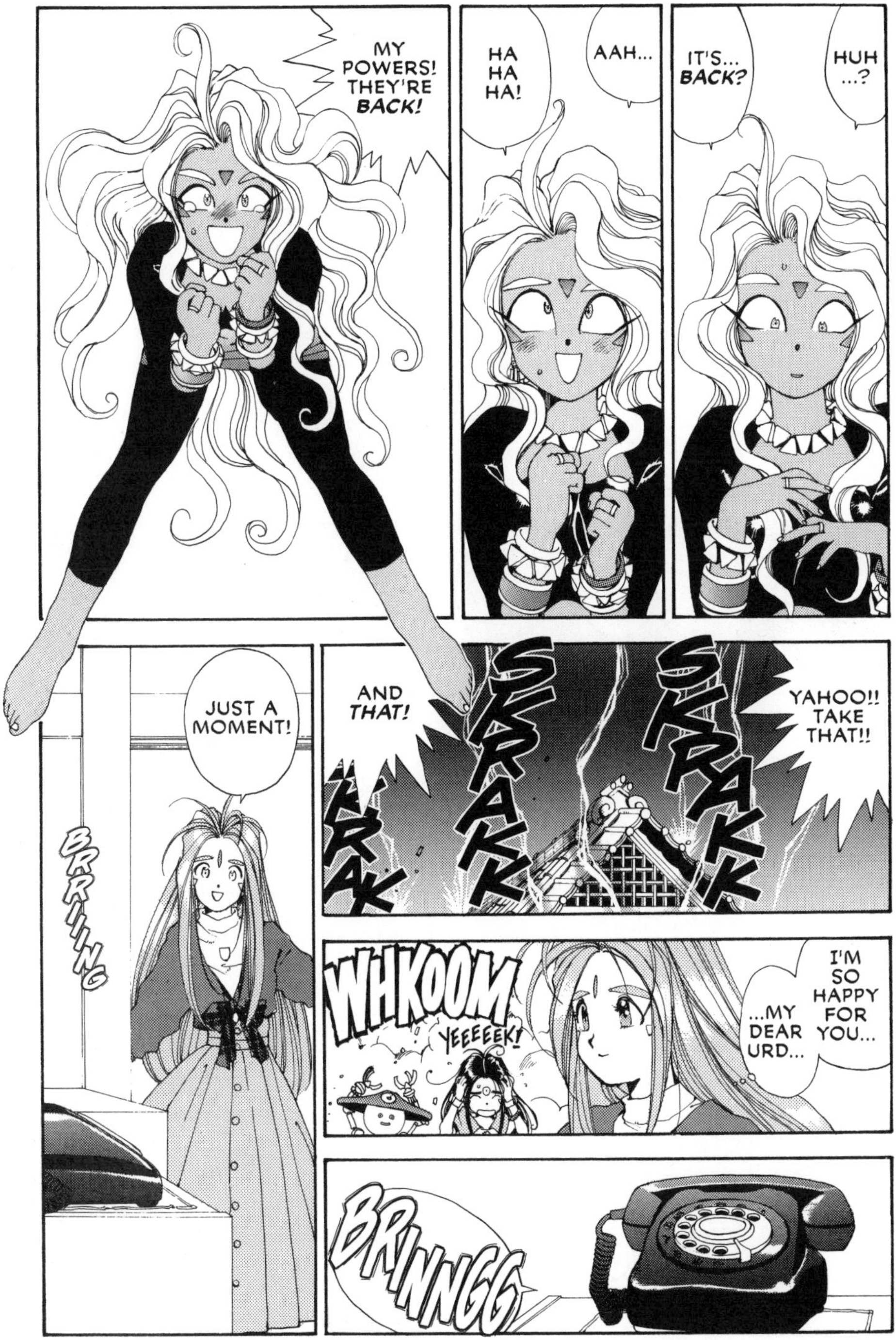
HUH ...?
IT'S... BACK?
AAH...
HA HA HA!
MY POWERS! THEY'RE BACK!
YAHOO!! TAKE THAT!!
SKRAKK
SKRAKK
AND THAT!
SKRAK
I'M SO HAPPY FOR YOU...
...MY DEAR URD...
YEEEEEK!
WHKOOM
BRINNGG
JUST A MOMENT!
BRRIIING

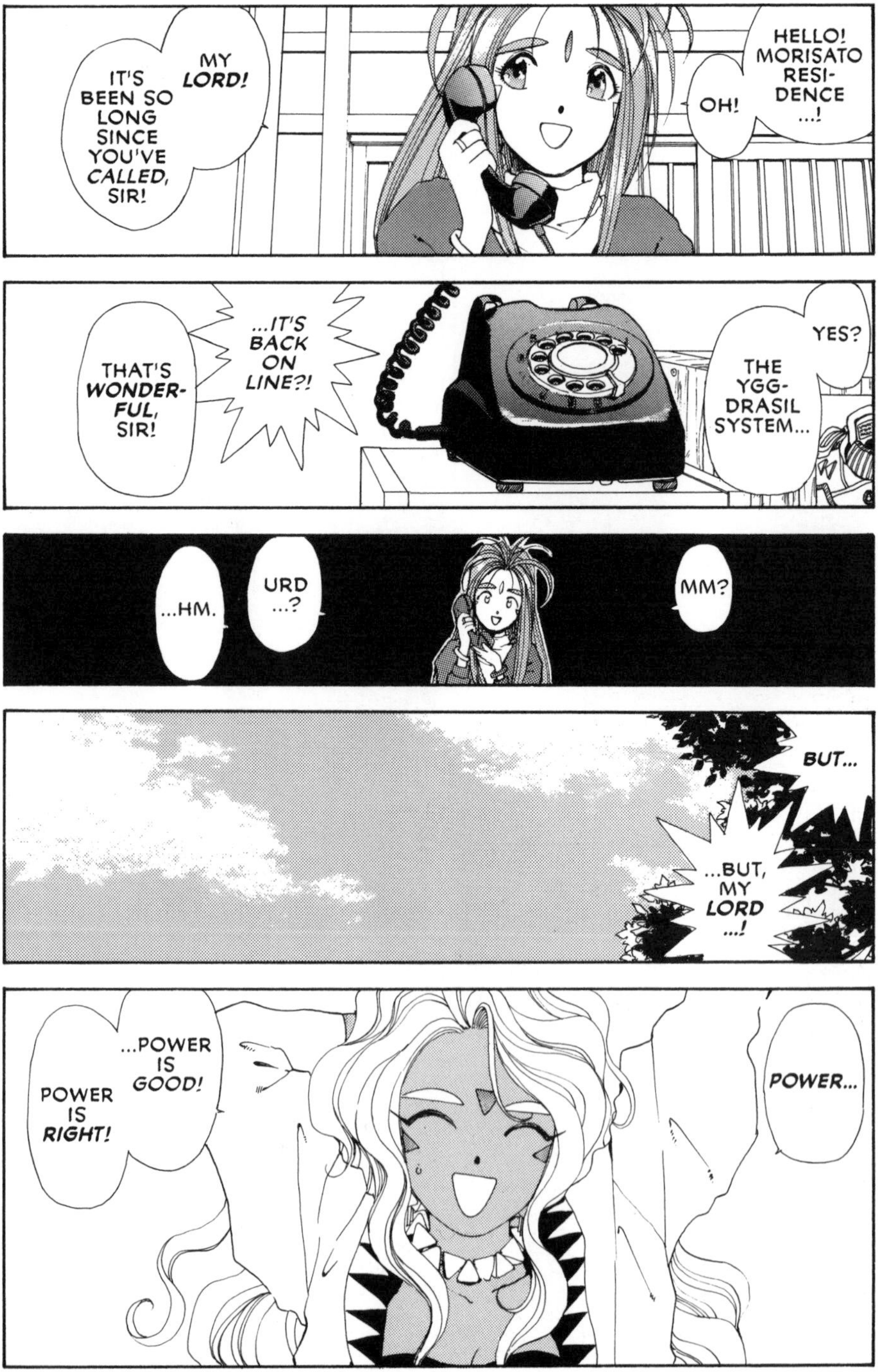
HELLO! MORISATO RESIDENCE ...!
OH!
MY LORD!
IT'S BEEN SO LONG SINCE YOU'VE CALLED, SIR!
YES?
THE YGGDRASIL SYSTEM...
...IT'S BACK ON LINE?!
THAT'S WONDERFUL, SIR!
MM?
URD ...?
...HM.
BUT...
...BUT, MY LORD ...!
POWER...
...POWER IS GOOD!
POWER IS RIGHT!

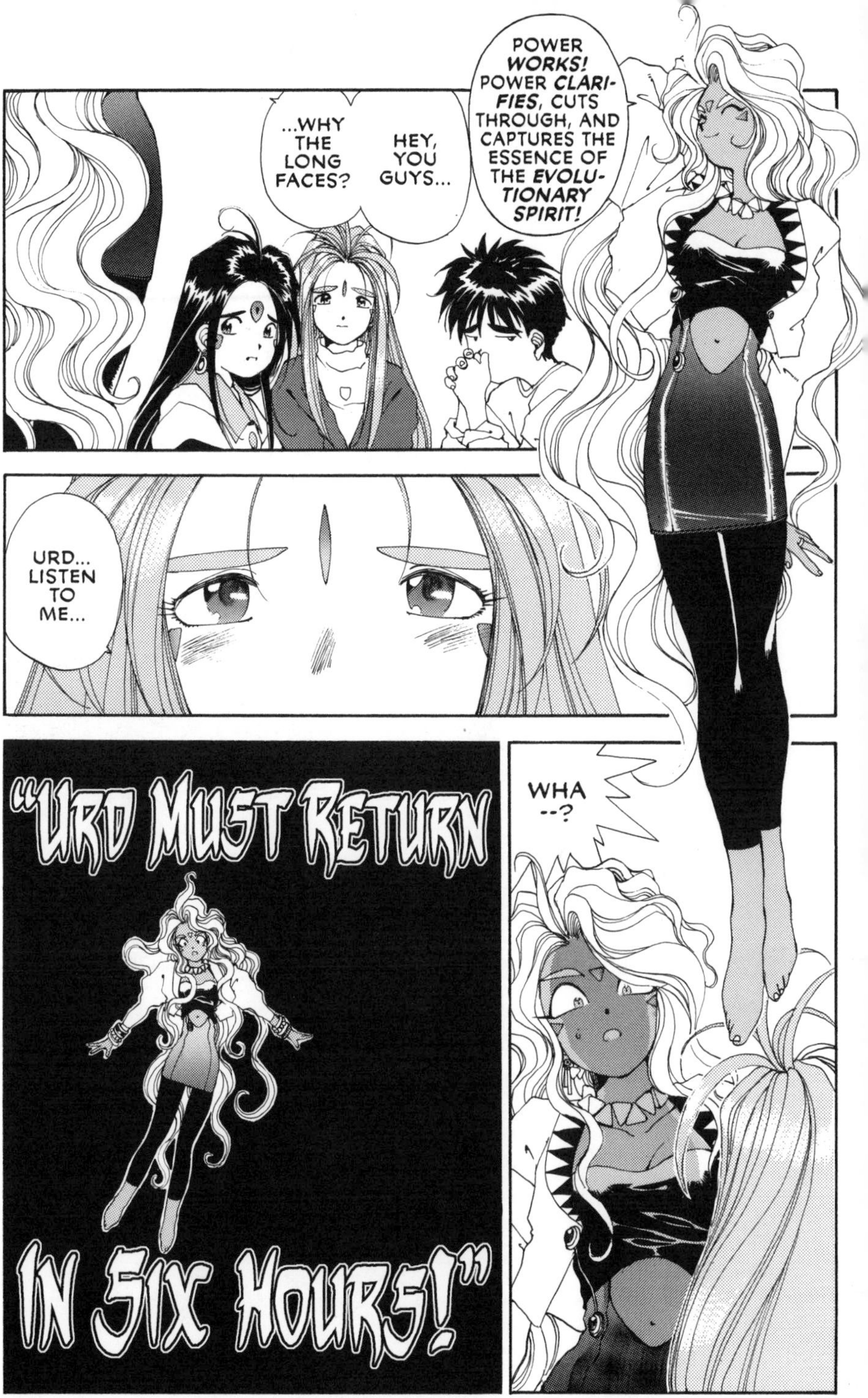
POWER WORKS! POWER CLARIFIES, CUTS THROUGH, AND CAPTURES THE ESSENCE OF THE EVOLUTIONARY SPIRIT!
HEY, YOU GUYS...
...WHY THE LONG FACES?
URD... LISTEN TO ME...
WHA --?
"URD MUST RETURN IN SIX HOURS!"

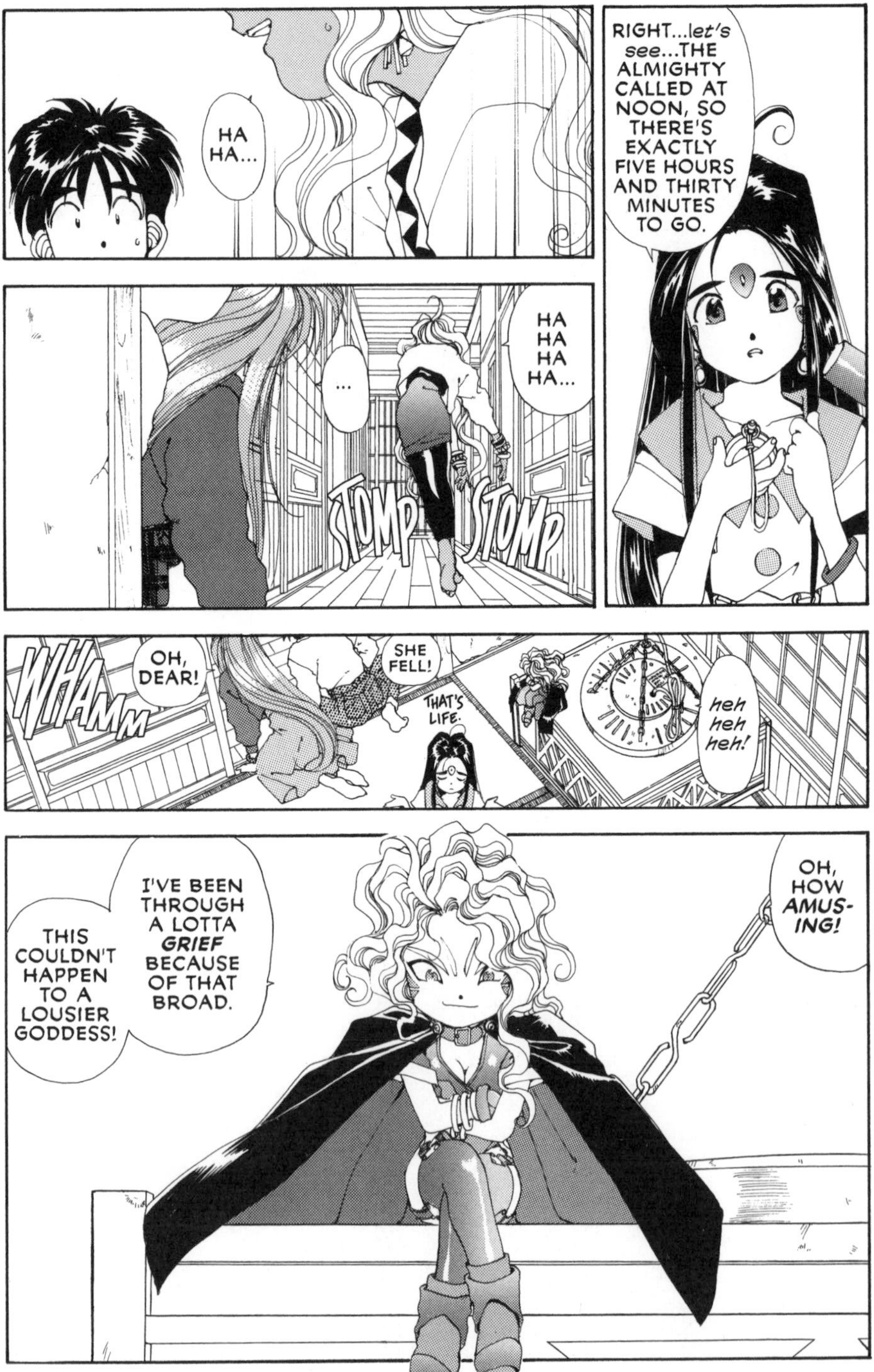
RIGHT...*let's see*...THE ALMIGHTY CALLED AT NOON, SO THERE'S EXACTLY FIVE HOURS AND THIRTY MINUTES TO GO.
HA HA...
HA HA HA HA...
...
STOMP
STOMP
heh heh heh!
THAT'S LIFE.
SHE FELL!
OH, DEAR!
WHAMM
OH, HOW *AMUSING!*
I'VE BEEN THROUGH A LOTTA ***GRIEF*** BECAUSE OF THAT BROAD.
THIS COULDN'T HAPPEN TO A LOUSIER GODDESS!

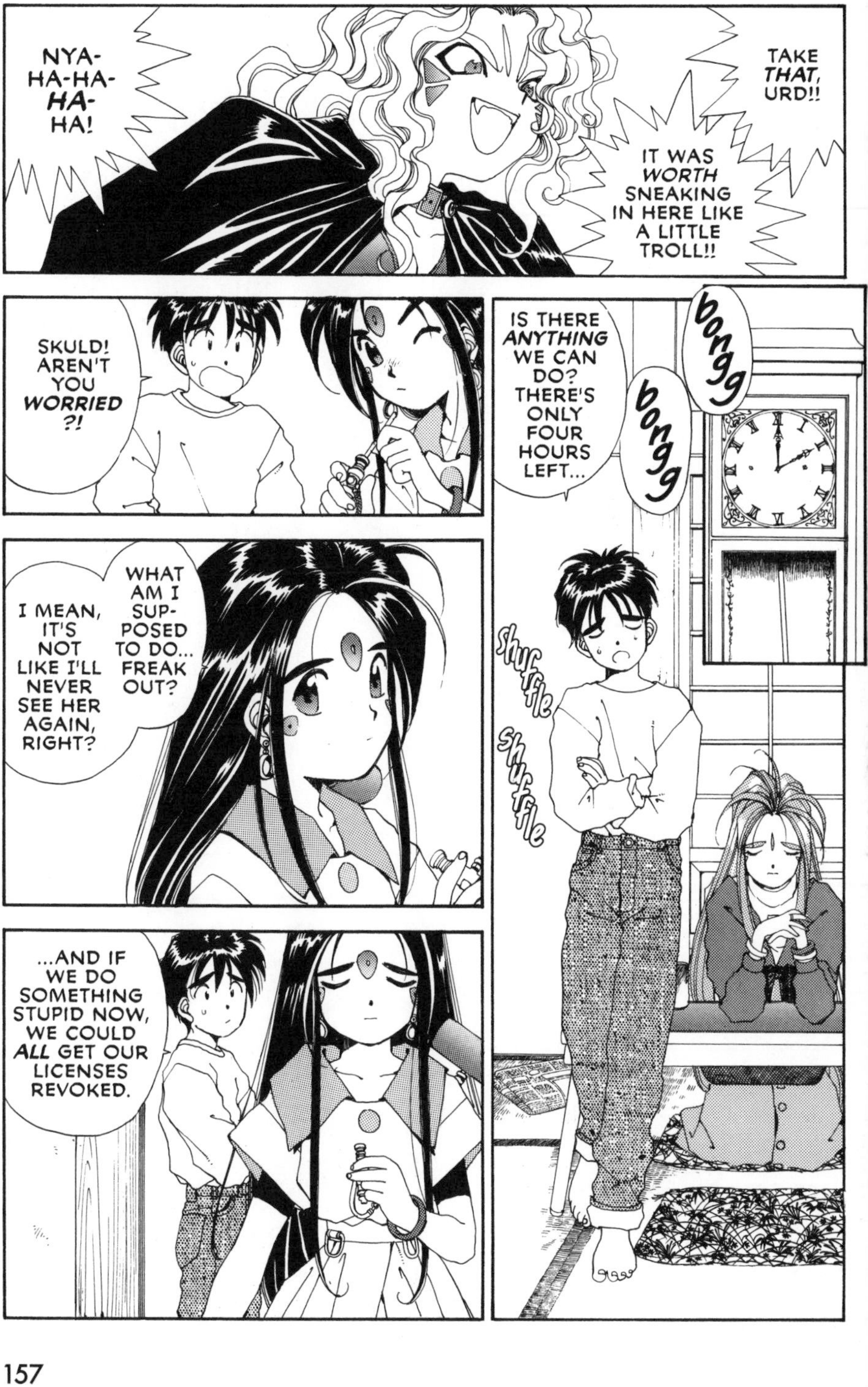
TAKE THAT, URD!!
IT WAS WORTH SNEAKING IN HERE LIKE A LITTLE TROLL!!
NYA-HA-HA-HA-HA!
bongg
bongg
IS THERE ANYTHING WE CAN DO? THERE'S ONLY FOUR HOURS LEFT...
shuffle
shuffle
SKULD! AREN'T YOU WORRIED?!
WHAT AM I SUPPOSED TO DO... FREAK OUT?
I MEAN, IT'S NOT LIKE I'LL NEVER SEE HER AGAIN, RIGHT?
...AND IF WE DO SOMETHING STUPID NOW, WE COULD ALL GET OUR LICENSES REVOKED.

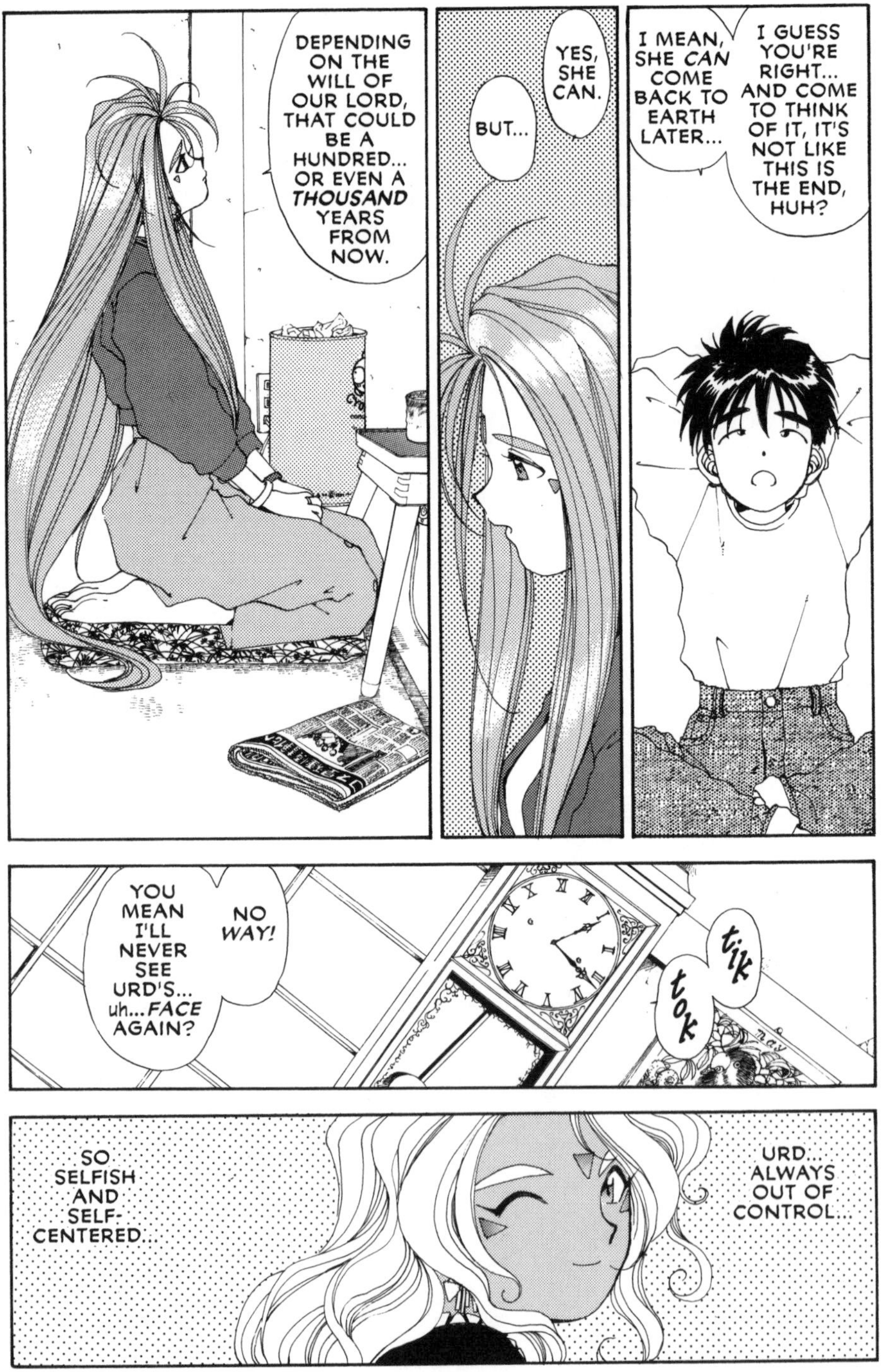
I GUESS YOU'RE RIGHT... AND COME TO THINK OF IT, IT'S NOT LIKE THIS IS THE END, HUH?
I MEAN, SHE *CAN* COME BACK TO EARTH LATER...
YES, SHE CAN.
BUT...
DEPENDING ON THE WILL OF OUR LORD, THAT COULD BE A HUNDRED... OR EVEN A *THOUSAND* YEARS FROM NOW.
tik
tok
NO *WAY!*
YOU MEAN I'LL NEVER SEE URD'S... uh...*FACE* AGAIN?
URD... ALWAYS OUT OF CONTROL...
SO SELFISH AND SELF-CENTERED...

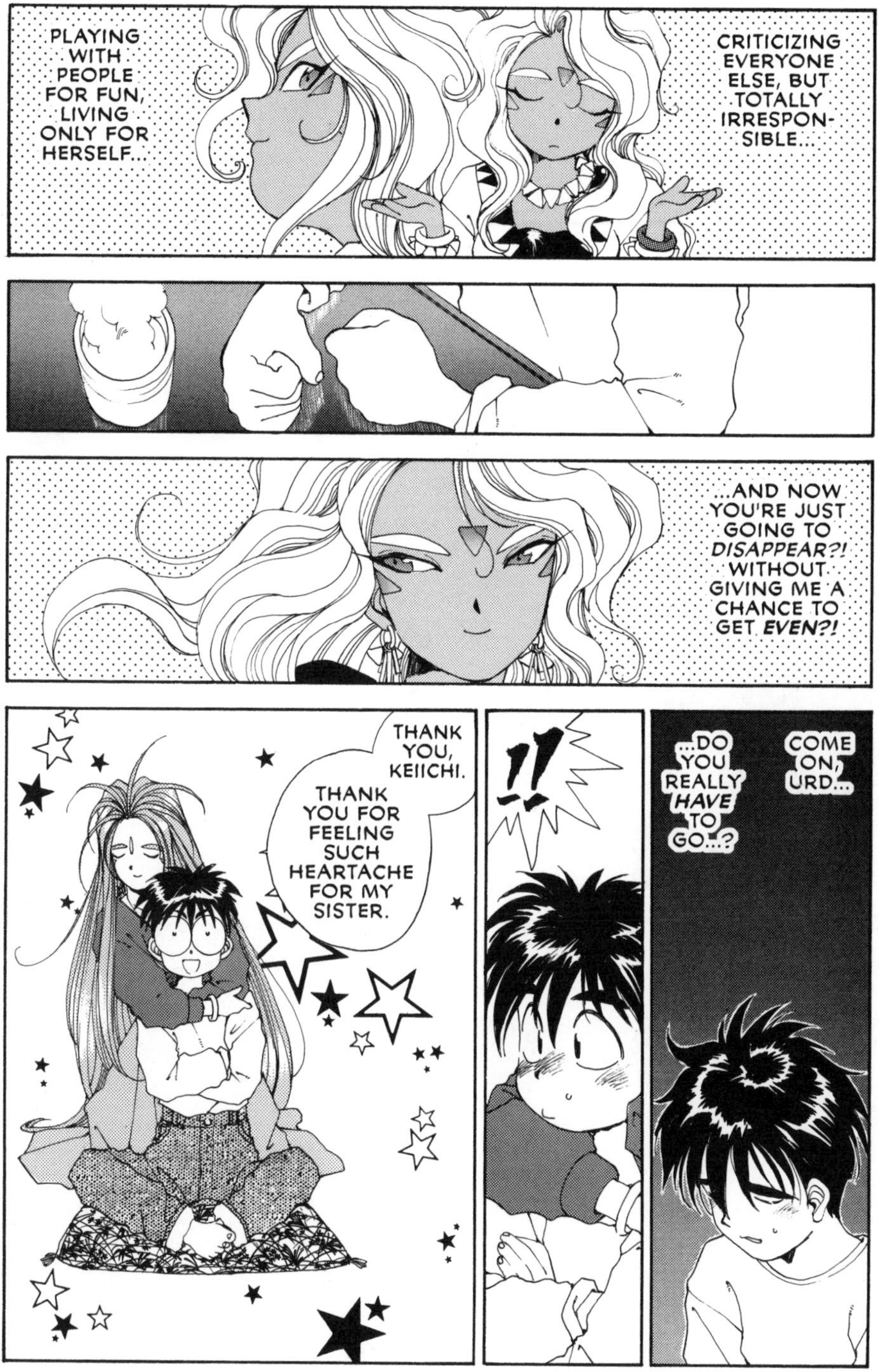
CRITICIZING EVERYONE ELSE, BUT TOTALLY IRRESPONSIBLE...
PLAYING WITH PEOPLE FOR FUN, LIVING ONLY FOR HERSELF...
...AND NOW YOU'RE JUST GOING TO *DISAPPEAR?!* WITHOUT GIVING ME A CHANCE TO GET ***EVEN?!***
COME ON, URD...
...DO YOU REALLY *HAVE* TO GO...?
!!
THANK YOU, KEIICHI.
THANK YOU FOR FEELING SUCH HEARTACHE FOR MY SISTER.

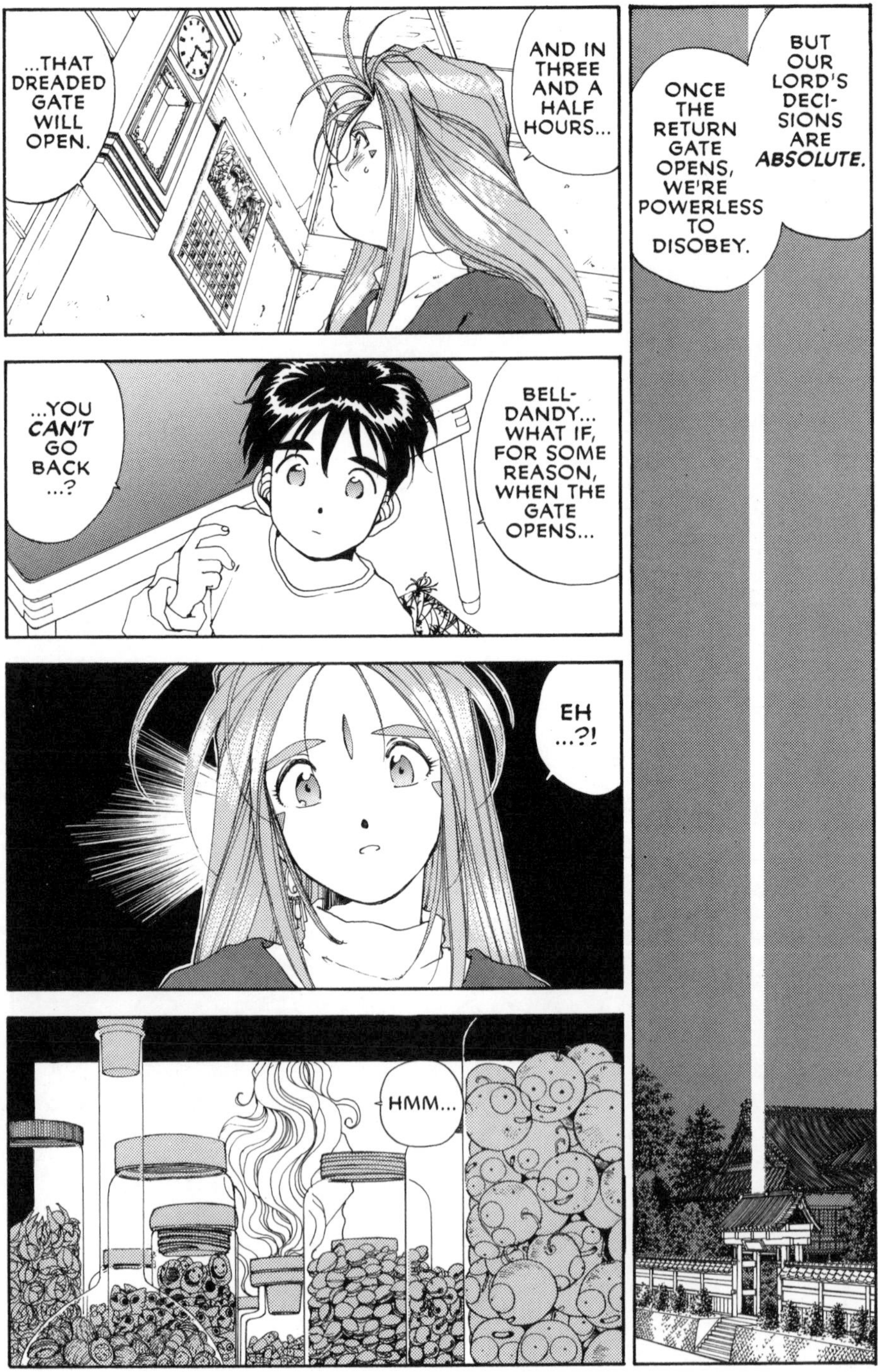
BUT OUR LORD'S DECI-SIONS ARE *ABSOLUTE.*
ONCE THE RETURN GATE OPENS, WE'RE POWERLESS TO DISOBEY.
AND IN THREE AND A HALF HOURS...
...THAT DREADED GATE WILL OPEN.
BELL-DANDY... WHAT IF, FOR SOME REASON, WHEN THE GATE OPENS...
...YOU *CAN'T* GO BACK ...?
EH ...?!
HMM...

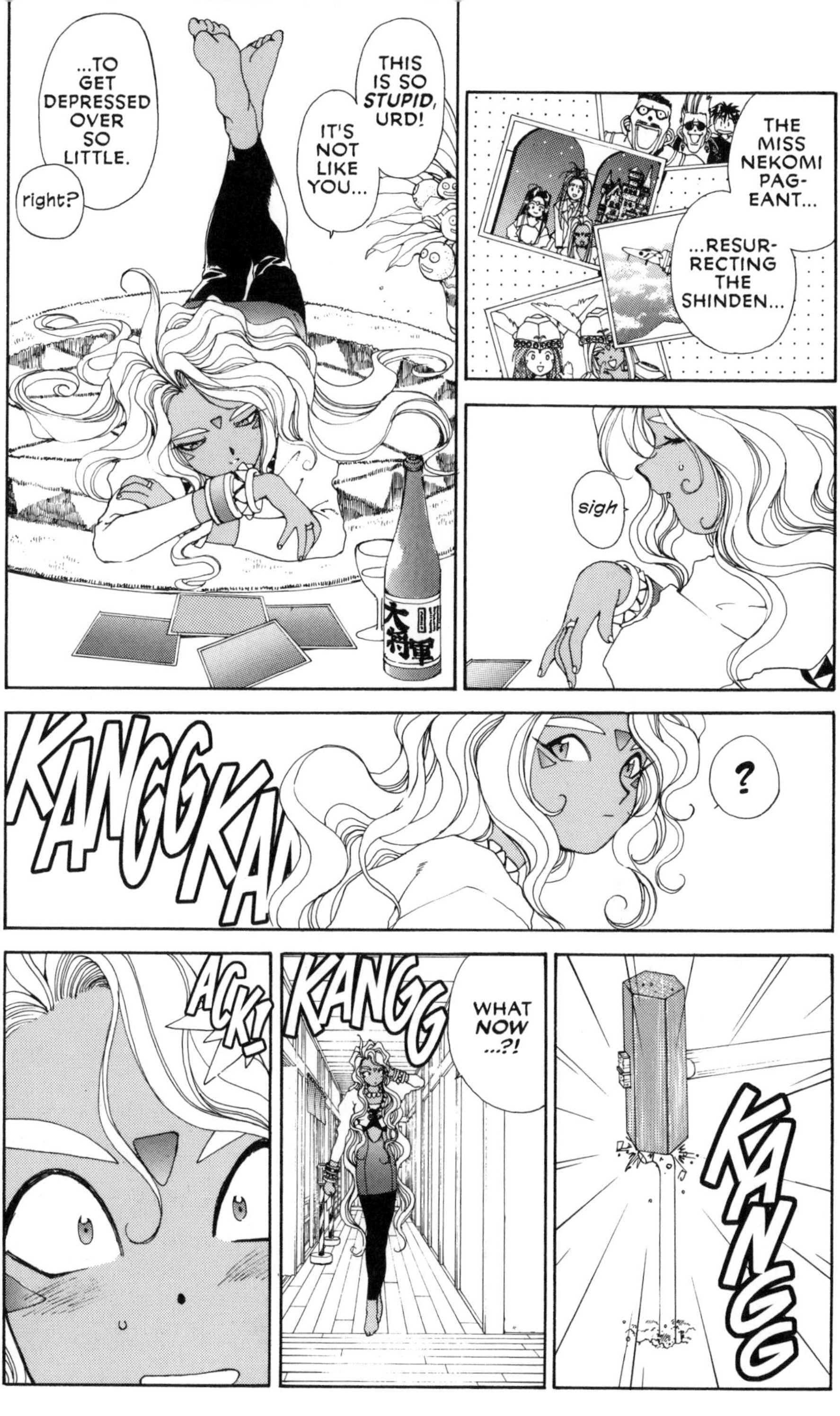
THE MISS NEKOMI PAGEANT...
...RESURRECTING THE SHINDEN...
sigh
THIS IS SO *STUPID*, URD!
IT'S NOT LIKE YOU...
...TO GET DEPRESSED OVER SO LITTLE.
right?
?
KANGGKA
KANNG
WHAT *NOW*...?!
KANGG
ACK!

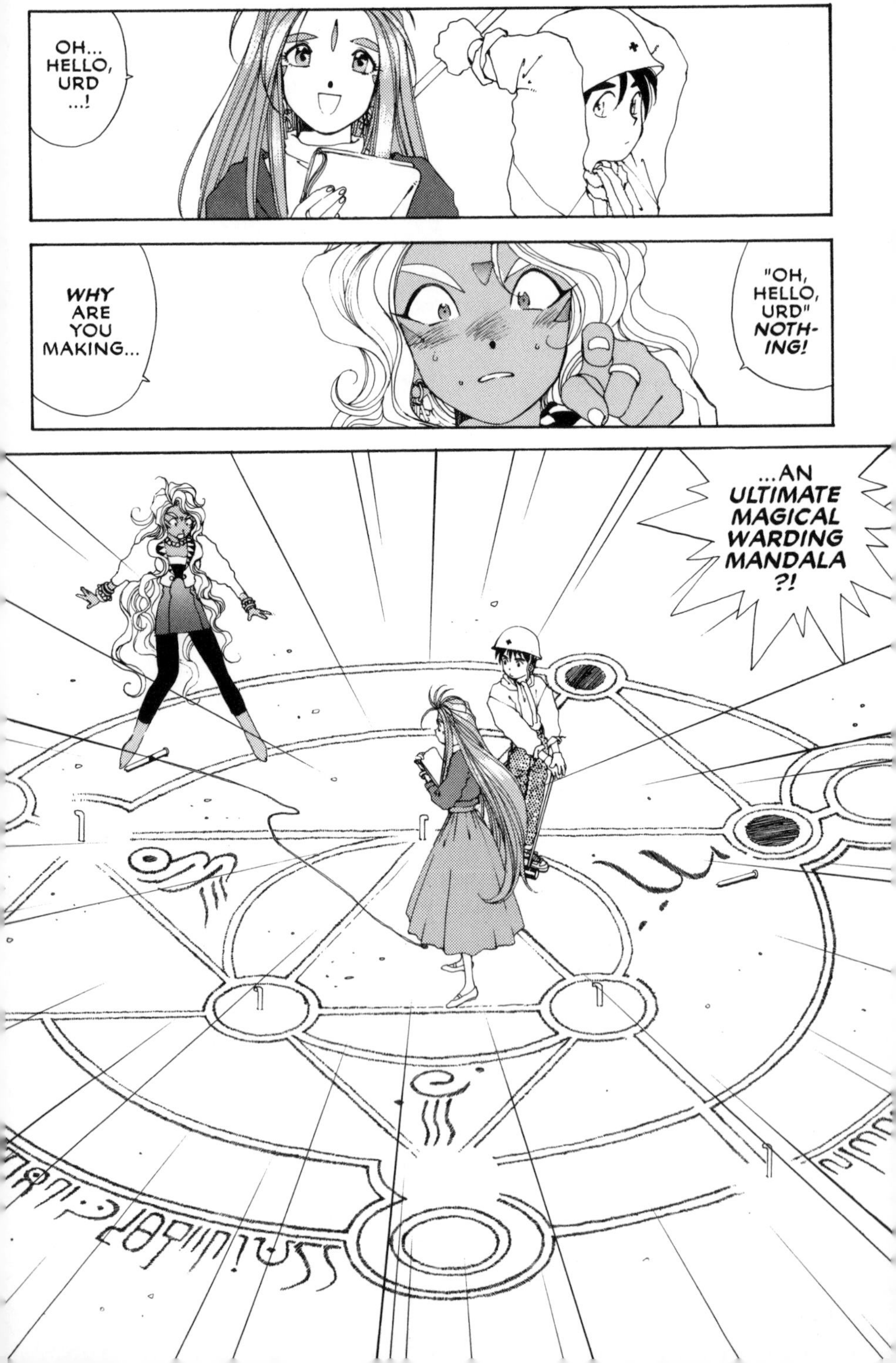
OH... HELLO, URD ...!
"OH, HELLO, URD" *NOTHING!*
WHY ARE YOU MAKING...
...AN *ULTIMATE* MAGICAL WARDING MANDALA ?!

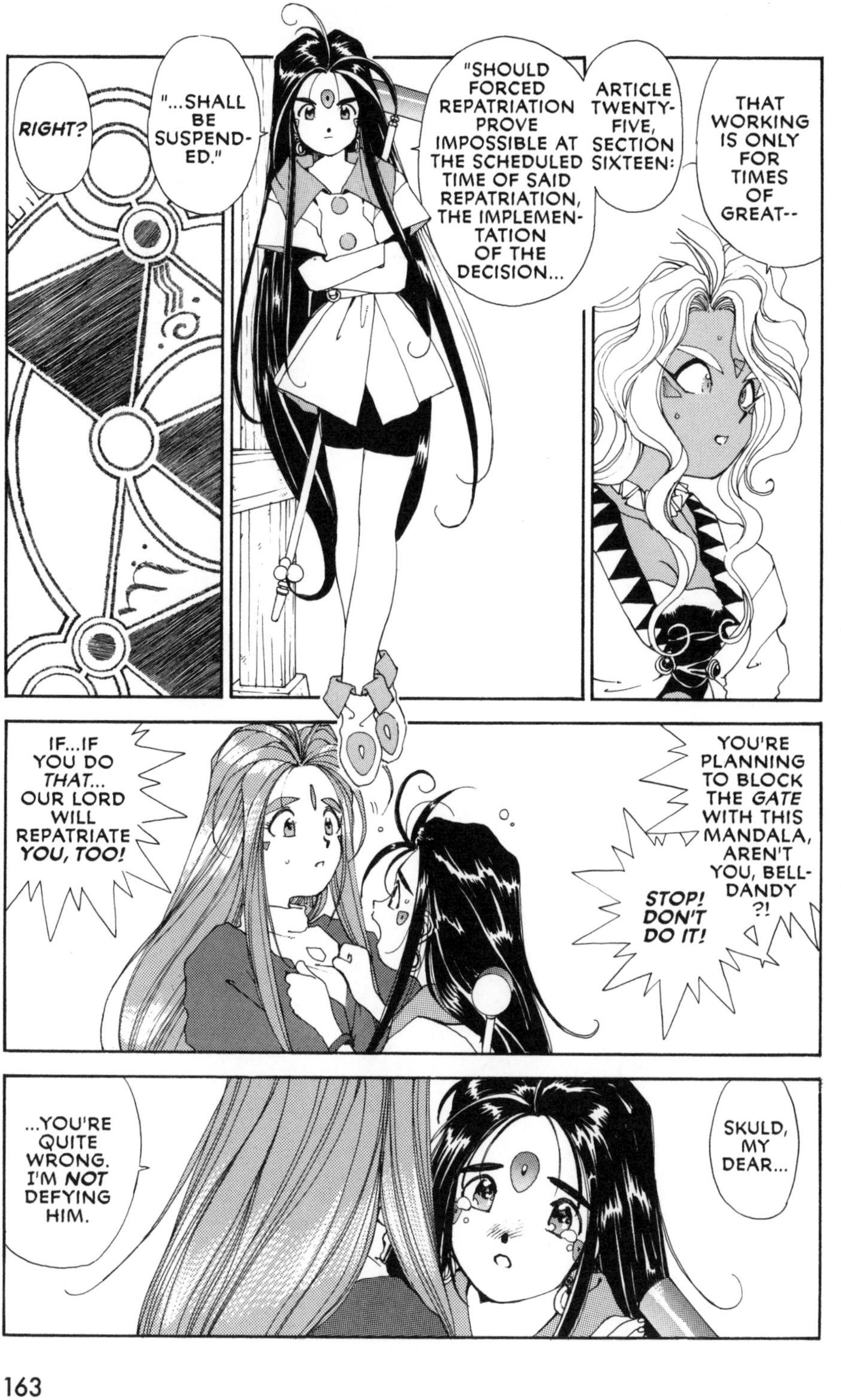
THAT WORKING IS ONLY FOR TIMES OF GREAT--
ARTICLE TWENTY-FIVE, SECTION SIXTEEN:
"SHOULD FORCED REPATRIATION PROVE IMPOSSIBLE AT THE SCHEDULED TIME OF SAID REPATRIATION, THE IMPLEMENTATION OF THE DECISION...
"...SHALL BE SUSPENDED."
RIGHT?
YOU'RE PLANNING TO BLOCK THE *GATE* WITH THIS MANDALA, AREN'T YOU, BELLDANDY?!
STOP! DON'T DO IT!
IF...IF YOU DO *THAT*... OUR LORD WILL REPATRIATE *YOU, TOO!*
SKULD, MY DEAR...
...YOU'RE QUITE WRONG. I'M *NOT* DEFYING HIM.

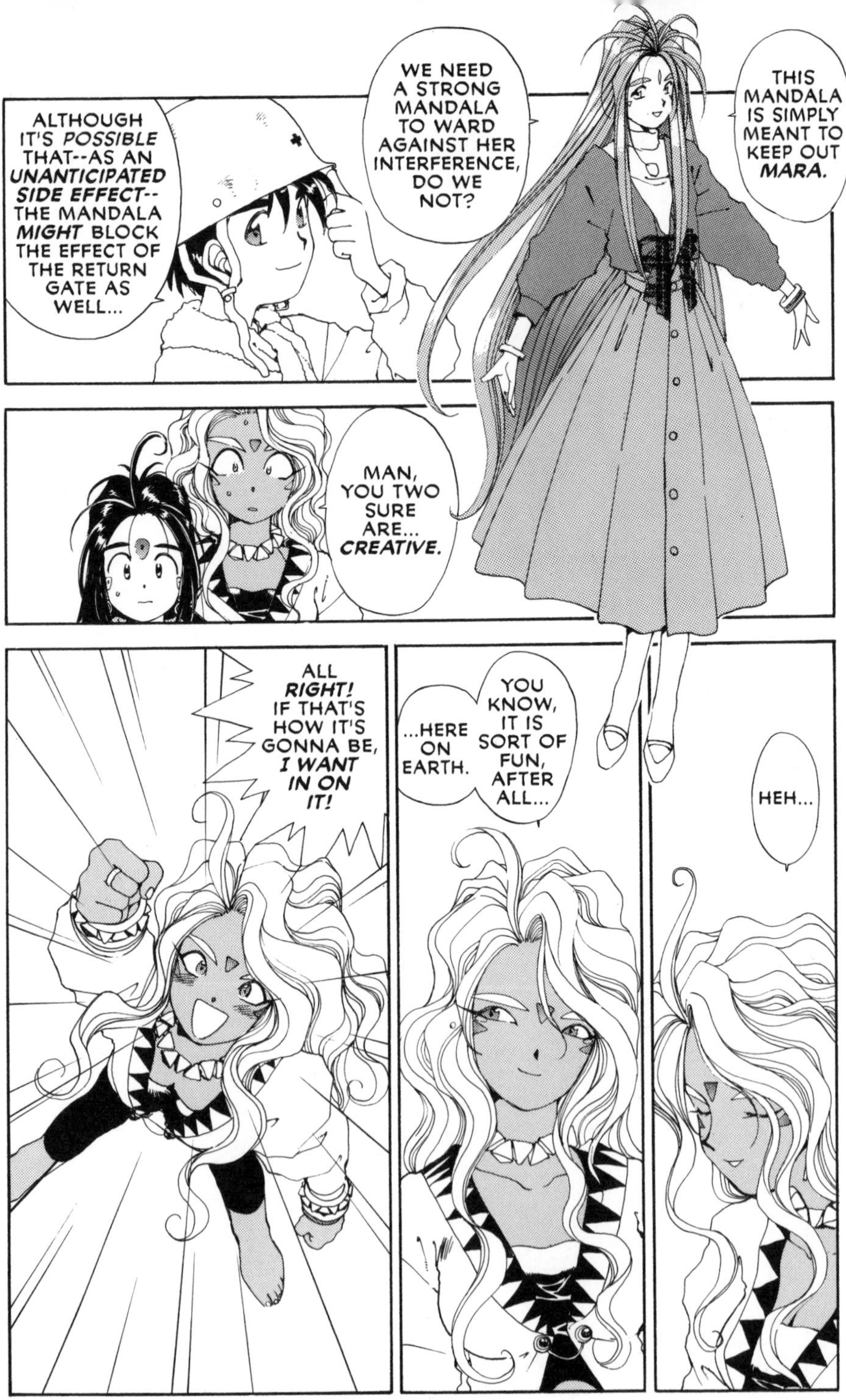
THIS MANDALA IS SIMPLY MEANT TO KEEP OUT *MARA.*
WE NEED A STRONG MANDALA TO WARD AGAINST HER INTERFERENCE, DO WE NOT?
ALTHOUGH IT'S *POSSIBLE* THAT--AS AN *UNANTICIPATED SIDE EFFECT*--THE MANDALA *MIGHT* BLOCK THE EFFECT OF THE RETURN GATE AS WELL...
MAN, YOU TWO SURE ARE... *CREATIVE.*
HEH...
YOU KNOW, IT IS SORT OF FUN, AFTER ALL...
...HERE ON EARTH.
ALL *RIGHT!* IF THAT'S HOW IT'S GONNA BE, *I WANT IN ON IT!*

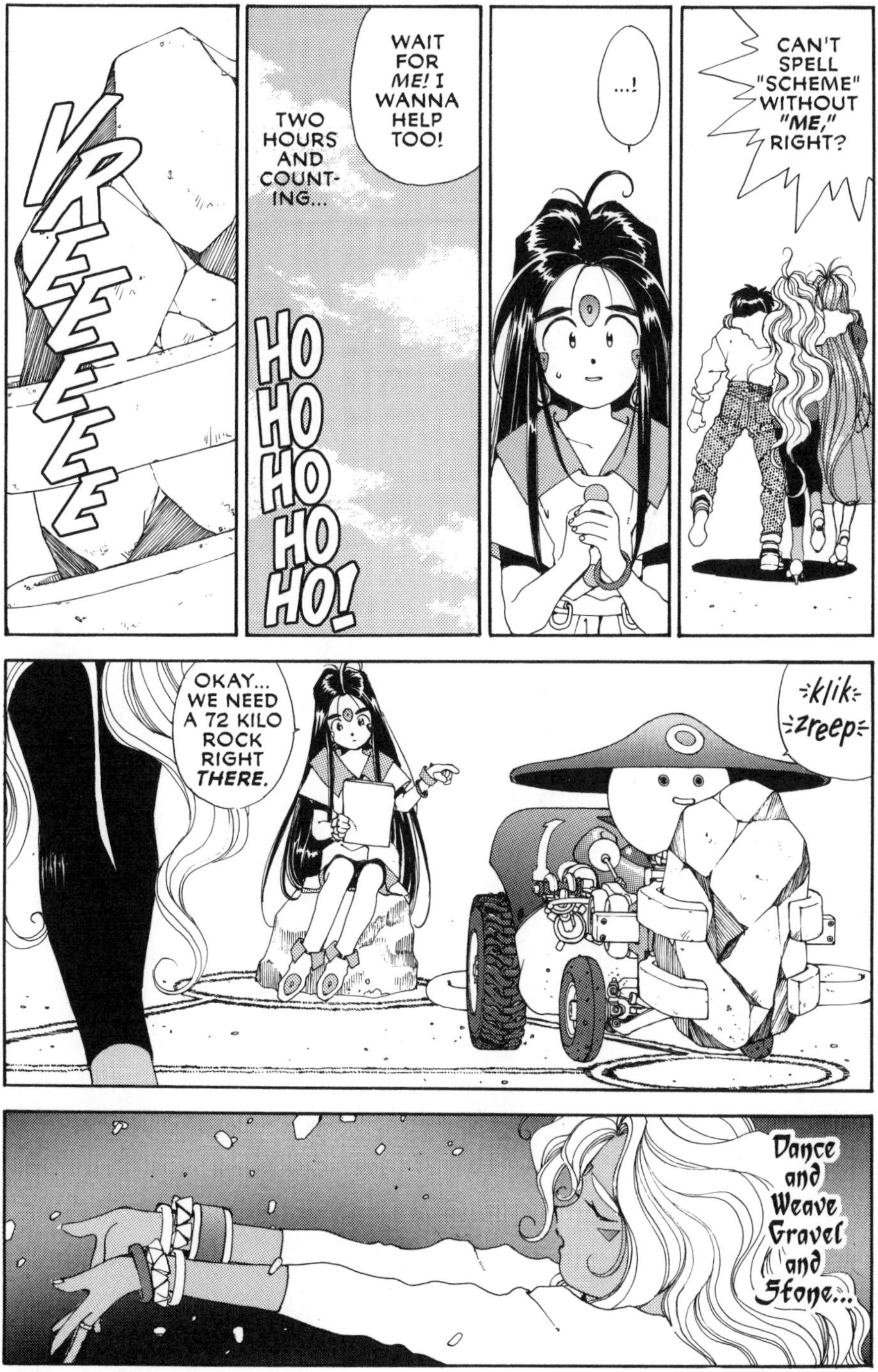
CAN'T SPELL "SCHEME" WITHOUT "ME," RIGHT?
...!
WAIT FOR ME! I WANNA HELP TOO!
TWO HOURS AND COUNT-ING...
HO HO HO HO HO HO!
VREEEEEE
klik zreep
OKAY... WE NEED A 72 KILO ROCK RIGHT THERE.
Dance and Weave Gravel and Stone...

Obey We
Goddesses
Three
Past,
Present,
and
Future...

...Hark
to the
Covenant
of Urd,
Belldandy,
and
Skuld...

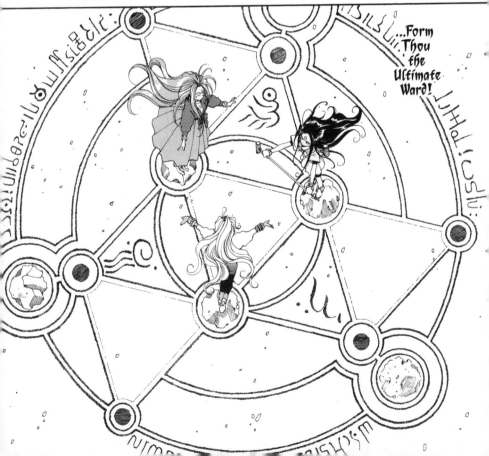

...Form
Thou
the
Ultimate
Ward!

gasp!
JUST IN THE NICK OF TIME!
WE DID IT!!
LET ME GUESS...
...THIS IS THE FIRST TIME YOU EVER COOPERATED?

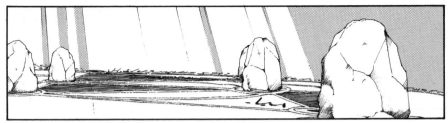

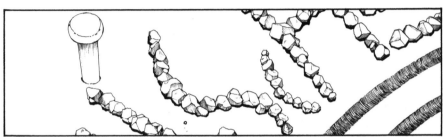

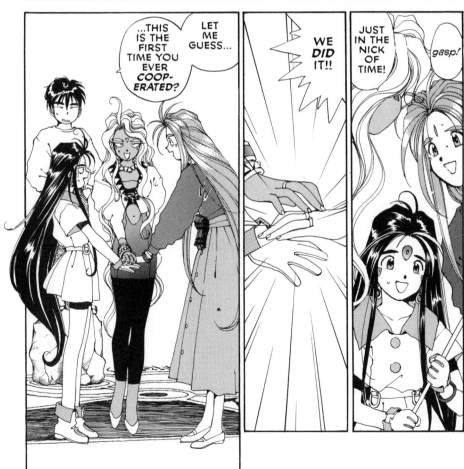

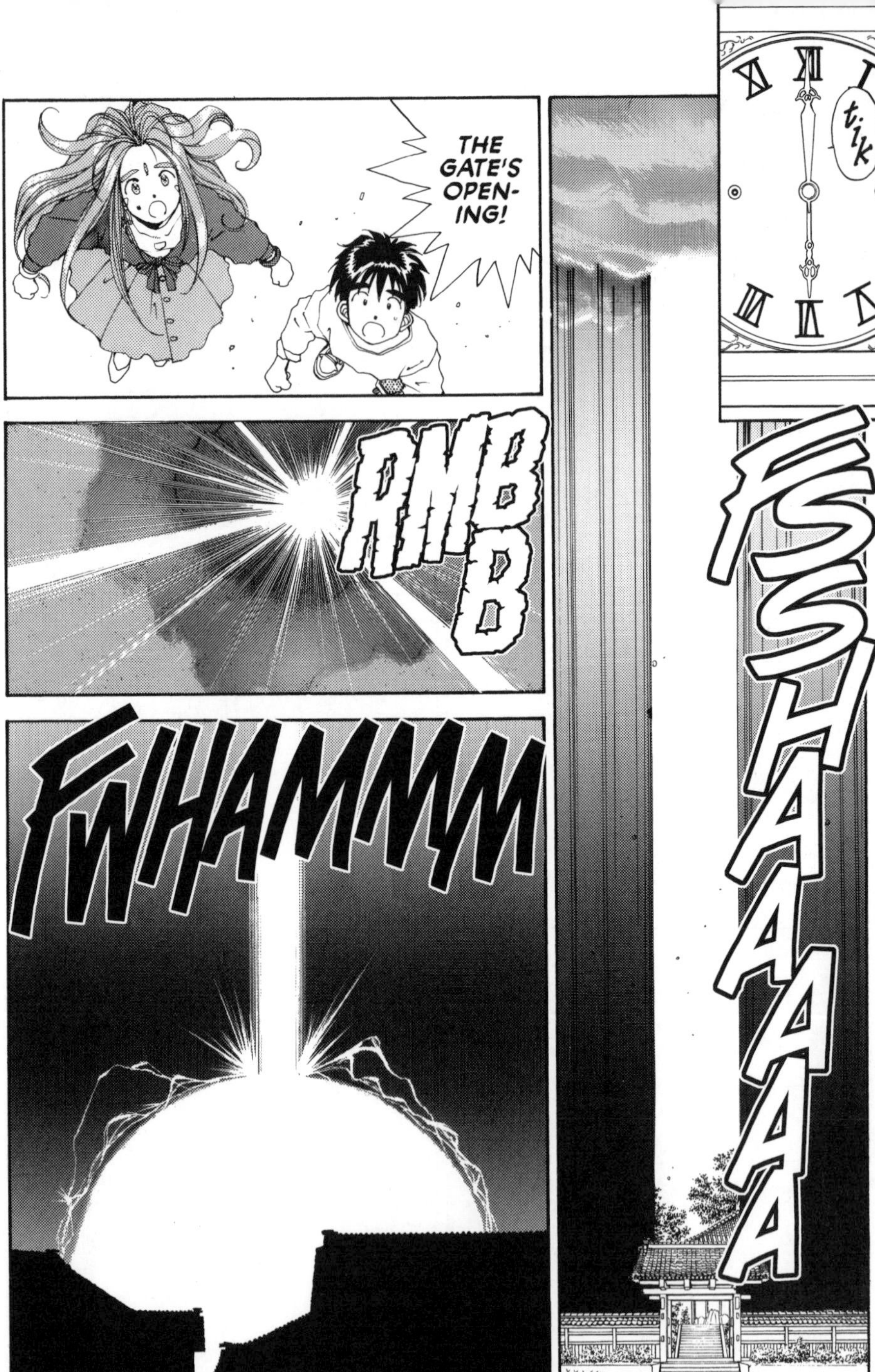
tik
FSHAAAAAA
THE GATE'S OPEN-ING!
RMBB
FWHAMMMM

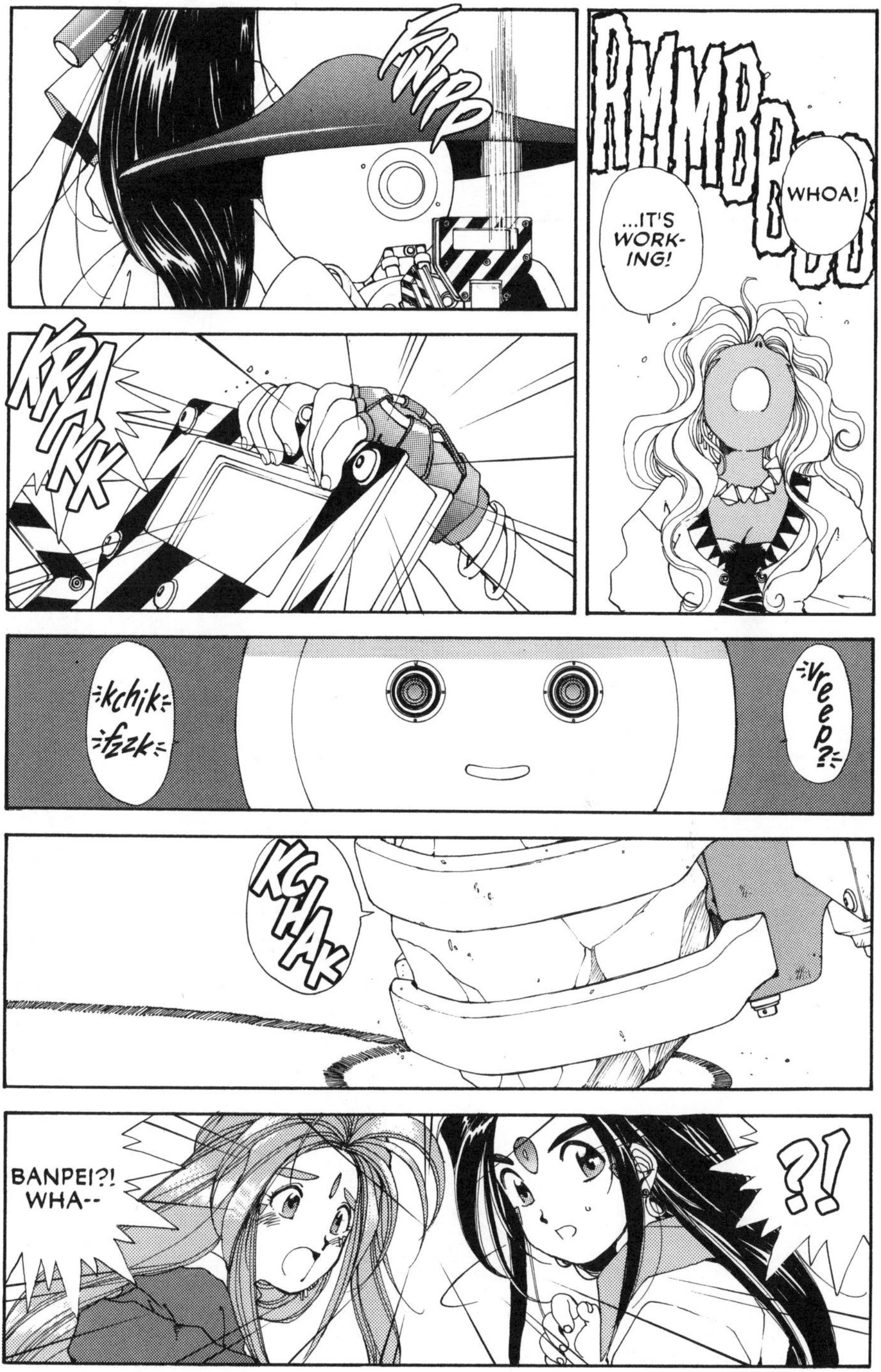

RMMBBOO
WHOA!
...IT'S WORKING!
KRAKK
vreep?
kchik
fzzk
KCHAK
?!
BANPEI?! WHA--

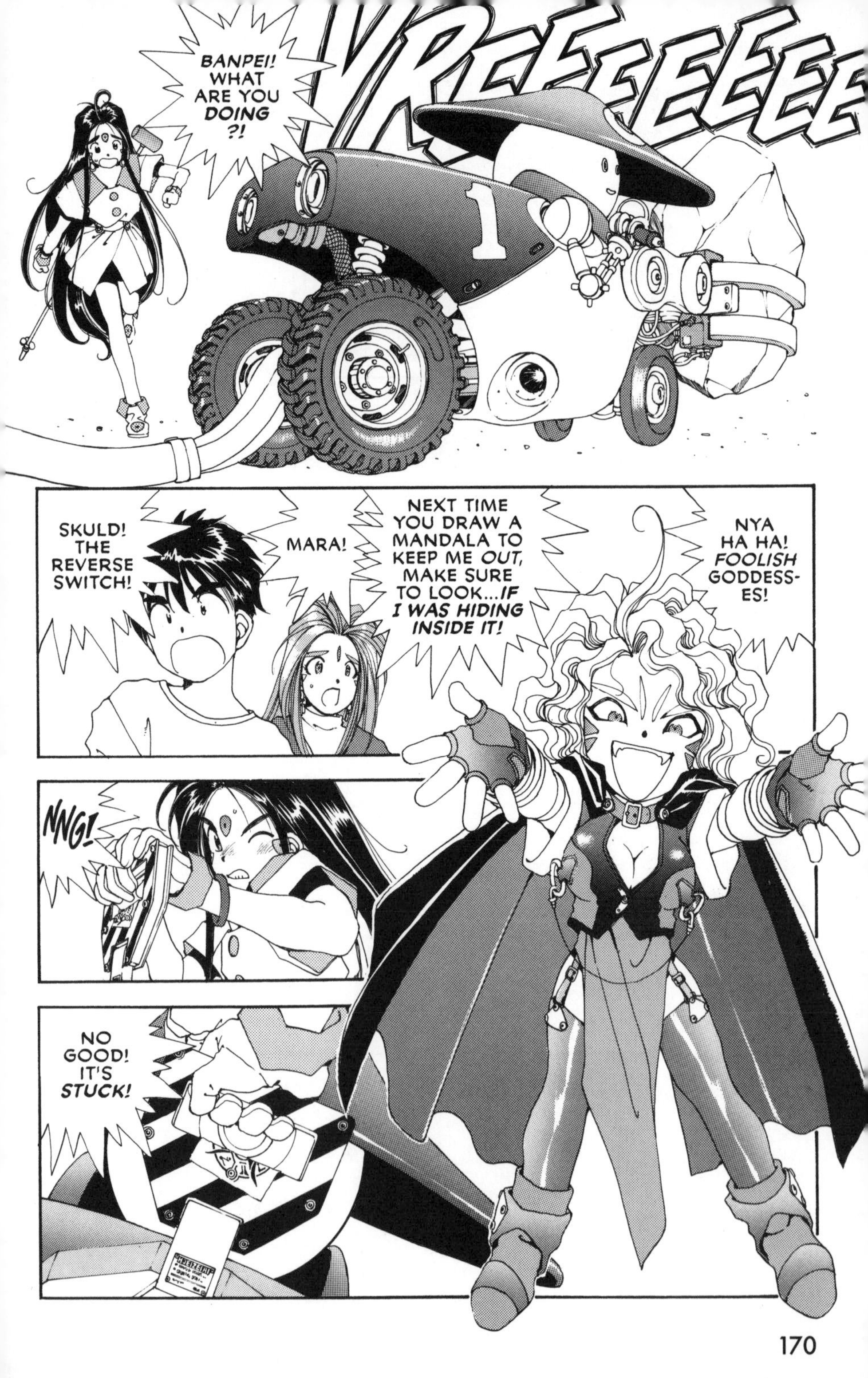
VREEEEEEE
BANPEI! WHAT ARE YOU DOING?!
NYA HA HA! FOOLISH GODDESS-ES!
NEXT TIME YOU DRAW A MANDALA TO KEEP ME OUT, MAKE SURE TO LOOK...IF I WAS HIDING INSIDE IT!
MARA!
SKULD! THE REVERSE SWITCH!
NNG!
NO GOOD! IT'S STUCK!

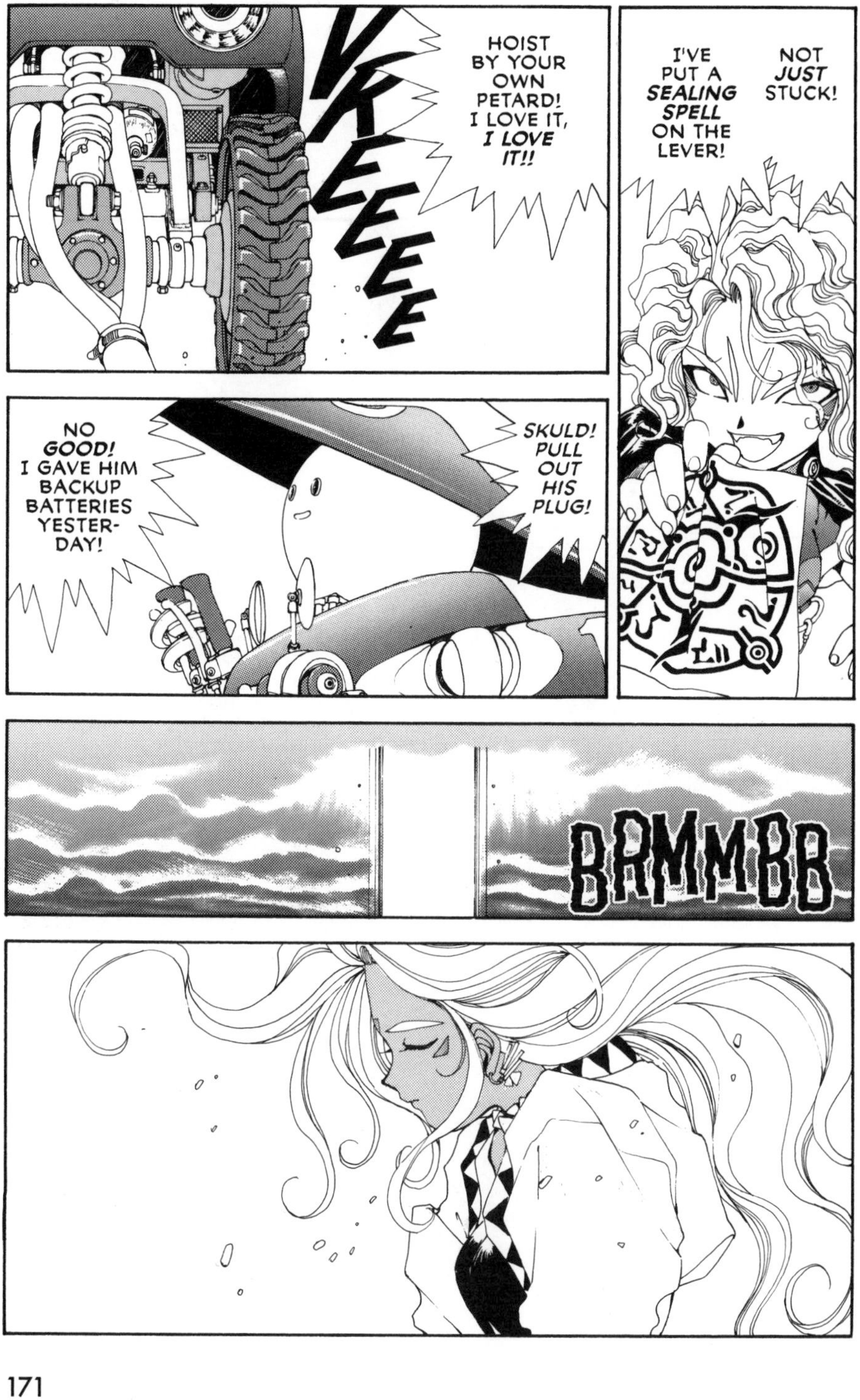
NOT JUST STUCK!
I'VE PUT A SEALING SPELL ON THE LEVER!
HOIST BY YOUR OWN PETARD! I LOVE IT, I LOVE IT!!
VKEEEEE
SKULD! PULL OUT HIS PLUG!
NO GOOD! I GAVE HIM BACKUP BATTERIES YESTER-DAY!
BRMMBB

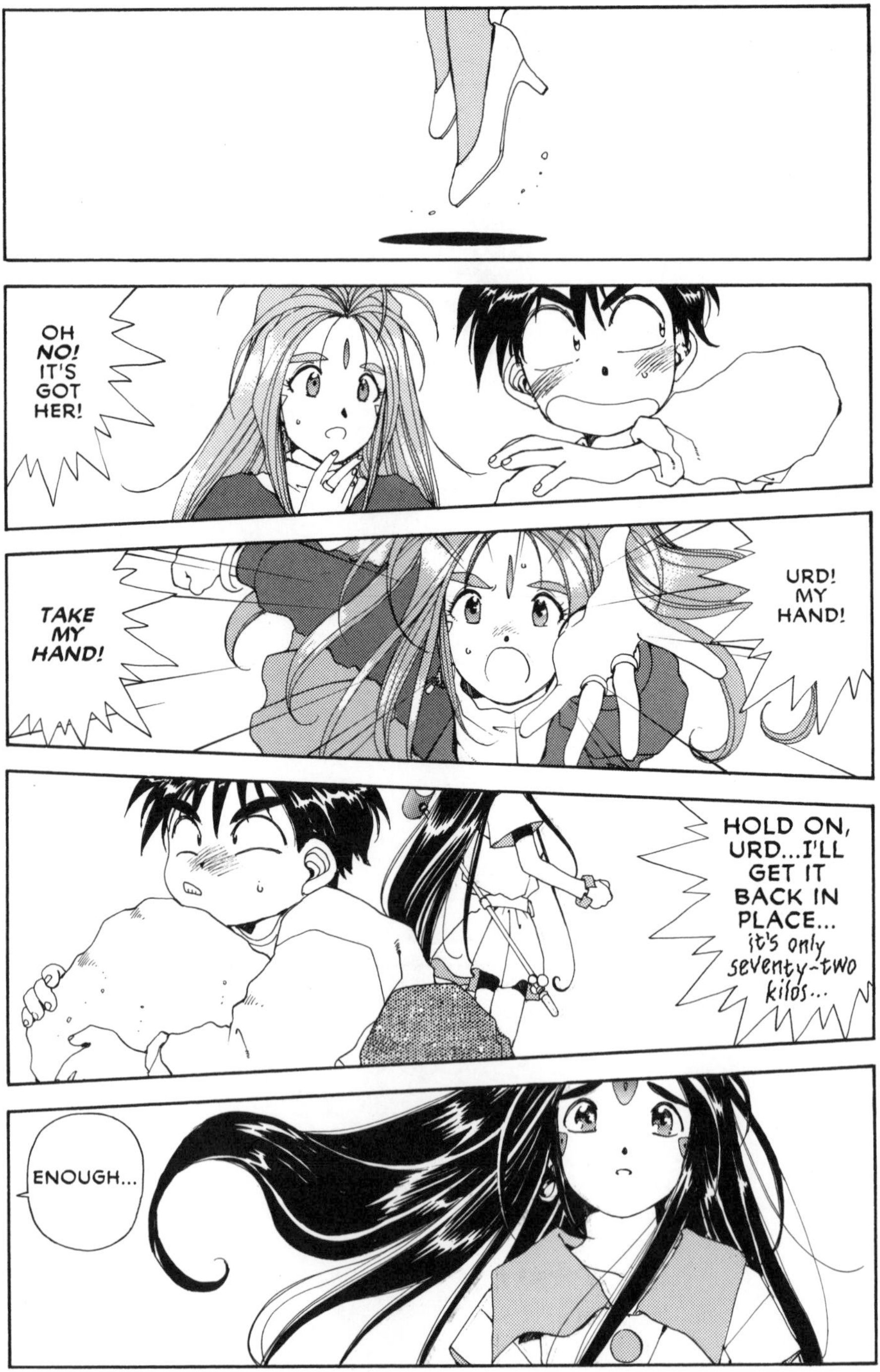
OH NO! IT'S GOT HER!
URD! MY HAND!
TAKE MY HAND!
HOLD ON, URD...I'LL GET IT BACK IN PLACE...
it's only seventy-two kilos...
ENOUGH...

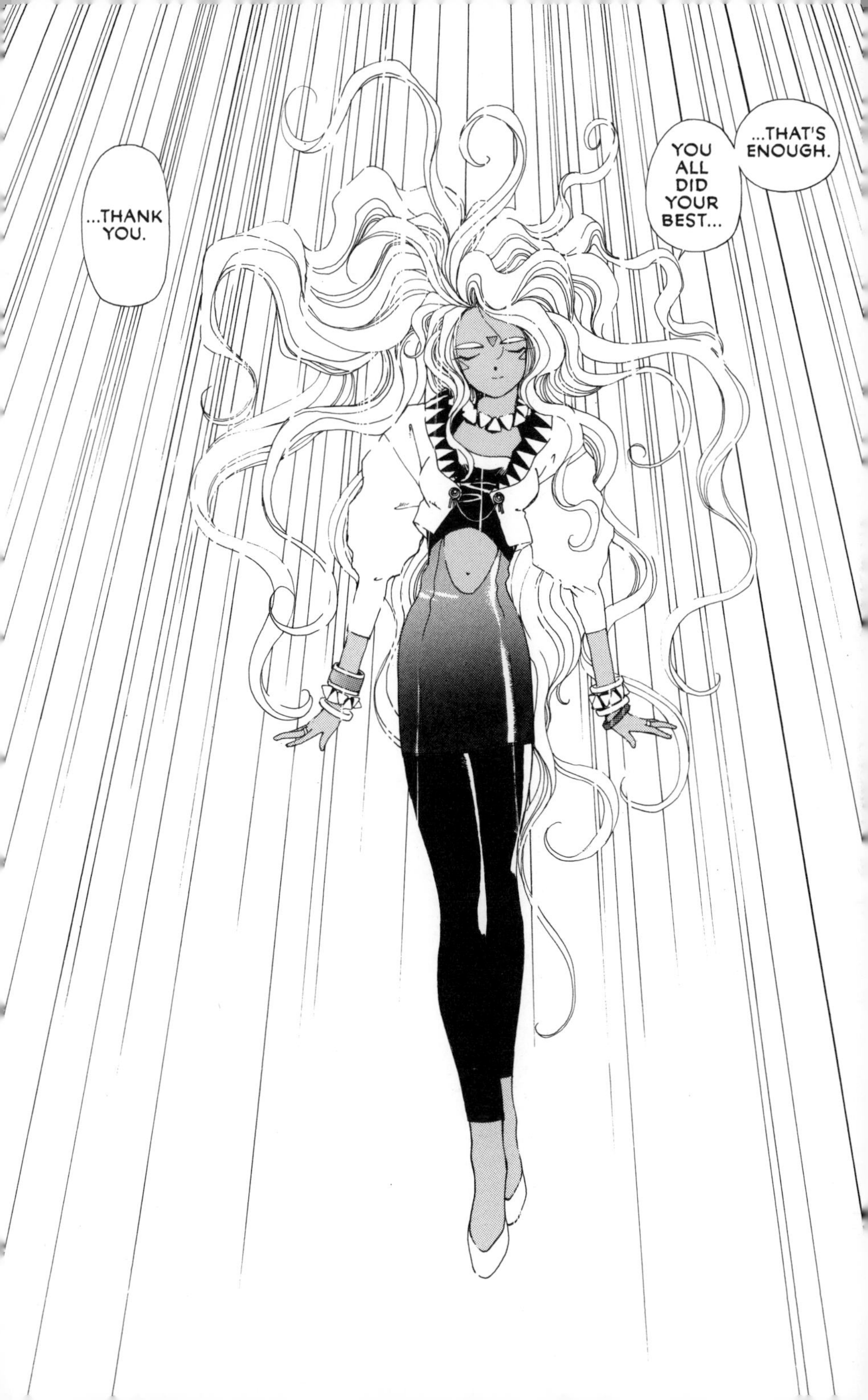
...THAT'S ENOUGH.
YOU ALL DID YOUR BEST...
...THANK YOU.

YOU CAN'T GIVE UP!

URD!!

WHUDD

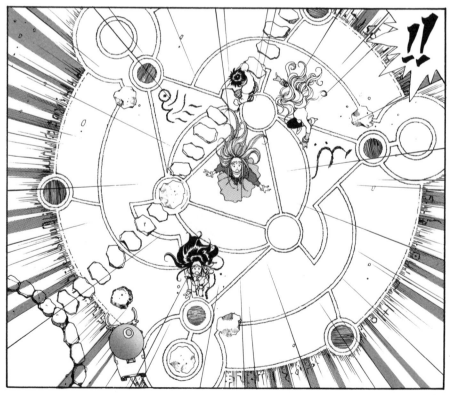

!!

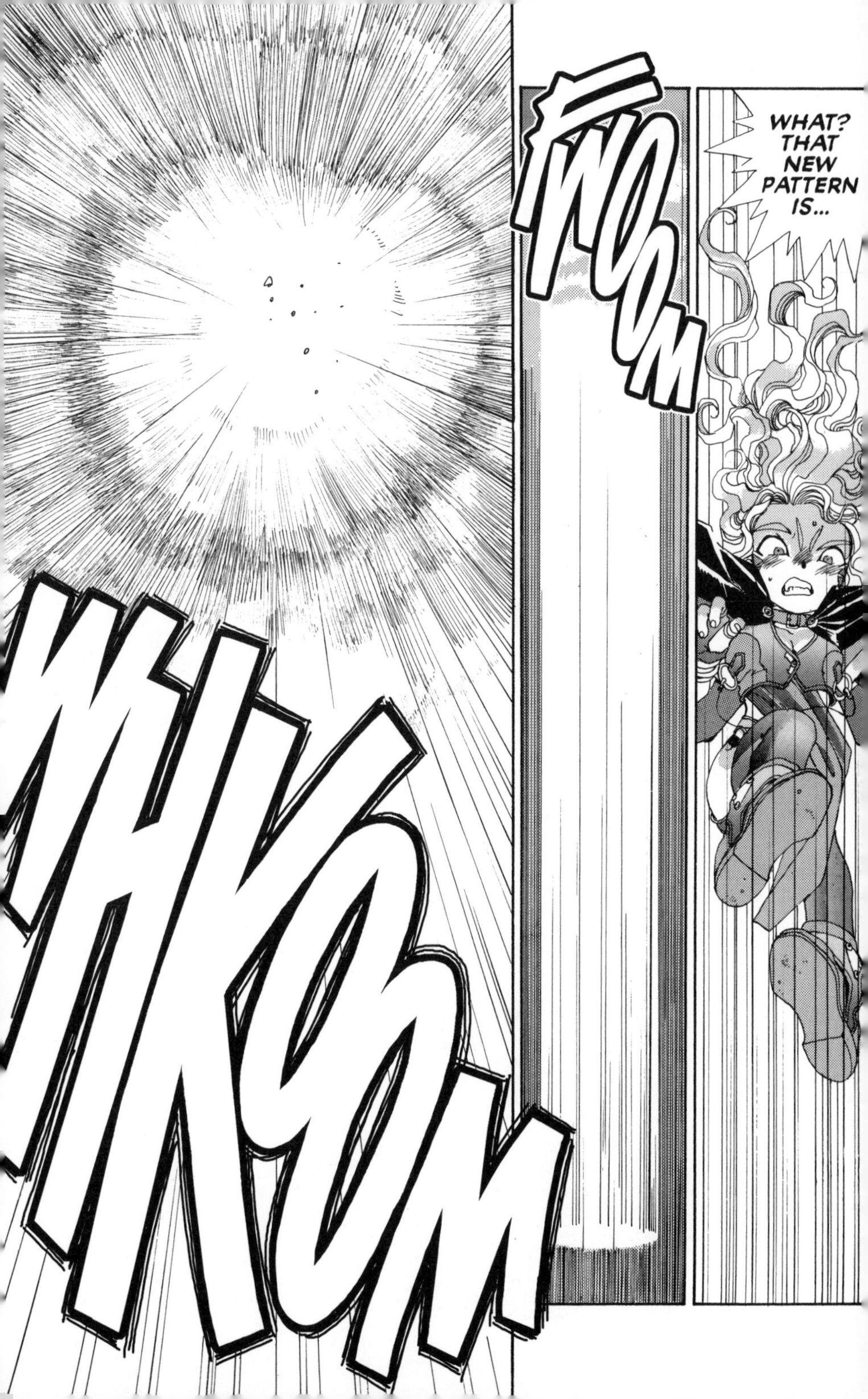
WHAT? THAT NEW PATTERN IS...
FWOOM

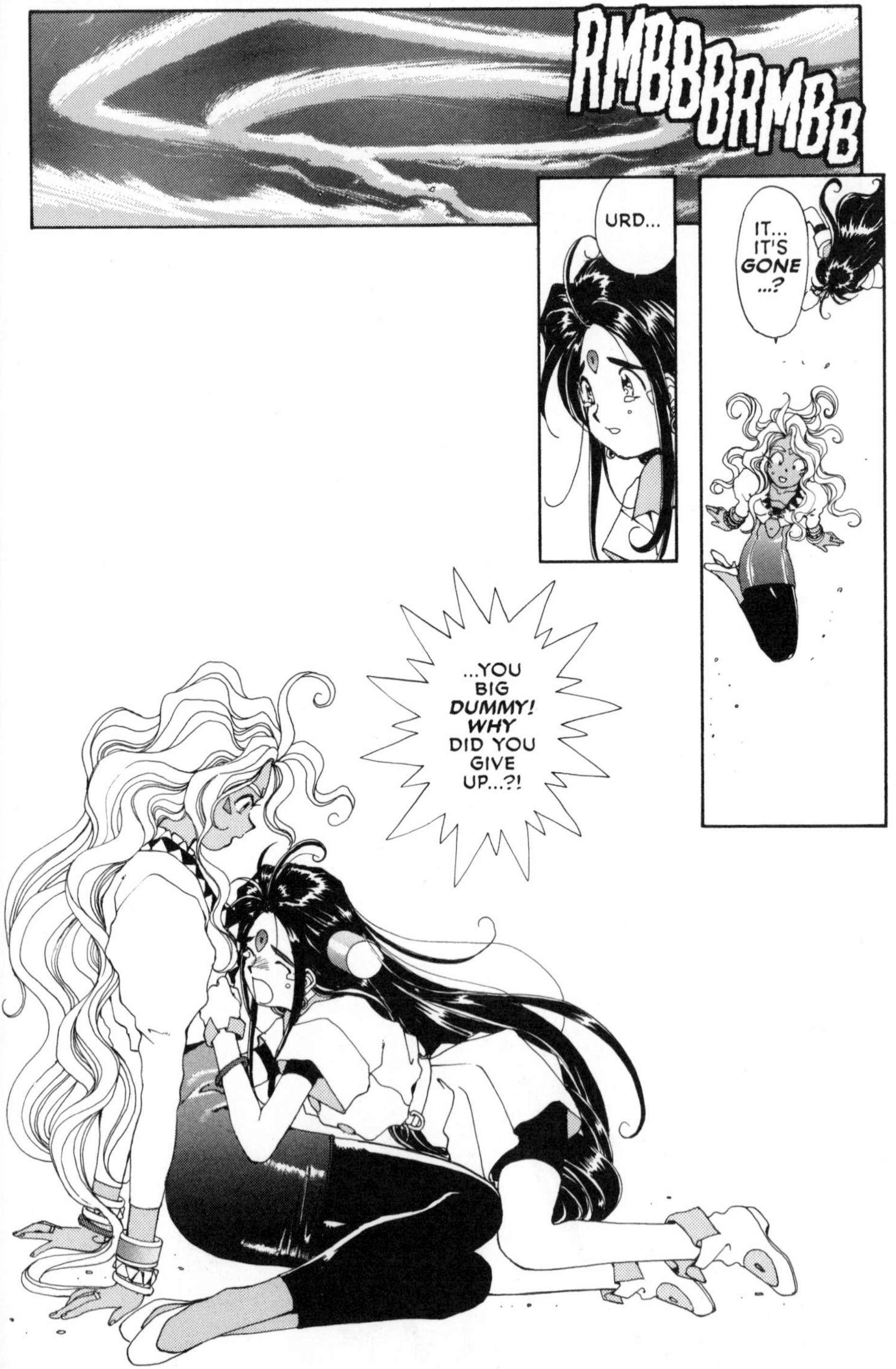
RMBBBRMBB
IT... IT'S GONE ...?
URD...
...YOU BIG DUMMY! WHY DID YOU GIVE UP...?!

WAAAH!

I KNOW YOU'RE *JUST A KID*... BUT STOP CRYING, OKAY?

AW, SKULD!

...WOULD CHANGE IT INTO A RETURN GATE *DESTRUCTION* MANDALA?! WHO'D A THUNK IT... MY LORD?! HA HA

PRETTY *WEIRD*, HUH? WHO'D HAVE THOUGHT THAT RETURNING THE STONES TO THEIR *ORIGINAL* POSITION...

LET US ACCEPT, IN OUR MERCY, THAT IT WAS SIMPLY AN ACCIDENT.

HMMM... WELL, WE SHALL LEAVE IT AT THAT.

...THIS IS *ALSO* THE FIRST TIME YOU ALL MESSED UP TOGETHER.

LET ME GUESS...

I CAN'T *UNDERSTAND* THAT *DIVINE* SPEECH, BUT THE *TONE'S* PRETTY CLEAR!..

--THE BACKLASH OF THE GATE SLAMMING SHUT CRASHED THE YGGDRASIL SYSTEM AGAIN!

BUT HOW WILL YE REPENT FOR *THIS*--

177

THE ADVENTURES OF MINI-URD

With the Miracle Ingredient: MINI-SKULD!

◆ FORWARD TO THE FUTURE! ◆

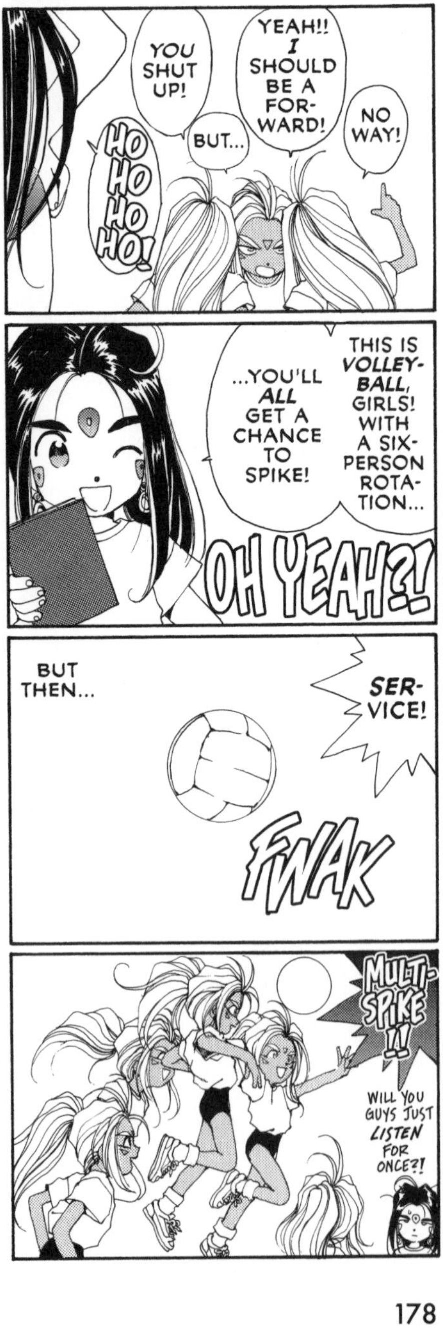
YEAH!! *I* SHOULD BE A FOR-WARD!
NO WAY!
YOU SHUT UP!
BUT...
HO HO HO HO!
THIS IS *VOLLEY-BALL*, GIRLS! WITH A SIX-PERSON ROTA-TION...
...YOU'LL *ALL* GET A CHANCE TO SPIKE!
OH YEAH?!
*SER-*VICE!
BUT THEN...
FWAK
MULTI-SPIKE!!
WILL YOU GUYS JUST *LISTEN* FOR ONCE?!

◆ BLOOMERS OF DOOM ◆

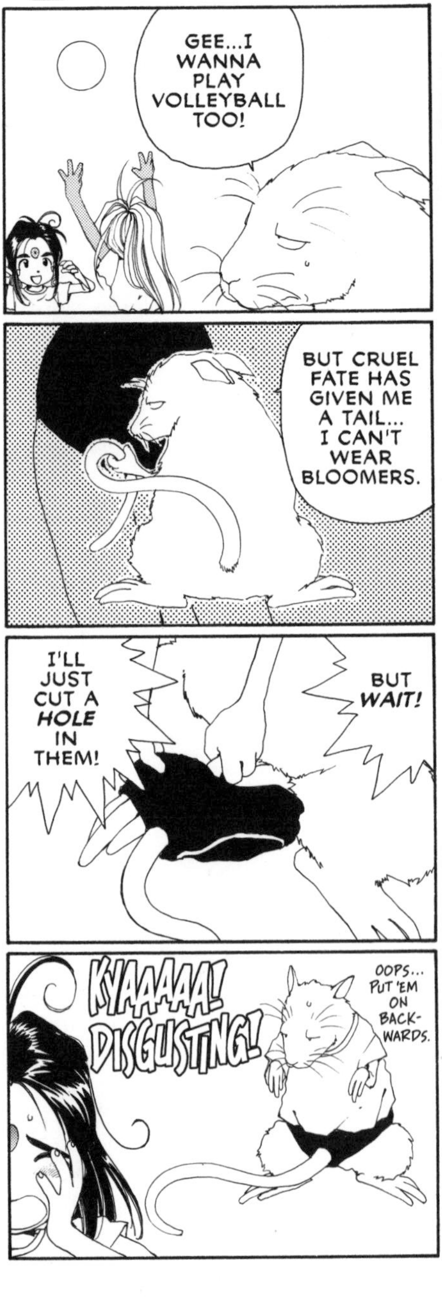
GEE...I WANNA PLAY VOLLEYBALL TOO!
BUT CRUEL FATE HAS GIVEN ME A TAIL... I CAN'T WEAR BLOOMERS.
BUT *WAIT!*
I'LL JUST CUT A *HOLE* IN THEM!
OOPS... PUT 'EM ON BACK-WARDS.
KYAAAAA! DISGUSTING!

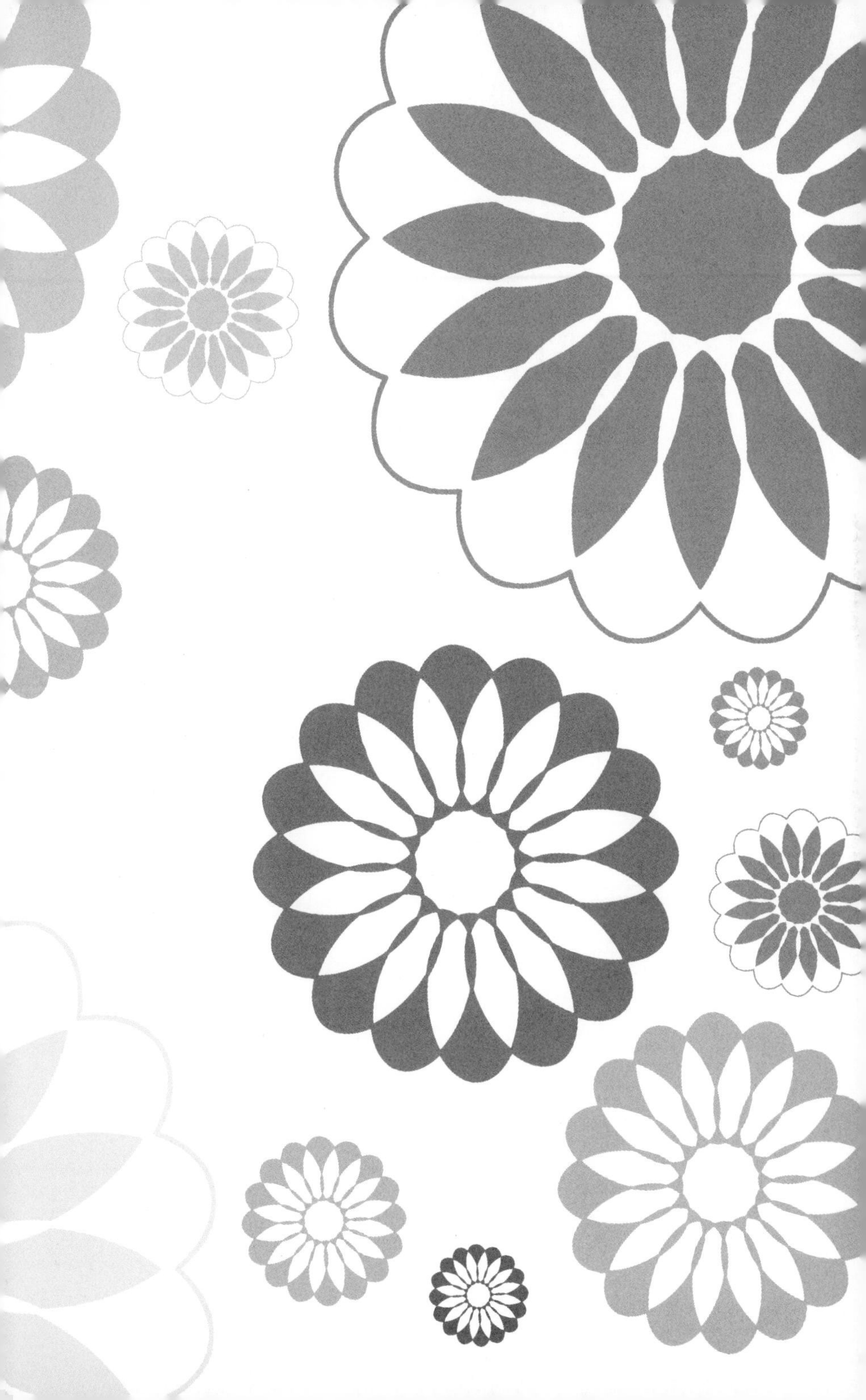

OH MY GODDESS!

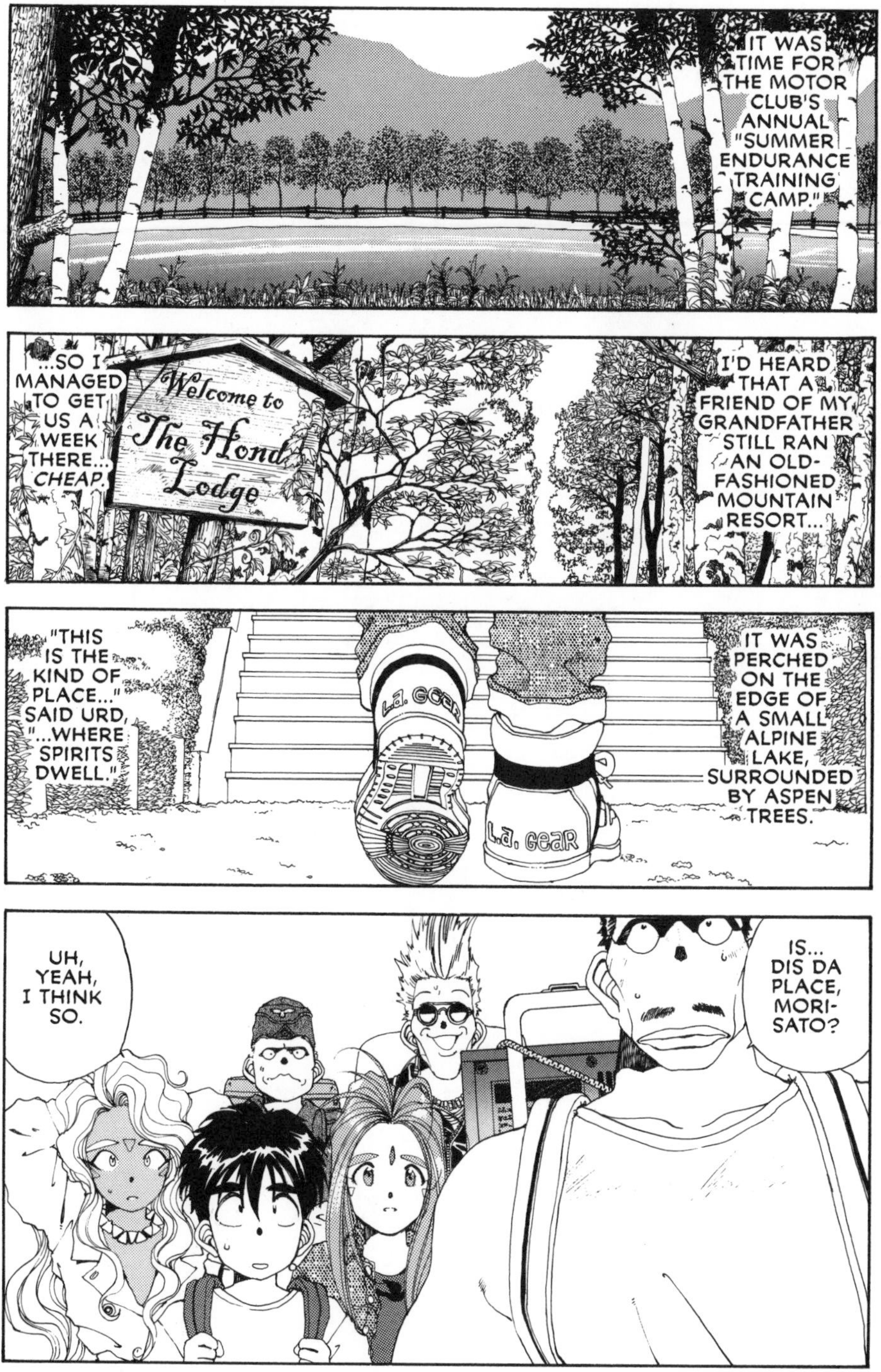
IT WAS TIME FOR THE MOTOR CLUB'S ANNUAL "SUMMER ENDURANCE TRAINING CAMP."
I'D HEARD THAT A FRIEND OF MY GRANDFATHER STILL RAN AN OLD-FASHIONED MOUNTAIN RESORT...
Welcome to The Hond Lodge
...SO I MANAGED TO GET US A WEEK THERE... *CHEAP.*
IT WAS PERCHED ON THE EDGE OF A SMALL ALPINE LAKE, SURROUNDED BY ASPEN TREES.
"THIS IS THE KIND OF PLACE..." SAID URD, "...WHERE SPIRITS DWELL."
L.A. GEAR
L.A. GEAR
IS... DIS DA PLACE, MORI-SATO?
UH, YEAH, I THINK SO.

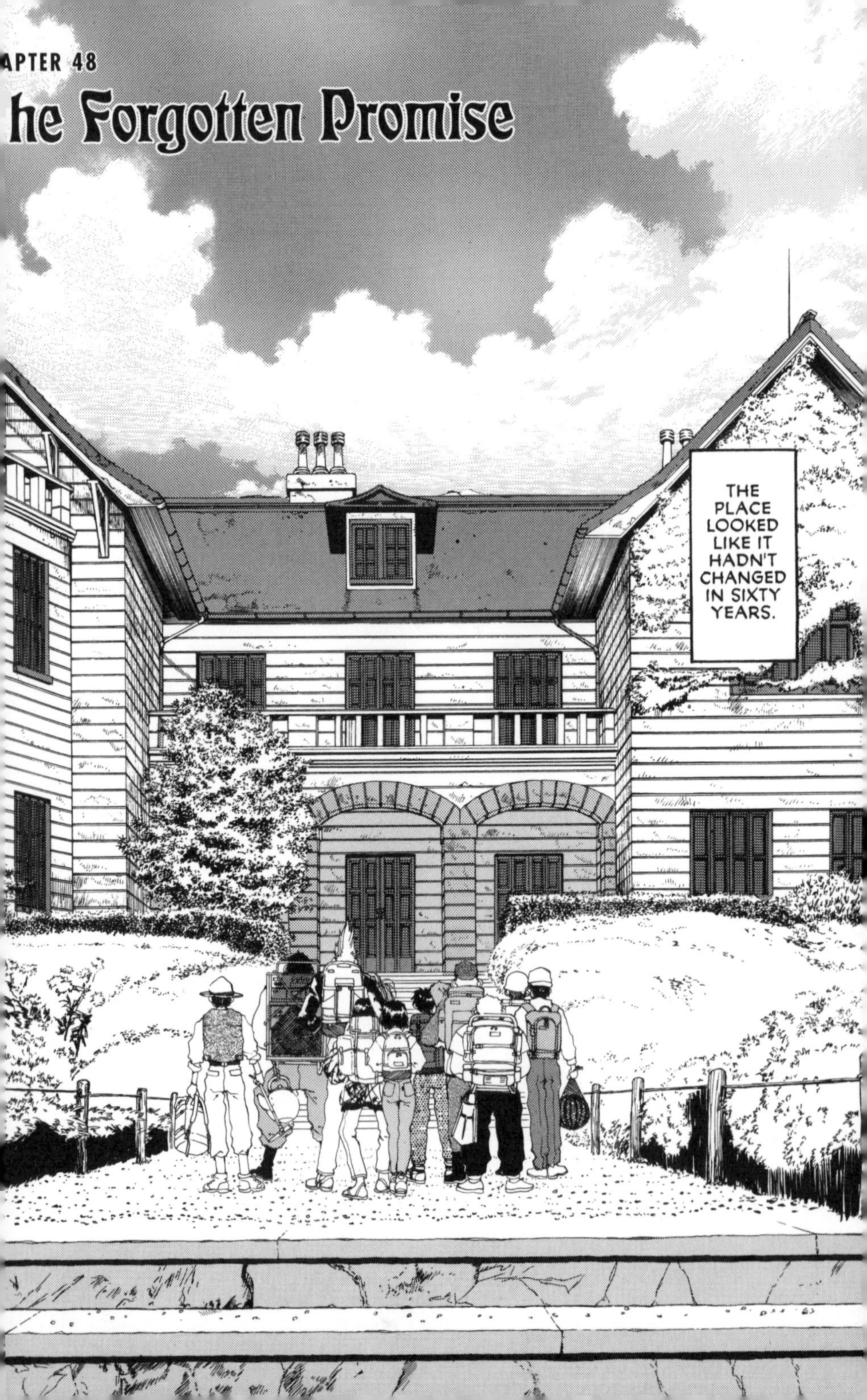
APTER 48
he Forgotten Promise
THE PLACE LOOKED LIKE IT HADN'T CHANGED IN SIXTY YEARS.

183

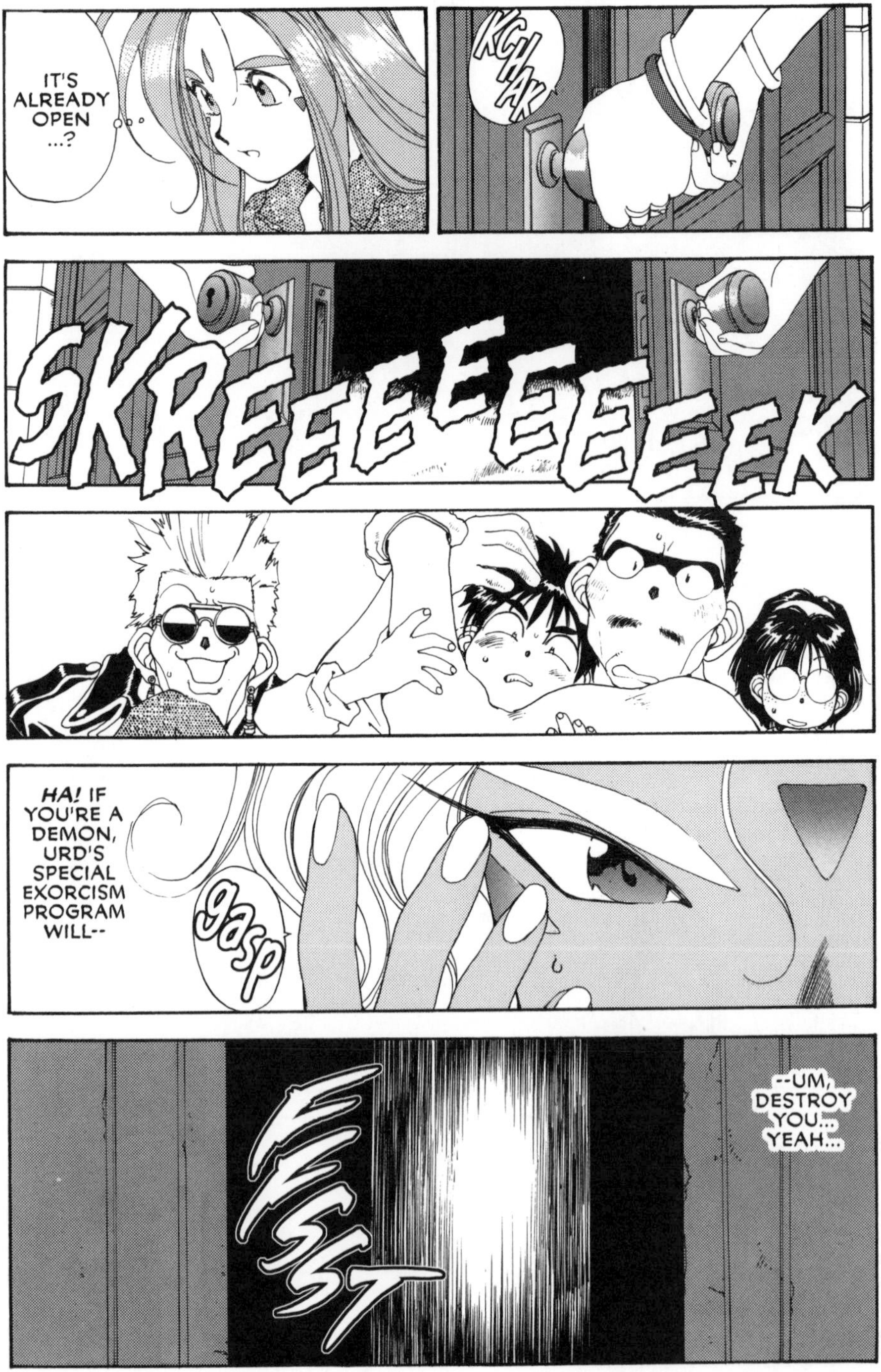
KCHAK
IT'S ALREADY OPEN ...?
SKREEEEEEEK
HA! IF YOU'RE A DEMON, URD'S SPECIAL EXORCISM PROGRAM WILL--
gasp
--UM, DESTROY YOU... YEAH...
FFSST

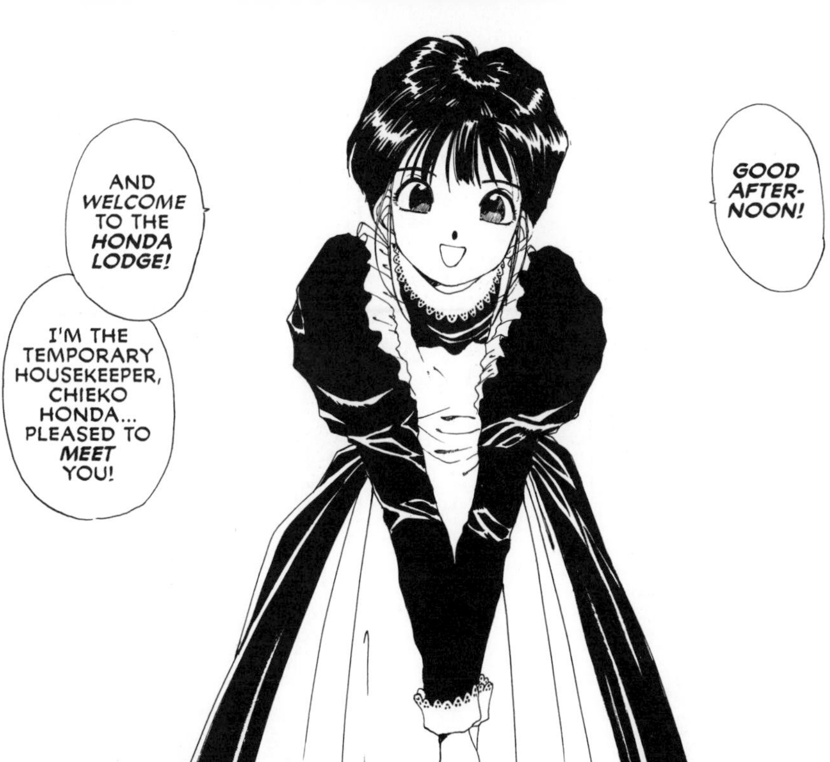
GOOD AFTERNOON!
AND WELCOME TO THE HONDA LODGE!
I'M THE TEMPORARY HOUSEKEEPER, CHIEKO HONDA... PLEASED TO MEET YOU!

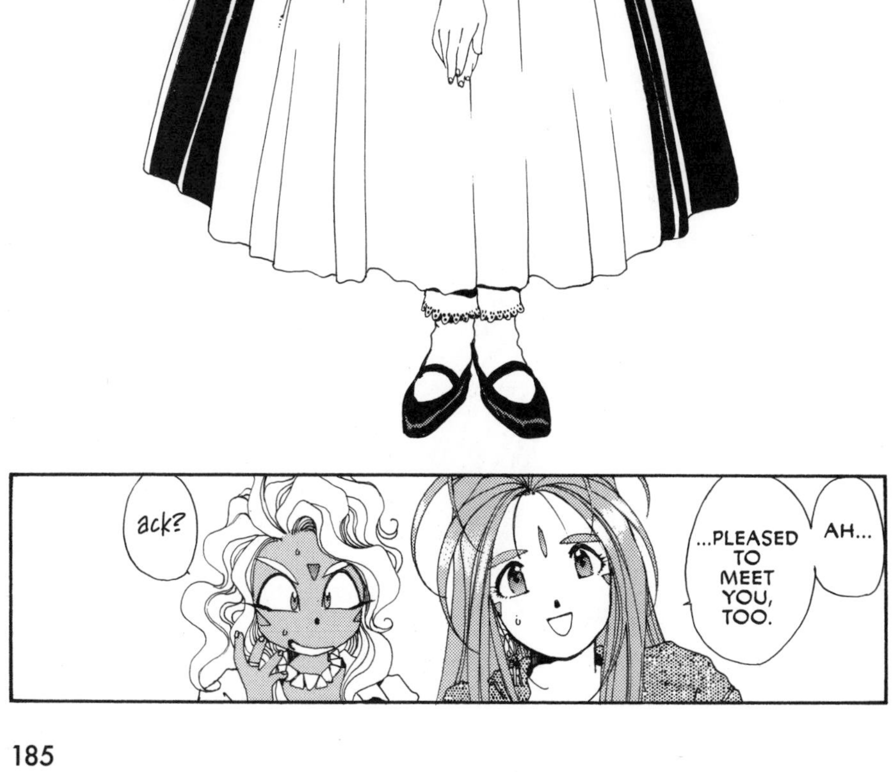
AH...
...PLEASED TO MEET YOU, TOO.
ack?

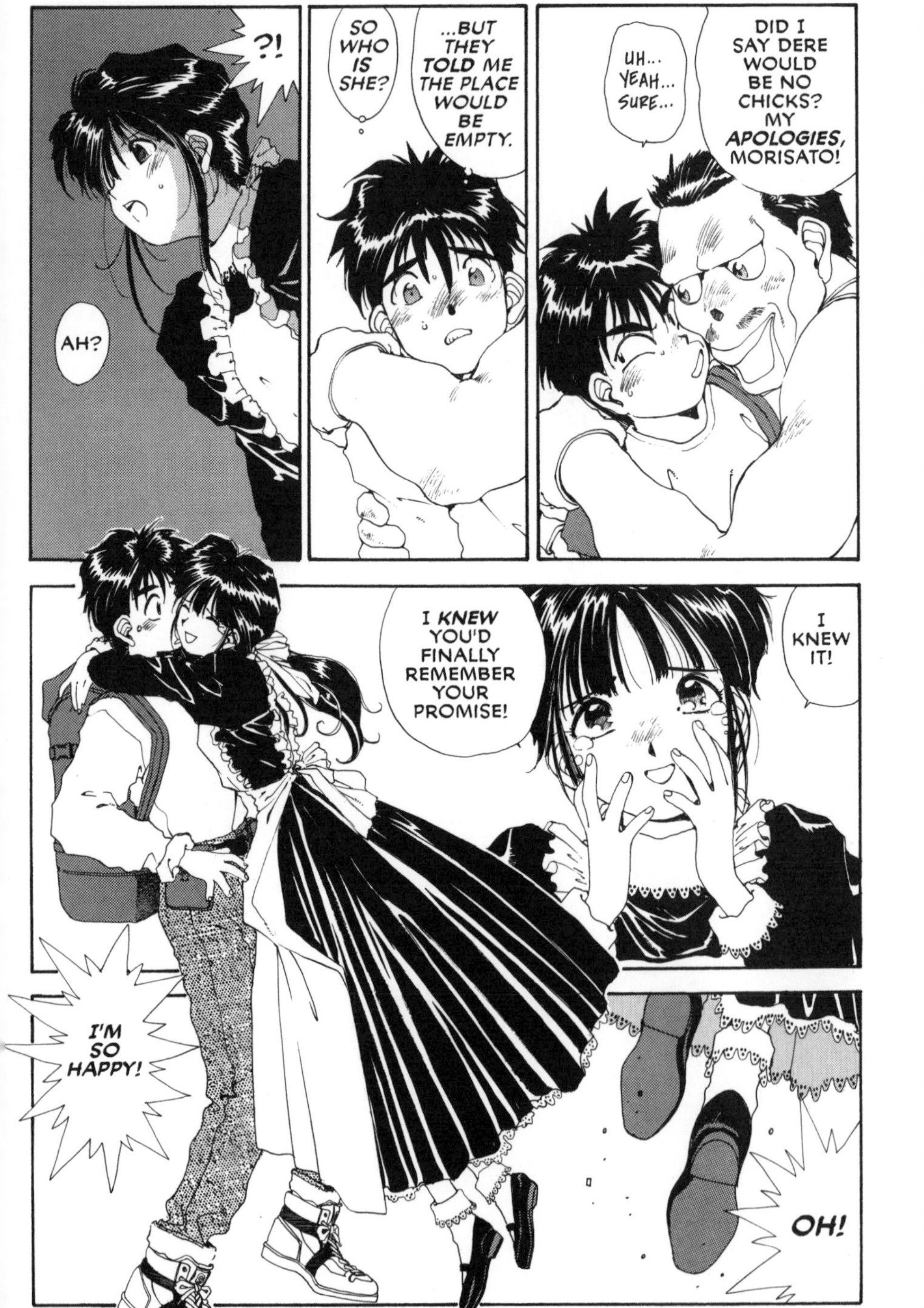
DID I SAY DERE WOULD BE NO CHICKS? MY APOLOGIES, MORISATO!
UH... YEAH... SURE...
...BUT THEY TOLD ME THE PLACE WOULD BE EMPTY.
SO WHO IS SHE?
?!
AH?
I KNEW IT!
I KNEW YOU'D FINALLY REMEMBER YOUR PROMISE!
OH!
I'M SO HAPPY!

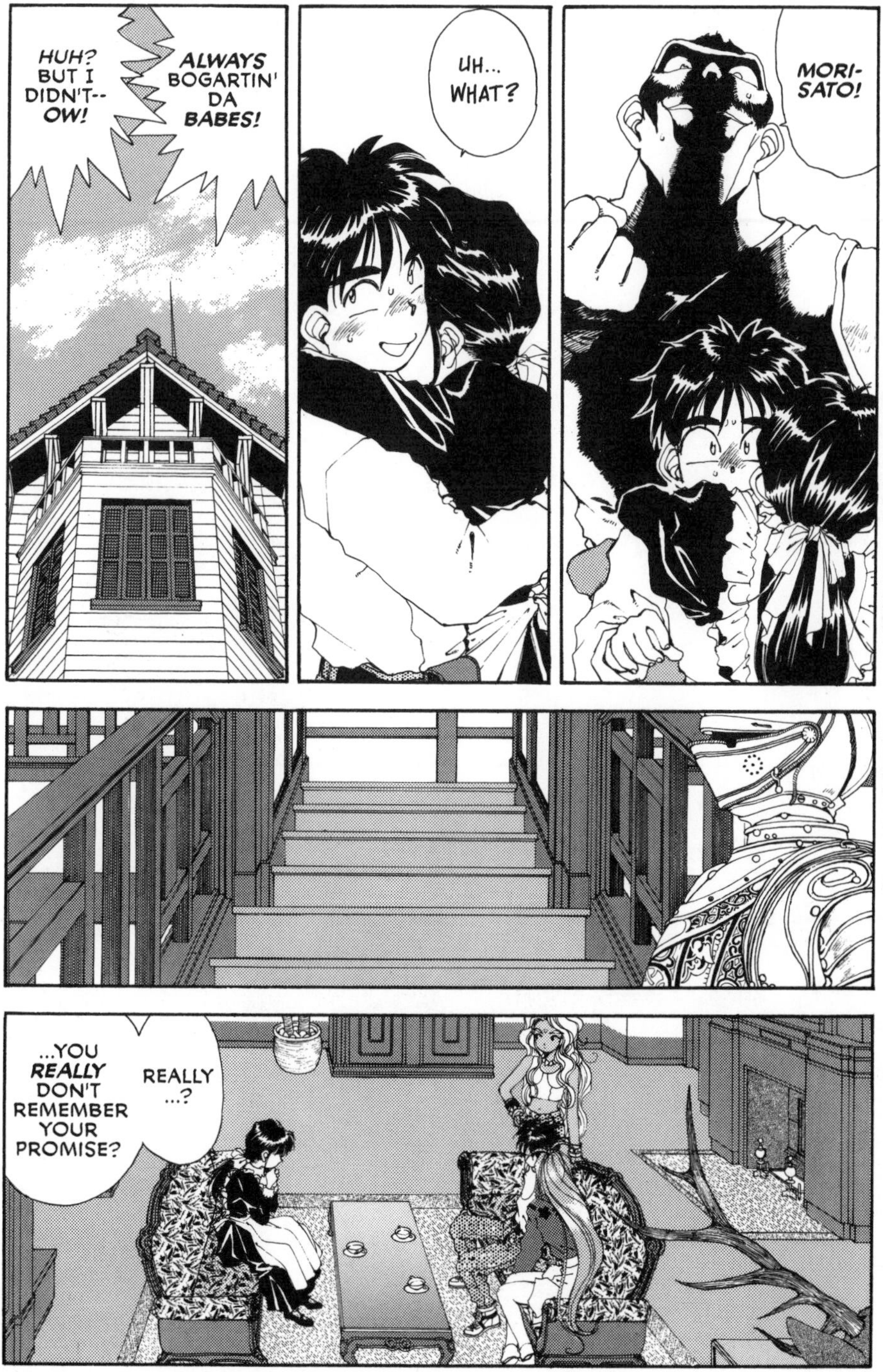
MORI-SATO!
UH... WHAT?
ALWAYS BOGARTIN' DA BABES!
HUH? BUT I DIDN'T-- OW!
...YOU REALLY DON'T REMEMBER YOUR PROMISE?
REALLY ...?

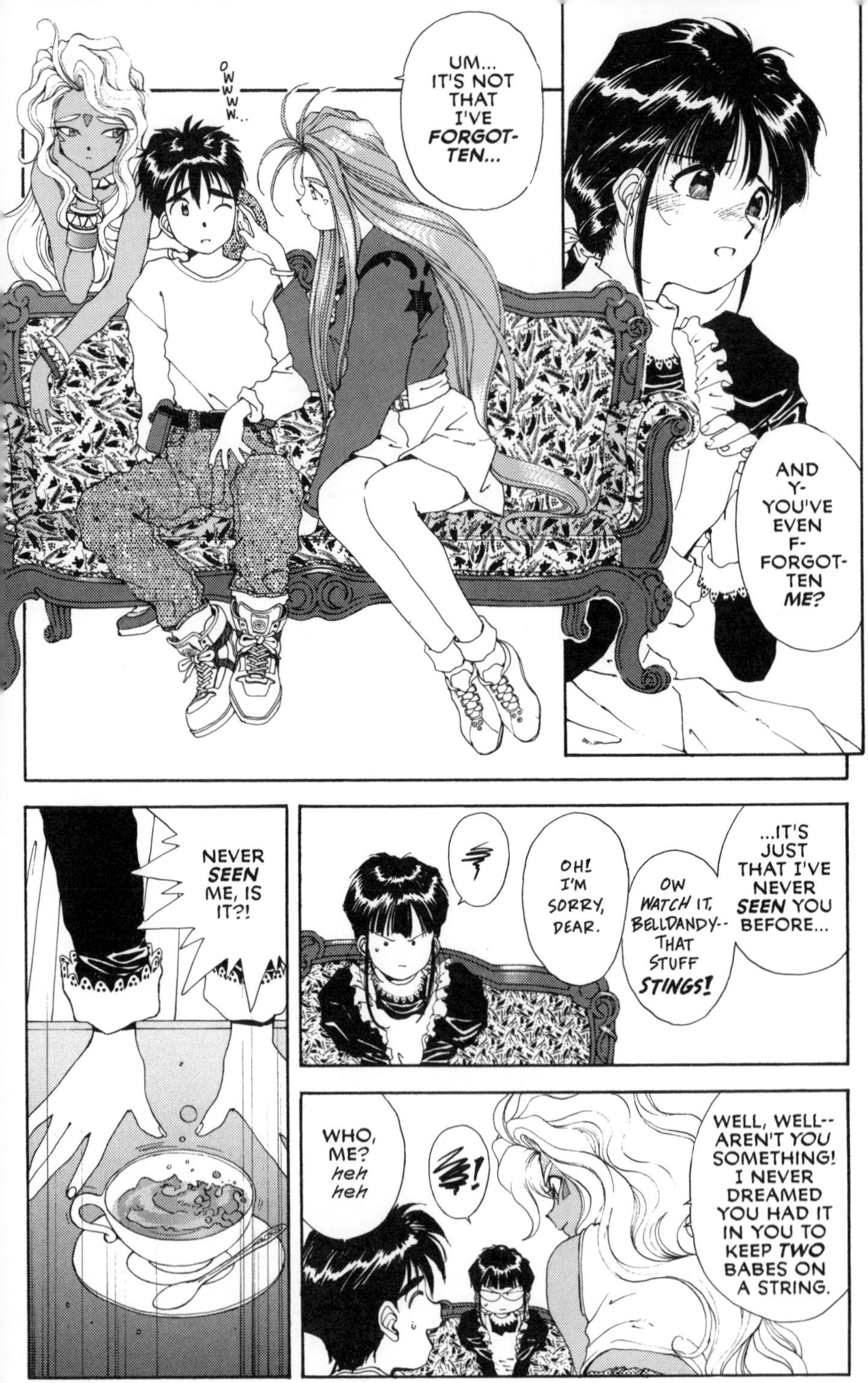
AND Y-YOU'VE EVEN F-FORGOTTEN ME?
UM... IT'S NOT THAT I'VE FORGOTTEN...
OWWWW...
...IT'S JUST THAT I'VE NEVER SEEN YOU BEFORE...
OW WATCH IT, BELLDANDY-- THAT STUFF STINGS!
OH! I'M SORRY, DEAR.
WELL, WELL-- AREN'T YOU SOMETHING! I NEVER DREAMED YOU HAD IT IN YOU TO KEEP TWO BABES ON A STRING.
WHO, ME? heh heh
NEVER SEEN ME, IS IT?!

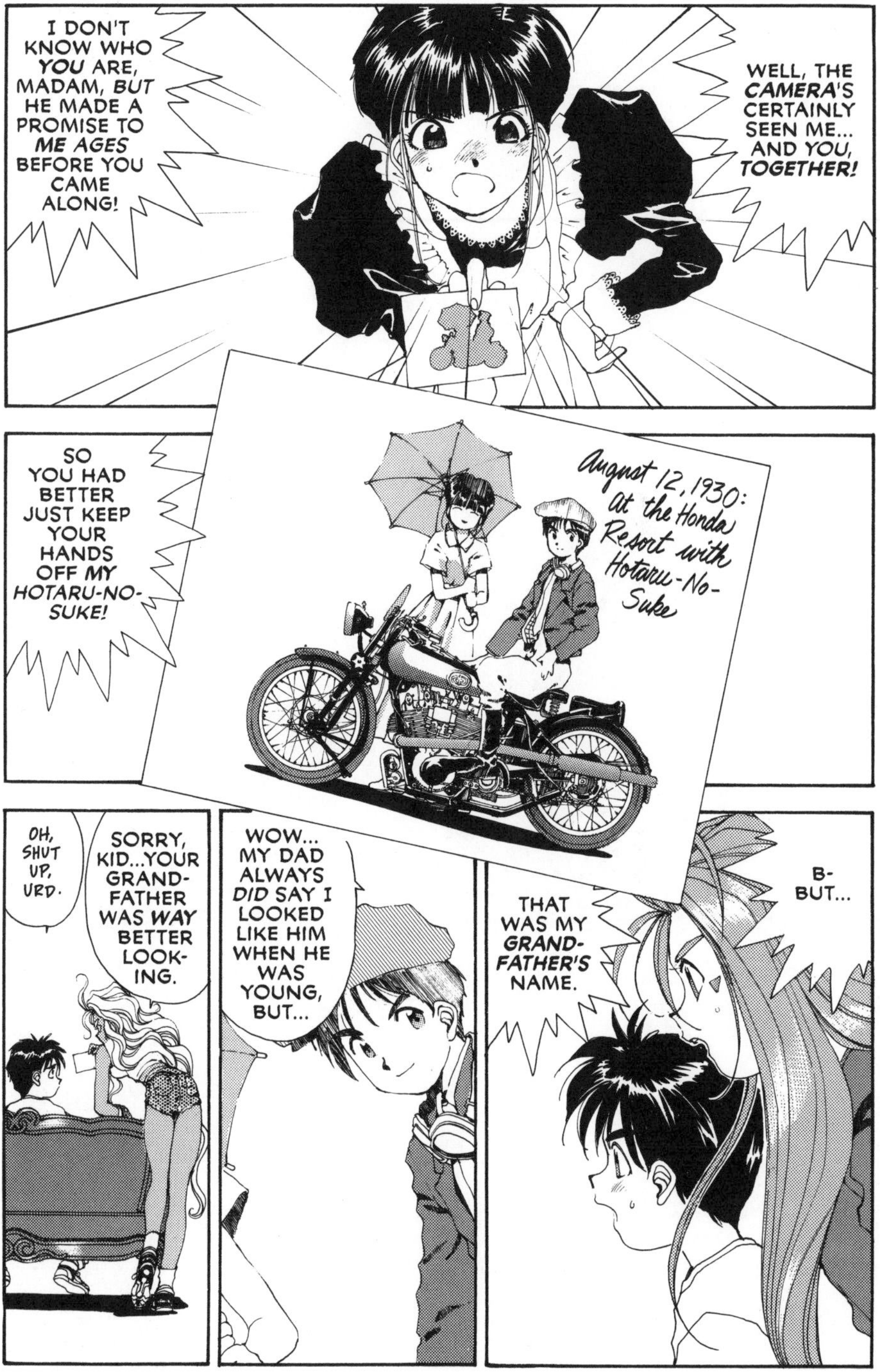
WELL, THE CAMERA'S CERTAINLY SEEN ME... AND YOU, TOGETHER!
I DON'T KNOW WHO YOU ARE, MADAM, BUT HE MADE A PROMISE TO ME AGES BEFORE YOU CAME ALONG!
August 12, 1930: At the Honda Resort with Hotaru-No-Suke
SO YOU HAD BETTER JUST KEEP YOUR HANDS OFF MY HOTARU-NO-SUKE!
B-BUT...
THAT WAS MY GRANDFATHER'S NAME.
WOW... MY DAD ALWAYS DID SAY I LOOKED LIKE HIM WHEN HE WAS YOUNG, BUT...
SORRY, KID...YOUR GRANDFATHER WAS WAY BETTER LOOKING.
OH, SHUT UP, URD.

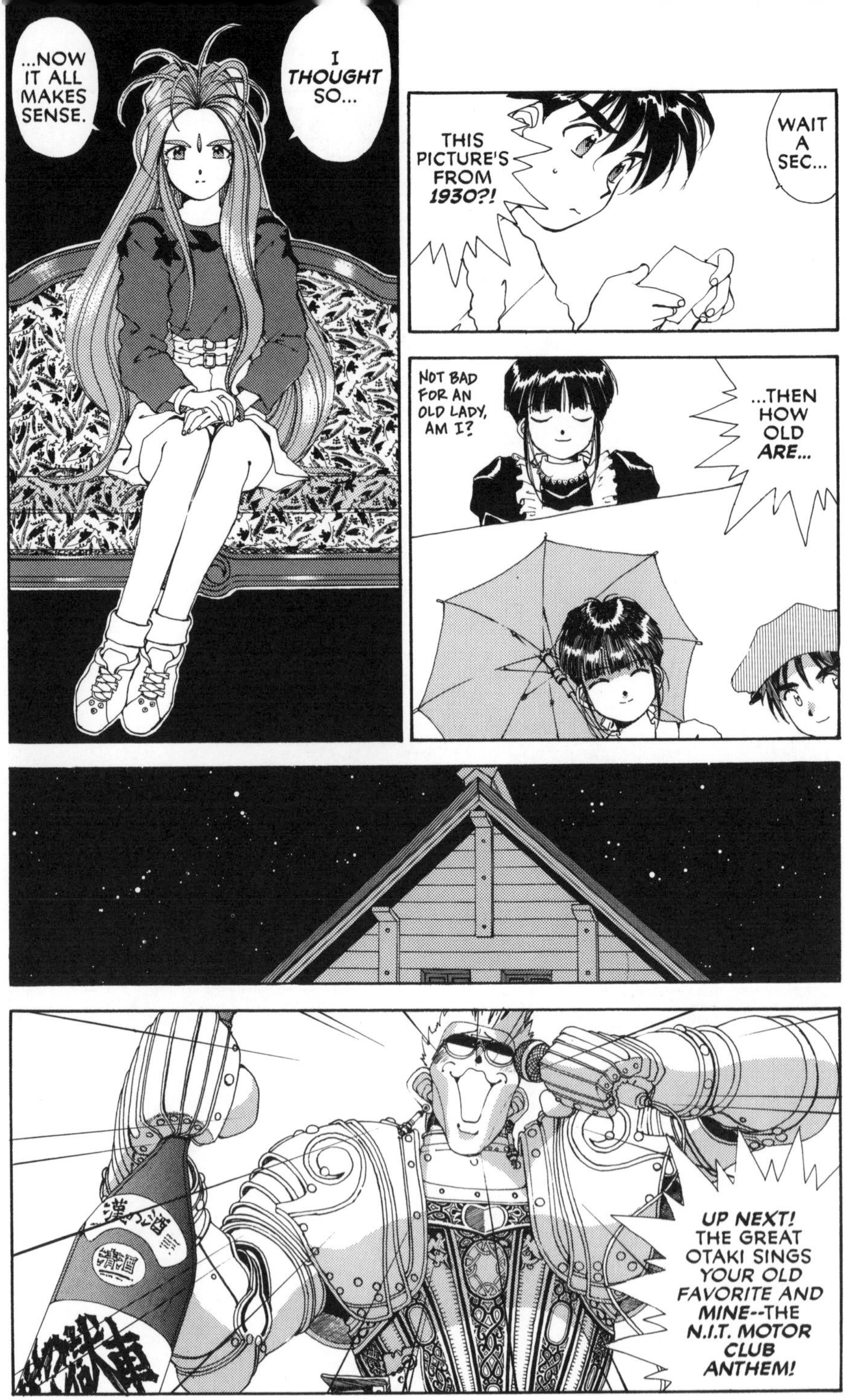
WAIT A SEC...
THIS PICTURE'S FROM *1930?!*
...THEN HOW OLD *ARE...*
NOT BAD FOR AN OLD LADY, AM I?
I *THOUGHT* SO...
...NOW IT ALL MAKES SENSE.
UP NEXT! THE GREAT OTAKI SINGS *YOUR OLD FAVORITE AND MINE*--THE *N.I.T. MOTOR CLUB ANTHEM!*

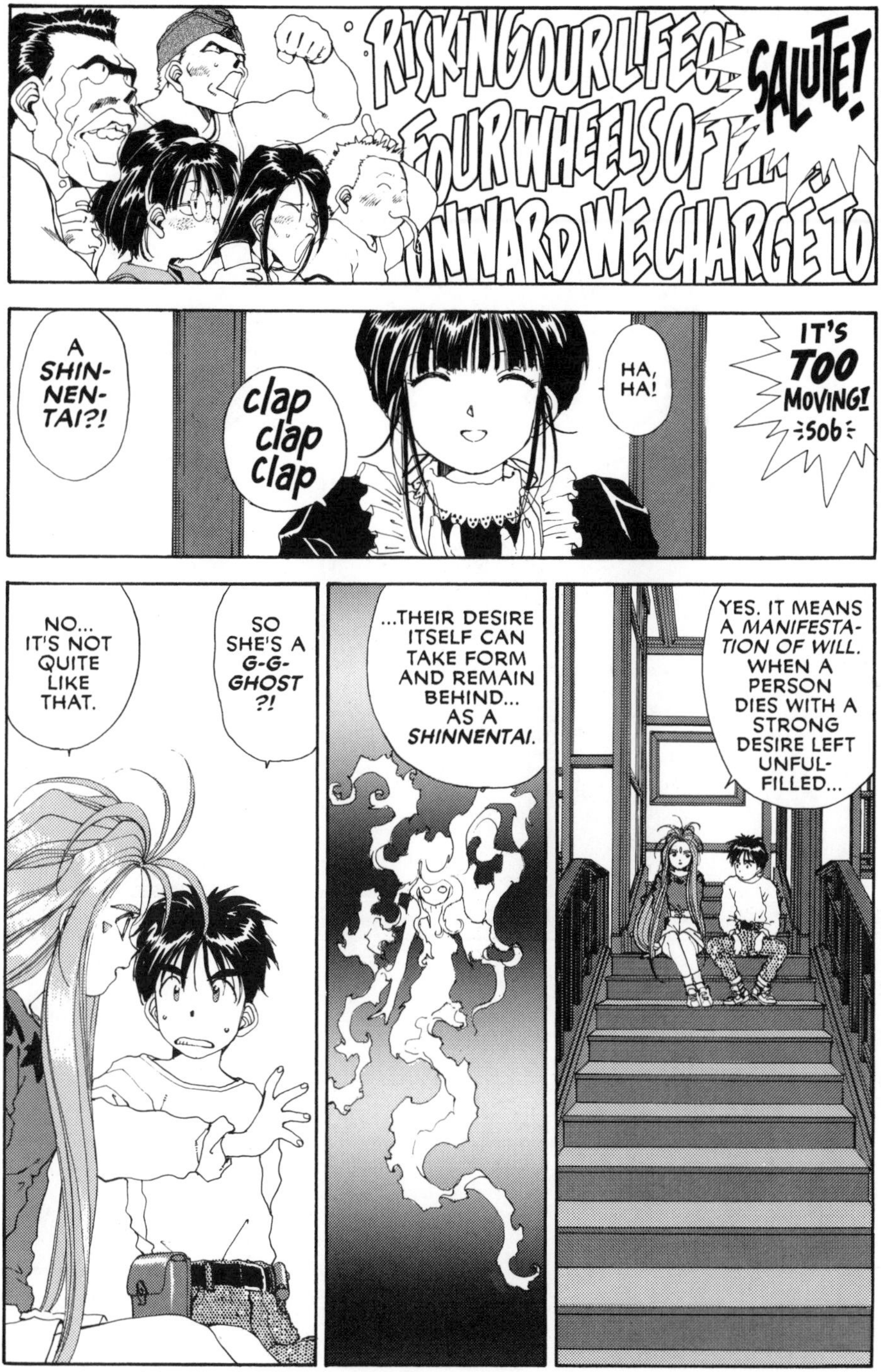
SALUTE!
RISKING OUR LIFE O
FOUR WHEELS OF
ONWARD WE CHARGE TO
IT'S TOO MOVING! sob
HA, HA!
clap clap clap
A SHIN-NEN-TAI?!
YES. IT MEANS A MANIFESTATION OF WILL. WHEN A PERSON DIES WITH A STRONG DESIRE LEFT UNFULFILLED...
...THEIR DESIRE ITSELF CAN TAKE FORM AND REMAIN BEHIND... AS A SHINNENTAI.
SO SHE'S A G-G-GHOST?!
NO... IT'S NOT QUITE LIKE THAT.

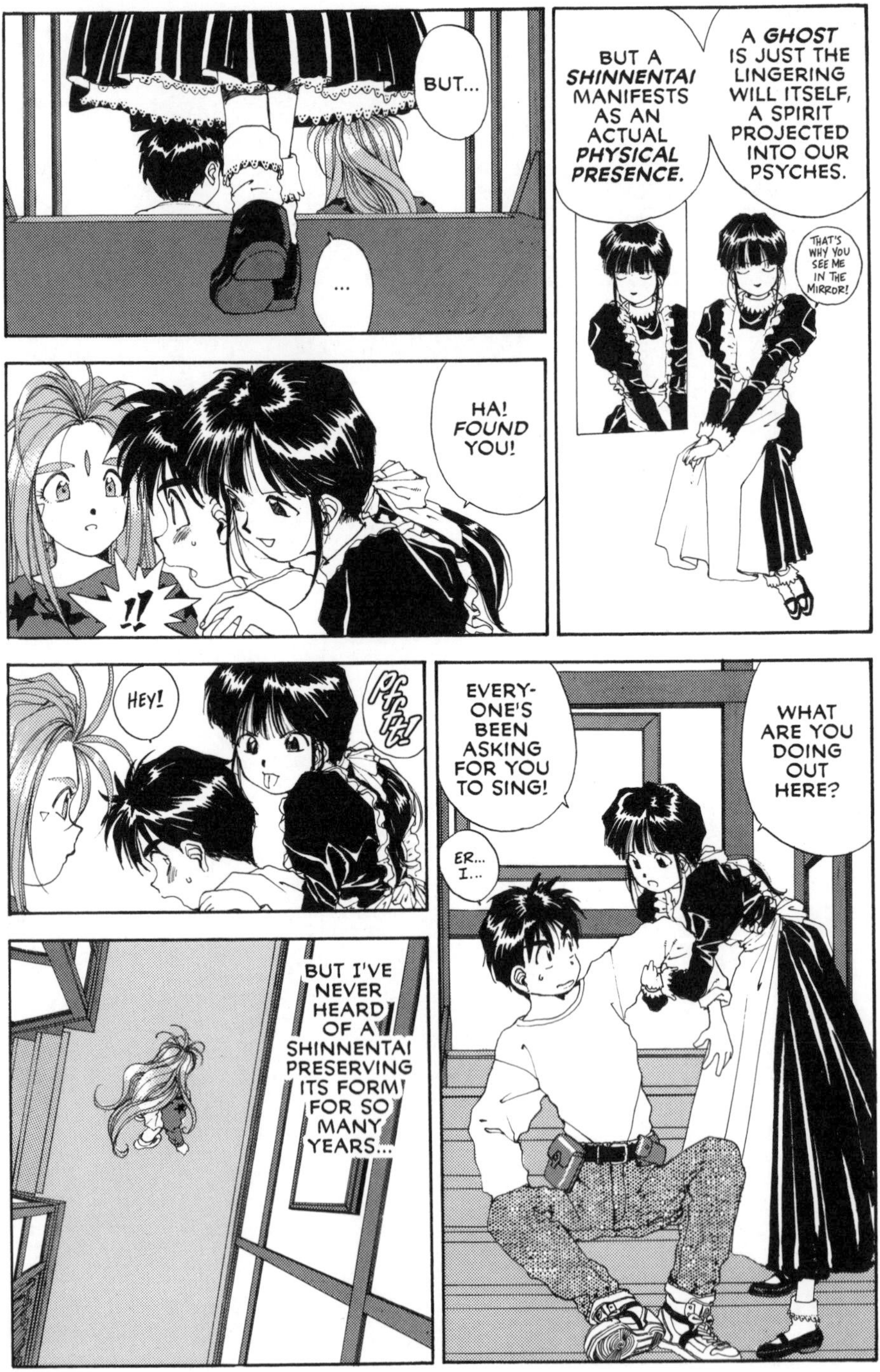
A GHOST IS JUST THE LINGERING WILL ITSELF, A SPIRIT PROJECTED INTO OUR PSYCHES.
BUT A SHINNENTAI MANIFESTS AS AN ACTUAL PHYSICAL PRESENCE.
THAT'S WHY YOU SEE ME IN THE MIRROR!
BUT...
...
HA! FOUND YOU!
!!
WHAT ARE YOU DOING OUT HERE?
EVERY-ONE'S BEEN ASKING FOR YOU TO SING!
ER... I...
Pfft!
HEY!
BUT I'VE NEVER HEARD OF A SHINNENTAI PRESERVING ITS FORM FOR SO MANY YEARS...

CALL ME QUEEN!

...WHAT CAN BE KEEPING HER BOUND TO THIS WORLD?

HURRAH!

ME FIRST!

WORSHIP ME AND LICK MY SNEAKERS!

URD, DIDN'T KEIICHI COME IN TO SING...?

HUH? NO...I HAVEN'T SEEN HIM ALL NIGHT.

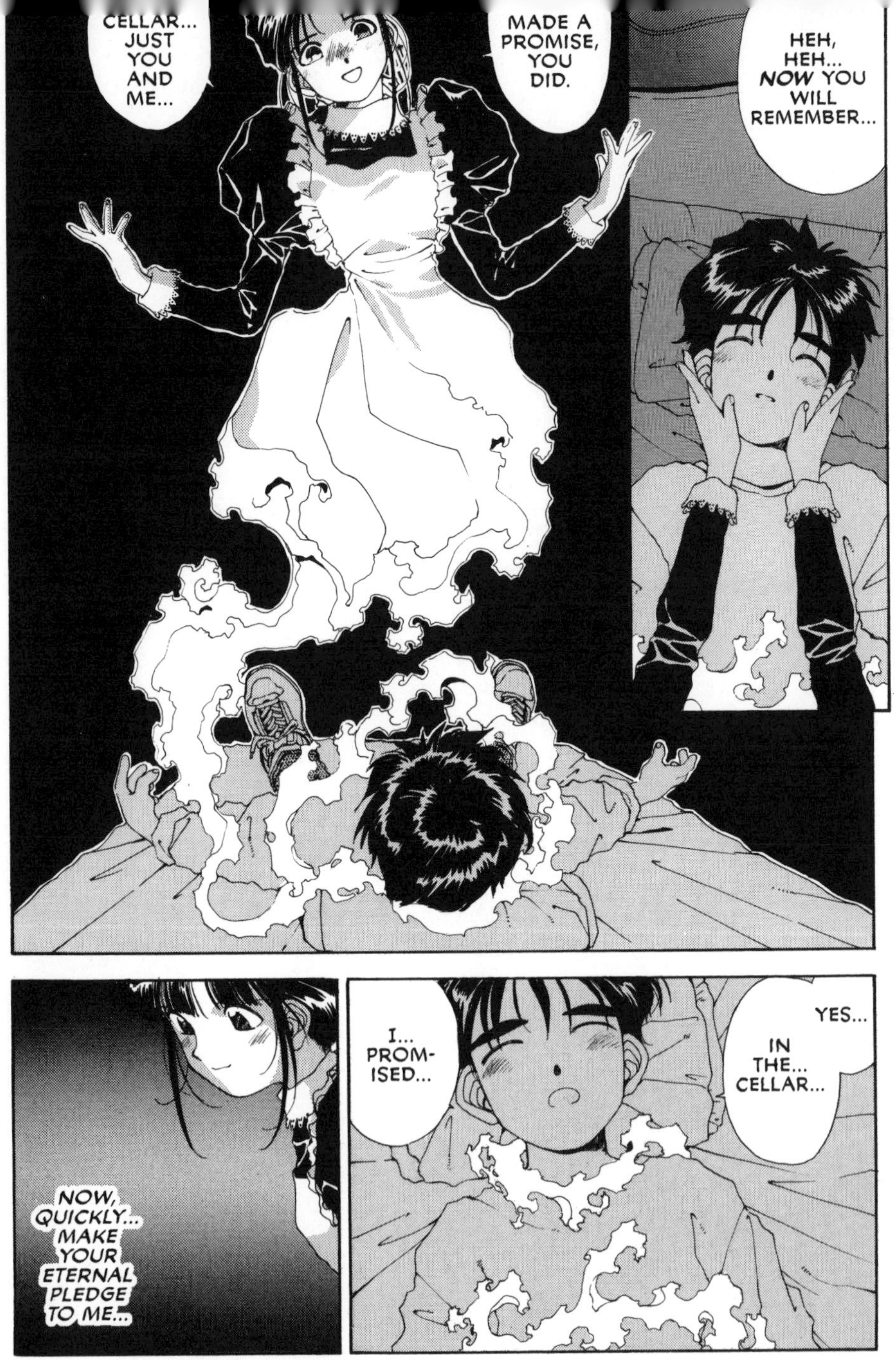
HEH, HEH... *NOW* YOU WILL REMEMBER...
MADE A PROMISE, YOU DID.
CELLAR... JUST YOU AND ME...
YES...
IN THE... CELLAR...
I... PROM-ISED...
NOW, QUICKLY... MAKE YOUR ETERNAL PLEDGE TO ME...

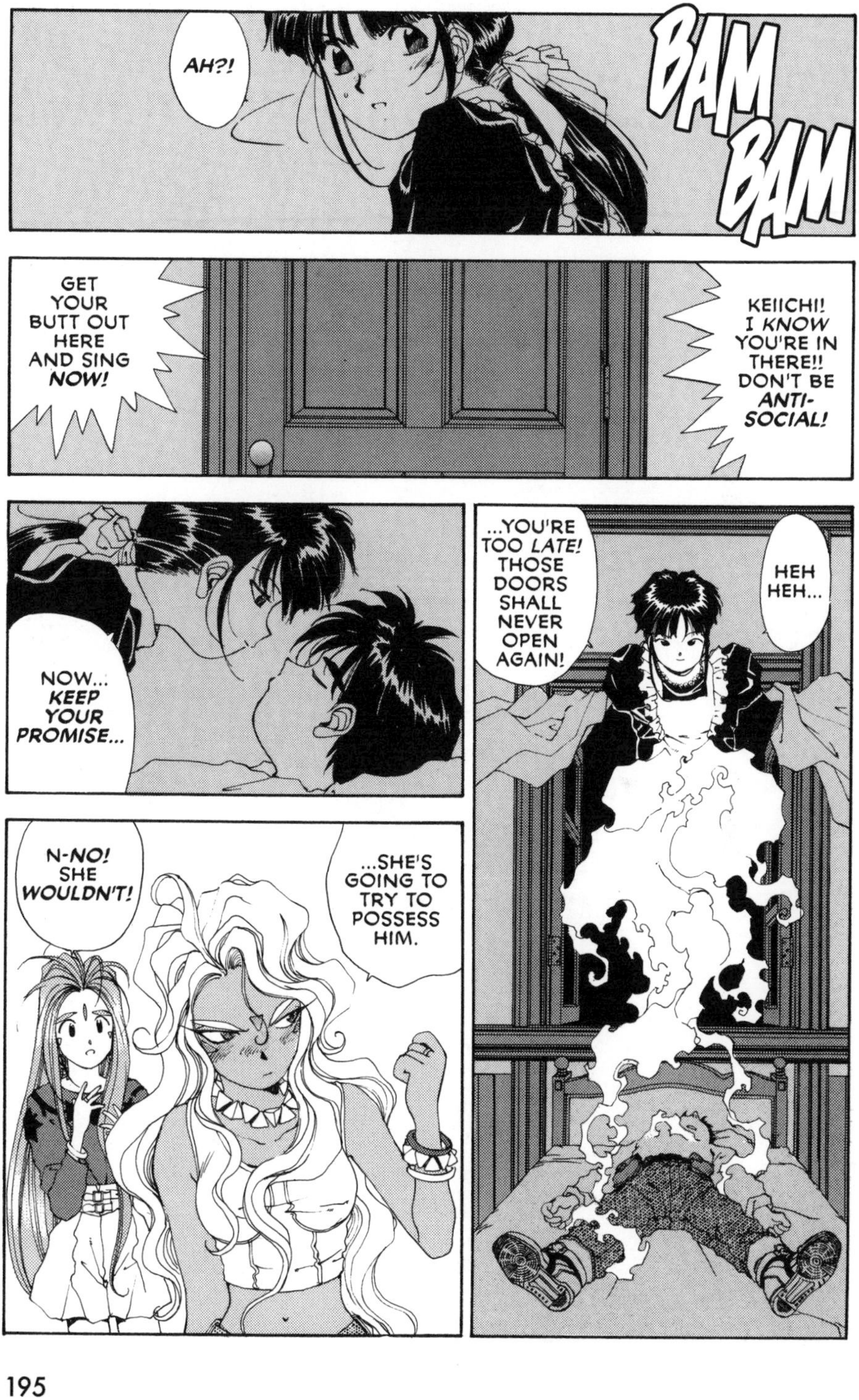
BAM BAM
AH?!
KEIICHI! I *KNOW* YOU'RE IN THERE!! DON'T BE **ANTI-SOCIAL!**
GET YOUR BUTT OUT HERE AND SING ***NOW!***
HEH HEH...
...YOU'RE TOO *LATE!* THOSE DOORS SHALL NEVER OPEN AGAIN!
NOW... ***KEEP YOUR PROMISE...***
...SHE'S GOING TO TRY TO POSSESS HIM.
N-*NO!* SHE ***WOULDN'T!***

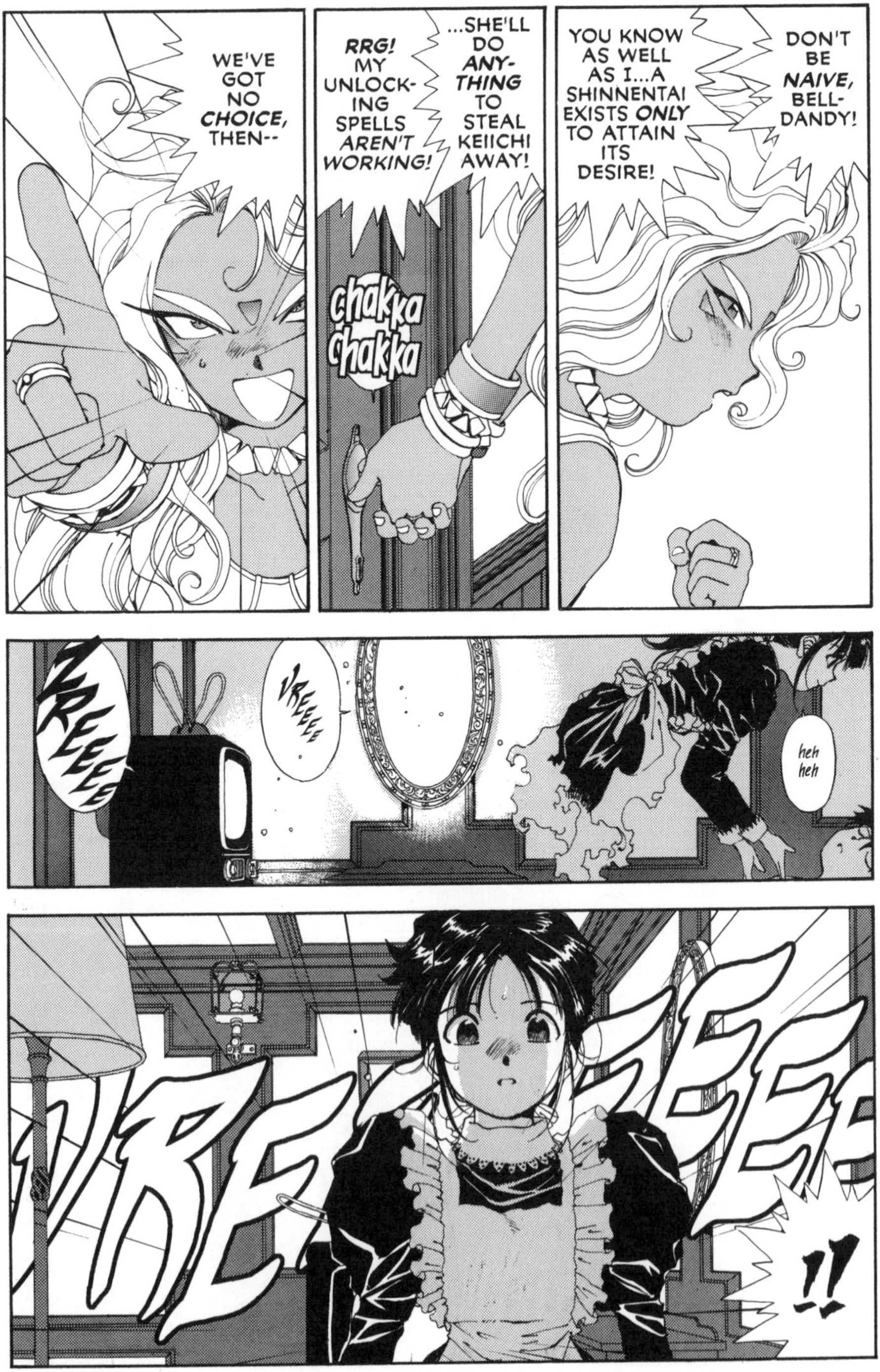
DON'T BE *NAIVE,* BELL-DANDY!
YOU KNOW AS WELL AS I...A SHINNENTAI EXISTS *ONLY* TO ATTAIN ITS DESIRE!
...SHE'LL DO *ANYTHING* TO STEAL KEIICHI AWAY!
RRG! MY UNLOCKING SPELLS *AREN'T WORKING!*
chakka chakka
WE'VE GOT NO *CHOICE,* THEN--
heh heh
VREEEE
VREEEE
!!
VREEEEEE

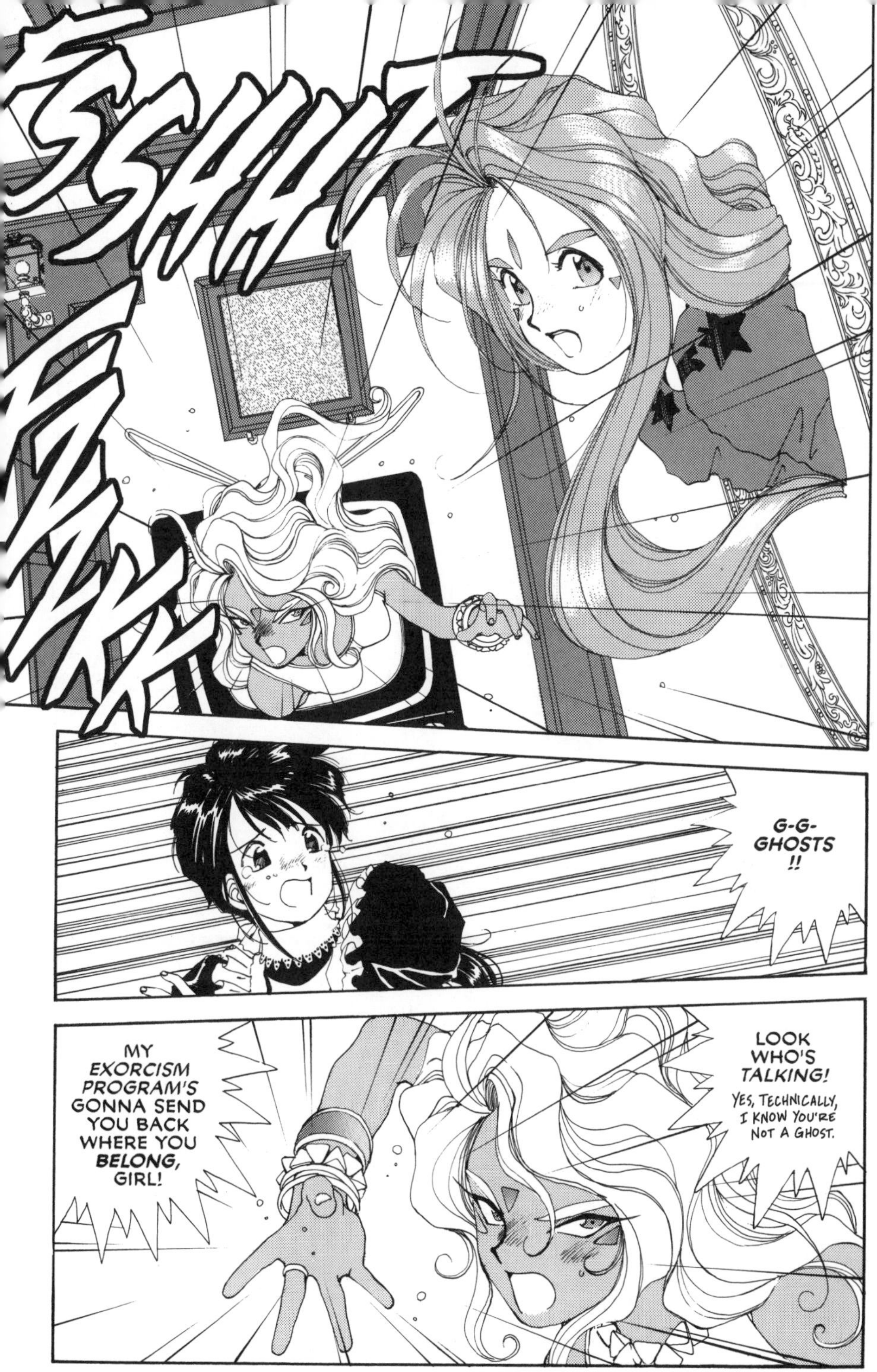
G-G-GHOSTS !!
LOOK WHO'S *TALKING!*
YES, TECHNICALLY, I KNOW YOU'RE NOT A GHOST.
MY *EXORCISM PROGRAM'S* GONNA SEND YOU BACK WHERE YOU **BELONG,** GIRL!

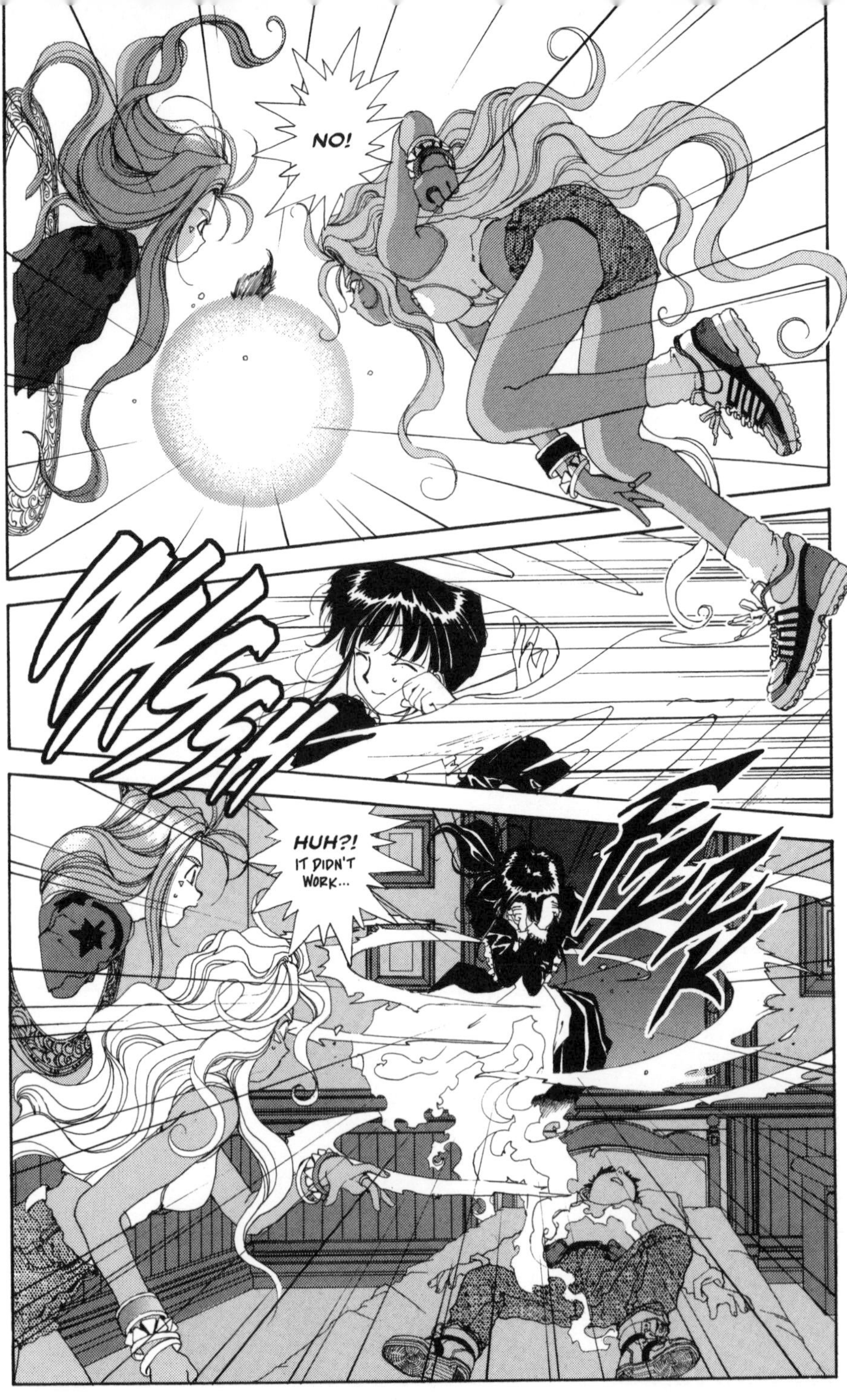
NO!
HUH?! IT DIDN'T WORK...

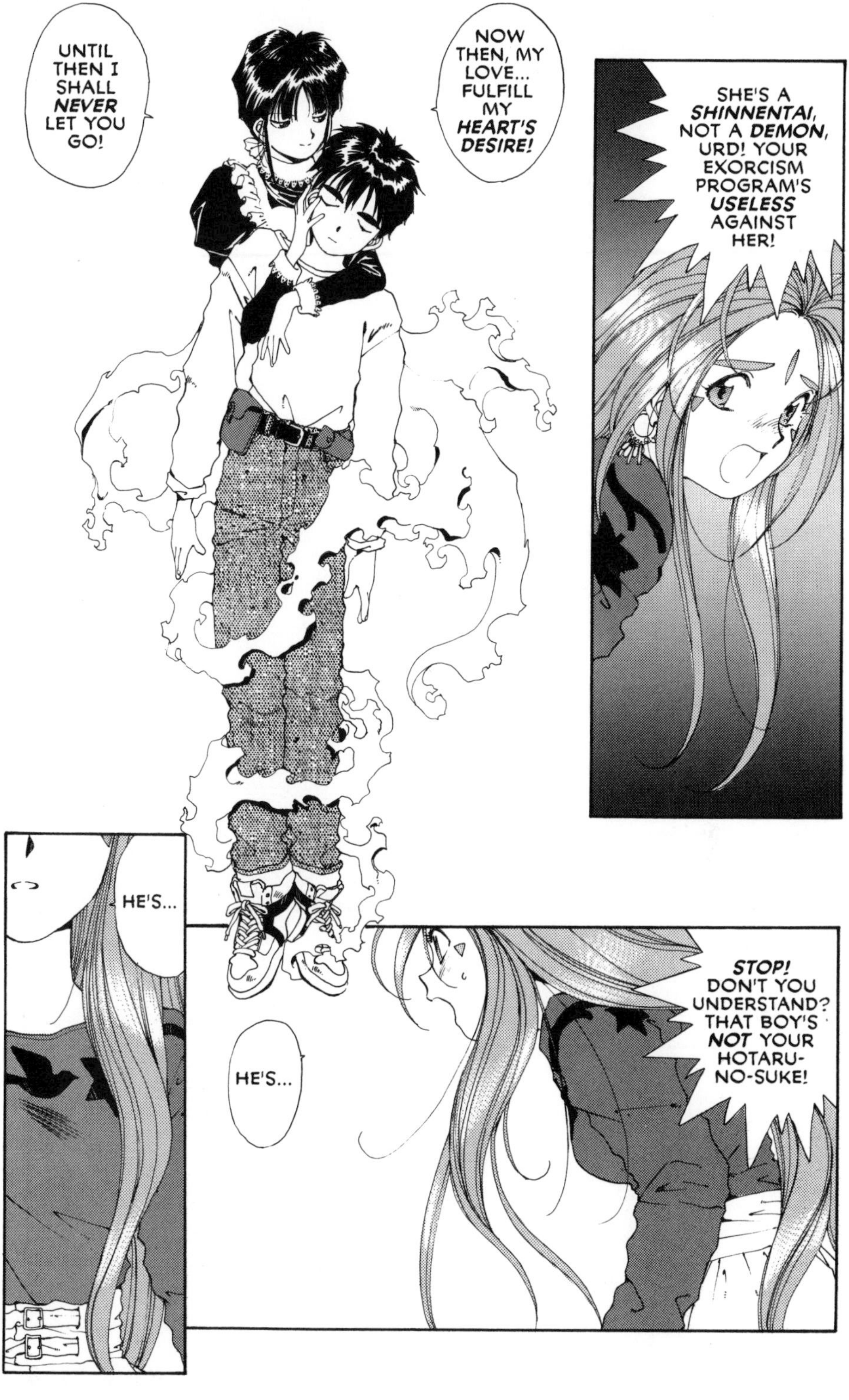
SHE'S A *SHINNENTAI*, NOT A *DEMON*, URD! YOUR EXORCISM PROGRAM'S *USELESS* AGAINST HER!
NOW THEN, MY LOVE... FULFILL MY *HEART'S DESIRE!*
UNTIL THEN I SHALL *NEVER* LET YOU GO!
STOP! DON'T YOU UNDERSTAND? THAT BOY'S *NOT* YOUR HOTARU-NO-SUKE!
HE'S...
HE'S...

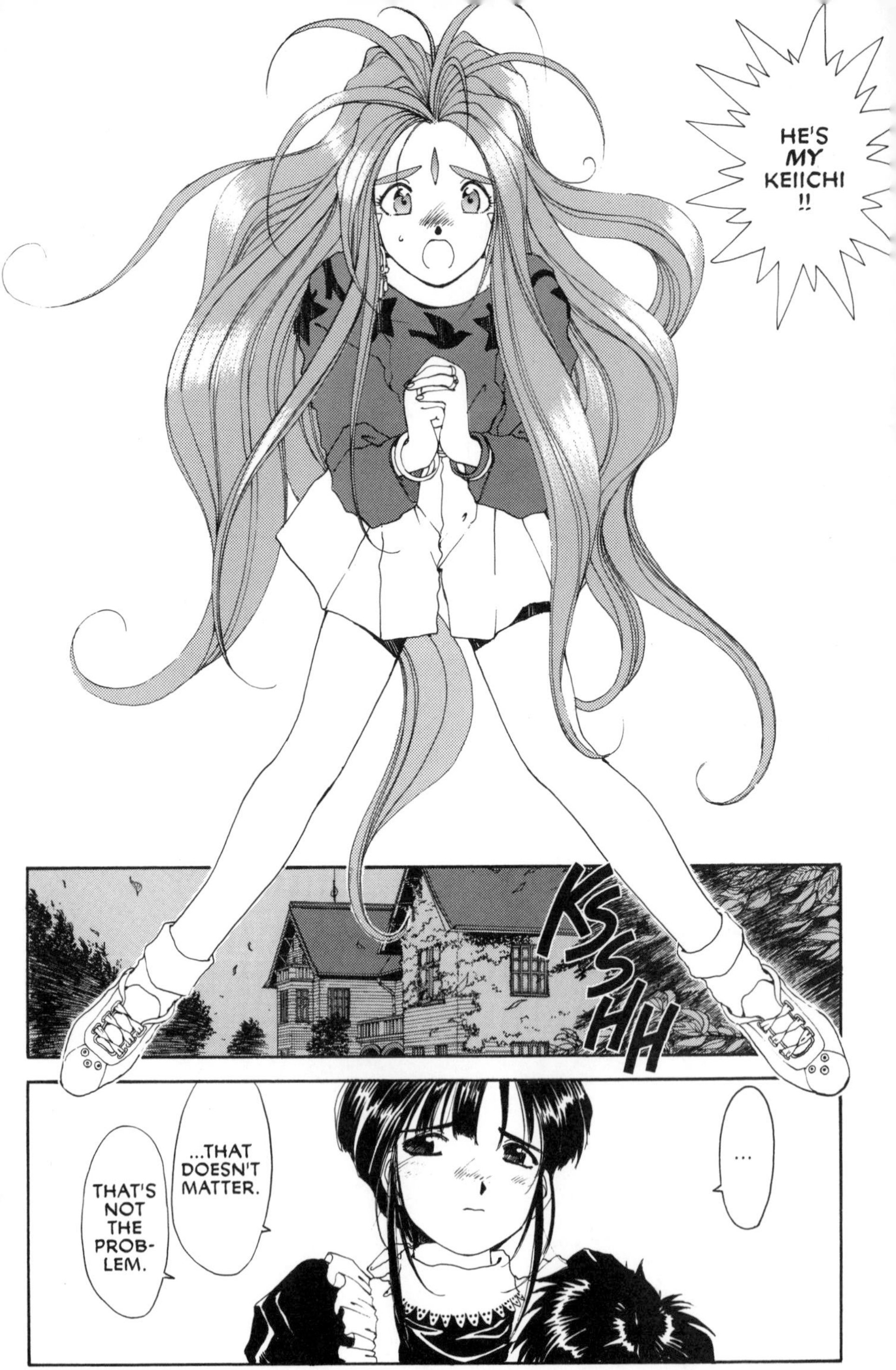
HE'S MY KEIICHI !!
KSSHH
...
...THAT DOESN'T MATTER.
THAT'S NOT THE PROB-LEM.

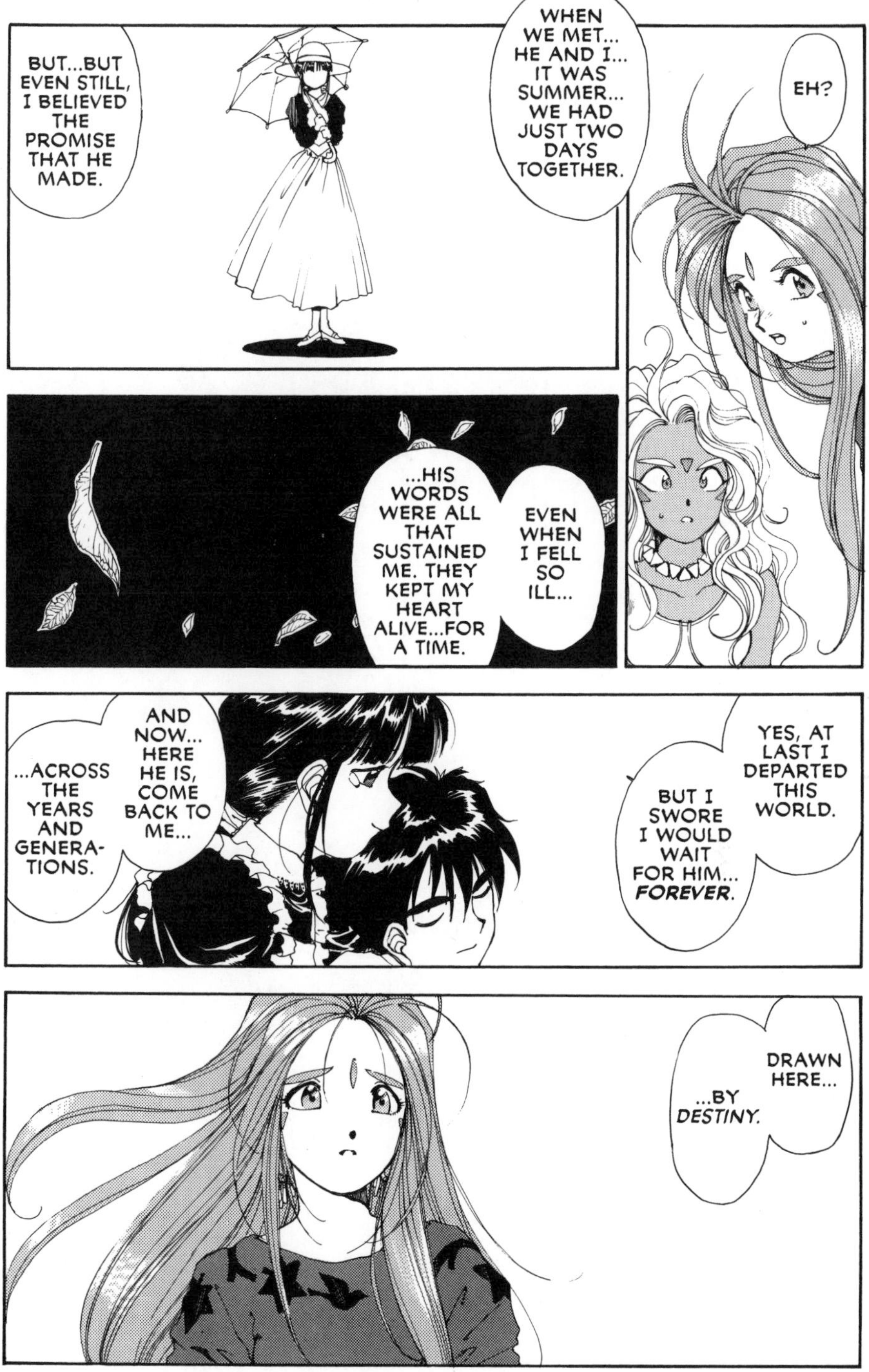
EH?
WHEN WE MET... HE AND I... IT WAS SUMMER... WE HAD JUST TWO DAYS TOGETHER.
BUT...BUT EVEN STILL, I BELIEVED THE PROMISE THAT HE MADE.
EVEN WHEN I FELL SO ILL...
...HIS WORDS WERE ALL THAT SUSTAINED ME. THEY KEPT MY HEART ALIVE...FOR A TIME.
YES, AT LAST I DEPARTED THIS WORLD.
BUT I SWORE I WOULD WAIT FOR HIM... *FOREVER*.
AND NOW... HERE HE IS, COME BACK TO ME...
...ACROSS THE YEARS AND GENERA-TIONS.
DRAWN HERE...
...BY *DESTINY*.

JUST TELL US ONE THING, DEAR...

WHAT EXACT-LY...

...WAS THE PROMISE ...?

GOOD *MORNING*, KEIICHI!

WHY AM I IN BED?

WHAT TH--?

?

?

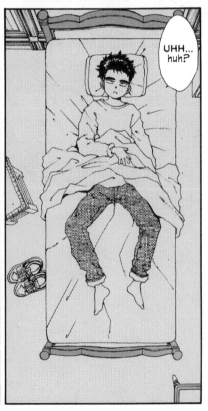

UHH... huh?

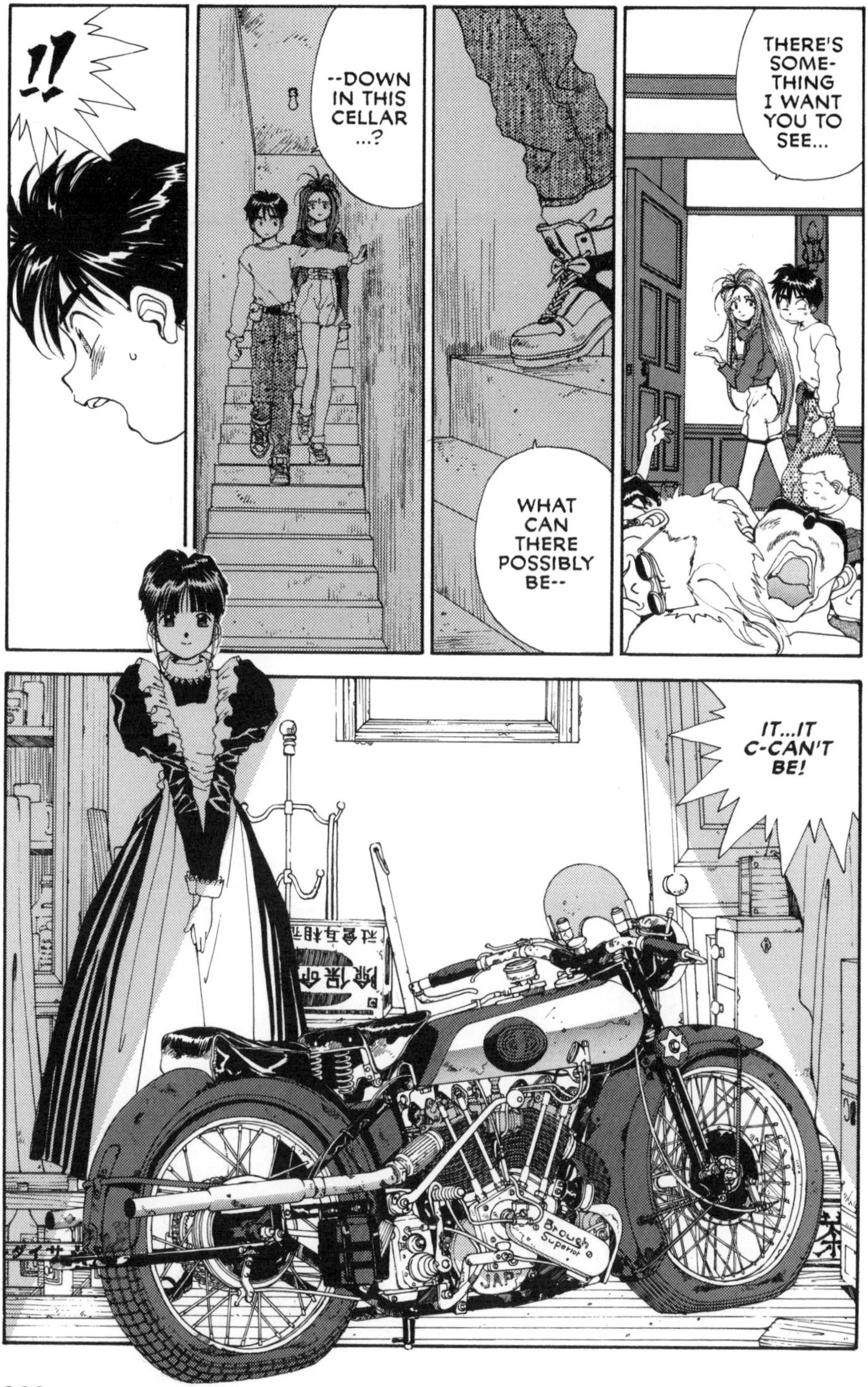
THERE'S SOMETHING I WANT YOU TO SEE...
WHAT CAN THERE POSSIBLY BE--
--DOWN IN THIS CELLAR ...?
!!
IT...IT C-CAN'T BE!
Brough Superior
JAP

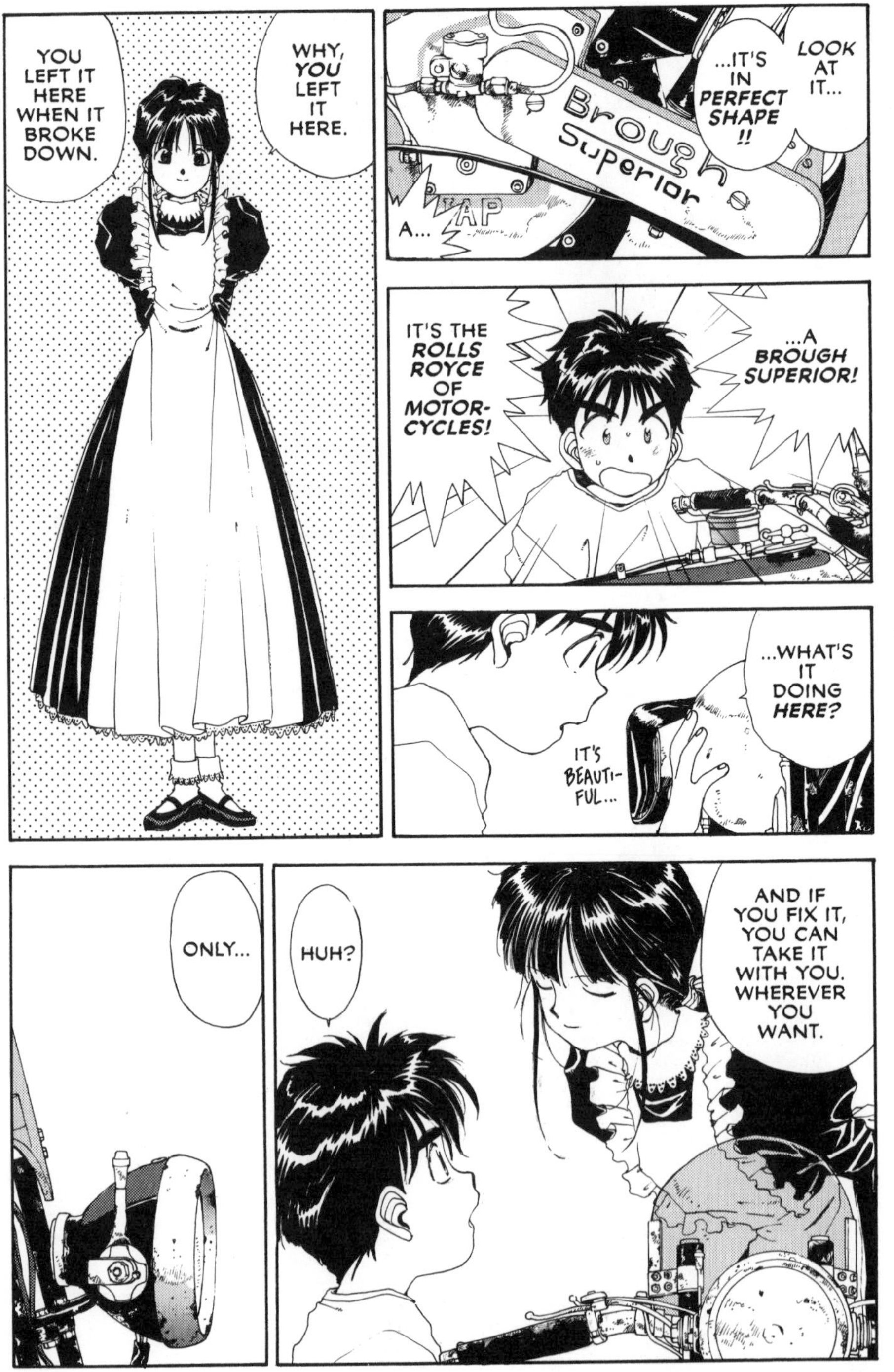
LOOK AT IT...
...IT'S IN PERFECT SHAPE !!
Brough Superior
A...
AP
...A BROUGH SUPERIOR!
IT'S THE ROLLS ROYCE OF MOTOR-CYCLES!
...WHAT'S IT DOING HERE?
IT'S BEAUTI-FUL...
WHY, YOU LEFT IT HERE.
YOU LEFT IT HERE WHEN IT BROKE DOWN.
AND IF YOU FIX IT, YOU CAN TAKE IT WITH YOU. WHEREVER YOU WANT.
HUH?
ONLY...

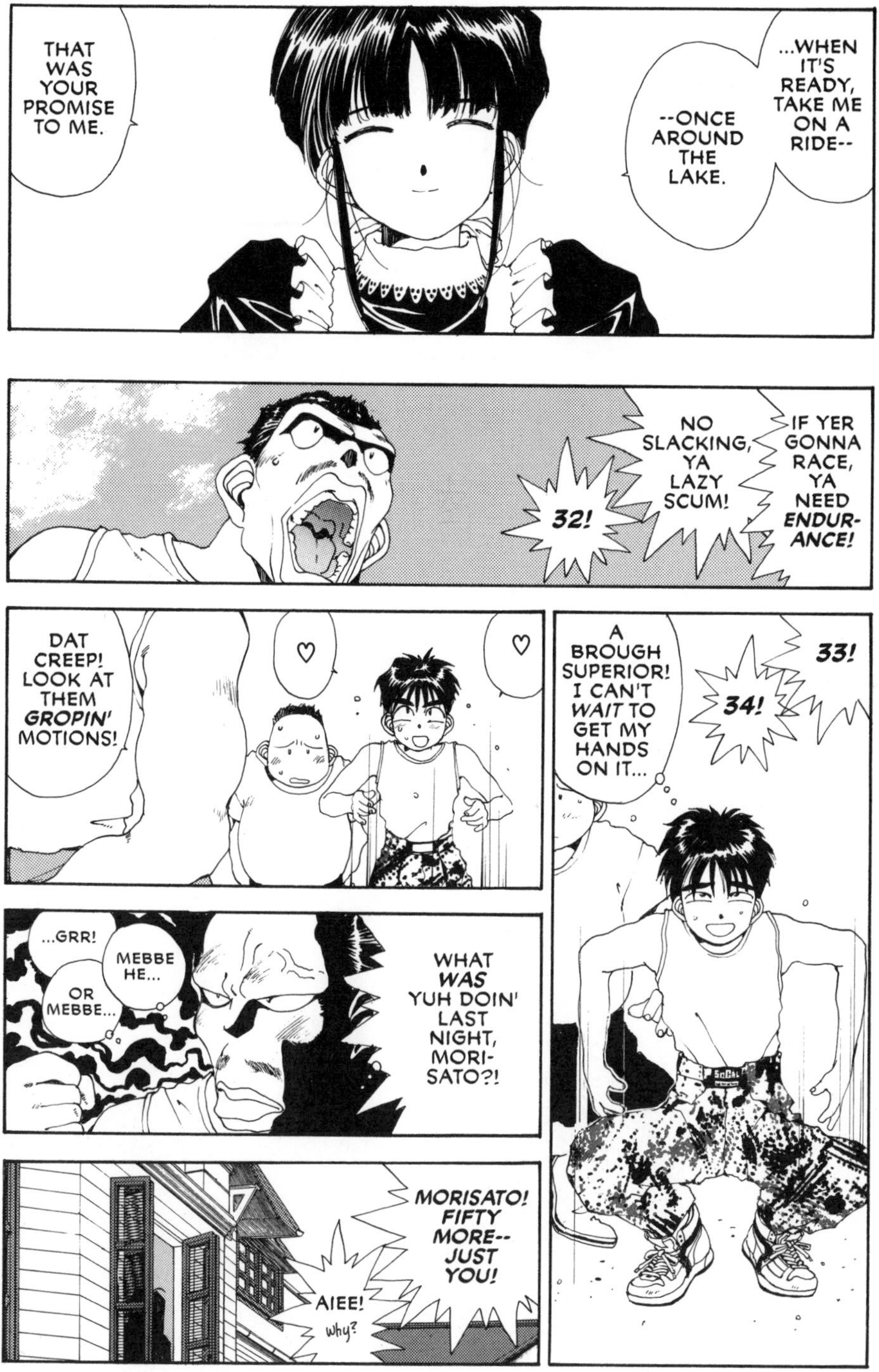
...WHEN IT'S READY, TAKE ME ON A RIDE--
--ONCE AROUND THE LAKE.
THAT WAS YOUR PROMISE TO ME.
IF YER GONNA RACE, YA NEED *ENDURANCE!*
NO SLACKING, YA LAZY SCUM!
32!
33!
34!
A BROUGH SUPERIOR! I CAN'T *WAIT* TO GET MY HANDS ON IT...
♡
♡
DAT CREEP! LOOK AT THEM *GROPIN'* MOTIONS!
WHAT *WAS* YUH DOIN' LAST NIGHT, MORISATO?!
...GRR!
MEBBE HE...
OR MEBBE...
MORISATO! FIFTY MORE-- JUST YOU!
AIEE!
why?

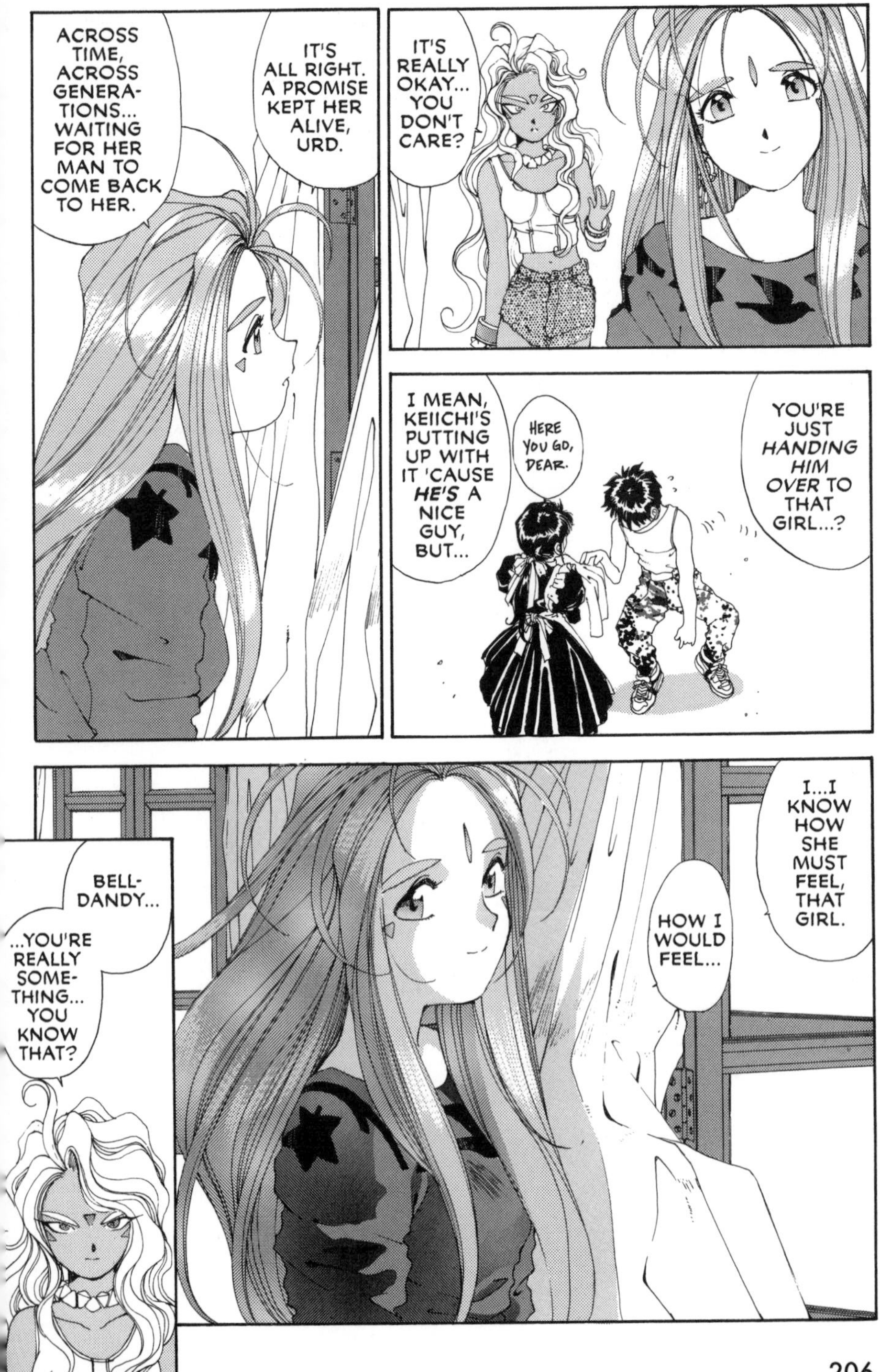
IT'S REALLY OKAY... YOU DON'T CARE?
YOU'RE JUST *HANDING HIM OVER* TO THAT GIRL...?
HERE YOU GO, DEAR.
I MEAN, KEIICHI'S PUTTING UP WITH IT 'CAUSE *HE'S* A NICE GUY, BUT...
IT'S ALL RIGHT. A PROMISE KEPT HER ALIVE, URD.
ACROSS TIME, ACROSS GENERATIONS... WAITING FOR HER MAN TO COME BACK TO HER.
I...I KNOW HOW SHE MUST FEEL, THAT GIRL.
HOW I WOULD FEEL...
BELLDANDY...
...YOU'RE REALLY SOMETHING... YOU KNOW THAT?

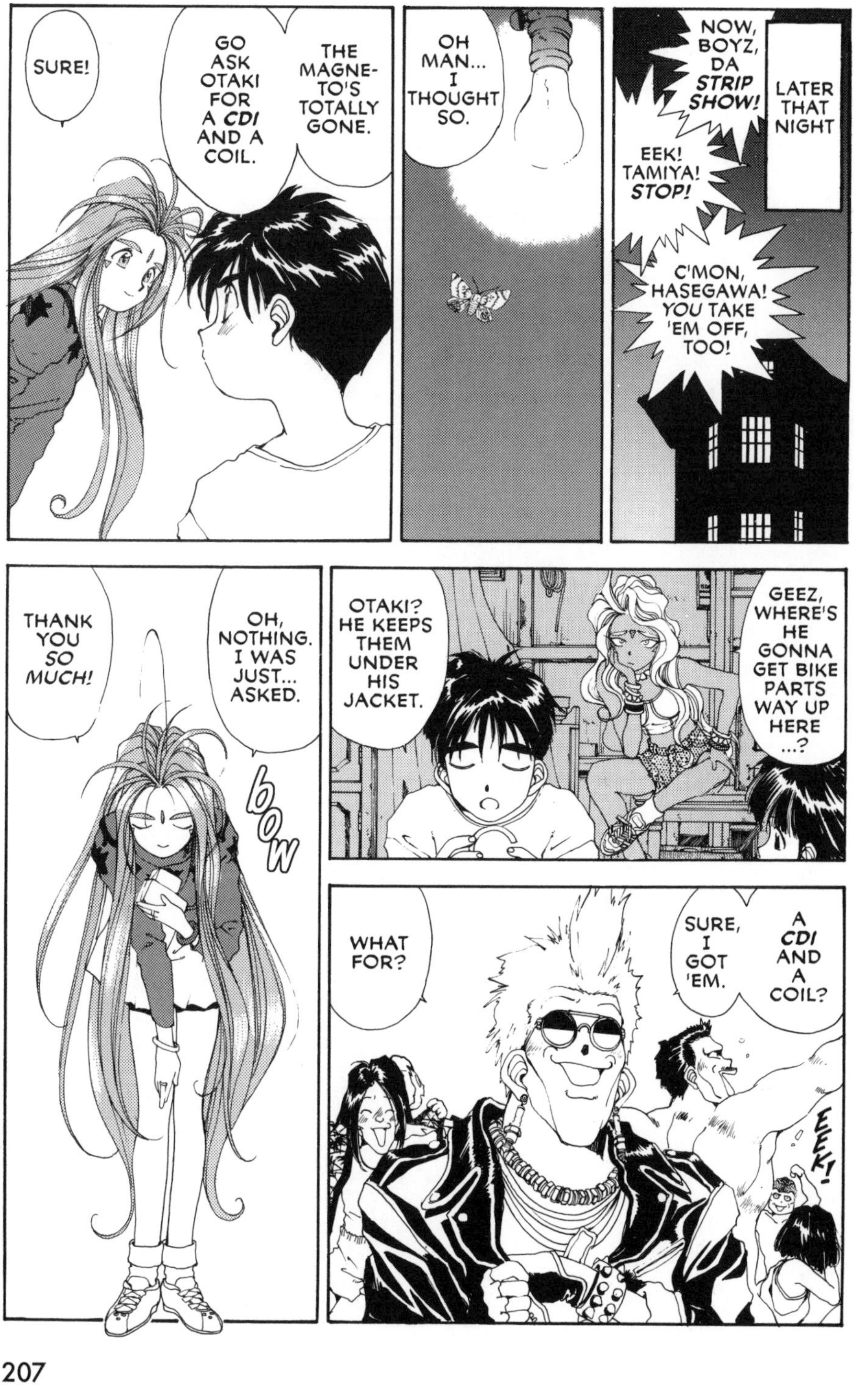
LATER THAT NIGHT
NOW, BOYZ, DA *STRIP SHOW!*
EEK! TAMIYA! *STOP!*
C'MON, HASEGAWA! *YOU* TAKE 'EM OFF, TOO!
OH MAN... I THOUGHT SO.
THE MAGNETO'S TOTALLY GONE.
GO ASK OTAKI FOR A *CDI* AND A COIL.
SURE!
GEEZ, WHERE'S HE GONNA GET BIKE PARTS WAY UP HERE ...?
OTAKI? HE KEEPS THEM UNDER HIS JACKET.
A *CDI* AND A COIL?
SURE, I GOT 'EM.
WHAT FOR?
EEK!
OH, NOTHING. I WAS JUST... ASKED.
THANK YOU *SO MUCH!*
BOW

YOU KNOW... TAMIYA WAS RIGHT.

BELL-DANDY... WHAT A *WOMAN*...

PAY! YOU'LL PAY!!

IT'S *VERY* IMPORTANT MORISATO *PAY* FOR HIS GOOD FORTUNE!

UNTIL FINALLY... ON THE LAST MORN-ING...

...WHILE THE NIGHTS WERE DEDICATED TO REPAIRING THE BROUGH.

AND THUS, DURING THE DAY THE BRUTAL (OR AS TAMIYA AND OTAKI WOULD PUT IT, "EQUITABLE AND REASONABLE") TRAINING DRAGGED ON...

MORI-SATO! FIVE MORE KM FOR YOU, SLACKER!

I'M ALMOST DEAD...

KCHNK

I'M ALMOST DONE...

BRMBBB

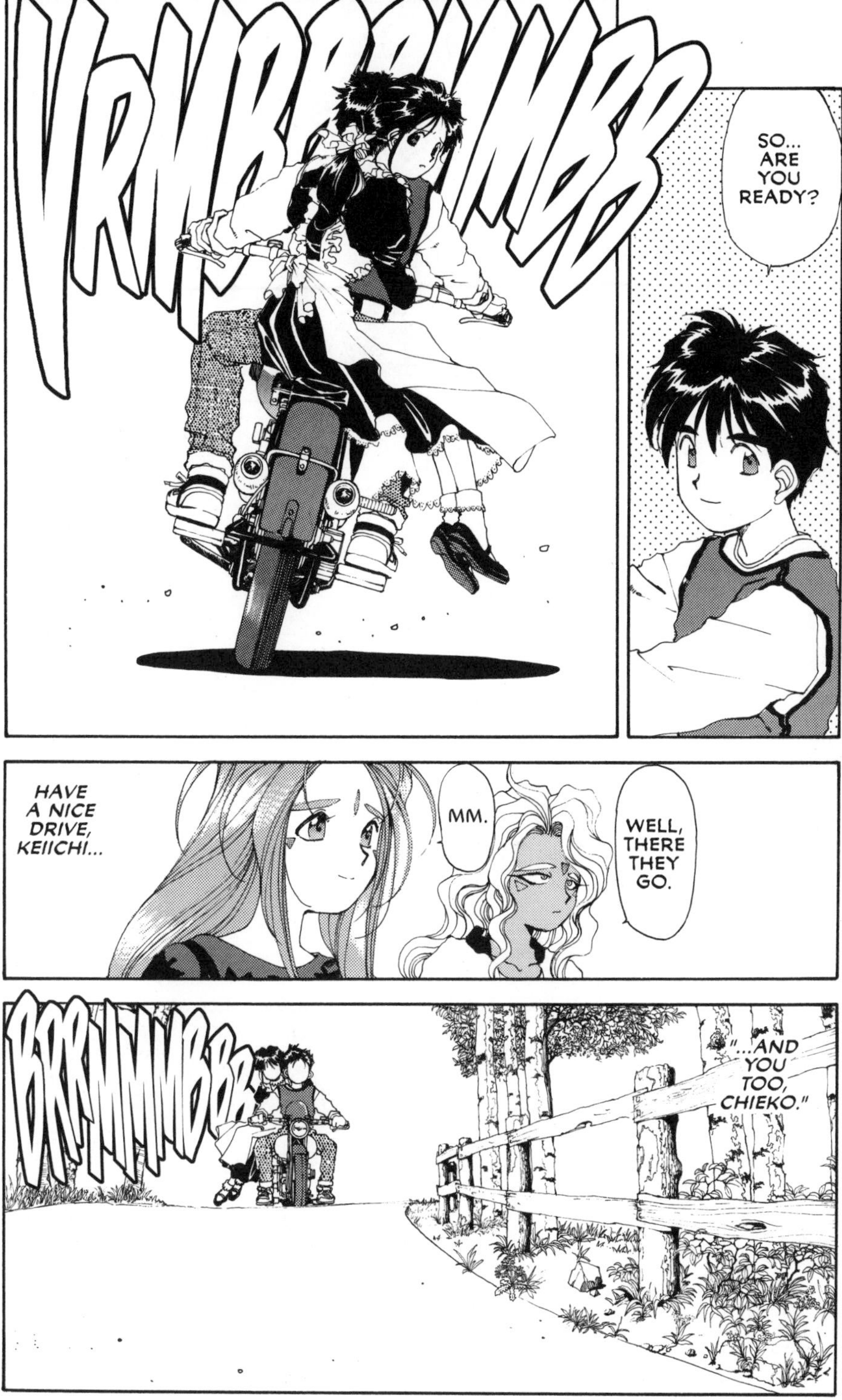
SO... ARE YOU READY?
WELL, THERE THEY GO.
MM.
HAVE A NICE DRIVE, KEIICHI...
"...AND YOU TOO, CHIEKO."

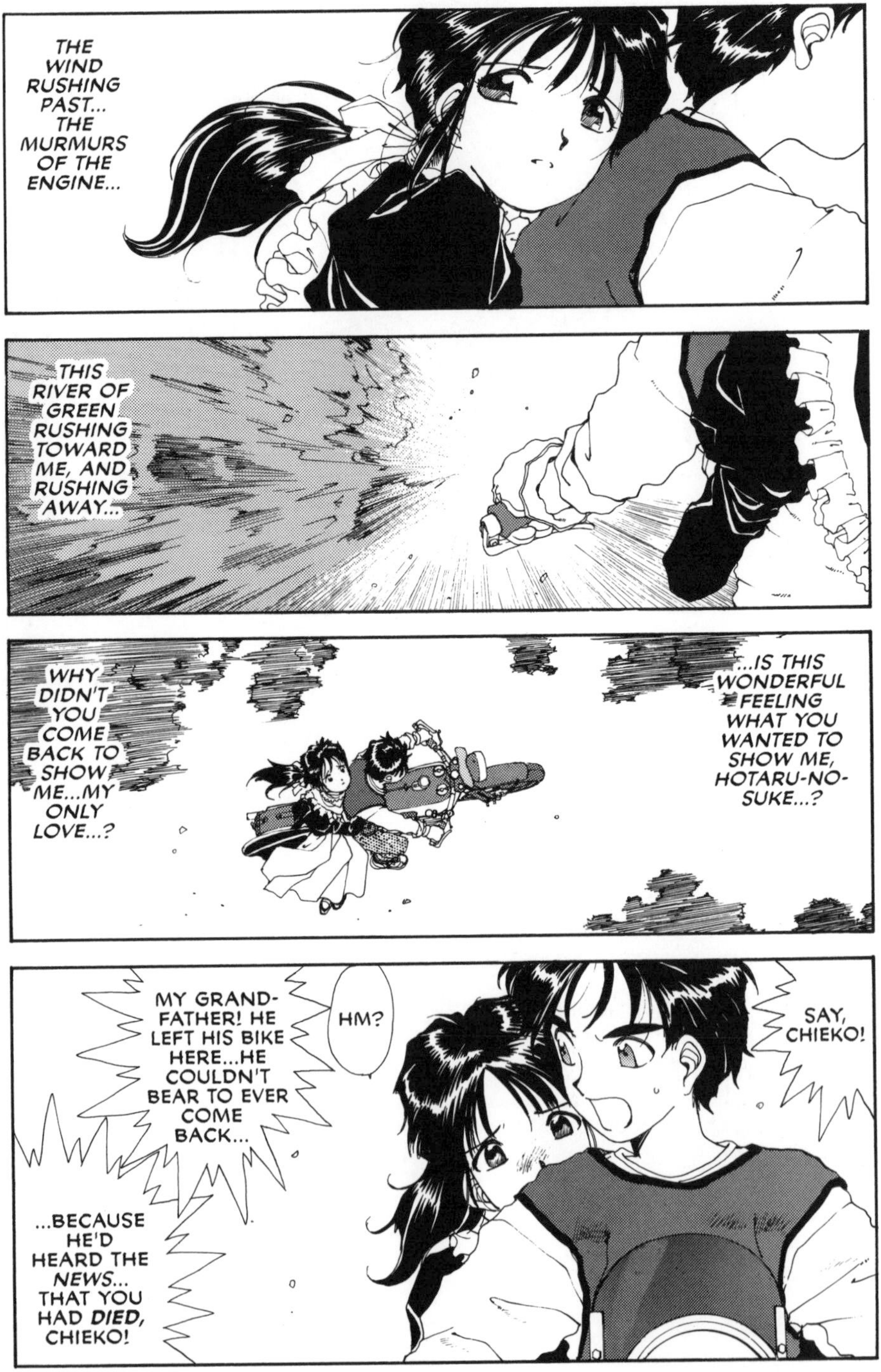
THE WIND RUSHING PAST... THE MURMURS OF THE ENGINE...
THIS RIVER OF GREEN RUSHING TOWARD ME, AND RUSHING AWAY...
...IS THIS WONDERFUL FEELING WHAT YOU WANTED TO SHOW ME, HOTARU-NO-SUKE...?
WHY DIDN'T YOU COME BACK TO SHOW ME...MY ONLY LOVE...?
SAY, CHIEKO!
HM?
MY GRAND-FATHER! HE LEFT HIS BIKE HERE...HE COULDN'T BEAR TO EVER COME BACK...
...BECAUSE HE'D HEARD THE *NEWS*... THAT YOU HAD ***DIED***, CHIEKO!

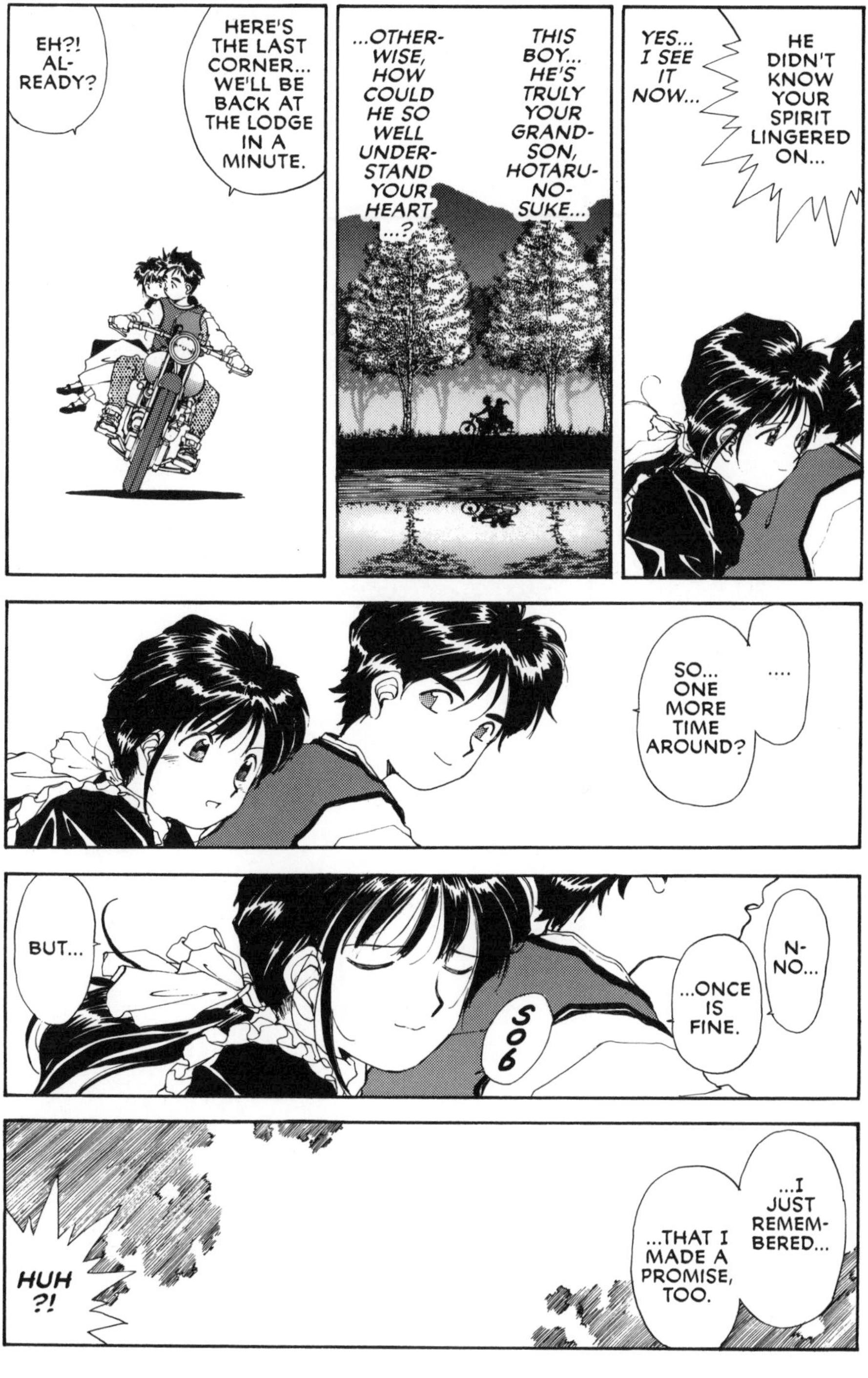

HE DIDN'T KNOW YOUR SPIRIT LINGERED ON...
YES... I SEE IT NOW...
THIS BOY... HE'S TRULY YOUR GRANDSON, HOTARU-NO-SUKE...
...OTHERWISE, HOW COULD HE SO WELL UNDERSTAND YOUR HEART...?
HERE'S THE LAST CORNER... WE'LL BE BACK AT THE LODGE IN A MINUTE.
EH?! ALREADY?
....
SO... ONE MORE TIME AROUND?
N-NO...
...ONCE IS FINE.
SOB
BUT...
...I JUST REMEMBERED...
...THAT I MADE A PROMISE, TOO.
HUH?!

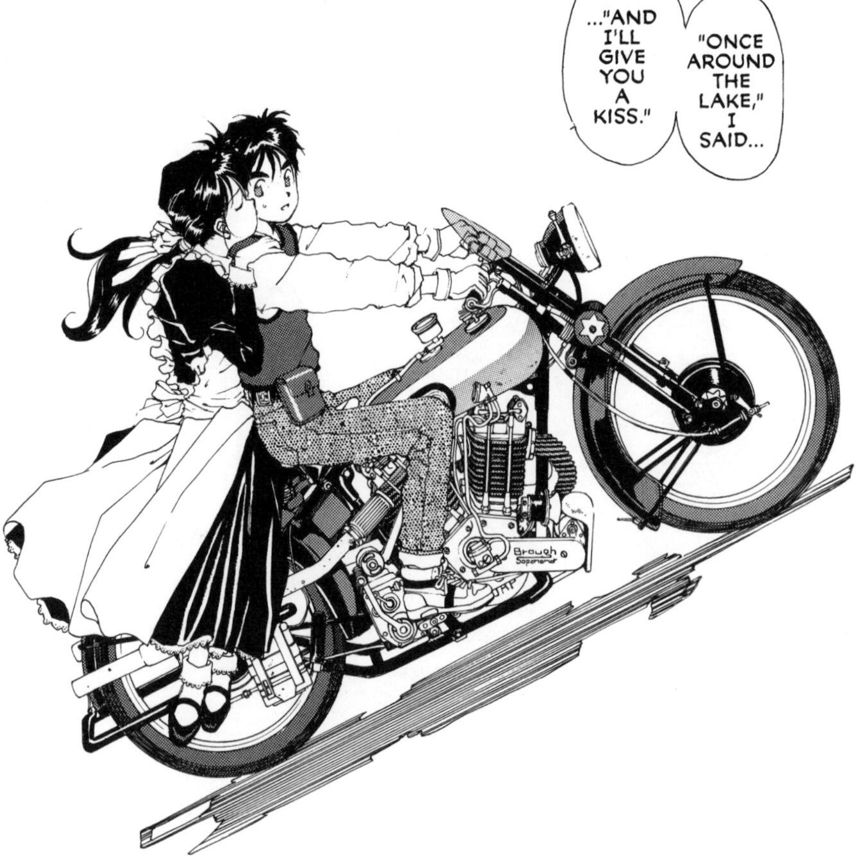
"ONCE AROUND THE LAKE," I SAID...
..."AND I'LL GIVE YOU A KISS."

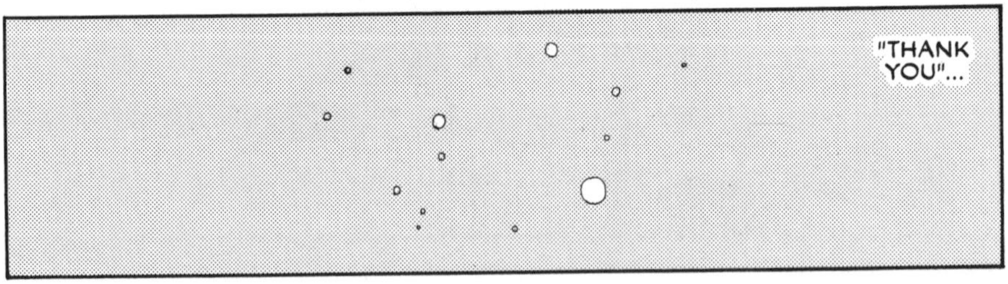
"THANK YOU"...

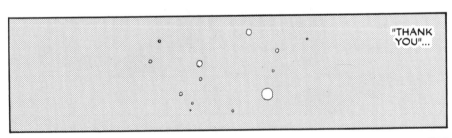

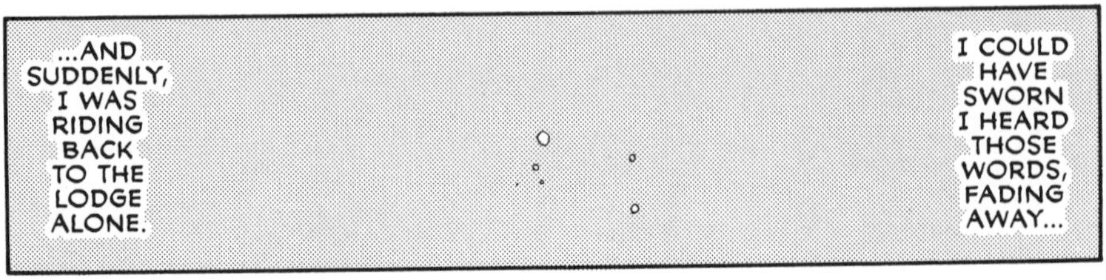
I COULD HAVE SWORN I HEARD THOSE WORDS, FADING AWAY...
...AND SUDDENLY, I WAS RIDING BACK TO THE LODGE ALONE.

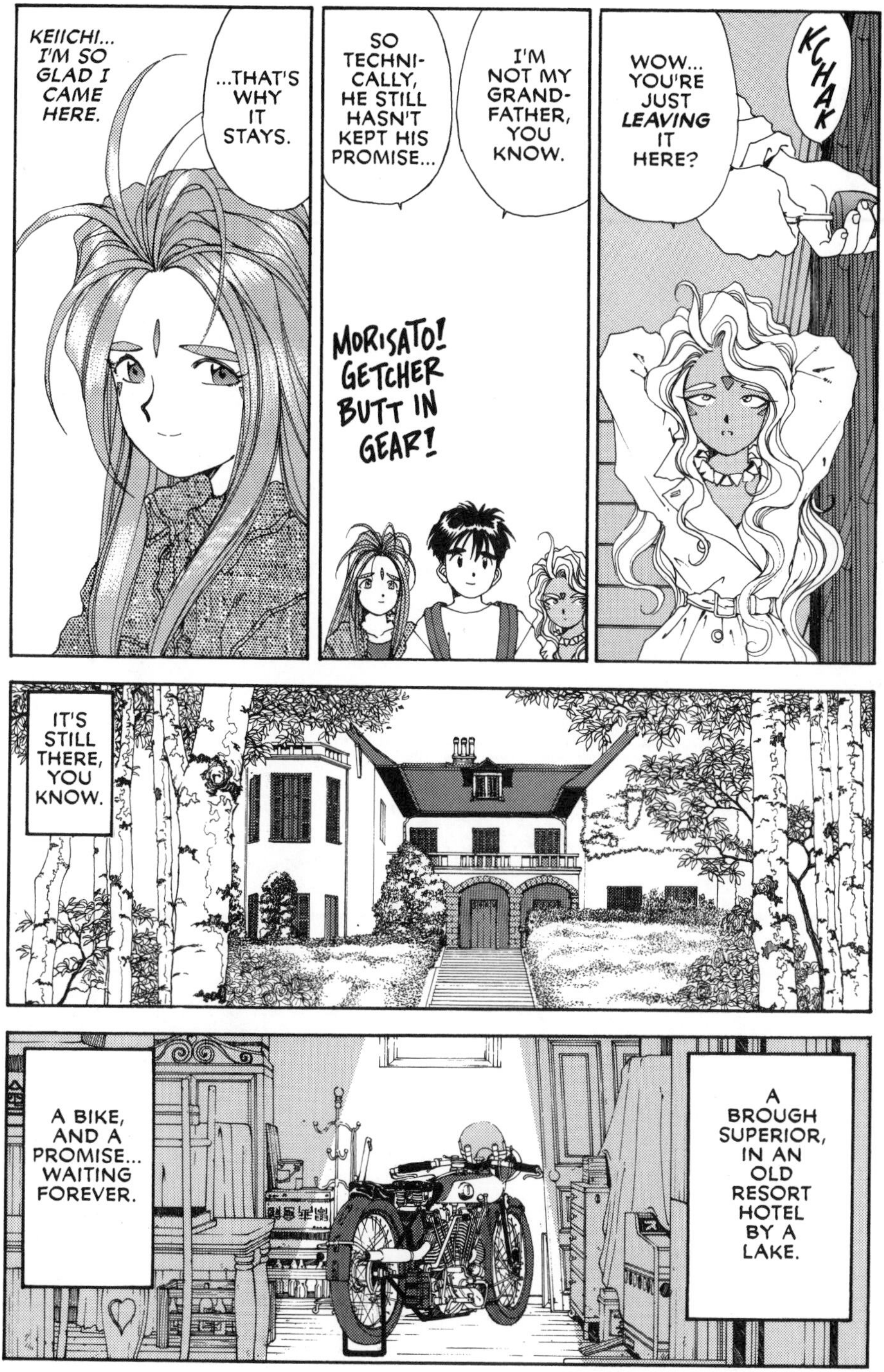
KCHAK
WOW... YOU'RE JUST *LEAVING* IT HERE?
I'M NOT MY GRANDFATHER, YOU KNOW.
SO TECHNICALLY, HE STILL HASN'T KEPT HIS PROMISE...
MORISATO! GETCHER BUTT IN GEAR!
...THAT'S WHY IT STAYS.
KEIICHI... I'M SO GLAD I CAME HERE.
IT'S STILL THERE, YOU KNOW.
A BROUGH SUPERIOR, IN AN OLD RESORT HOTEL BY A LAKE.
A BIKE, AND A PROMISE... WAITING FOREVER.

THE ADVENTURES OF MINI-URD

Now with added MINI-SKULD!

◆ SUPER SPIKE! ◆

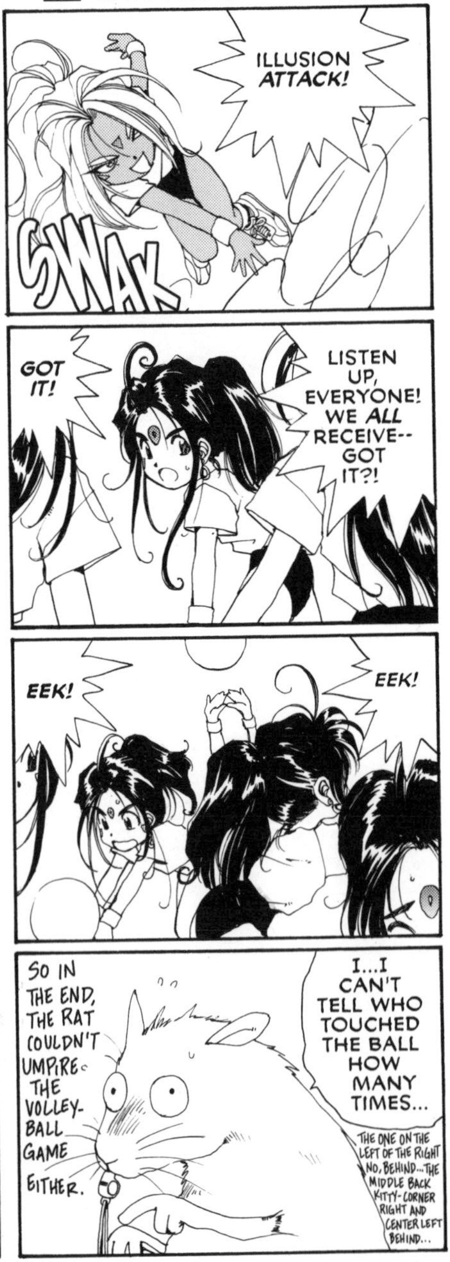
ILLUSION ATTACK!
SWAK
LISTEN UP, EVERYONE! WE ALL RECEIVE--GOT IT?!
GOT IT!
EEK!
EEK!
I...I CAN'T TELL WHO TOUCHED THE BALL HOW MANY TIMES...
THE ONE ON THE LEFT OF THE RIGHT NO, BEHIND...THE MIDDLE BACK KITTY-CORNER RIGHT AND CENTER LEFT BEHIND...
SO IN THE END, THE RAT COULDN'T UMPIRE THE VOLLEY-BALL GAME EITHER.

◆ ATTACKING FURIES ◆

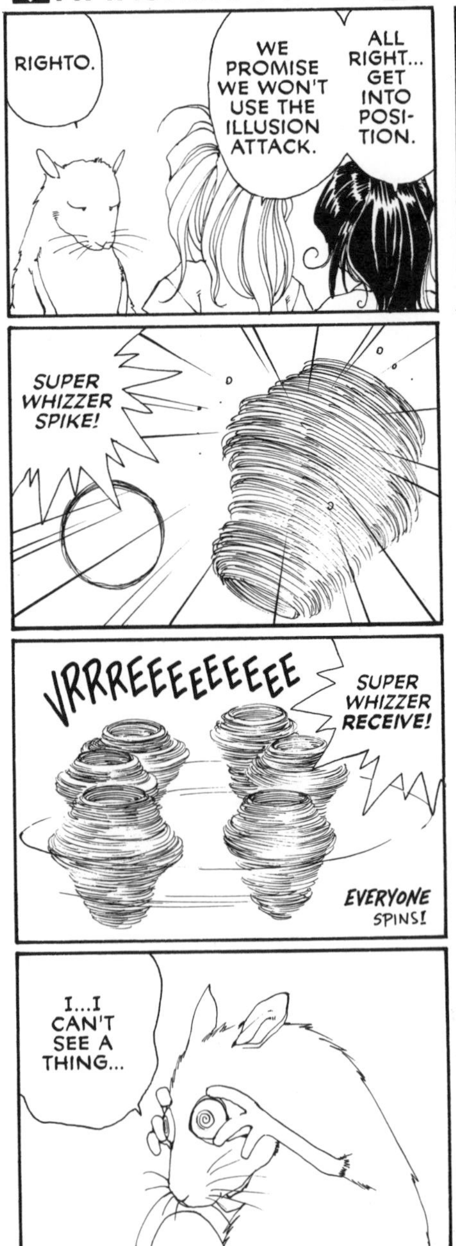
ALL RIGHT... GET INTO POSI-TION.
WE PROMISE WE WON'T USE THE ILLUSION ATTACK.
RIGHTO.
SUPER WHIZZER SPIKE!
SUPER WHIZZER RECEIVE!
VRRREEEEEEEEE
EVERYONE SPINS!
I...I CAN'T SEE A THING...

◆ IT HAS ITS ADVANTAGES ◆

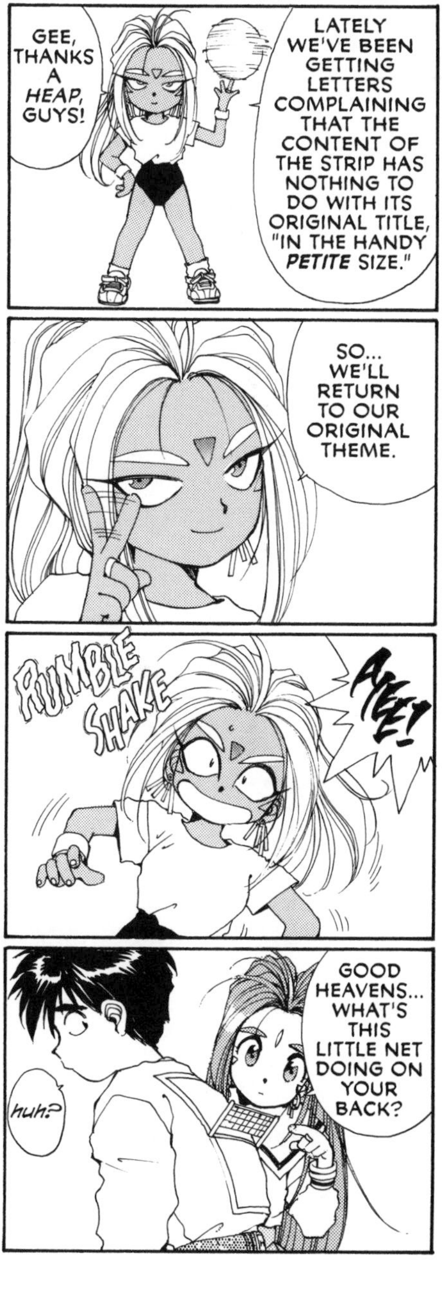
LATELY WE'VE BEEN GETTING LETTERS COMPLAINING THAT THE CONTENT OF THE STRIP HAS NOTHING TO DO WITH ITS ORIGINAL TITLE, "IN THE HANDY *PETITE* SIZE."
GEE, THANKS A *HEAP*, GUYS!
SO... WE'LL RETURN TO OUR ORIGINAL THEME.
AIEE!
RUMBLE
SHAKE
GOOD HEAVENS... WHAT'S THIS LITTLE NET DOING ON YOUR BACK?
huh?

◆ AN IDOL APPEARS— ◆ INTRODUCING THE NEW URD!

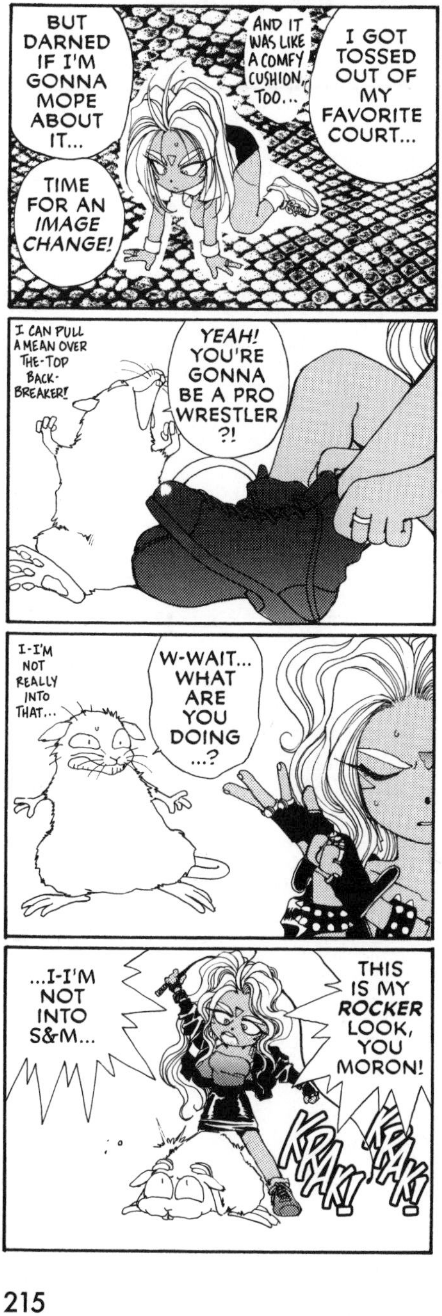
I GOT TOSSED OUT OF MY FAVORITE COURT...
AND IT WAS LIKE A COMFY CUSHION, TOO...
BUT DARNED IF I'M GONNA MOPE ABOUT IT...
TIME FOR AN *IMAGE CHANGE!*
YEAH! YOU'RE GONNA BE A PRO WRESTLER?!
I CAN PULL A MEAN OVER-THE-TOP BACK-BREAKER!
W-WAIT... WHAT ARE YOU DOING...?
I-I'M NOT REALLY INTO THAT...
THIS IS MY *ROCKER* LOOK, YOU MORON!
...I-I'M NOT INTO S&M...
KRAK!
KRAK!

◆ IT'S THE NON-STOP ROCK SHOW! ◆

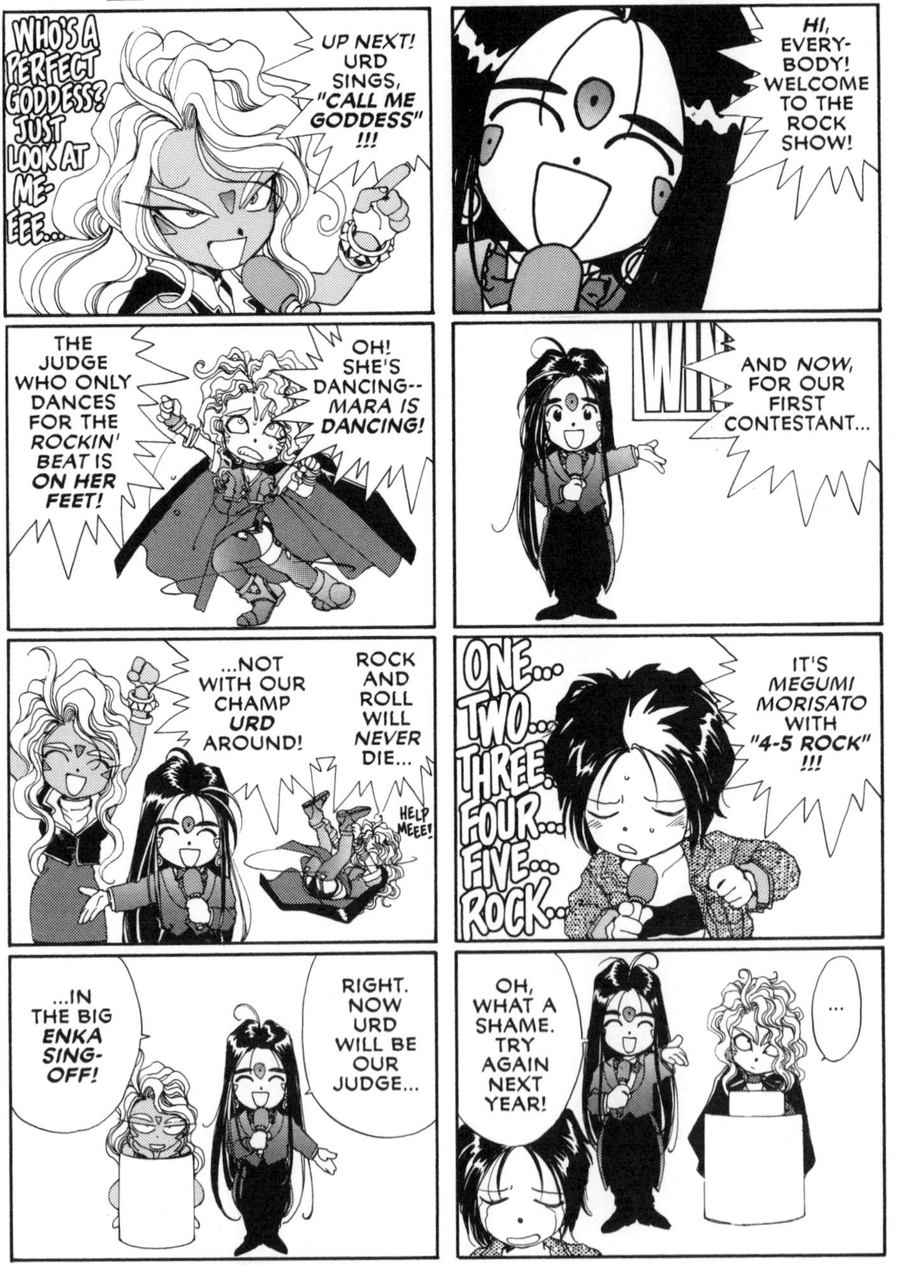
HI, EVERY-BODY! WELCOME TO THE ROCK SHOW!
UP NEXT! URD SINGS, "CALL ME GODDESS" !!!
WHO'S A PERFECT GODDESS? JUST LOOK AT ME-EEE...
AND NOW, FOR OUR FIRST CONTESTANT...
OH! SHE'S DANCING-- MARA IS DANCING!
THE JUDGE WHO ONLY DANCES FOR THE ROCKIN' BEAT IS ON HER FEET!
IT'S MEGUMI MORISATO WITH "4-5 ROCK" !!!
ONE... TWO... THREE... FOUR... FIVE... ROCK...
ROCK AND ROLL WILL NEVER DIE...
...NOT WITH OUR CHAMP URD AROUND!
HELP MEEE!
...
OH, WHAT A SHAME. TRY AGAIN NEXT YEAR!
RIGHT. NOW URD WILL BE OUR JUDGE...
...IN THE BIG ENKA SING-OFF!

CHAPTER 49

Lunchbox with Love

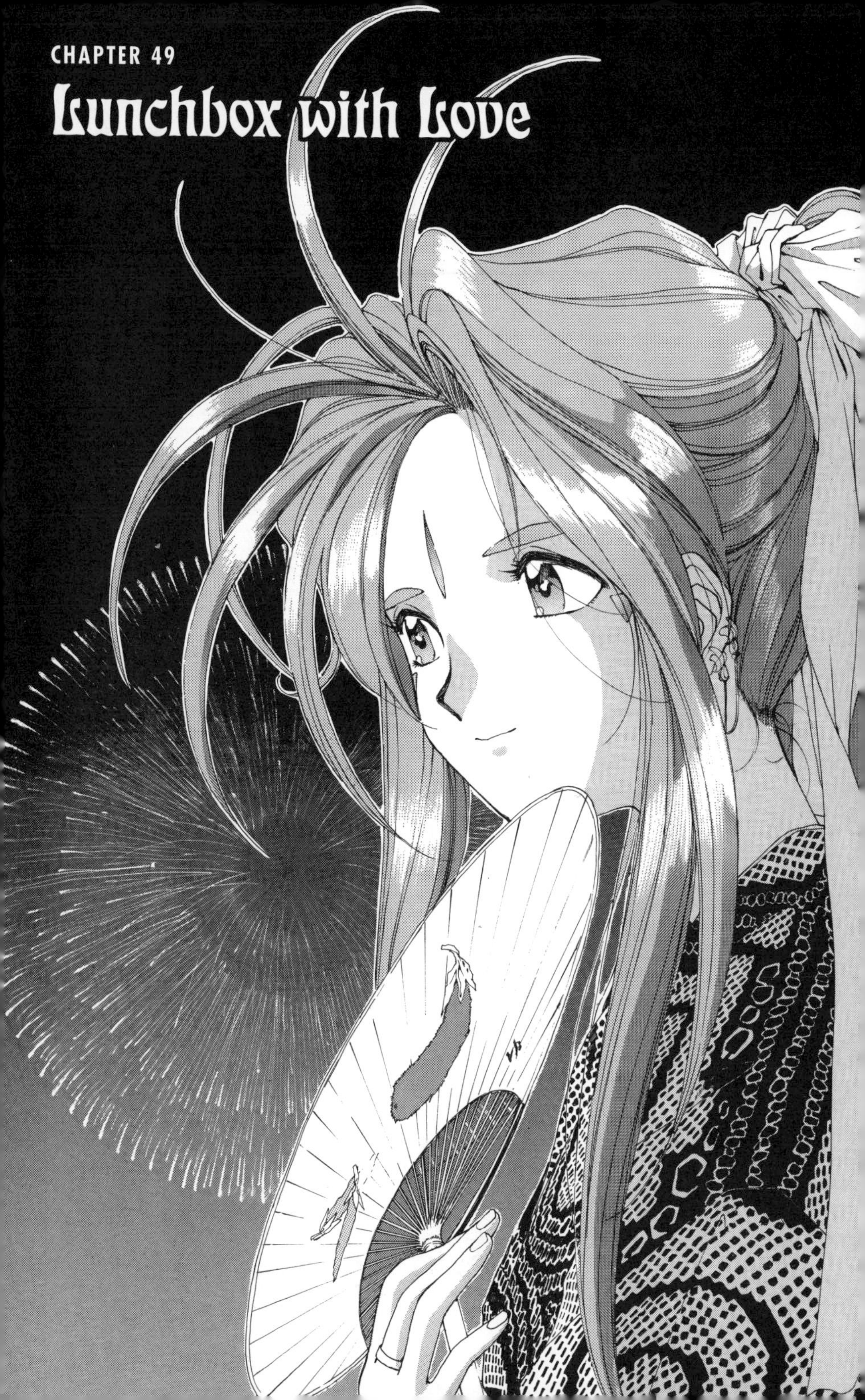

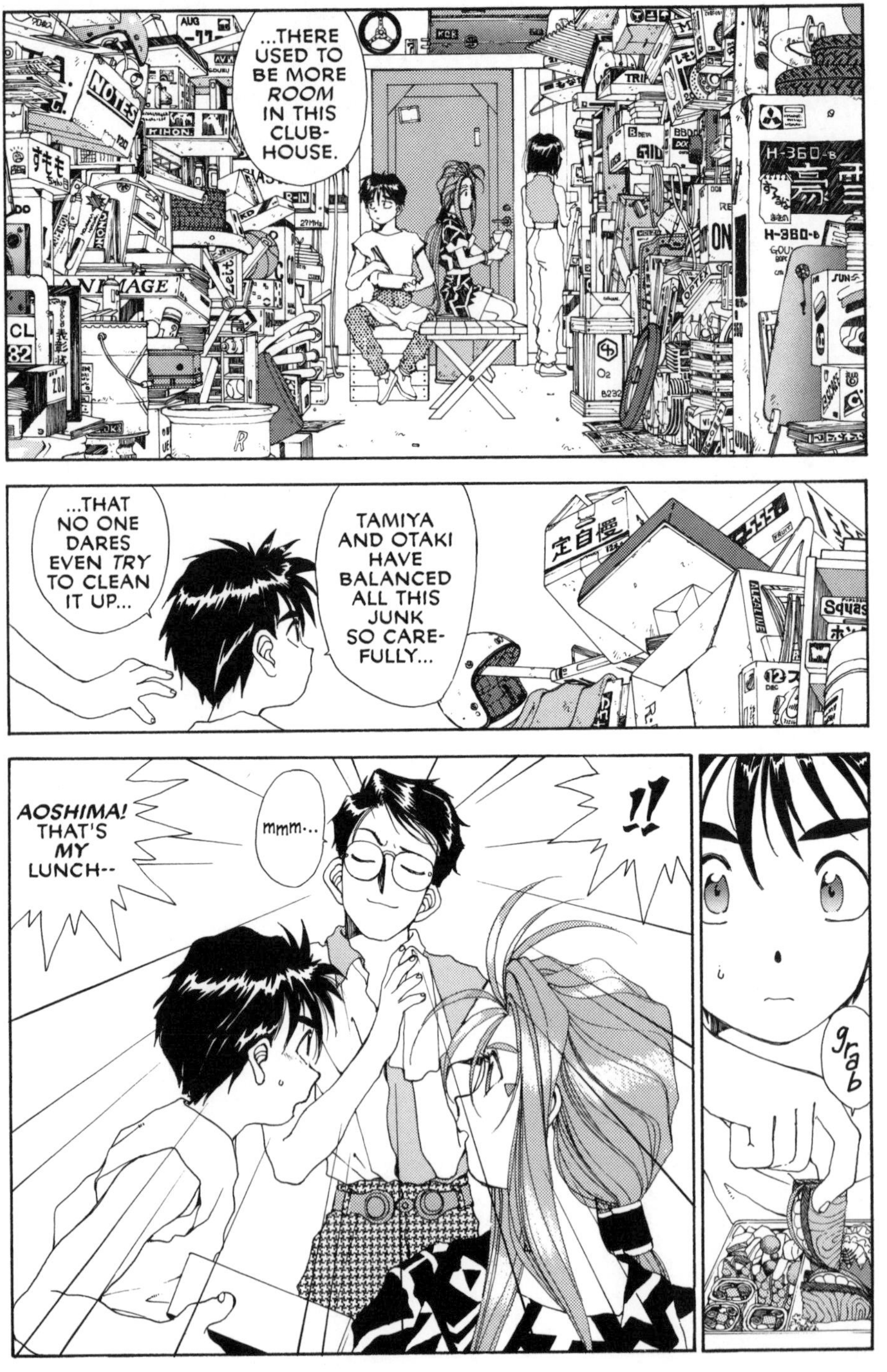
...THERE USED TO BE MORE ROOM IN THIS CLUB-HOUSE.
TAMIYA AND OTAKI HAVE BALANCED ALL THIS JUNK SO CARE-FULLY...
...THAT NO ONE DARES EVEN TRY TO CLEAN IT UP...
grab
!!
mmm...
AOSHIMA! THAT'S MY LUNCH--

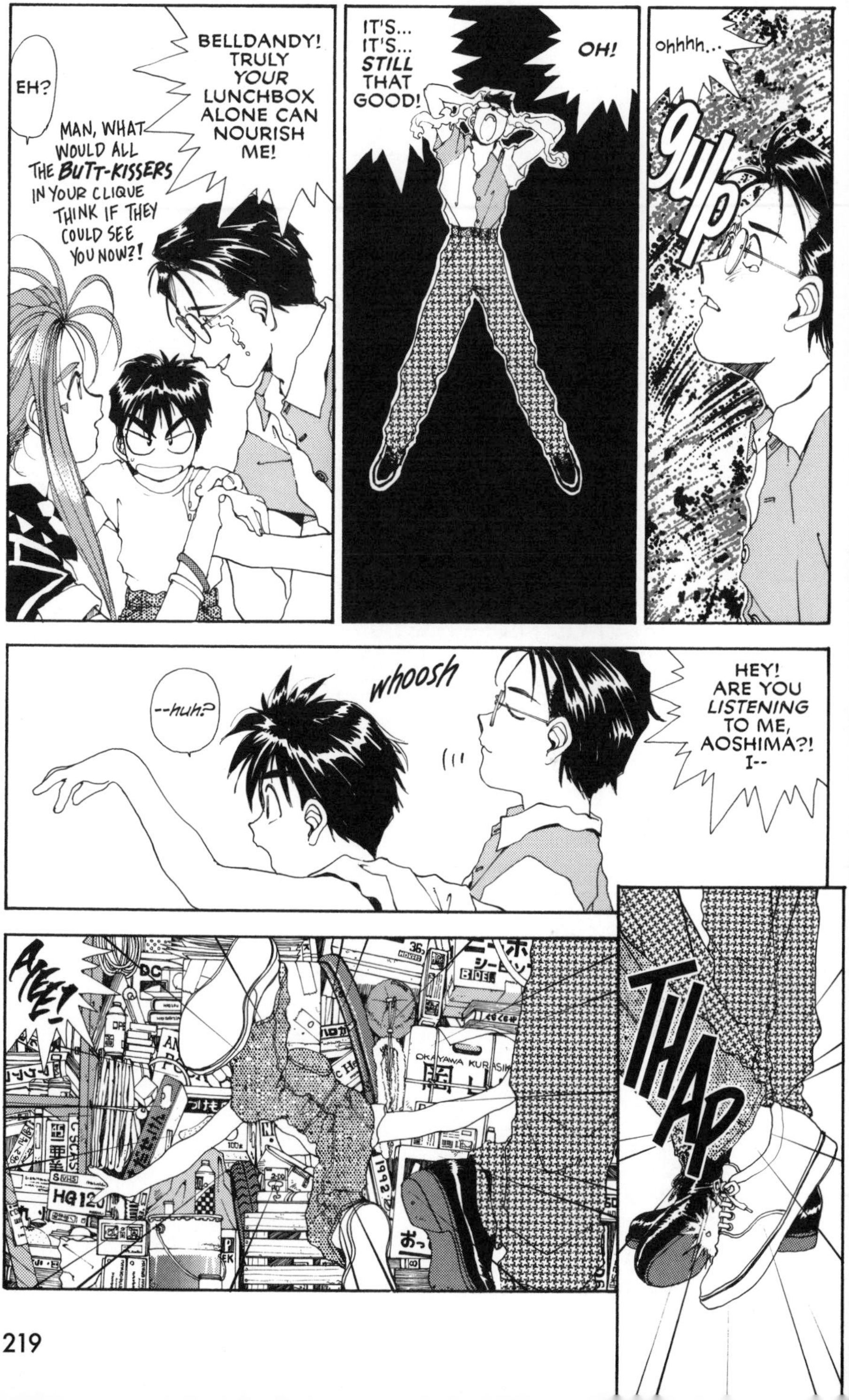
ohhhh...
gulp
IT'S... IT'S... STILL THAT GOOD!
OH!
BELLDANDY! TRULY YOUR LUNCHBOX ALONE CAN NOURISH ME!
EH?
MAN, WHAT WOULD ALL THE BUTT-KISSERS IN YOUR CLIQUE THINK IF THEY COULD SEE YOU NOW?!
HEY! ARE YOU LISTENING TO ME, AOSHIMA?! I--
whoosh
--huh?
THAP!
AIEEE!

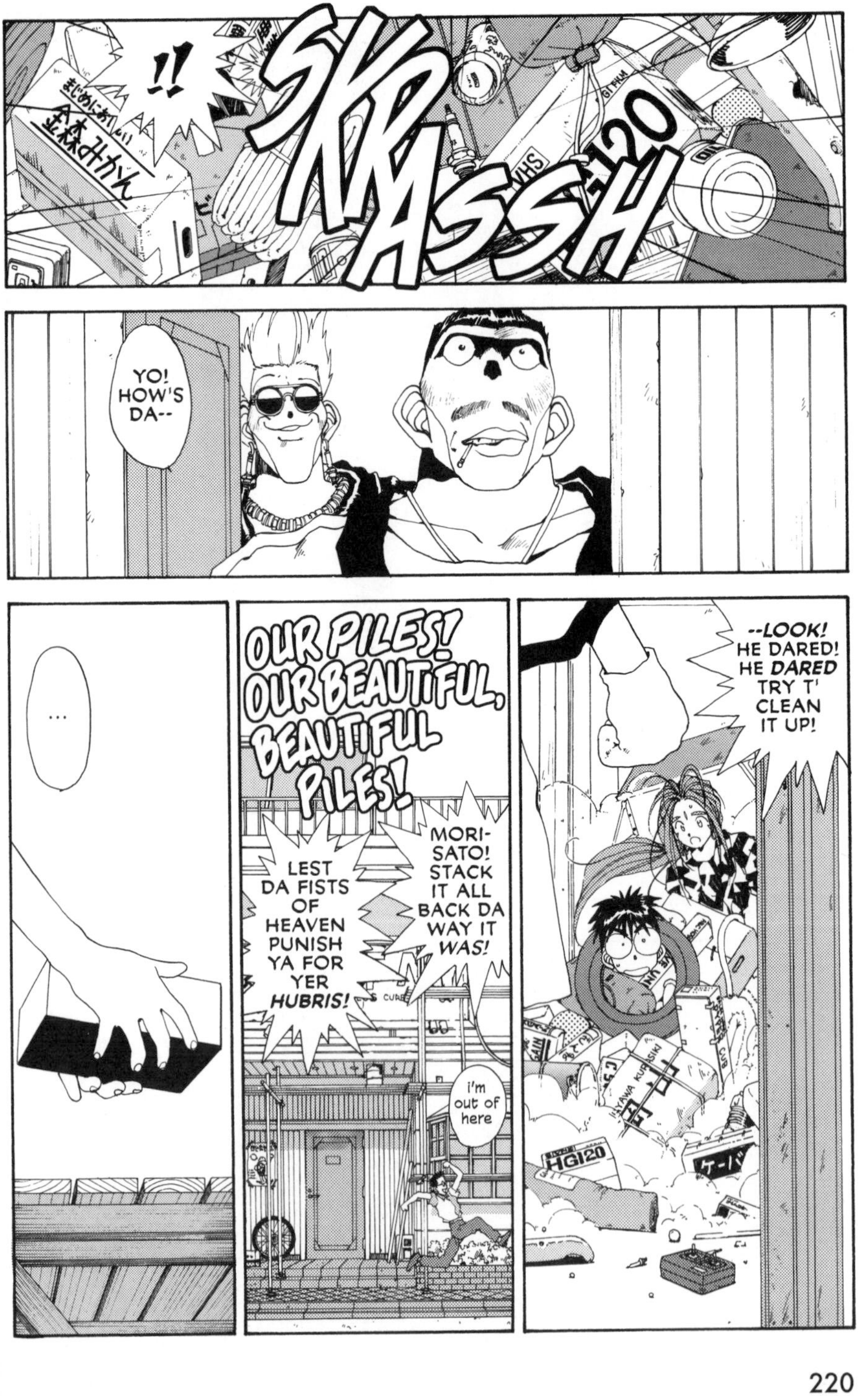
!!
SKRASSH
YO! HOW'S DA--
--LOOK! HE DARED! HE DARED TRY T' CLEAN IT UP!
OUR PILES! OUR BEAUTIFUL, BEAUTIFUL PILES!
MORI-SATO! STACK IT ALL BACK DA WAY IT WAS!
LEST DA FISTS OF HEAVEN PUNISH YA FOR YER HUBRIS!
i'm out of here
...

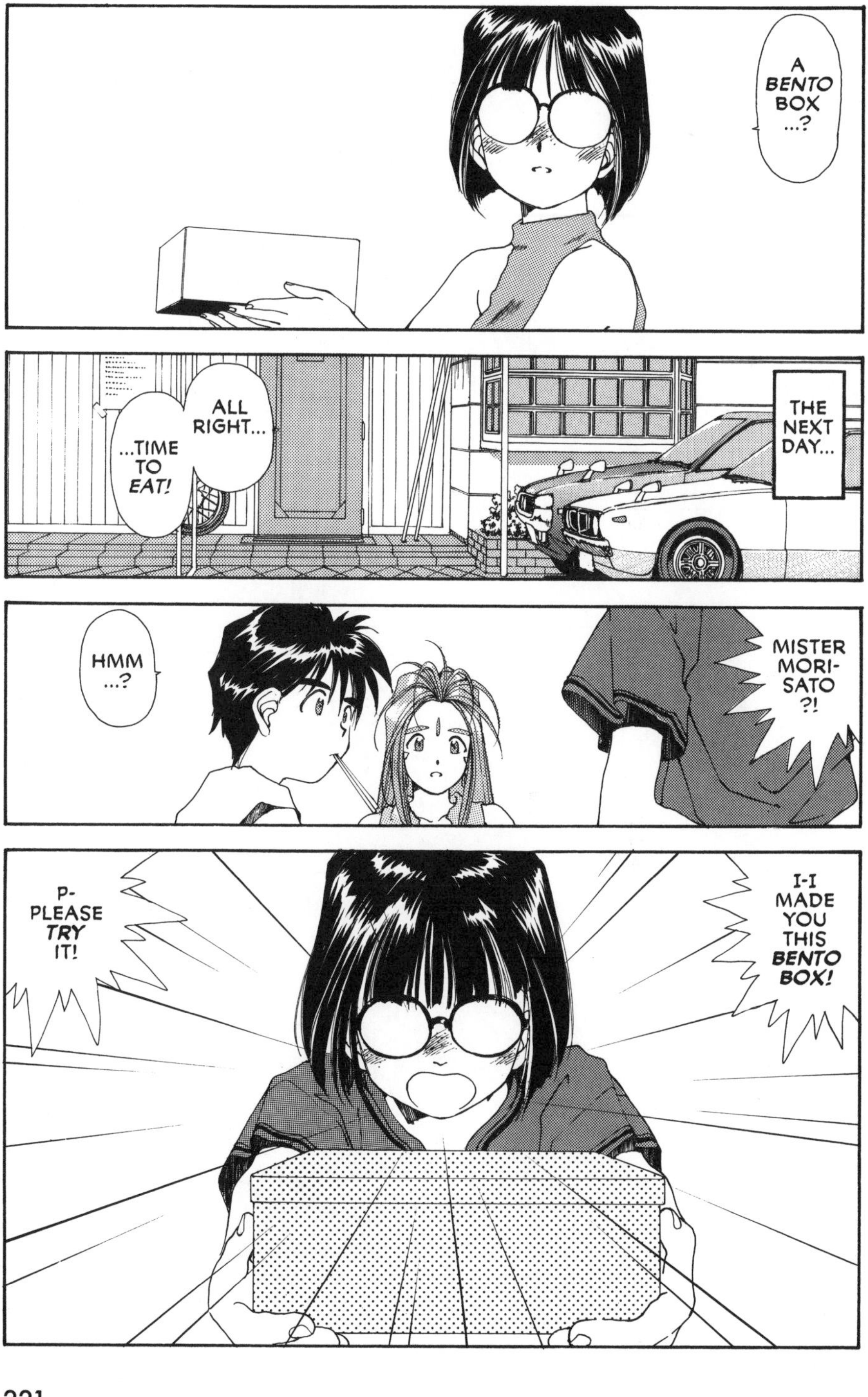
A BENTO BOX ...?
THE NEXT DAY...
ALL RIGHT...
...TIME TO EAT!
MISTER MORI-SATO?!
HMM ...?
I-I MADE YOU THIS BENTO BOX!
P-PLEASE TRY IT!

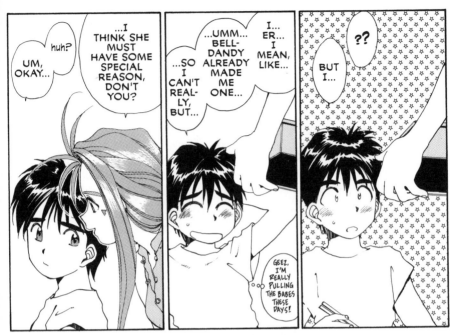

UM, OKAY...

huh?

...I THINK SHE MUST HAVE SOME SPECIAL REASON, DON'T YOU?

...SO I CAN'T REALLY, BUT...

...UMM... BELL-DANDY ALREADY MADE ME ONE...

I... ER... I MEAN, LIKE...

??

BUT I...

GEEZ, I'M REALLY PULLING THE BABES THESE DAYS!

OKAY. UNDERSTOOD. I'LL EAT IT.

I CAN TAKE A HINT WHEN IT'S APPLIED WITH A SLEDGE-HAMMER.

LOVE NOT AM IN I!

NO! NOT THAT I'M IN LOVE!

um

YES! BUT IT'S NOT THAT I'M IN LOVE WITH YOU, SIR!

SO DON'T GO GIVING IT TO AOSHIMA... OKAY?

...BUT BELLDANDY, I'LL HAVE YOURS RIGHT AFTERWARDS.

222

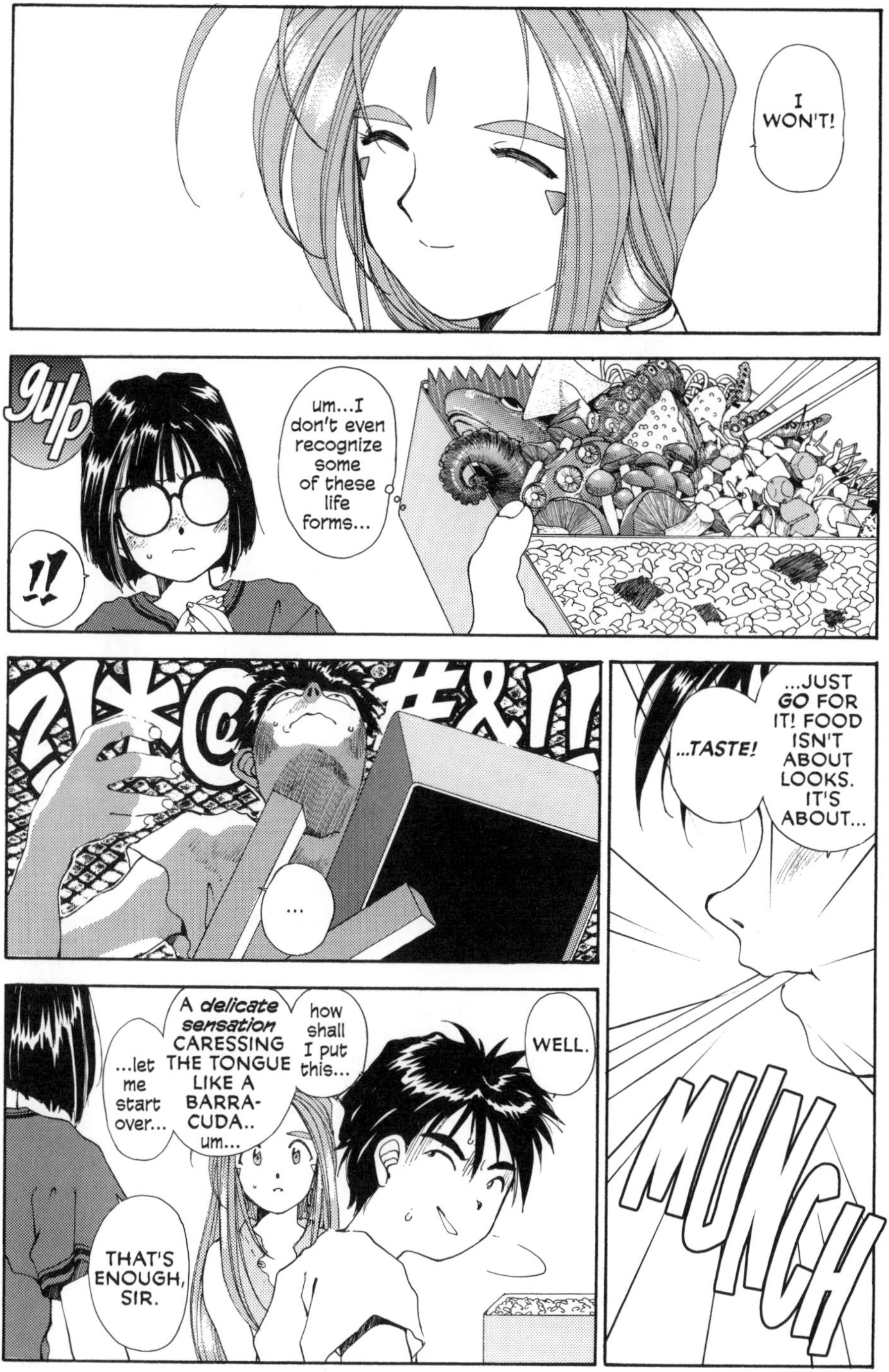
I WON'T!
um...I don't even recognize some of these life forms...
gulp
!!
...JUST *GO* FOR IT! FOOD ISN'T ABOUT LOOKS. IT'S ABOUT...
...*TASTE!*
MUNCH
...
WELL.
how shall I put this...
A *delicate sensation* CARESSING THE TONGUE LIKE A BARRA-CUDA.. um...
...let me start over...
THAT'S ENOUGH, SIR.

AND ON MY REPORT CARDS, MY TEACHERS ALWAYS WROTE... H-HORRIBLE THINGS...

Perhaps Sora would benefit from practicing her cooking at home. Preferably in an air lock.

She's poison.

EVER SINCE ELEMENTARY SCHOOL I'VE GOTTEN FAILING GRADES IN HOME ECONOMICS!

...MY COOKING IS *AWFUL.*

I KNOW... I KNOW AL-READY...

I MEAN...

...HOW-*HOW* MUCH OF THAT DID I EAT...?

AND Y-YET... AND YET I WANT...

THEY CALLED ME... HASEGAWA... *THE CHEF ASSASSIN...*

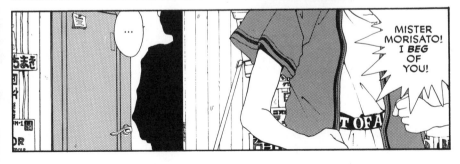

...

MISTER MORISATO! I *BEG* OF YOU!

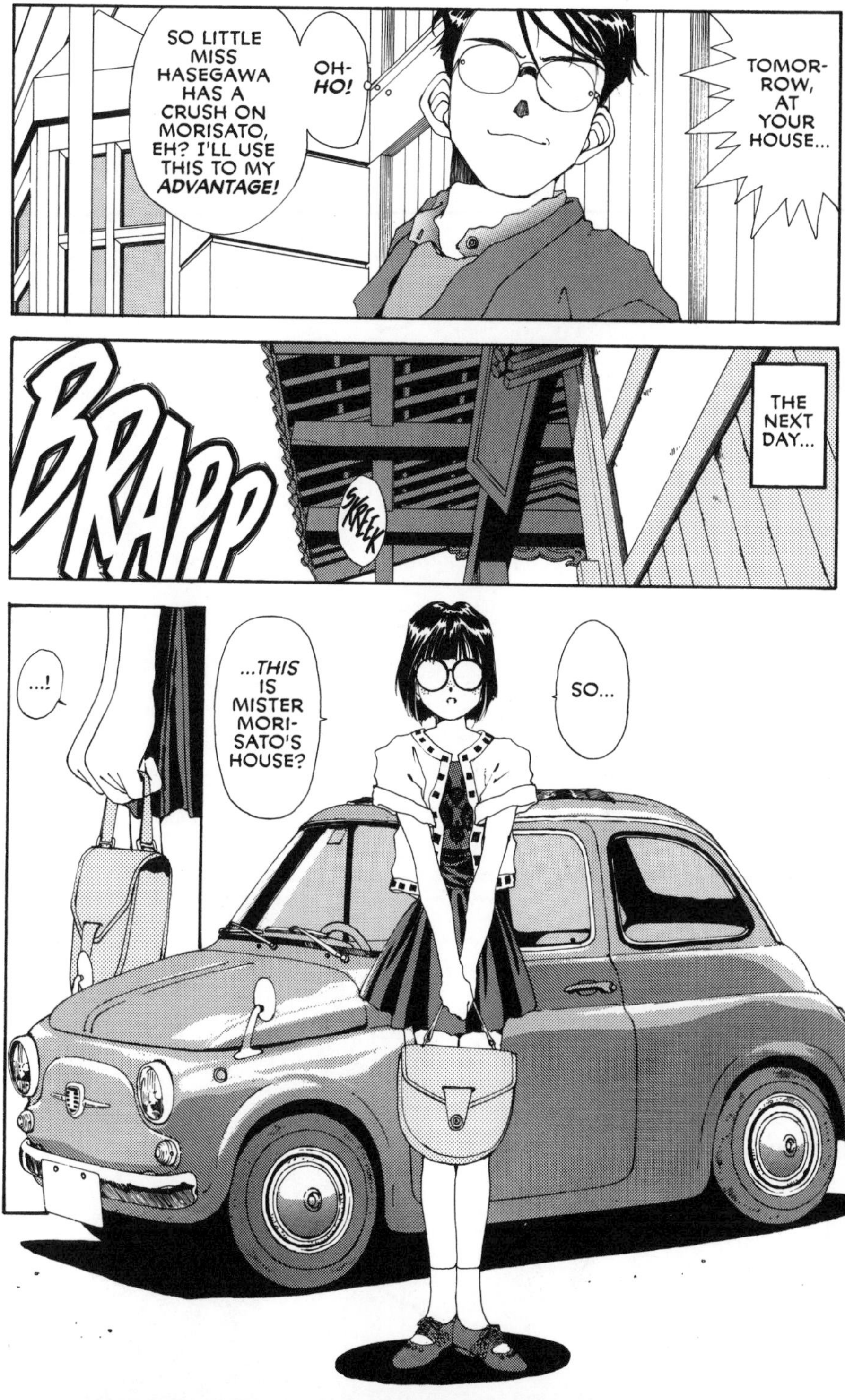
TOMORROW, AT YOUR HOUSE...
OH-HO!
SO LITTLE MISS HASEGAWA HAS A CRUSH ON MORISATO, EH? I'LL USE THIS TO MY *ADVANTAGE!*
THE NEXT DAY...
SKREEK
BRAPP
SO...
...*THIS* IS MISTER MORISATO'S HOUSE?
...!

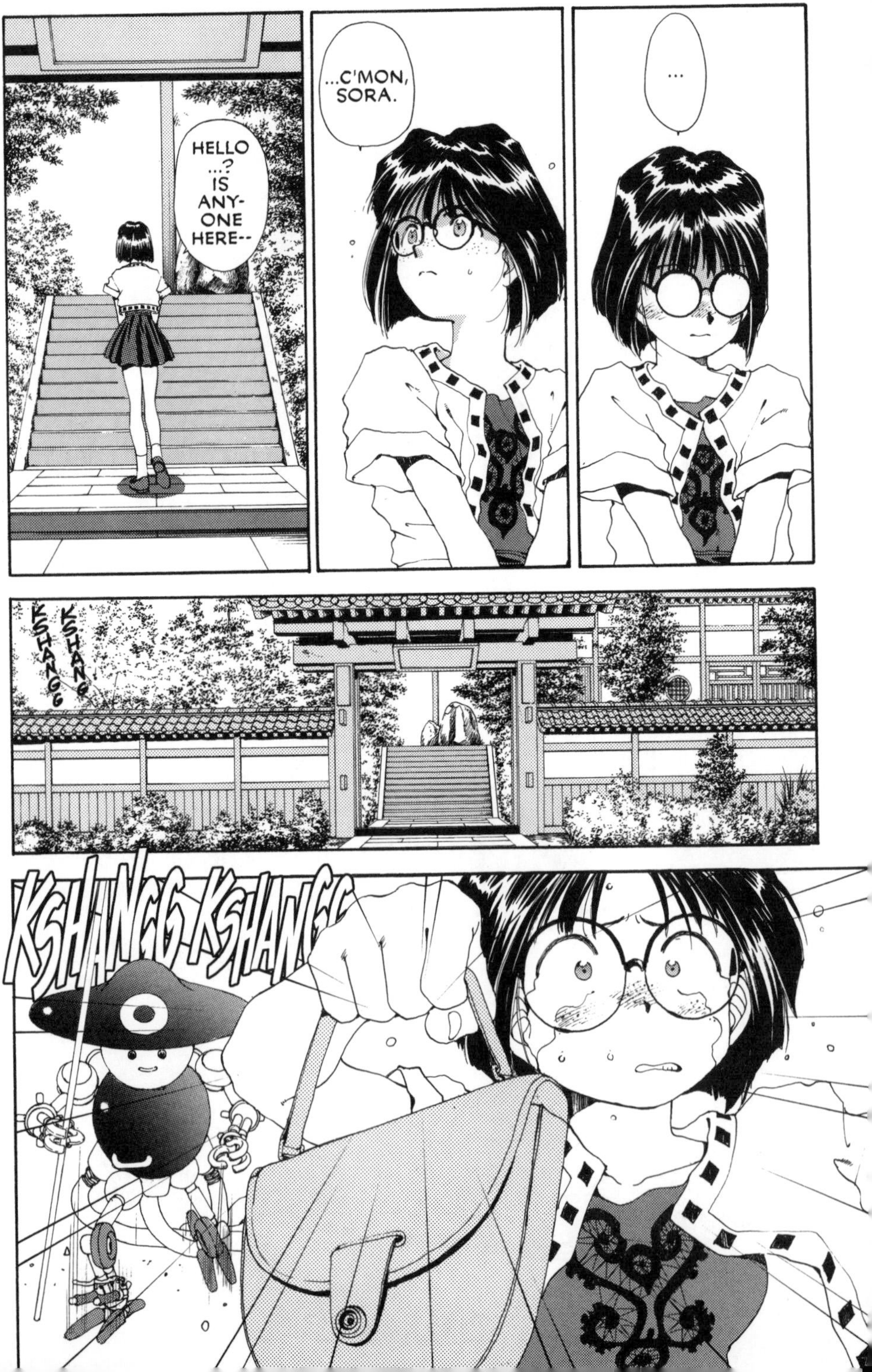
...
...C'MON, SORA.
HELLO ...? IS ANY-ONE HERE--
KSHANG!
KSHANGG
KSHANGG KSHANG

SHRIIIREEK!

OH *NO!* THAT'S *RIGHT!!* BELLDANDY *DID* ASK ME TO TURN HIM OFF THIS MORNING!

FOR CRYING OUT LOUD, SKULD... WHY DON'T YOU JUST TURN THAT THING *OFF?*

k..iink

HMM... SOUNDS LIKE BANPEI'S CAUGHT SOME- ONE.

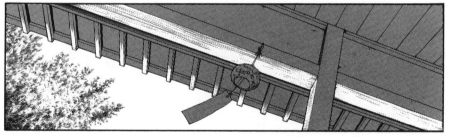

YEAH... um... SORRY.

I'M VERY SORRY ABOUT YOUR ENCOUNTER, SORA.

227

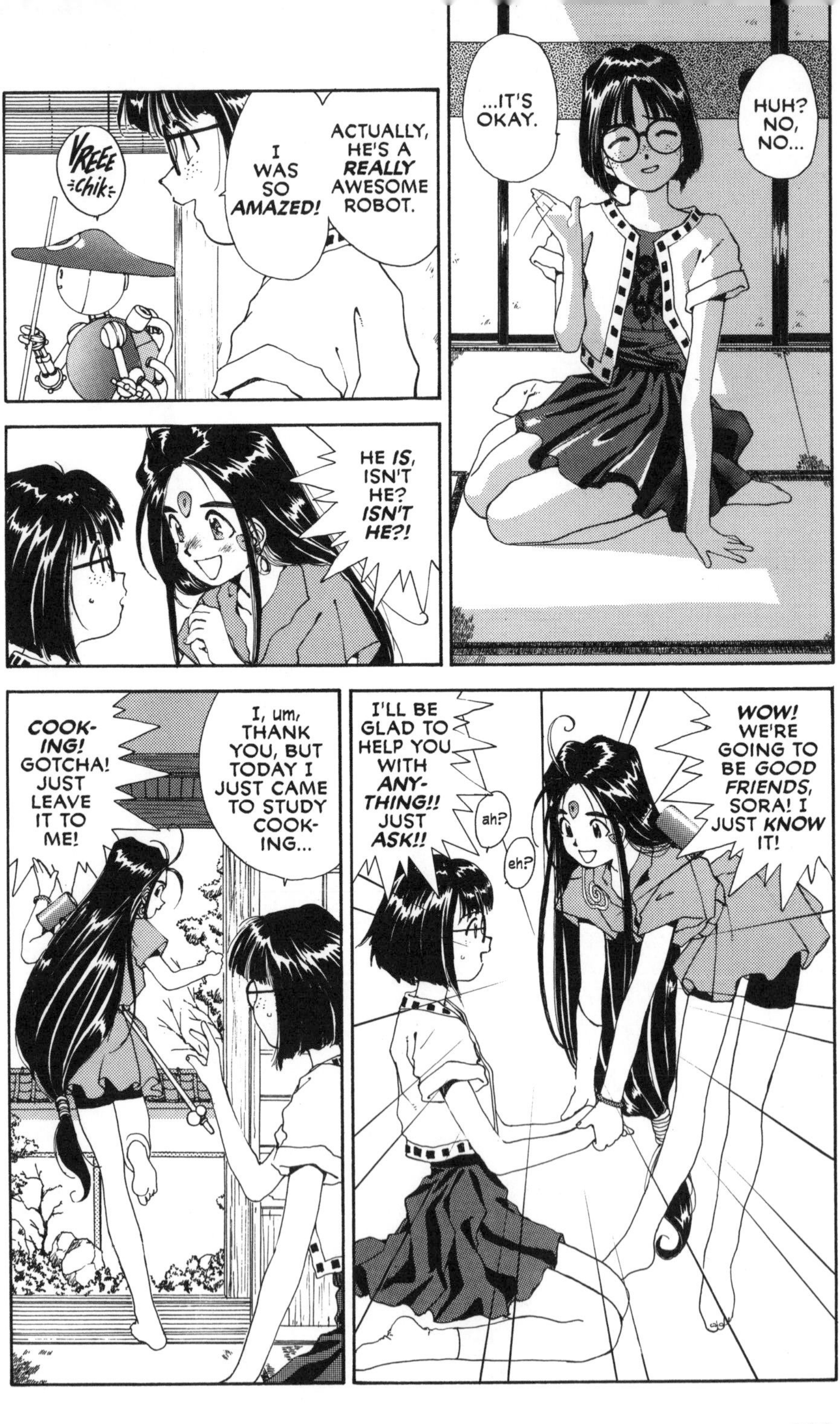

HUH? NO, NO...
...IT'S OKAY.
ACTUALLY, HE'S A REALLY AWESOME ROBOT.
I WAS SO AMAZED!
VREEE chik
HE IS, ISN'T HE? ISN'T HE?!
WOW! WE'RE GOING TO BE GOOD FRIENDS, SORA! I JUST KNOW IT!
I'LL BE GLAD TO HELP YOU WITH ANYTHING!! JUST ASK!!
ah?
eh?
I, um, THANK YOU, BUT TODAY I JUST CAME TO STUDY COOKING...
COOKING! GOTCHA! JUST LEAVE IT TO ME!

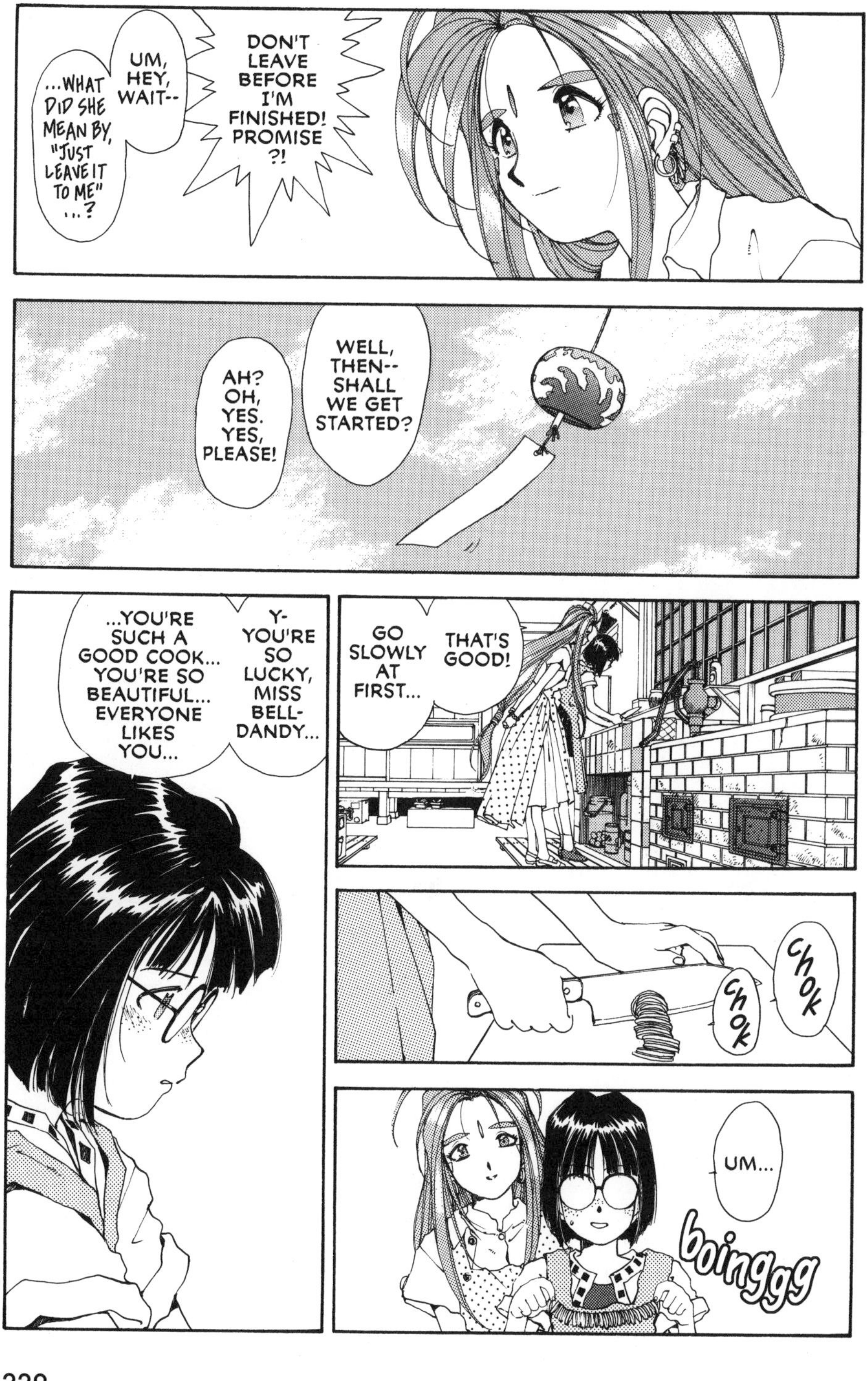
DON'T LEAVE BEFORE I'M FINISHED! PROMISE?!
UM, HEY, WAIT--
...WHAT DID SHE MEAN BY, "JUST LEAVE IT TO ME"...?
WELL, THEN--SHALL WE GET STARTED?
AH? OH, YES. YES, PLEASE!
THAT'S GOOD!
GO SLOWLY AT FIRST...
chok
chok
UM...
boinggg
Y-YOU'RE SO LUCKY, MISS BELL-DANDY...
...YOU'RE SUCH A GOOD COOK... YOU'RE SO BEAUTIFUL... EVERYONE LIKES YOU...

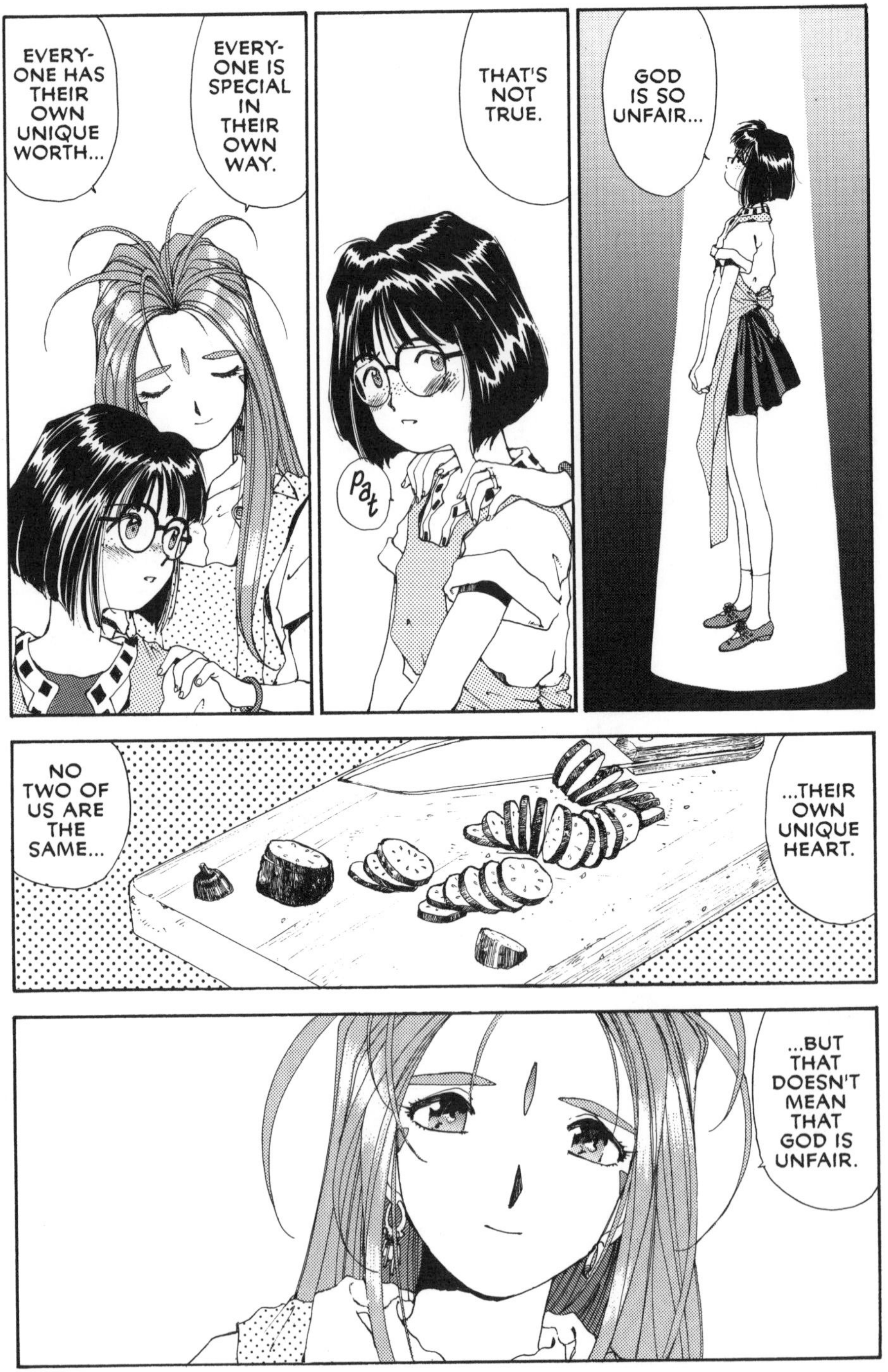
GOD IS SO UNFAIR...
THAT'S NOT TRUE.
pat
EVERY-ONE IS SPECIAL IN THEIR OWN WAY.
EVERY-ONE HAS THEIR OWN UNIQUE WORTH...
...THEIR OWN UNIQUE HEART.
NO TWO OF US ARE THE SAME...
...BUT THAT DOESN'T MEAN THAT GOD IS UNFAIR.

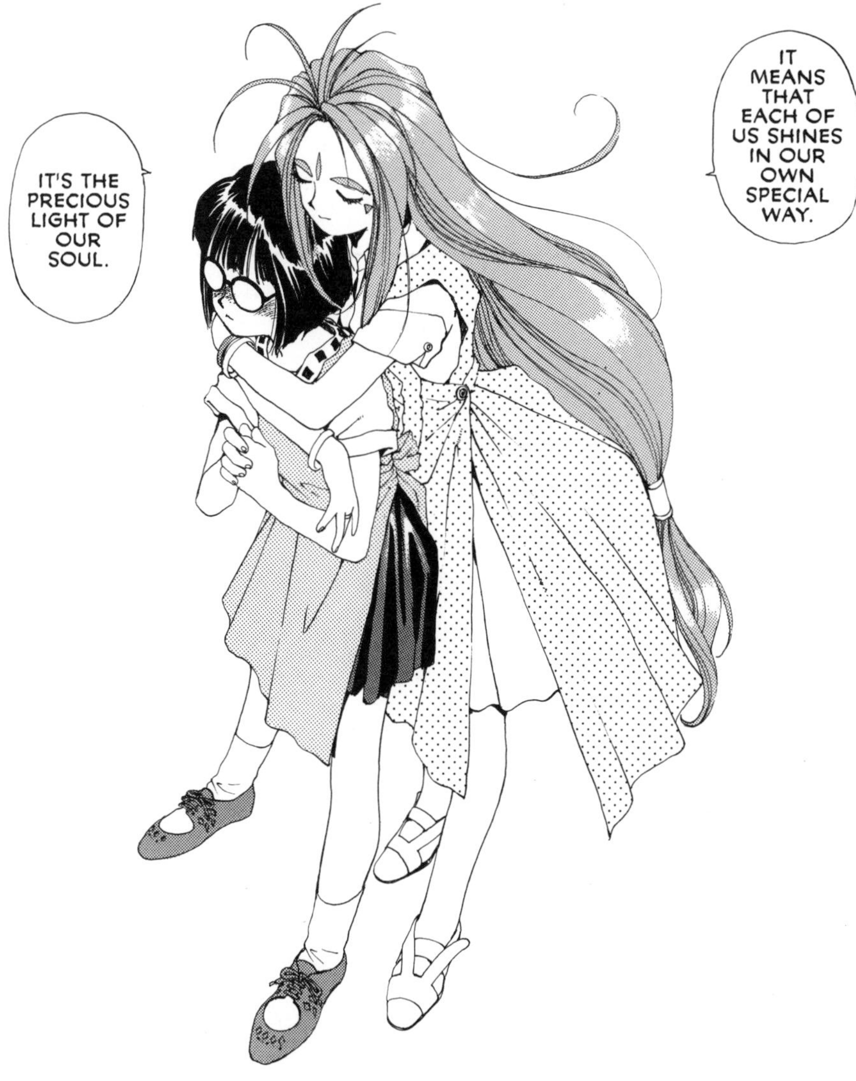
IT MEANS THAT EACH OF US SHINES IN OUR OWN SPECIAL WAY.
IT'S THE PRECIOUS LIGHT OF OUR SOUL.

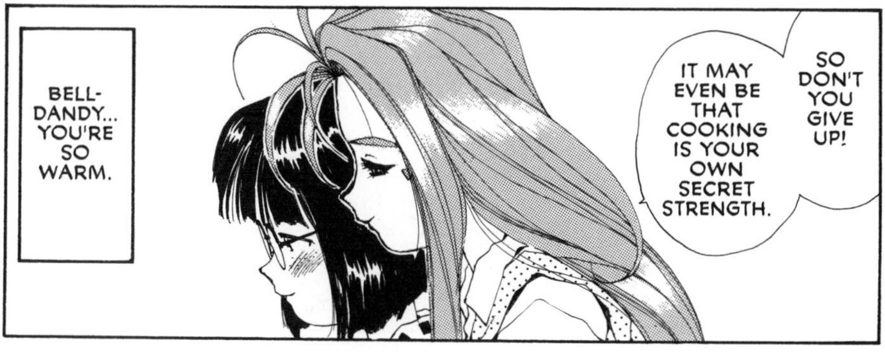
SO DON'T YOU GIVE UP!
IT MAY EVEN BE THAT COOKING IS YOUR OWN SECRET STRENGTH.
BELL-DANDY... YOU'RE SO WARM.

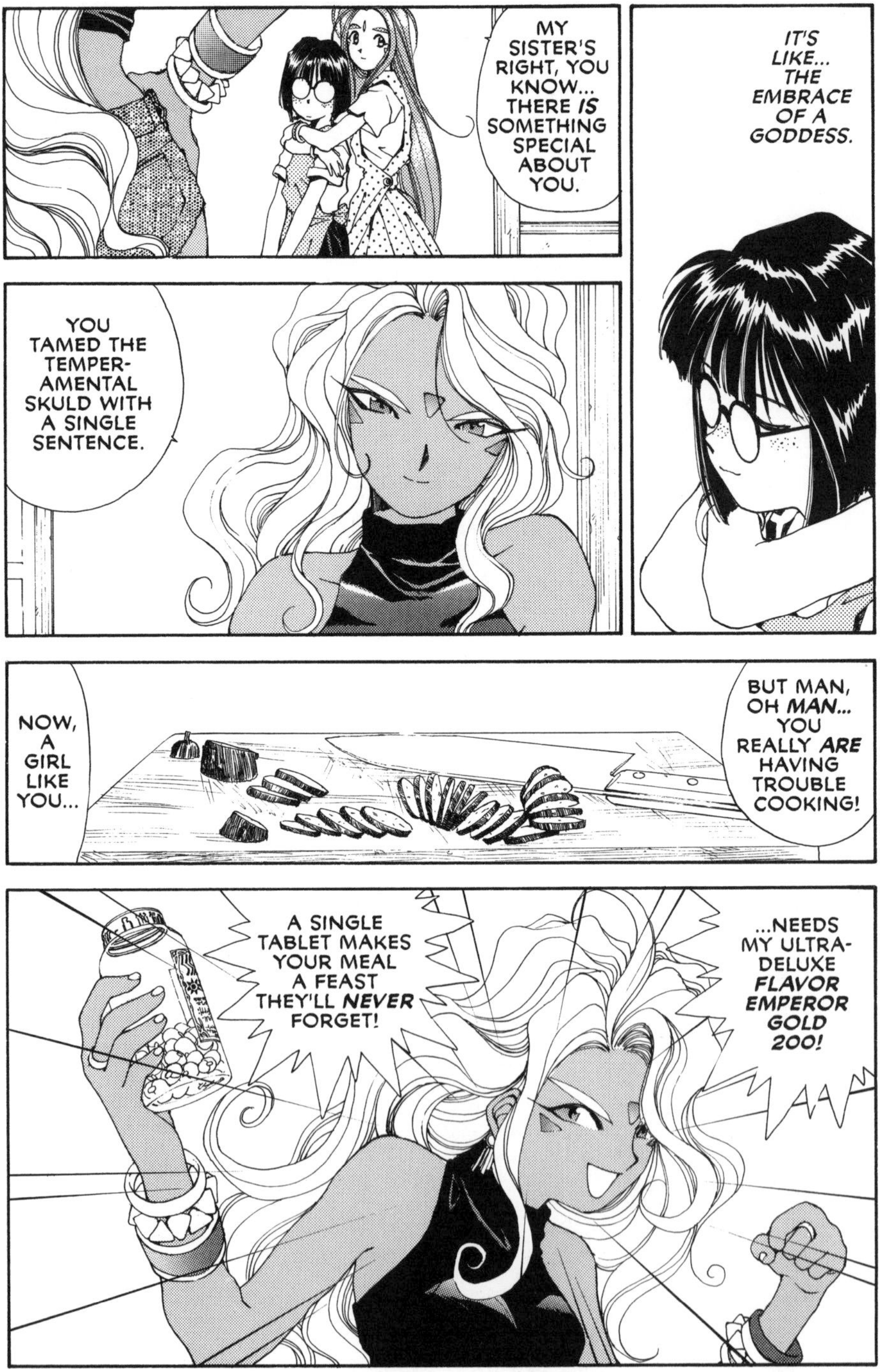
IT'S LIKE... THE EMBRACE OF A GODDESS.
MY SISTER'S RIGHT, YOU KNOW... THERE *IS* SOMETHING SPECIAL ABOUT YOU.
YOU TAMED THE TEMPER-AMENTAL SKULD WITH A SINGLE SENTENCE.
BUT MAN, OH *MAN*... YOU REALLY *ARE* HAVING TROUBLE COOKING!
NOW, A GIRL LIKE YOU...
...NEEDS MY ULTRA-DELUXE *FLAVOR EMPEROR GOLD 200!*
A SINGLE TABLET MAKES YOUR MEAL A FEAST THEY'LL *NEVER* FORGET!

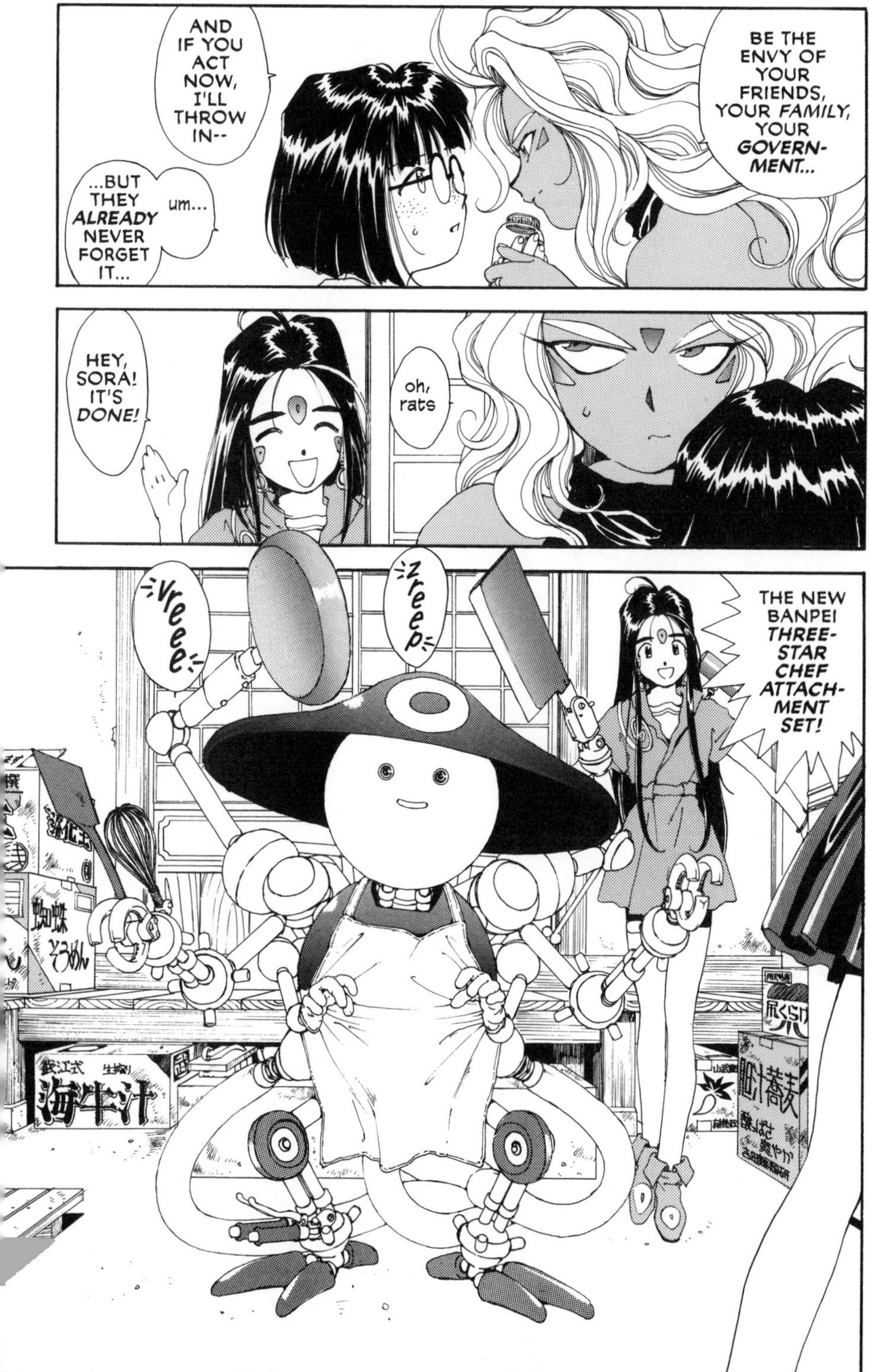
BE THE ENVY OF YOUR FRIENDS, YOUR FAMILY, YOUR GOVERNMENT...
AND IF YOU ACT NOW, I'LL THROW IN--
um...
...BUT THEY ALREADY NEVER FORGET IT...
oh, rats
HEY, SORA! IT'S DONE!
THE NEW BANPEI THREE-STAR CHEF ATTACHMENT SET!
zreep
vreeee

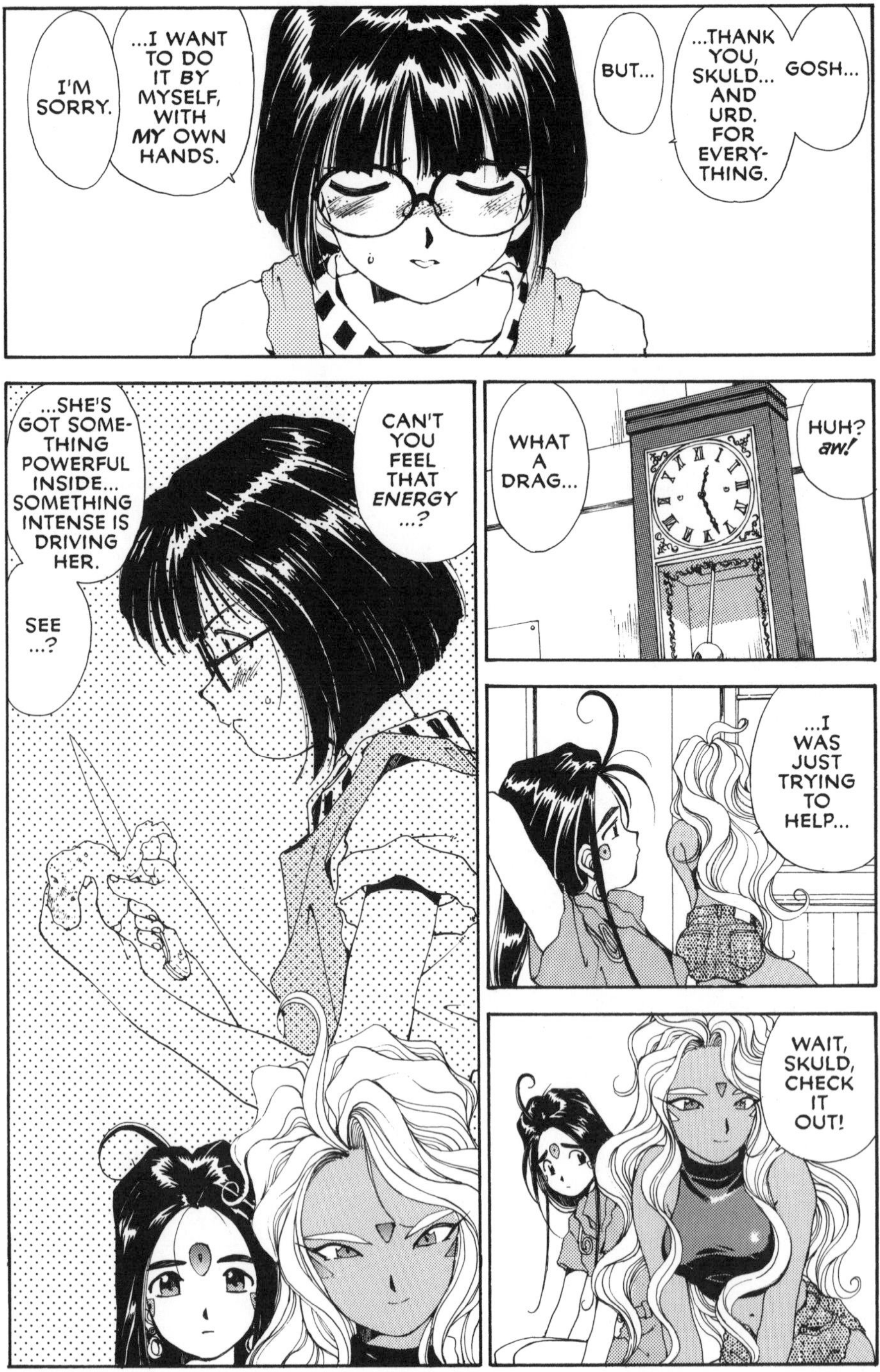
GOSH...
...THANK YOU, SKULD... AND URD. FOR EVERYTHING.
BUT...
...I WANT TO DO IT BY MYSELF, WITH MY OWN HANDS.
I'M SORRY.
HUH? aw!
WHAT A DRAG...
...I WAS JUST TRYING TO HELP...
WAIT, SKULD, CHECK IT OUT!
CAN'T YOU FEEL THAT ENERGY ...?
...SHE'S GOT SOMETHING POWERFUL INSIDE... SOMETHING INTENSE IS DRIVING HER.
SEE ...?

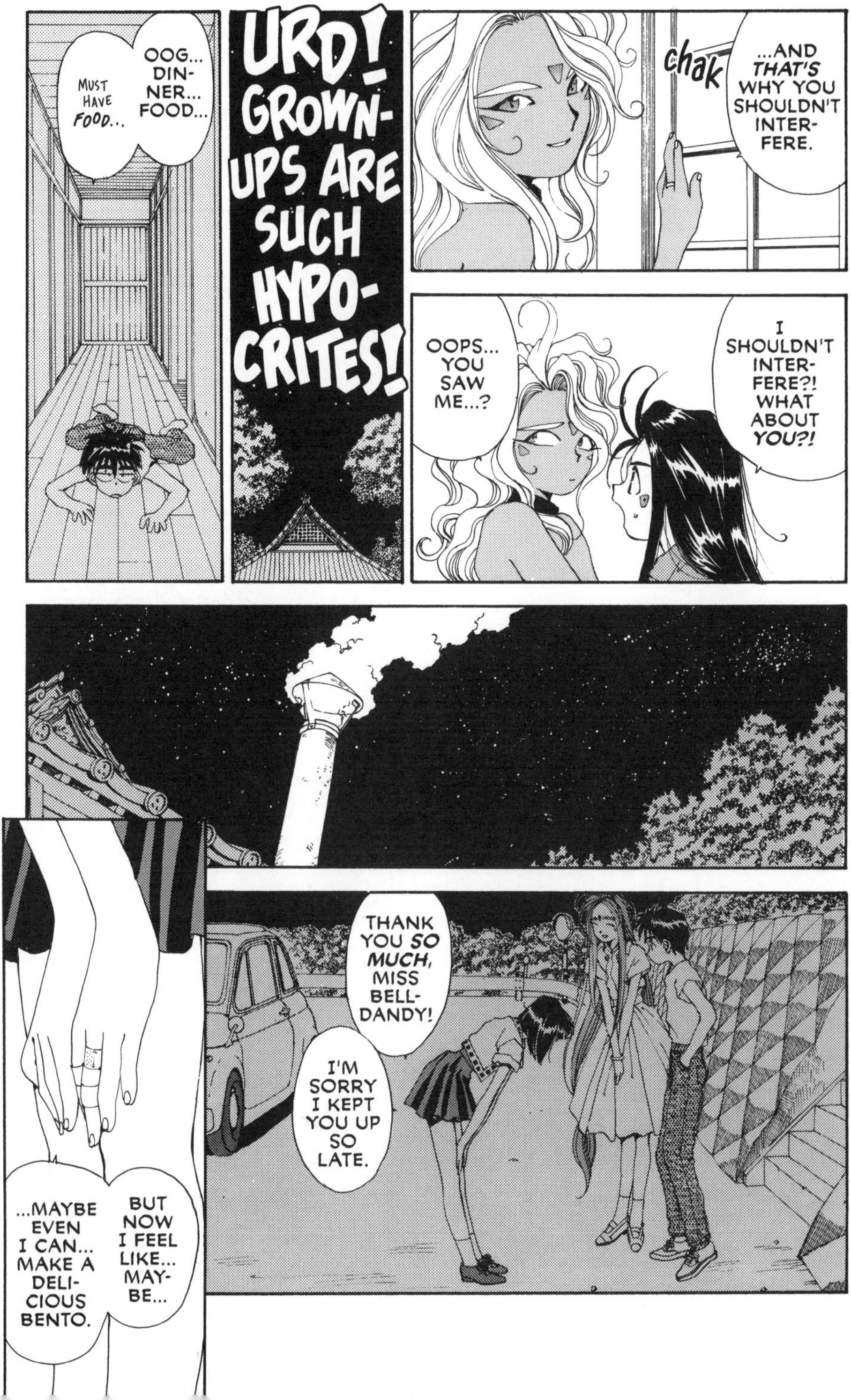
...AND THAT'S WHY YOU SHOULDN'T INTER-FERE.
chak
I SHOULDN'T INTER-FERE?! WHAT ABOUT YOU?!
OOPS... YOU SAW ME...?
URD! GROWN-UPS ARE SUCH HYPO-CRITES!
OOG... DIN-NER... FOOD...
MUST HAVE FOOD...
THANK YOU SO MUCH, MISS BELL-DANDY!
I'M SORRY I KEPT YOU UP SO LATE.
BUT NOW I FEEL LIKE... MAY-BE...
...MAYBE EVEN I CAN... MAKE A DELI-CIOUS BENTO.

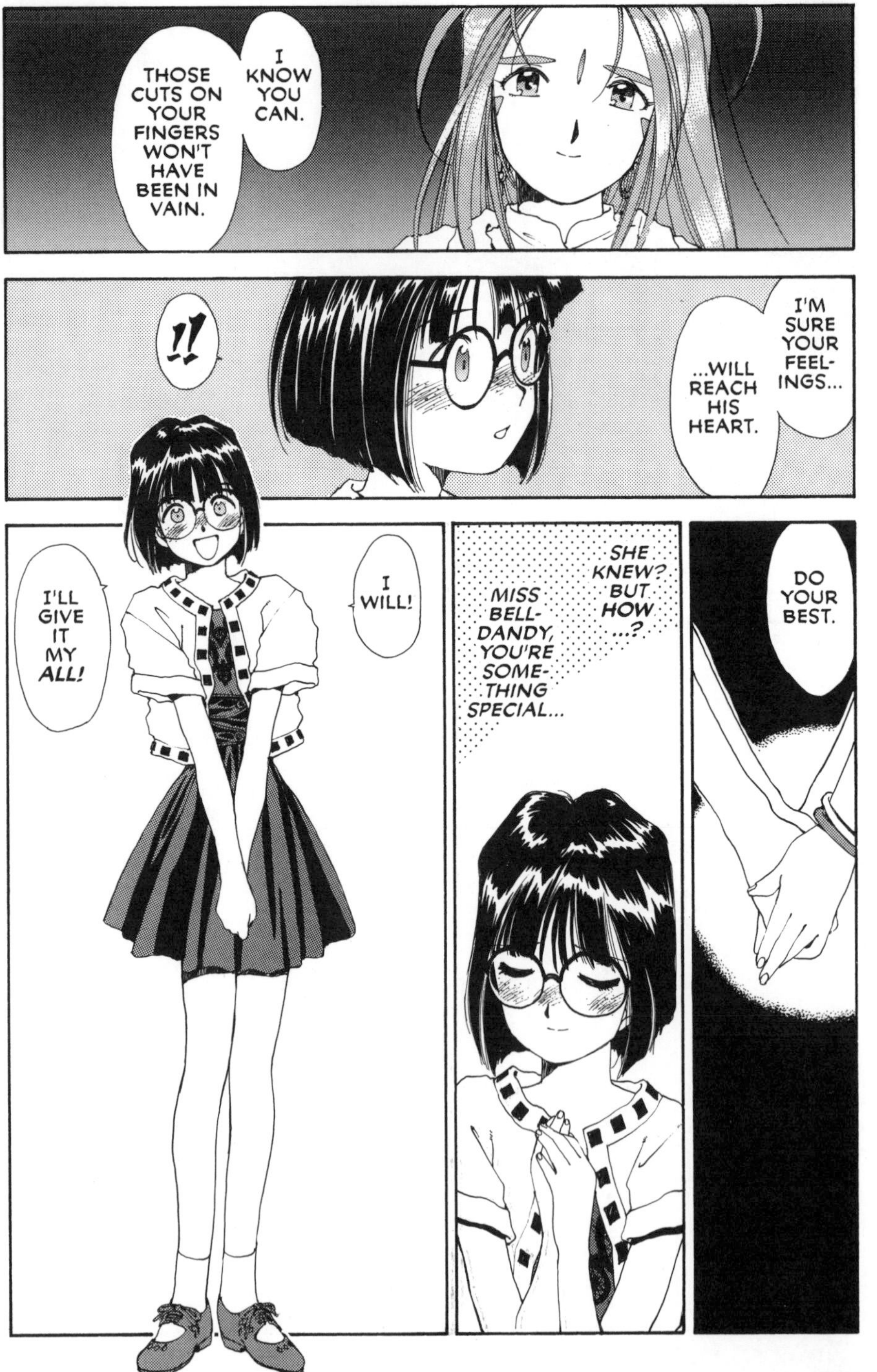
I KNOW YOU CAN.
THOSE CUTS ON YOUR FINGERS WON'T HAVE BEEN IN VAIN.
I'M SURE YOUR FEEL-INGS...
...WILL REACH HIS HEART.
!!
DO YOUR BEST.
SHE KNEW? BUT *HOW* ...?
MISS BELL-DANDY, YOU'RE SOME-THING SPECIAL...
I WILL!
I'LL GIVE IT MY *ALL!*

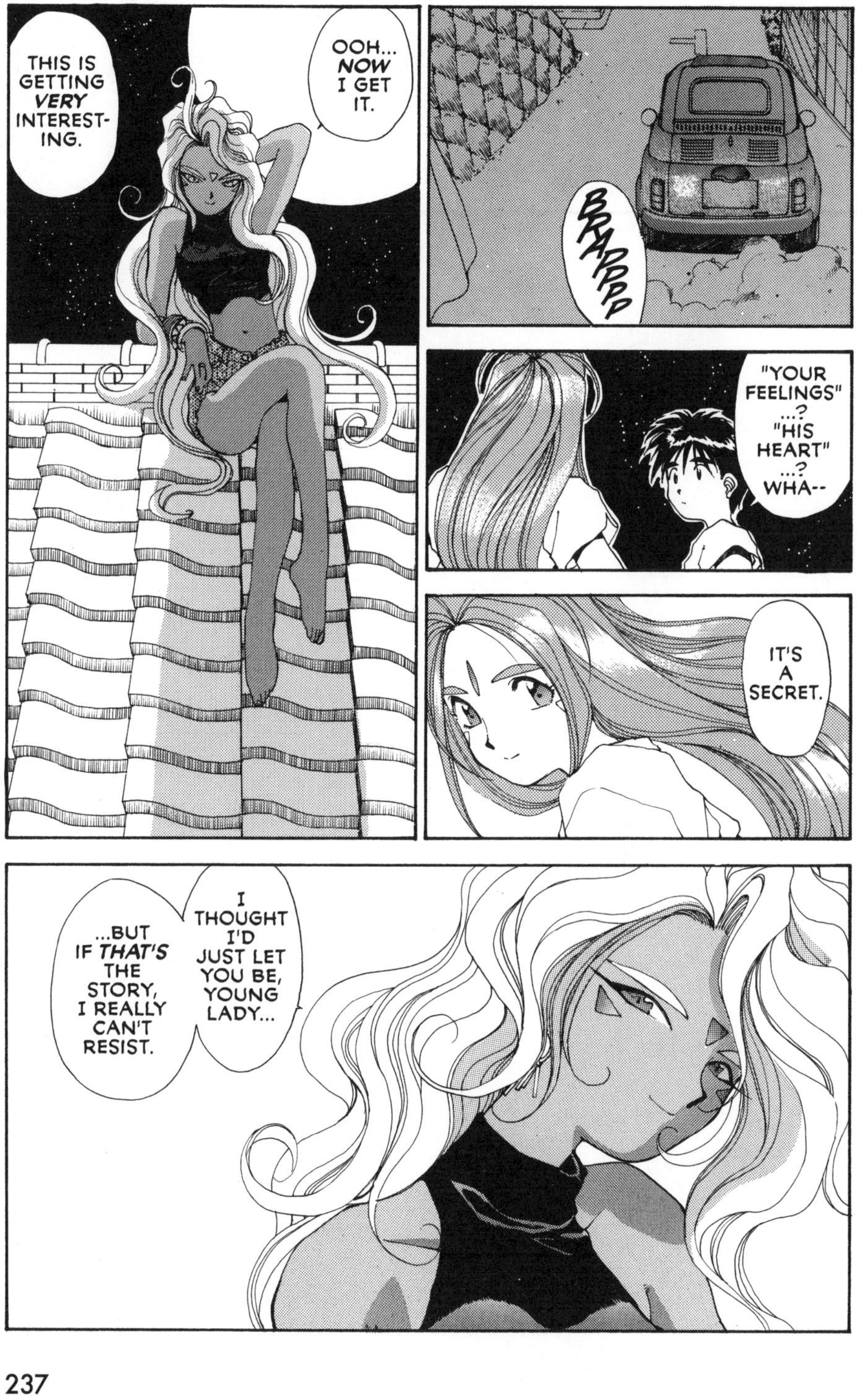
BRMPPPP
"YOUR FEELINGS"...? "HIS HEART"...? WHA--
IT'S A SECRET.
OOH... *NOW* I GET IT.
THIS IS GETTING *VERY* INTERESTING.
I THOUGHT I'D JUST LET YOU BE, YOUNG LADY...
...BUT IF *THAT'S* THE STORY, I REALLY CAN'T RESIST.

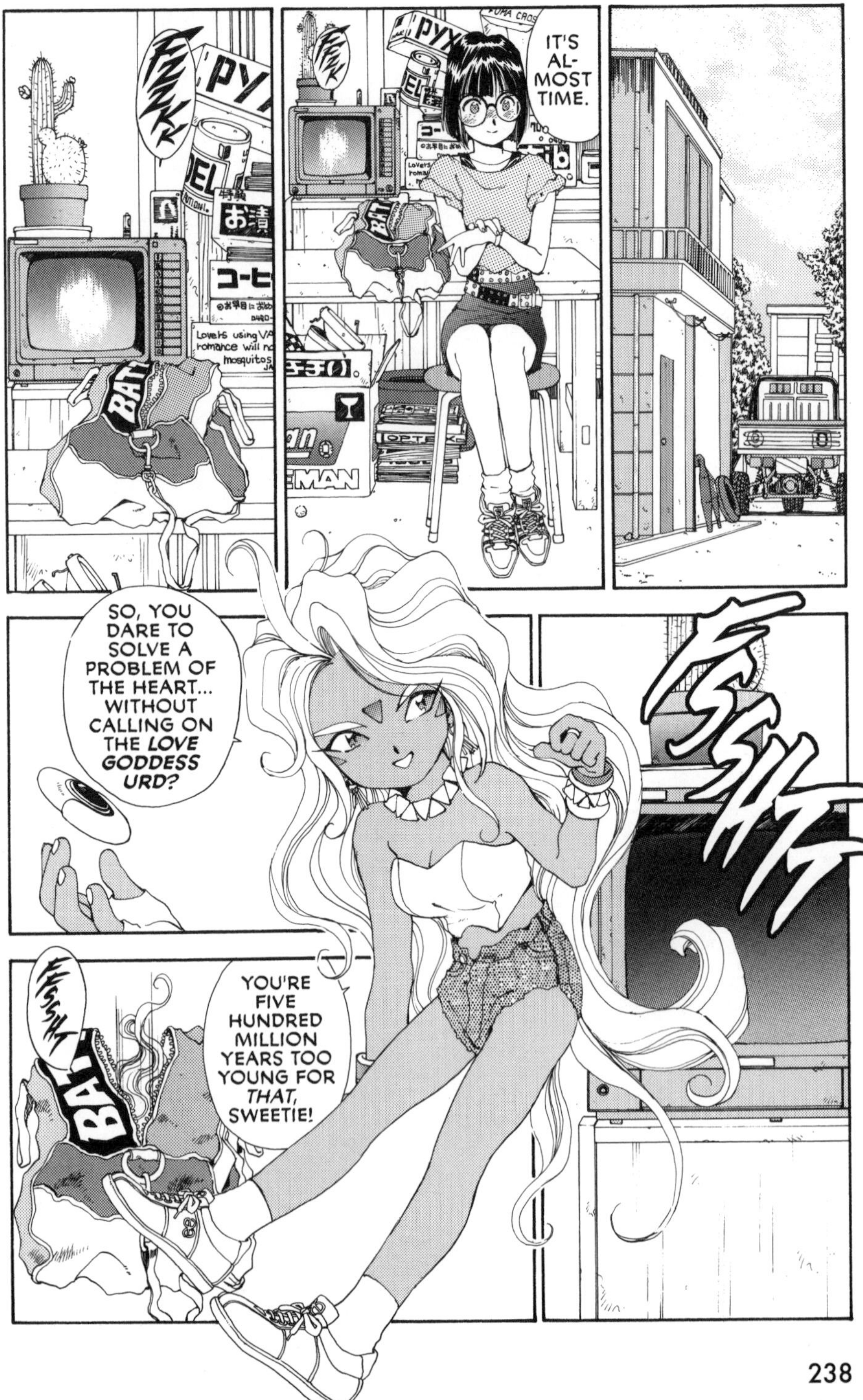
IT'S AL-MOST TIME.
SO, YOU DARE TO SOLVE A PROBLEM OF THE HEART... WITHOUT CALLING ON THE *LOVE GODDESS URD?*
YOU'RE FIVE HUNDRED MILLION YEARS TOO YOUNG FOR *THAT,* SWEETIE!

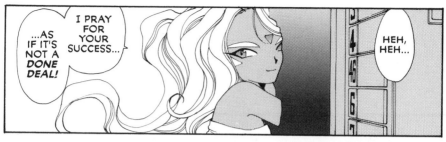

HEH, HEH...
I PRAY FOR YOUR SUCCESS...
...AS IF IT'S NOT A DONE DEAL!
...SORRY WE'RE SO LATE!
OH, HI!
ALL MY PRACTICE WENT INTO THIS...
...SO HERE-- PLEASE TRY A BITE.
...WHAT IS IT, BELLDANDY?
I THOUGHT I REMEMBERED SEEING SOME TEA HERE BEFORE...
TEA? I DON'T REMEMBER SEEING ANY. ARE YOU SURE?

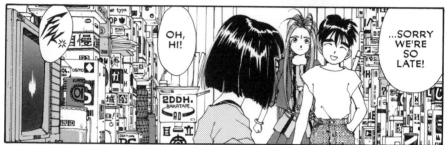

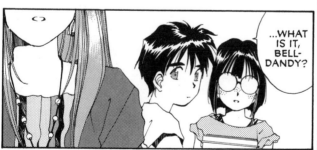

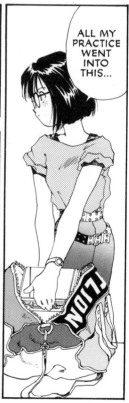

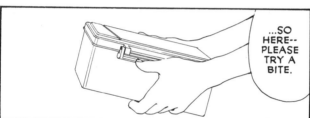

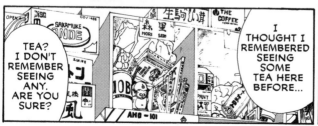

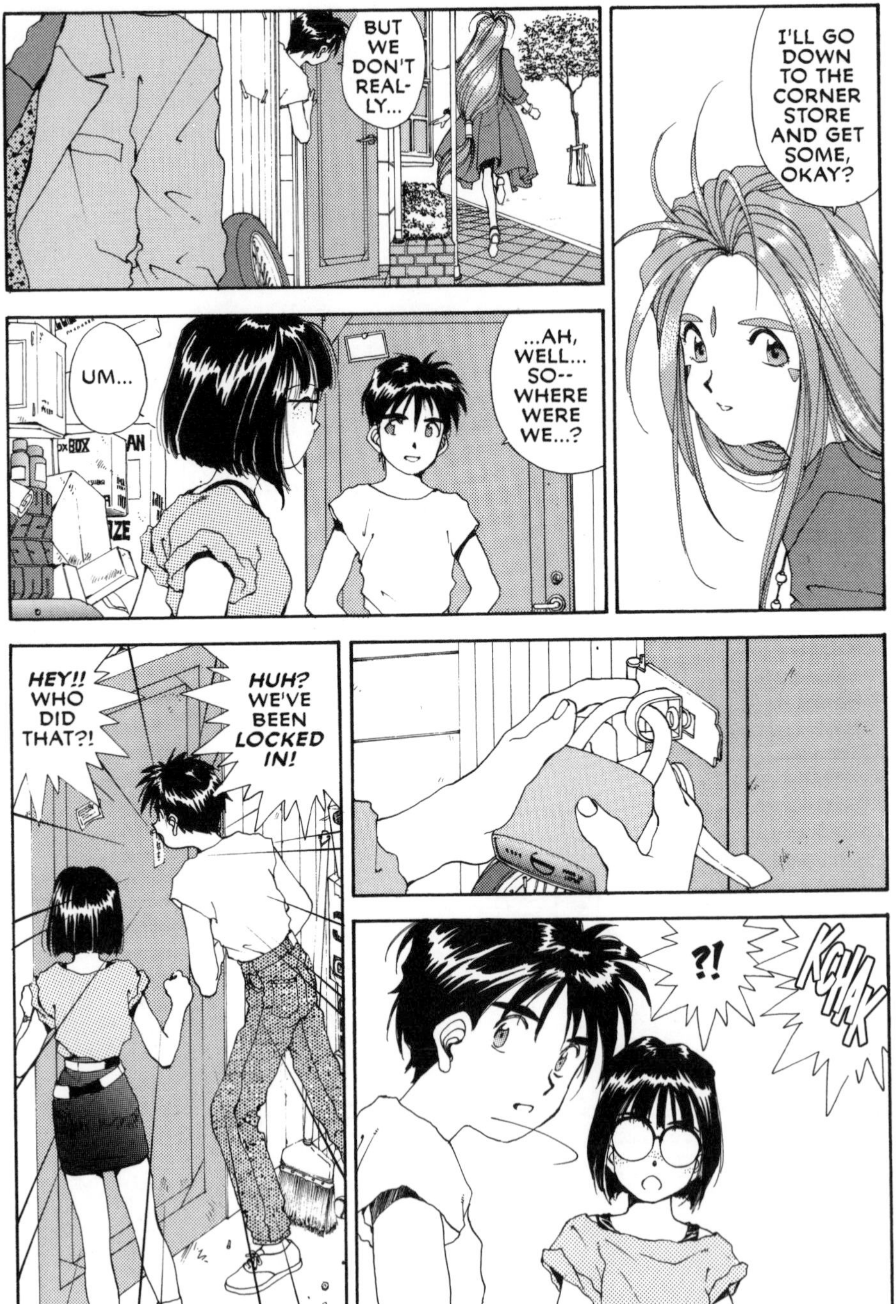
I'LL GO DOWN TO THE CORNER STORE AND GET SOME, OKAY?
BUT WE DON'T REALLY...
...AH, WELL... SO-- WHERE WERE WE...?
UM...
?!
KCHAK
HUH? WE'VE BEEN *LOCKED IN!*
HEY!! WHO DID THAT?!

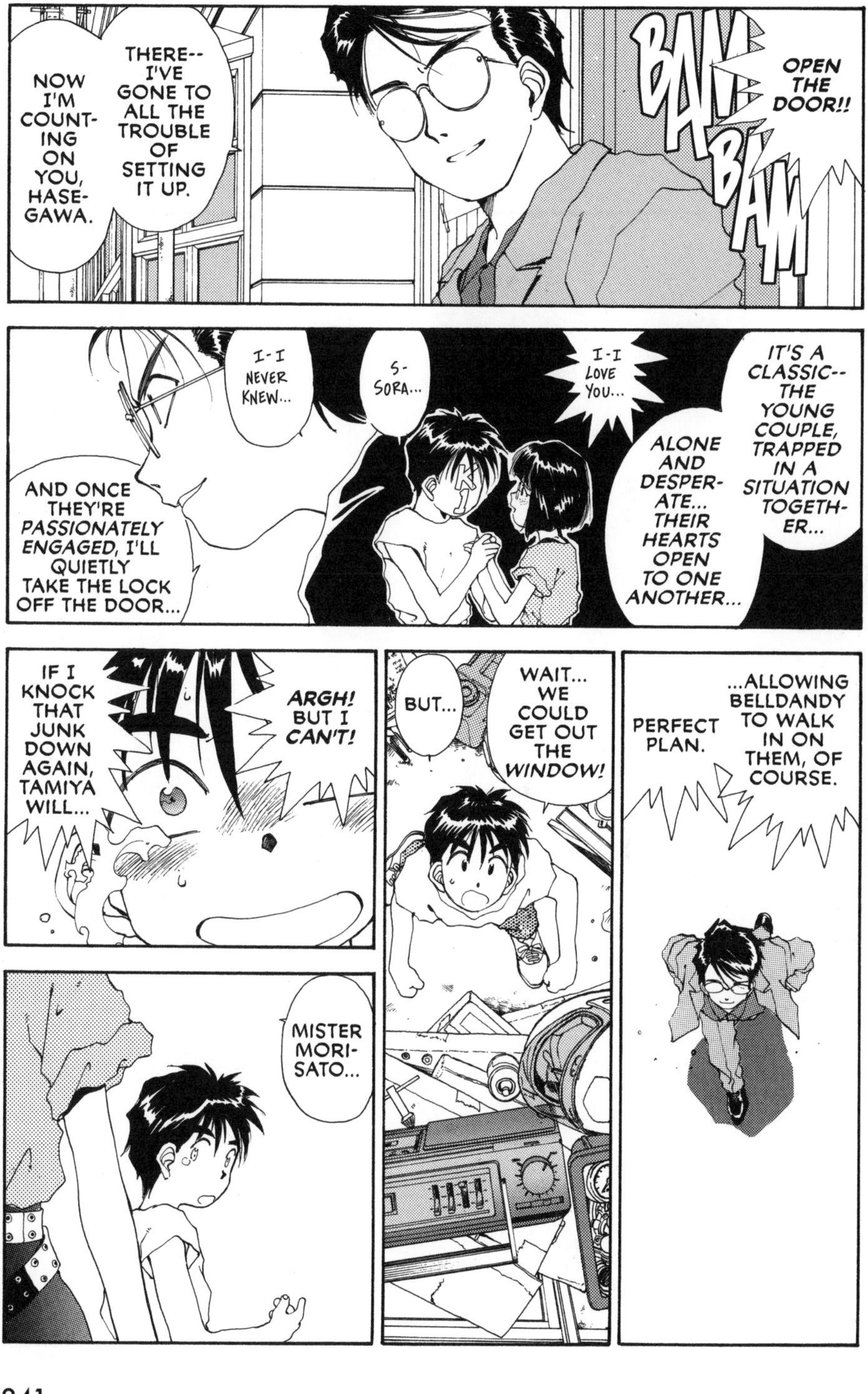
BAM BAM BAM
OPEN THE DOOR!!
THERE-- I'VE GONE TO ALL THE TROUBLE OF SETTING IT UP.
NOW I'M COUNTING ON YOU, HASEGAWA.
IT'S A CLASSIC-- THE YOUNG COUPLE, TRAPPED IN A SITUATION TOGETHER...
ALONE AND DESPERATE... THEIR HEARTS OPEN TO ONE ANOTHER...
I-I LOVE YOU...
S-SORA...
I-I NEVER KNEW...
AND ONCE THEY'RE *PASSIONATELY ENGAGED*, I'LL QUIETLY TAKE THE LOCK OFF THE DOOR...
...ALLOWING BELLDANDY TO WALK IN ON THEM, OF COURSE.
PERFECT PLAN.
WAIT... WE COULD GET OUT THE *WINDOW!*
BUT...
ARGH! BUT I *CAN'T!*
IF I KNOCK THAT JUNK DOWN AGAIN, TAMIYA WILL...
MISTER MORISATO...

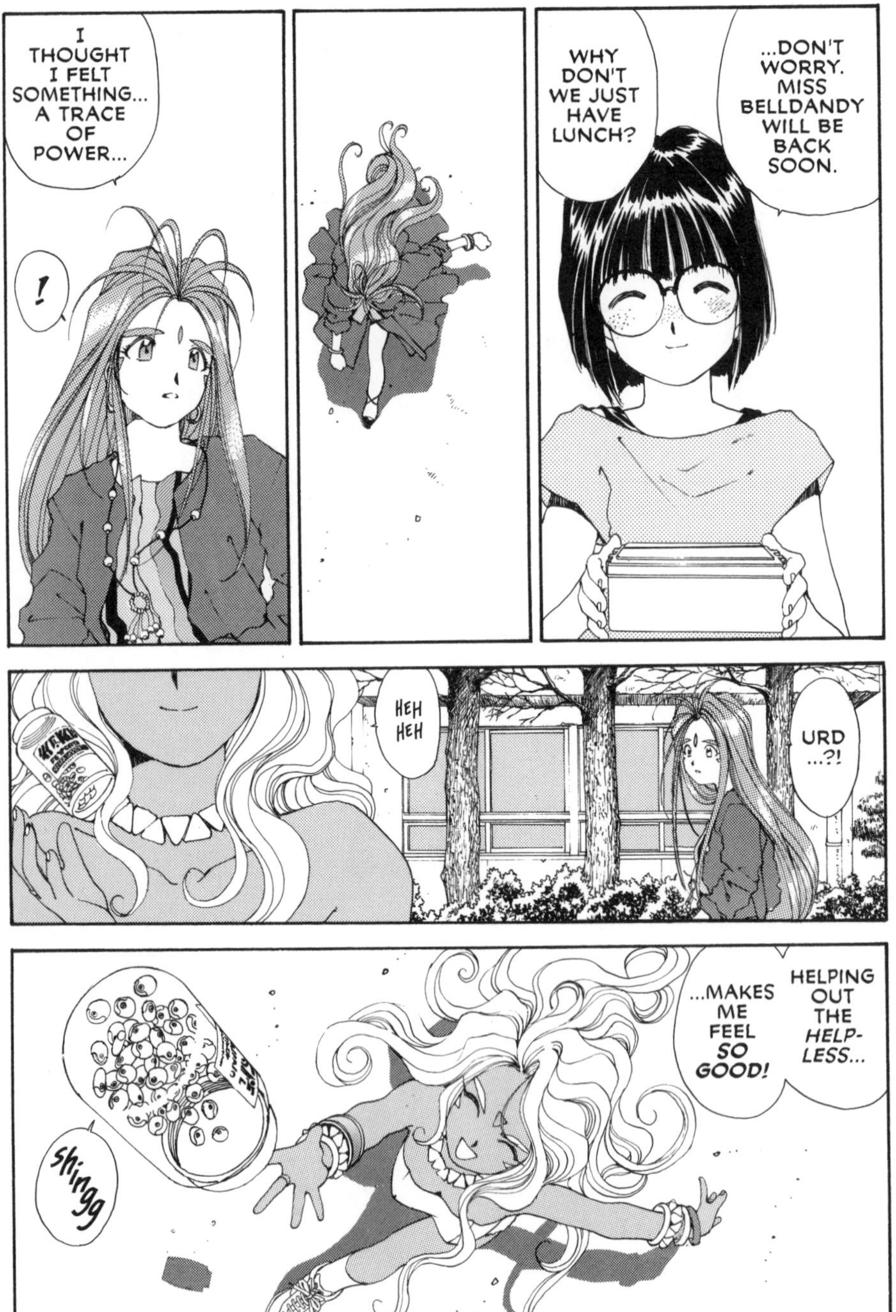
...DON'T WORRY. MISS BELLDANDY WILL BE BACK SOON.
WHY DON'T WE JUST HAVE LUNCH?
I THOUGHT I FELT SOMETHING... A TRACE OF POWER...
!
URD ...?!
HEH HEH
HELPING OUT THE HELP-LESS...
...MAKES ME FEEL SO GOOD!
shingg

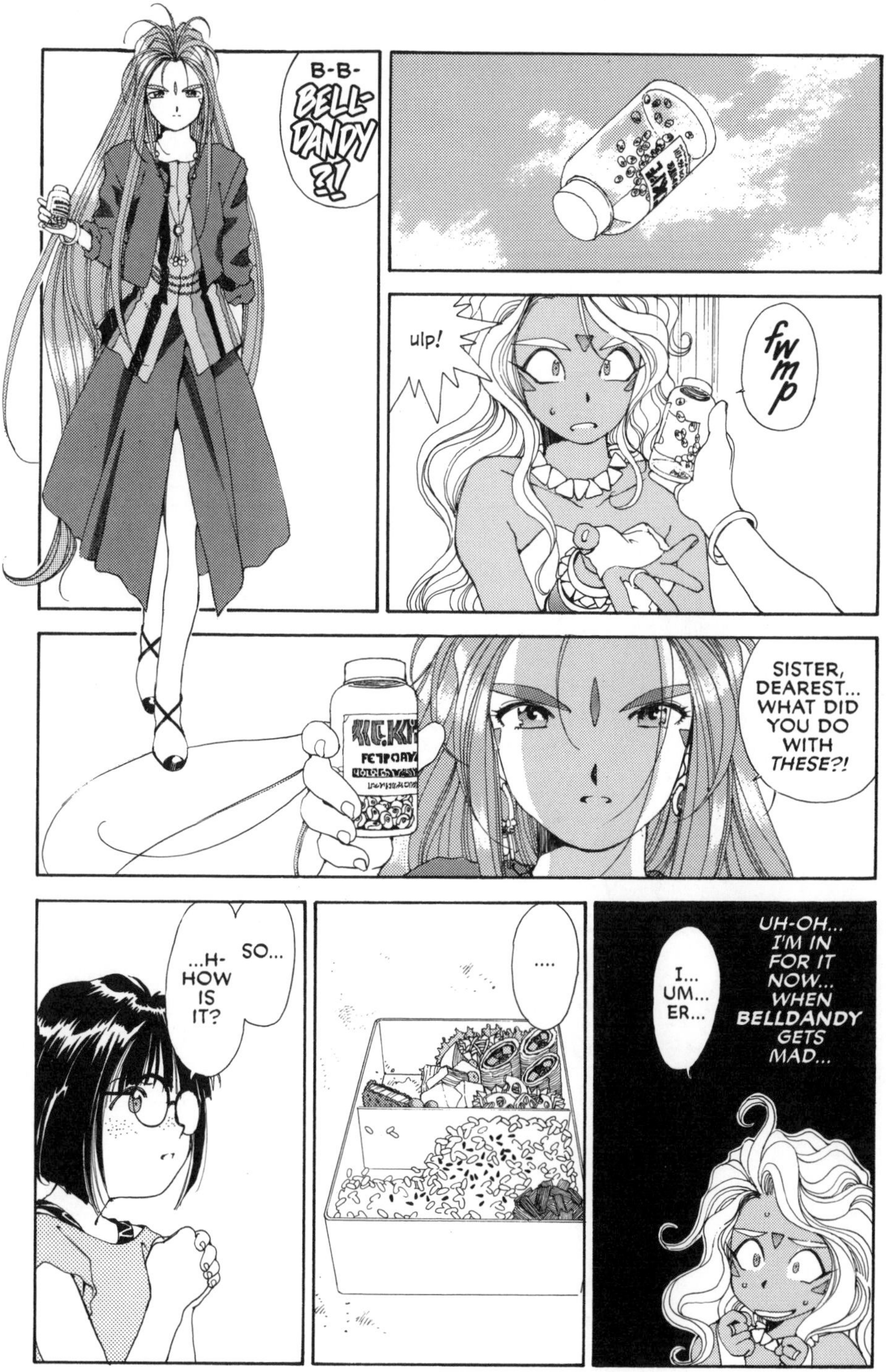
fwmp
ulp!
B-B-BELL-DANDY?!
SISTER, DEAREST... WHAT DID YOU DO WITH *THESE?!*
UH-OH... I'M IN FOR IT NOW... WHEN BELLDANDY GETS MAD...
I... UM... ER...
....
SO...
...H-HOW IS IT?

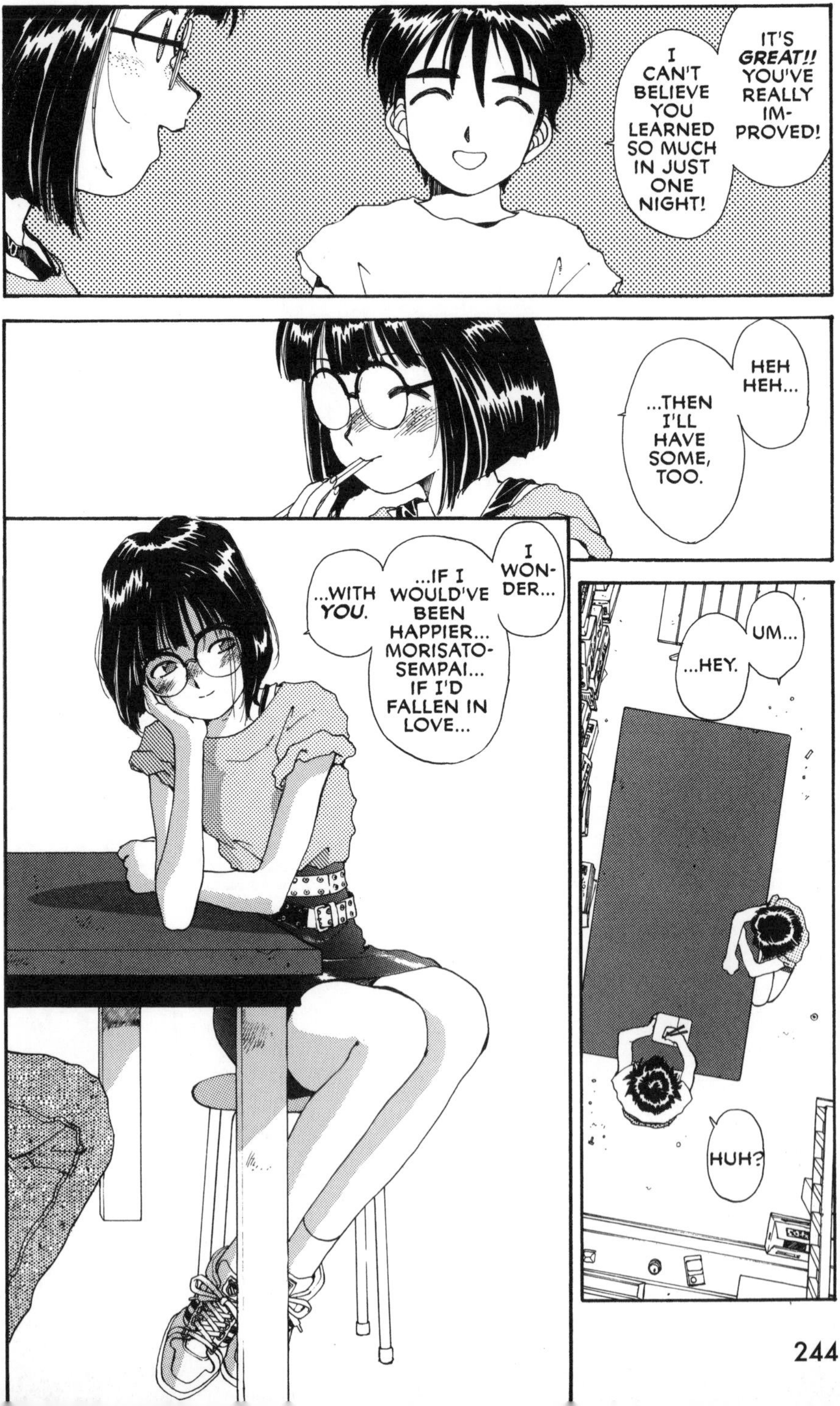
IT'S GREAT!! YOU'VE REALLY IM-PROVED!
I CAN'T BELIEVE YOU LEARNED SO MUCH IN JUST ONE NIGHT!
HEH HEH...
...THEN I'LL HAVE SOME, TOO.
UM...
...HEY.
HUH?
I WON-DER...
...IF I WOULD'VE BEEN HAPPIER... MORISATO-SEMPAI... IF I'D FALLEN IN LOVE...
...WITH YOU.

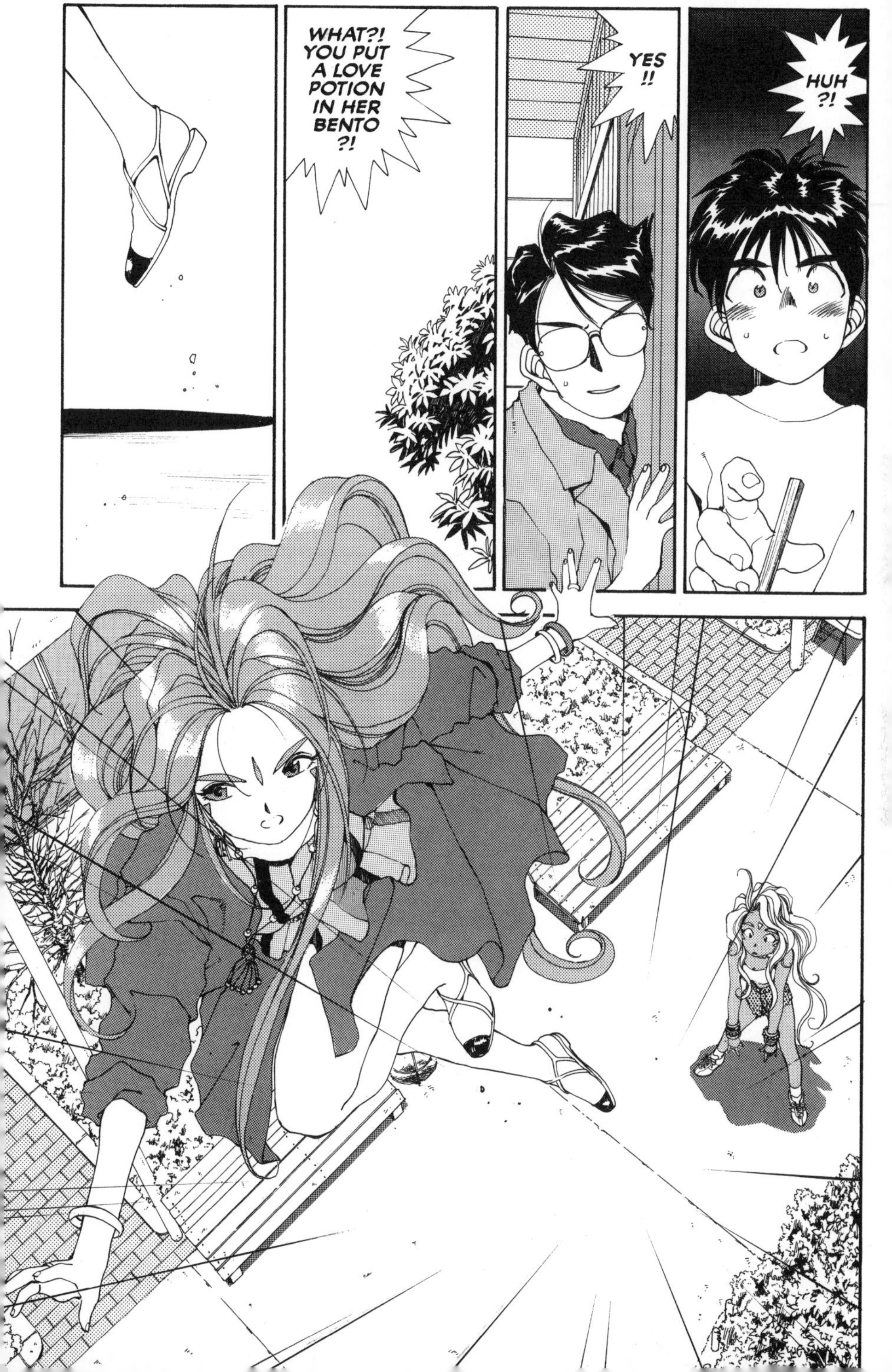
HUH?!
YES!!
WHAT?! YOU PUT A LOVE POTION IN HER BENTO?!

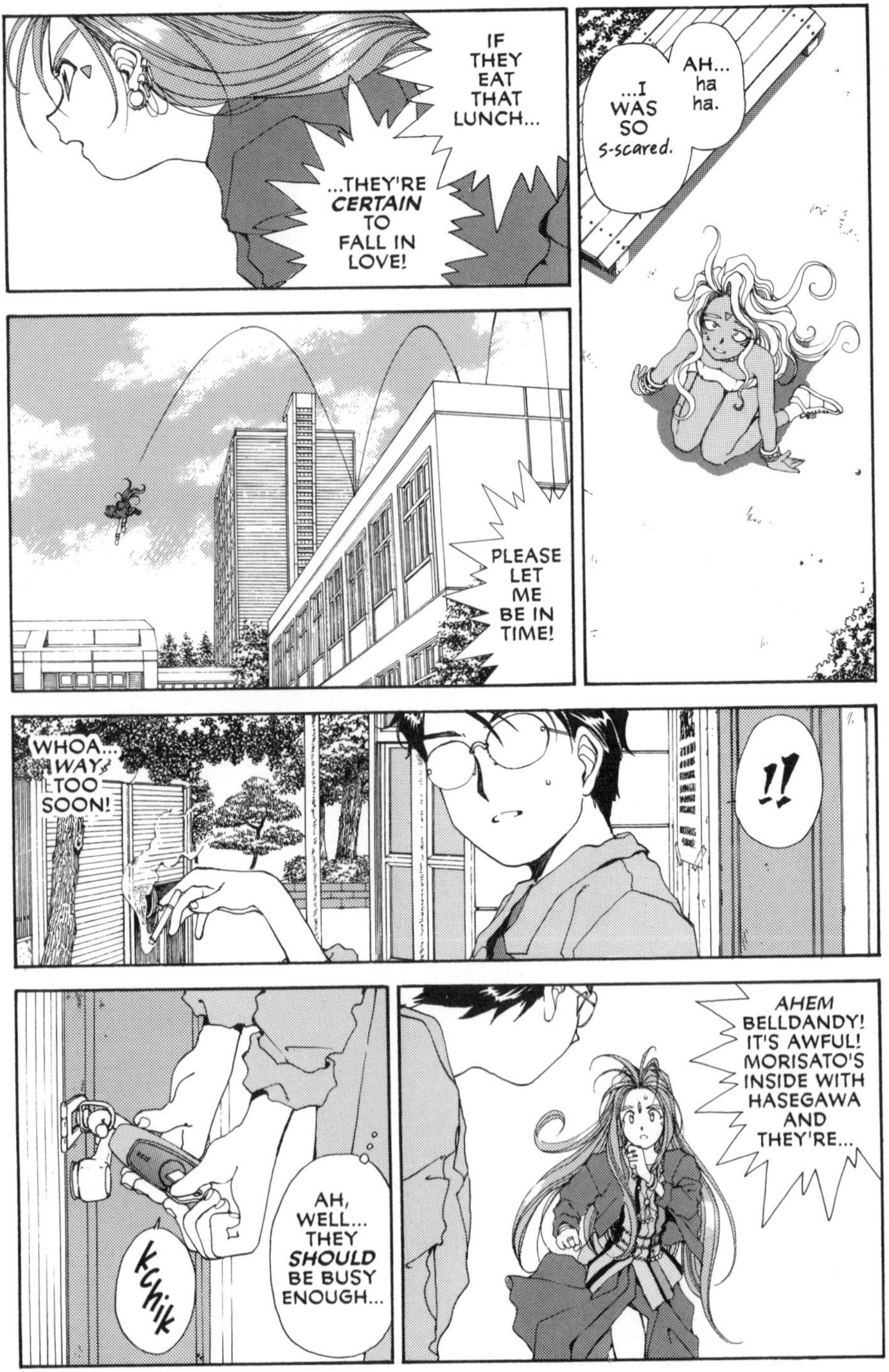
AH... ha ha.
...I WAS SO s-scared.
IF THEY EAT THAT LUNCH...
...THEY'RE *CERTAIN* TO FALL IN LOVE!
PLEASE LET ME BE IN TIME!
!!
WHOA... WAY TOO SOON!
AHEM BELLDANDY! IT'S AWFUL! MORISATO'S INSIDE WITH HASEGAWA AND THEY'RE...
AH, WELL... THEY *SHOULD* BE BUSY ENOUGH...
kchik

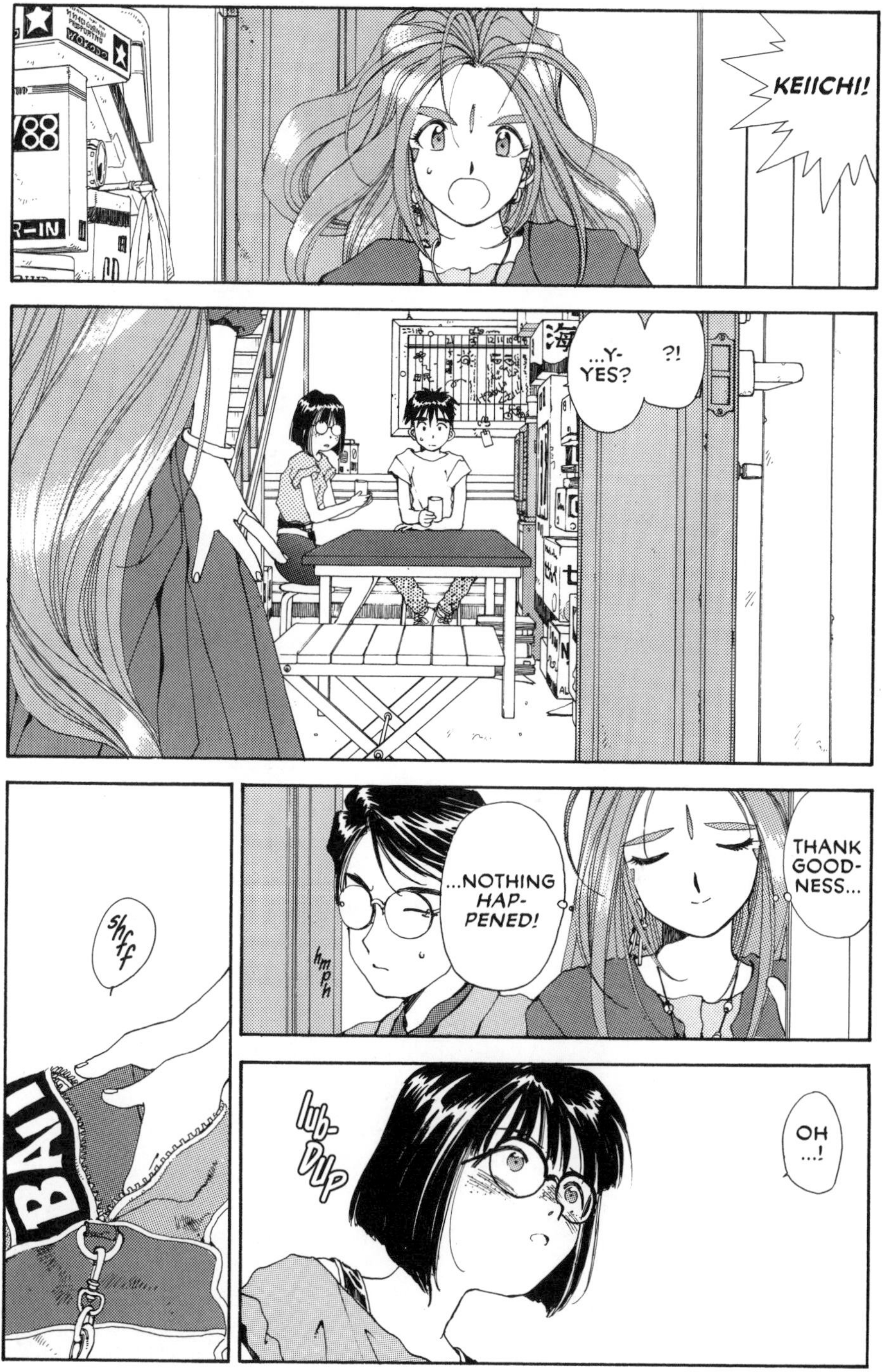
KEIICHI!
?!
...Y-YES?
THANK GOODNESS...
...NOTHING HAPPENED!
hmph
OH ...!
lub-DUP
shff

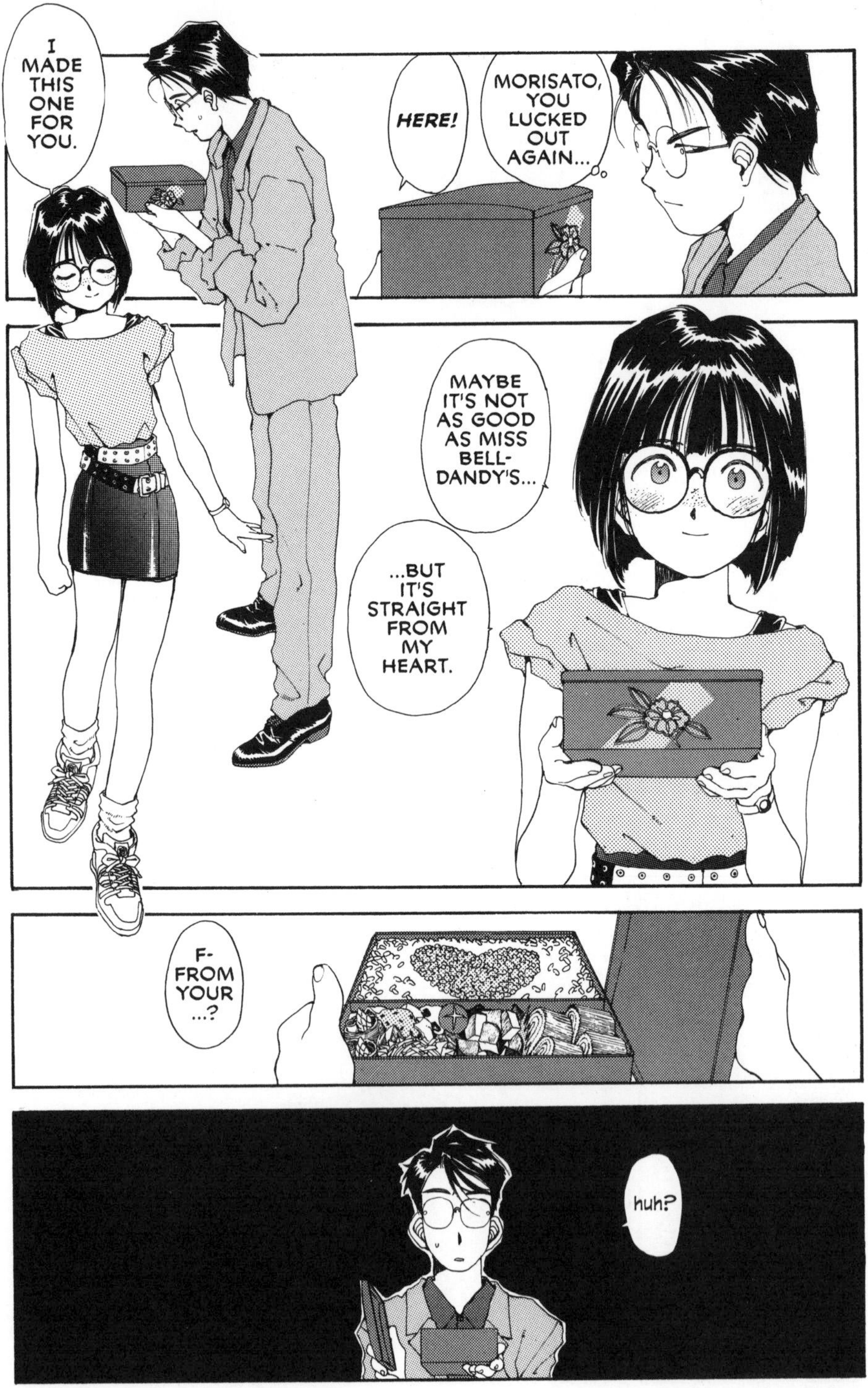

MORISATO, YOU LUCKED OUT AGAIN...
HERE!
I MADE THIS ONE FOR YOU.
MAYBE IT'S NOT AS GOOD AS MISS BELL-DANDY'S...
...BUT IT'S STRAIGHT FROM MY HEART.
F-FROM YOUR ...?
huh?

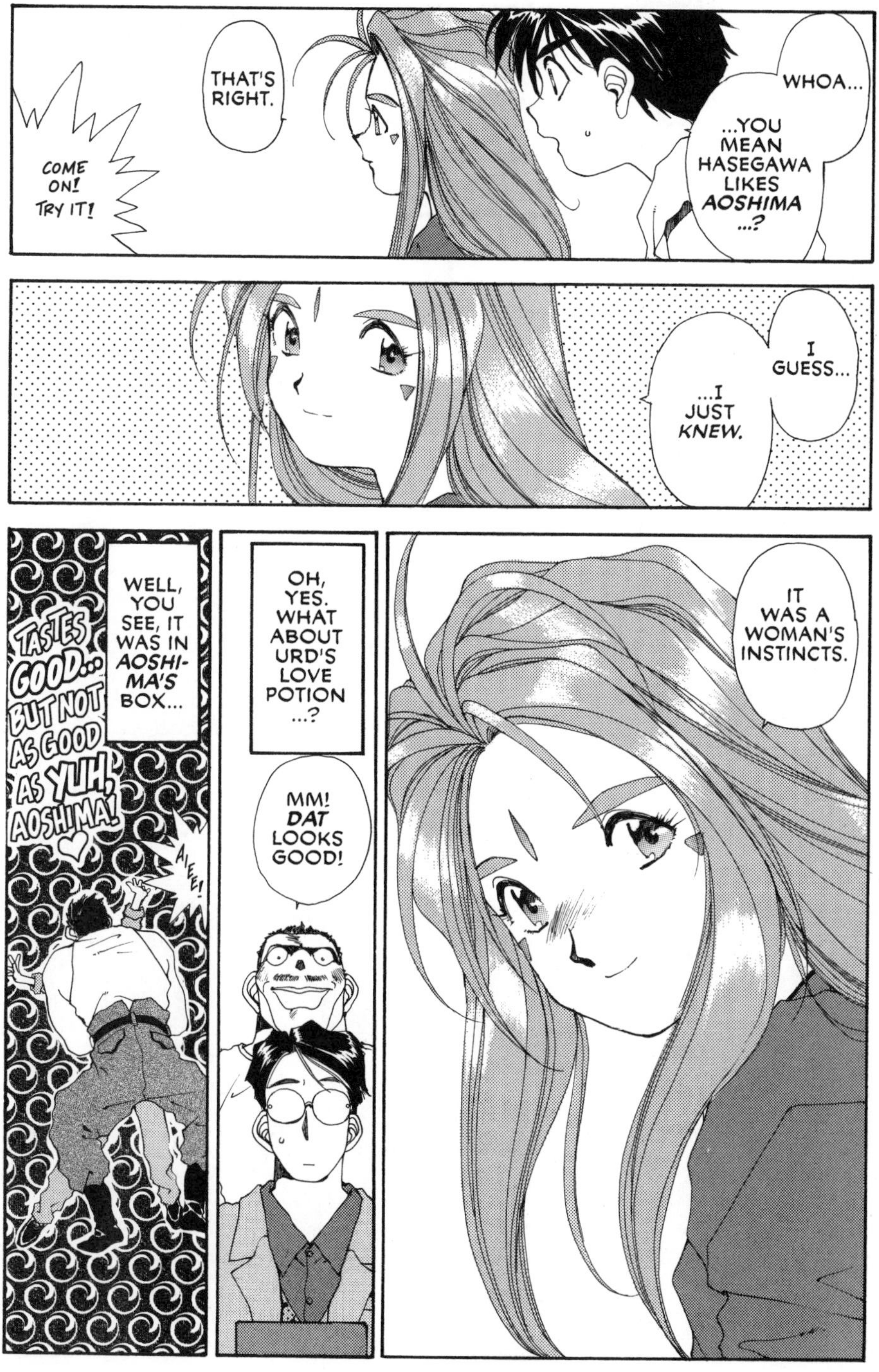
WHOA...
...YOU MEAN HASEGAWA LIKES AOSHIMA ...?
THAT'S RIGHT.
COME ON! TRY IT!
I GUESS...
...I JUST KNEW.
IT WAS A WOMAN'S INSTINCTS.
OH, YES. WHAT ABOUT URD'S LOVE POTION ...?
MM! DAT LOOKS GOOD!
WELL, YOU SEE, IT WAS IN AOSHIMA'S BOX...
TASTES GOOD... BUT NOT AS GOOD AS YUH, AOSHIMA! ♥
AIEEE!

THE ADVENTURES OF MINI-URD

◆ (INSERT DRUMMER JOKE HERE) ◆

◆ LET'S START A BAND! ◆

◆ YOU TOO CAN PLAY DRUMS! ◆

RIGHT PAW MOVING IN SYNC WITH LEFT PAW...

ALL RIGHT-- I RECOGNIZE YOUR BURNING PASSION FOR THE DRUMS!

THEN... THE LEFT PAW ONE HUNDRED TIMES...

NOW! RIGHT PAW ALONE ONE HUNDRED TIMES...

BUT *WAIT!* FIRST, YOU HAVE TO PROVE YOU'RE *QUALIFIED* TO BE A DRUMMER.

THNK THNK

I *DID* IT! I'M A *DRUM-MER!*

skssh skssh

IF YOU CAN'T DO *THAT*, YOU DON'T MAKE THE CUT.

OKAY-- MOVE YOUR RIGHT PAW UP AND DOWN, WHILE MOV-ING YOUR LEFT PAW SIDE TO SIDE.

FREAKING OUT TOTALLY

...

NOW DO IT WITH YOUR PAWS IN THE AIR.

RIGHT PAW MAKING LEFT PAW MOVE AT AN ANGLE.

◆ SPECIAL TRAINING: OBSERVATIONS ON PRACTICAL TECHNIQUE ◆

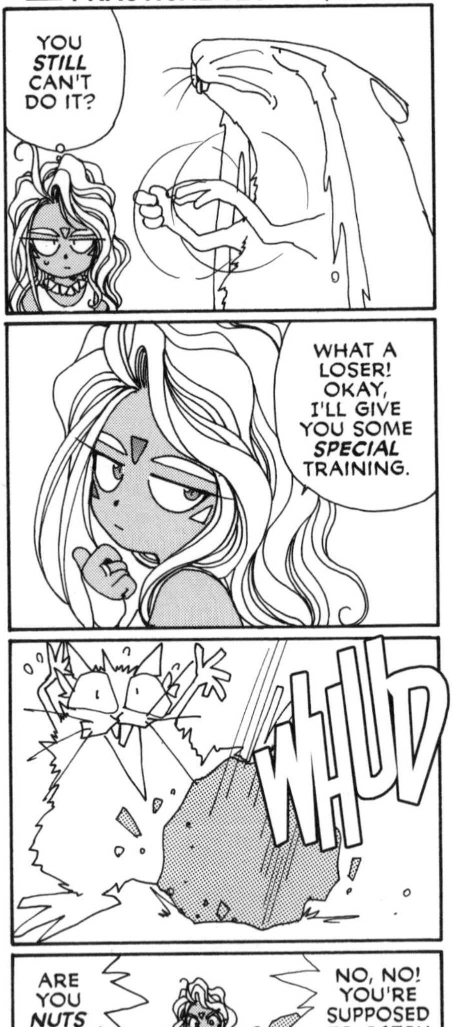
YOU *STILL* CAN'T DO IT?
WHAT A LOSER! OKAY, I'LL GIVE YOU SOME *SPECIAL* TRAINING.
WHUD
NO, NO! YOU'RE SUPPOSED TO *CATCH IT,* YOU DUMB RAT!
ARE YOU *NUTS* ?!

◆ SPECIAL TRAINING VERSUS RESULTS: A STUDY IN NON-CAUSALITY ◆

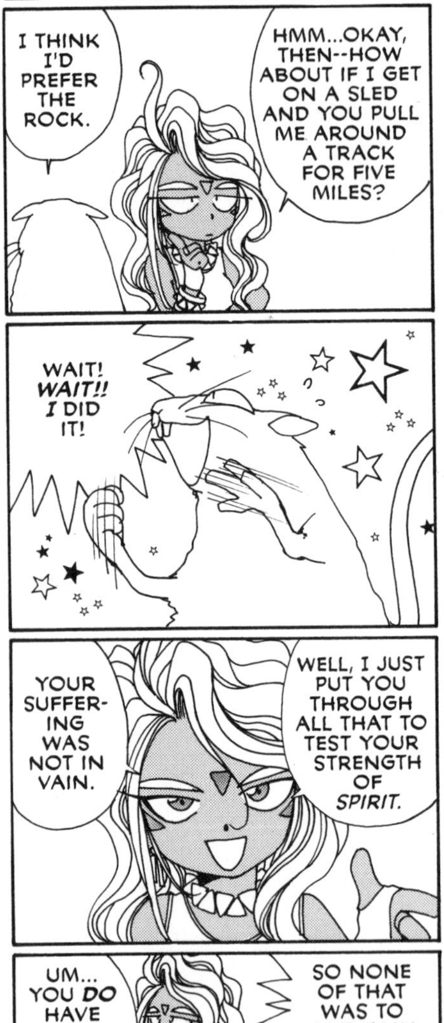
HMM...OKAY, THEN--HOW ABOUT IF I GET ON A SLED AND YOU PULL ME AROUND A TRACK FOR FIVE MILES?
I THINK I'D PREFER THE ROCK.
WAIT! *WAIT!! I* DID IT!
WELL, I JUST PUT YOU THROUGH ALL THAT TO TEST YOUR STRENGTH OF *SPIRIT.*
YOUR SUFFERING WAS NOT IN VAIN.
SO NONE OF THAT WAS TO ACTUALLY HELP ME BE A BETTER *DRUMMER* ...?!
UM... YOU *DO* HAVE SOME STRENGTH OF SPIRIT, RIGHT?

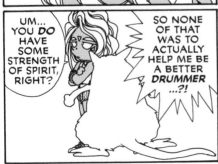

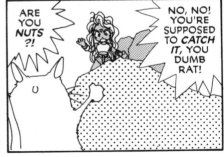

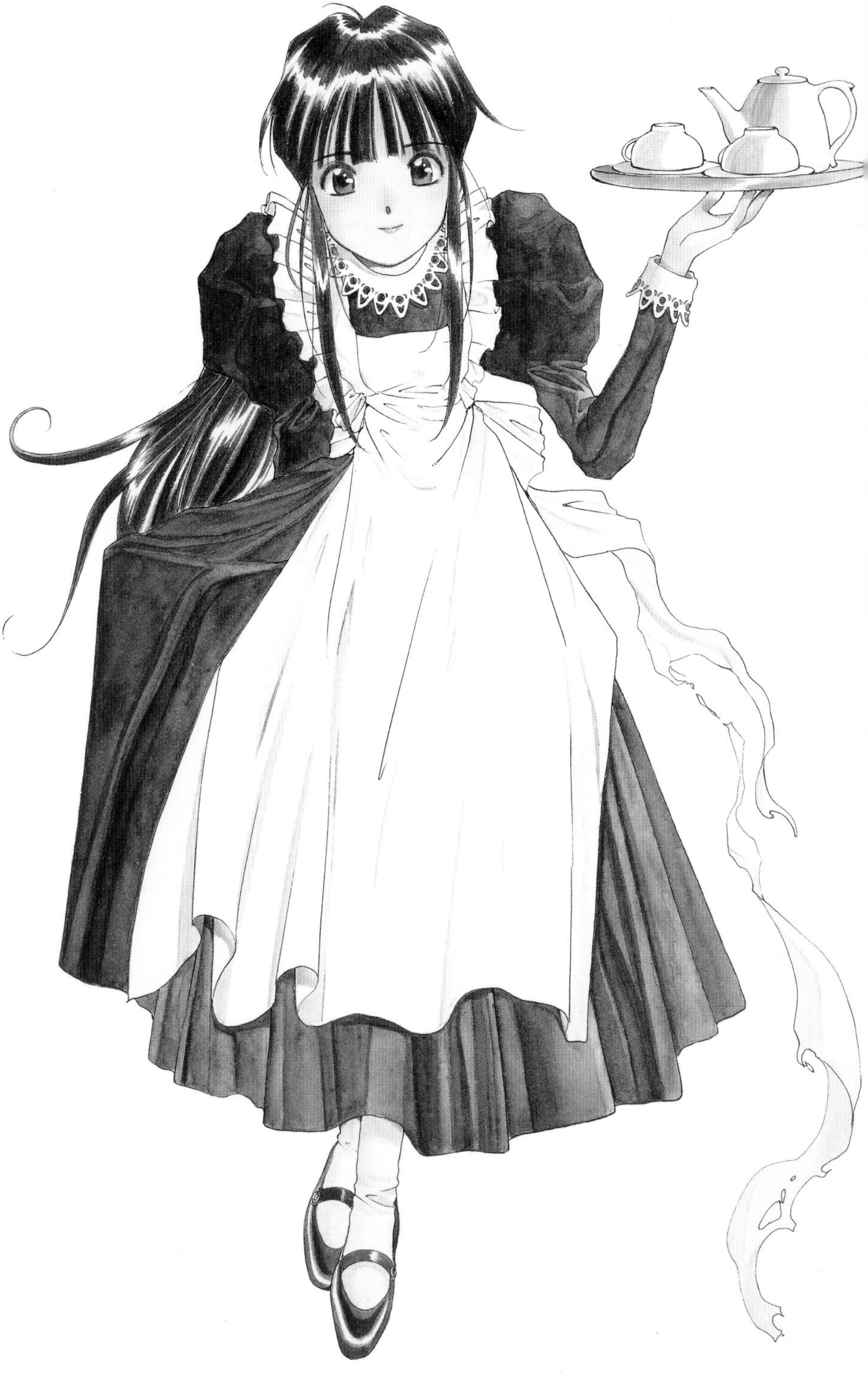

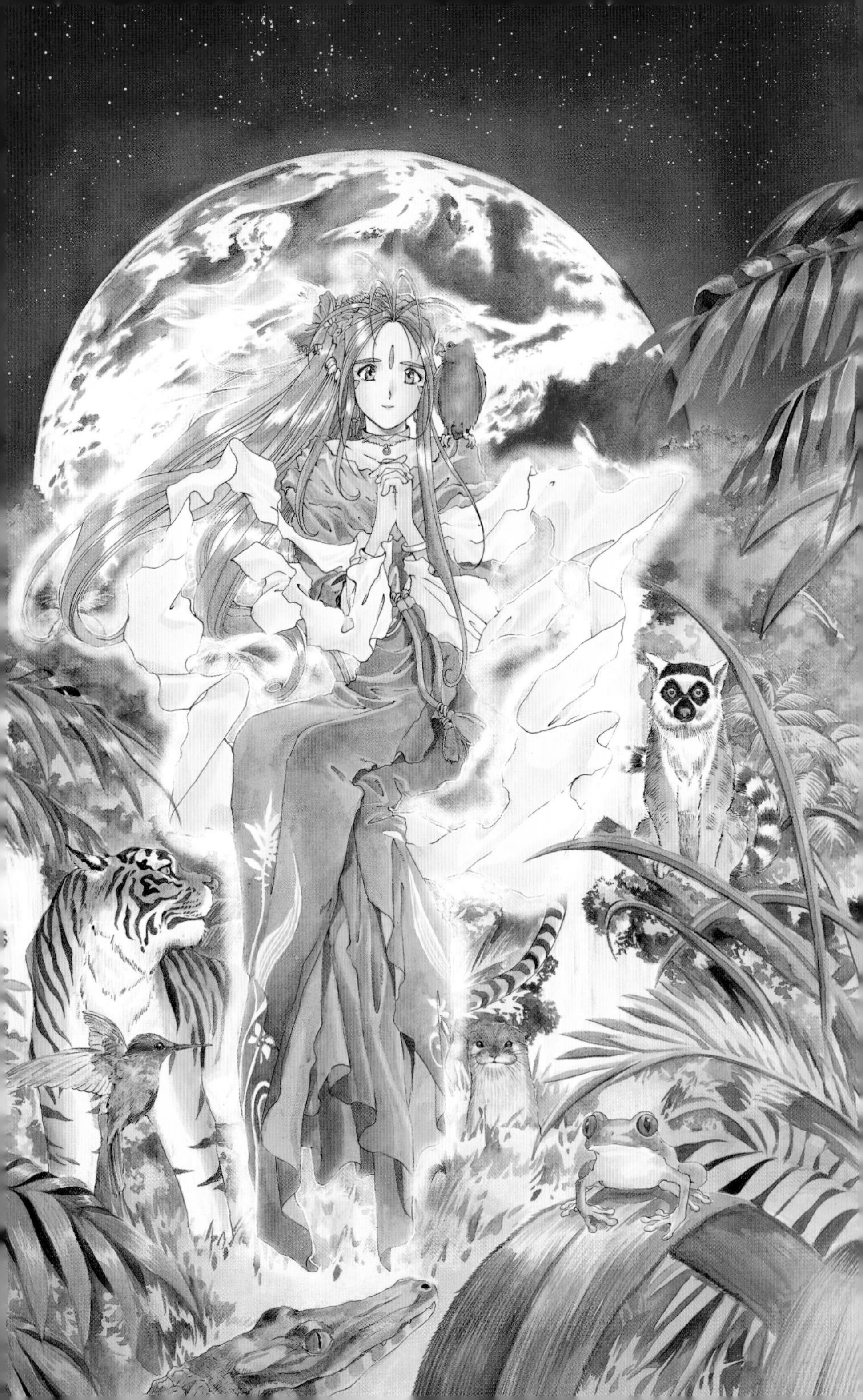

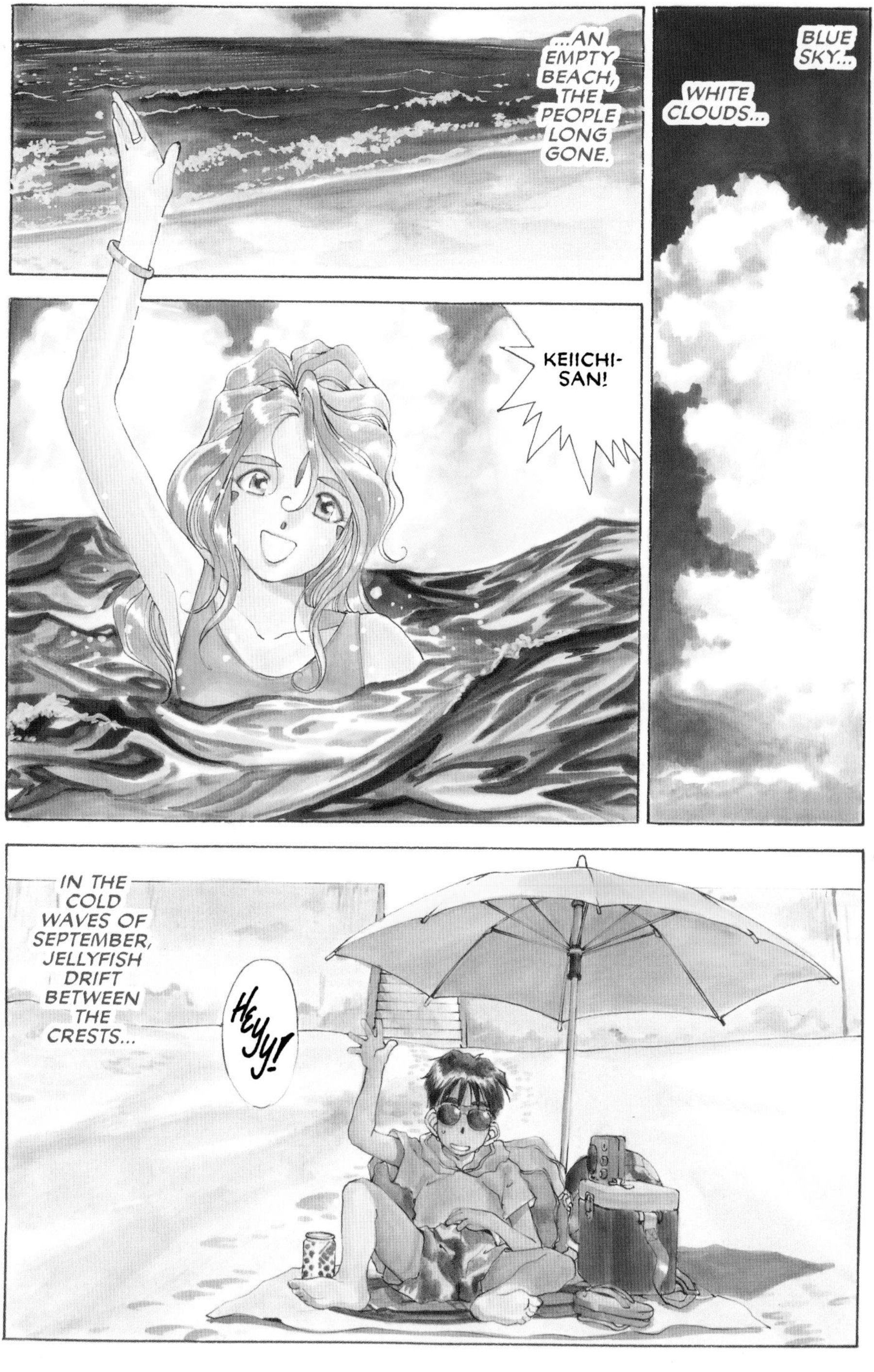
BLUE SKY...
WHITE CLOUDS...
...AN EMPTY BEACH, THE PEOPLE LONG GONE.
KEIICHI-SAN!
IN THE COLD WAVES OF SEPTEMBER, JELLYFISH DRIFT BETWEEN THE CRESTS...
HEYY!

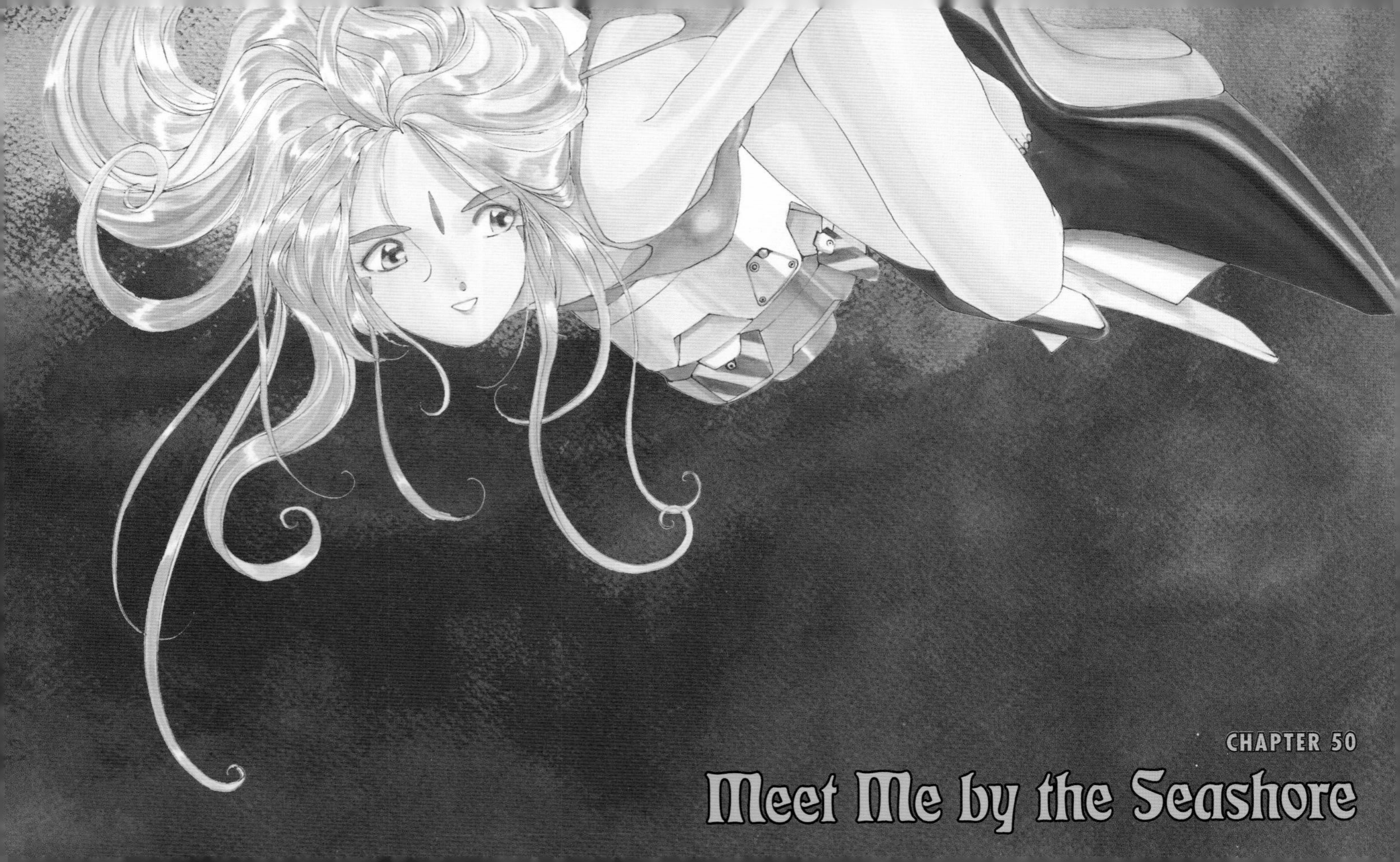
CHAPTER 50
Meet Me by the Seashore

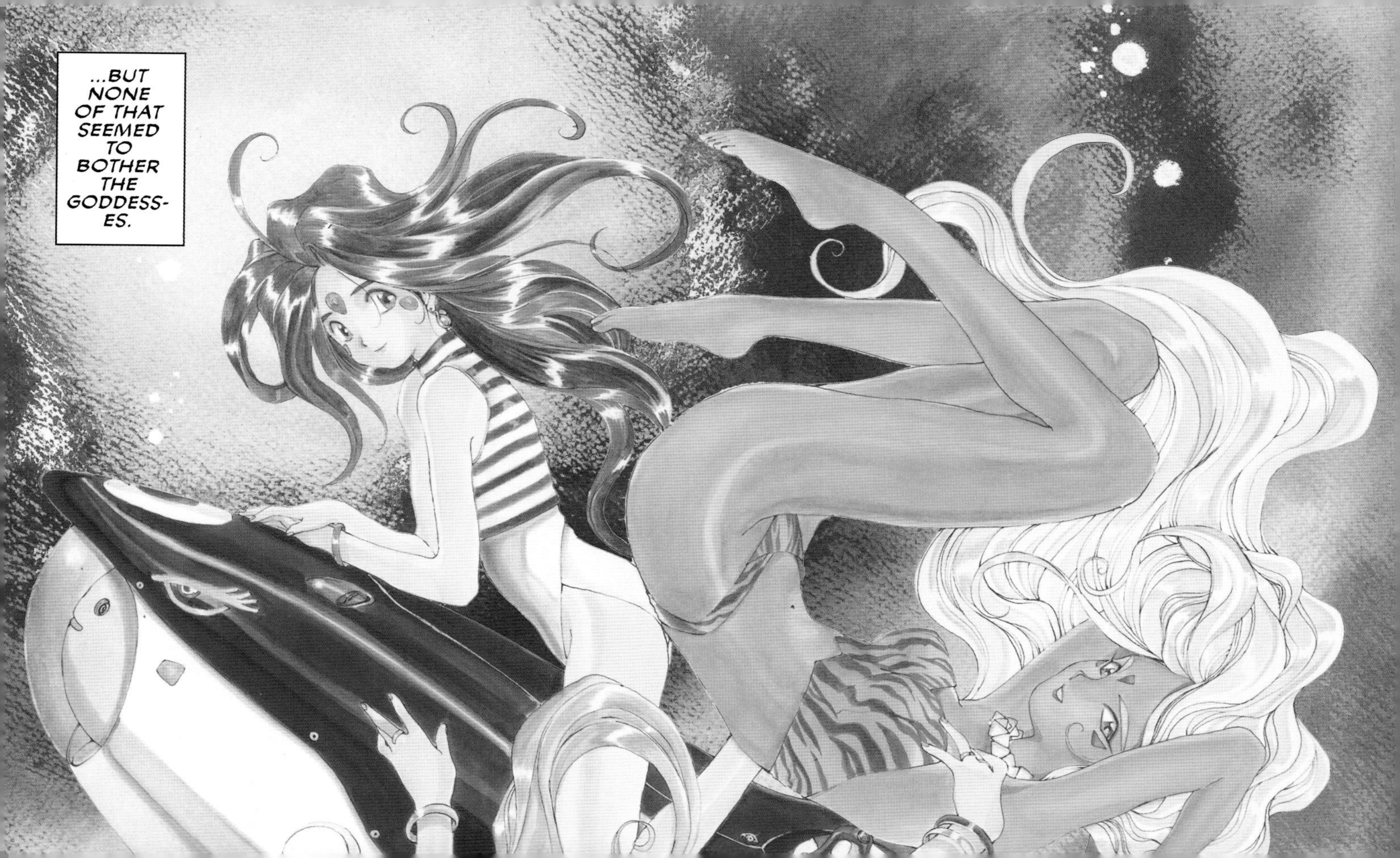
...BUT NONE OF THAT SEEMED TO BOTHER THE GODDESS-ES.

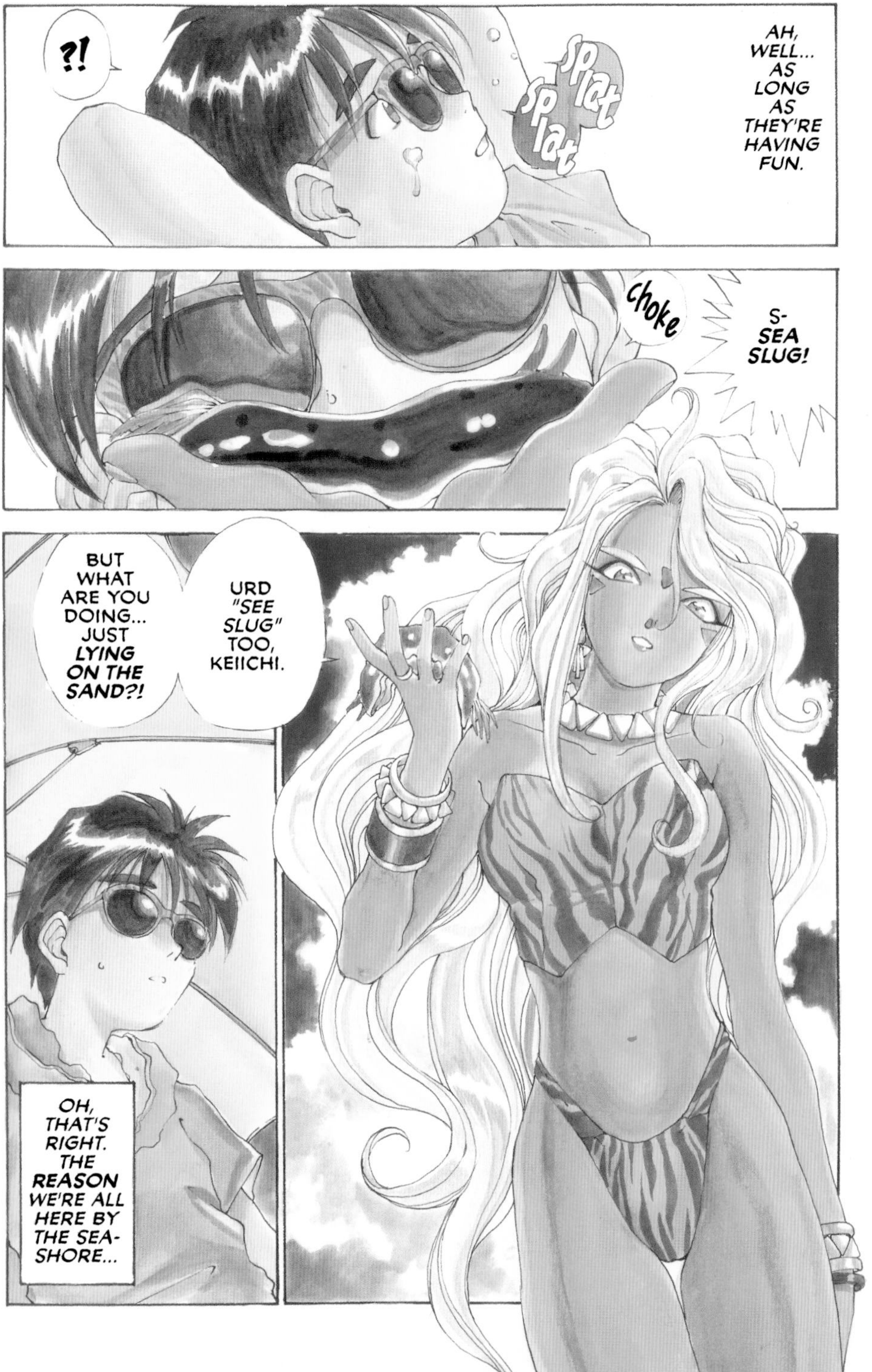
AH, WELL... AS LONG AS THEY'RE HAVING FUN.
splat
splat
?!
S- SEA SLUG!
choke
URD "SEE SLUG" TOO, KEIICHI.
BUT WHAT ARE YOU DOING... JUST LYING ON THE SAND?!
OH, THAT'S RIGHT. THE REASON WE'RE ALL HERE BY THE SEA-SHORE...

...WHEN URD SUDDENLY ANNOUNCED SHE WOULD CAST MY FORTUNE.

SILENCE! I MUST CONCENTRATE...

BUT I DON'T **WANT** TO KNOW THE FUTURE, URD...

...WAS BECAUSE OF SOMETHING SHE TOLD ME YESTERDAY...

KEIICHI! TOMORROW... YOU MUST **GO TO THE BEACH!**

HMMM... I CAN **SEE** IT!

THAT THOU AND THY **PARTNER STAR** WAX BRIGHT, DRAWN INEXORABLY TOWARD ONE ANOTHER?

THAT THE TIME DRAWS NIGH FOR THOU BOTH TO BURN WITH **ETERNAL LIGHT?**

KNOW YE NOT THAT THY BIRTH PLANET TRANSITS THROUGH THE PROTECTION OF THE MOON?

WHAT KIND OF FORTUNE IS **THAT?**

HUH?

...WILL BE BOUND TOGETHER FOREVER!

THOSE WHO PLEDGE THEIR LOVE UPON THAT ROCK, BENEATH THE FULL MOON...

Nope. Not a word.

...dost thou get it?!

I'M STUDYING *ENGINEERING*, NOT *ASTROLOGY*...

ON THE COAST-LINE SOUTH OF HERE...

WELL, LISTEN *UP!*

...STANDS THE *ROCK OF THE THREE SISTERS.*

NOW DOST THOU GET IT?

FOR-EVER!

IT IS FATE... KISMET... *DESTINY* !!

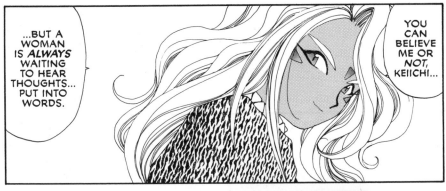

YOU CAN BELIEVE ME OR *NOT*, KEIICHI...
...BUT A WOMAN IS ***ALWAYS*** WAITING TO HEAR THOUGHTS... PUT INTO WORDS.
AND YOU'LL TURN UP BY THE SEA-SHORE... I KNOW IT.
JUST ANOTHER ONE OF HER LOONY-TUNE STORIES.
OR... SO I THOUGHT.
BUT OF COURSE, HERE I AM-- BY THE SEA-SHORE... LIKE A SUCKER.
THAT SLUG GOES ON YOUR HEAD, TO HELP YOU THINK. THE NEXT ONE GOES DOWN YOUR PANTS.
PLEASE DON'T.
WHERE DOES SHE *FIND* THESE THINGS?
KEIICHI ...?

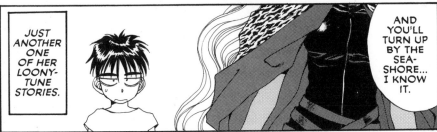

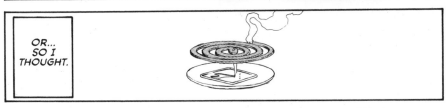

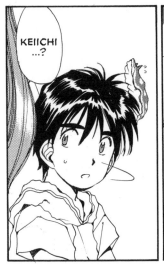

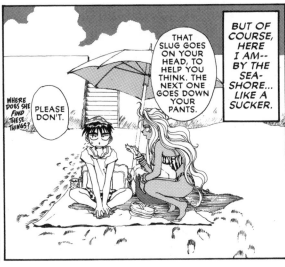

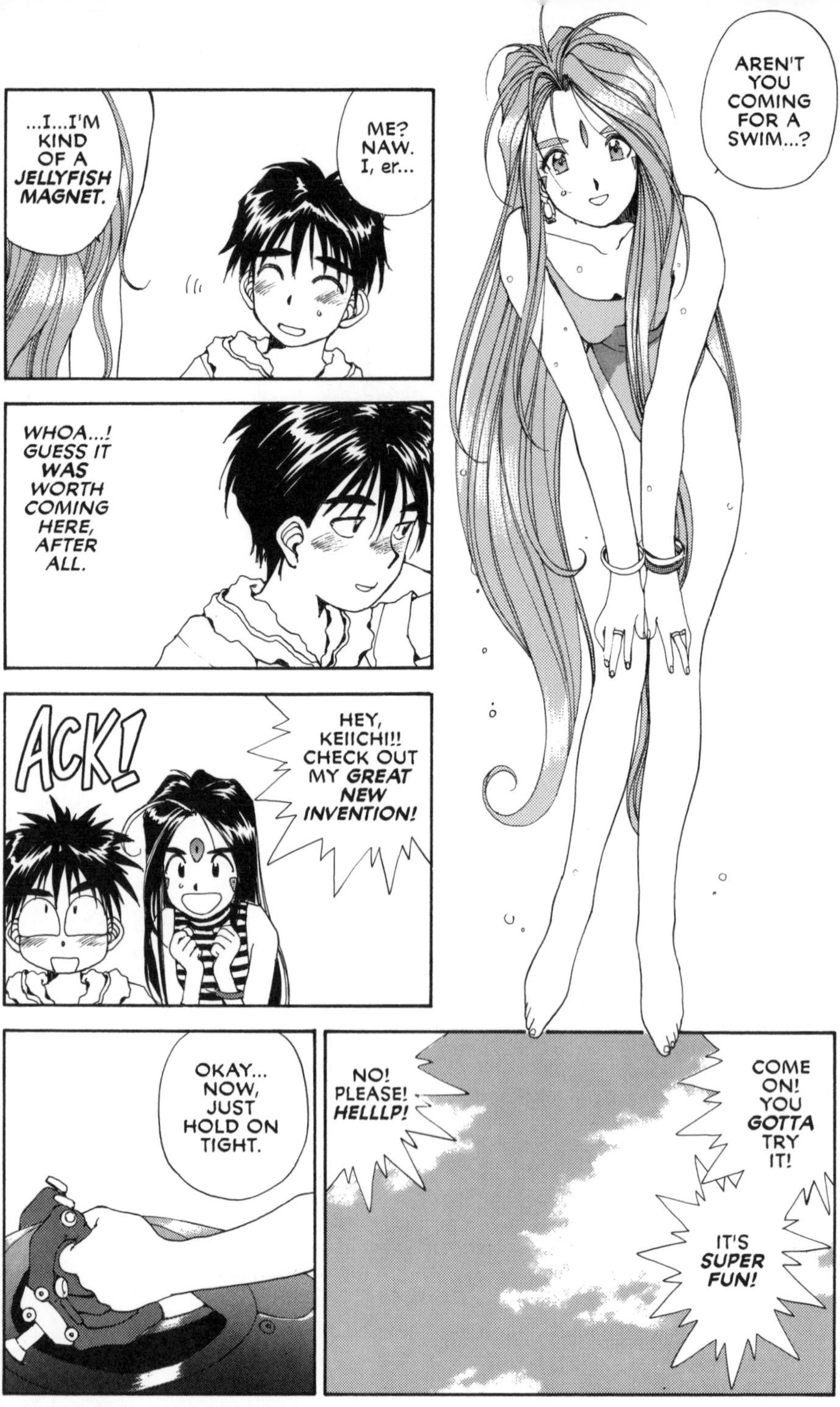
AREN'T YOU COMING FOR A SWIM...?
ME? NAW. I, er...
...I...I'M KIND OF A *JELLYFISH* MAGNET.
*WHOA...! GUESS IT **WAS** WORTH COMING HERE, AFTER ALL.*
HEY, KEIICHI!!! CHECK OUT MY ***GREAT NEW INVENTION!***
ACK!
COME ON! YOU ***GOTTA*** TRY IT!
NO! PLEASE! ***HELLLP!***
IT'S ***SUPER FUN!***
OKAY... NOW, JUST HOLD ON TIGHT.

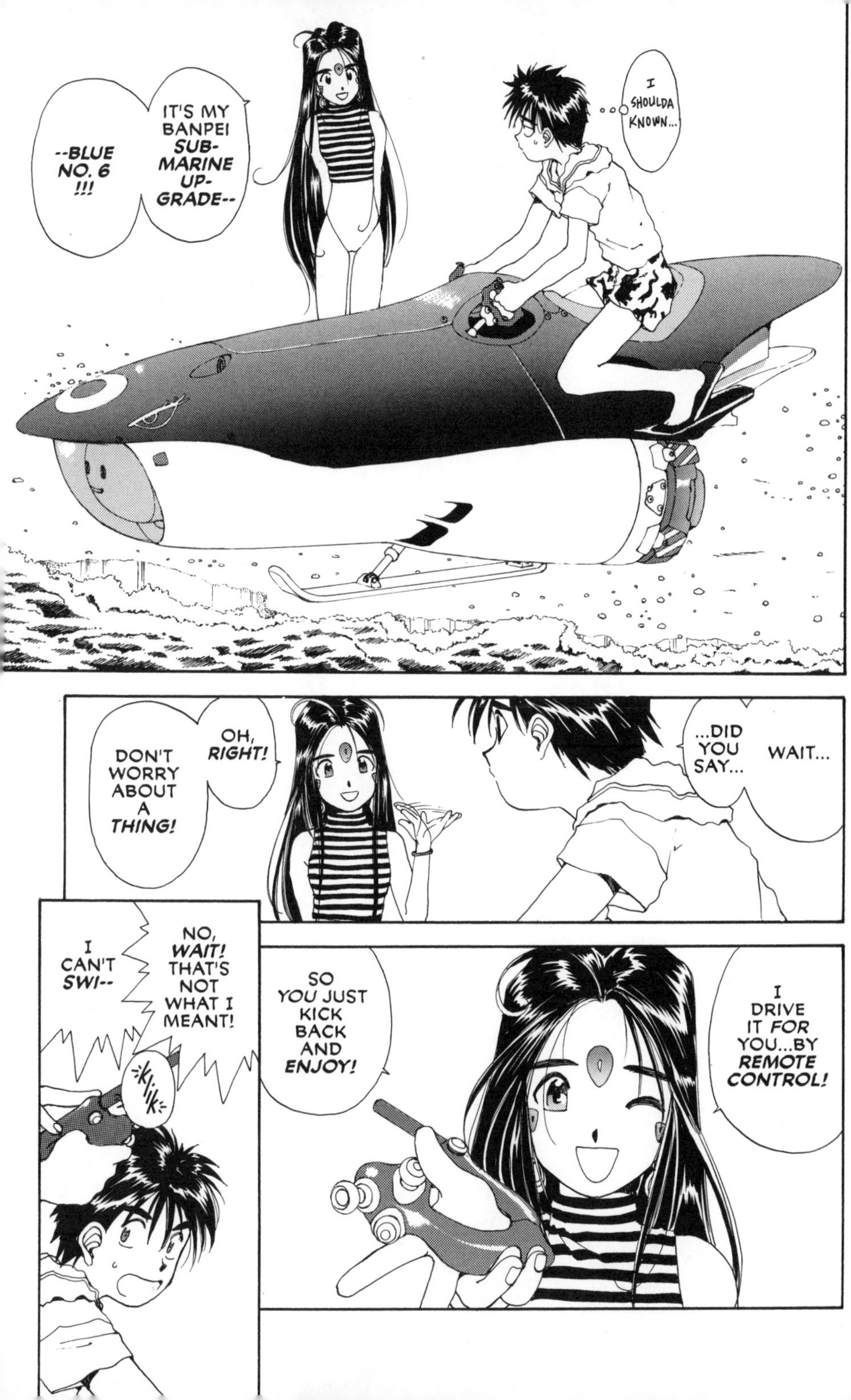
I SHOULDA KNOWN...
IT'S MY BANPEI SUB-MARINE UP-GRADE--
--BLUE NO. 6 !!!
WAIT...
...DID YOU SAY...
OH, RIGHT!
DON'T WORRY ABOUT A THING!
I DRIVE IT FOR YOU...BY REMOTE CONTROL!
SO YOU JUST KICK BACK AND ENJOY!
NO, WAIT! THAT'S NOT WHAT I MEANT!
I CAN'T SWI--
KLIK

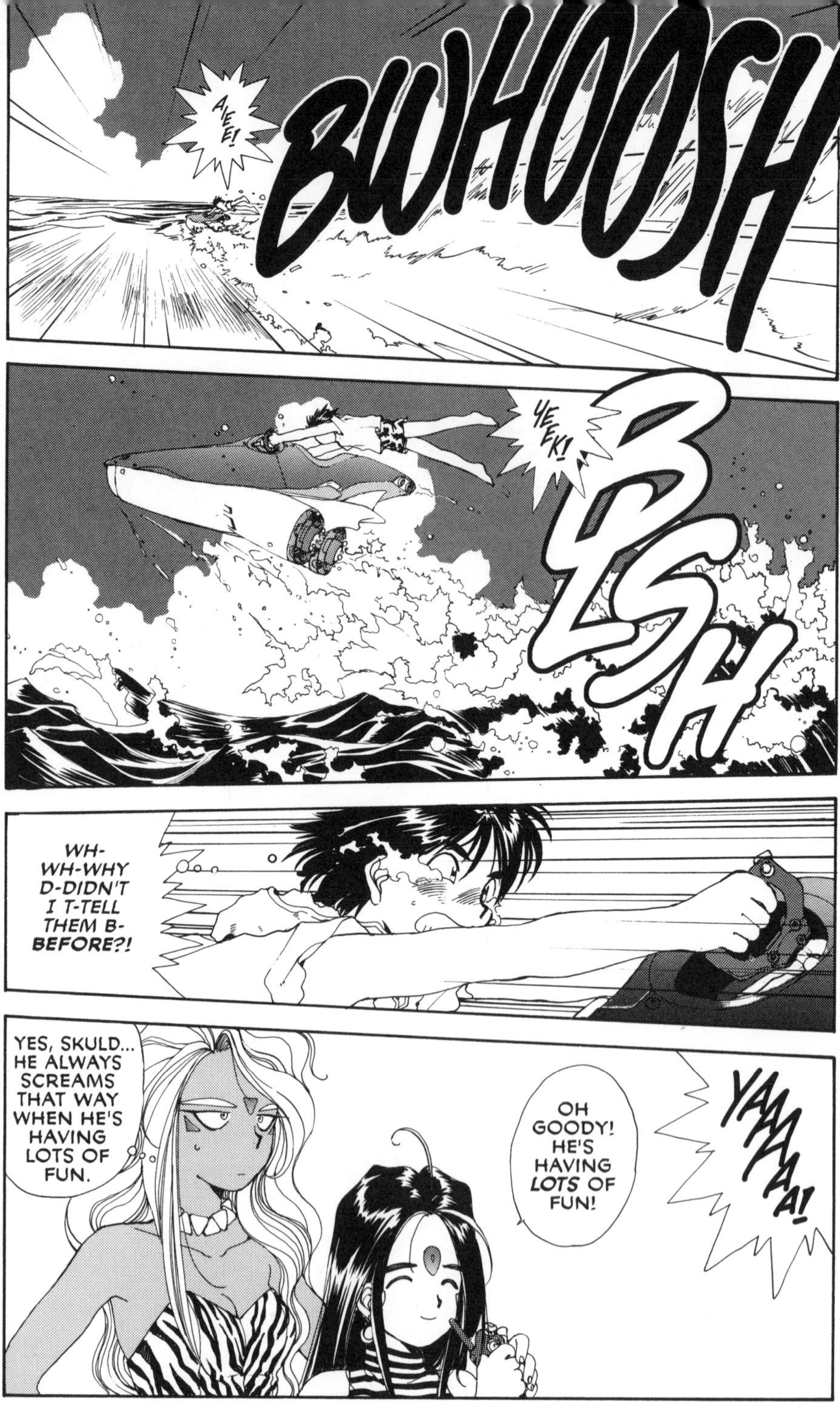
AIEE!
BWHOOSH
YEEK!
WH-WH-WHY D-DIDN'T I T-TELL THEM B-BEFORE?!
YAAAAA!
OH GOODY! HE'S HAVING *LOTS* OF FUN!
YES, SKULD... HE ALWAYS SCREAMS THAT WAY WHEN HE'S HAVING LOTS OF FUN.

265

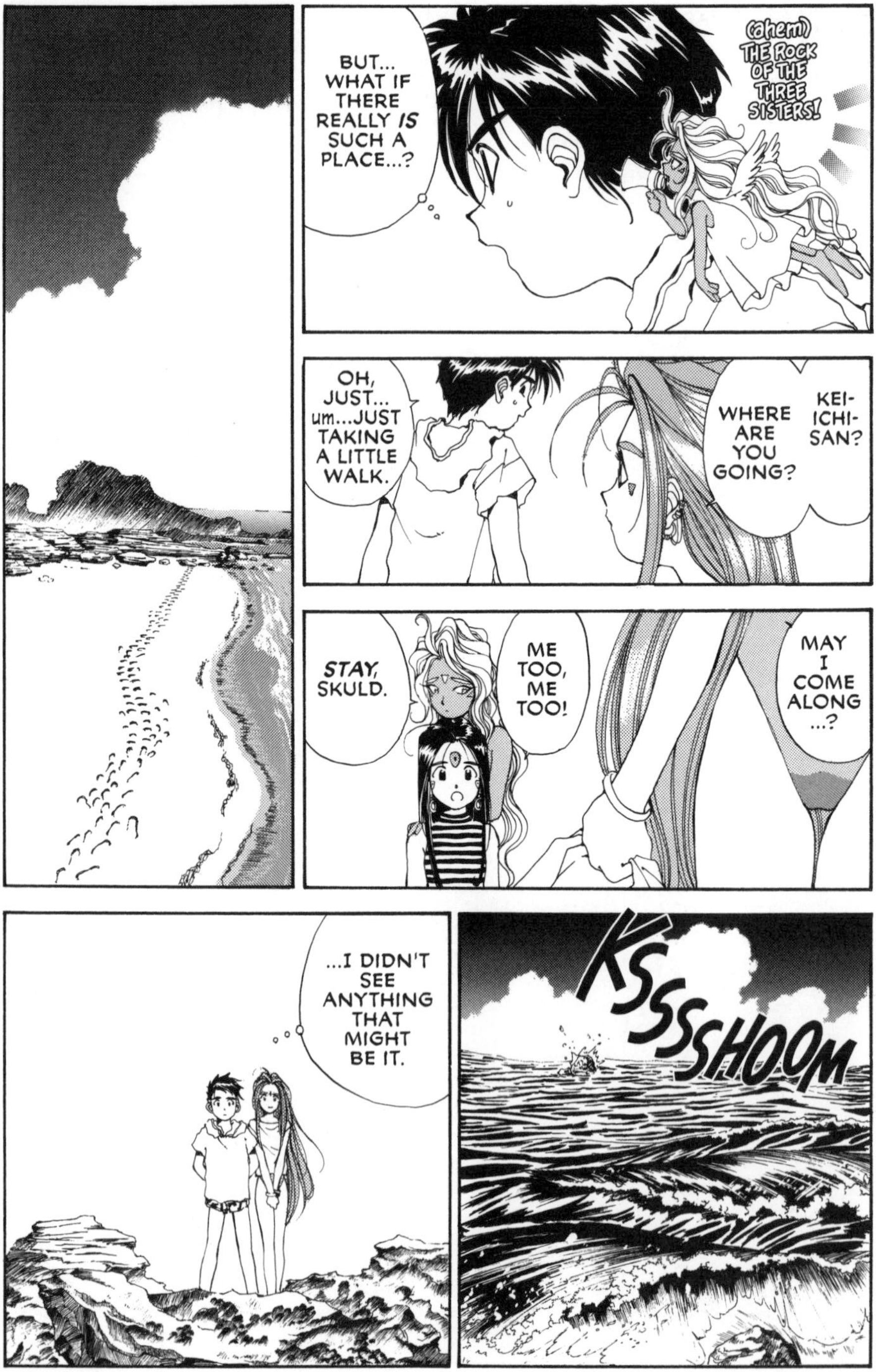
(ahem) THE ROCK OF THE THREE SISTERS!
BUT... WHAT IF THERE REALLY *IS* SUCH A PLACE...?
KEI-ICHI-SAN?
WHERE ARE YOU GOING?
OH, JUST... um...JUST TAKING A LITTLE WALK.
MAY I COME ALONG ...?
ME TOO, ME TOO!
STAY, SKULD.
KSSSSHOOM
...I DIDN'T SEE ANYTHING THAT MIGHT BE IT.

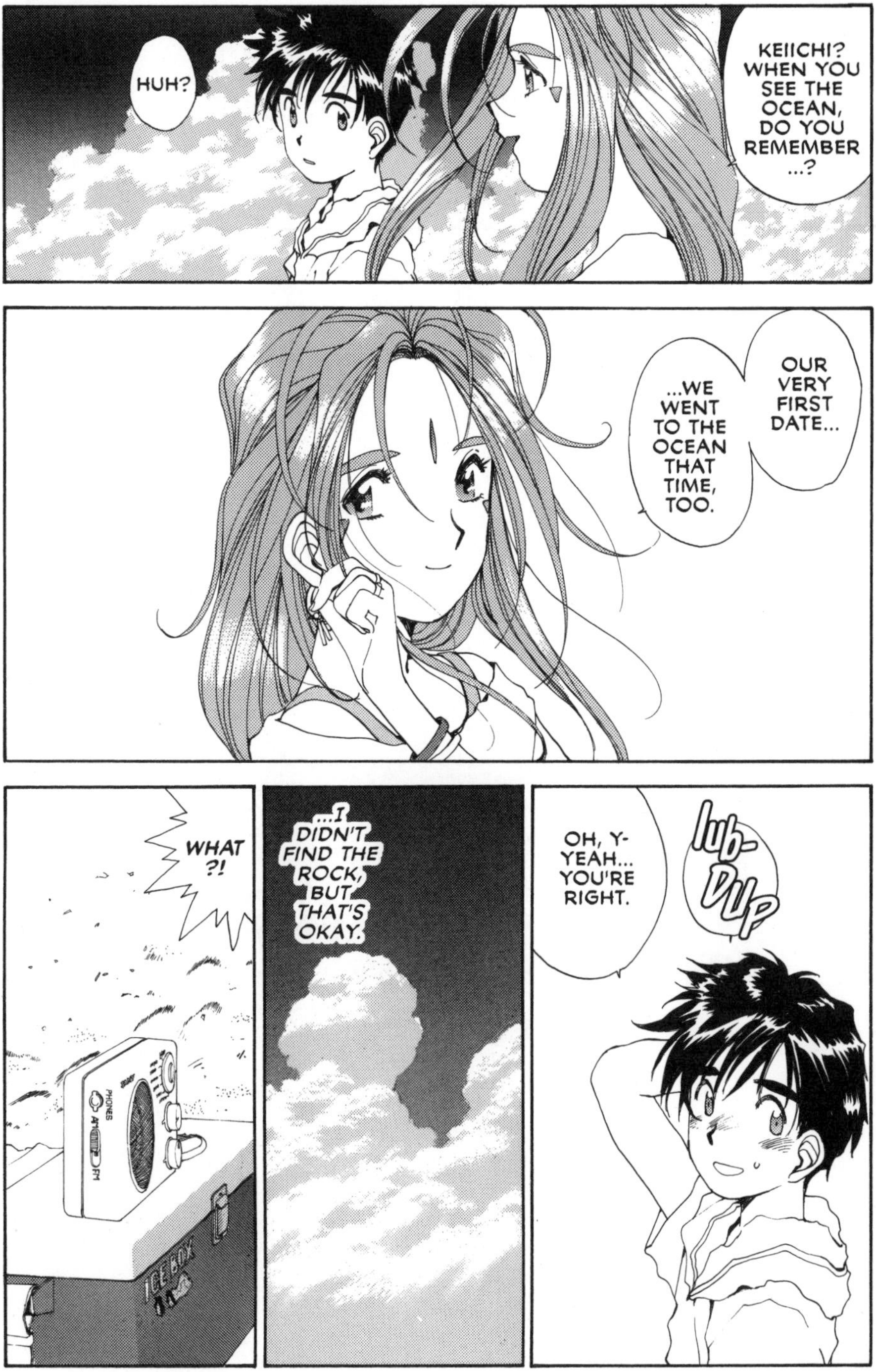
KEIICHI? WHEN YOU SEE THE OCEAN, DO YOU REMEMBER ...?
HUH?
OUR VERY FIRST DATE...
...WE WENT TO THE OCEAN THAT TIME, TOO.
lub-DUP
OH, Y-YEAH... YOU'RE RIGHT.
...I DIDN'T FIND THE ROCK, BUT THAT'S OKAY.
WHAT ?!
PHONES
AM
FM
ICE BOX

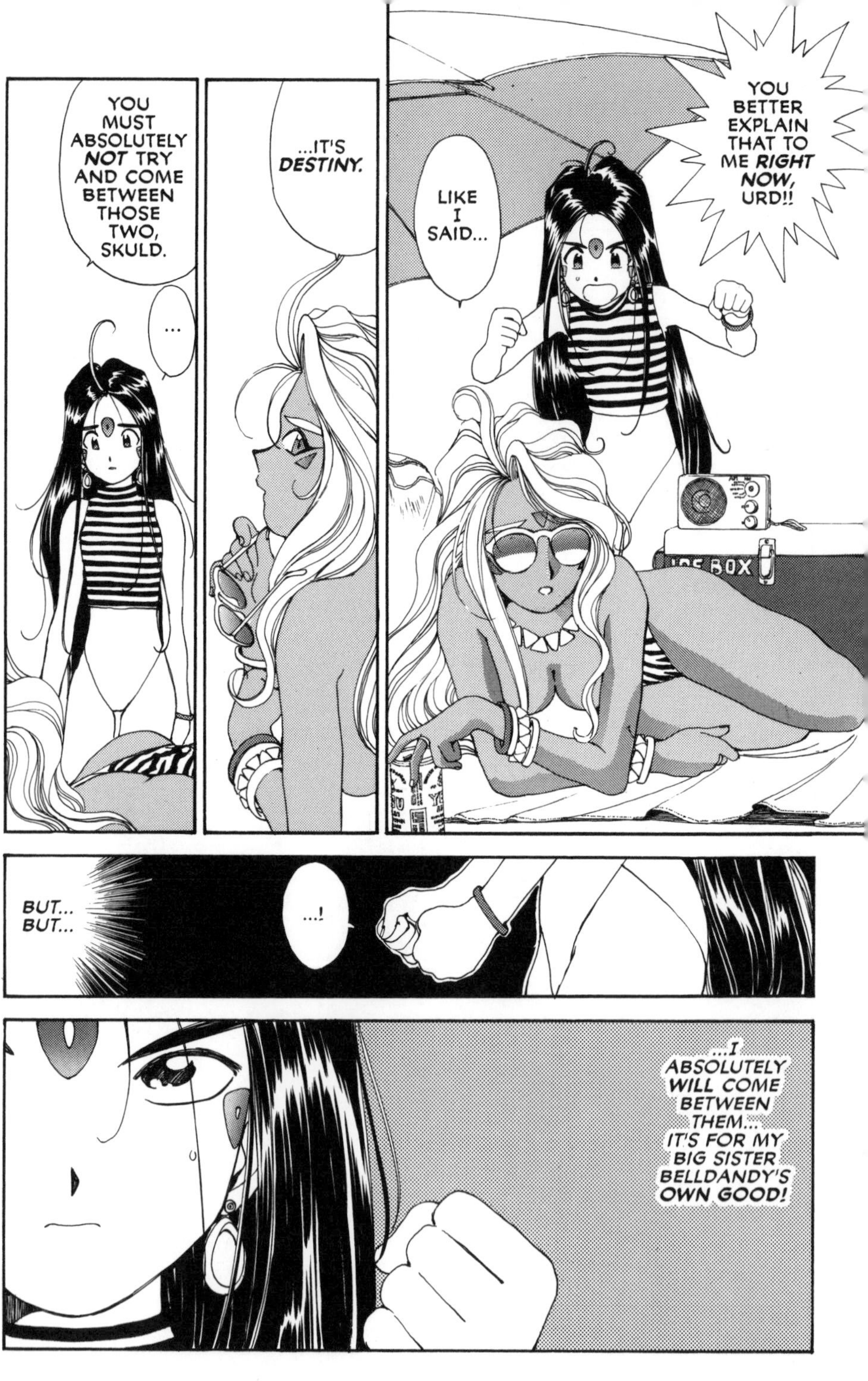
YOU BETTER EXPLAIN THAT TO ME *RIGHT NOW*, URD!!
LIKE I SAID...
...IT'S *DESTINY.*
YOU MUST ABSOLUTELY *NOT* TRY AND COME BETWEEN THOSE TWO, SKULD.
...
...!
BUT... BUT...
...I ABSOLUTELY WILL COME BETWEEN THEM... IT'S FOR MY BIG SISTER BELLDANDY'S OWN GOOD!

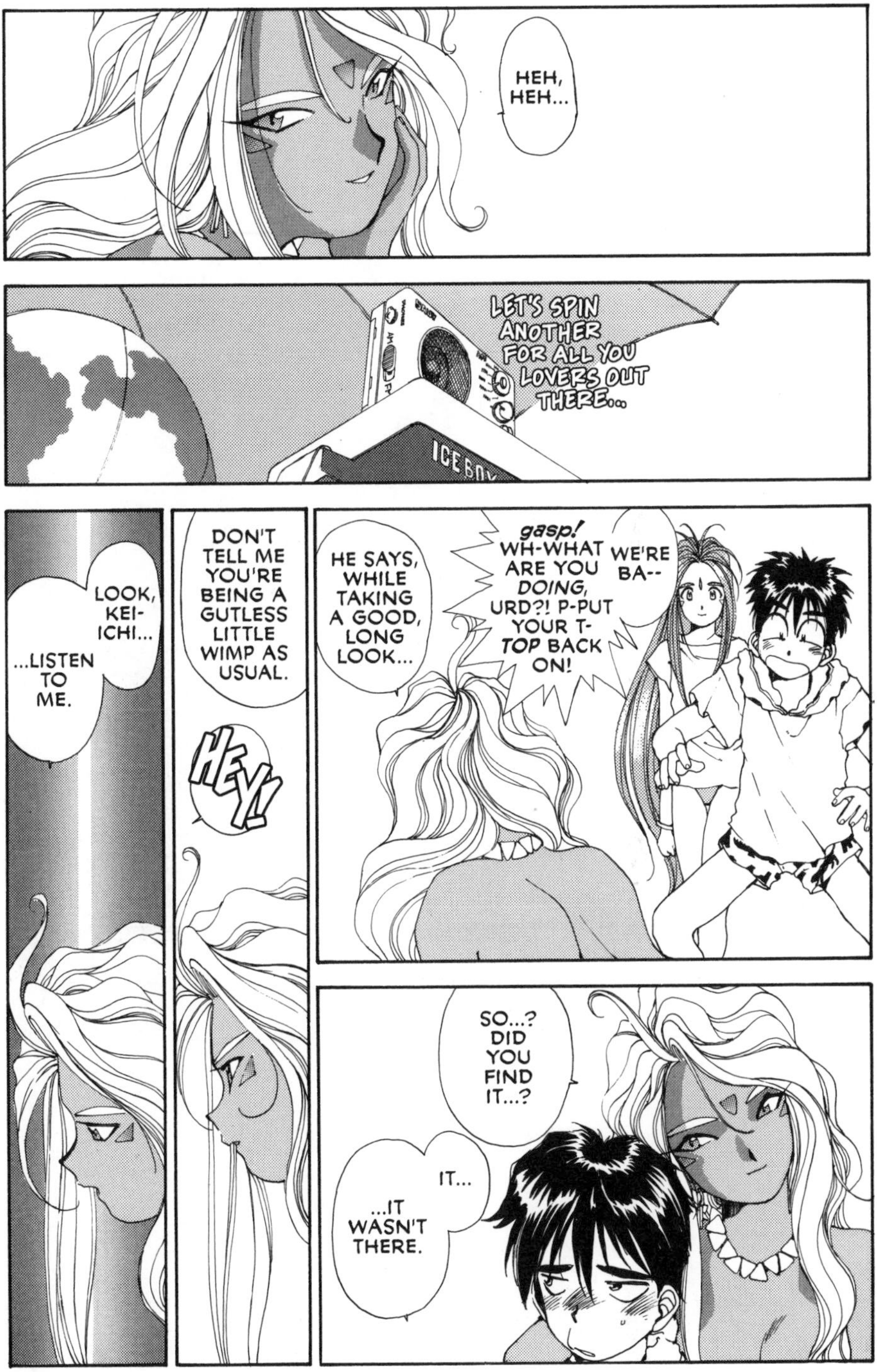
HEH, HEH...
LET'S SPIN ANOTHER FOR ALL YOU LOVERS OUT THERE...
ICE BOX
WE'RE BA--
gasp! WH-WHAT ARE YOU DOING, URD?! P-PUT YOUR T-TOP BACK ON!
HE SAYS, WHILE TAKING A GOOD, LONG LOOK...
SO...? DID YOU FIND IT...?
IT...
...IT WASN'T THERE.
DON'T TELL ME YOU'RE BEING A GUTLESS LITTLE WIMP AS USUAL.
HEY!
LOOK, KEI-ICHI...
...LISTEN TO ME.

SOME THINGS ARE ONLY VISIBLE... TO THOSE WITH FAITH TO SEE THEM.

KEIICHI... ARE YOU REALLY GOING TO THROW AWAY THIS CHANCE YOU *KNOW* ABOUT...?

BECAUSE THEY USUALLY DON'T REALIZE WHEN AND WHERE *THEIR* CHANCE WILL COME.

THERE ARE AS MANY CHANCES FOR HAPPINESS AS THERE ARE STARS TWINKLING IN THE SKY.

BUT ONLY A HANDFUL OF PEOPLE EVER REACH OUT AND SEIZE THEM.

DO YOU KNOW *WHY*?

AND, OH... IF YOU RUN INTO TROUBLE, JUST CALL.

GO LOOK. ONE MORE TIME.

UM... ER...

...GOOD QUES-TION.

WHAT WAS THAT ABOUT?

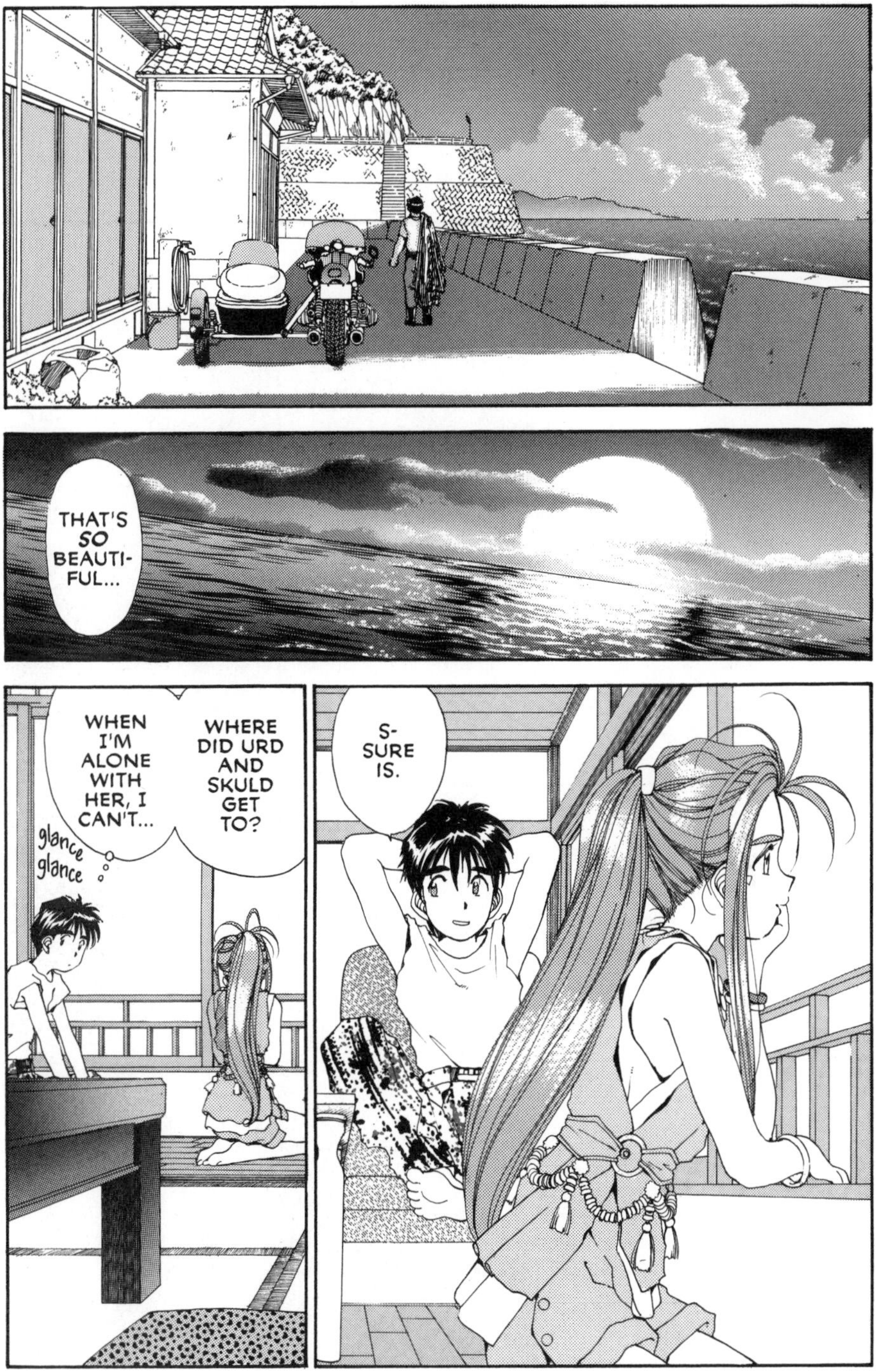
THAT'S *SO* BEAUTIFUL...
S-SURE IS.
WHERE DID URD AND SKULD GET TO?
WHEN I'M ALONE WITH HER, I CAN'T...
glance glance

SHE'S WAITING!

TELL HER!

...DO I *REALLY* HAVE TO SPELL IT OUT FOR HER... AFTER ALL THIS TIME...?

I MEAN...

TAKEN ABACK, SHE HESITATES...

I LOVE YOU, MY DARLING.

WHAT WOULD IT BE LIKE? THE TWO OF US UPON THE ROCK, UNDER THE FULL MOON...

BELL-DANDY...

YES, DEAR?

I LOVE YOU, TOO...

...A SHY SMILE STEALS ACROSS HER FACE. AND THEN--

STOP! *STOP!* NOW THINGS ARE HAPPENING *FAST!*

HEY! I DIDN'T SAY NOTHIN' ABOUT THAT!

YEAH! DON'T GET CARRIED *AWAY!*

272

lub-DUP

um

OH NO! IT'S *NOTHING!* I'M *FINE!*

I...WE... SHE... he...it... they... *ha ha!*

SCOOT SCOOT scoot

YOUR FACE IS SO RED. DID YOU GET A SUN-BURN...?

KEIICHI ...?

IT SEEMS LIKE... EVER SINCE WE AR-RIVED...

...YOUR MIND'S BEEN SOME-WHERE ELSE.

UM... KEIICHI... ARE YOU SORRY YOU CAME TO THE SEASHORE WITH ME...?

NO! ABSOLUTELY NOT! *NOT* TRUE!

273

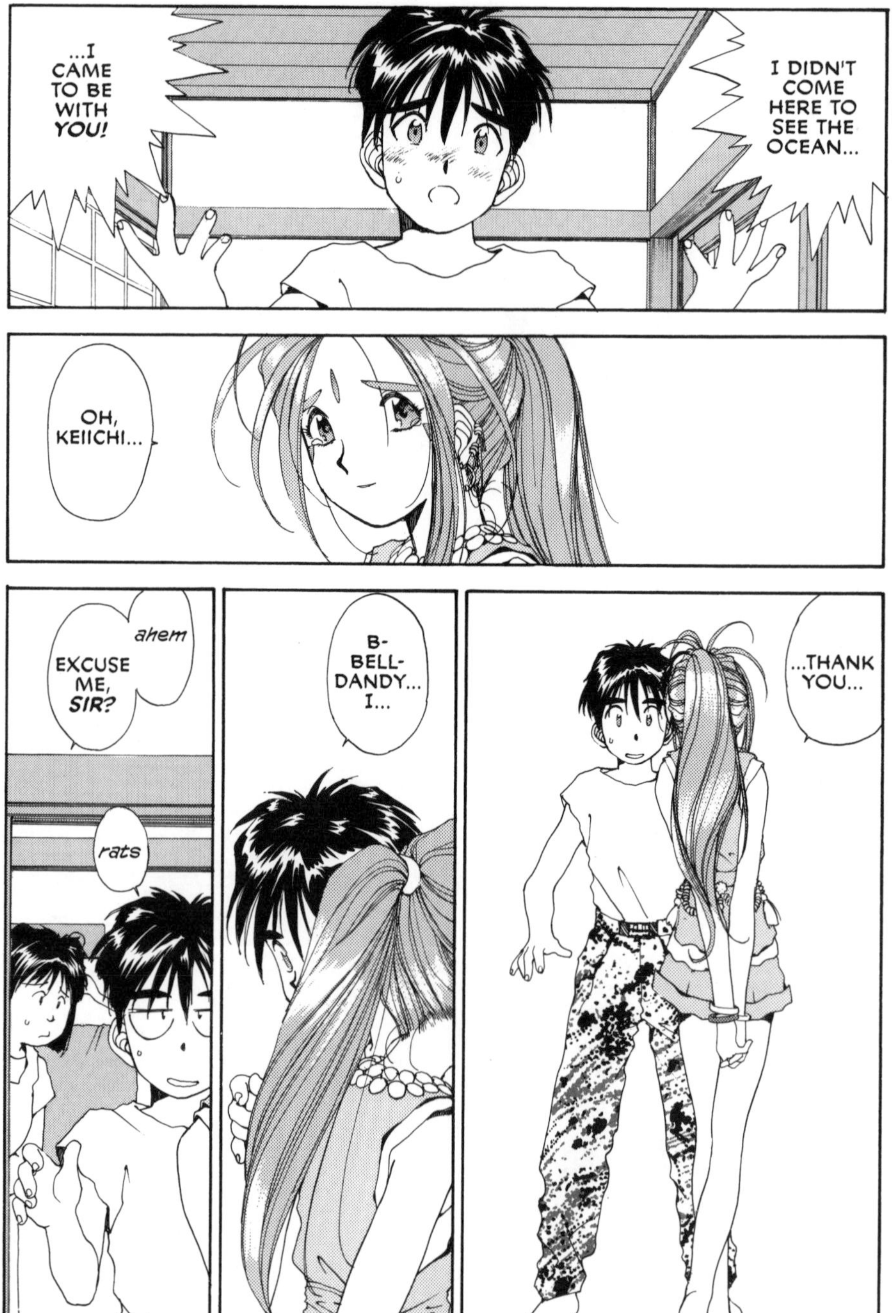
I DIDN'T COME HERE TO SEE THE OCEAN...
...I CAME TO BE WITH *YOU!*
OH, KEIICHI...
...THANK YOU...
B-BELL-DANDY... I...
ahem
EXCUSE ME, *SIR?*
rats

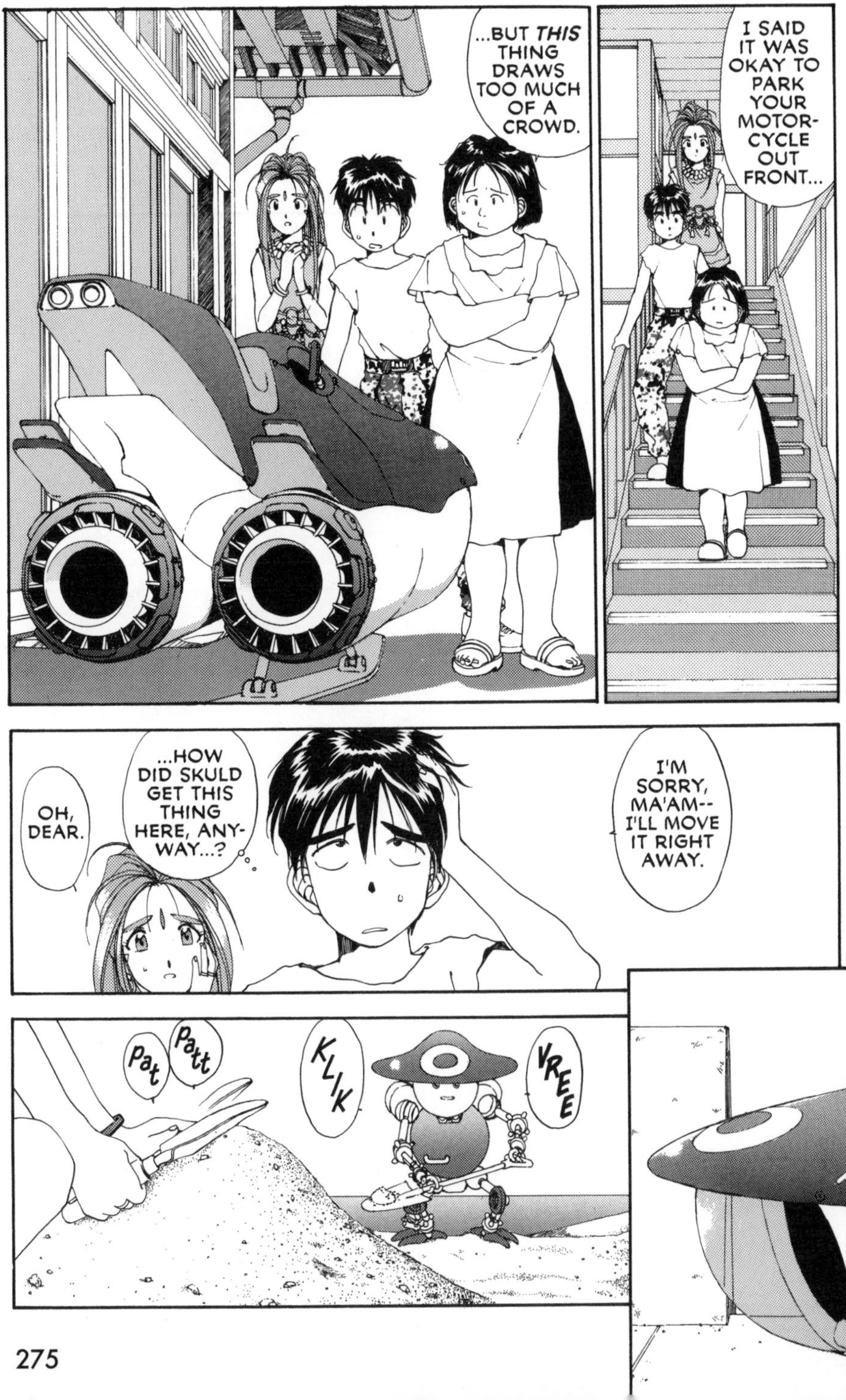
I SAID IT WAS OKAY TO PARK YOUR MOTORCYCLE OUT FRONT...
...BUT *THIS* THING DRAWS TOO MUCH OF A CROWD.
I'M SORRY, MA'AM-- I'LL MOVE IT RIGHT AWAY.
...HOW DID SKULD GET THIS THING HERE, ANYWAY...?
OH, DEAR.
VREE
KLIK
patt
pat

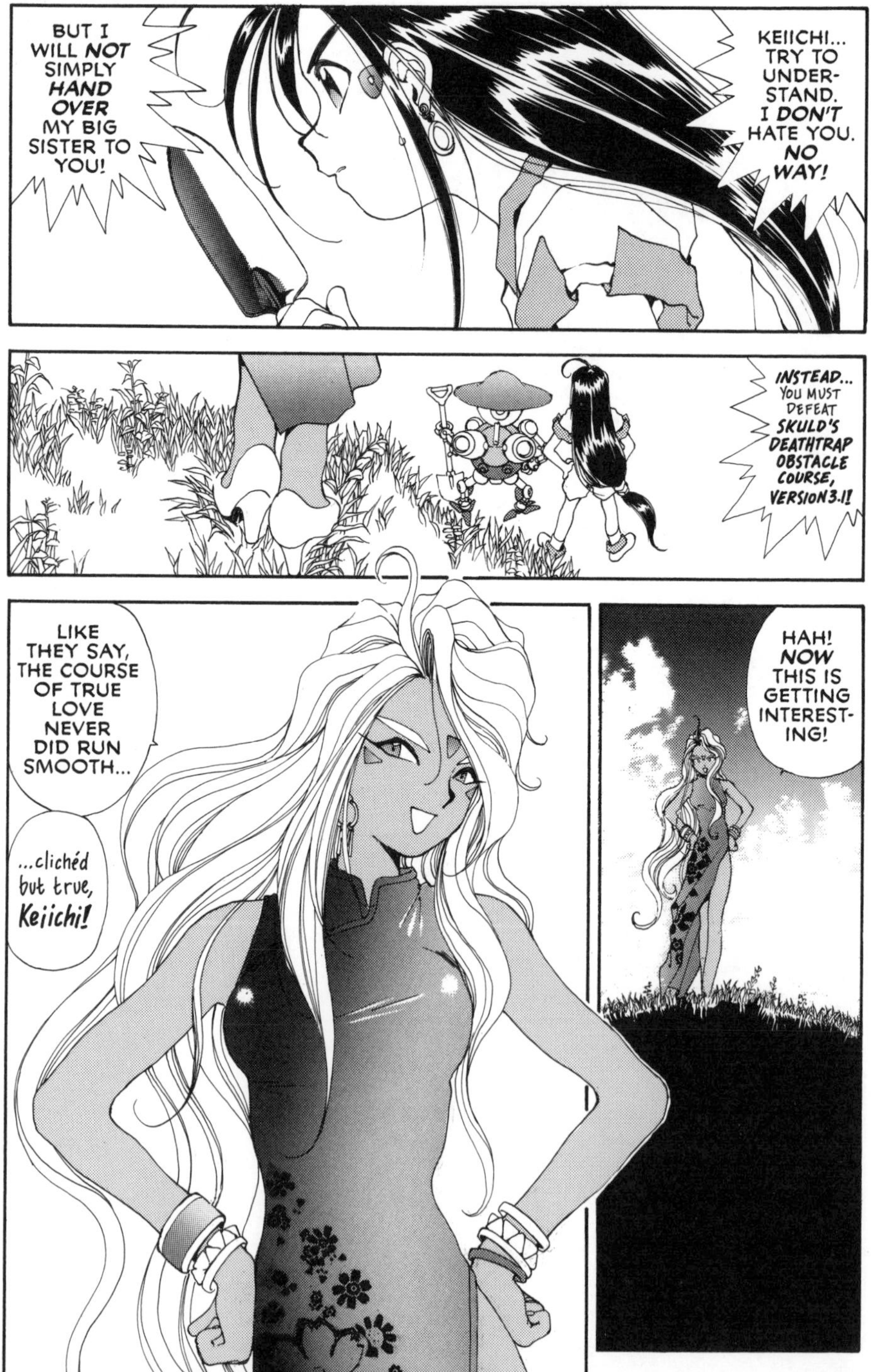
KEIICHI... TRY TO UNDER-STAND. I DON'T HATE YOU. NO WAY!
BUT I WILL NOT SIMPLY HAND OVER MY BIG SISTER TO YOU!
INSTEAD... YOU MUST DEFEAT SKULD'S DEATHTRAP OBSTACLE COURSE, VERSION 3.1!
HAH! NOW THIS IS GETTING INTEREST-ING!
LIKE THEY SAY, THE COURSE OF TRUE LOVE NEVER DID RUN SMOOTH...
...clichéd but true, Keiichi!

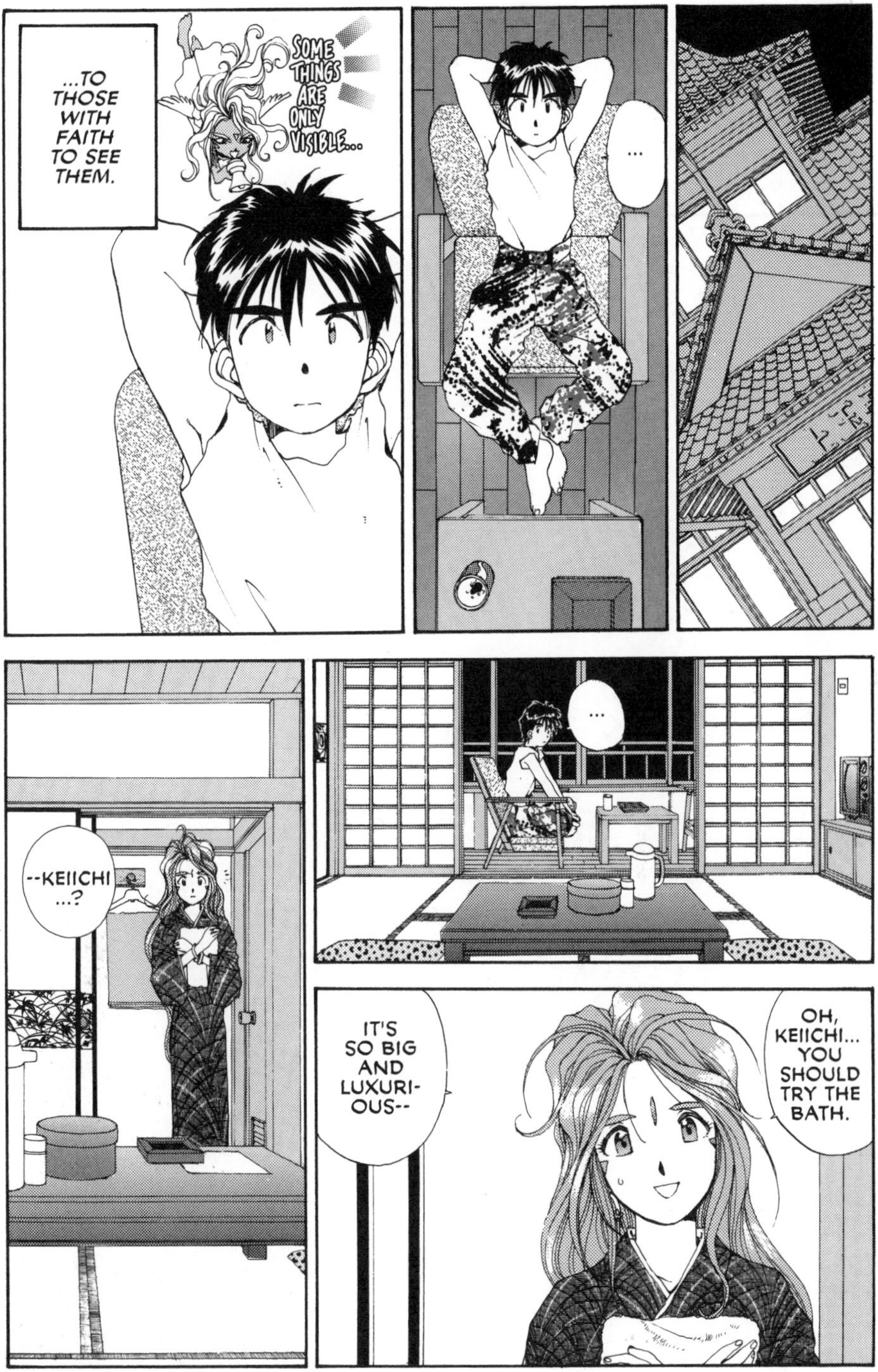
...
SOME THINGS ARE ONLY VISIBLE...
...TO THOSE WITH FAITH TO SEE THEM.
...
OH, KEIICHI... YOU SHOULD TRY THE BATH.
IT'S SO BIG AND LUXURI-OUS--
--KEIICHI ...?

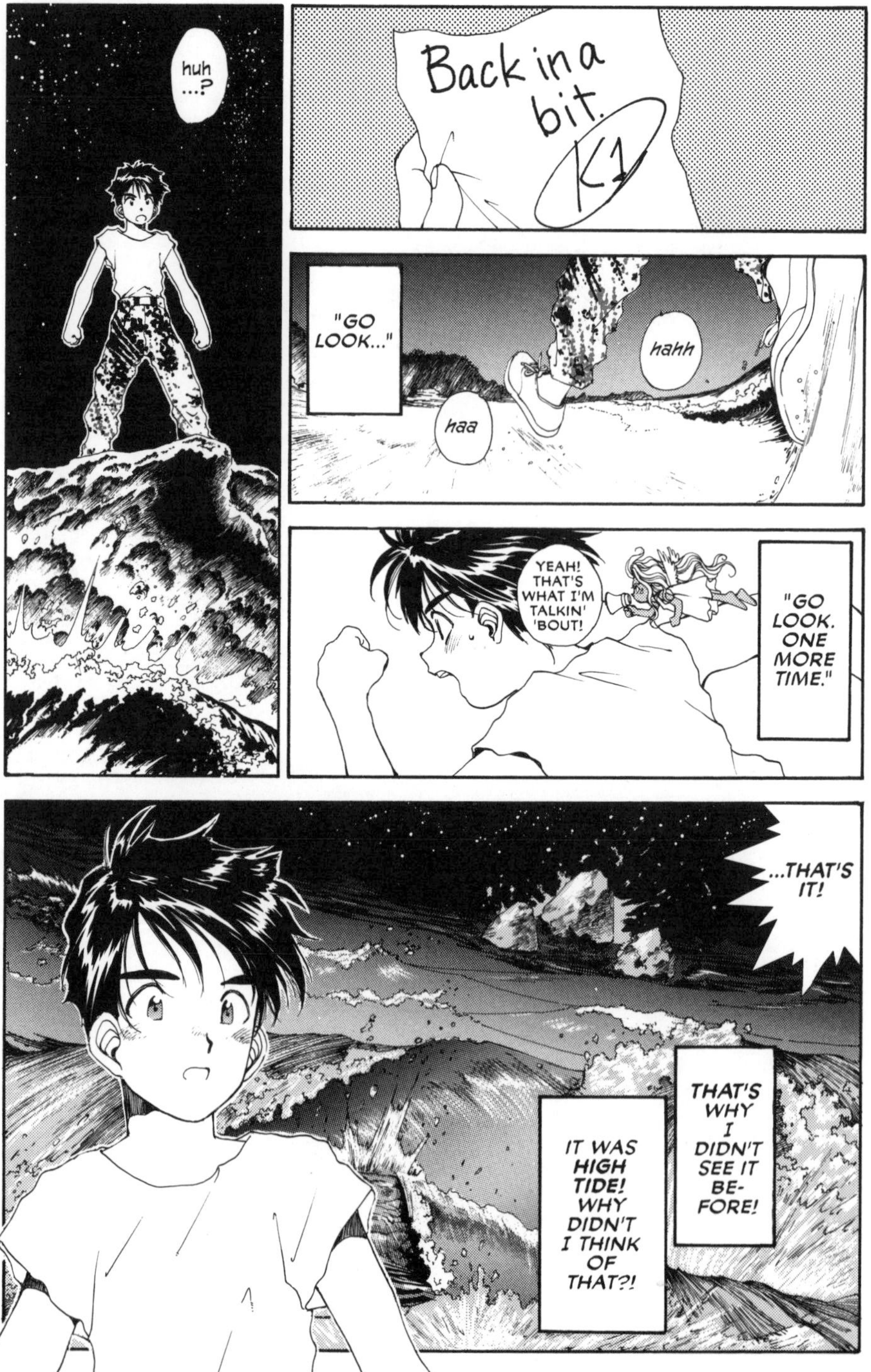
Back in a bit. K1
hahh
"GO LOOK..."
haa
"GO LOOK. ONE MORE TIME."
YEAH! THAT'S WHAT I'M TALKIN' 'BOUT!
huh ...?
...THAT'S IT!
THAT'S WHY I DIDN'T SEE IT BE-FORE!
IT WAS HIGH TIDE! WHY DIDN'T I THINK OF THAT?!

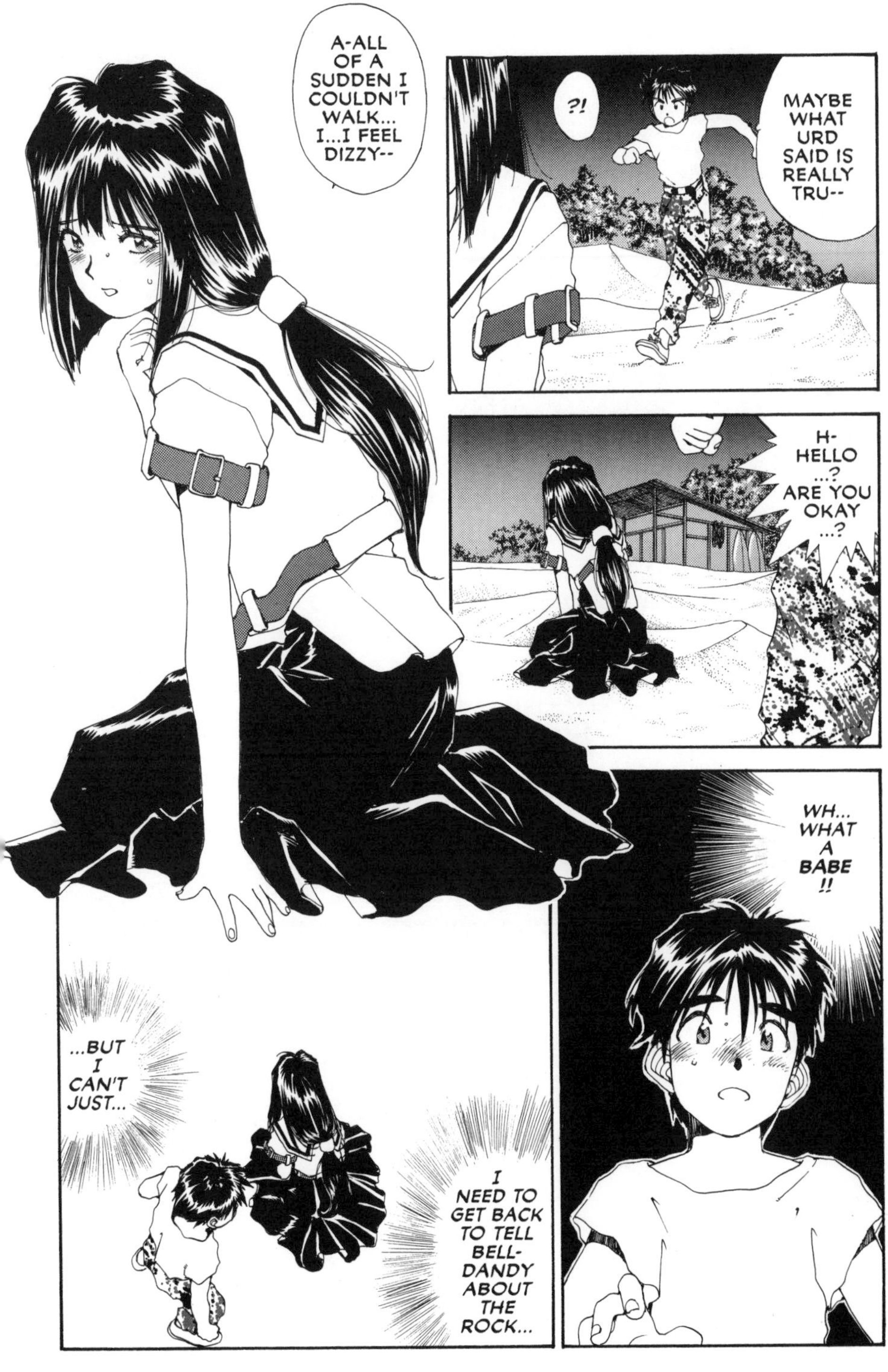
MAYBE WHAT URD SAID IS REALLY TRU--
?!
H-HELLO ...? ARE YOU OKAY ...?
A-ALL OF A SUDDEN I COULDN'T WALK... I...I FEEL DIZZY--
WH... WHAT A BABE !!
I NEED TO GET BACK TO TELL BELL-DANDY ABOUT THE ROCK...
...BUT I CAN'T JUST...

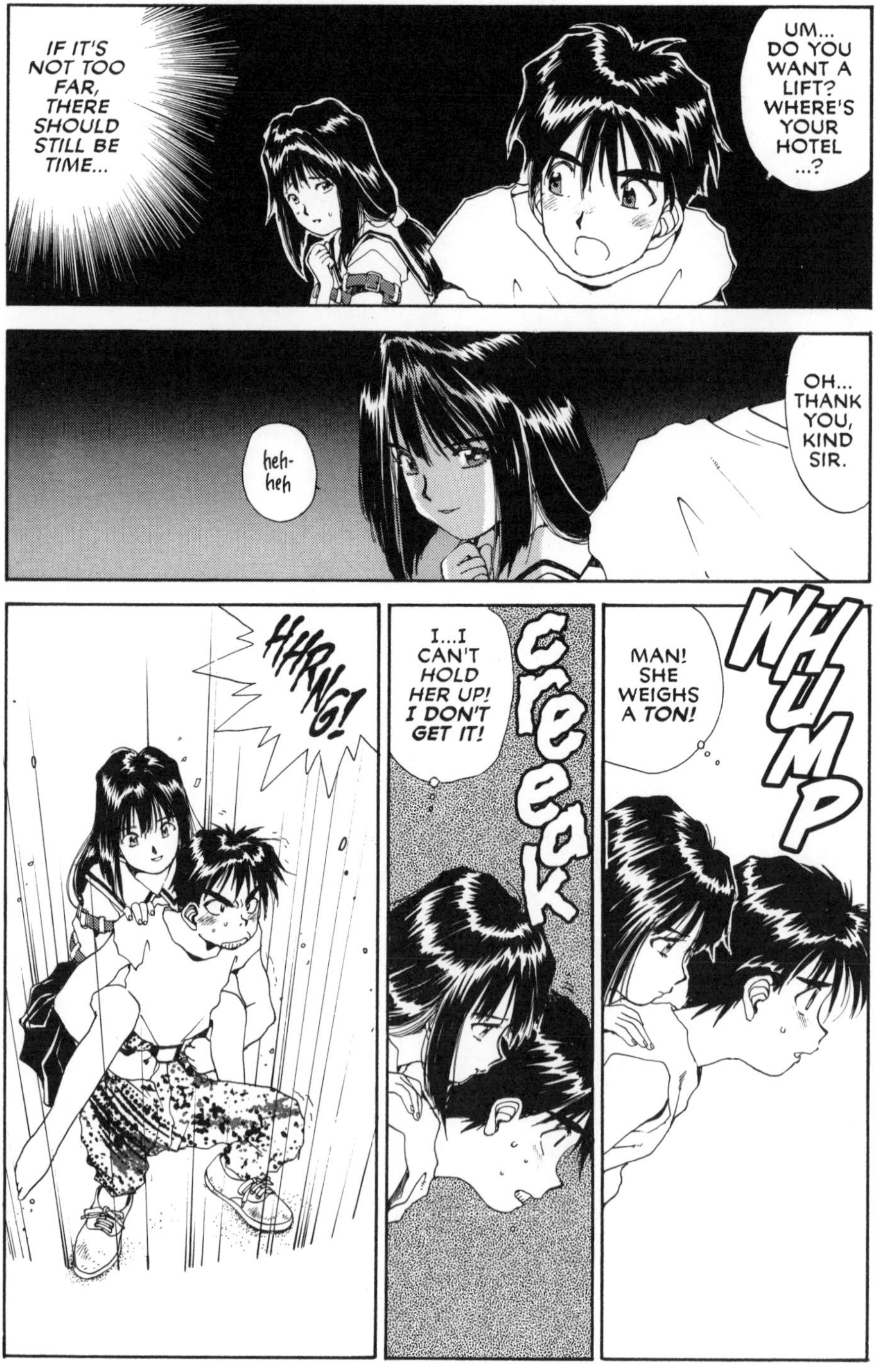
UM... DO YOU WANT A LIFT? WHERE'S YOUR HOTEL ...?
IF IT'S NOT TOO FAR, THERE SHOULD STILL BE TIME...
OH... THANK YOU, KIND SIR.
heh-heh
WHUMP
MAN! SHE WEIGHS A *TON!*
creak
I...I CAN'T HOLD HER UP! I DON'T GET IT!
HHRNG!

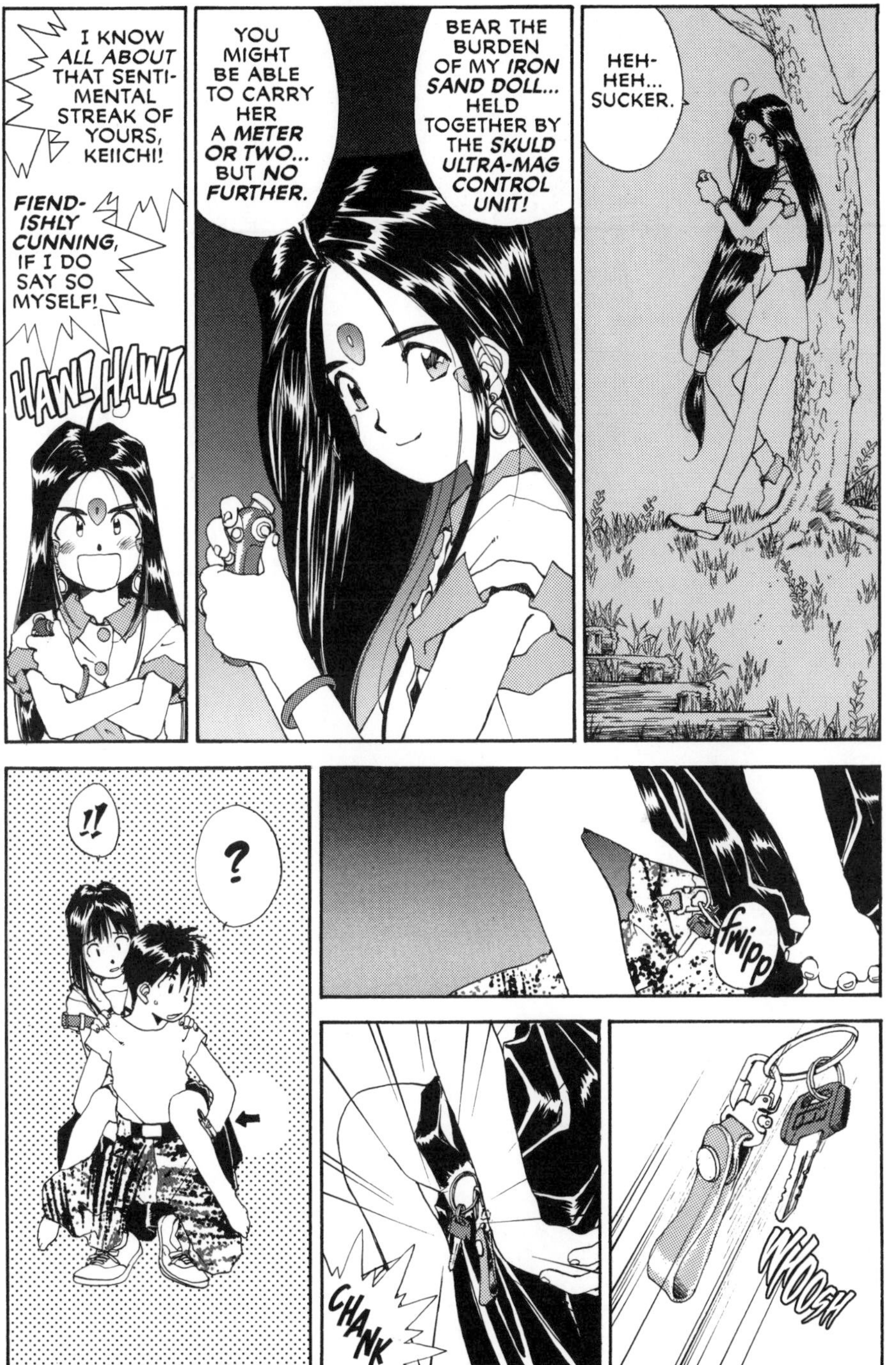
HEH-HEH... SUCKER.
BEAR THE BURDEN OF MY IRON SAND DOLL... HELD TOGETHER BY THE SKULD ULTRA-MAG CONTROL UNIT!
YOU MIGHT BE ABLE TO CARRY HER A METER OR TWO... BUT NO FURTHER.
I KNOW ALL ABOUT THAT SENTI-MENTAL STREAK OF YOURS, KEIICHI!
FIEND-ISHLY CUNNING, IF I DO SAY SO MYSELF!
HAW! HAW!
fwipp
WHOOSH
CHANK
?
!!

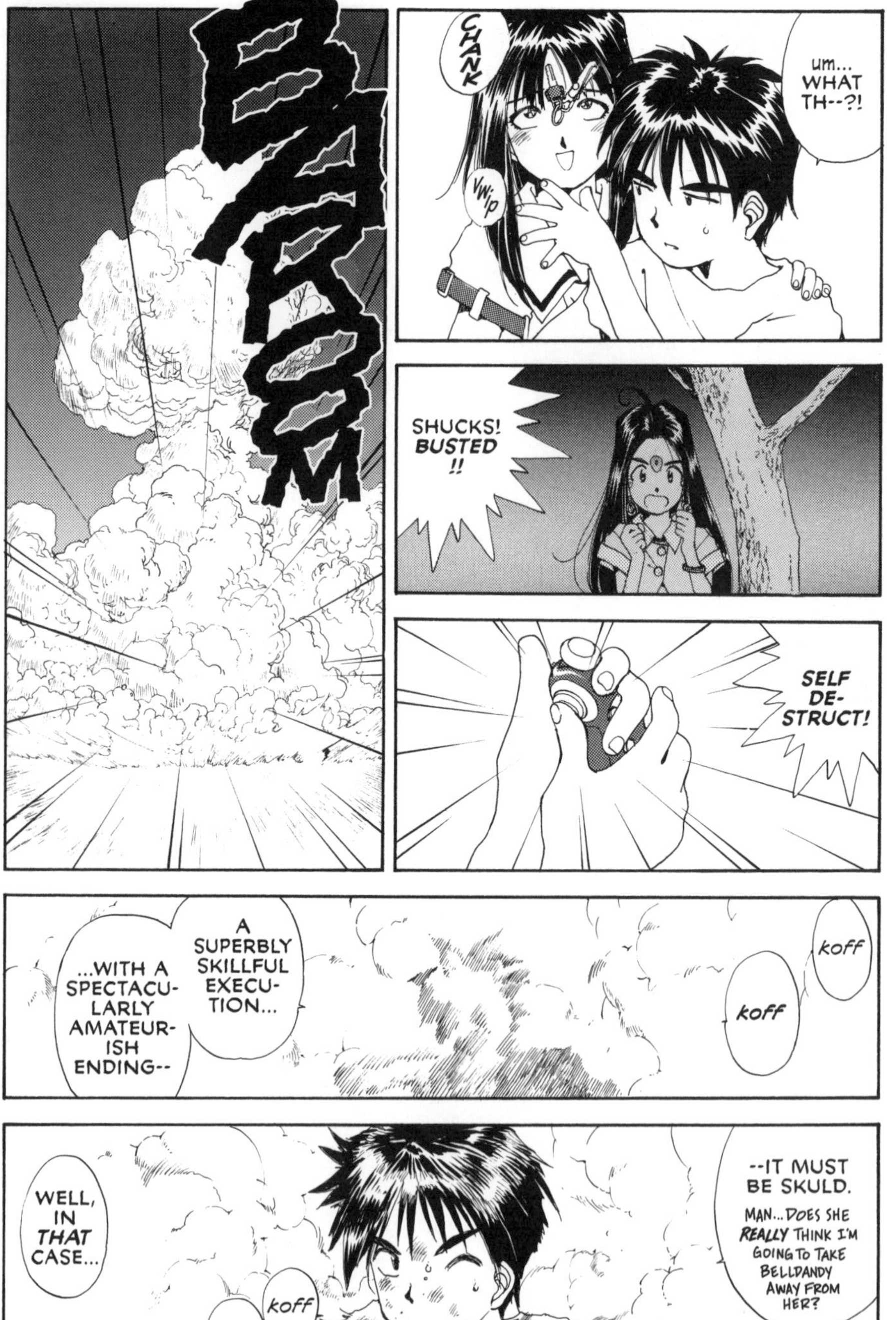
um... WHAT TH--?!
CHANK
VWip
SHUCKS! BUSTED !!
SELF DE-STRUCT!
koff
koff
A SUPERBLY SKILLFUL EXECU-TION...
...WITH A SPECTACU-LARLY AMATEUR-ISH ENDING--
--IT MUST BE SKULD.
MAN... DOES SHE REALLY THINK I'M GOING TO TAKE BELLDANDY AWAY FROM HER?
WELL, IN THAT CASE...
koff
koff

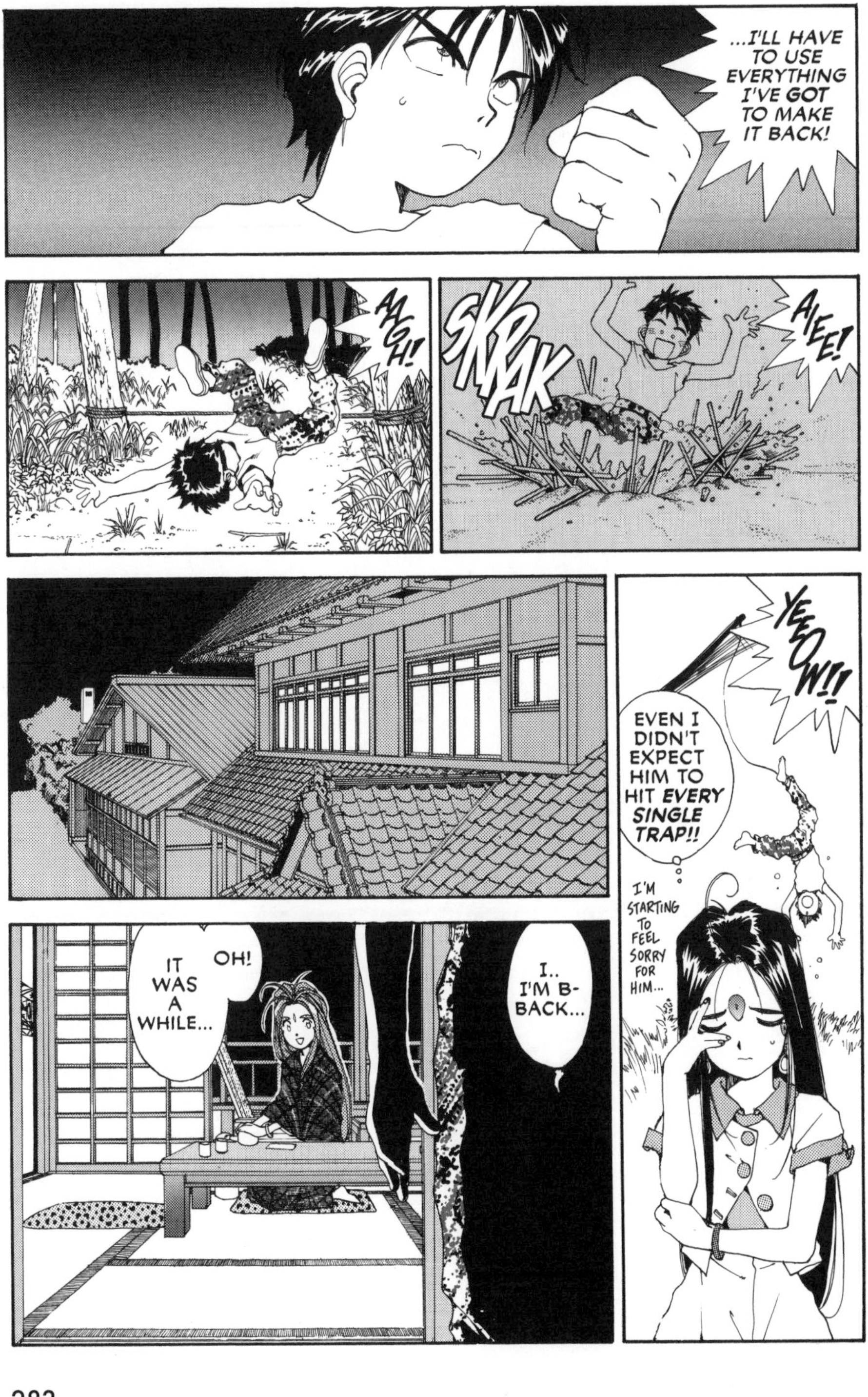
...I'LL HAVE TO USE EVERYTHING I'VE GOT TO MAKE IT BACK!
AIEEE!
SKRAK
AAAGH!
YEEOW!!
EVEN I DIDN'T EXPECT HIM TO HIT EVERY SINGLE TRAP!!
I'M STARTING TO FEEL SORRY FOR HIM...
I.. I'M B-BACK...
OH! IT WAS A WHILE...

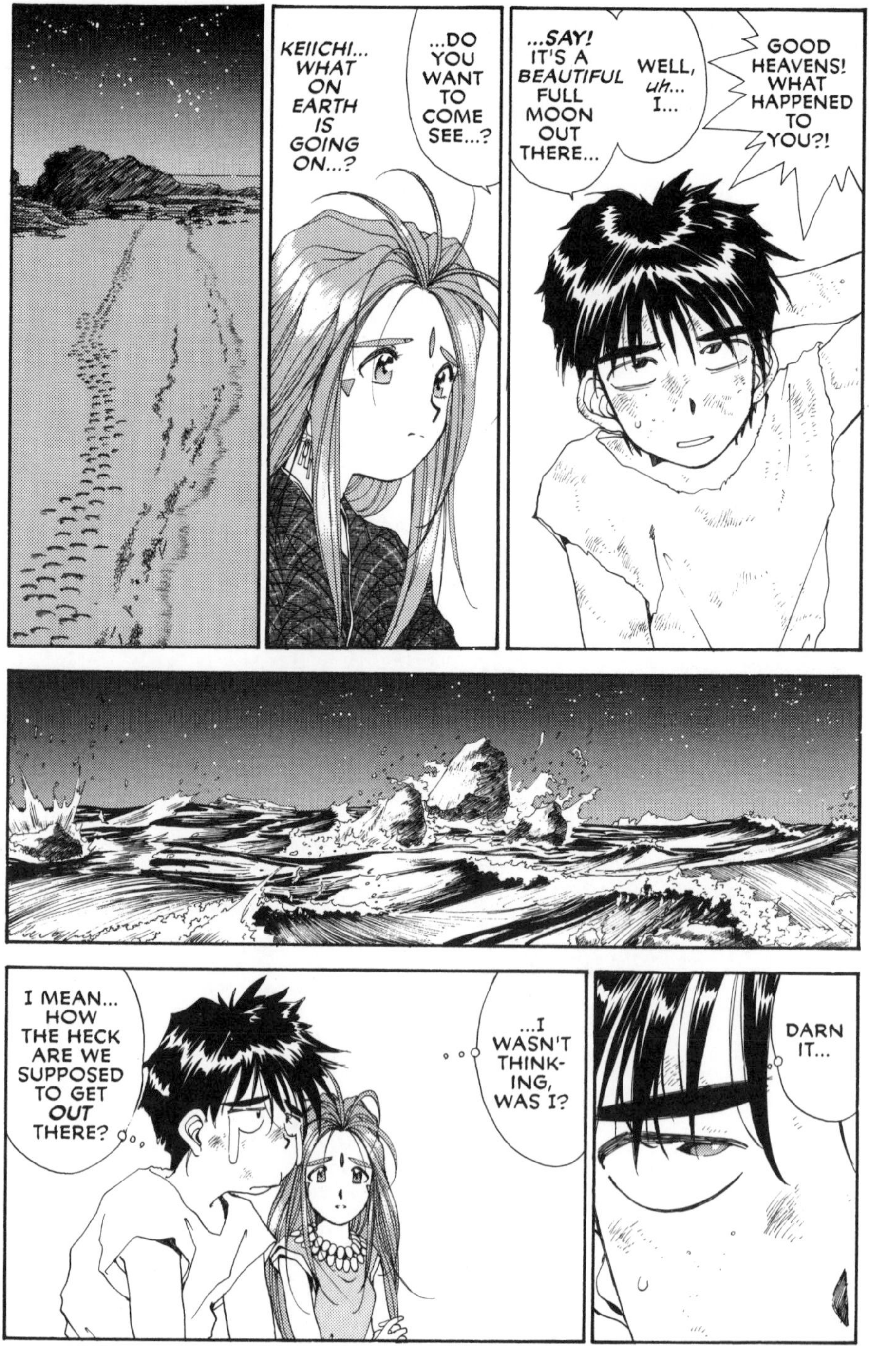
GOOD HEAVENS! WHAT HAPPENED TO YOU?!
WELL, *uh*... I...
...*SAY!* IT'S A *BEAUTIFUL* FULL MOON OUT THERE...
...DO YOU WANT TO COME SEE...?
KEIICHI... WHAT ON EARTH IS GOING ON...?
DARN IT...
...I WASN'T THINKING, WAS I?
I MEAN... HOW THE HECK ARE WE SUPPOSED TO GET *OUT* THERE?

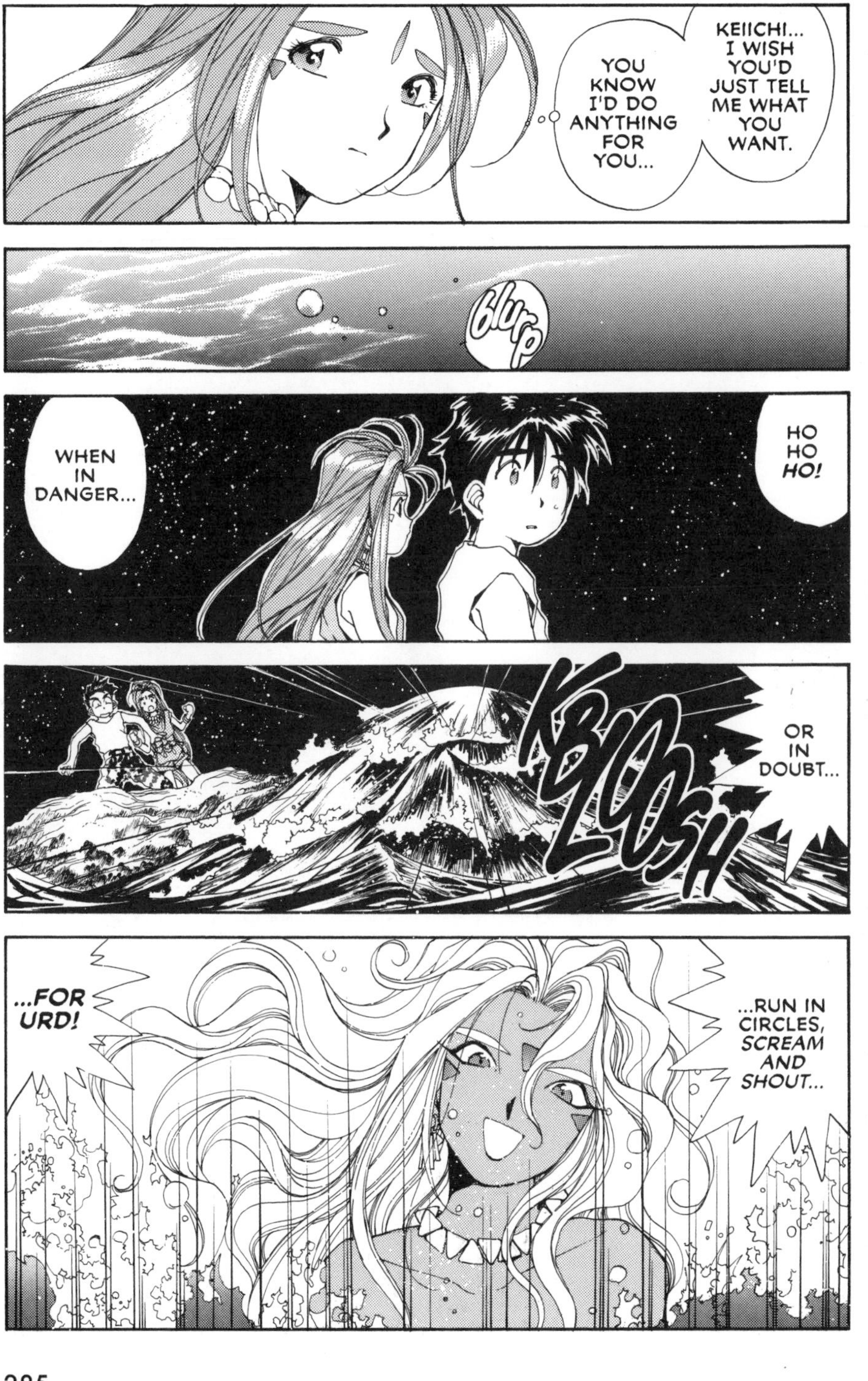

KEIICHI... I WISH YOU'D JUST TELL ME WHAT YOU WANT.
YOU KNOW I'D DO ANYTHING FOR YOU...
blurp
HO HO *HO!*
WHEN IN DANGER...
OR IN DOUBT...
KBLOOSH
...RUN IN CIRCLES, *SCREAM* AND *SHOUT...*
...FOR URD!

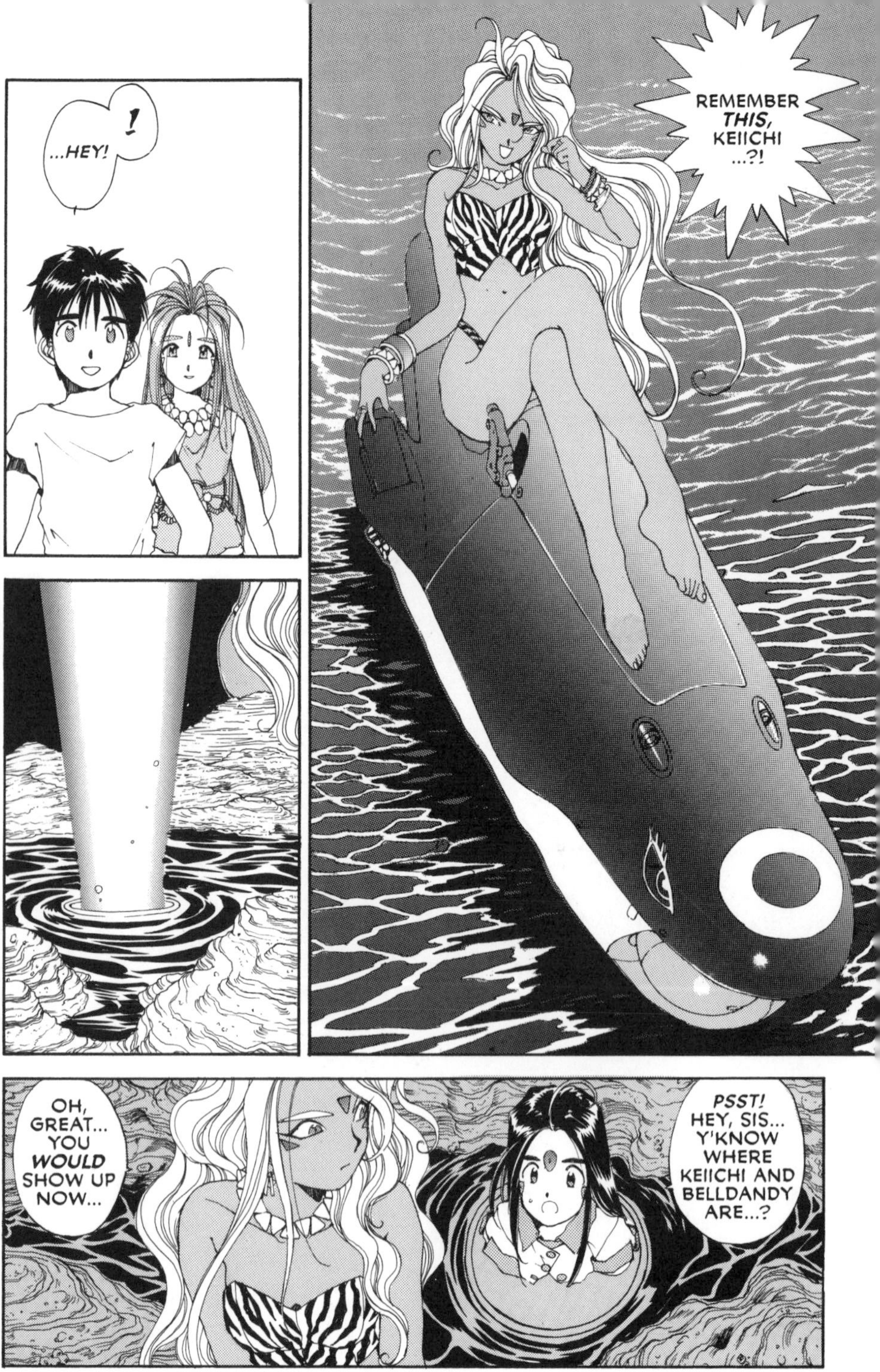
REMEMBER THIS, KEIICHI ...?!
!
...HEY!
PSST! HEY, SIS... Y'KNOW WHERE KEIICHI AND BELLDANDY ARE...?
OH, GREAT... YOU WOULD SHOW UP NOW...

...THAT'S THEM!

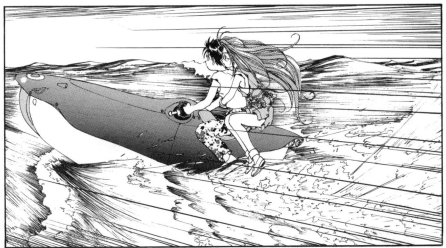

BLUE NO. 6... *DIVE!!*

klick

OH *NO*, YOU *DON'T!*

...ALMOST THERE...

ALMOST THERE...

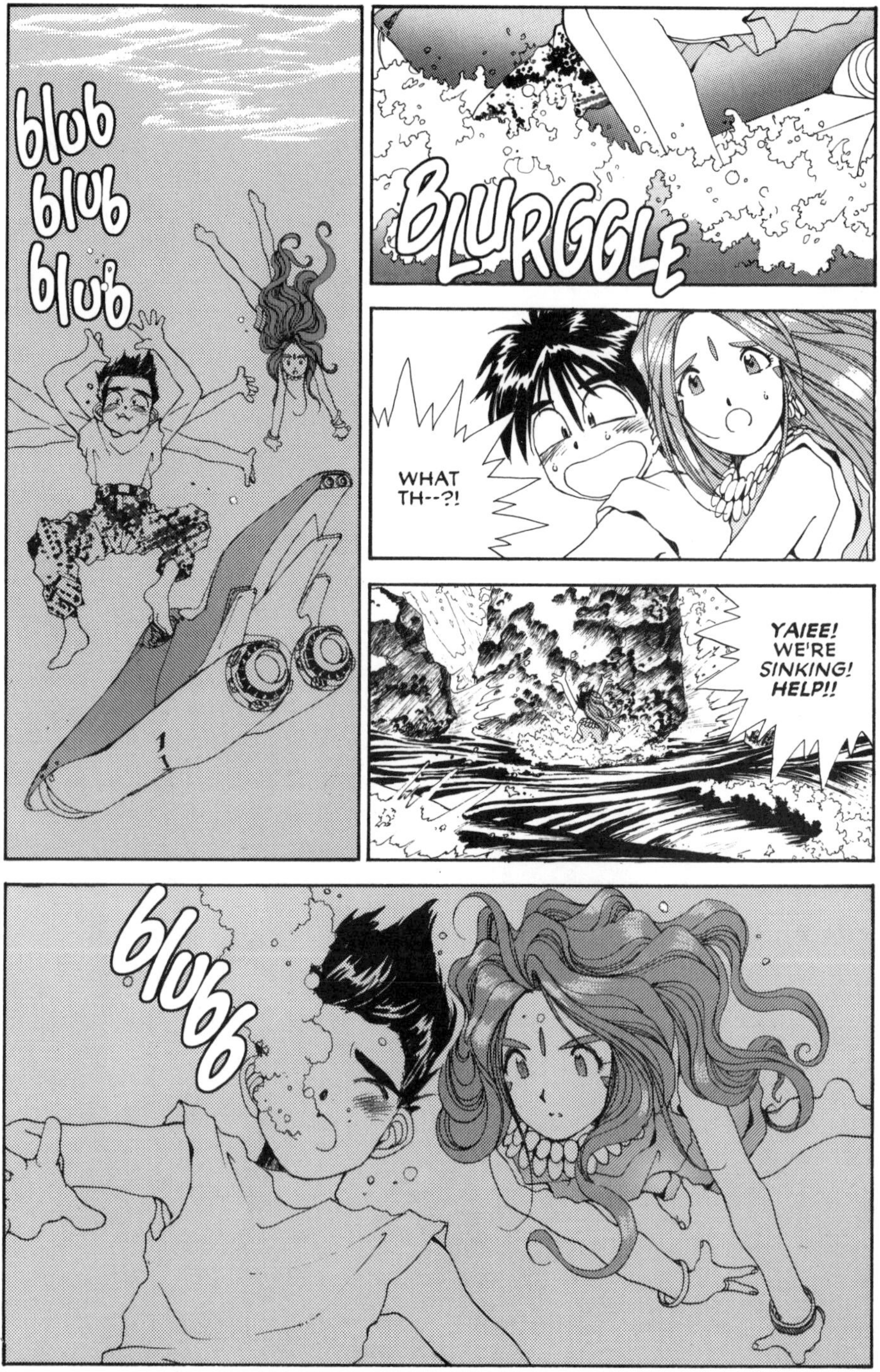

BLURGGLE
WHAT TH--?!
YAIEE! WE'RE SINKING! HELP!!
blub blub blub
blubb

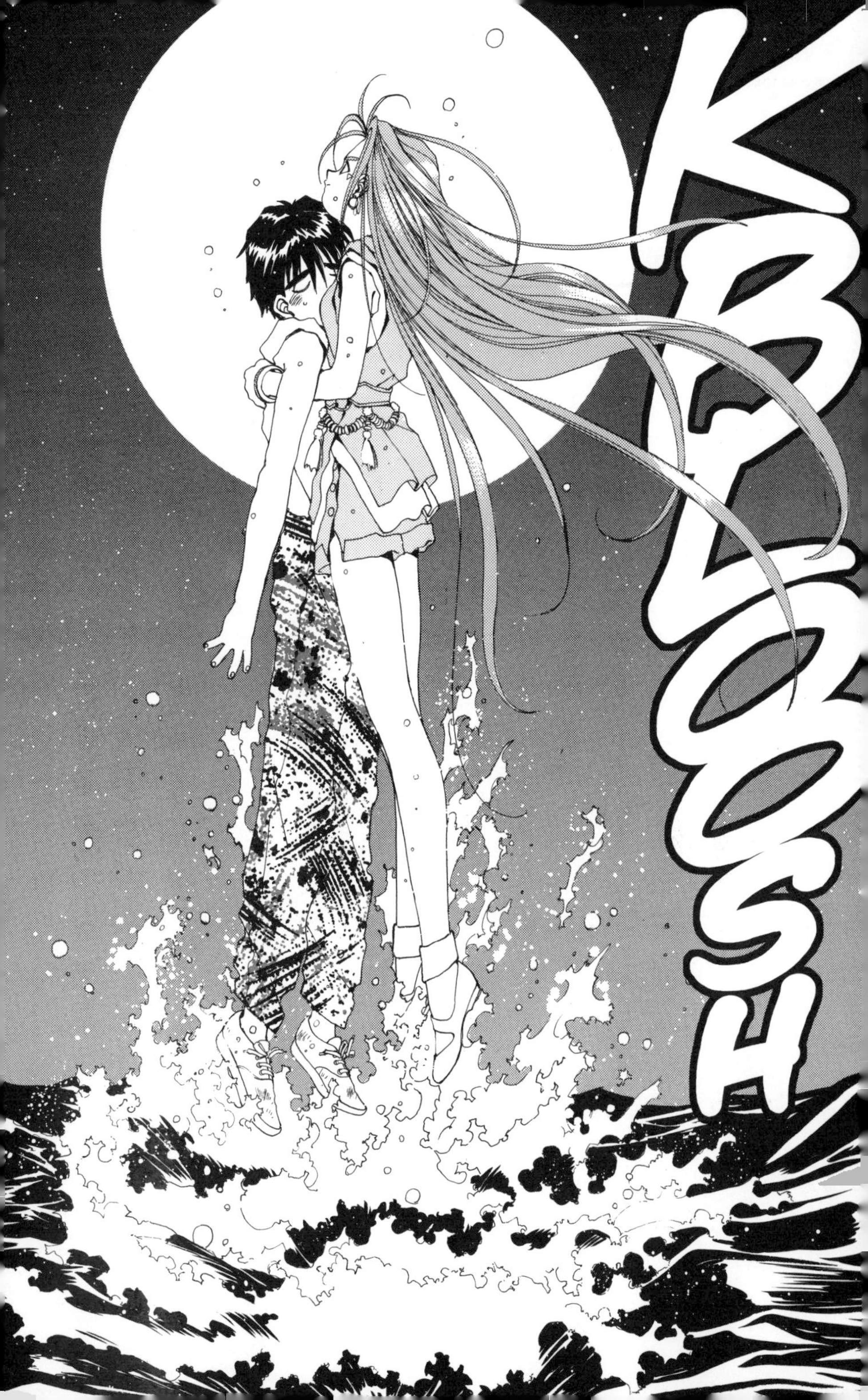
KPLOOSH

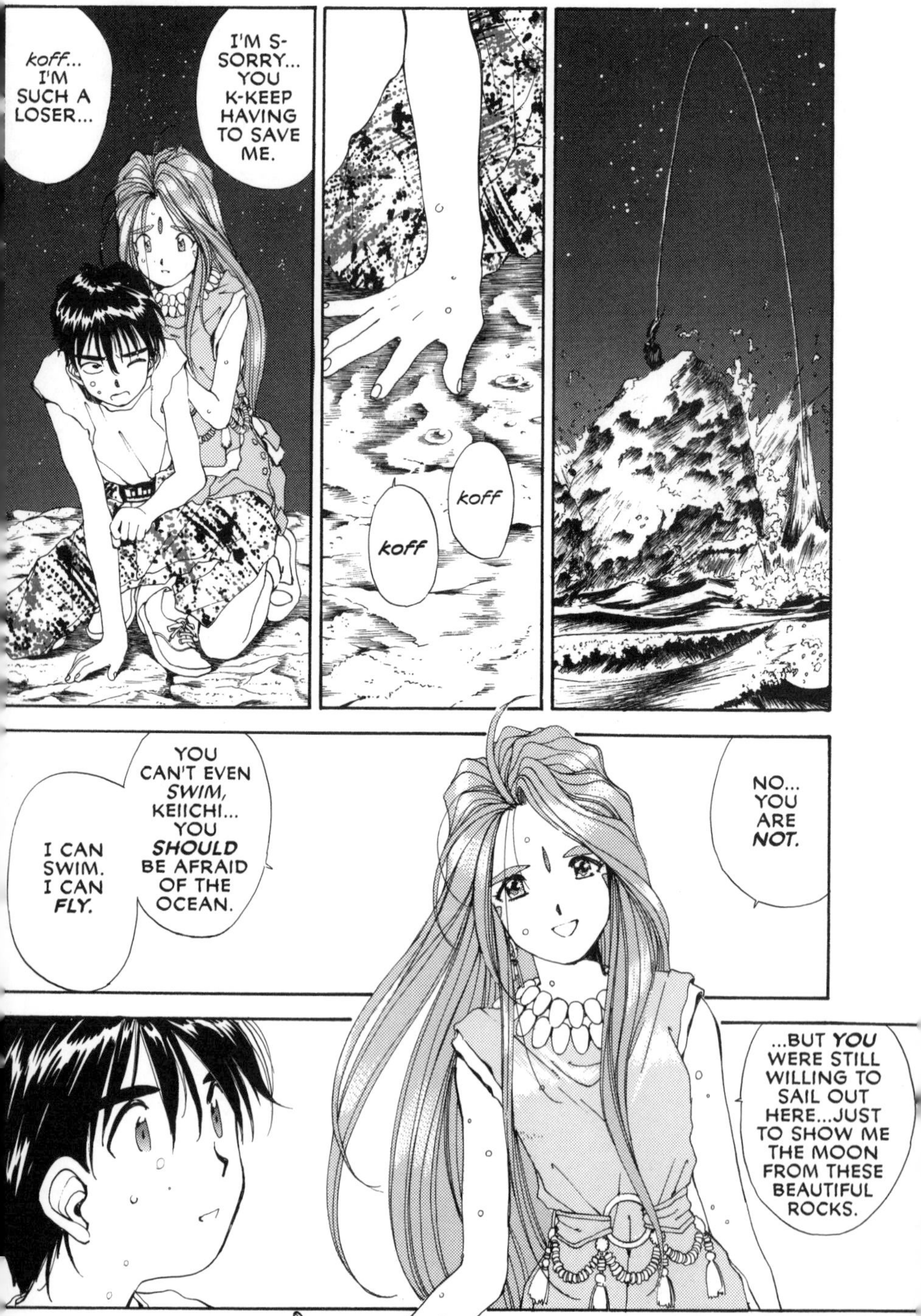
koff
koff
I'M S-SORRY... YOU K-KEEP HAVING TO SAVE ME.
koff... I'M SUCH A LOSER...
NO... YOU ARE ***NOT.***
YOU CAN'T EVEN *SWIM*, KEIICHI... YOU ***SHOULD*** BE AFRAID OF THE OCEAN.
I CAN SWIM. I CAN ***FLY.***
...BUT ***YOU*** WERE STILL WILLING TO SAIL OUT HERE...JUST TO SHOW ME THE MOON FROM THESE BEAUTIFUL ROCKS.

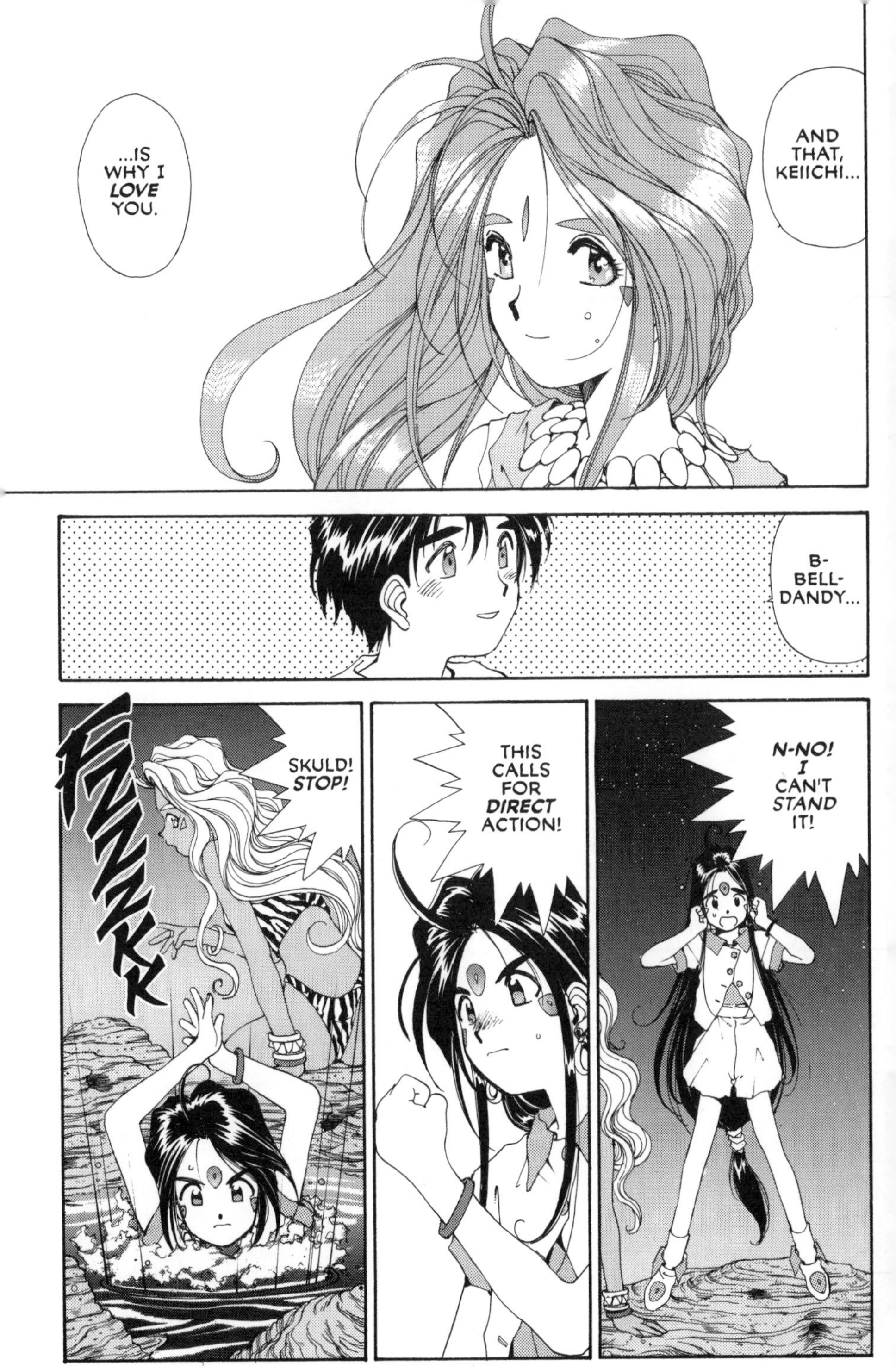
AND THAT, KEIICHI...
...IS WHY I *LOVE* YOU.
B-BELL-DANDY...
N-NO! I CAN'T *STAND* IT!
THIS CALLS FOR *DIRECT* ACTION!
SKULD! *STOP!*

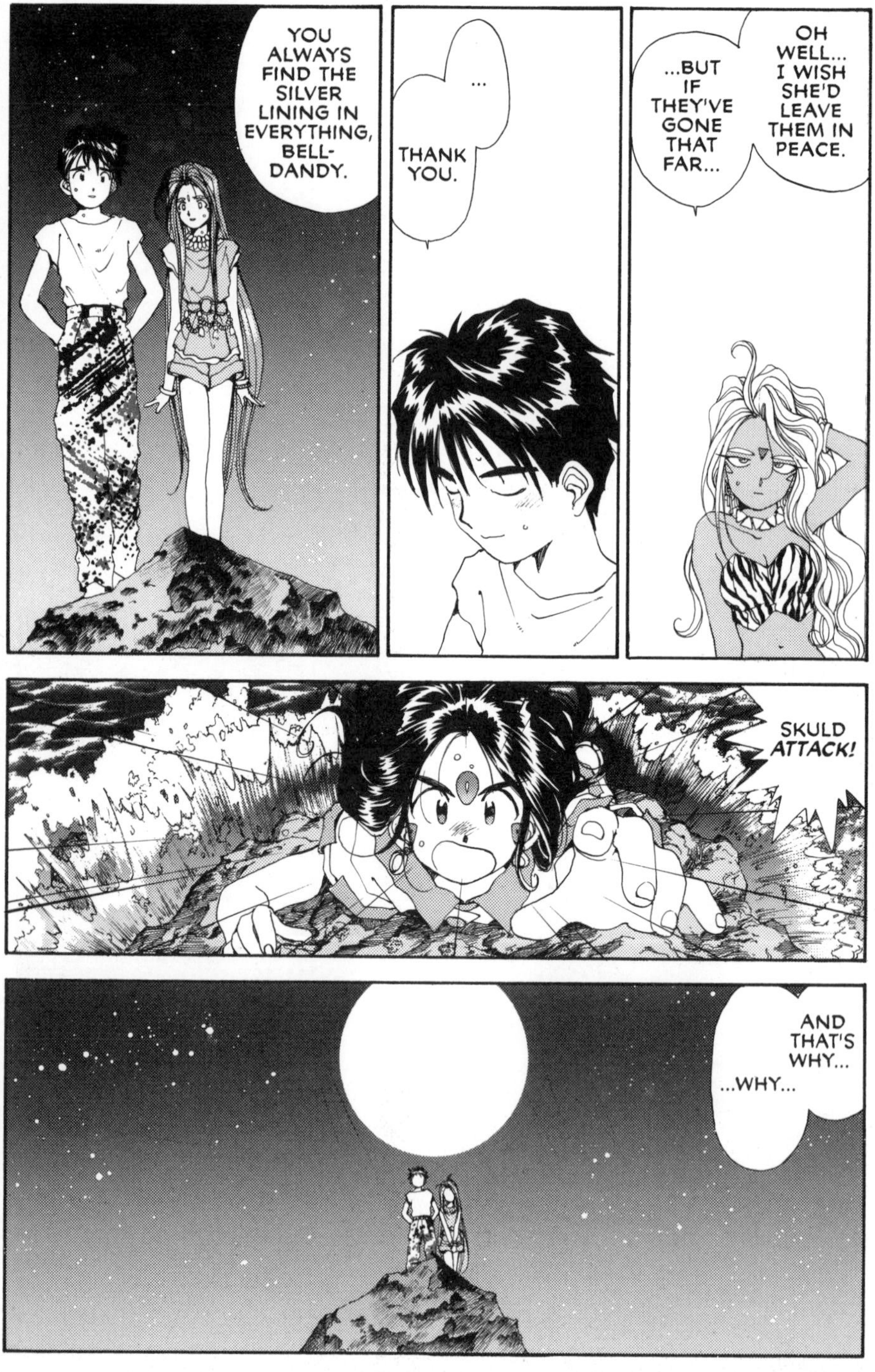
OH WELL... I WISH SHE'D LEAVE THEM IN PEACE.
...BUT IF THEY'VE GONE THAT FAR...
...
THANK YOU.
YOU ALWAYS FIND THE SILVER LINING IN EVERYTHING, BELL-DANDY.
SKULD ATTACK!
AND THAT'S WHY...
...WHY...

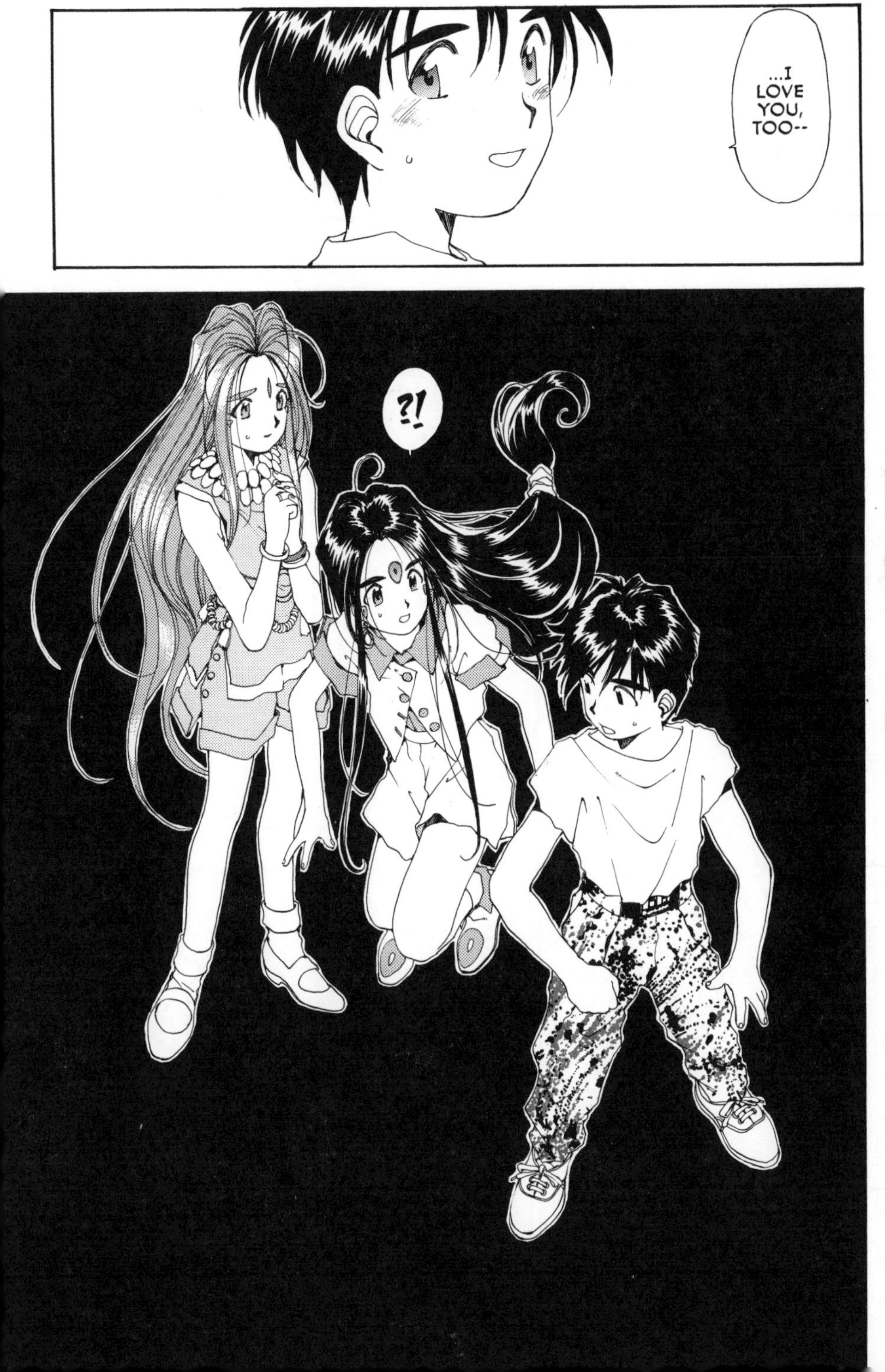
...I LOVE YOU, TOO--
?!

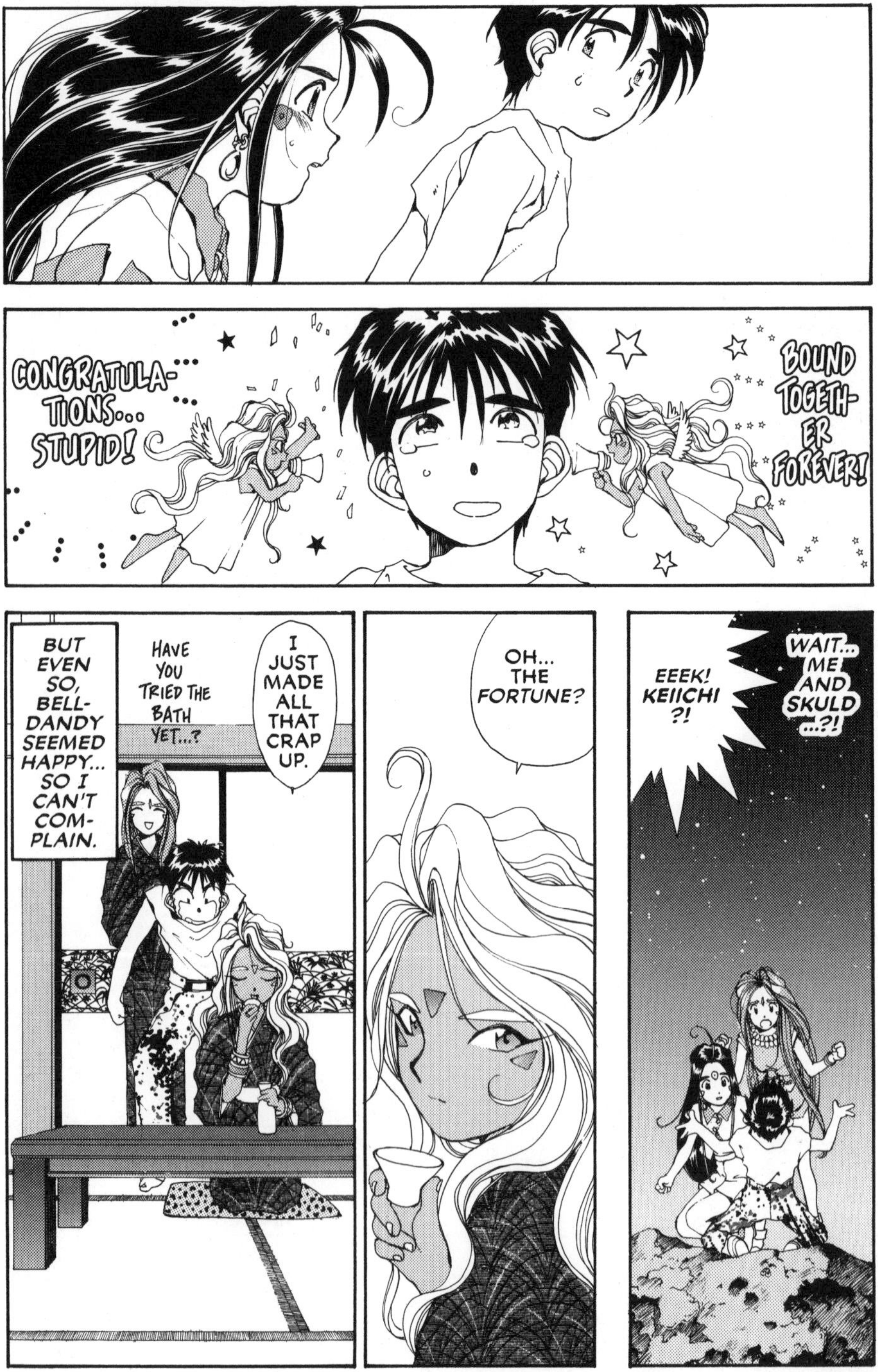
BOUND TOGETHER FOREVER!
CONGRATULATIONS... STUPID!
WAIT... ME AND SKULD ...?!
EEEK! KEIICHI ?!
OH... THE FORTUNE?
I JUST MADE ALL THAT CRAP UP.
HAVE YOU TRIED THE BATH YET...?
BUT EVEN SO, BELLDANDY SEEMED HAPPY... SO I CAN'T COMPLAIN.

CHAPTER 51

No, Sweetie

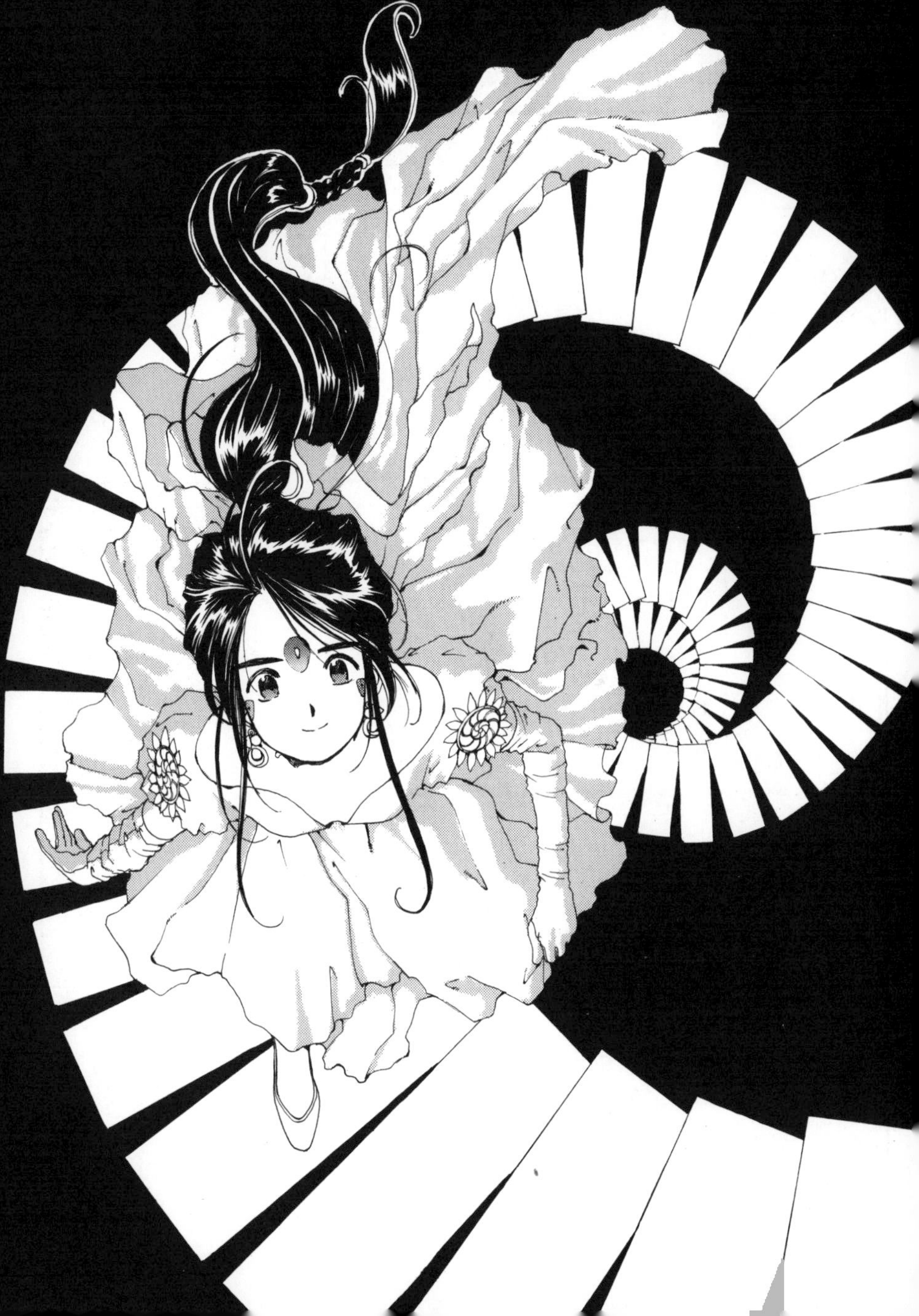

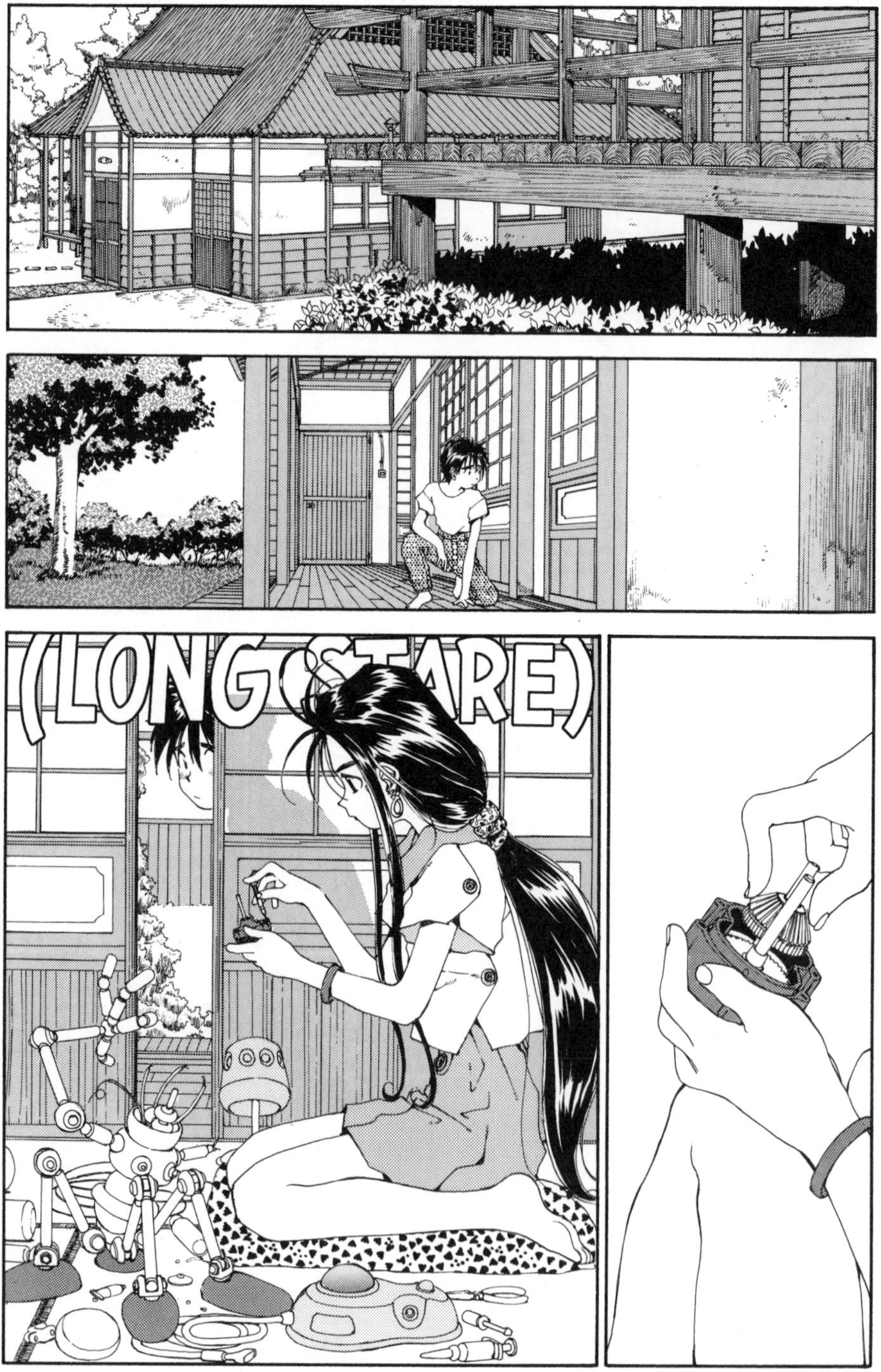
(LONG STARE)

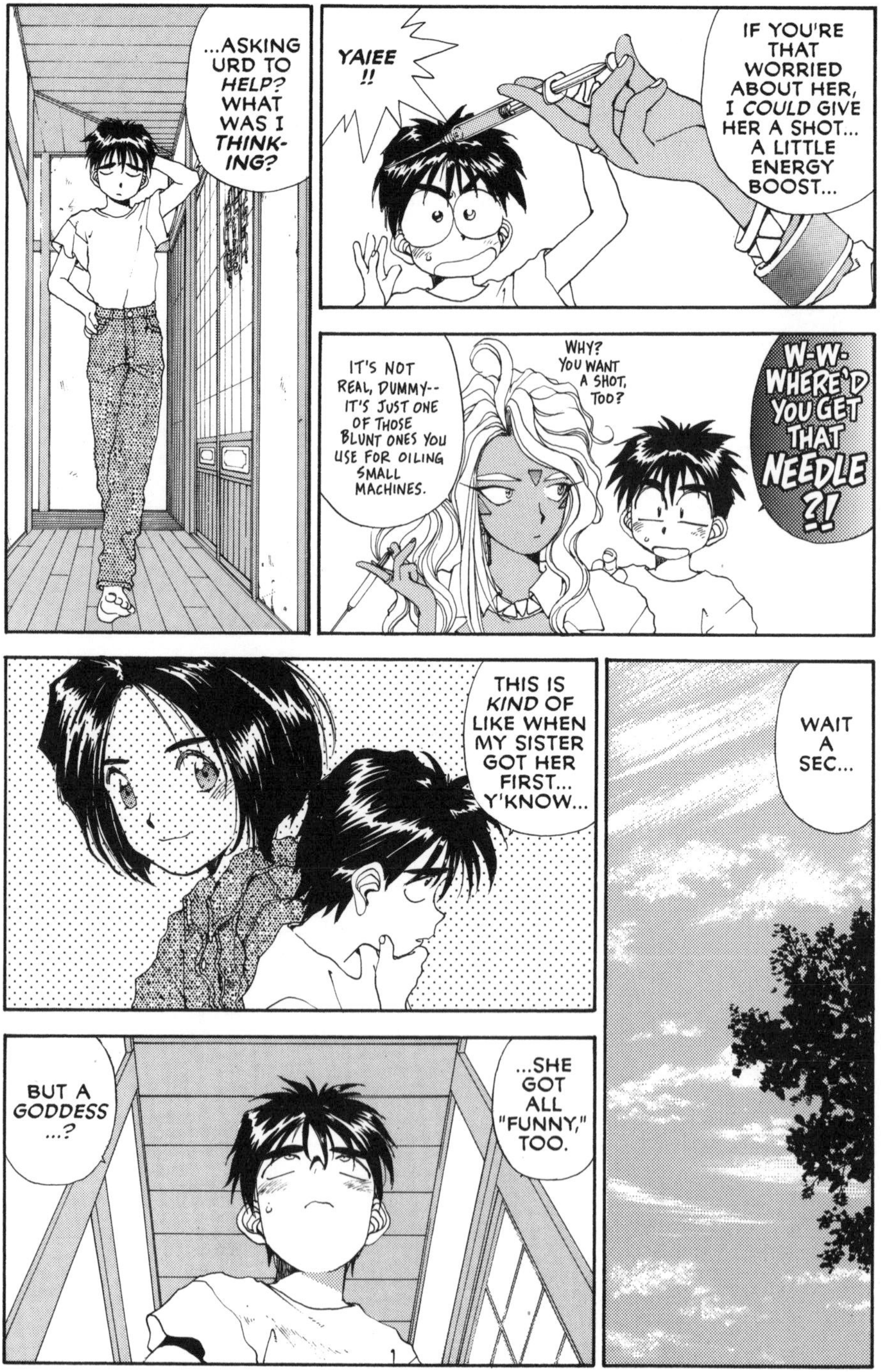
IF YOU'RE THAT WORRIED ABOUT HER, I COULD GIVE HER A SHOT... A LITTLE ENERGY BOOST...
YAIEE !!
W-W-WHERE'D YOU GET THAT NEEDLE ?!
WHY? YOU WANT A SHOT, TOO?
IT'S NOT REAL, DUMMY-- IT'S JUST ONE OF THOSE BLUNT ONES YOU USE FOR OILING SMALL MACHINES.
...ASKING URD TO HELP? WHAT WAS I THINKING?
WAIT A SEC...
THIS IS KIND OF LIKE WHEN MY SISTER GOT HER FIRST... Y'KNOW...
...SHE GOT ALL "FUNNY," TOO.
BUT A GODDESS ...?

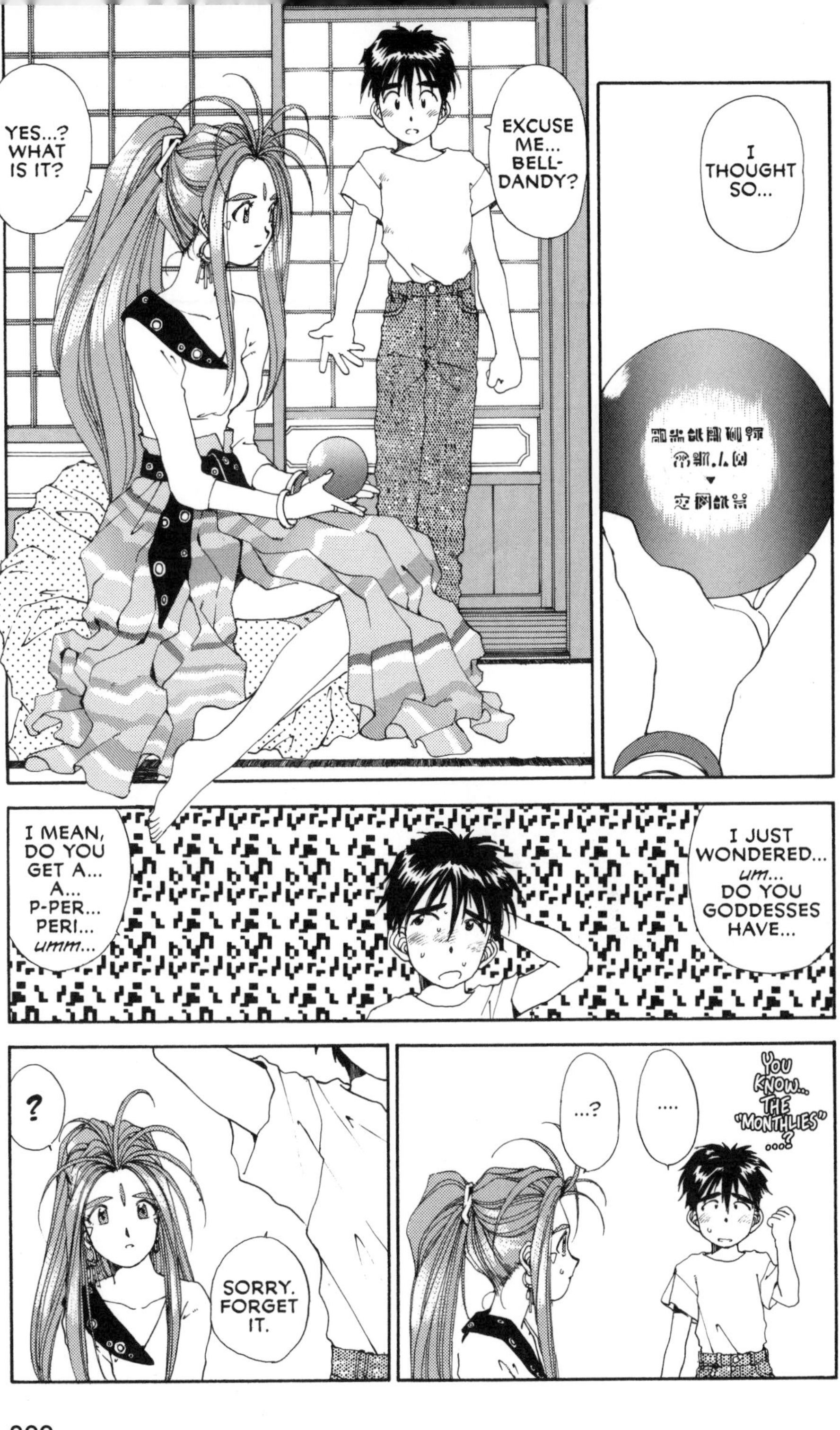
I THOUGHT SO...
EXCUSE ME... BELL-DANDY?
YES...? WHAT IS IT?
I JUST WONDERED... *um*... DO YOU GODDESSES HAVE...
I MEAN, DO YOU GET A... A... P-PER... PERI... *umm*...
YOU KNOW... THE "MONTHLIES" ...?
....
...?
?
SORRY. FORGET IT.

STILL, I BET THAT'S IT. SHE LOOKS LIKE SHE'S THE RIGHT AGE.
IN THAT CASE...
KASUGANO PHARMACY
I *TOLD* YOU, I DON'T NEED YOUR "HAPPY FAMILY PLANNING" KIT!
WELL, YOU SEEMED SO *NERVOUS*, YOUNG MAN...I JUST ASSUMED...
...
sighh
HMM...
MAYBE LIKE... SO...
squeek
squeek

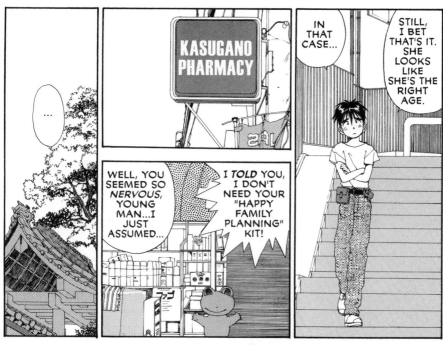

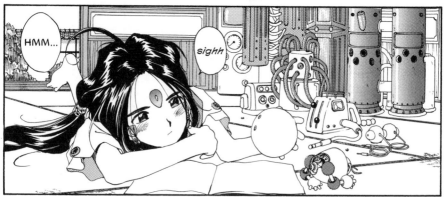

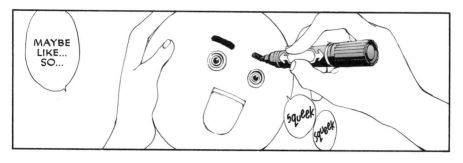

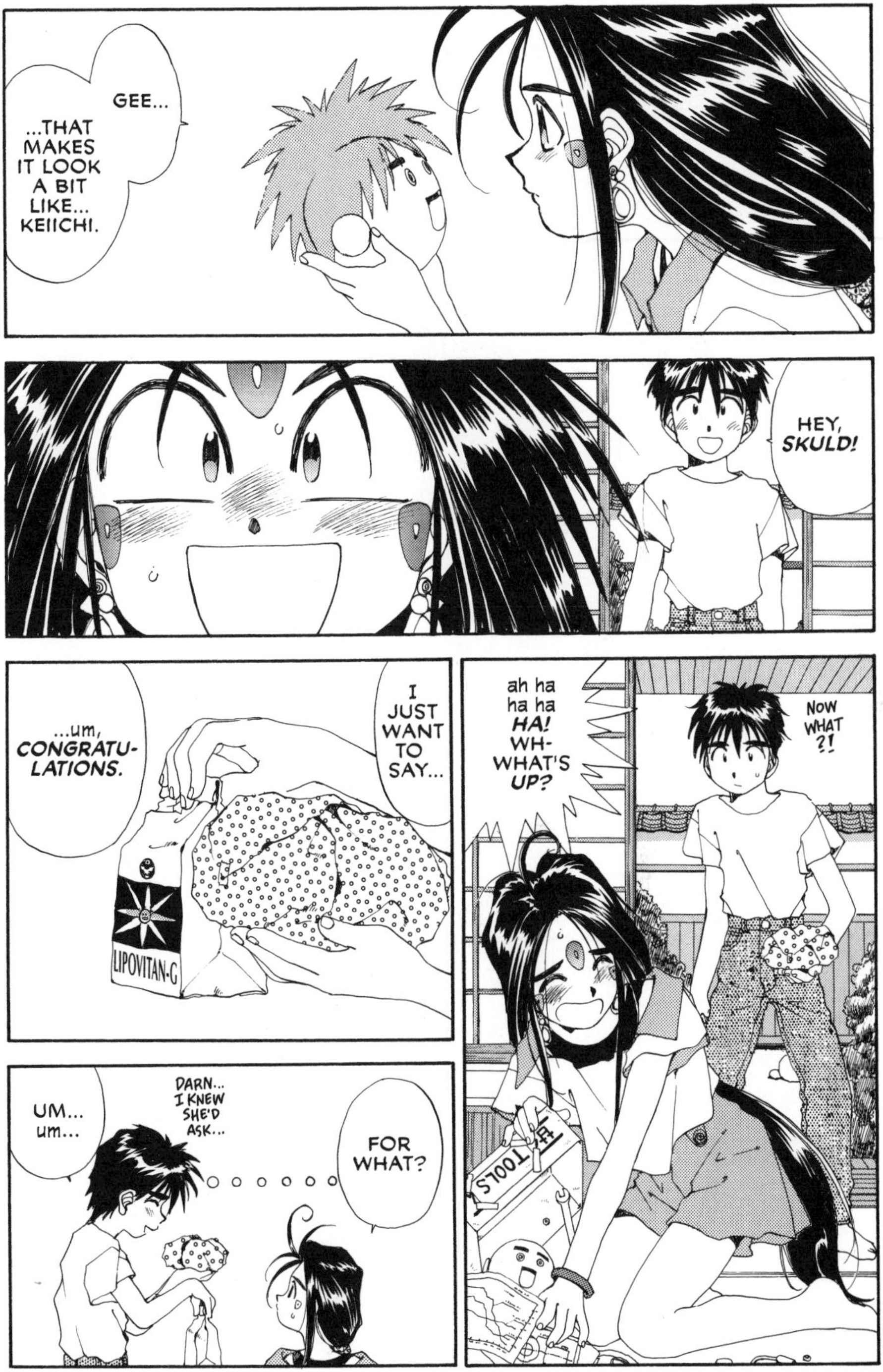
GEE...
...THAT MAKES IT LOOK A BIT LIKE... KEIICHI.
HEY, SKULD!
NOW WHAT?!
ah ha ha ha HA! WH- WHAT'S UP?
TOOLS
I JUST WANT TO SAY...
...um, CONGRATU- LATIONS.
LIPOVITAN-G
FOR WHAT?
DARN... I KNEW SHE'D ASK...
UM... um...

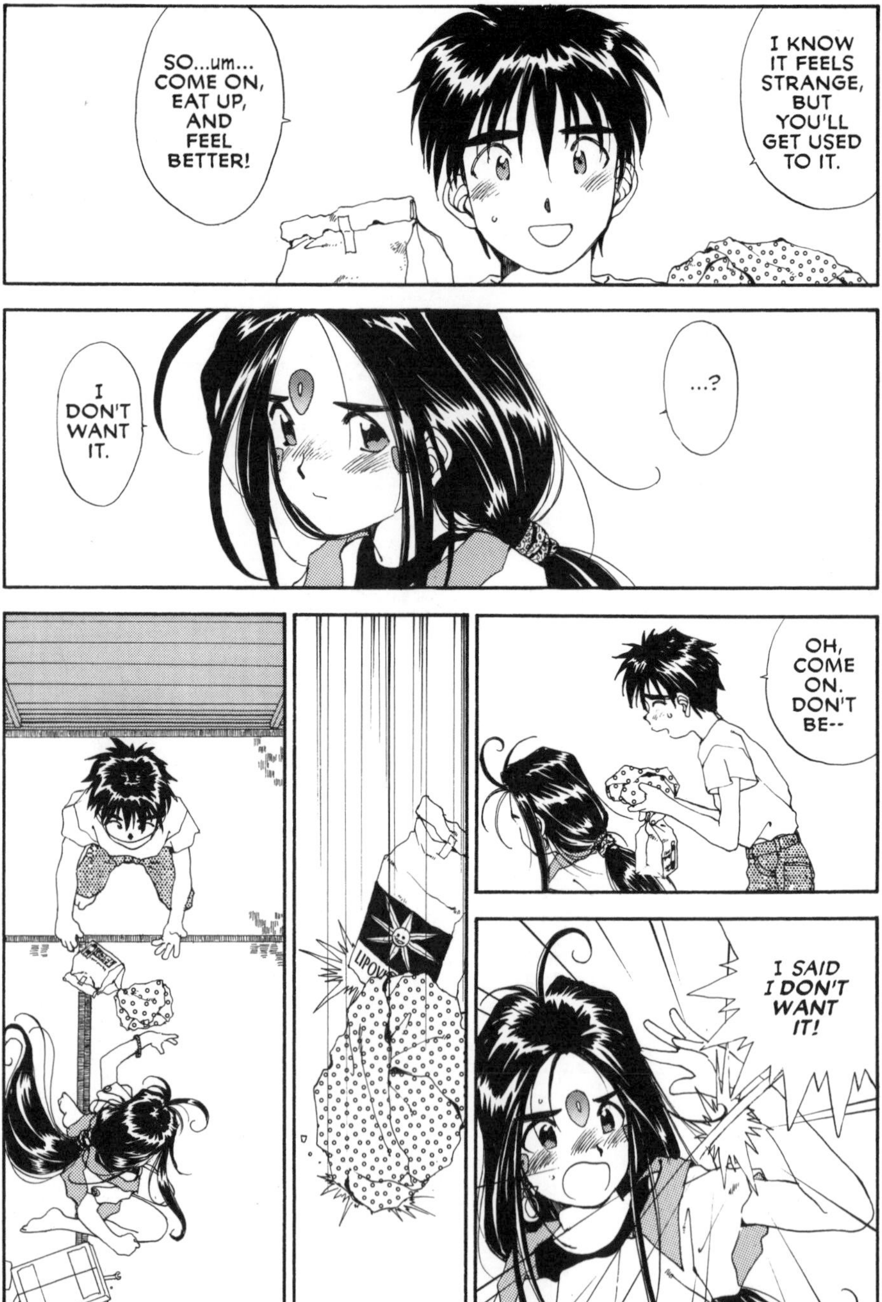
I KNOW IT FEELS STRANGE, BUT YOU'LL GET USED TO IT.
SO...um... COME ON, EAT UP, AND FEEL BETTER!
...?
I DON'T WANT IT.
OH, COME ON. DON'T BE--
I *SAID* I DON'T WANT IT!

Y'*KNOW*, YOU CAN ALWAYS TALK TO BELL-DANDY ABOUT IT...

KEIICHI! WAI--

...WELL, MAYBE I SHOULDN'T HAVE BARGED IN.

UH... *HA HA!*... YEAH, GUESS YOU CAN'T HELP FEELING KINDA IRRITABLE RIGHT NOW...

OH ...!

I'M STILL RATTLED ABOUT THAT OLD COOT AT THE PHARMACY... TRYING TO MAKE ME BUY...

"HAPPY FAMILY PLANNING" ...right.

Ice cream isn't good for your tummy right now. These sweet cakes are called "tai-yaki". Try them instead!

303

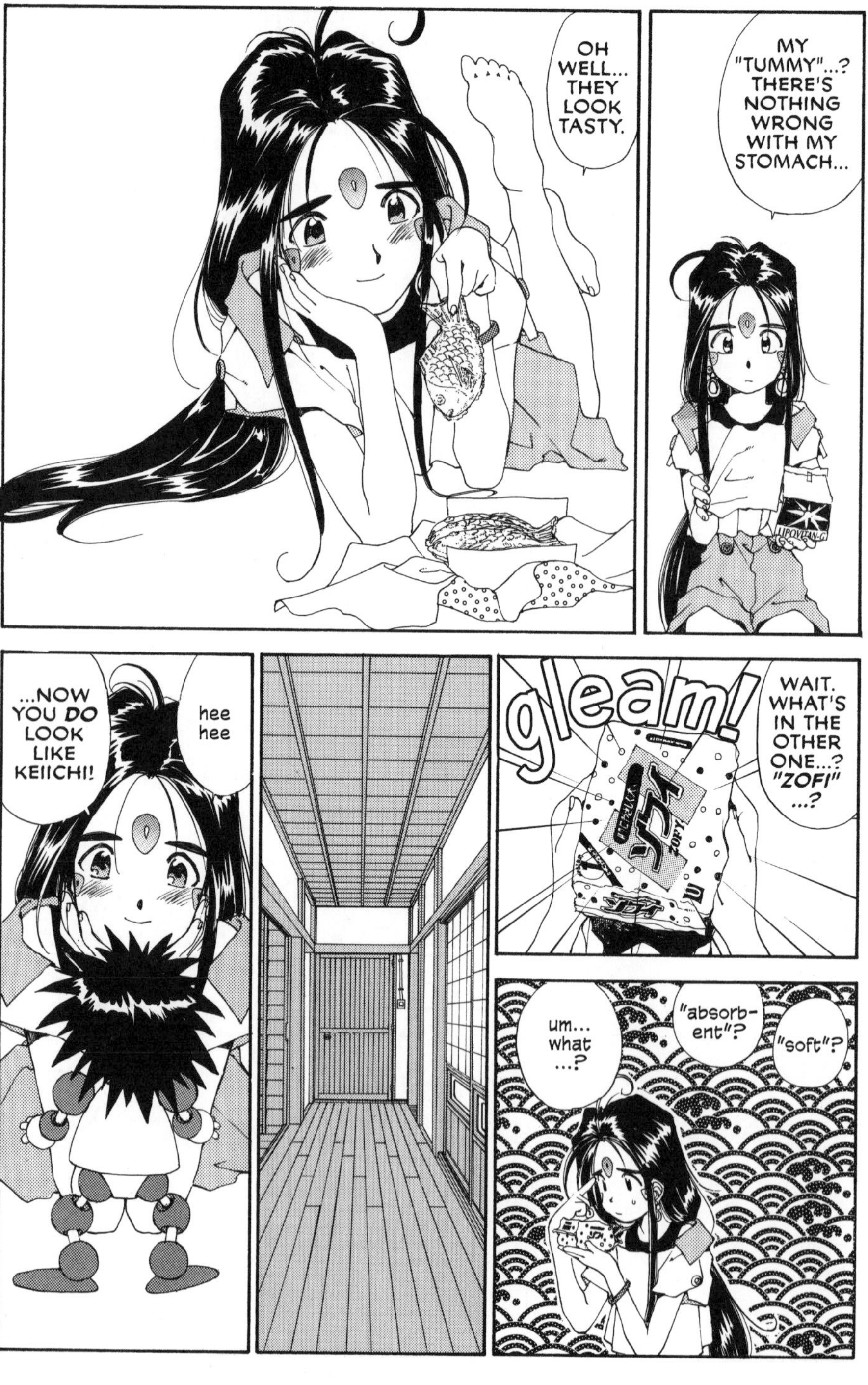
MY "TUMMY"...? THERE'S NOTHING WRONG WITH MY STOMACH...
LIPOVITAN-G
OH WELL... THEY LOOK TASTY.
WAIT. WHAT'S IN THE OTHER ONE...? "ZOFI" ...?
gleam!
"soft"?
"absorb-ent"?
um... what ...?
hee hee
...NOW YOU DO LOOK LIKE KEIICHI!

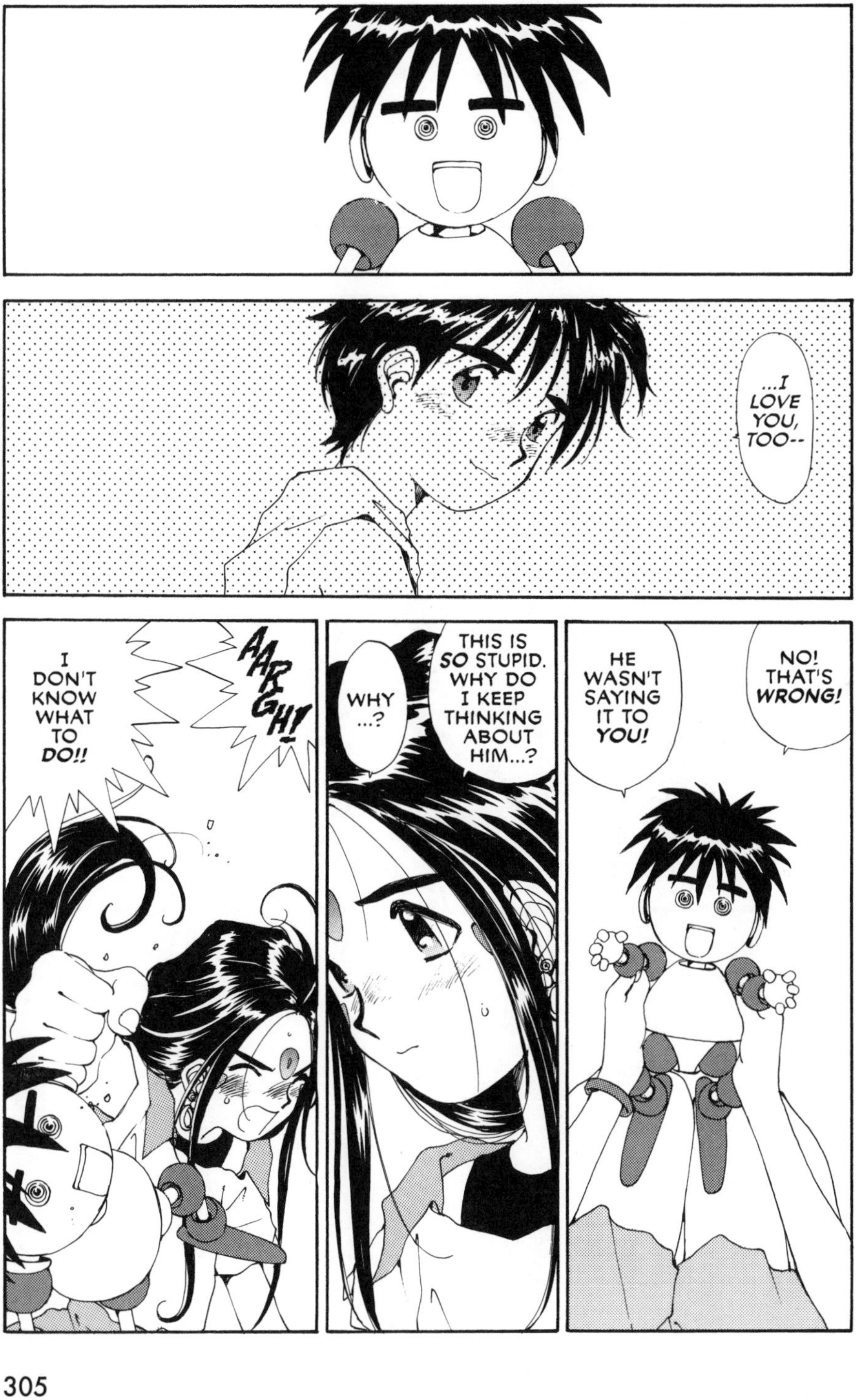
...I LOVE YOU, TOO--
NO! THAT'S *WRONG!*
HE WASN'T SAYING IT TO *YOU!*
THIS IS *SO* STUPID. WHY DO I KEEP THINKING ABOUT HIM...?
WHY ...?
AARGH!
I DON'T KNOW WHAT TO *DO!!*

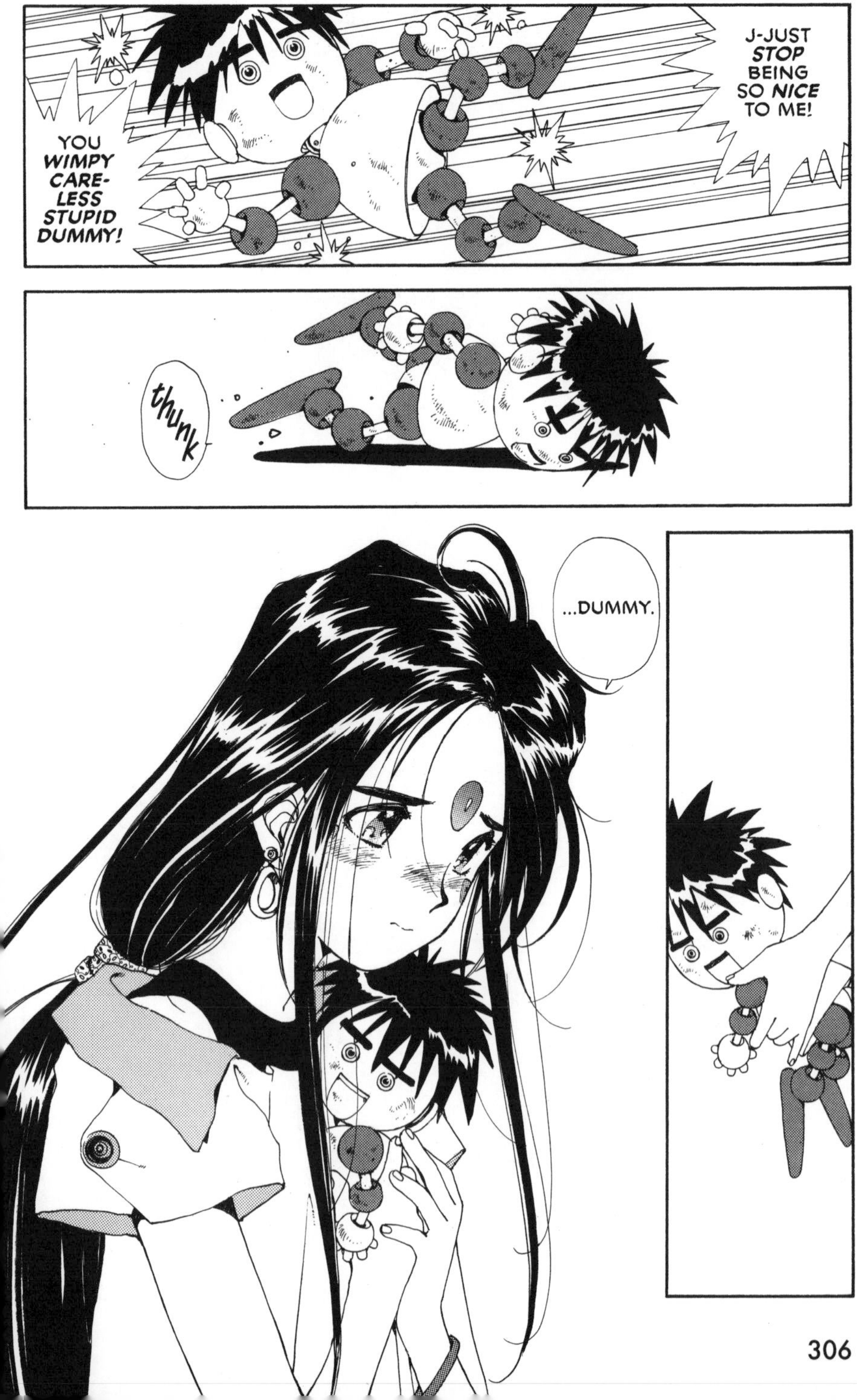
J-JUST STOP BEING SO NICE TO ME!
YOU WIMPY CARE-LESS STUPID DUMMY!
thunk
...DUMMY.

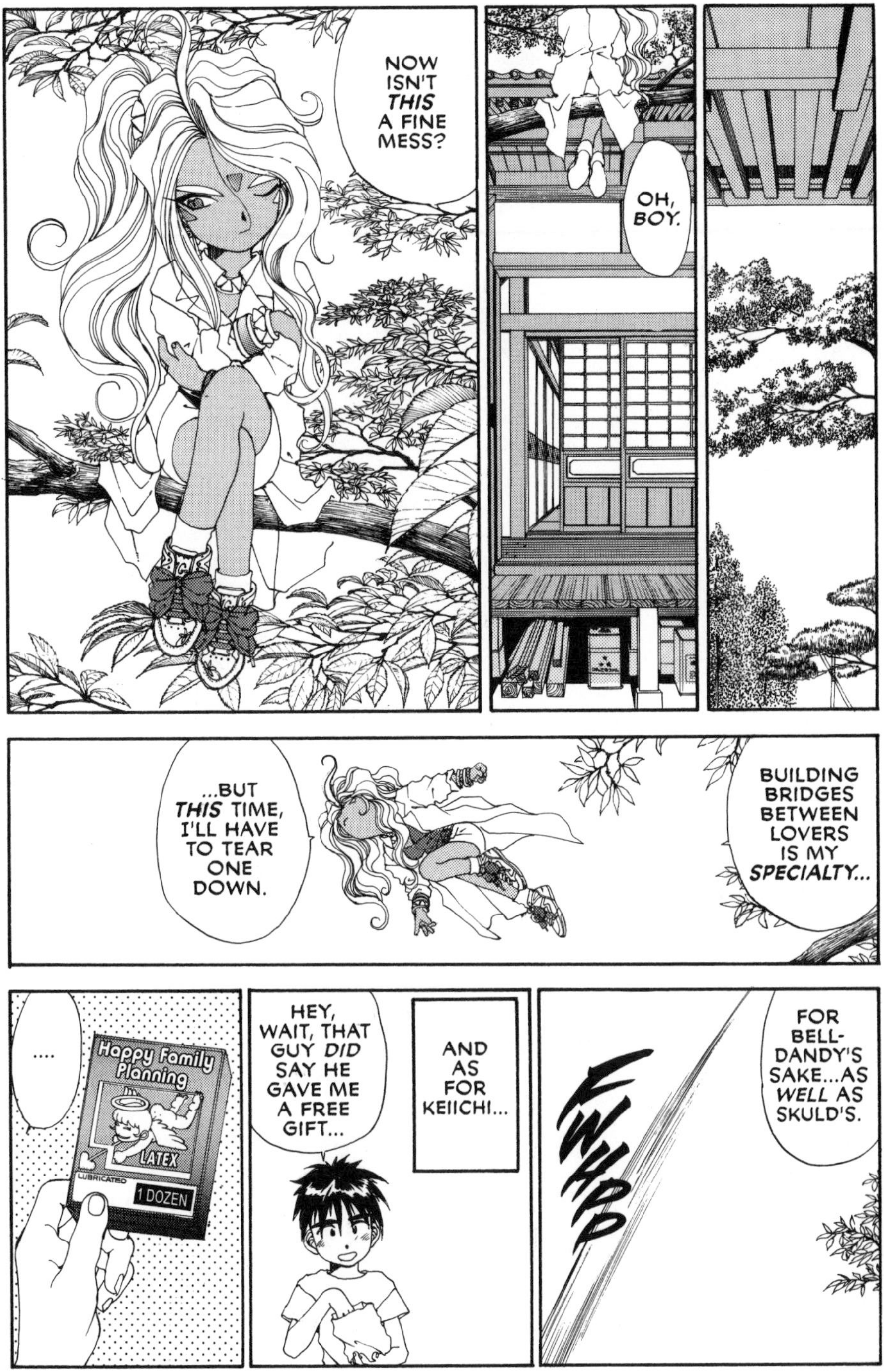
OH, BOY.
NOW ISN'T THIS A FINE MESS?
BUILDING BRIDGES BETWEEN LOVERS IS MY SPECIALTY...
...BUT THIS TIME, I'LL HAVE TO TEAR ONE DOWN.
FOR BELL-DANDY'S SAKE...AS WELL AS SKULD'S.
AND AS FOR KEIICHI...
HEY, WAIT, THAT GUY DID SAY HE GAVE ME A FREE GIFT...
....
Happy Family Planning
LATEX
LUBRICATED
1 DOZEN

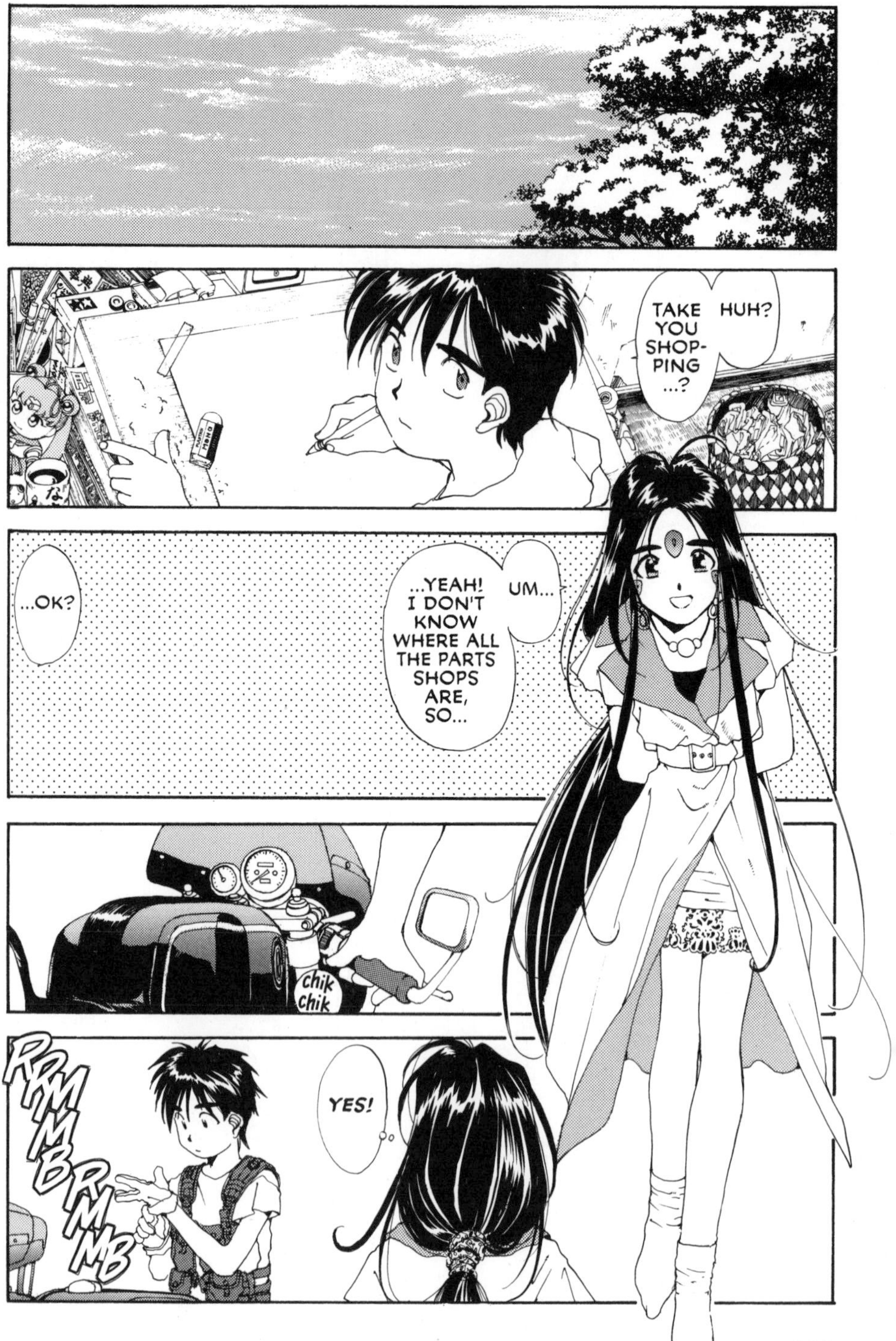
HUH?
TAKE YOU SHOPPING ...?
UM...
...YEAH! I DON'T KNOW WHERE ALL THE PARTS SHOPS ARE, SO...
...OK?
chik chik
YES!
RMMMBRMMB

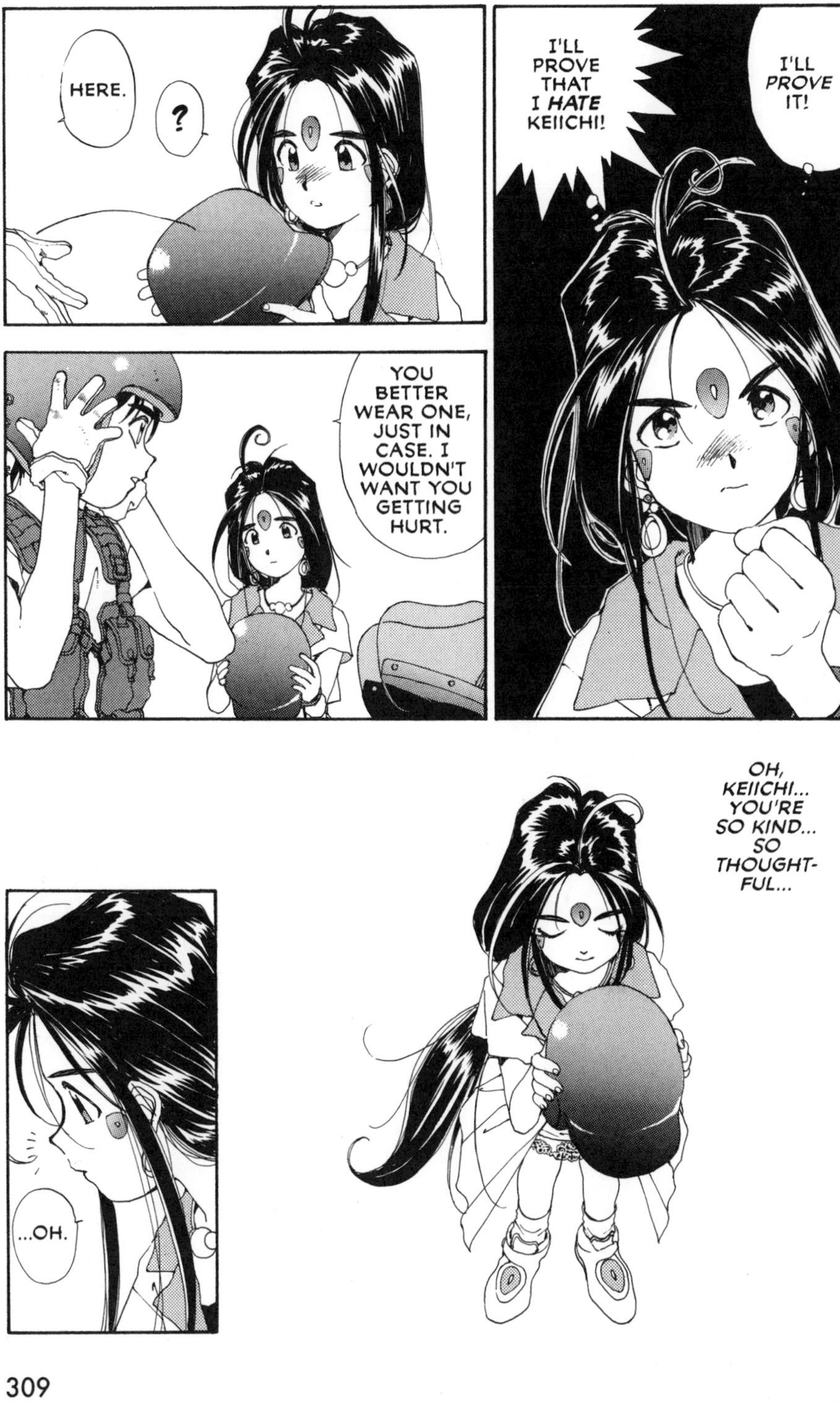
I'LL PROVE IT!
I'LL PROVE THAT I HATE KEIICHI!
?
HERE.
YOU BETTER WEAR ONE, JUST IN CASE. I WOULDN'T WANT YOU GETTING HURT.
OH, KEIICHI... YOU'RE SO KIND... SO THOUGHTFUL...
...OH.

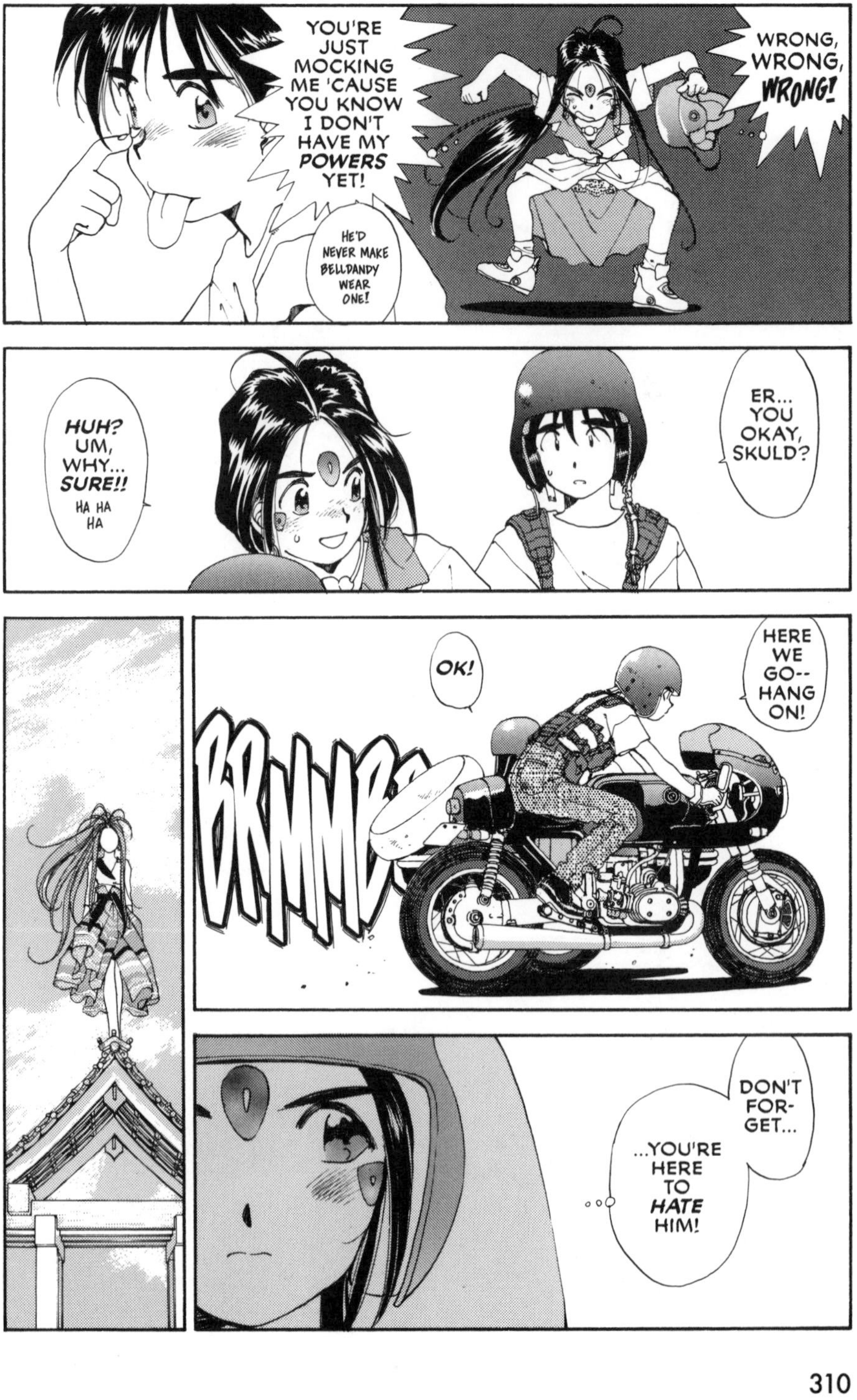
WRONG, WRONG, WRONG!
YOU'RE JUST MOCKING ME 'CAUSE YOU KNOW I DON'T HAVE MY POWERS YET!
HE'D NEVER MAKE BELLDANDY WEAR ONE!
ER... YOU OKAY, SKULD?
HUH? UM, WHY... SURE!! HA HA HA
HERE WE GO-- HANG ON!
OK!
BRMMB
DON'T FOR- GET...
...YOU'RE HERE TO HATE HIM!

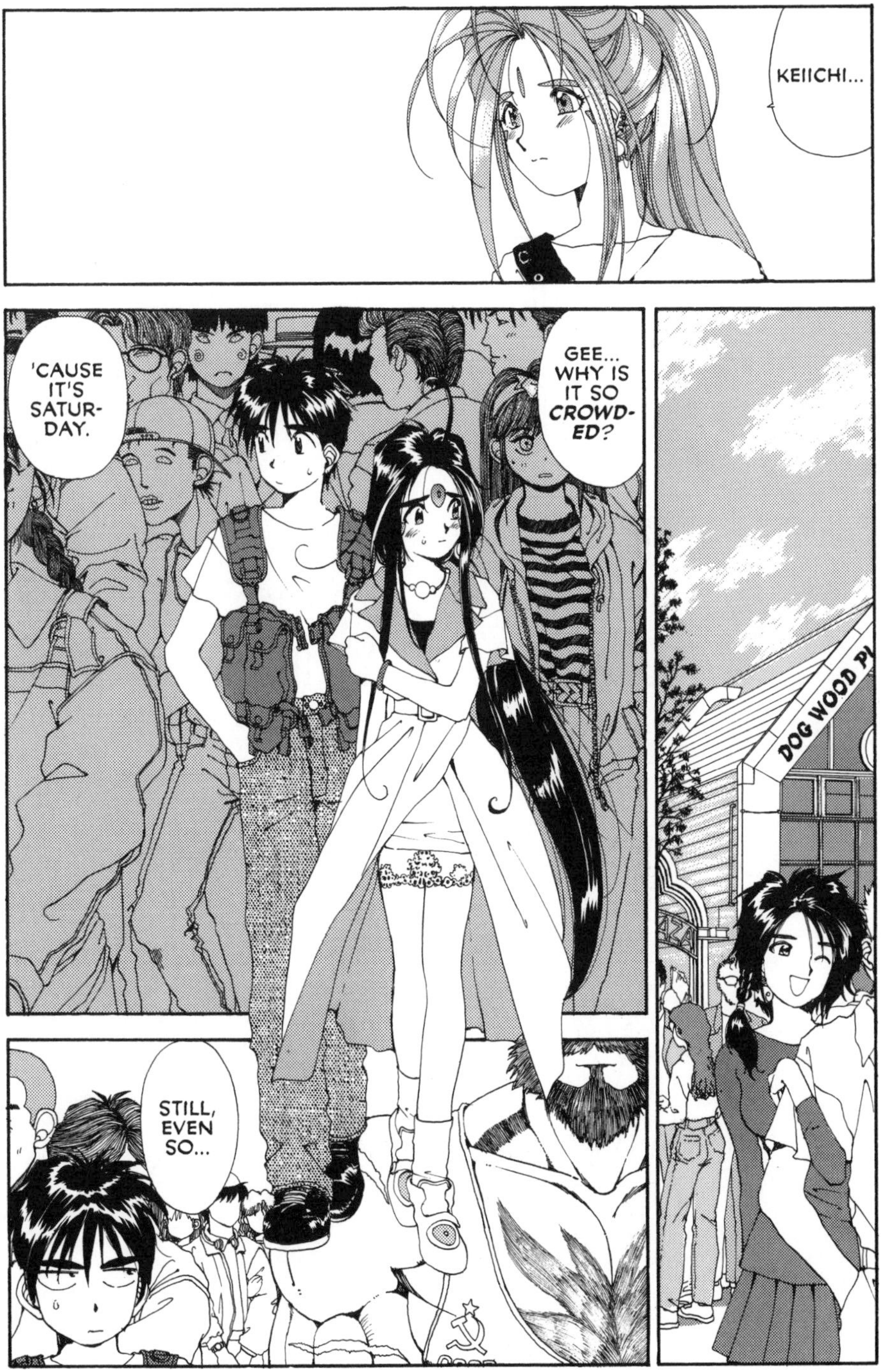
KEIICHI...
DOG WOOD PL
GEE... WHY IS IT SO CROWDED?
'CAUSE IT'S SATURDAY.
STILL, EVEN SO...

IT'S URD'S *MOSH PIT HELL SPELL!*

AND NOW FOR THE *FUN* PART... AT LEAST, FOR ME.

HEH, HEH...

THIS IS A *LOT* WORSE THAN NORMAL...

SQWRRSSH

HERP

...I *SHOVE* THOSE TWO TOGETHER!

...ADD A TAD OF POWER... AND THEN, BY JUST DEFLECTING THEM A *LITTLE*...

HOW DOES IT *WORK*, YOU ASK? I MERELY TAKE THE NORMAL VECTORS OF HUMAN CROWD MOVEMENT...

I'M SORRY, SKULD... FORGIVE YOUR LOVING SISTER...

KABOOM

HOW *DARE* YOU TOUCH ME!

WHEN KEIICHI GETS MASHED UP AGAINST HER BY THE CROWD... HEH, HEH...

312

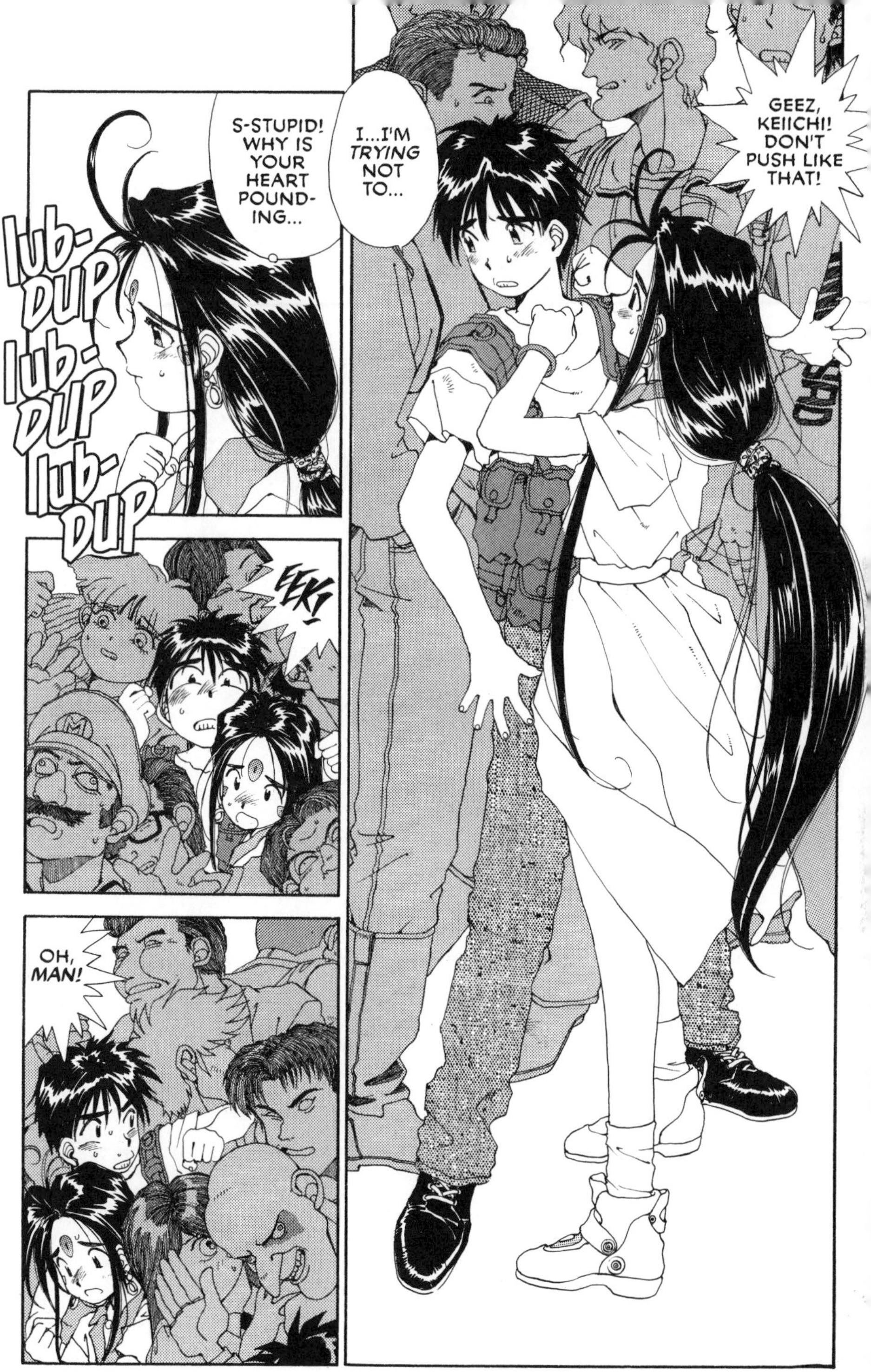
GEEZ, KEIICHI! DON'T PUSH LIKE THAT!
I...I'M *TRYING* NOT TO...
S-STUPID! WHY IS YOUR HEART POUNDING...
lub-DUP lub-DUP DUP lub-DUP
EEK!
OH, *MAN!*

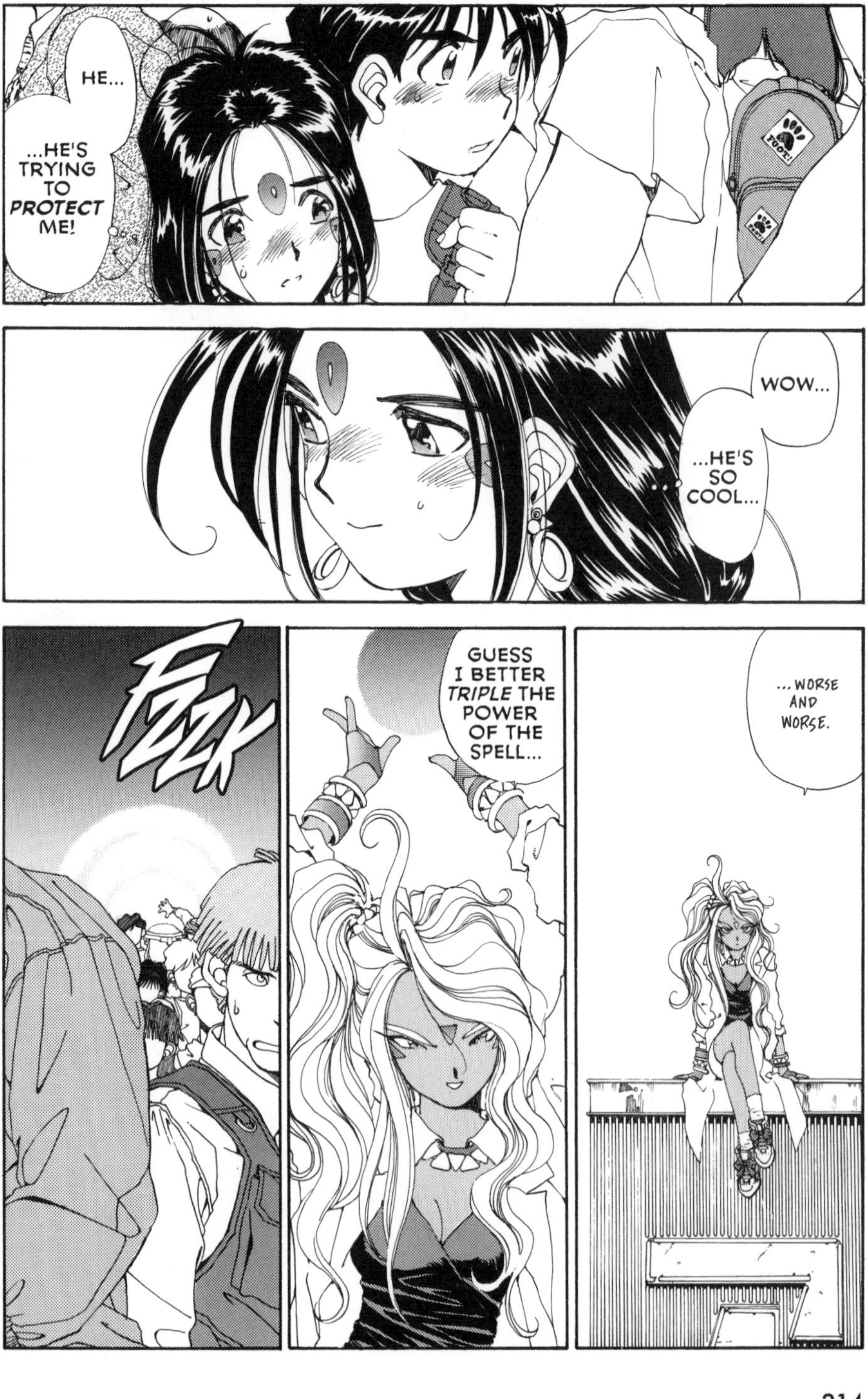
HE...
...HE'S TRYING TO *PROTECT* ME!
WOW...
...HE'S SO COOL...
...WORSE AND WORSE.
GUESS I BETTER *TRIPLE* THE POWER OF THE SPELL...
FZZK

315

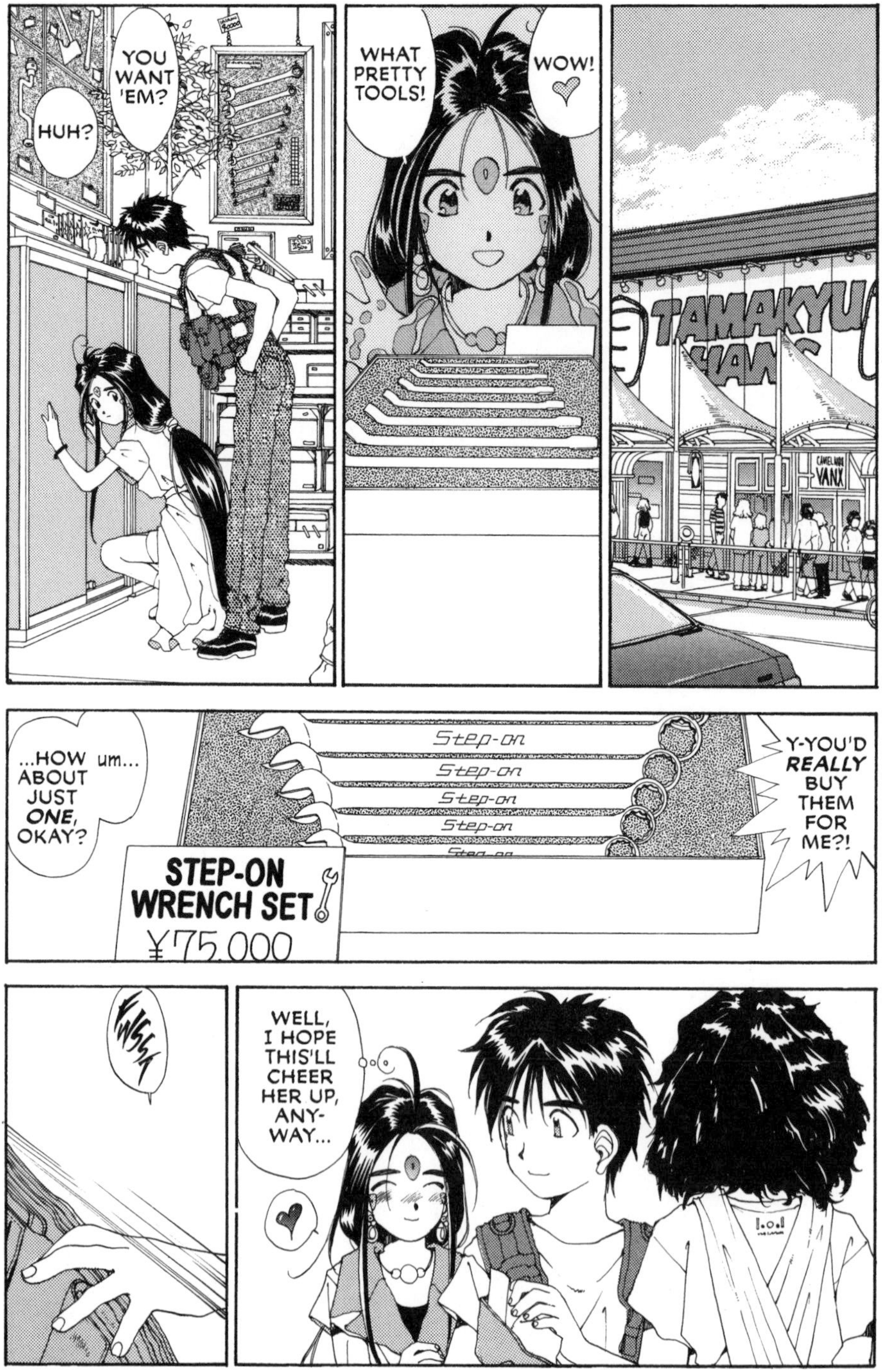
TAMAKYU
VANX
WOW!
WHAT PRETTY TOOLS!
YOU WANT 'EM?
HUH?
Y-YOU'D *REALLY* BUY THEM FOR ME?!
Step-on
Step-on
Step-on
Step-on
STEP-ON WRENCH SET
¥75,000
...HOW ABOUT JUST *ONE*, OKAY?
um...
WELL, I HOPE THIS'LL CHEER HER UP, ANY-WAY...

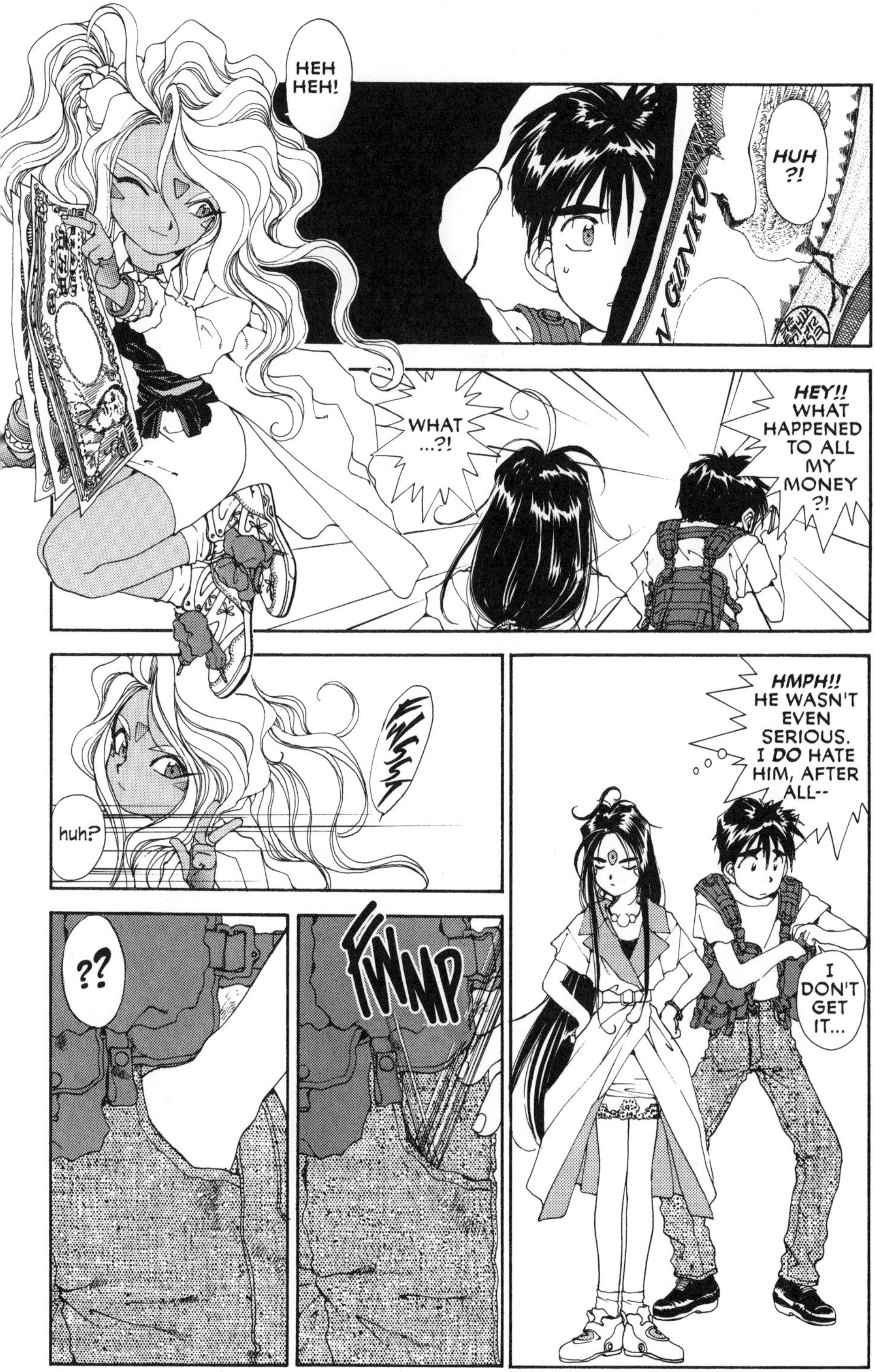
HUH ?!
HEH HEH!
HEY!! WHAT HAPPENED TO ALL MY MONEY ?!
WHAT ...?!
HMPH!! HE WASN'T EVEN SERIOUS. I DO HATE HIM, AFTER ALL--
I DON'T GET IT...
huh?
FWMP
??

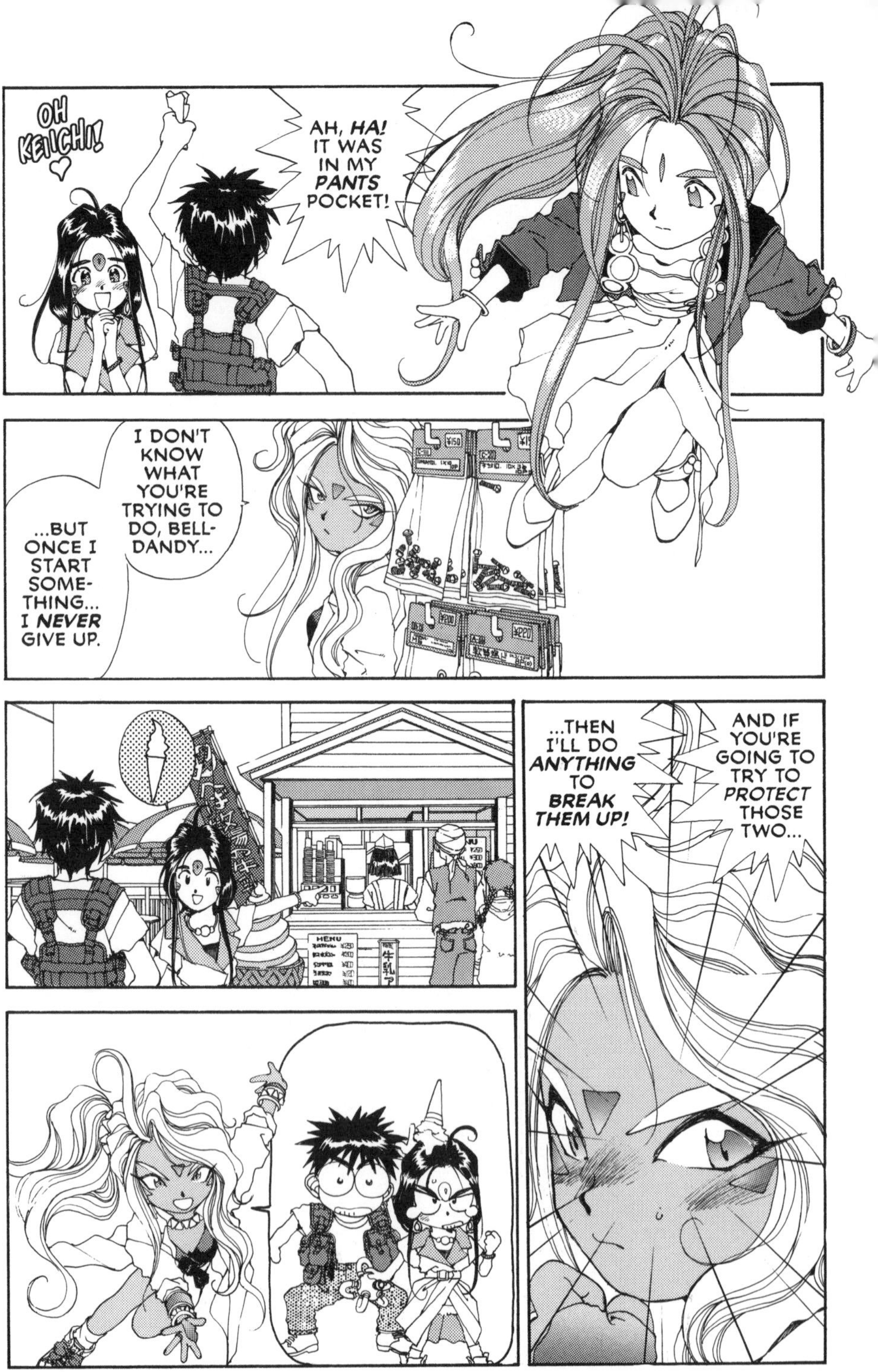
AH, HA! IT WAS IN MY PANTS POCKET!
OH KEIICHI! ♡
I DON'T KNOW WHAT YOU'RE TRYING TO DO, BELL-DANDY...
...BUT ONCE I START SOME-THING... I NEVER GIVE UP.
AND IF YOU'RE GOING TO TRY TO PROTECT THOSE TWO...
...THEN I'LL DO ANYTHING TO BREAK THEM UP!
MENU

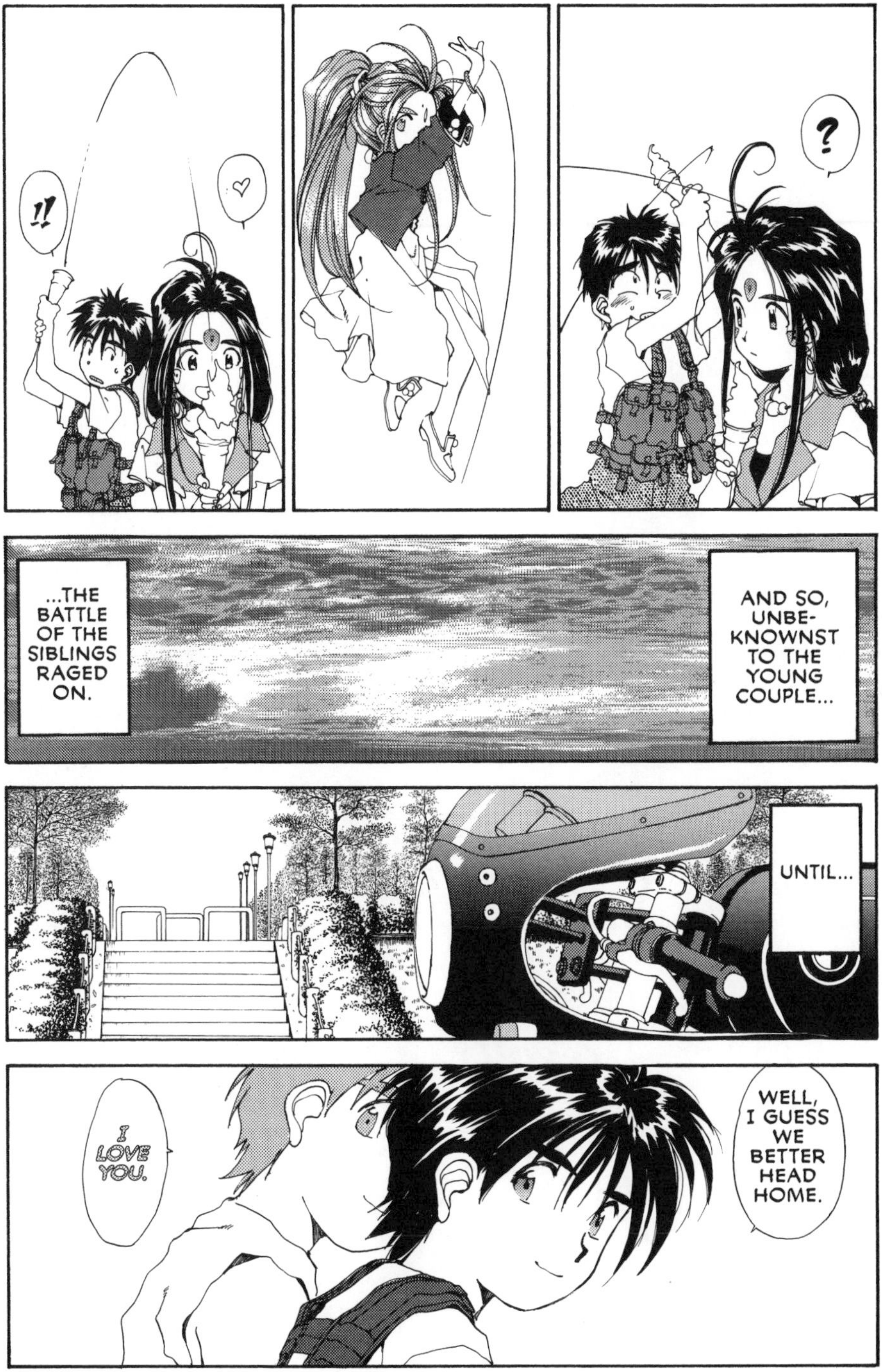
?
!!
♡
AND SO, UNBE-KNOWNST TO THE YOUNG COUPLE...
...THE BATTLE OF THE SIBLINGS RAGED ON.
UNTIL...
WELL, I GUESS WE BETTER HEAD HOME.
I LOVE YOU.

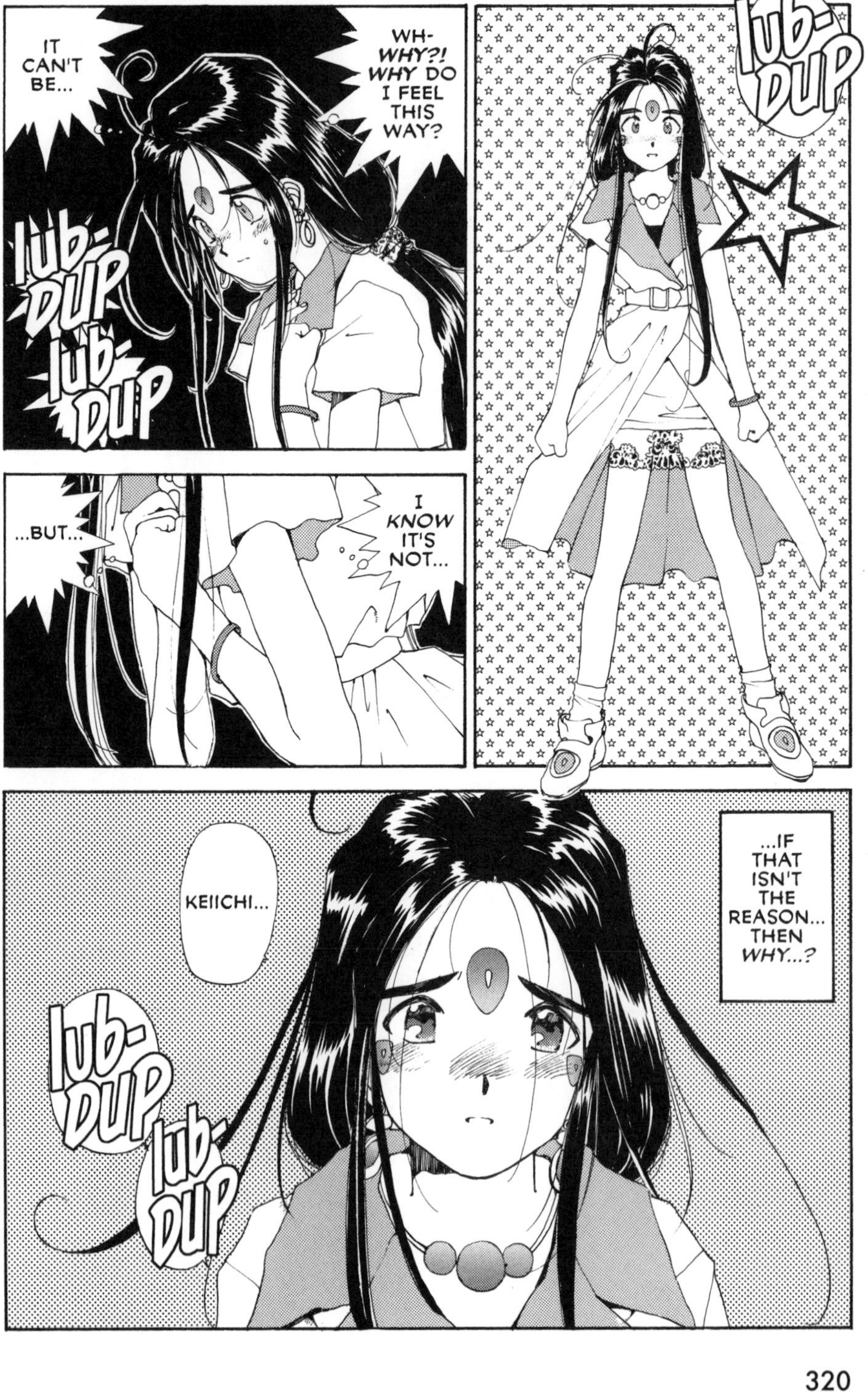
lub-DUP
WH- WHY?! WHY DO I FEEL THIS WAY?
IT CAN'T BE...
lub-DUP lub-DUP
I KNOW IT'S NOT...
...BUT...
...IF THAT ISN'T THE REASON... THEN WHY...?
KEIICHI...
lub-DUP lub-DUP

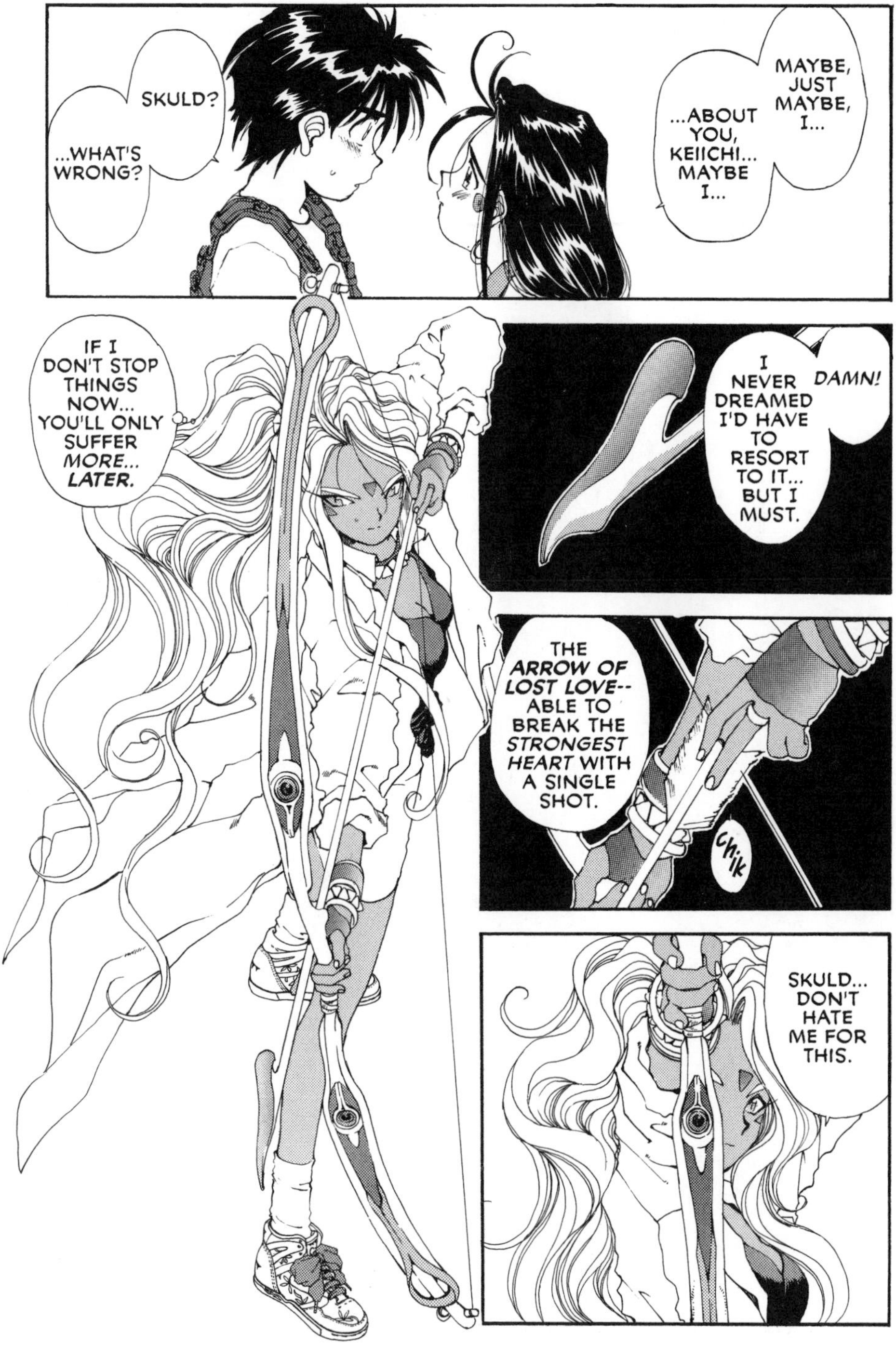
MAYBE, JUST MAYBE, I...
...ABOUT YOU, KEIICHI... MAYBE I...
SKULD?
...WHAT'S WRONG?
DAMN!
I NEVER DREAMED I'D HAVE TO RESORT TO IT... BUT I MUST.
THE *ARROW OF LOST LOVE*-- ABLE TO BREAK THE *STRONGEST HEART* WITH A SINGLE SHOT.
Chik
SKULD... DON'T HATE ME FOR THIS.
IF I DON'T STOP THINGS NOW... YOU'LL ONLY SUFFER *MORE*... ***LATER.***

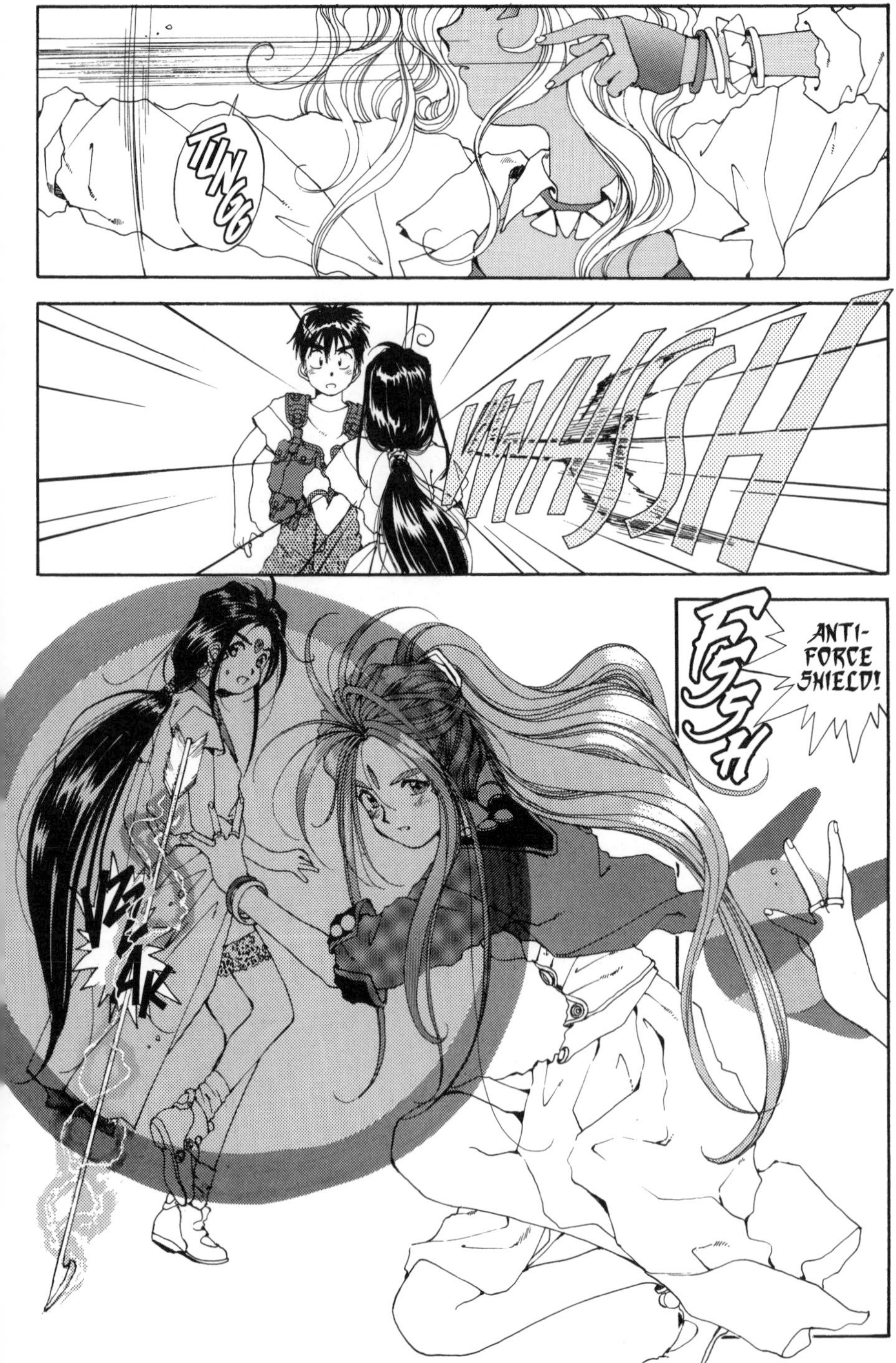
TUNGG
WHISH
FSSH
ANTI-FORCE SHIELD!
VZZAK

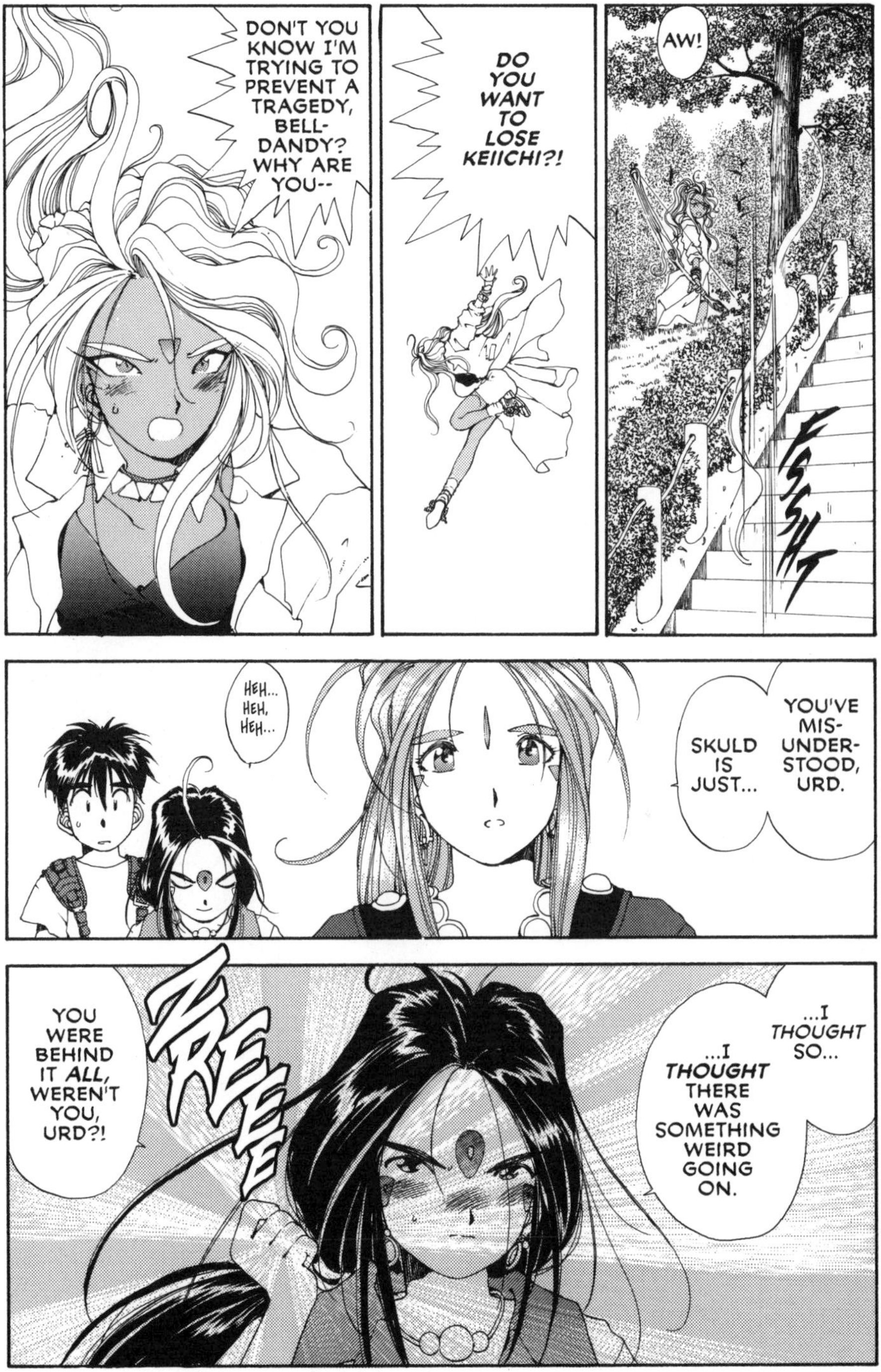
AW!
FSSHT
DO YOU WANT TO LOSE KEIICHI?!
DON'T YOU KNOW I'M TRYING TO PREVENT A TRAGEDY, BELL-DANDY? WHY ARE YOU--
YOU'VE MIS-UNDER-STOOD, URD.
SKULD IS JUST...
HEH... HEH, HEH...
...I THOUGHT SO...
...I THOUGHT THERE WAS SOMETHING WEIRD GOING ON.
ZREEE
YOU WERE BEHIND IT ALL, WEREN'T YOU, URD?!

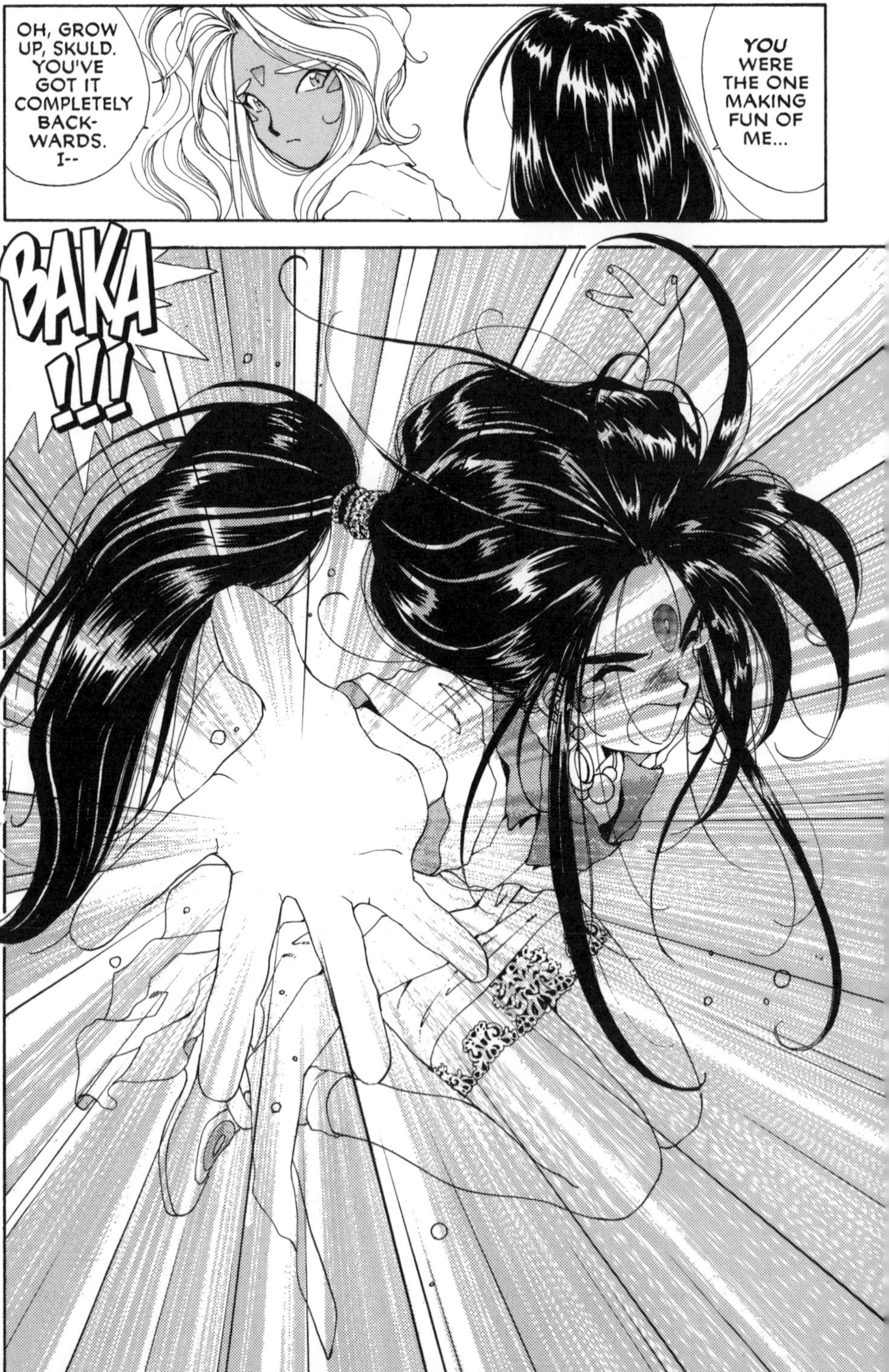
YOU WERE THE ONE MAKING FUN OF ME...
OH, GROW UP, SKULD. YOU'VE GOT IT COMPLETELY BACK-WARDS. I--
BAKA !!!

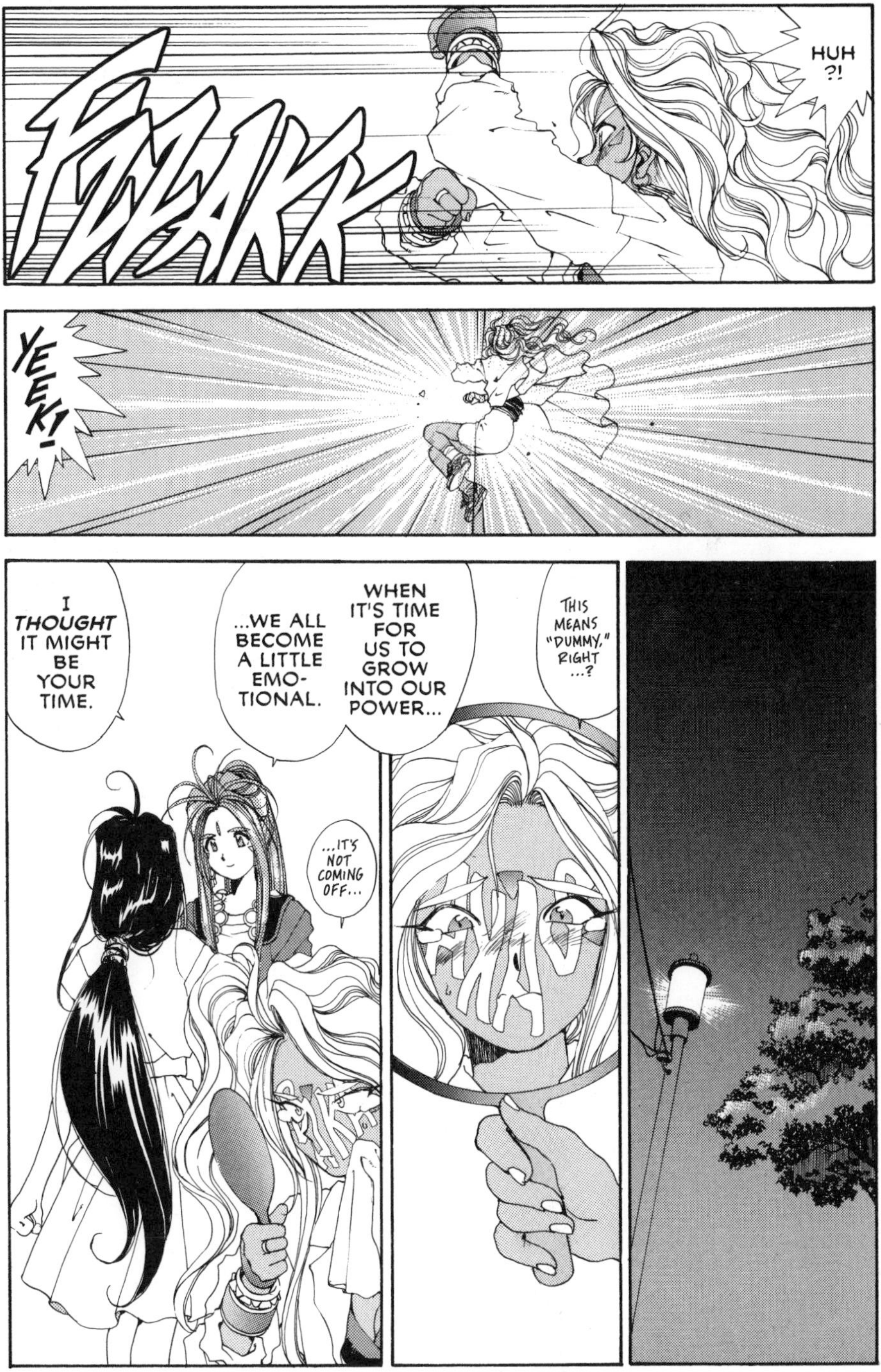
HUH?!
FZZAKK
YEEK!
THIS MEANS "DUMMY," RIGHT ...?
WHEN IT'S TIME FOR US TO GROW INTO OUR POWER...
...WE ALL BECOME A LITTLE EMO-TIONAL.
I *THOUGHT* IT MIGHT BE YOUR TIME.
...IT'S NOT COMING OFF...

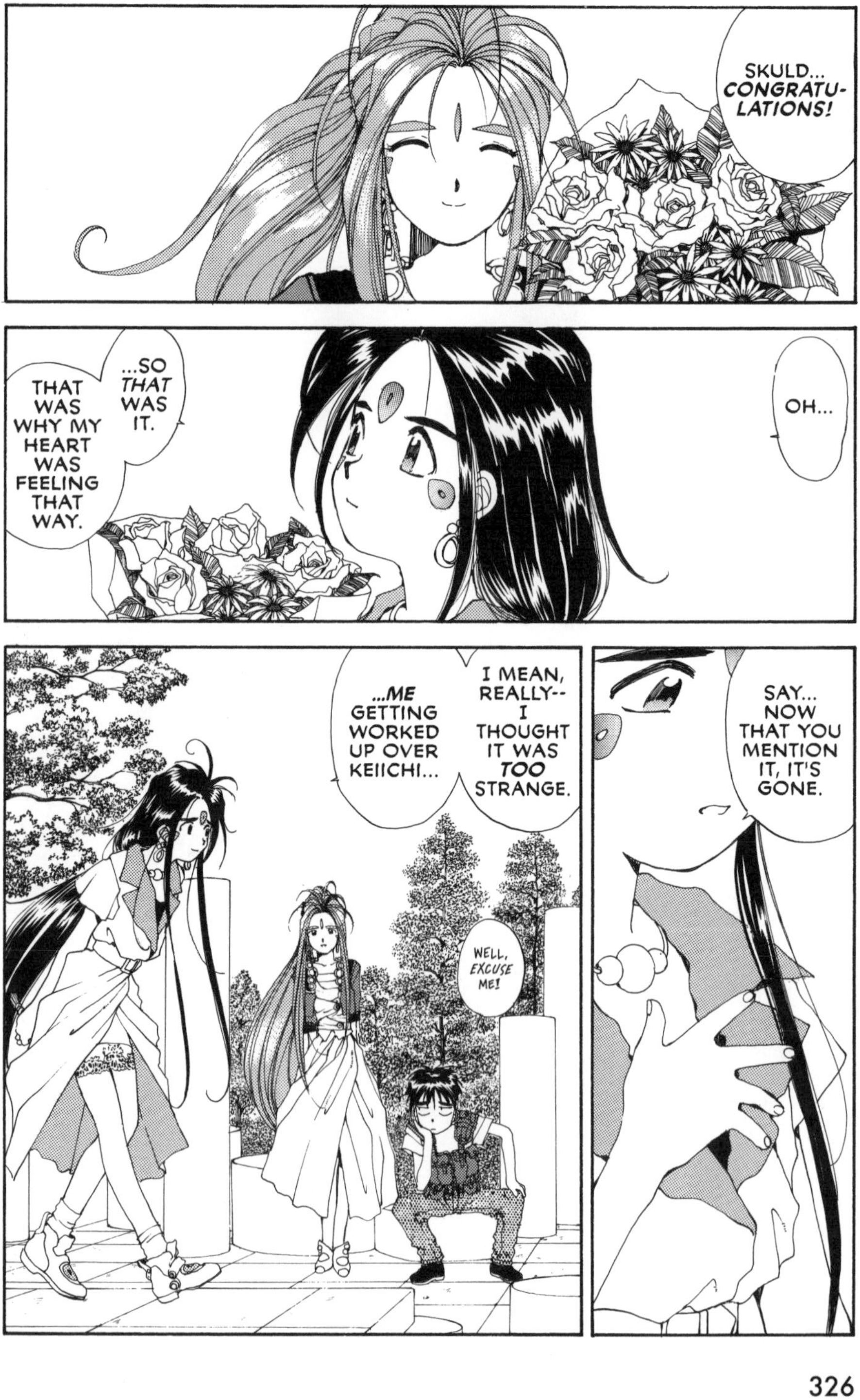
SKULD... CONGRATULATIONS!
OH...
...SO THAT WAS IT.
THAT WAS WHY MY HEART WAS FEELING THAT WAY.
SAY... NOW THAT YOU MENTION IT, IT'S GONE.
I MEAN, REALLY-- I THOUGHT IT WAS TOO STRANGE.
...ME GETTING WORKED UP OVER KEIICHI...
WELL, EXCUSE ME!

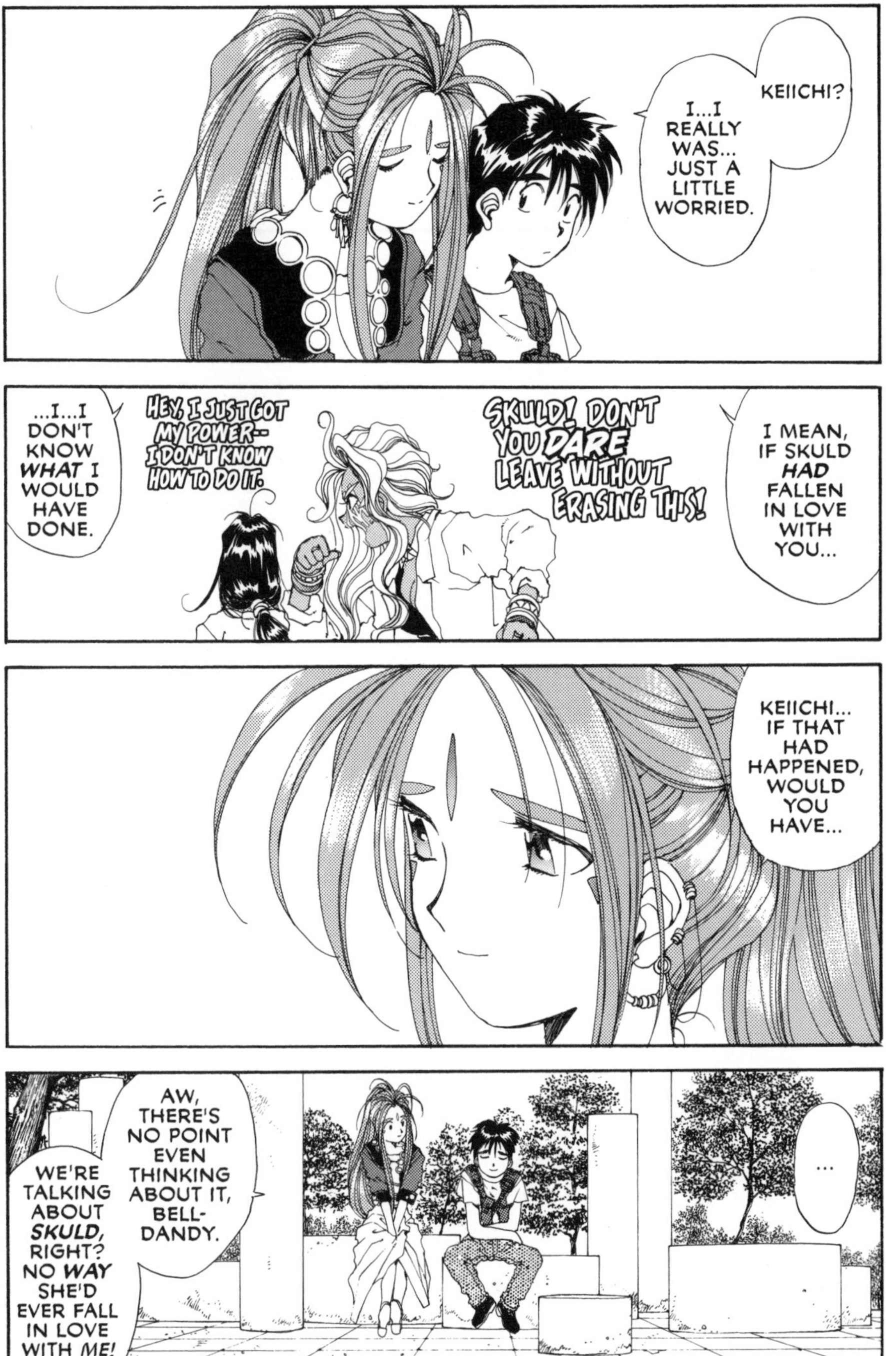
KEIICHI?
I...I REALLY WAS... JUST A LITTLE WORRIED.
I MEAN, IF SKULD HAD FALLEN IN LOVE WITH YOU...
SKULD! DON'T YOU DARE LEAVE WITHOUT ERASING THIS!
HEY, I JUST GOT MY POWER-- I DON'T KNOW HOW TO DO IT.
...I...I DON'T KNOW WHAT I WOULD HAVE DONE.
KEIICHI... IF THAT HAD HAPPENED, WOULD YOU HAVE...
...
AW, THERE'S NO POINT EVEN THINKING ABOUT IT, BELL-DANDY.
WE'RE TALKING ABOUT SKULD, RIGHT? NO WAY SHE'D EVER FALL IN LOVE WITH ME!

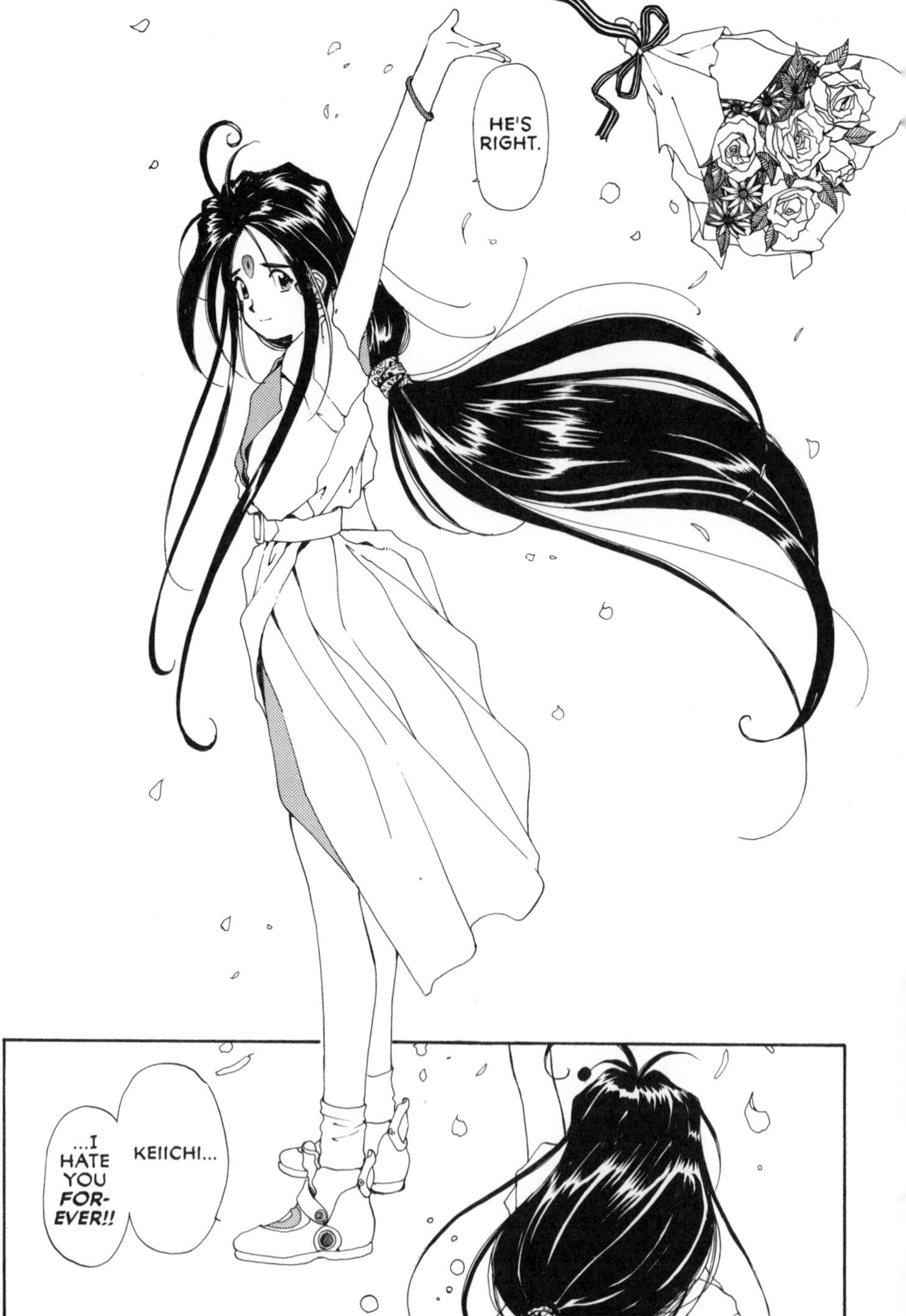
HE'S RIGHT.
KEIICHI...
...I HATE YOU *FOREVER!!*

CHAPTER 52

Ninja Master

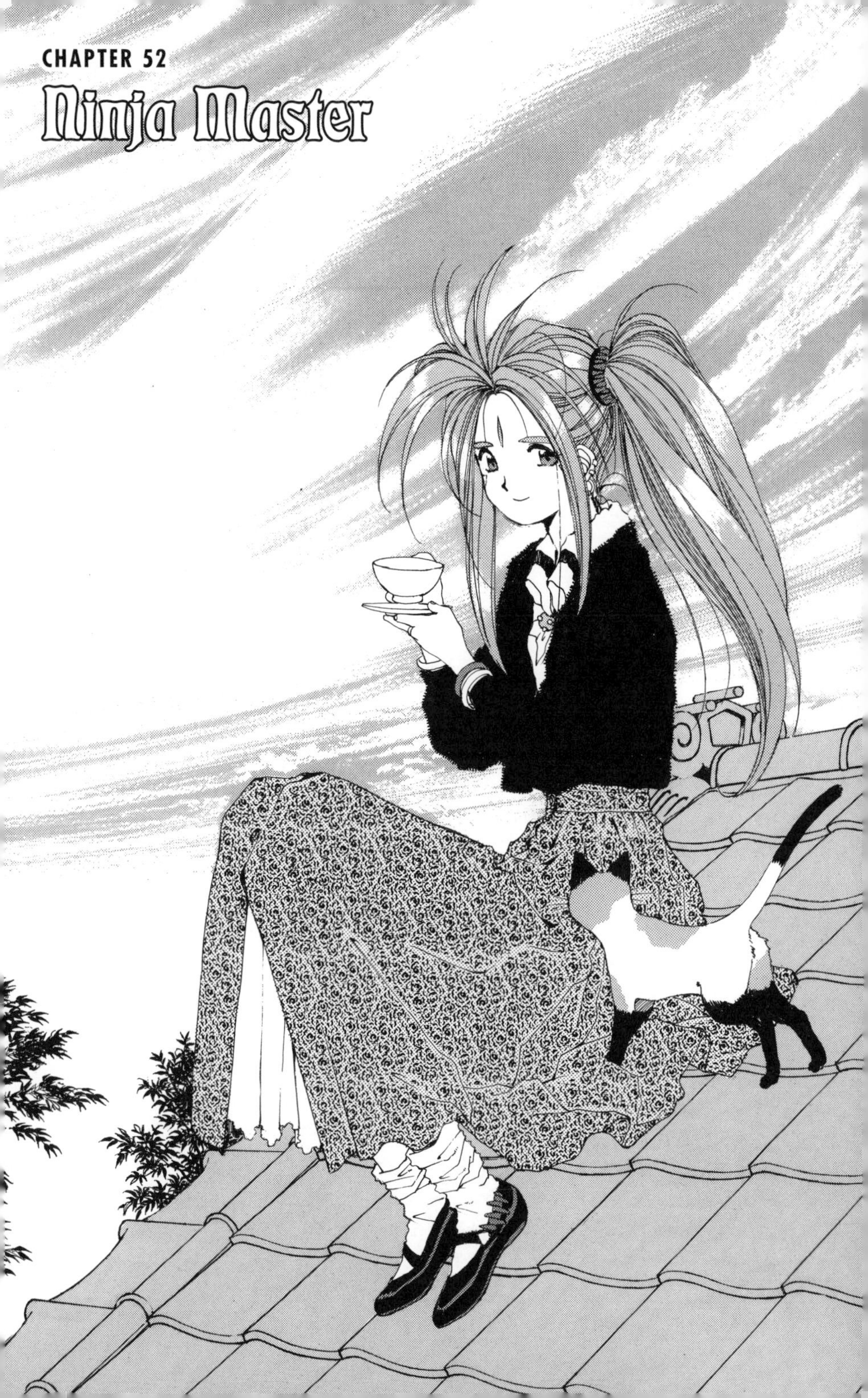

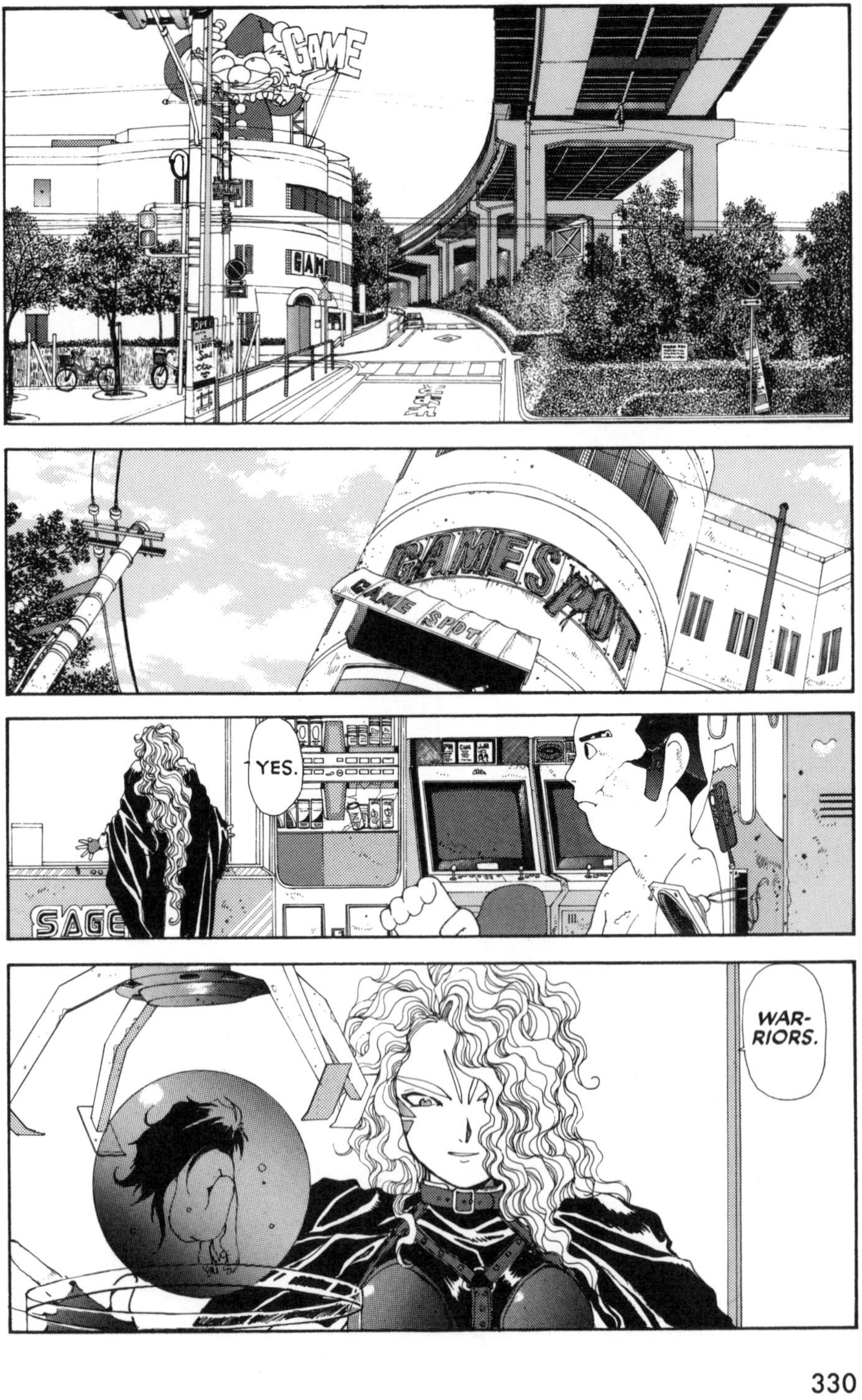
GAME
GAMESPOT
YES.
WAR-
RIORS.

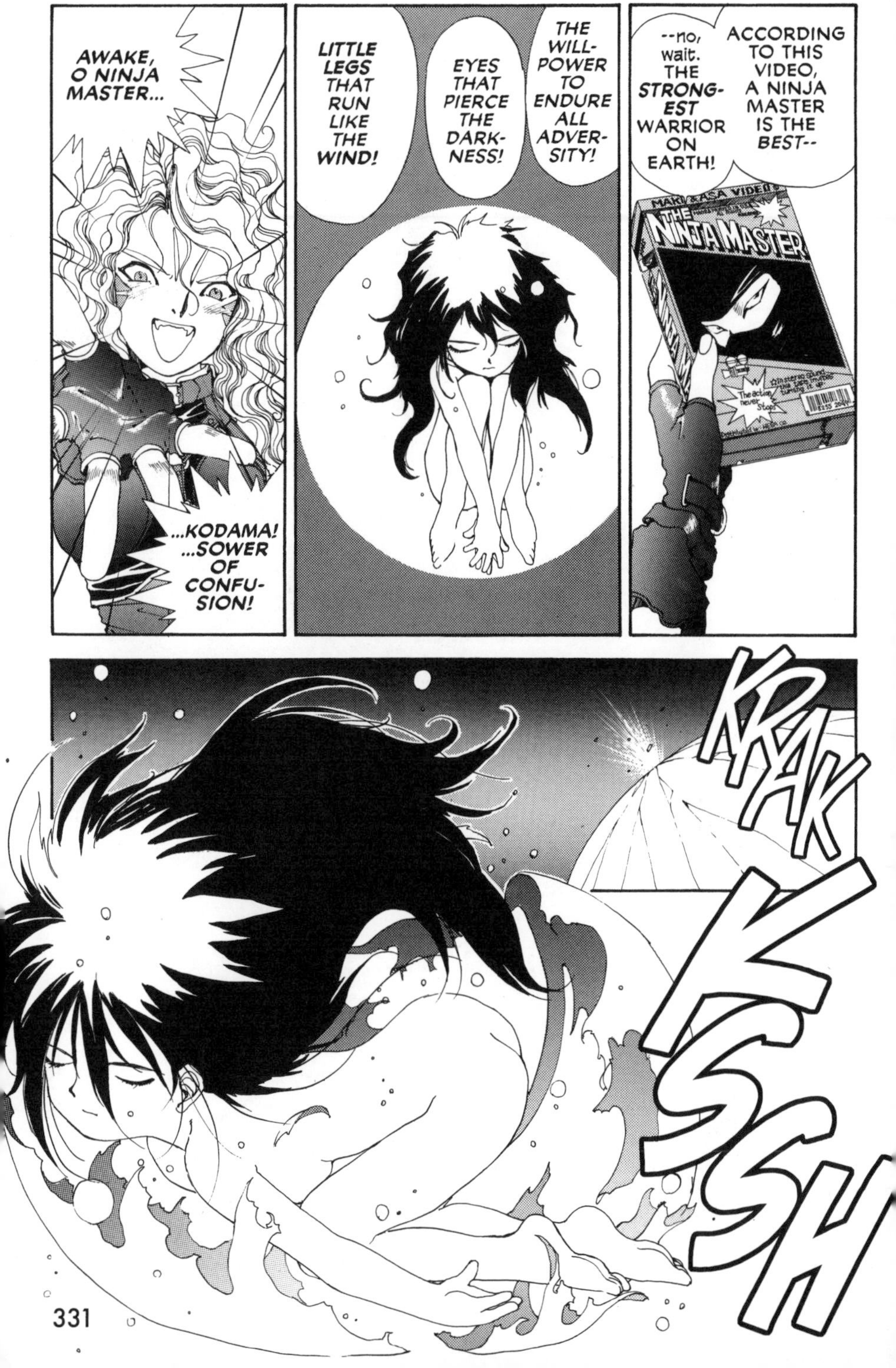
ACCORDING TO THIS VIDEO, A NINJA MASTER IS THE BEST--
--no, wait. THE STRONG-EST WARRIOR ON EARTH!
MARI & ASA VIDEO
THE NINJA MASTER
The action never stops
THE WILL-POWER TO ENDURE ALL ADVER-SITY!
EYES THAT PIERCE THE DARK-NESS!
LITTLE LEGS THAT RUN LIKE THE WIND!
AWAKE, O NINJA MASTER...
...KODAMA! ...SOWER OF CONFU-SION!
KRAKAK
KSSSH

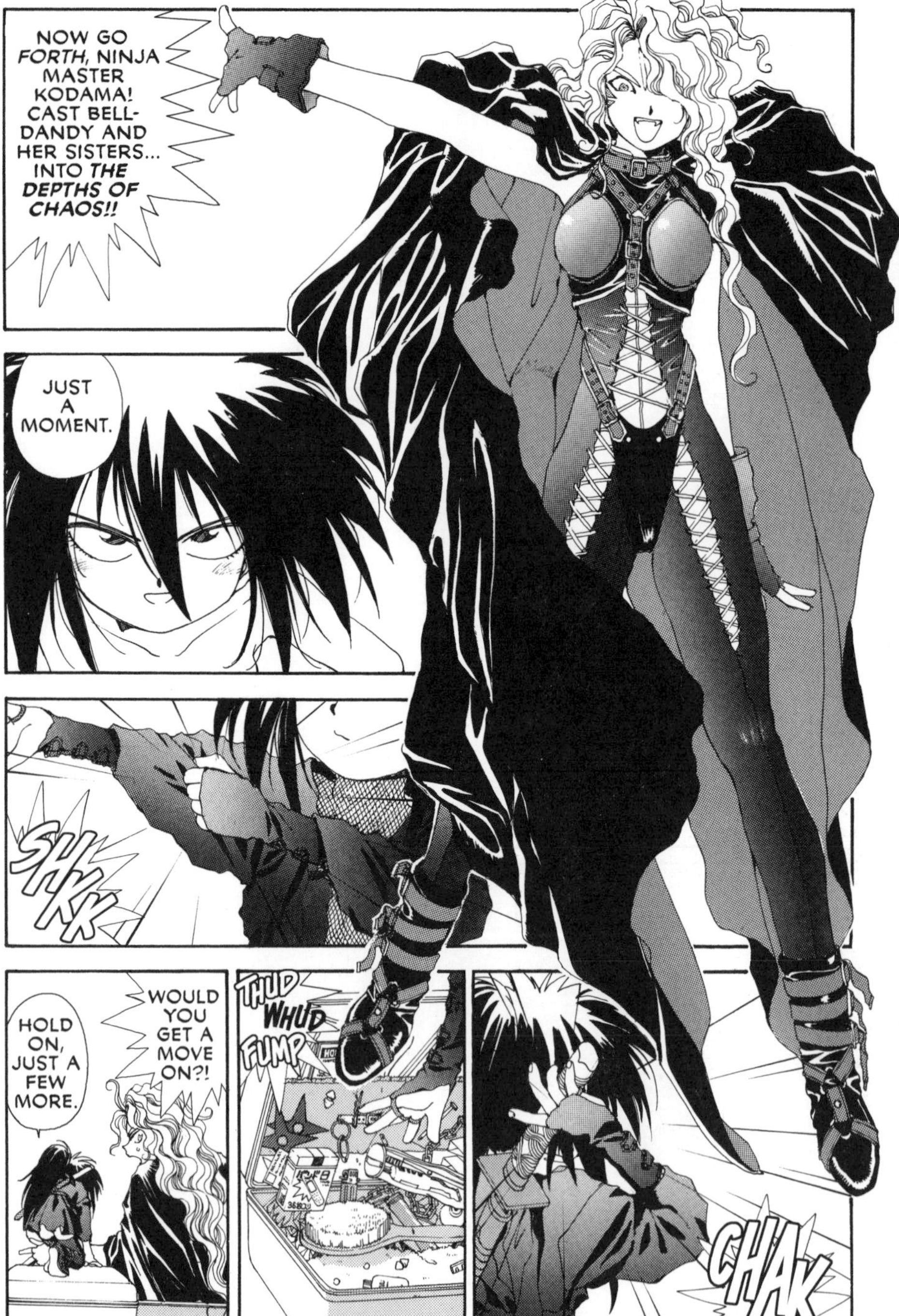
NOW GO FORTH, NINJA MASTER KODAMA! CAST BELL-DANDY AND HER SISTERS... INTO THE DEPTHS OF CHAOS!!
JUST A MOMENT.
SHKK
WOULD YOU GET A MOVE ON?!
HOLD ON, JUST A FEW MORE.
THUD WHUD FUMP
CHAK

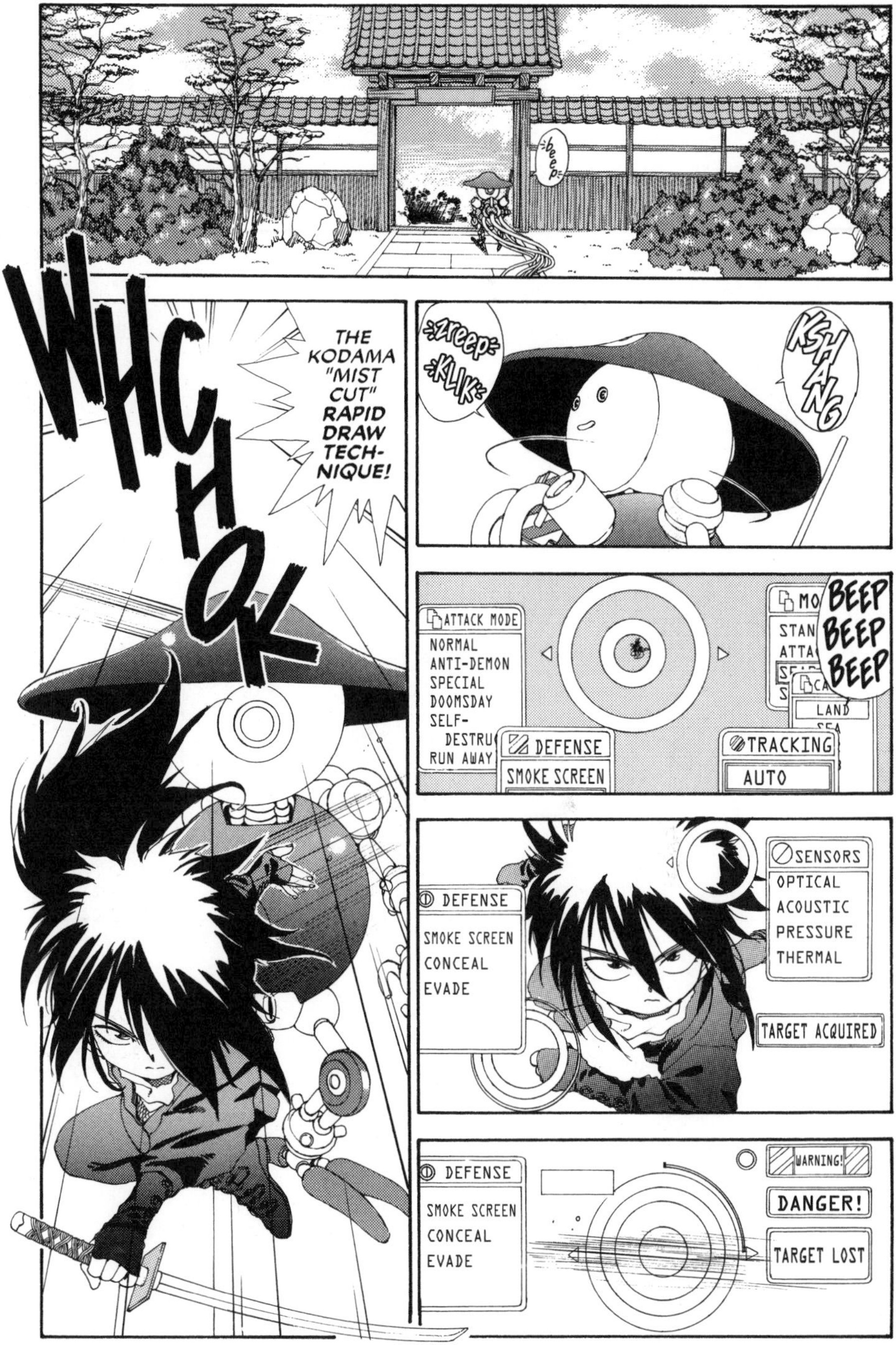
beep
zreep
KLIK
KSHANG
BEEP BEEP BEEP
ATTACK MODE
NORMAL
ANTI-DEMON
SPECIAL
DOOMSDAY
RUN AWAY
LAND
DEFENSE
SMOKE SCREEN
TRACKING
AUTO
SENSORS
OPTICAL
ACOUSTIC
PRESSURE
THERMAL
TARGET ACQUIRED
DEFENSE
SMOKE SCREEN
CONCEAL
EVADE
WARNING!
DANGER!
TARGET LOST
DEFENSE
SMOKE SCREEN
CONCEAL
EVADE
WHCHOK
THE KODAMA "MIST CUT" RAPID DRAW TECHNIQUE!

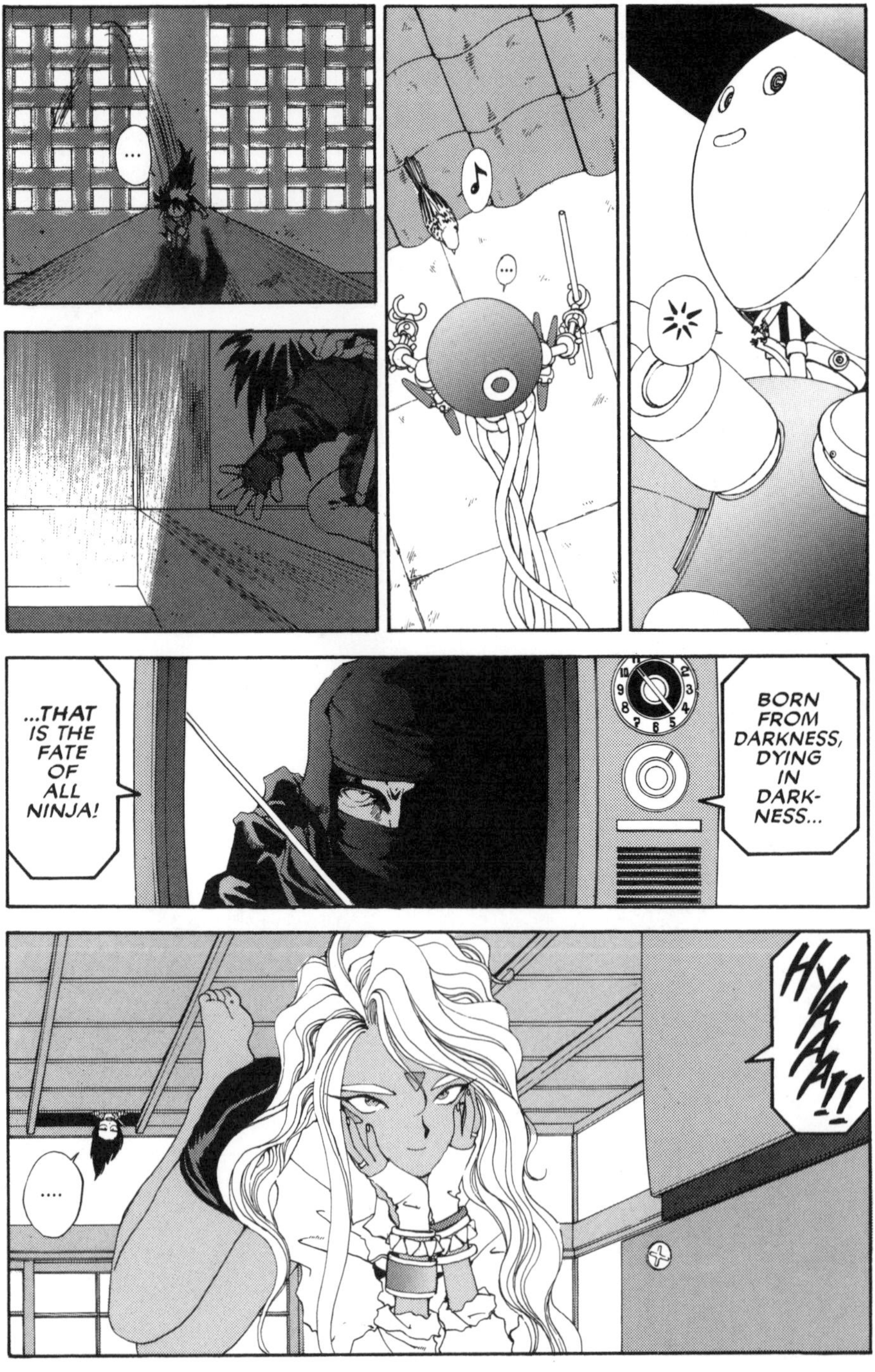
♪
...
...
BORN FROM DARKNESS, DYING IN DARKNESS...
...THAT IS THE FATE OF ALL NINJA!
HYAAA!!
....

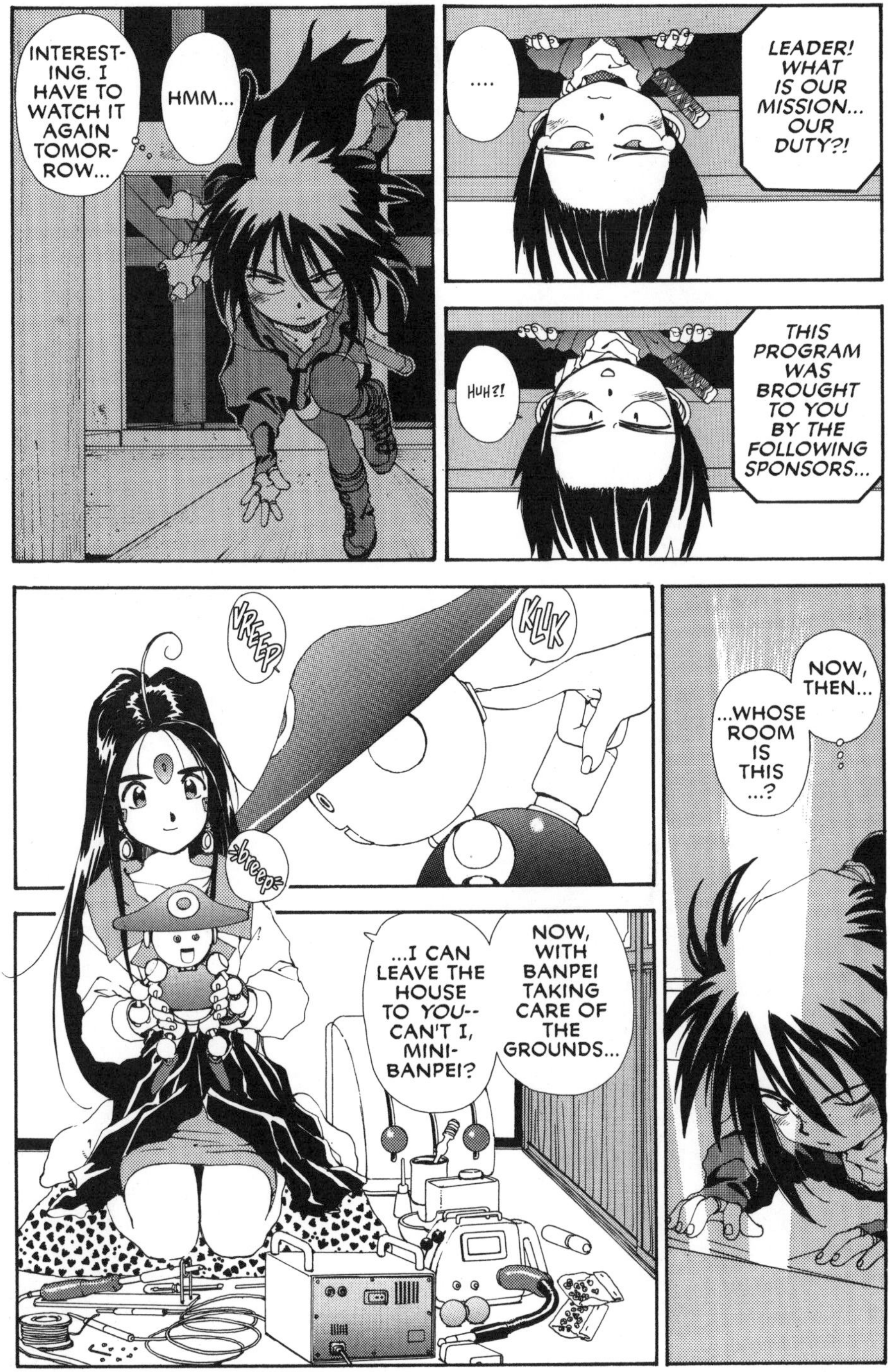
LEADER! WHAT IS OUR MISSION... OUR DUTY?!
....
THIS PROGRAM WAS BROUGHT TO YOU BY THE FOLLOWING SPONSORS...
HUH?!
HMM...
INTERESTING. I HAVE TO WATCH IT AGAIN TOMORROW...
NOW, THEN...
...WHOSE ROOM IS THIS ...?
KLIK
VREEP
NOW, WITH BANPEI TAKING CARE OF THE GROUNDS...
...I CAN LEAVE THE HOUSE TO *YOU*-- CAN'T I, MINI-BANPEI?
breep

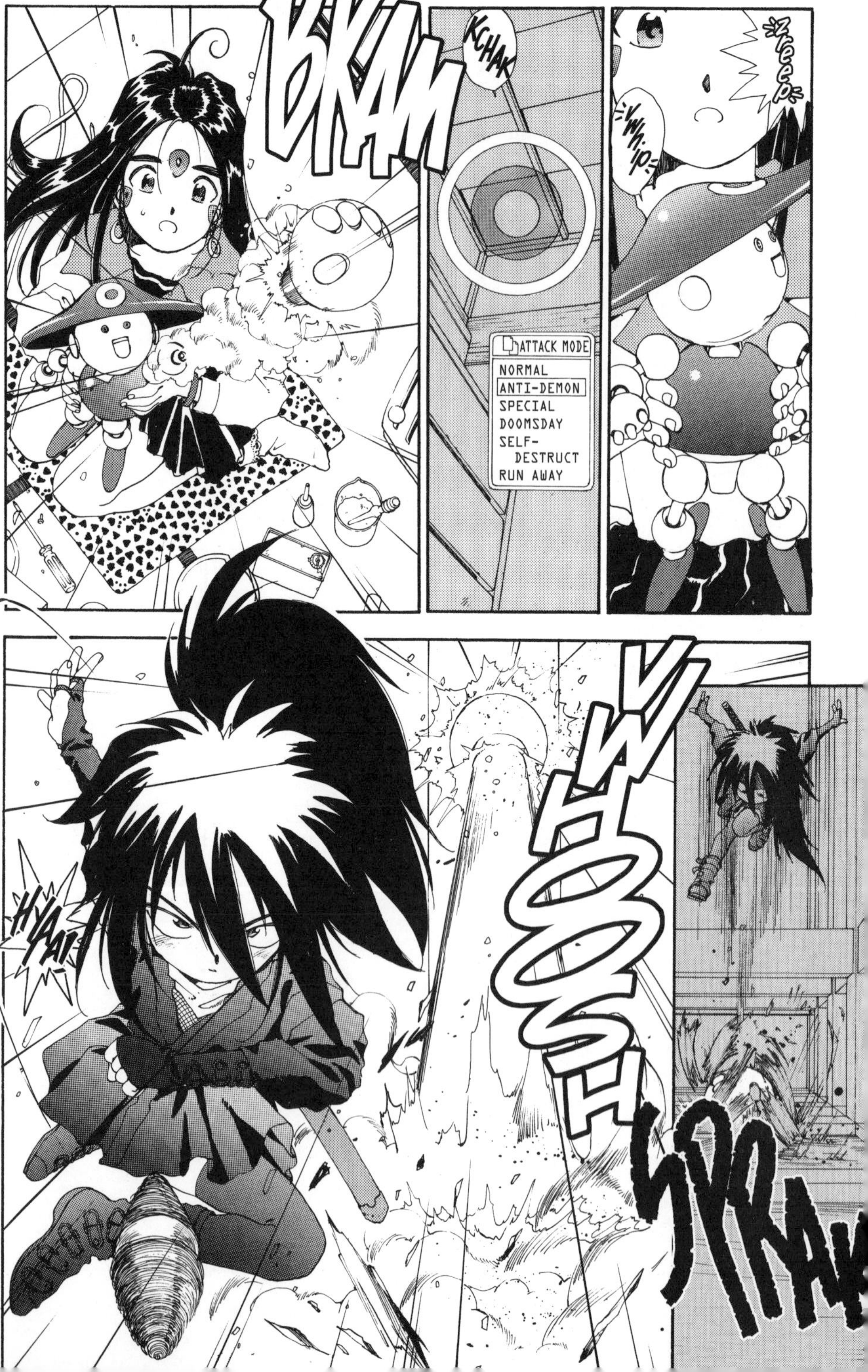
zreep
vwhip
KCHAK
ATTACK MODE
NORMAL
ANTI-DEMON
SPECIAL
DOOMSDAY
SELF-DESTRUCT
RUN AWAY
BKAM
SPRAK
VWHOOSH
HYAAA!

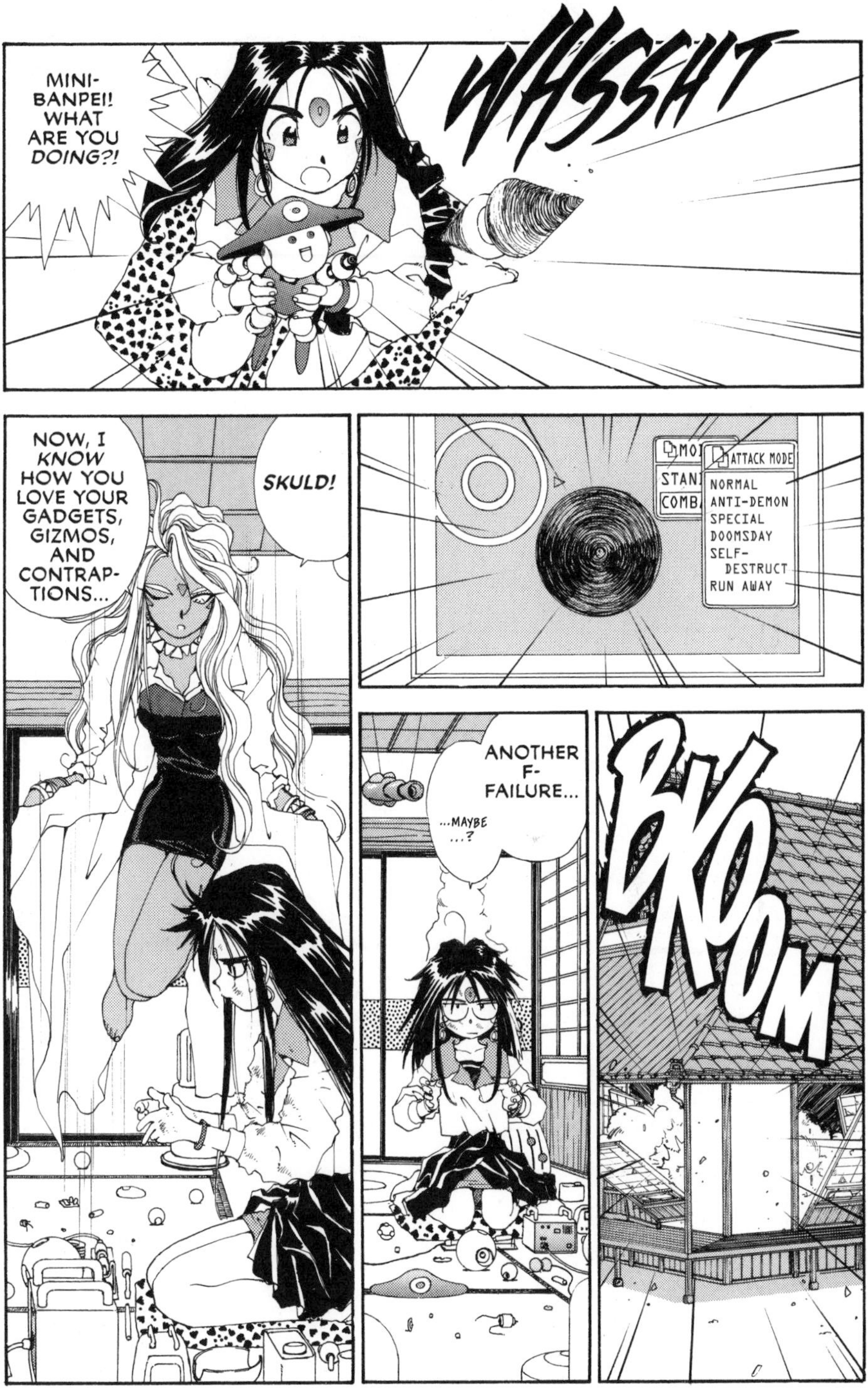
WHSSHT
MINI-BANPEI! WHAT ARE YOU *DOING?!*
ATTACK MODE
NORMAL
ANTI-DEMON
SPECIAL
DOOMSDAY
SELF-DESTRUCT
RUN AWAY
BKOOM
ANOTHER F-FAILURE...
...MAYBE ...?
SKULD!
NOW, I *KNOW* HOW YOU LOVE YOUR GADGETS, GIZMOS, AND CONTRAPTIONS...

YOU MADE ME DROP THE ONLY SAMPLE OF MY LATEST DRUG!

YOU'RE HAVING A HARD TIME?!

HEY...

BUT I'LL SAY THIS FOR THE LAST TIME... KEEP THEM TO YOURSELF!

...I'M HAVING A HARD TIME HERE!

HOW DARE YOU!

HOW DARE I?!

GOOD! AT LEAST THAT'S ONE POTION THAT WON'T BE MESSING UP ANYONE'S LIFE!

KEIICHI'S SHOP

SO... THESE TWO ARE BITTER ENEMIES.

ONE ADDICTED TO DRUGS...

...AND THE OTHER TO THING-A-MA-JIGS.

HMM.

BZZT

BZZT

338

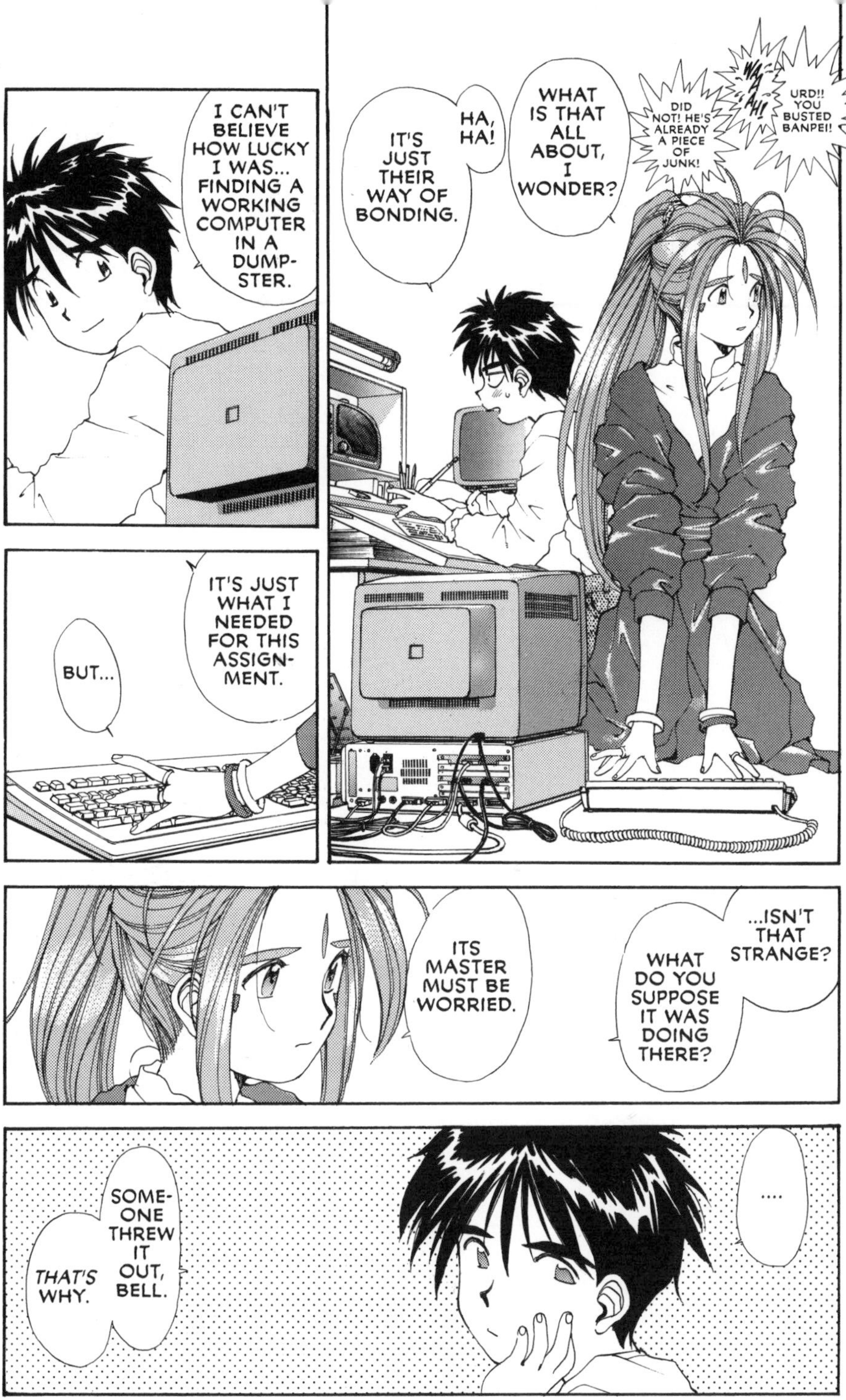
URD!! YOU BUSTED BANPEI!!
WA-A-AH!
DID NOT! HE'S ALREADY A PIECE OF JUNK!
WHAT IS THAT ALL ABOUT, I WONDER?
HA, HA!
IT'S JUST THEIR WAY OF BONDING.
I CAN'T BELIEVE HOW LUCKY I WAS... FINDING A WORKING COMPUTER IN A DUMP-STER.
IT'S JUST WHAT I NEEDED FOR THIS ASSIGN-MENT.
BUT...
...ISN'T THAT STRANGE?
WHAT DO YOU SUPPOSE IT WAS DOING THERE?
ITS MASTER MUST BE WORRIED.
....
SOME-ONE THREW IT OUT, BELL.
THAT'S WHY.

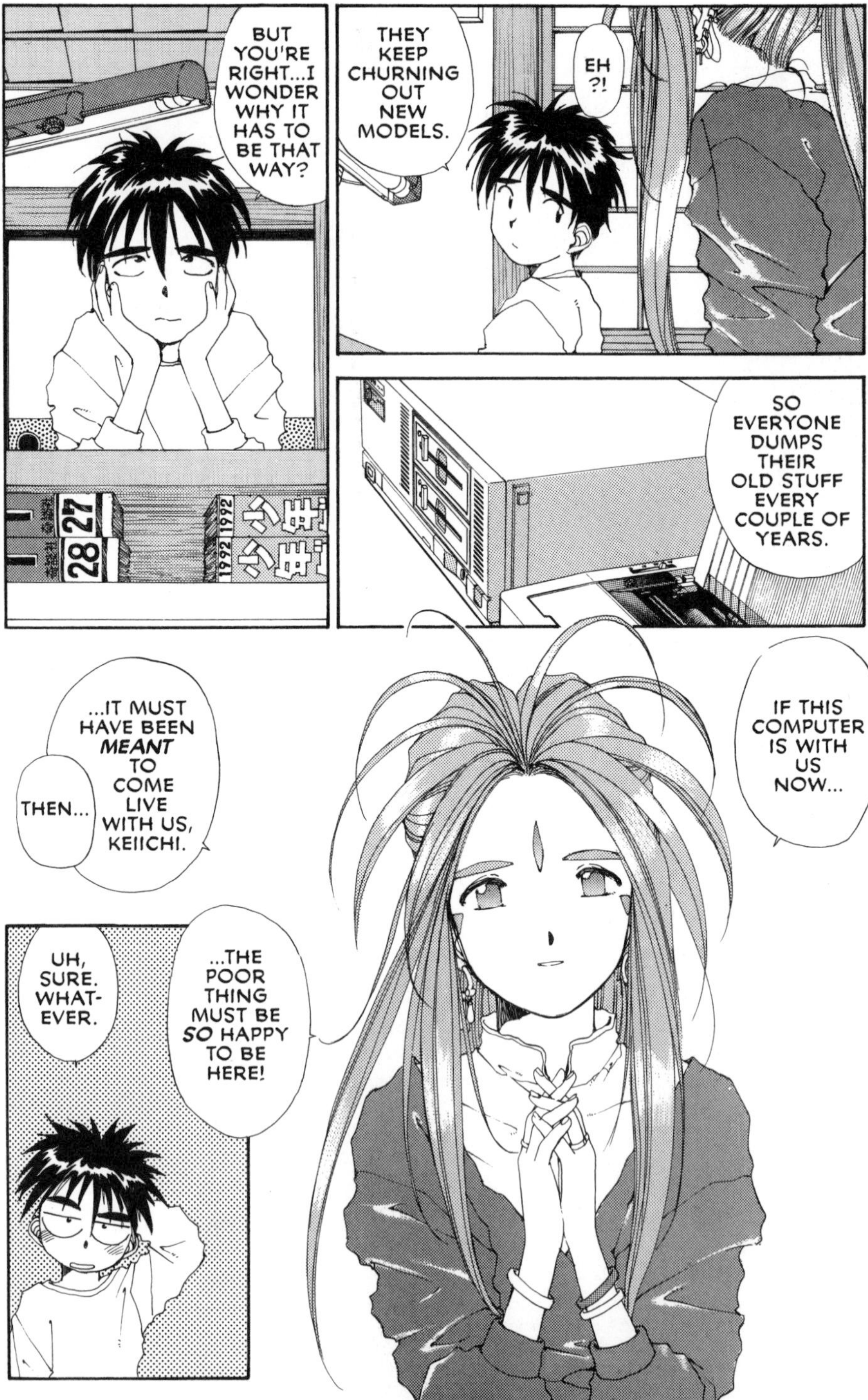
EH ?!
THEY KEEP CHURNING OUT NEW MODELS.
SO EVERYONE DUMPS THEIR OLD STUFF EVERY COUPLE OF YEARS.
BUT YOU'RE RIGHT...I WONDER WHY IT HAS TO BE THAT WAY?
IF THIS COMPUTER IS WITH US NOW...
...IT MUST HAVE BEEN *MEANT* TO COME LIVE WITH US, KEIICHI.
THEN...
...THE POOR THING MUST BE *SO* HAPPY TO BE HERE!
UH, SURE. WHAT-EVER.

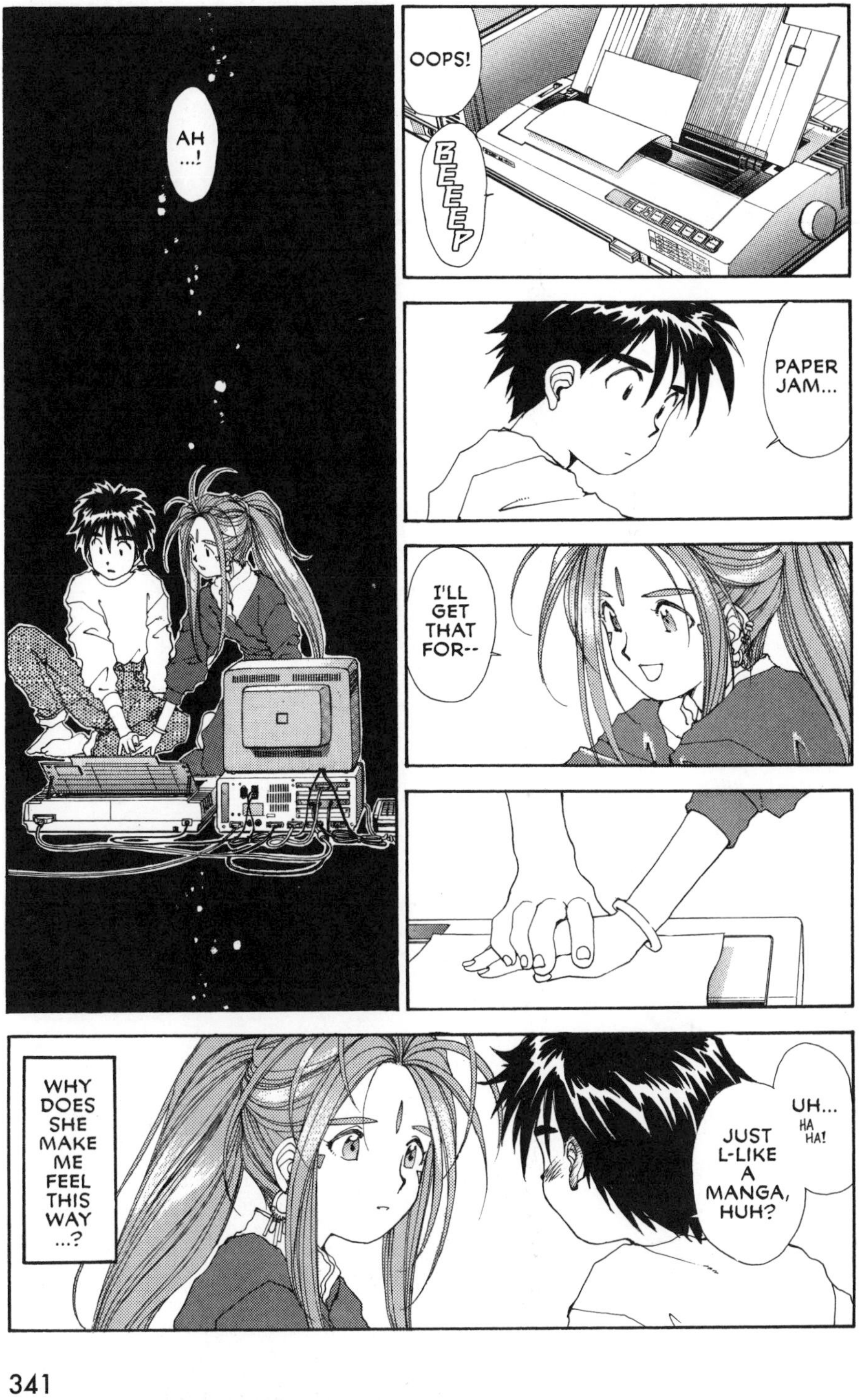
OOPS!
BEEEP
PAPER JAM...
I'LL GET THAT FOR--
AH ...!
UH...
HA HA!
JUST L-LIKE A MANGA, HUH?
WHY DOES SHE MAKE ME FEEL THIS WAY ...?

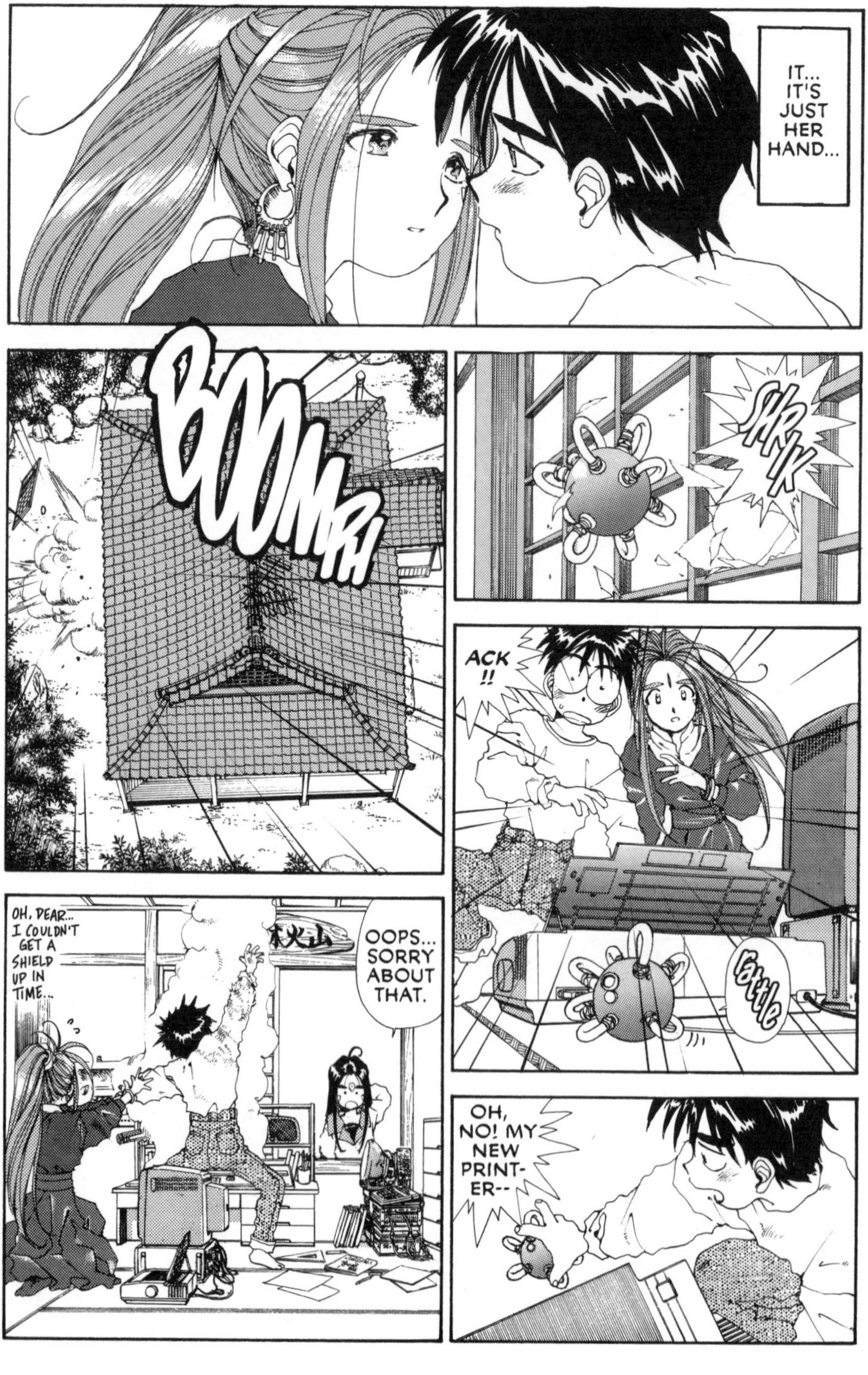
IT... IT'S JUST HER HAND...
BOOMM
SHRIK
ACK !!
rattle
OH, DEAR... I COULDN'T GET A SHIELD UP IN TIME...
OOPS... SORRY ABOUT THAT.
OH, NO! MY NEW PRINTER--

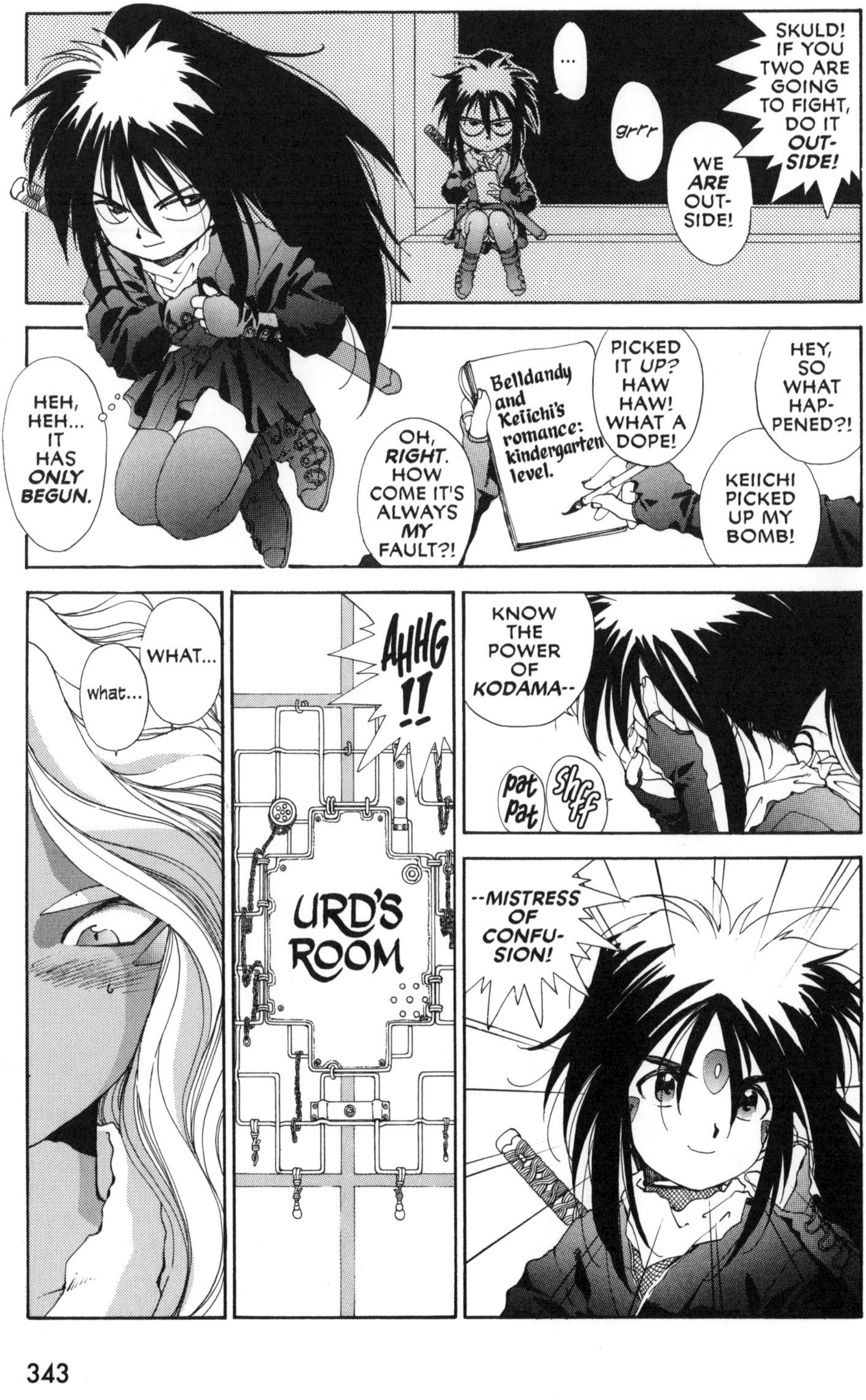
SKULD! IF YOU TWO ARE GOING TO FIGHT, DO IT OUTSIDE!
...
grrr
WE ARE OUTSIDE!
HEY, SO WHAT HAPPENED?!
KEIICHI PICKED UP MY BOMB!
PICKED IT UP? HAW HAW! WHAT A DOPE!
Belldandy and Keiichi's romance: kindergarten level.
OH, RIGHT. HOW COME IT'S ALWAYS MY FAULT?!
HEH, HEH... IT HAS ONLY BEGUN.
KNOW THE POWER OF KODAMA--
shfff
pat pat
--MISTRESS OF CONFUSION!
AHHG!!
URD'S ROOM
WHAT...
what...

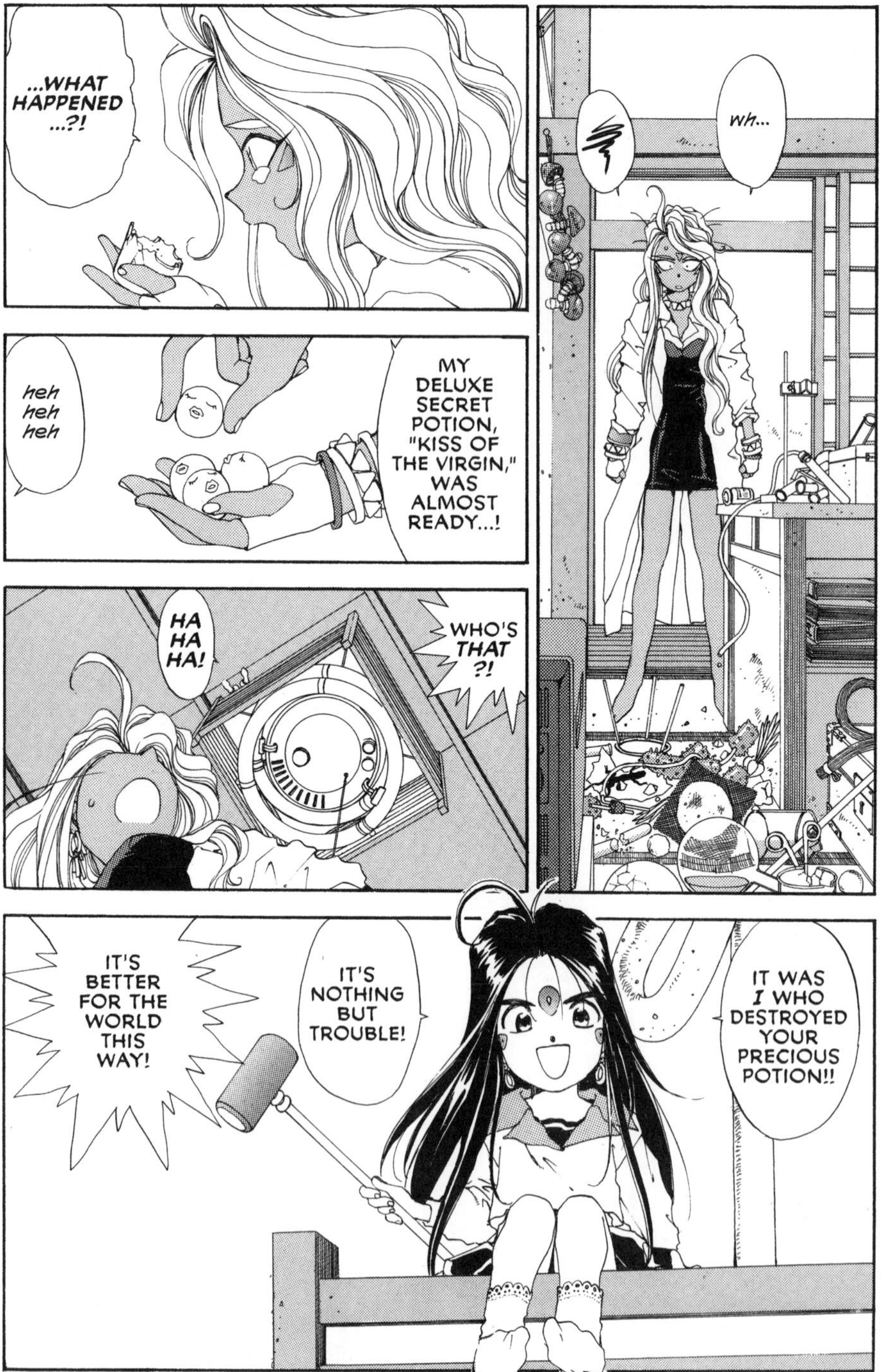
wh...
...WHAT HAPPENED ...?!
MY DELUXE SECRET POTION, "KISS OF THE VIRGIN," WAS ALMOST READY...!
heh heh heh
WHO'S THAT ?!
HA HA HA!
IT WAS I WHO DESTROYED YOUR PRECIOUS POTION!!
IT'S NOTHING BUT TROUBLE!
IT'S BETTER FOR THE WORLD THIS WAY!

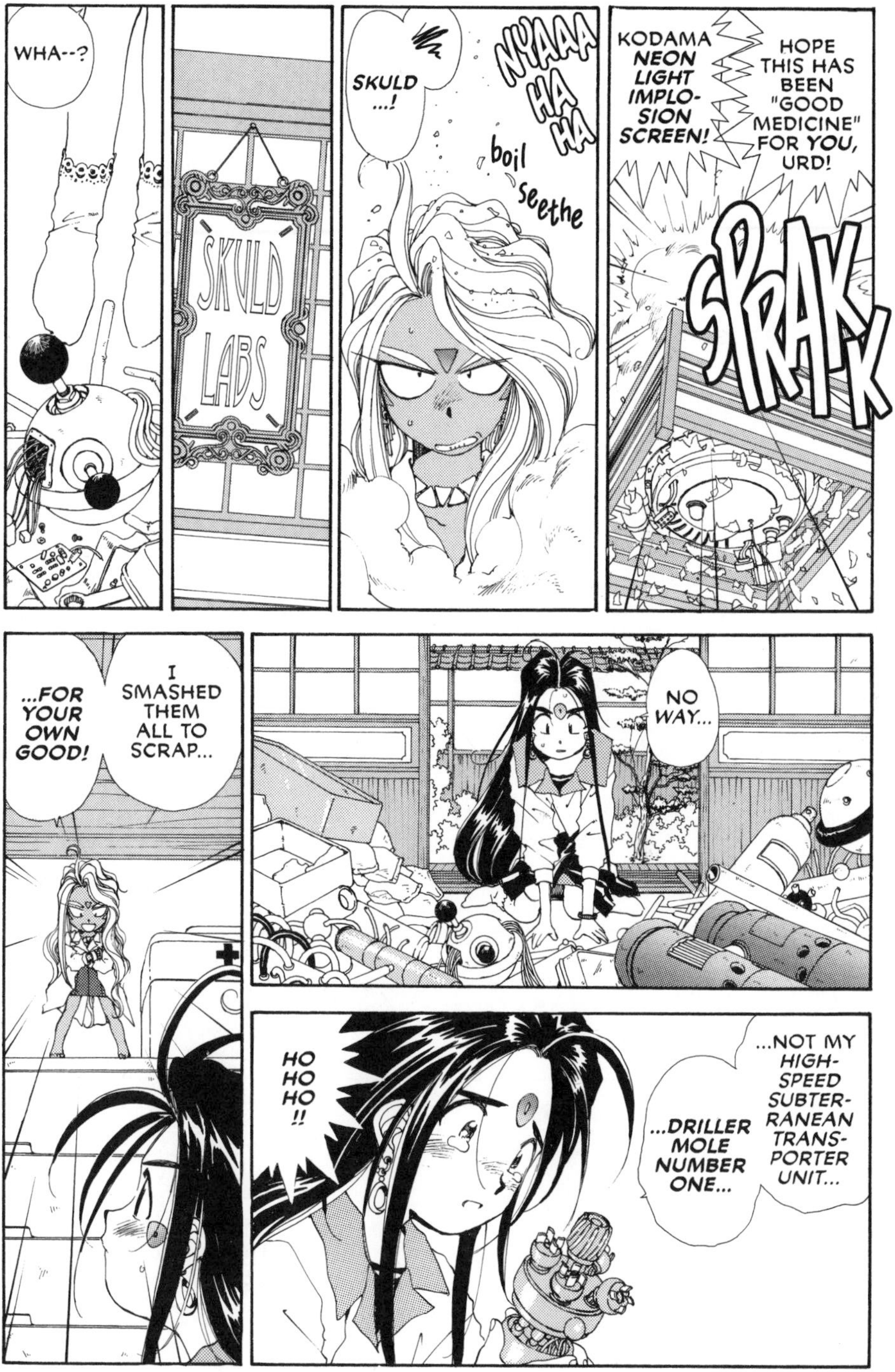
HOPE THIS HAS BEEN "GOOD MEDICINE" FOR YOU, URD!
KODAMA NEON LIGHT IMPLOSION SCREEN!
SPRAKK
NYAAA HA HA
SKULD ...!
boil
seethe
SKULD LABS
WHA--?
NO WAY...
...NOT MY HIGH-SPEED SUBTERRANEAN TRANS-PORTER UNIT...
HO HO HO!!
...DRILLER MOLE NUMBER ONE...
I SMASHED THEM ALL TO SCRAP...
...FOR YOUR OWN GOOD!

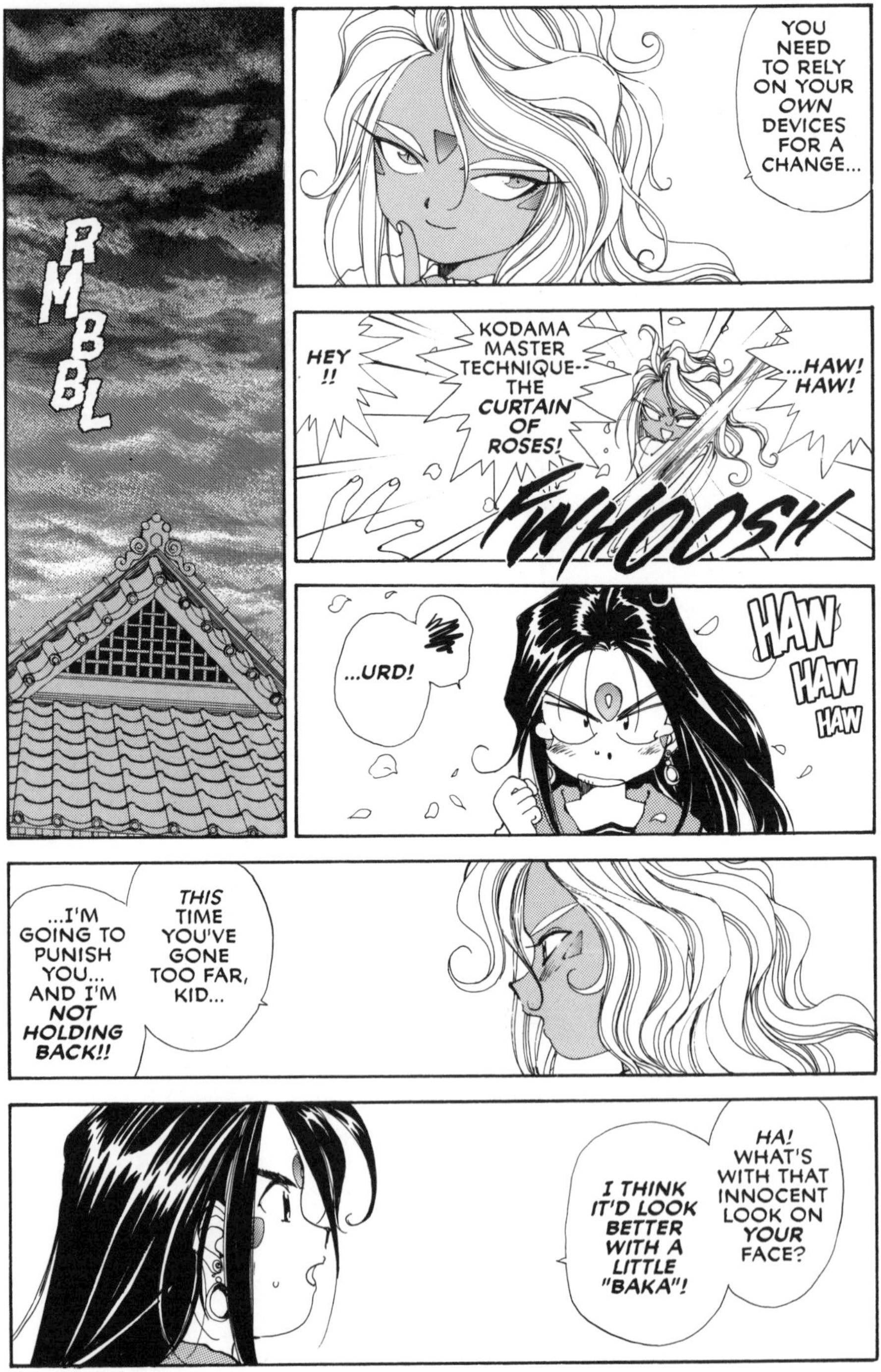
YOU NEED TO RELY ON YOUR *OWN* DEVICES FOR A CHANGE...
...HAW! HAW!
KODAMA MASTER TECHNIQUE-- THE *CURTAIN OF ROSES!*
HEY !!
FWHOOSH
HAW HAW HAW
...URD!
RMMBL
THIS TIME YOU'VE GONE TOO FAR, KID...
...I'M GOING TO PUNISH YOU... AND I'M *NOT HOLDING BACK!!*
HA! WHAT'S WITH THAT INNOCENT LOOK ON *YOUR* FACE?
I THINK IT'D LOOK BETTER WITH A LITTLE "BAKA"!

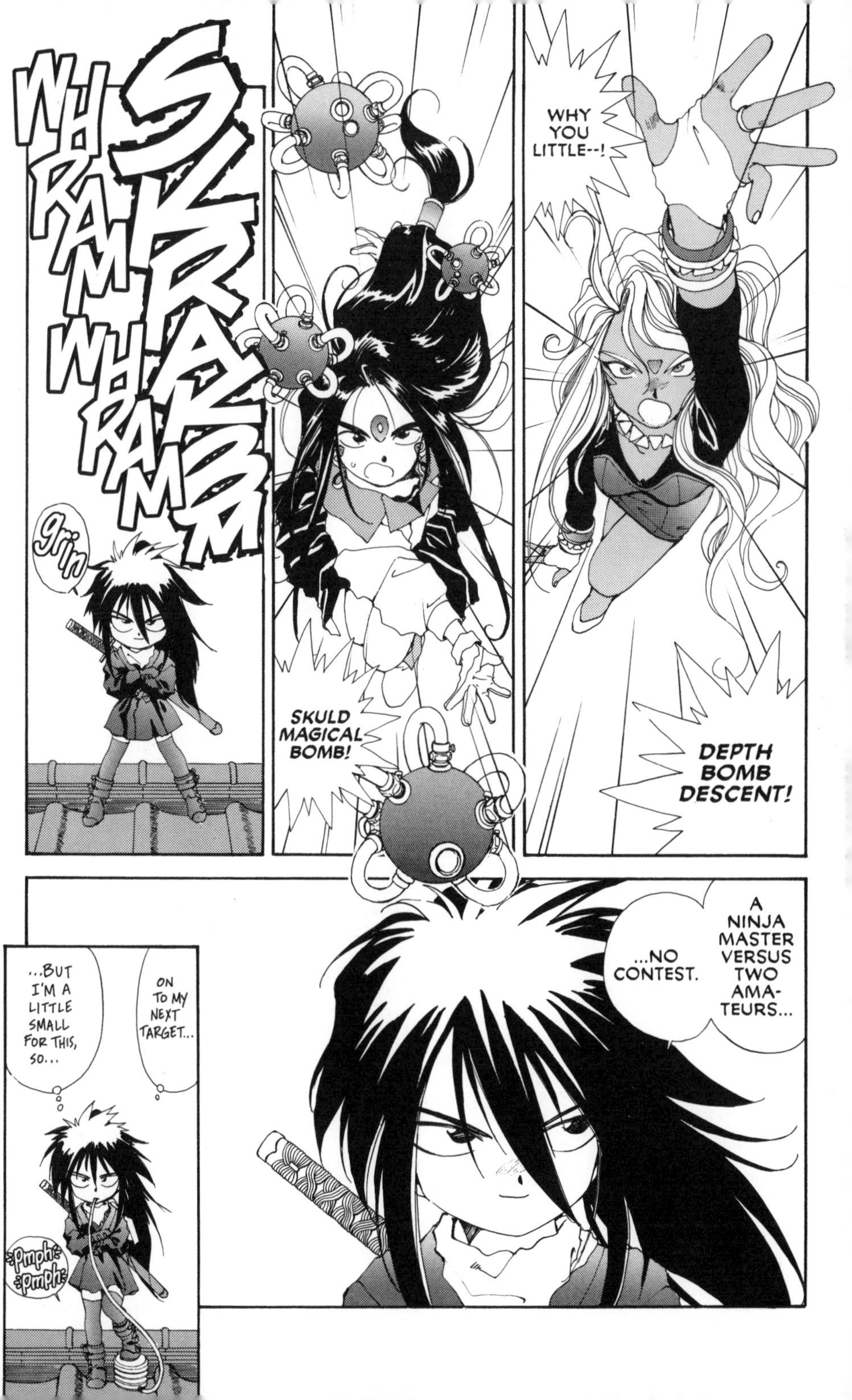

WHY YOU LITTLE--!
DEPTH BOMB DESCENT!
SKULD MAGICAL BOMB!
SKRABOOM
WHRAM WHRAM
grin
A NINJA MASTER VERSUS TWO AMATEURS...
...NO CONTEST.
ON TO MY NEXT TARGET...
...BUT I'M A LITTLE SMALL FOR THIS, SO...
pmph pmph

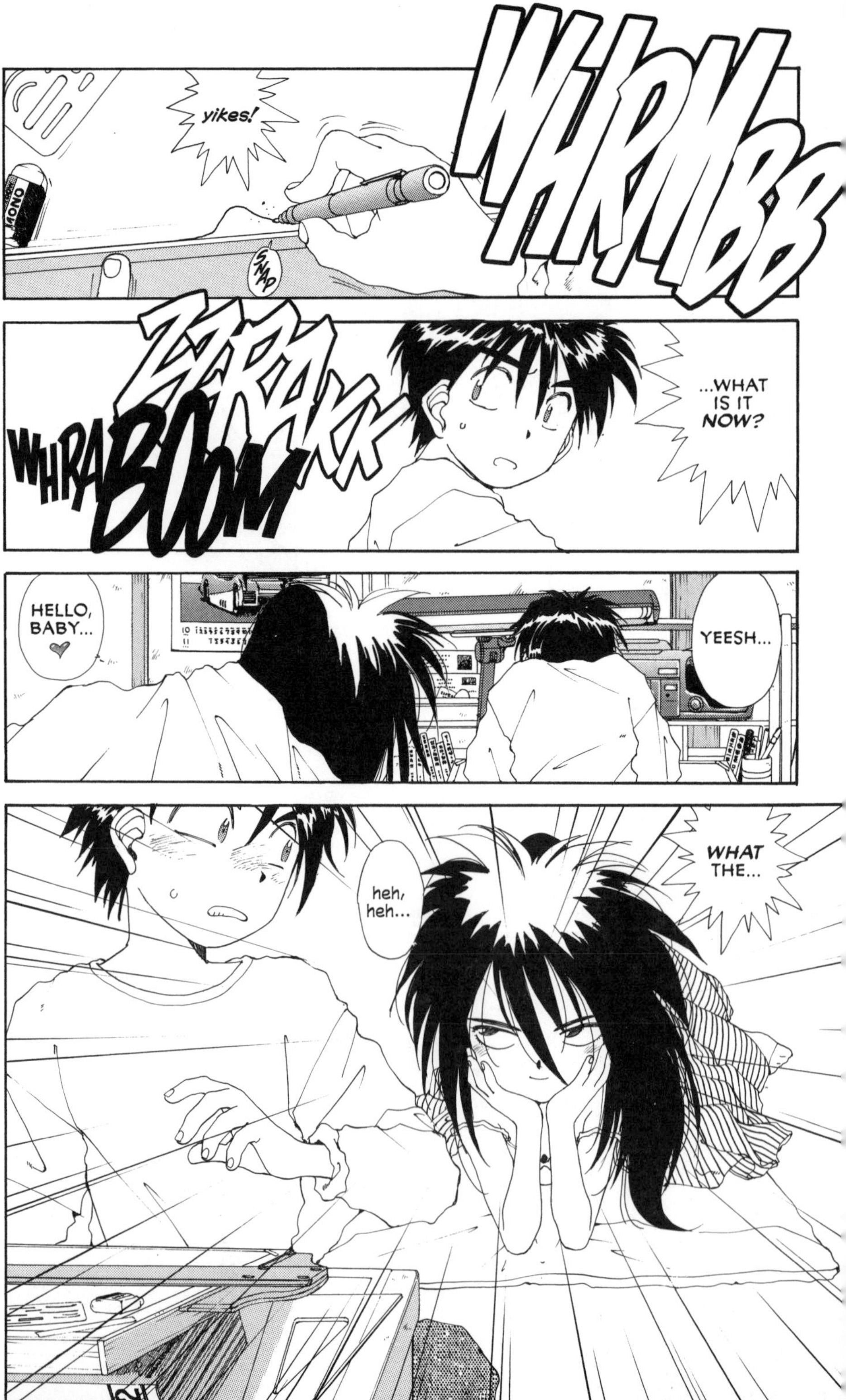
WHRMBB
yikes!
SNAP
...WHAT IS IT NOW?
ZZRAKK
WHRABOOM
YEESH...
HELLO, BABY... ♥
WHAT THE...
heh, heh...

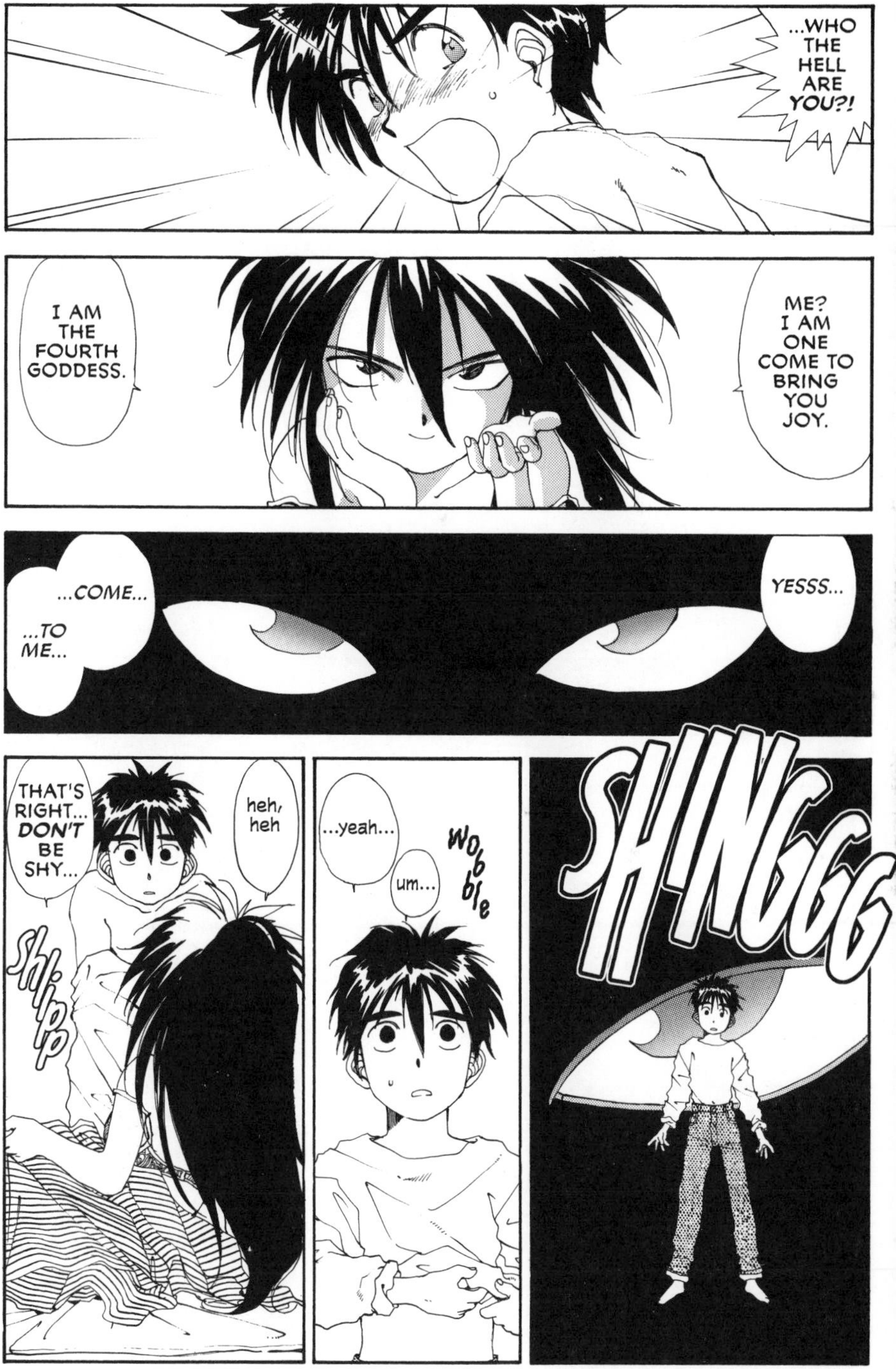
...WHO THE HELL ARE *YOU?!*
ME? I AM ONE COME TO BRING YOU JOY.
I AM THE FOURTH GODDESS.
YESSS...
...COME...
...TO ME...
SHINGGG
wobble
...yeah...
um...
heh, heh
THAT'S RIGHT... *DON'T* BE SHY...
shipp

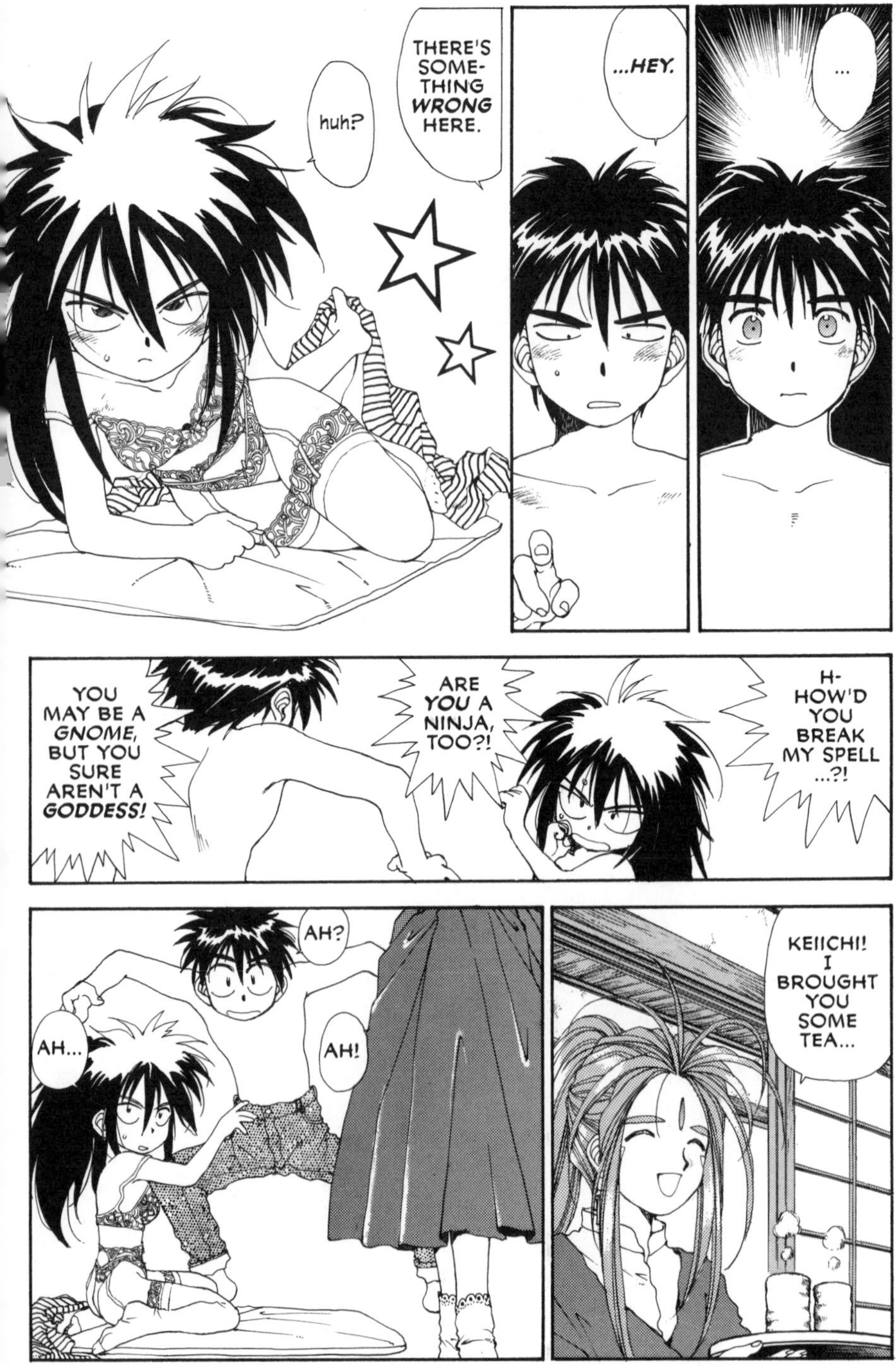
...
...HEY.
THERE'S SOME-THING WRONG HERE.
huh?
H-HOW'D YOU BREAK MY SPELL ...?!
ARE YOU A NINJA, TOO?!
YOU MAY BE A GNOME, BUT YOU SURE AREN'T A GODDESS!
KEIICHI! I BROUGHT YOU SOME TEA...
AH?
AH!
AH...

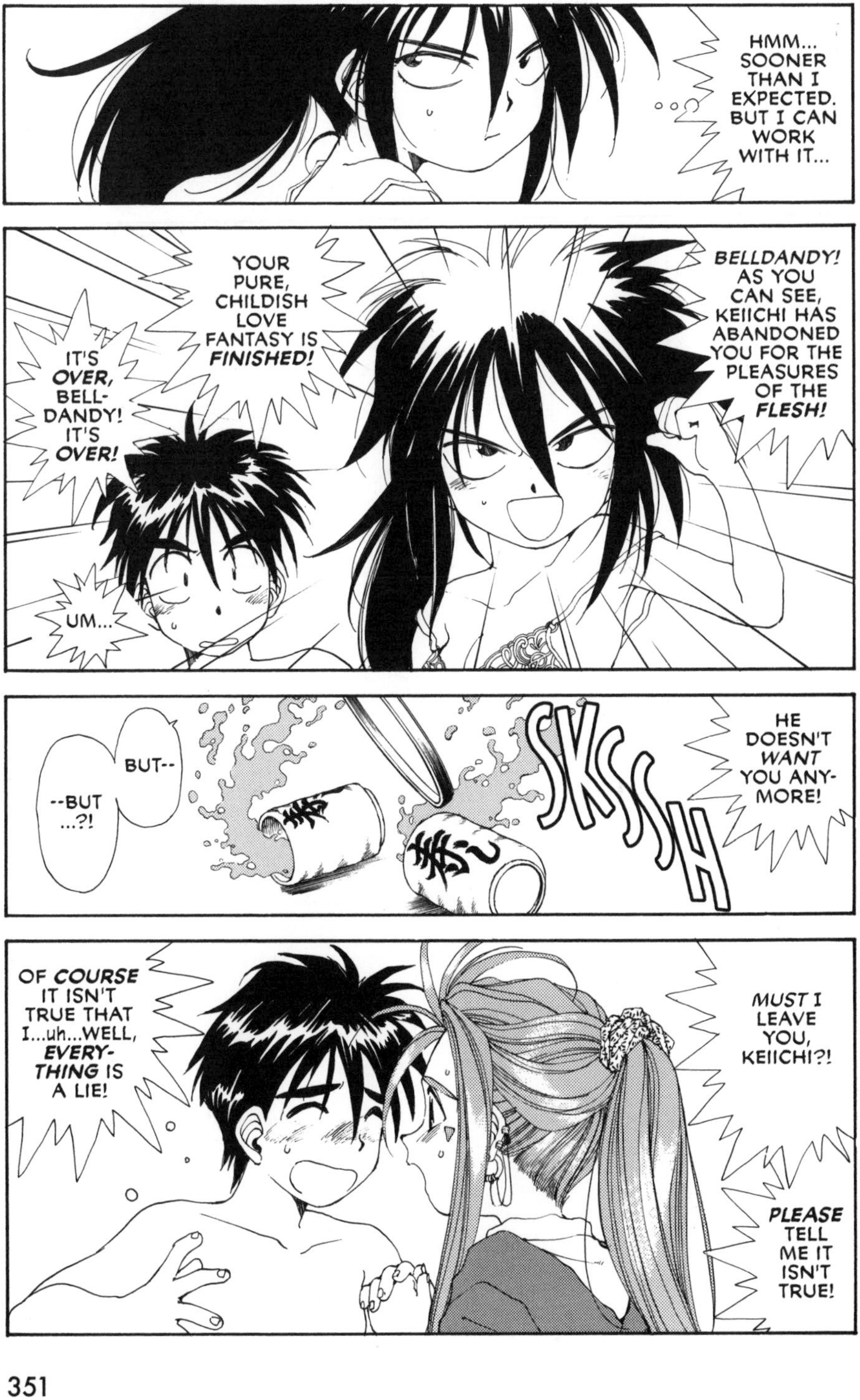
HMM... SOONER THAN I EXPECTED. BUT I CAN WORK WITH IT...
BELLDANDY! AS YOU CAN SEE, KEIICHI HAS ABANDONED YOU FOR THE PLEASURES OF THE FLESH!
YOUR PURE, CHILDISH LOVE FANTASY IS FINISHED!
IT'S OVER, BELL-DANDY! IT'S OVER!
UM...
HE DOESN'T WANT YOU ANY-MORE!
SKSSSH
BUT--
--BUT ...?!
MUST I LEAVE YOU, KEIICHI?!
PLEASE TELL ME IT ISN'T TRUE!
OF COURSE IT ISN'T TRUE THAT I...uh...WELL, EVERY-THING IS A LIE!

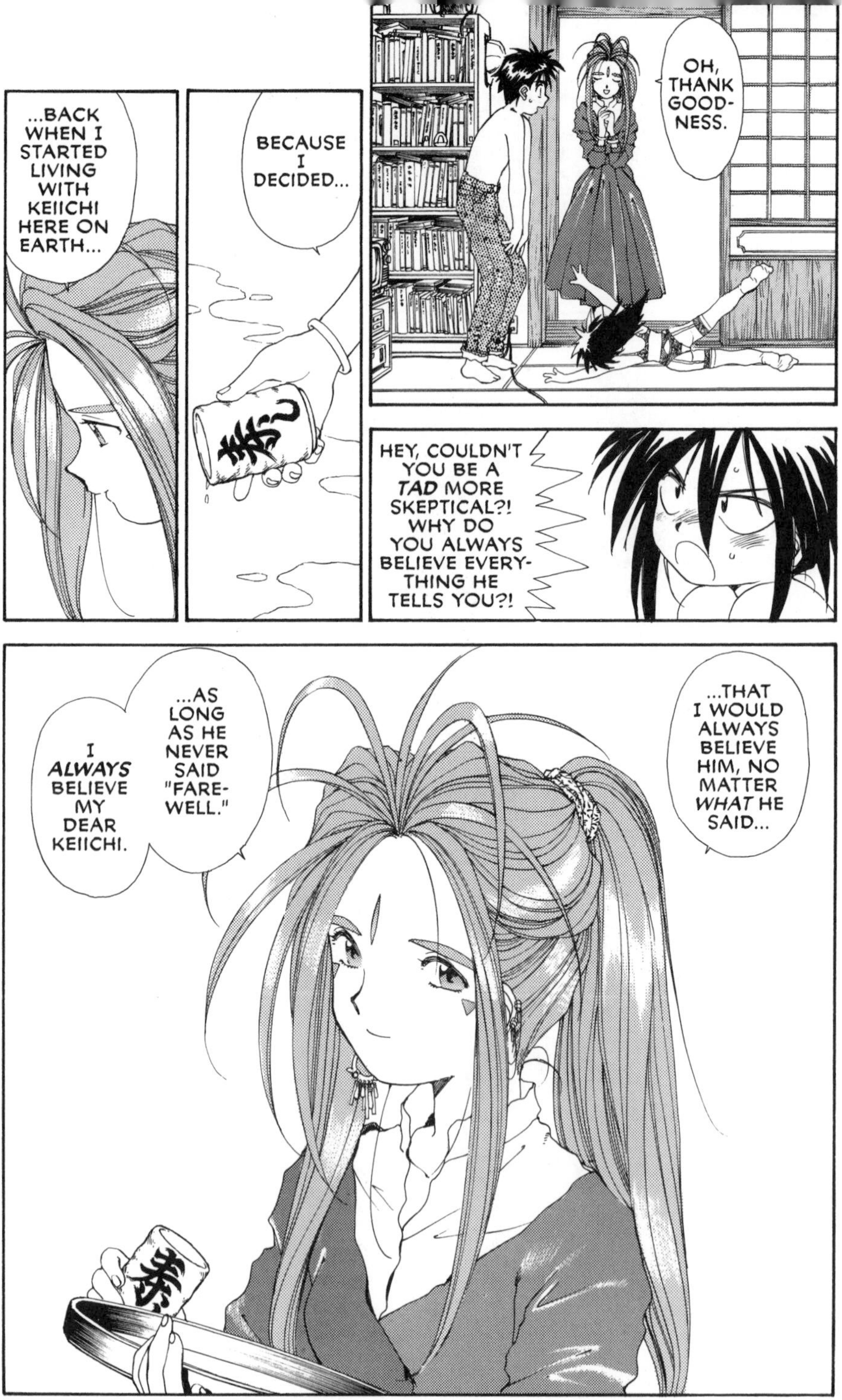
OH, THANK GOODNESS.
HEY, COULDN'T YOU BE A *TAD* MORE SKEPTICAL?! WHY DO YOU ALWAYS BELIEVE EVERYTHING HE TELLS YOU?!
BECAUSE I DECIDED...
...BACK WHEN I STARTED LIVING WITH KEIICHI HERE ON EARTH...
...THAT I WOULD ALWAYS BELIEVE HIM, NO MATTER *WHAT* HE SAID...
...AS LONG AS HE NEVER SAID "FAREWELL."
I *ALWAYS* BELIEVE MY DEAR KEIICHI.

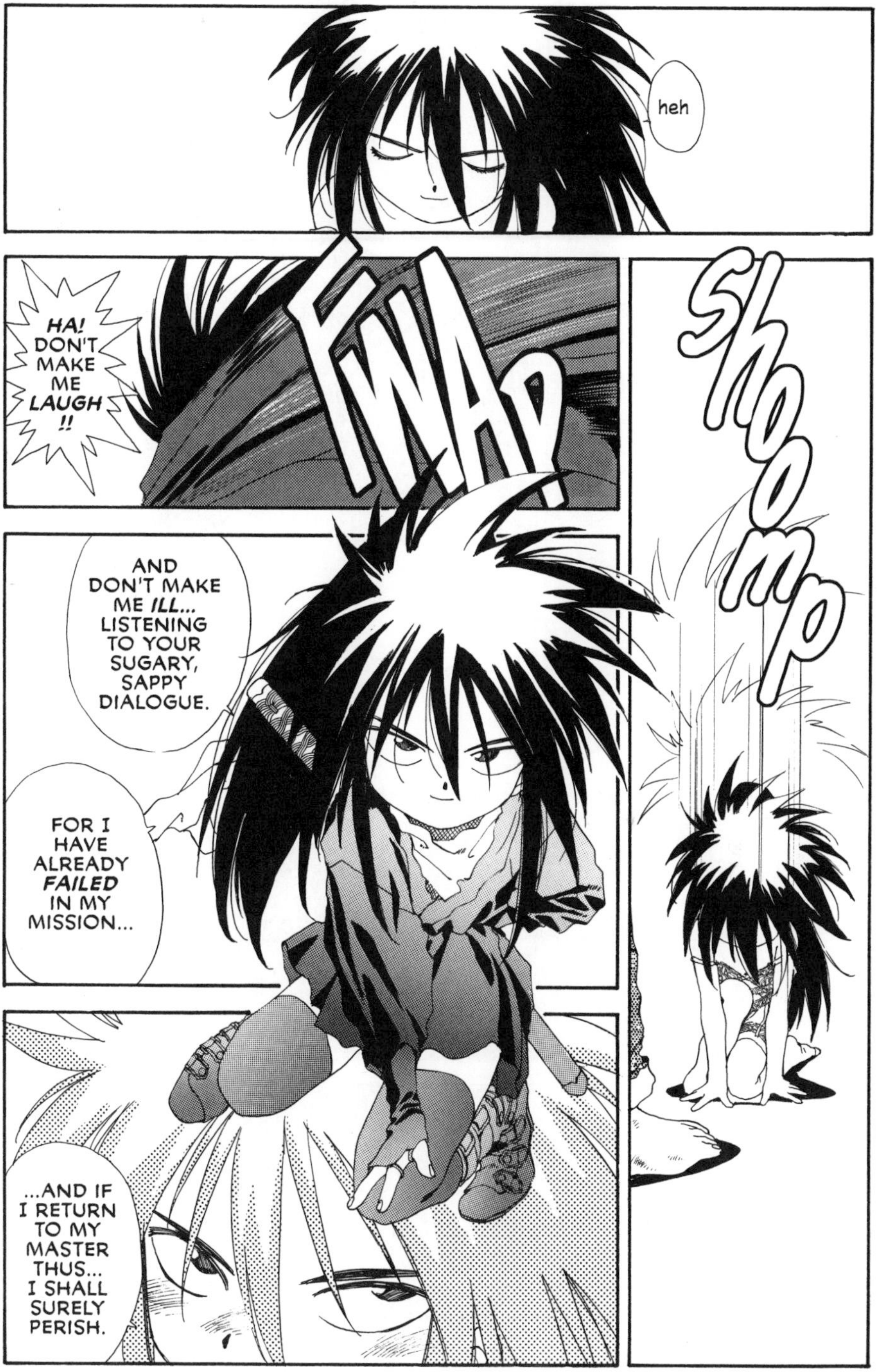
heh
SHOOOMP
FWAP
HA! DON'T MAKE ME LAUGH!!
AND DON'T MAKE ME ILL... LISTENING TO YOUR SUGARY, SAPPY DIALOGUE.
FOR I HAVE ALREADY FAILED IN MY MISSION...
...AND IF I RETURN TO MY MASTER THUS... I SHALL SURELY PERISH.

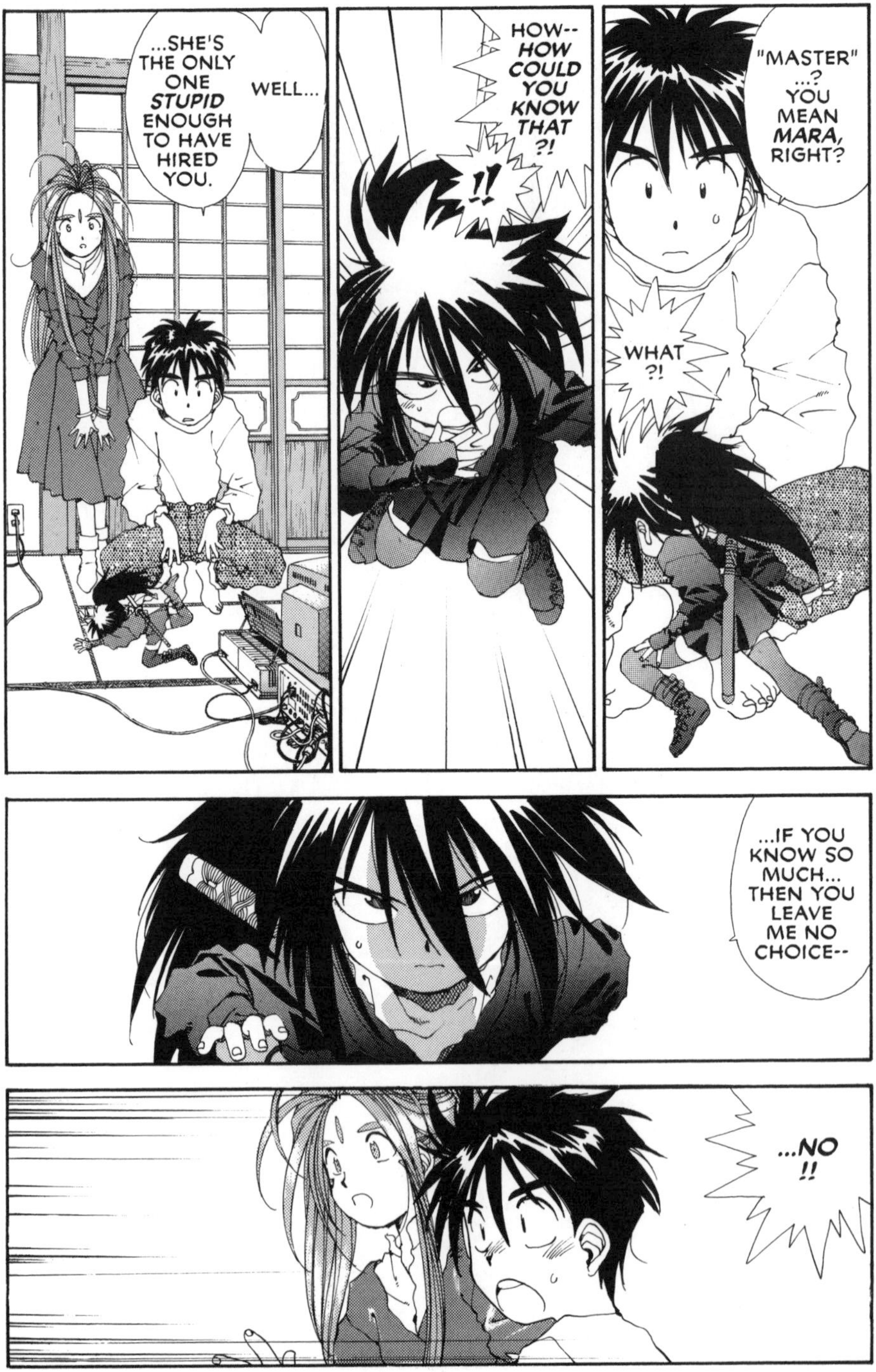
"MASTER" ...? YOU MEAN MARA, RIGHT?
WHAT ?!
HOW-- HOW COULD YOU KNOW THAT ?!
!!
WELL...
...SHE'S THE ONLY ONE STUPID ENOUGH TO HAVE HIRED YOU.
...IF YOU KNOW SO MUCH... THEN YOU LEAVE ME NO CHOICE--
...NO !!

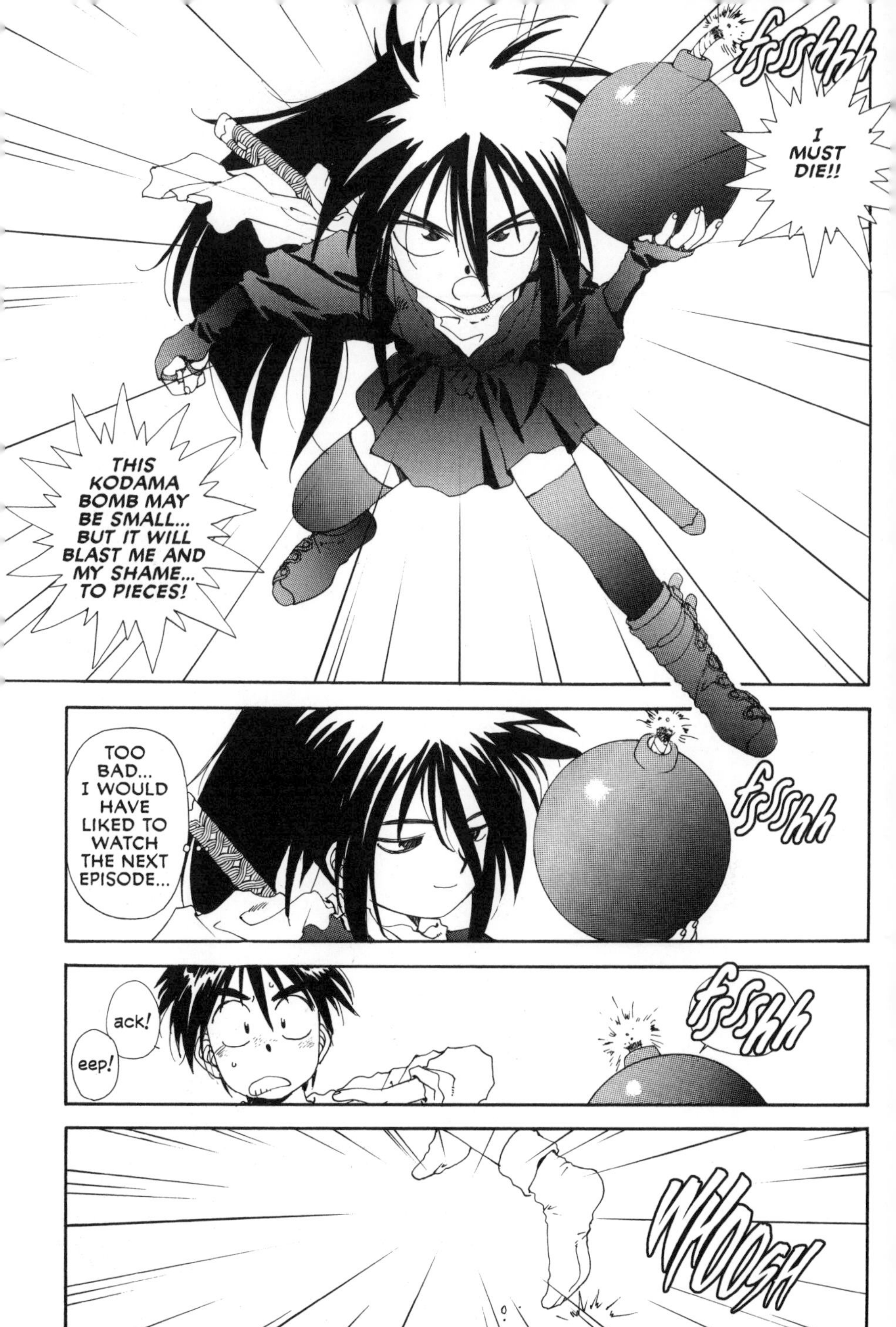
fsshhh
I MUST DIE!!
THIS KODAMA BOMB MAY BE SMALL... BUT IT WILL BLAST ME AND MY SHAME... TO PIECES!
fssshh
TOO BAD... I WOULD HAVE LIKED TO WATCH THE NEXT EPISODE...
fsshh
ack!
eep!
WHOOSH

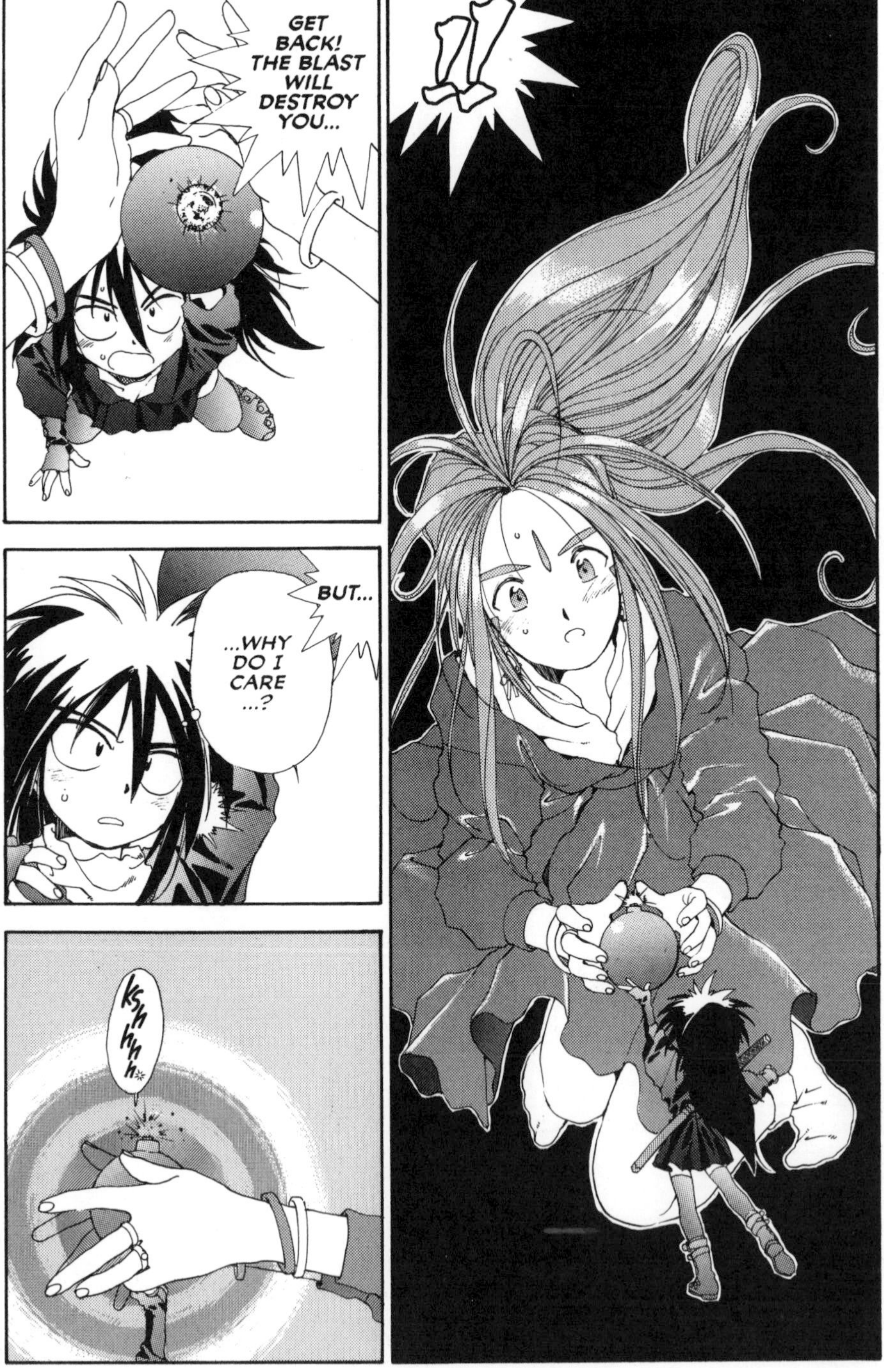
!!
GET BACK! THE BLAST WILL DESTROY YOU...
BUT...
...WHY DO I CARE ...?
kshhhh

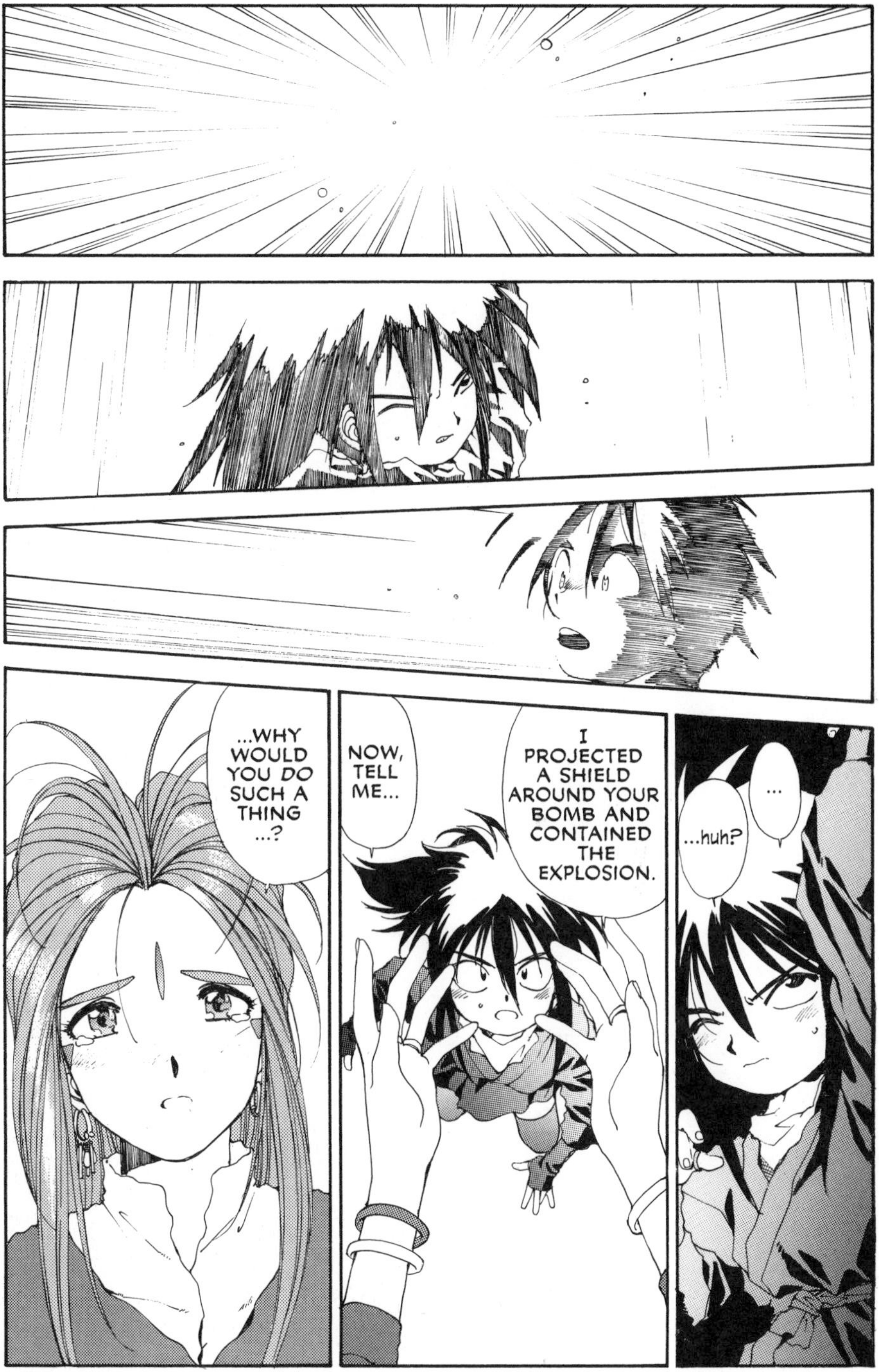
...
...huh?
I PROJECTED A SHIELD AROUND YOUR BOMB AND CONTAINED THE EXPLOSION.
NOW, TELL ME...
...WHY WOULD YOU *DO* SUCH A THING ...?

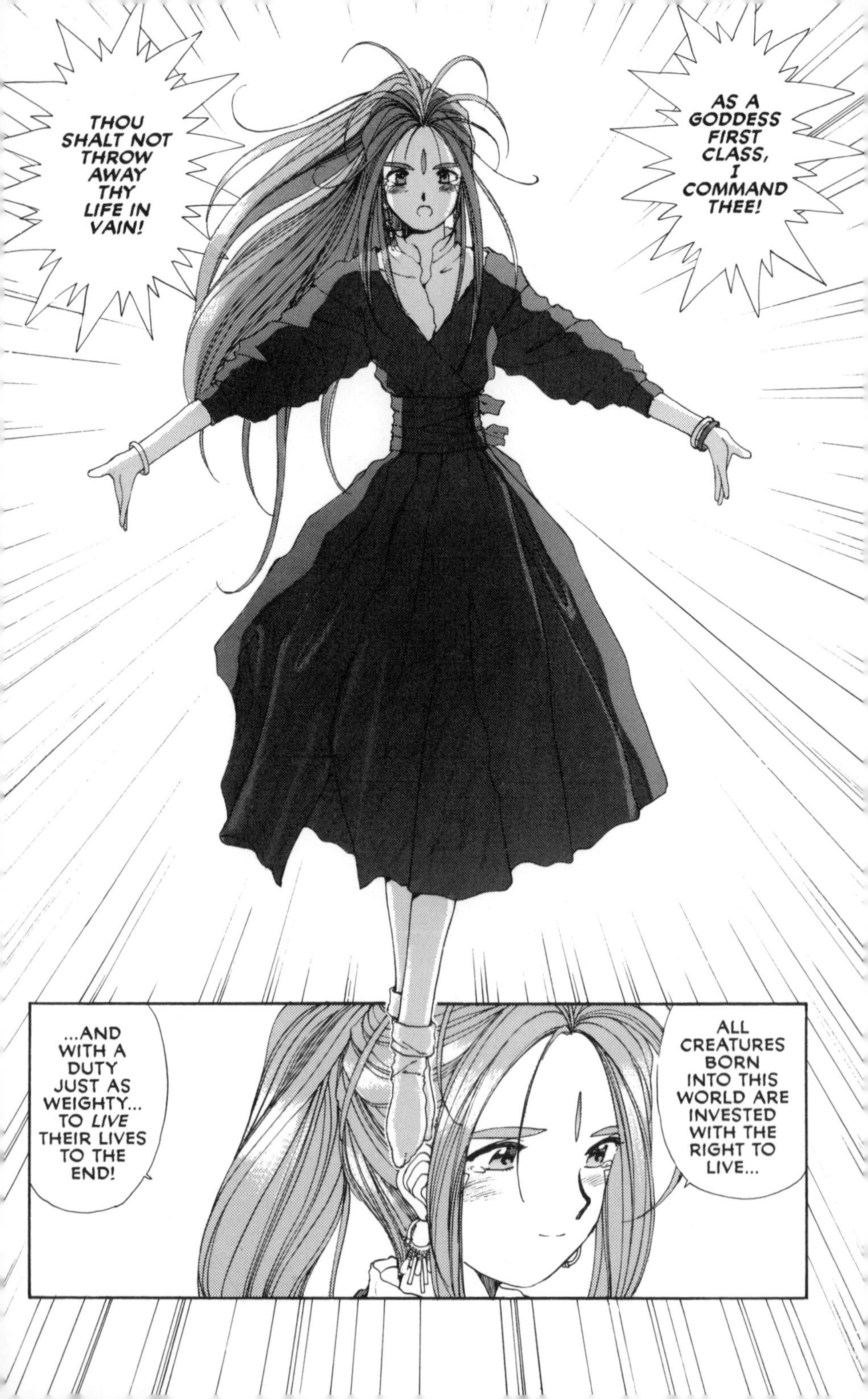
AS A GODDESS FIRST CLASS, I COMMAND THEE!
THOU SHALT NOT THROW AWAY THY LIFE IN VAIN!
ALL CREATURES BORN INTO THIS WORLD ARE INVESTED WITH THE RIGHT TO LIVE...
...AND WITH A DUTY JUST AS WEIGHTY... TO *LIVE* THEIR LIVES TO THE END!

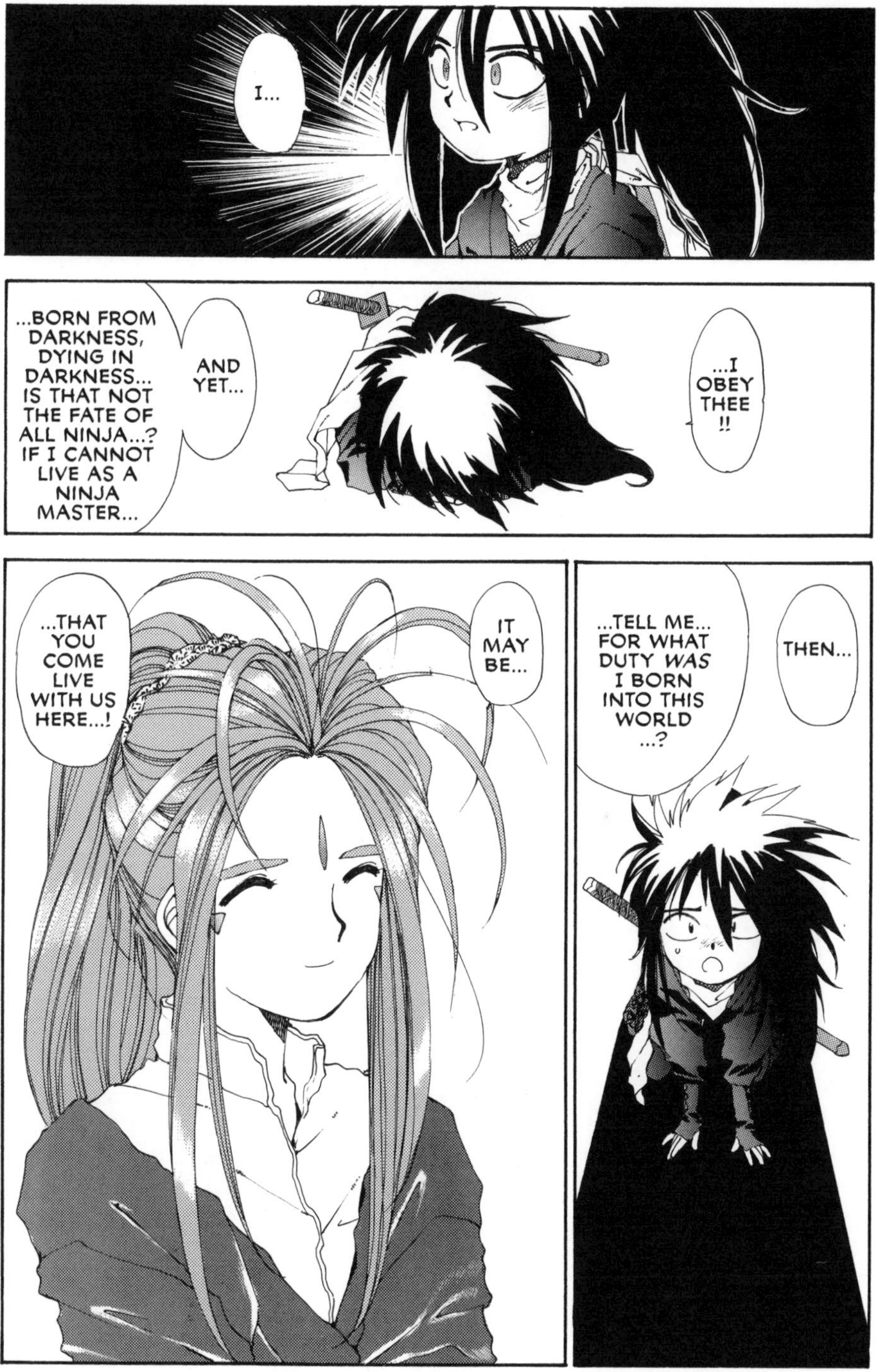
I...
...I OBEY THEE !!
AND YET...
...BORN FROM DARKNESS, DYING IN DARKNESS... IS THAT NOT THE FATE OF ALL NINJA...? IF I CANNOT LIVE AS A NINJA MASTER...
THEN...
...TELL ME... FOR WHAT DUTY *WAS* I BORN INTO THIS WORLD ...?
IT MAY BE...
...THAT YOU COME LIVE WITH US HERE...!

...HAD DETERIORATED INTO A SIMPLE CATFIGHT.

MEANWHILE, URD AND SKULD'S *BATTLE TO THE DEATH...*

YOU BETTER FIX MY *MACHINES*, URD!

OWWWWW! YOU'RE PULLING MY *HAIR!!*

NOT UNTIL YOU GIVE ME BACK MY *POTIONS*, BRAT!!

PLEASE DON'T *GIGGLE* LIKE THAT, MARA-- IT'S *TOO CREEPY!*

OOH, I CAN'T *WAIT* UNTIL KO-DAMA GETS BACK!

tee hee!

AND AS FOR MA-RA...

"MACHINES"...?

"POTIONS"...?

OH MY GODDESS!

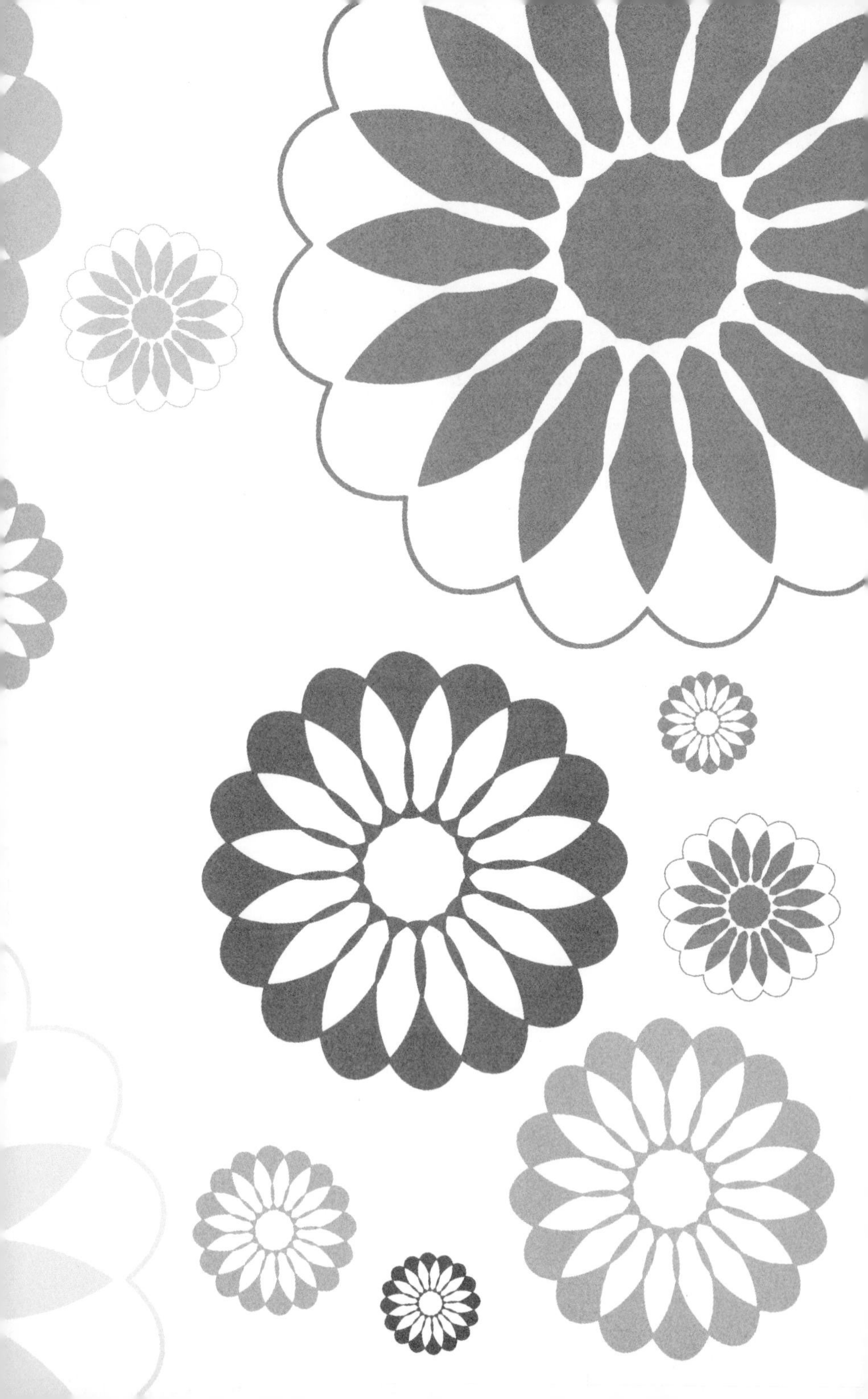

CHAPTER 53

Law of the Ninja

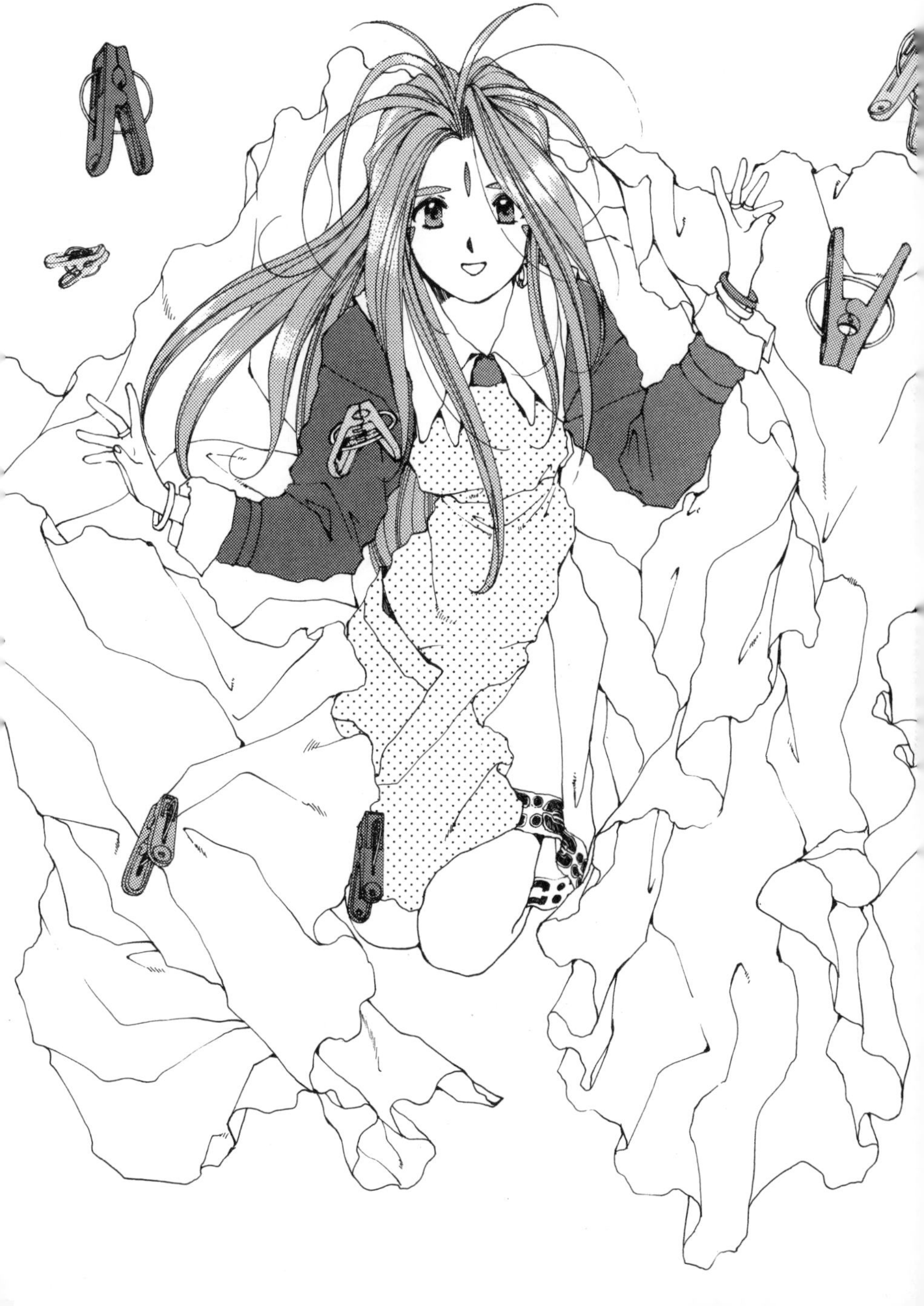

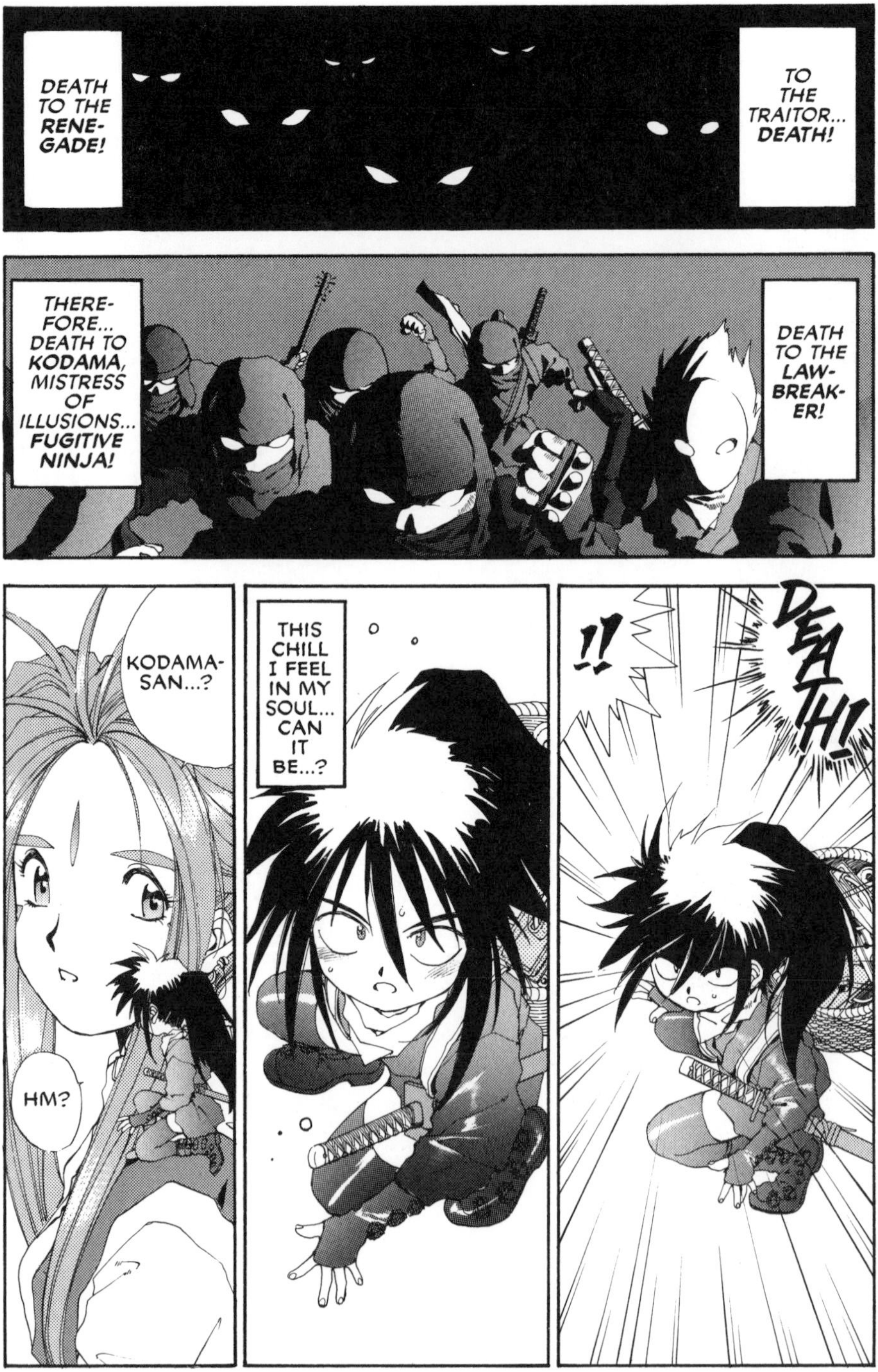
TO THE TRAITOR... DEATH!
DEATH TO THE RENEGADE!
DEATH TO THE LAWBREAKER!
THEREFORE... DEATH TO KODAMA, MISTRESS OF ILLUSIONS... FUGITIVE NINJA!
DEATH!
!!
THIS CHILL I FEEL IN MY SOUL... CAN IT BE...?
KODAMA-SAN...?
HM?

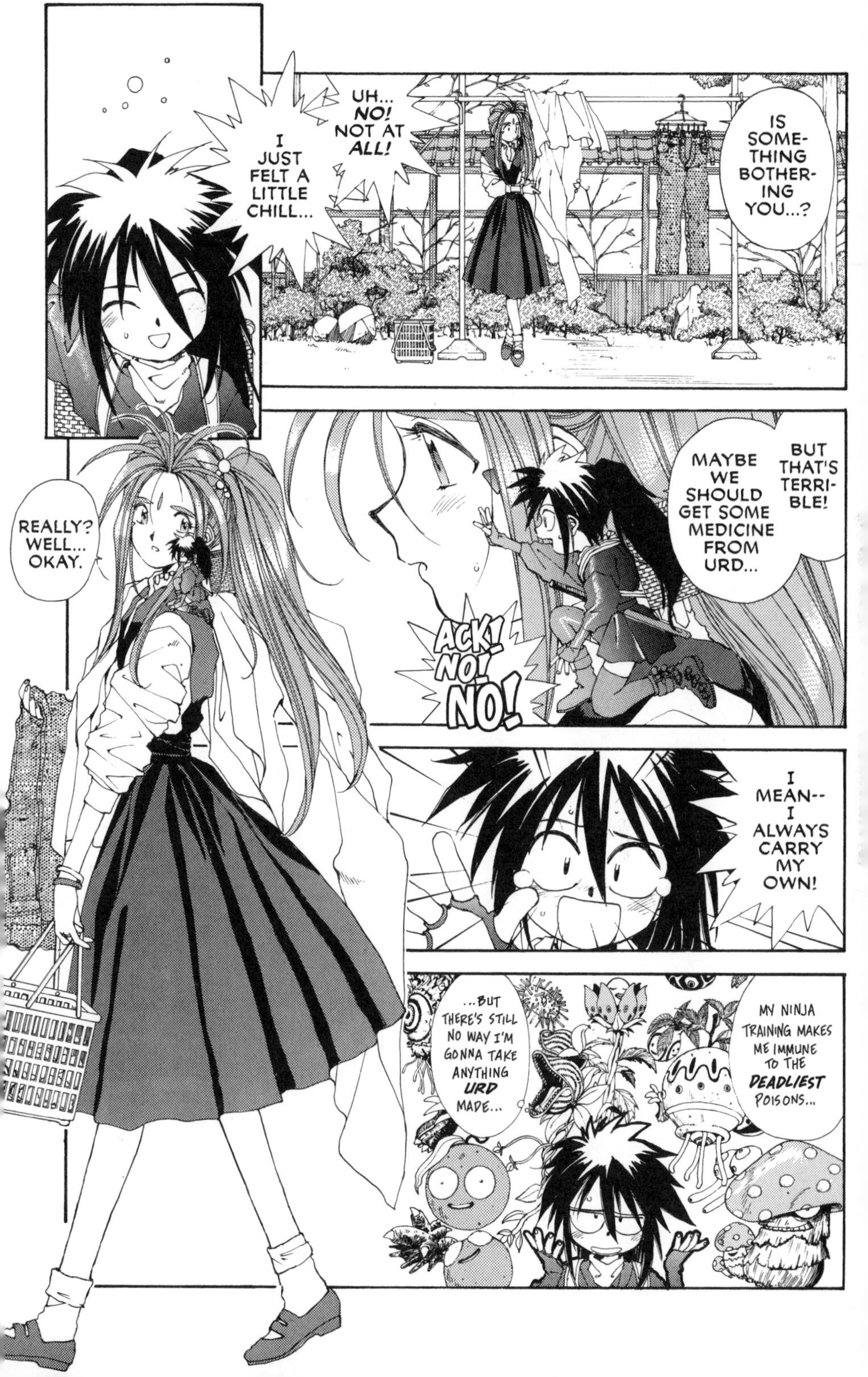
IS SOMETHING-THING BOTHERING YOU...?
UH... NO! NOT AT ALL!
I JUST FELT A LITTLE CHILL...
BUT THAT'S TERRIBLE!
MAYBE WE SHOULD GET SOME MEDICINE FROM URD...
ACK! NO! NO!
I MEAN-- I ALWAYS CARRY MY OWN!
MY NINJA TRAINING MAKES ME IMMUNE TO THE DEADLIEST POISONS...
...BUT THERE'S STILL NO WAY I'M GONNA TAKE ANYTHING URD MADE...
REALLY? WELL... OKAY.

LET'S GO INSIDE AND GET YOU SOME NICE, HOT TEA RIGHT NOW.

BUT DO BE CAREFUL, KODAMA. IT'S HARD TO GET RID OF A COLD AT THIS TIME OF YEAR.

AH, TO THINK MERE WORDS COULD BE SO...SO *WARMING*...

SUCH TENDER-NESS... OVER-FLOWING MY HEART...

...

YOU ALWAYS *WERE* THE SENTIMENTAL ONE, KODAMA DEAR.

I CAN SENSE YOU, EVEN FROM OVER HERE.

"♥♥," IS IT?

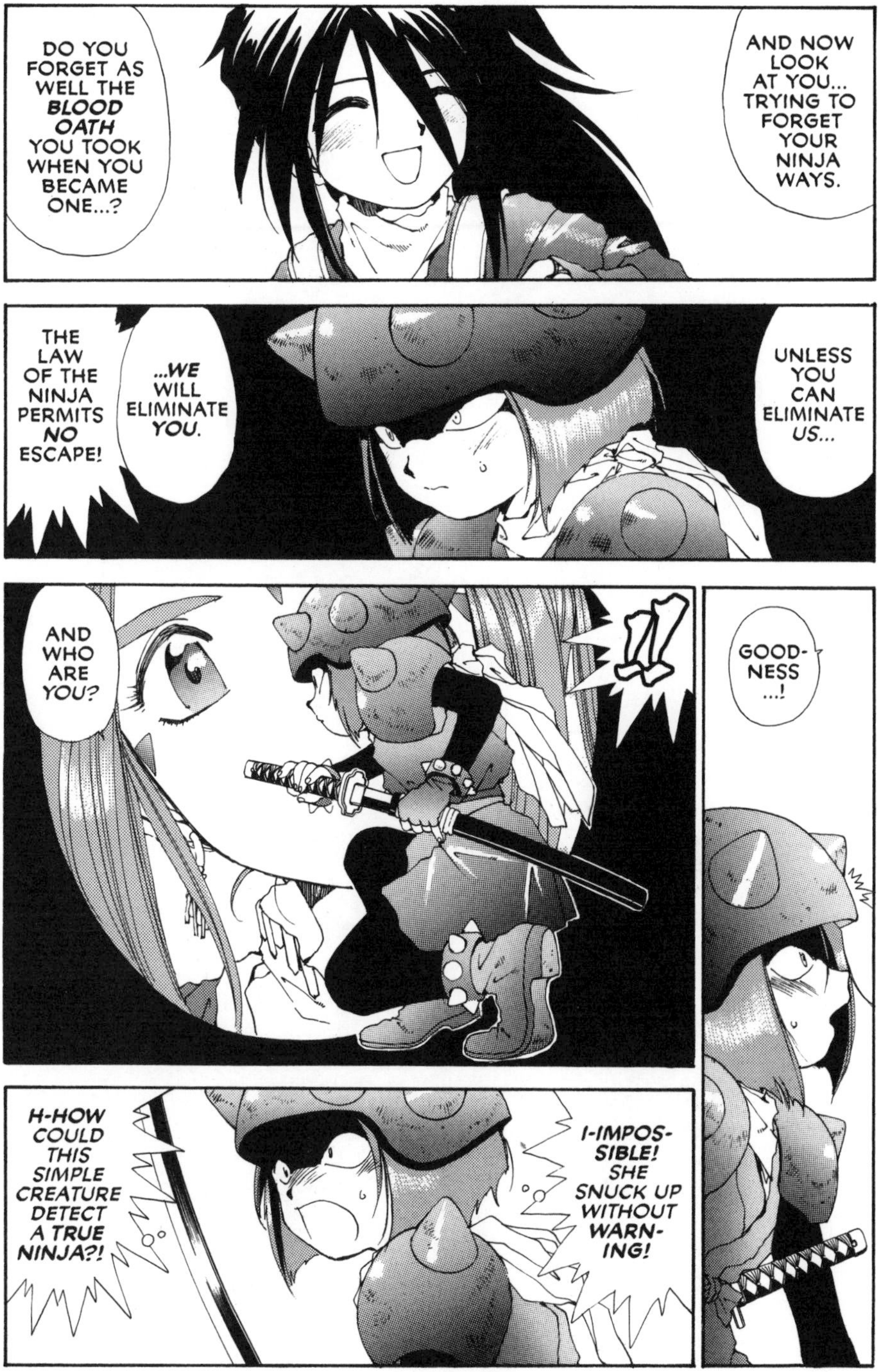
AND NOW LOOK AT YOU... TRYING TO FORGET YOUR NINJA WAYS.
DO YOU FORGET AS WELL THE ***BLOOD OATH*** YOU TOOK WHEN YOU BECAME ONE...?
UNLESS YOU CAN ELIMINATE *US*...
...WE WILL ELIMINATE ***YOU***.
THE LAW OF THE NINJA PERMITS ***NO*** ESCAPE!
AND WHO ARE *YOU?*
GOOD-NESS ...!
I-IMPOS-SIBLE! SHE SNUCK UP WITHOUT WARN-ING!
H-HOW COULD THIS SIMPLE CREATURE DETECT A TRUE NINJA?!

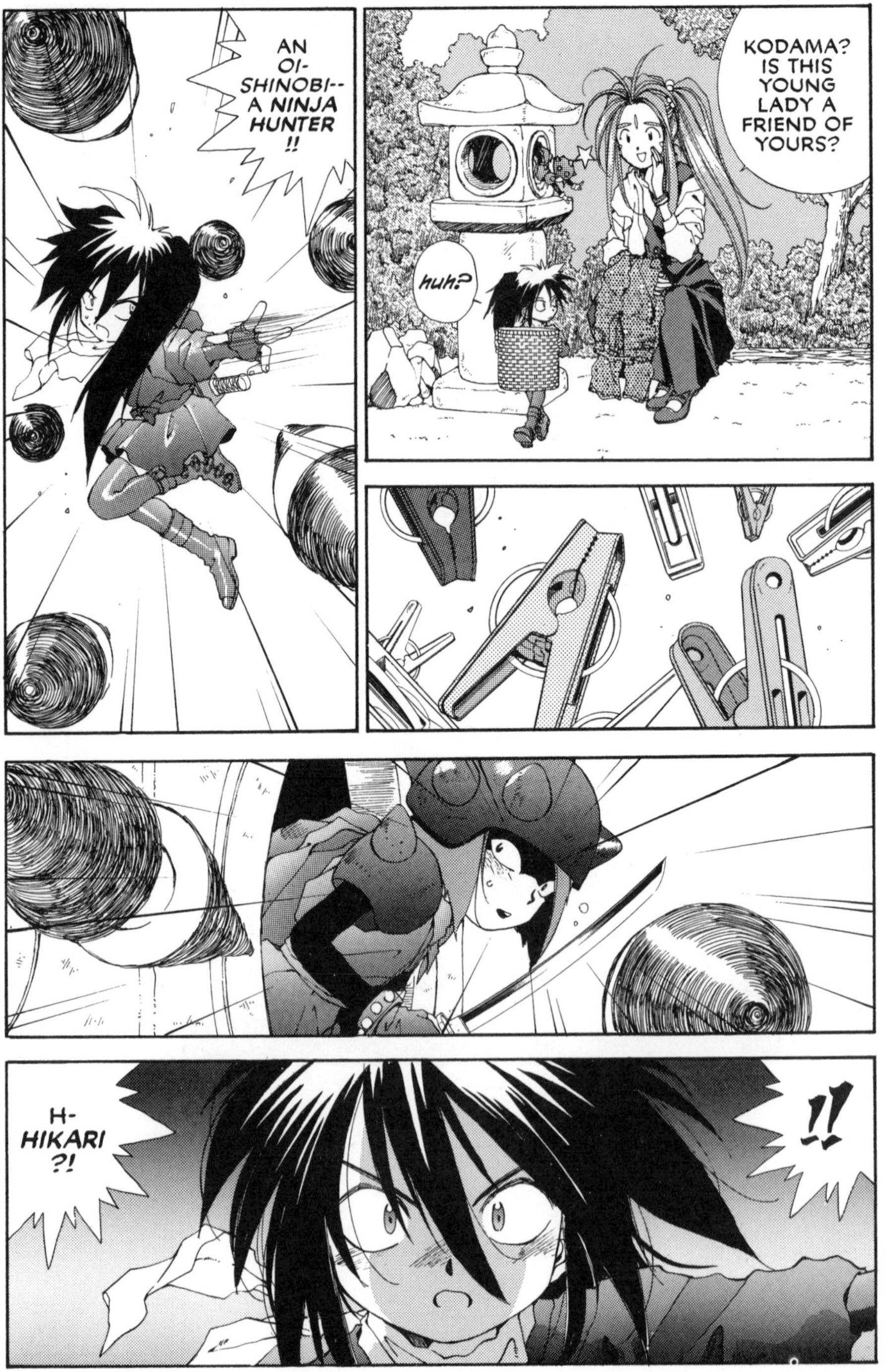
KODAMA? IS THIS YOUNG LADY A FRIEND OF YOURS?
huh?
AN OI-SHINOBI-- A NINJA HUNTER !!
!!
H-HIKARI ?!

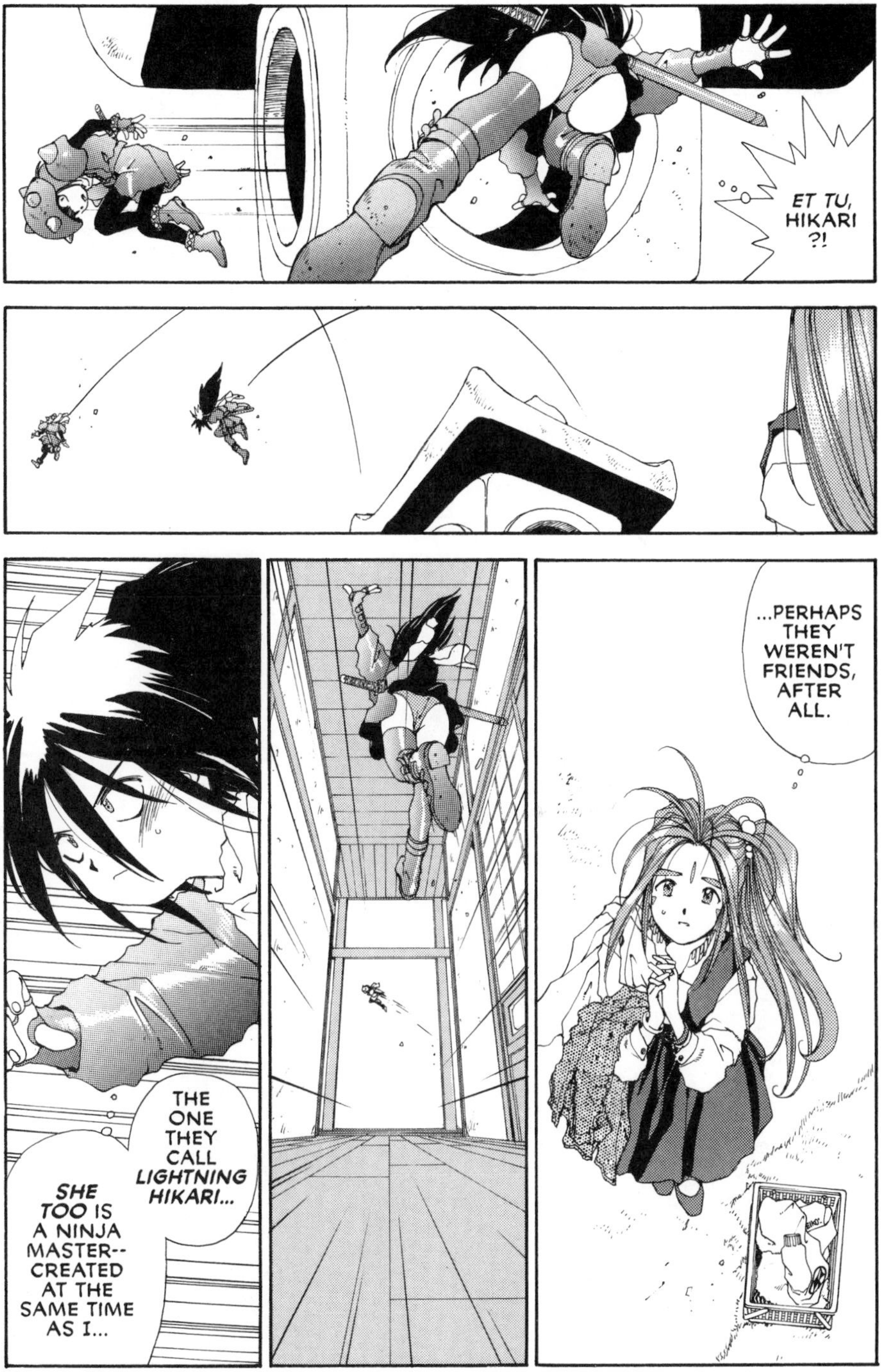
ET TU, HIKARI ?!
...PERHAPS THEY WEREN'T FRIENDS, AFTER ALL.
THE ONE THEY CALL *LIGHTNING HIKARI...*
SHE TOO IS A NINJA MASTER-- CREATED AT THE SAME TIME AS I...

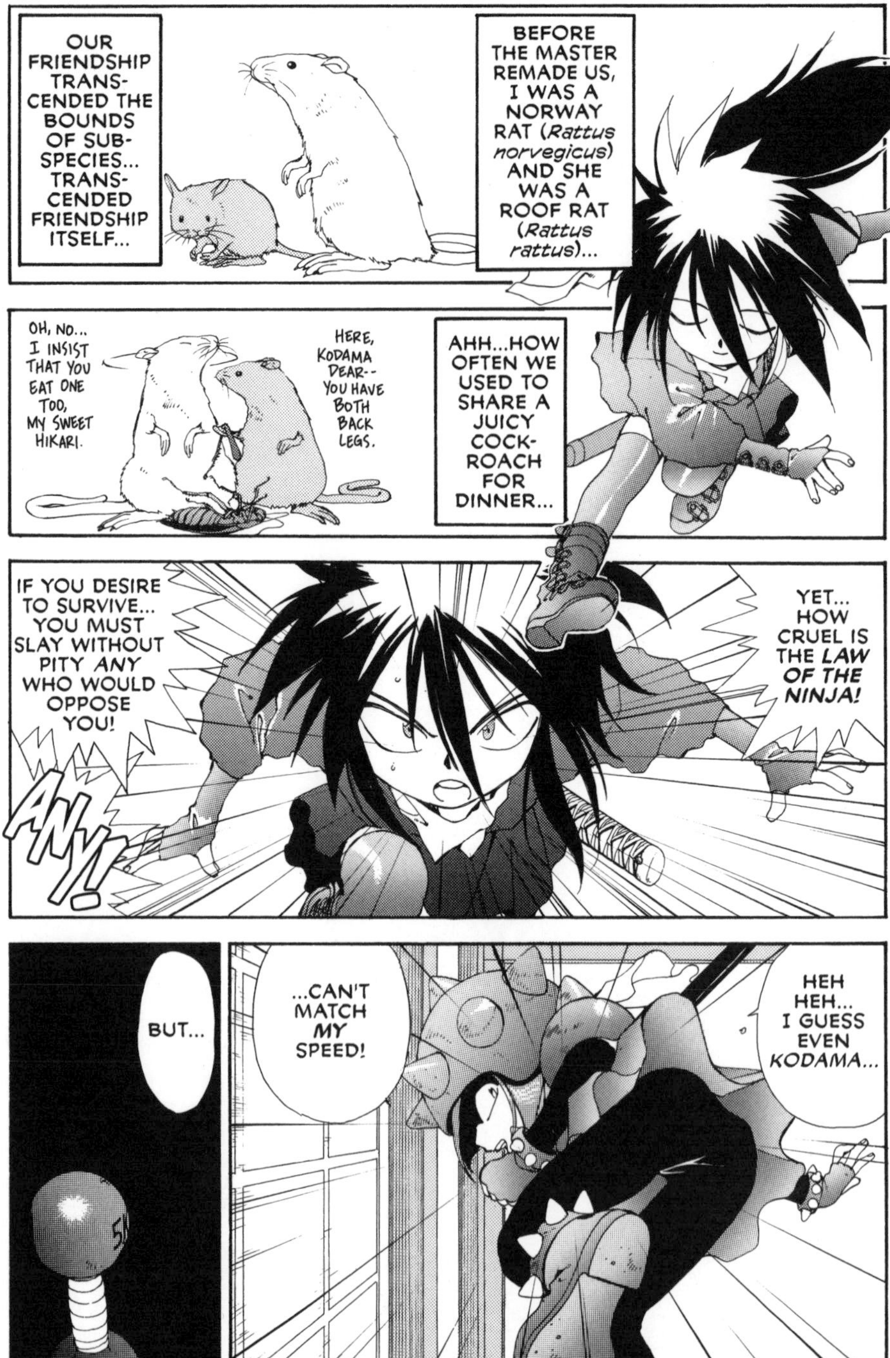
BEFORE THE MASTER REMADE US, I WAS A NORWAY RAT (*Rattus norvegicus*) AND SHE WAS A ROOF RAT (*Rattus rattus*)...
OUR FRIENDSHIP TRANSCENDED THE BOUNDS OF SUBSPECIES... TRANSCENDED FRIENDSHIP ITSELF...
AHH...HOW OFTEN WE USED TO SHARE A JUICY COCKROACH FOR DINNER...
HERE, KODAMA DEAR-- YOU HAVE BOTH BACK LEGS.
OH, NO... I INSIST THAT YOU EAT ONE TOO, MY SWEET HIKARI.
YET... HOW CRUEL IS THE *LAW OF THE NINJA!*
IF YOU DESIRE TO SURVIVE... YOU MUST SLAY WITHOUT PITY *ANY* WHO WOULD OPPOSE YOU!
ANY!
HEH HEH... I GUESS EVEN *KODAMA*...
...CAN'T MATCH *MY* SPEED!
BUT...

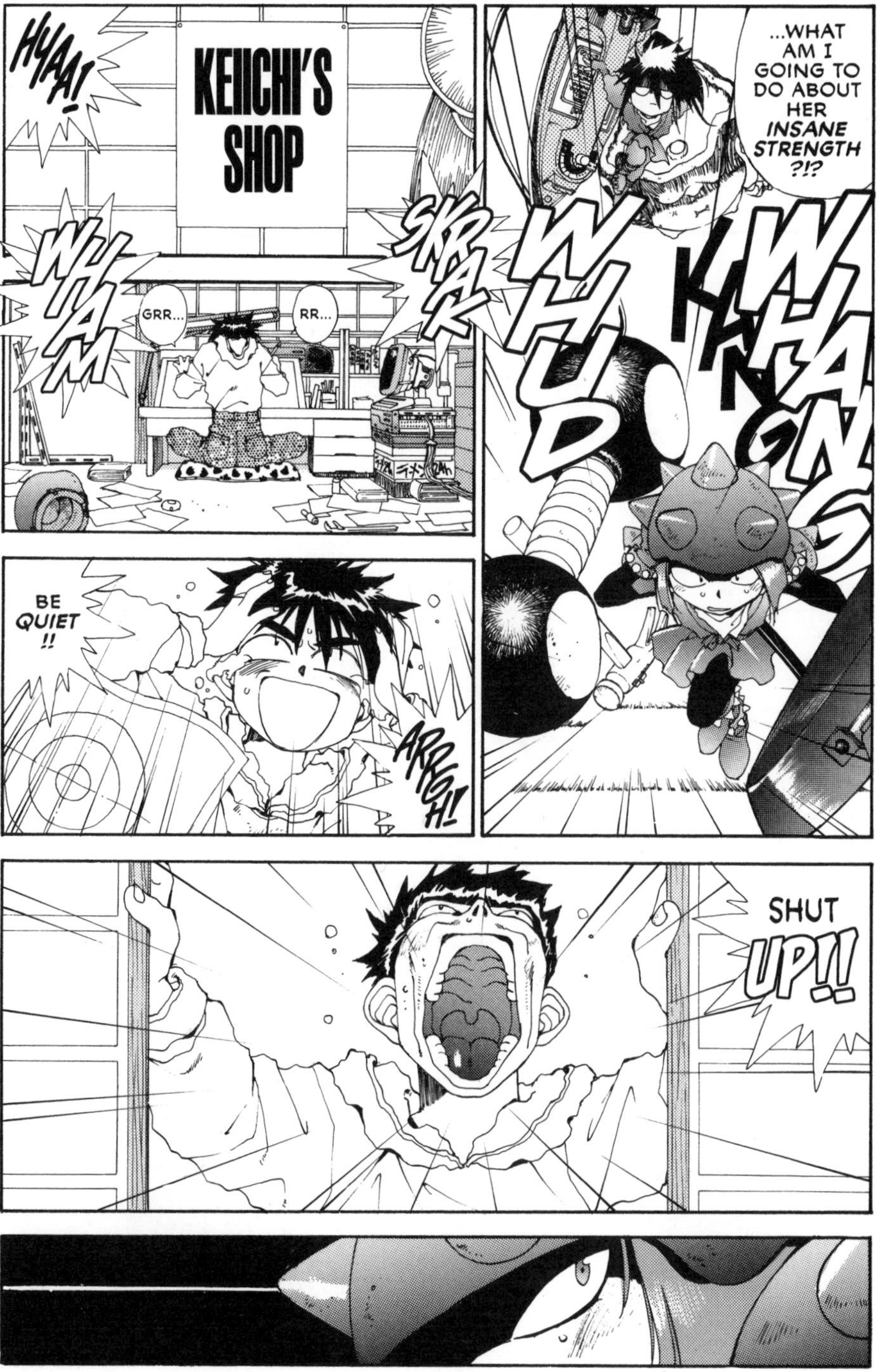
...WHAT AM I GOING TO DO ABOUT HER *INSANE STRENGTH* ?!?
WHUD
WHANGS
KEIICHI'S SHOP
HYAAA!
WHAM
SKRAK
GRR...
RR...
BE *QUIET* !!
ARRGH!
SHUT *UP!!*

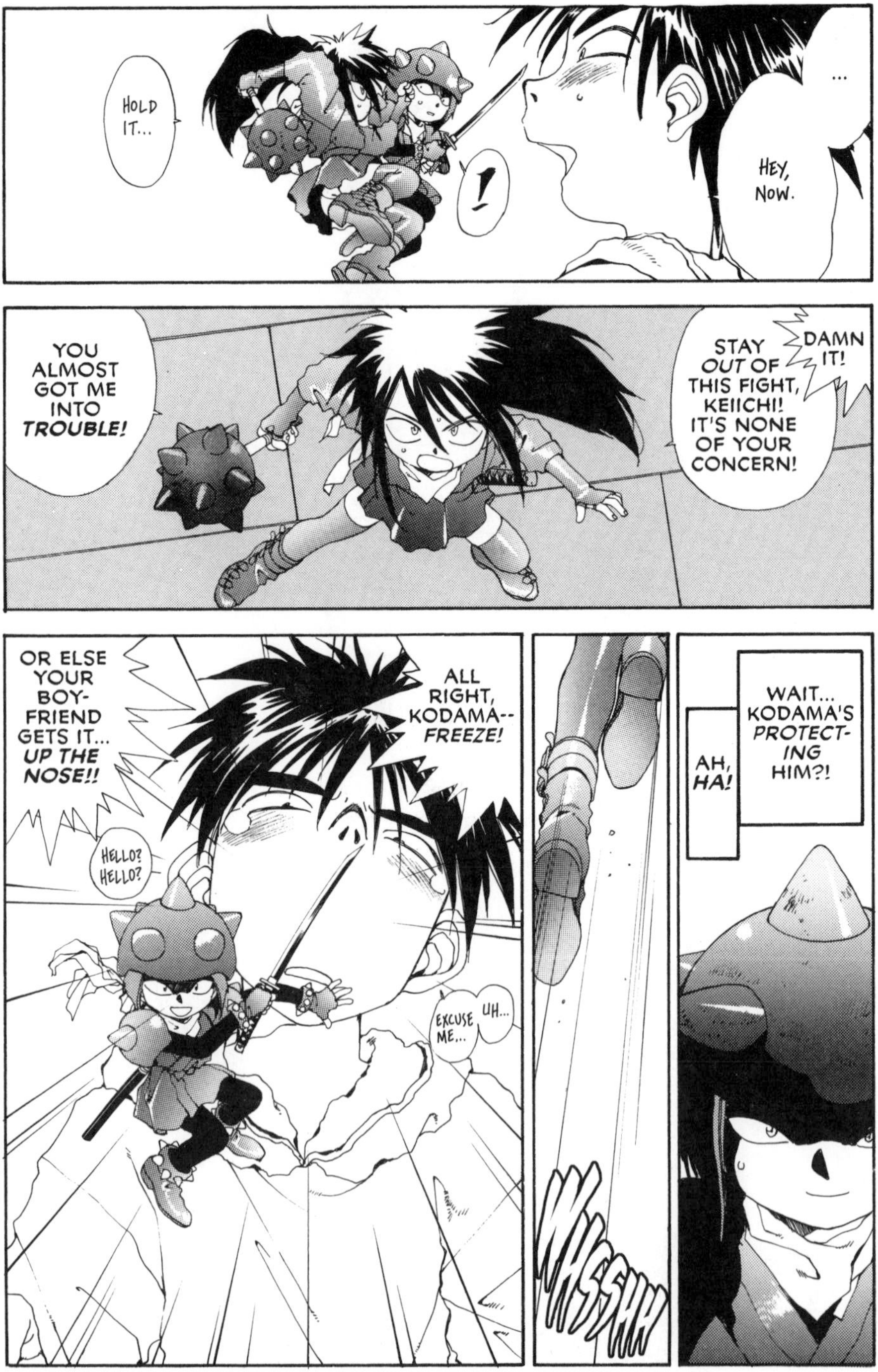
...
HEY, NOW.
!
HOLD IT...
DAMN IT!
STAY *OUT* OF THIS FIGHT, KEIICHI! IT'S NONE OF YOUR CONCERN!
YOU ALMOST GOT ME INTO ***TROUBLE!***
WAIT... KODAMA'S *PROTECTING* HIM?!
AH, *HA!*
WHSSHH
ALL RIGHT, KODAMA-- *FREEZE!*
OR ELSE YOUR BOY-FRIEND GETS IT... ***UP THE NOSE!!***
HELLO? HELLO?
UH...
EXCUSE ME...

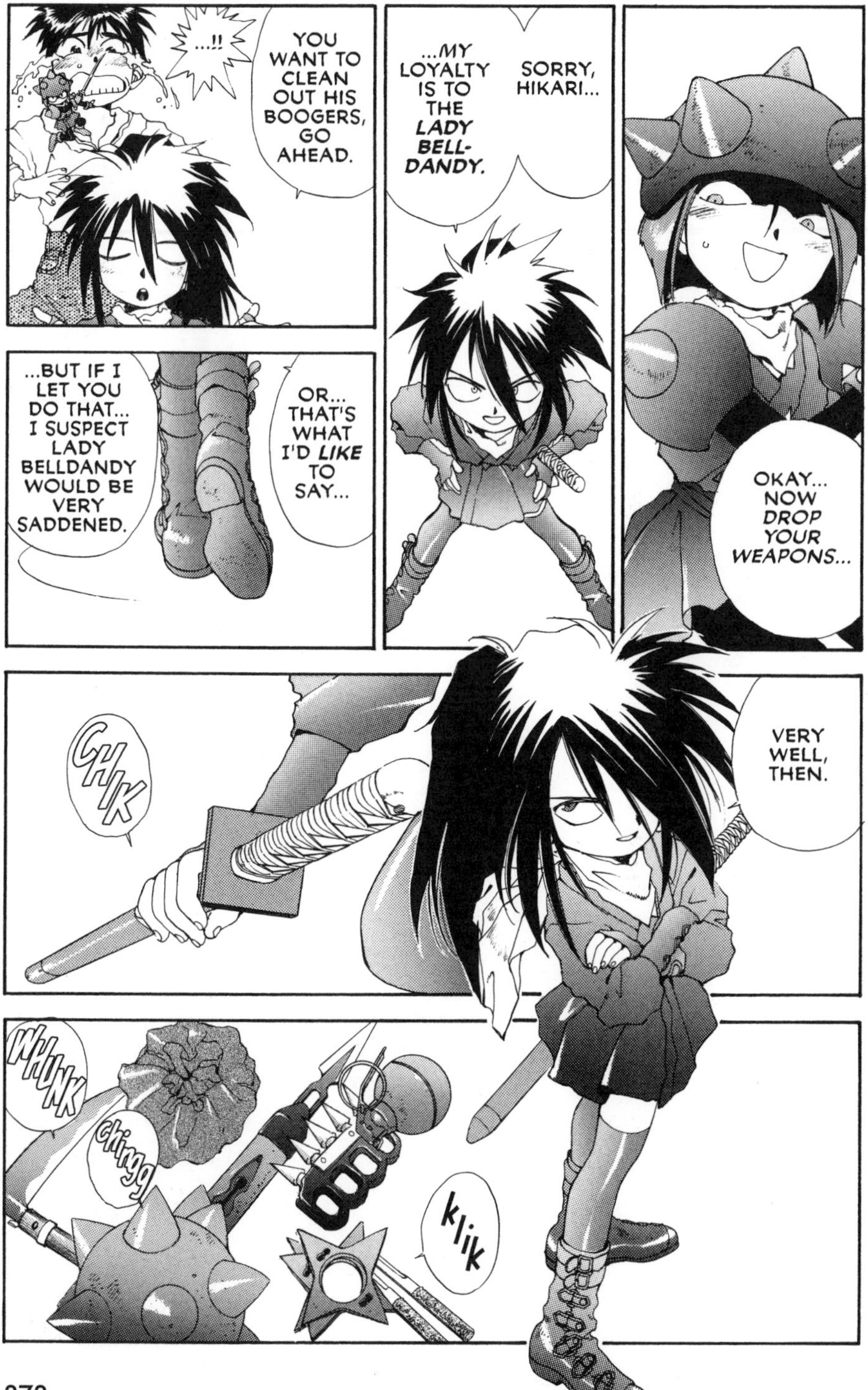
OKAY... NOW *DROP YOUR WEAPONS*...
SORRY, HIKARI...
...MY LOYALTY IS TO THE *LADY BELL-DANDY*.
...!!
YOU WANT TO CLEAN OUT HIS BOOGERS, GO AHEAD.
OR... THAT'S WHAT I'D *LIKE* TO SAY...
...BUT IF I LET YOU DO THAT... I SUSPECT LADY BELLDANDY WOULD BE VERY SADDENED.
VERY WELL, THEN.
CHIK
WHUNK
chingg
klik

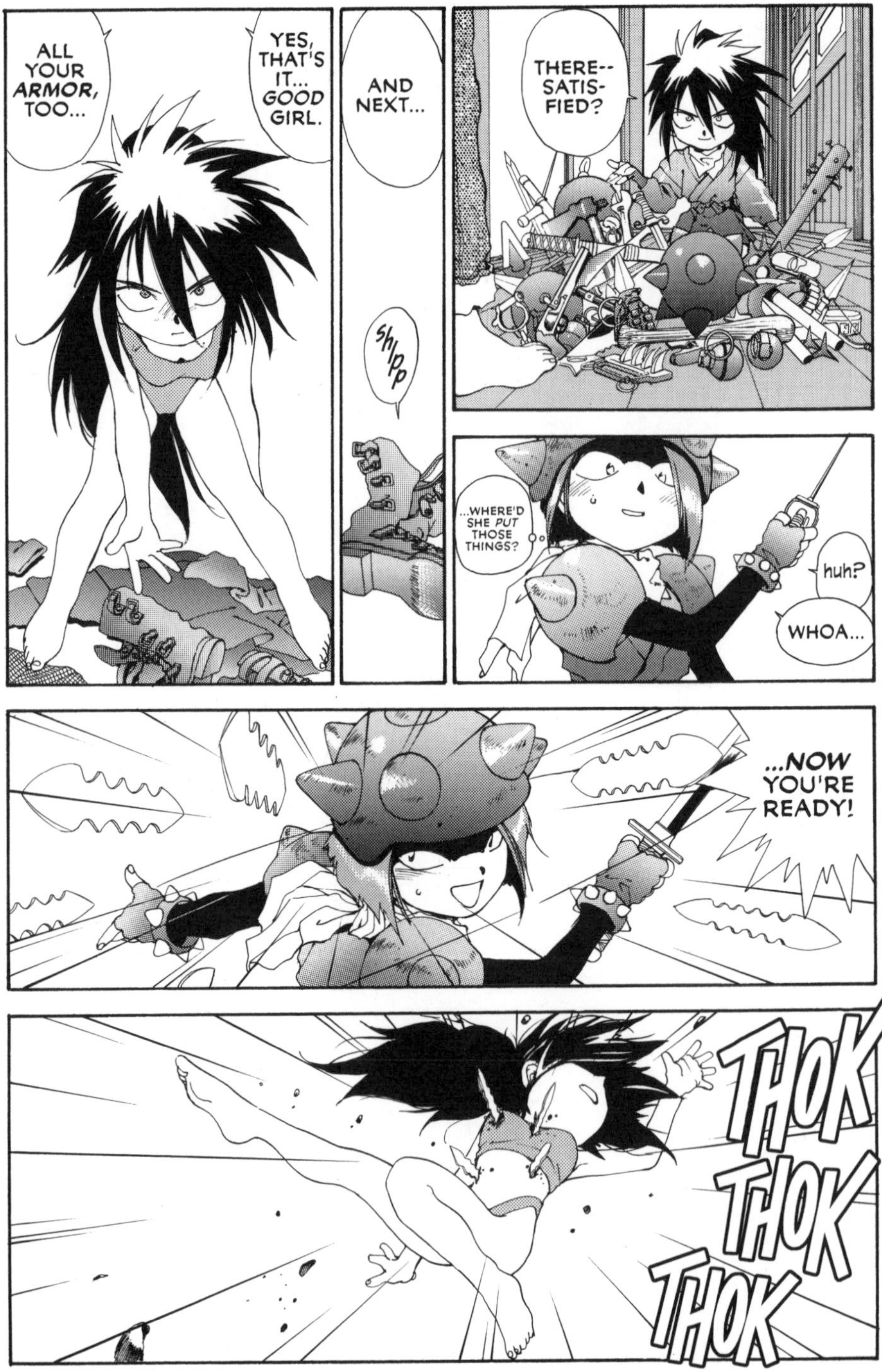
THERE-- SATISFIED?
...WHERE'D SHE *PUT* THOSE THINGS?
huh?
WHOA...
AND NEXT...
shlpp
YES, THAT'S IT... *GOOD* GIRL.
ALL YOUR *ARMOR,* TOO...
...*NOW* YOU'RE READY!
THOK
THOK
THOK

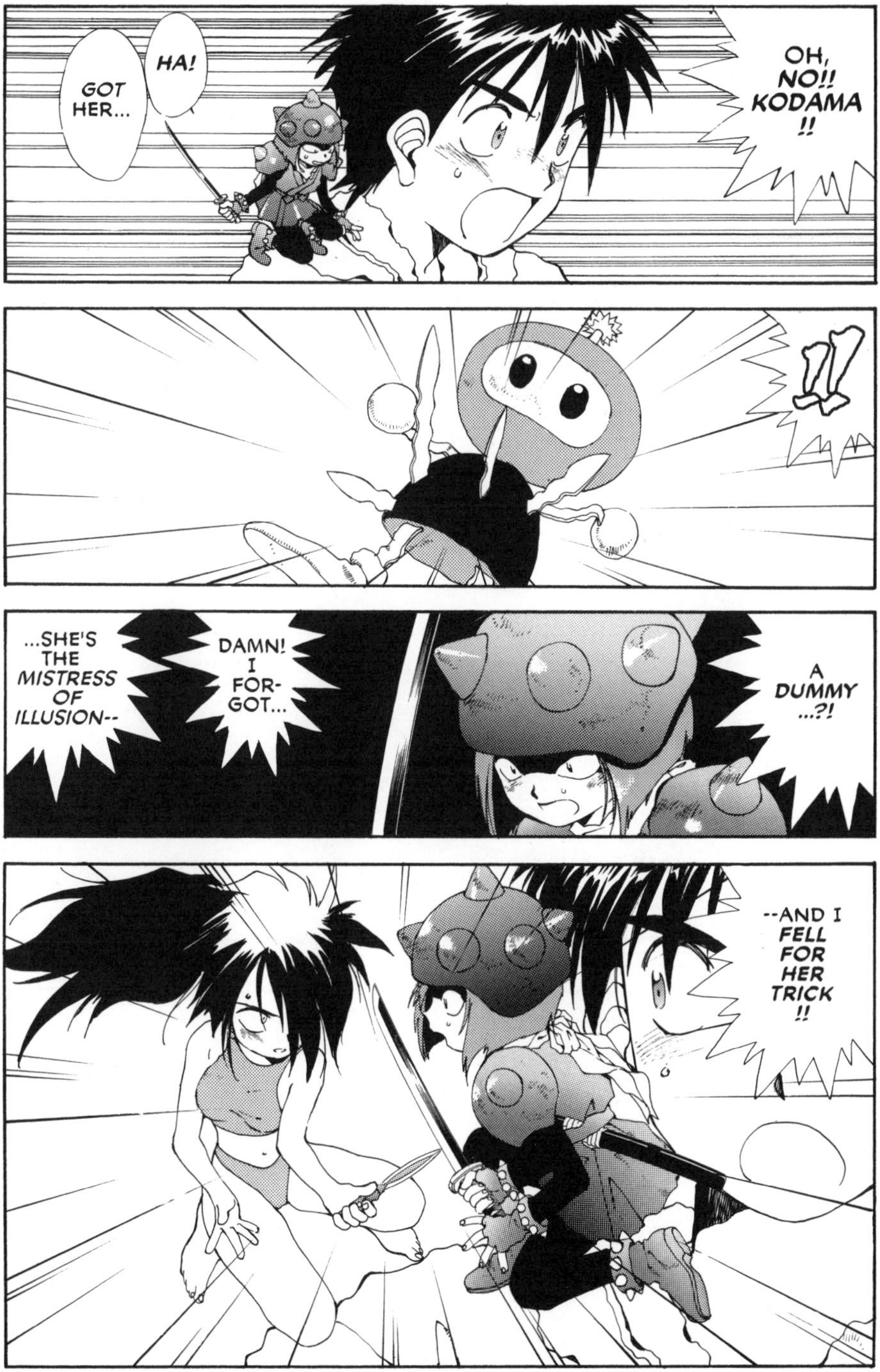
OH, NO!! KODAMA !!
HA!
GOT HER...
!!
A DUMMY ...?!
DAMN! I FOR-GOT...
...SHE'S THE MISTRESS OF ILLUSION--
--AND I FELL FOR HER TRICK !!

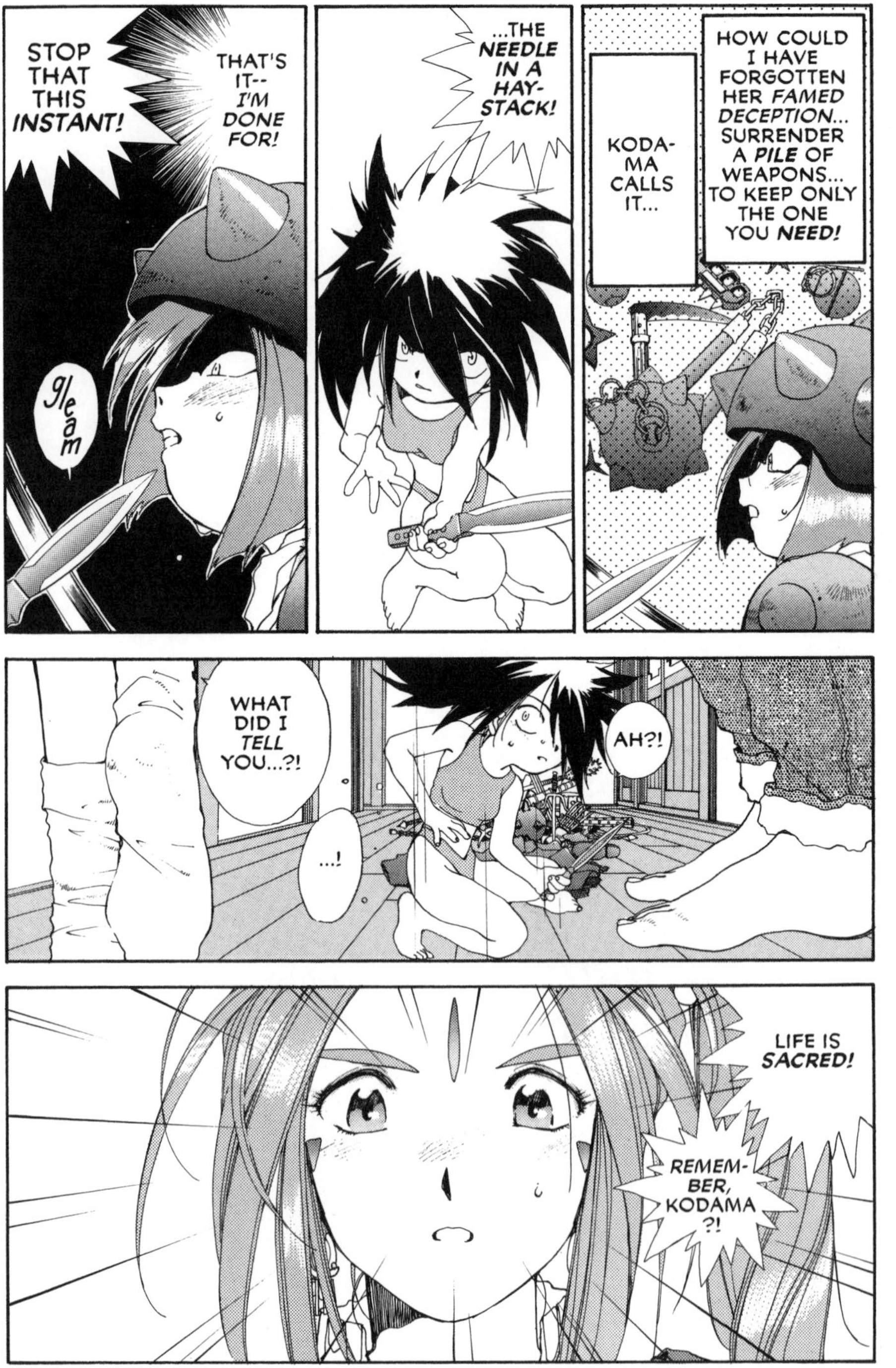
HOW COULD I HAVE FORGOTTEN HER FAMED DECEPTION... SURRENDER A PILE OF WEAPONS... TO KEEP ONLY THE ONE YOU NEED!
KODAMA CALLS IT...
...THE NEEDLE IN A HAYSTACK!
THAT'S IT-- I'M DONE FOR!
STOP THAT THIS INSTANT!
gleam
AH?!
WHAT DID I TELL YOU...?!
...!
LIFE IS SACRED!
REMEMBER, KODAMA?!

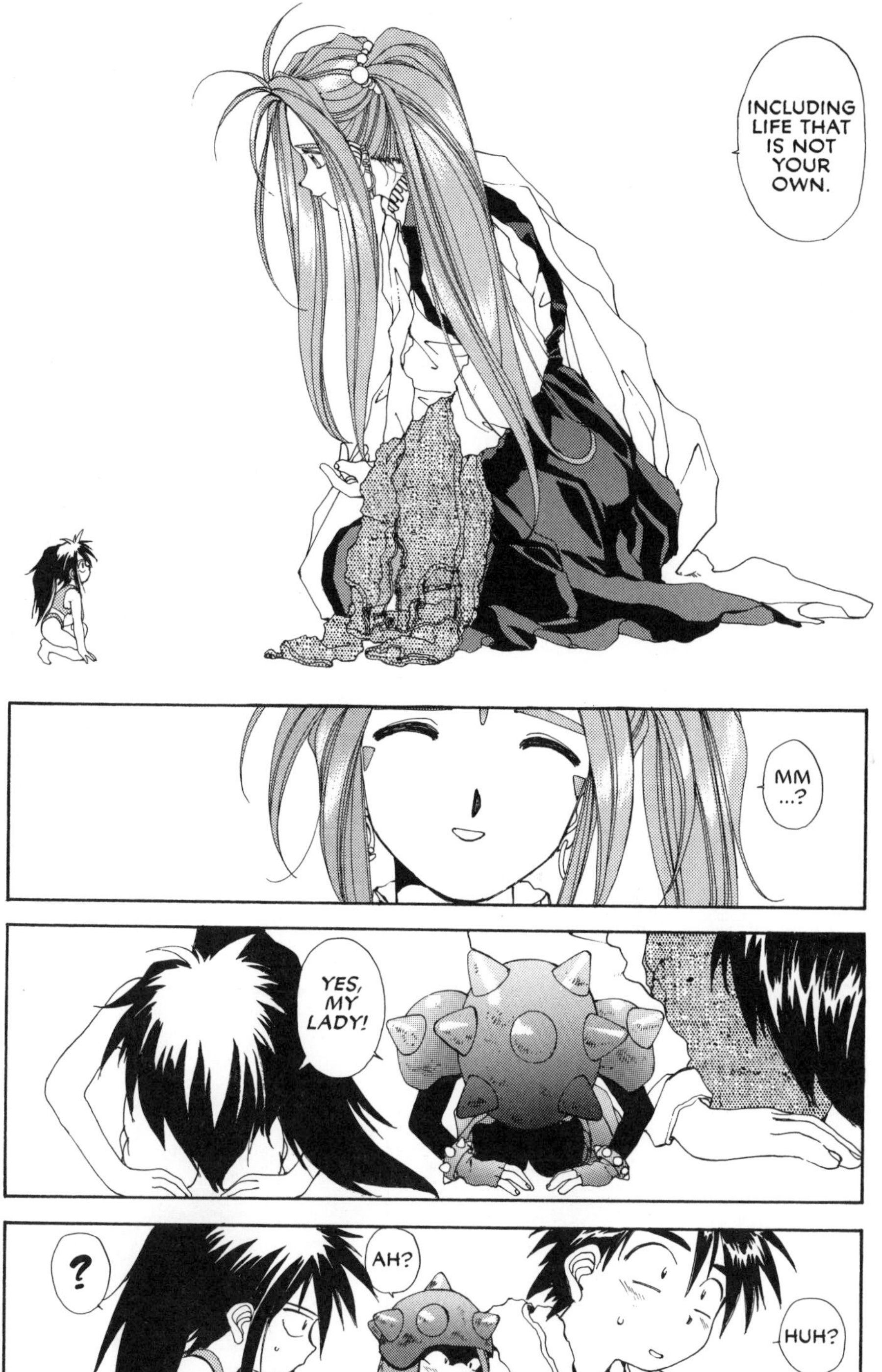
INCLUDING LIFE THAT IS NOT YOUR OWN.
MM ...?
YES, MY LADY!
HUH?
AH?
?

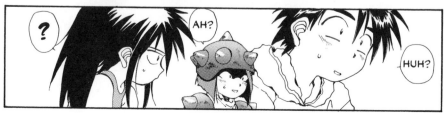

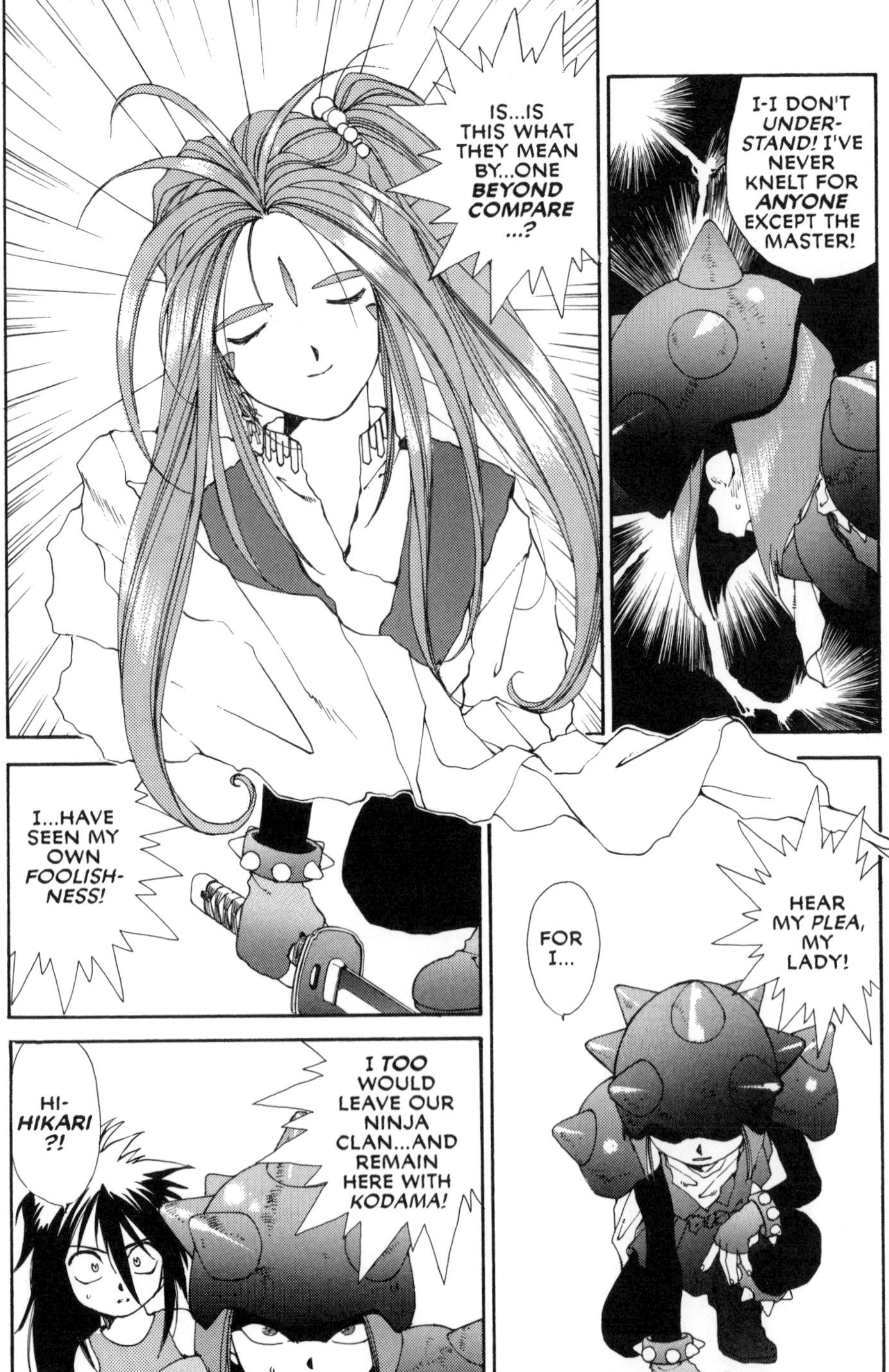
I-I DON'T *UNDERSTAND!* I'VE NEVER KNELT FOR *ANYONE* EXCEPT THE MASTER!
IS...IS THIS WHAT THEY MEAN BY...ONE *BEYOND COMPARE* ...?
HEAR MY *PLEA*, MY LADY!
FOR I...
I...HAVE SEEN MY OWN *FOOLISHNESS!*
I *TOO* WOULD LEAVE OUR NINJA CLAN...AND REMAIN HERE WITH *KODAMA!*
HI-*HIKARI* ?!

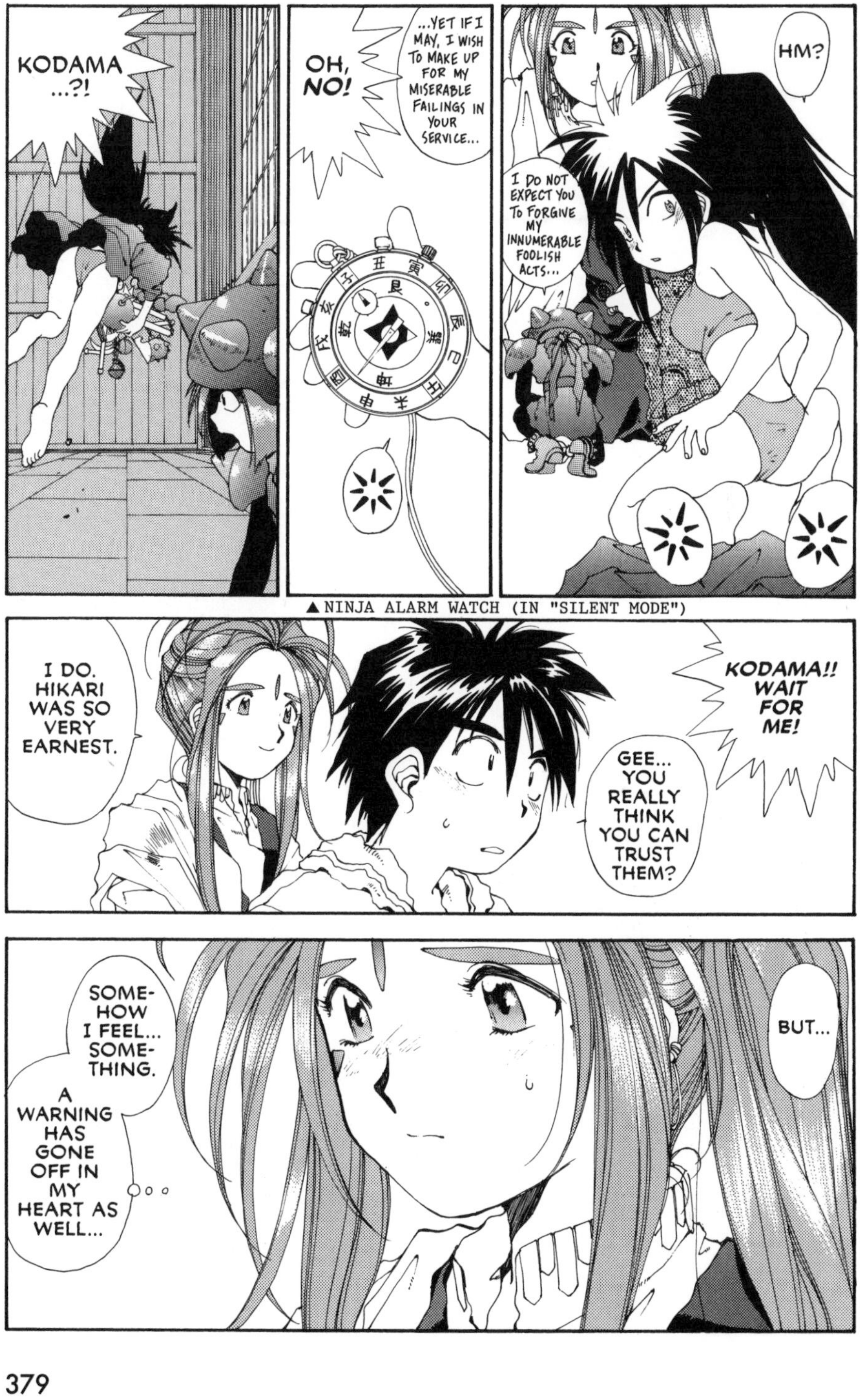
HM?
I DO NOT EXPECT YOU TO FORGIVE MY INNUMERABLE FOOLISH ACTS...
...YET IF I MAY, I WISH TO MAKE UP FOR MY MISERABLE FAILINGS IN YOUR SERVICE...
OH, NO!
KODAMA ...?!
▲NINJA ALARM WATCH (IN "SILENT MODE")
KODAMA!! WAIT FOR ME!
GEE... YOU REALLY THINK YOU CAN TRUST THEM?
I DO. HIKARI WAS SO VERY EARNEST.
BUT...
SOME-HOW I FEEL... SOME-THING.
A WARNING HAS GONE OFF IN MY HEART AS WELL...

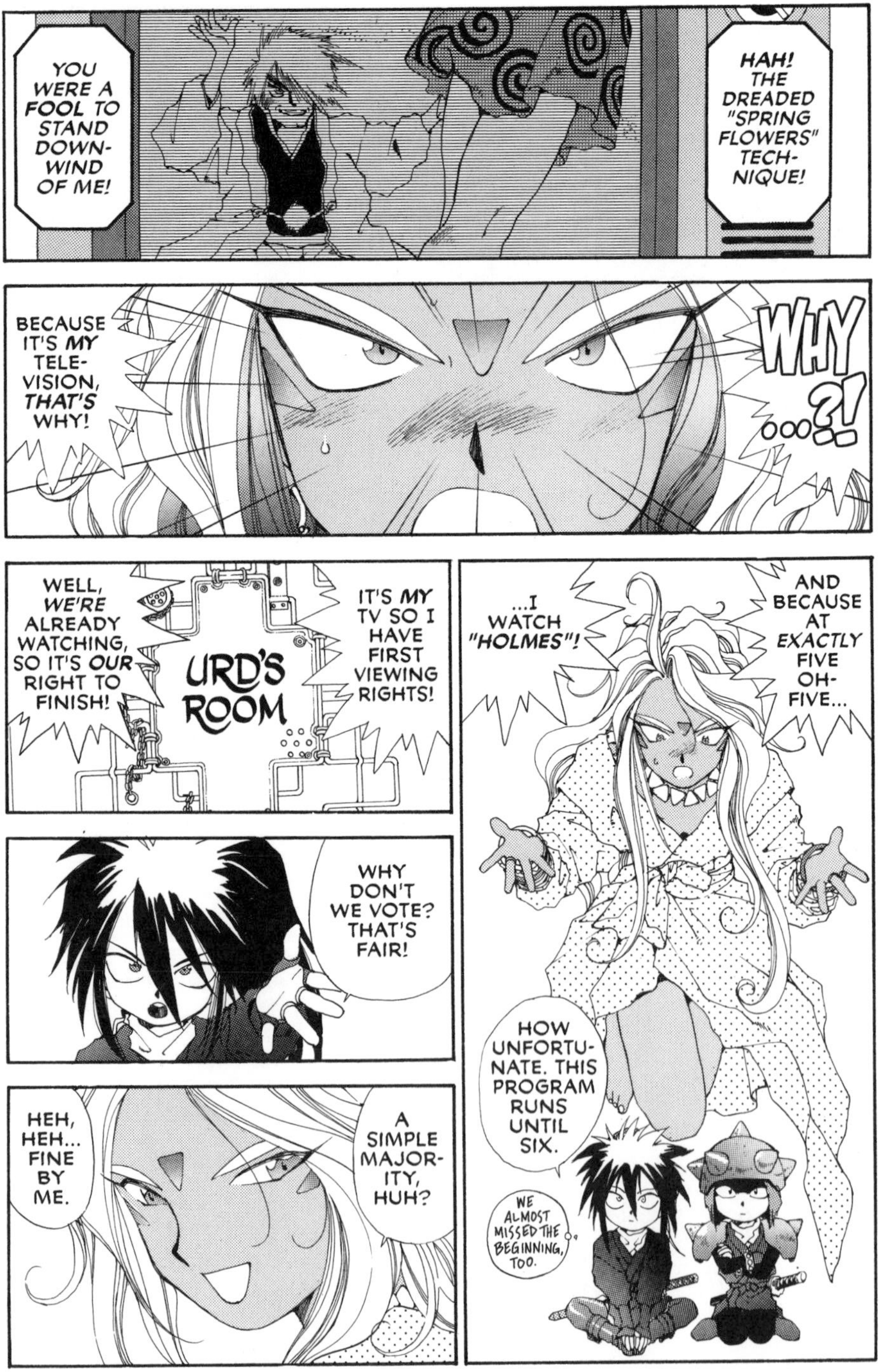
HAH! THE DREADED "SPRING FLOWERS" TECHNIQUE!
YOU WERE A FOOL TO STAND DOWNWIND OF ME!
WHY ooo?!
BECAUSE IT'S MY TELEVISION, THAT'S WHY!
AND BECAUSE AT EXACTLY FIVE OH-FIVE...
...I WATCH "HOLMES"!
HOW UNFORTUNATE. THIS PROGRAM RUNS UNTIL SIX.
WE ALMOST MISSED THE BEGINNING, TOO.
IT'S MY TV SO I HAVE FIRST VIEWING RIGHTS!
URD'S ROOM
WELL, WE'RE ALREADY WATCHING, SO IT'S OUR RIGHT TO FINISH!
WHY DON'T WE VOTE? THAT'S FAIR!
A SIMPLE MAJORITY, HUH?
HEH, HEH... FINE BY ME.

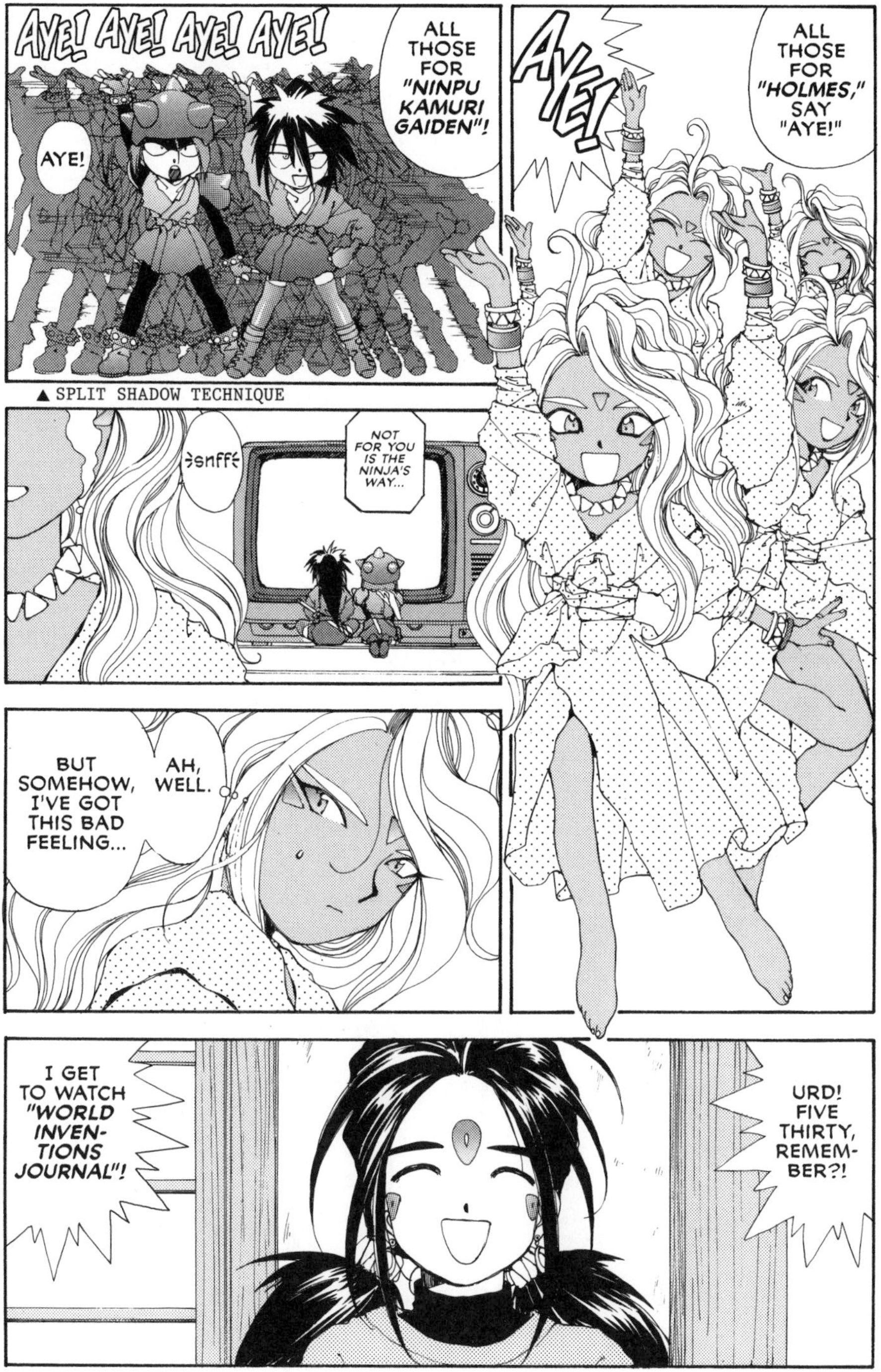
AYE!
ALL THOSE FOR "HOLMES," SAY "AYE!"
AYE! AYE! AYE! AYE!
ALL THOSE FOR "NINPU KAMURI GAIDEN"!
AYE!
▲SPLIT SHADOW TECHNIQUE
NOT FOR YOU IS THE NINJA'S WAY...
snff
AH, WELL.
BUT SOMEHOW, I'VE GOT THIS BAD FEELING...
URD! FIVE THIRTY, REMEMBER?!
I GET TO WATCH "WORLD INVENTIONS JOURNAL"!

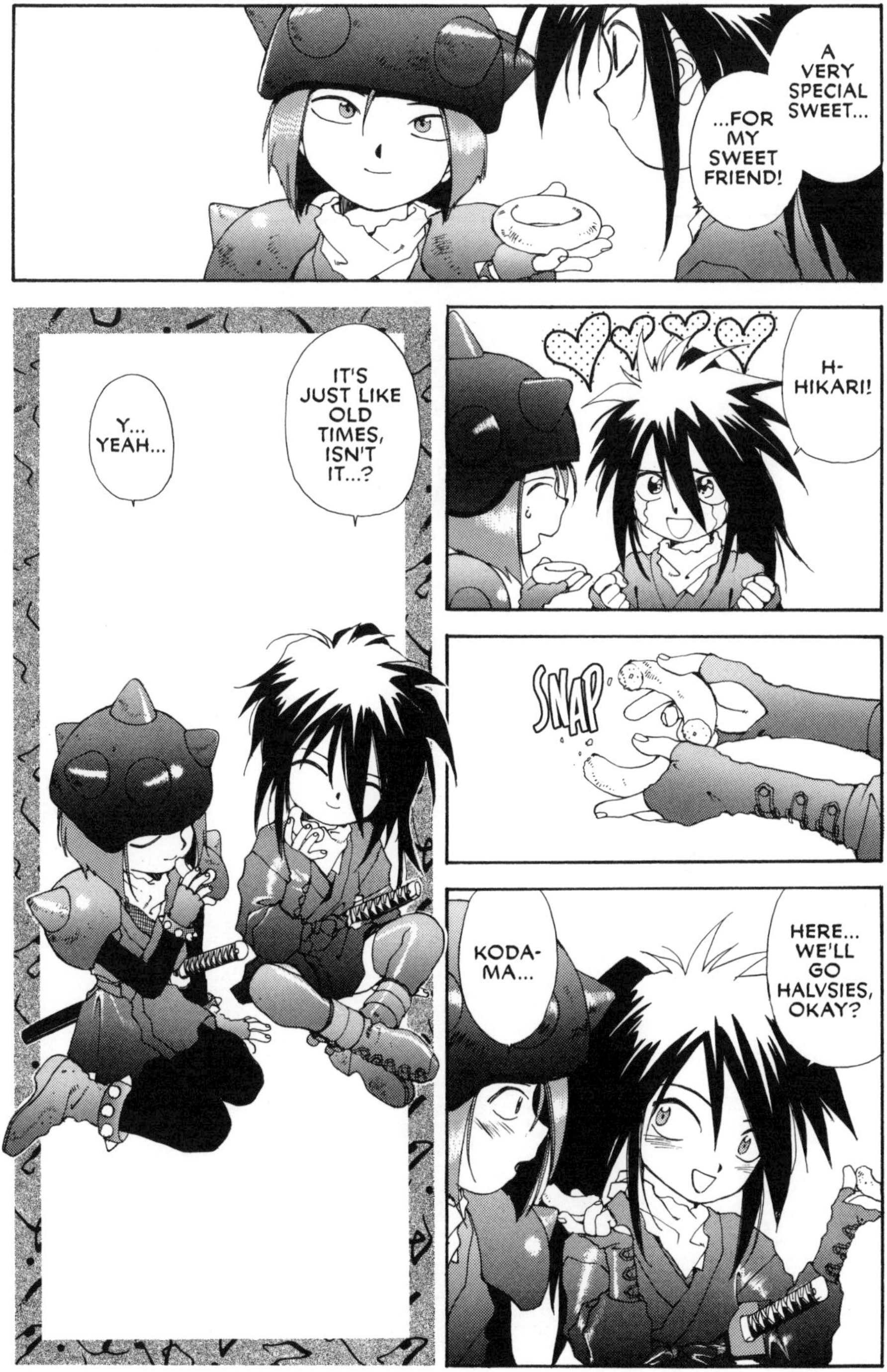
A VERY SPECIAL SWEET...
...FOR MY SWEET FRIEND!
H-HIKARI!
SNAP
HERE... WE'LL GO HALVSIES, OKAY?
KODA-MA...
IT'S JUST LIKE OLD TIMES, ISN'T IT...?
Y... YEAH...

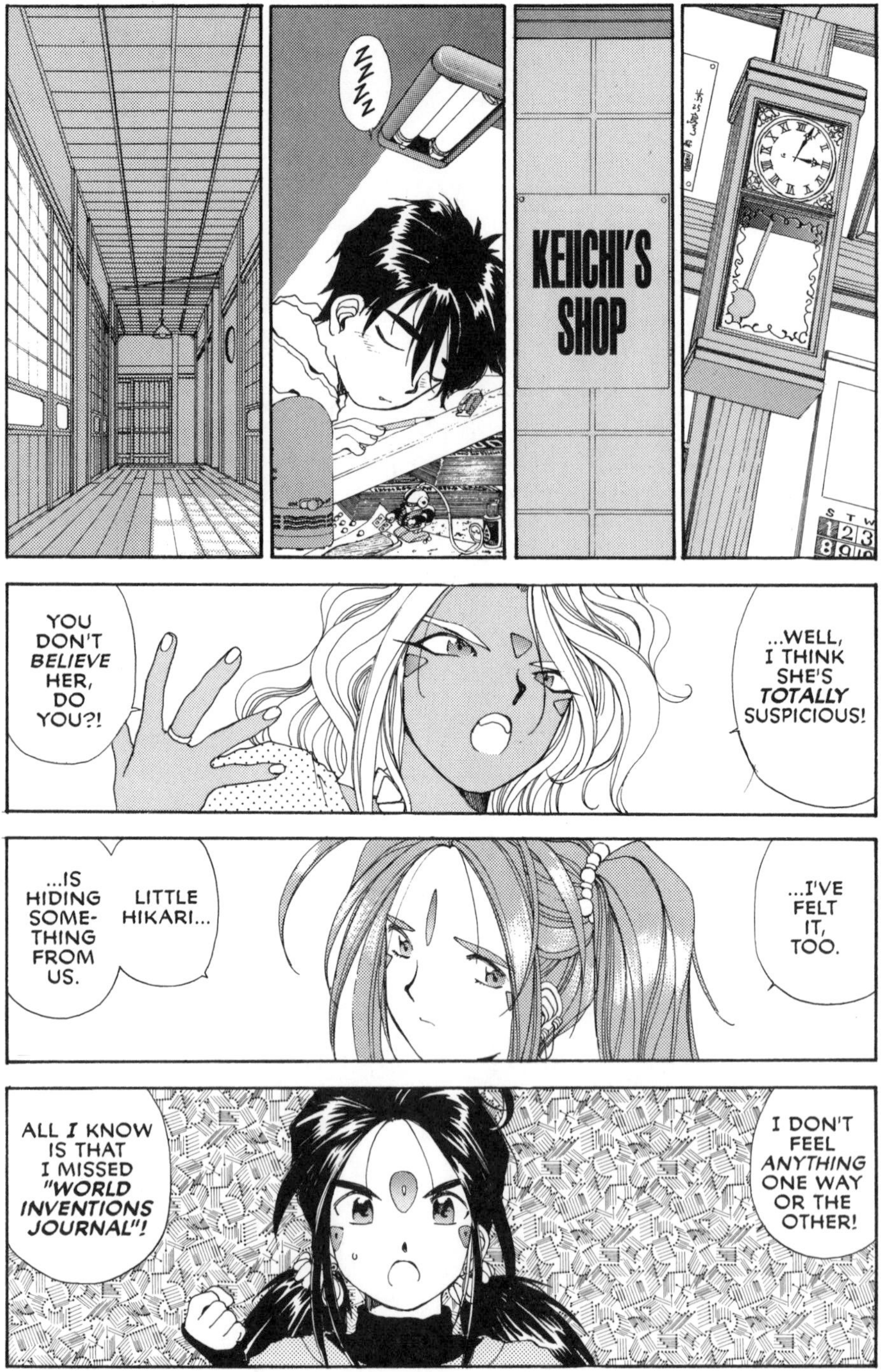
KEIICHI'S SHOP
ZZZZ
...WELL, I THINK SHE'S *TOTALLY* SUSPICIOUS!
YOU DON'T *BELIEVE* HER, DO YOU?!
...I'VE FELT IT, TOO.
LITTLE HIKARI...
...IS HIDING SOME-THING FROM US.
I DON'T FEEL *ANYTHING* ONE WAY OR THE OTHER!
ALL *I* KNOW IS THAT I MISSED *"WORLD INVENTIONS JOURNAL"*!

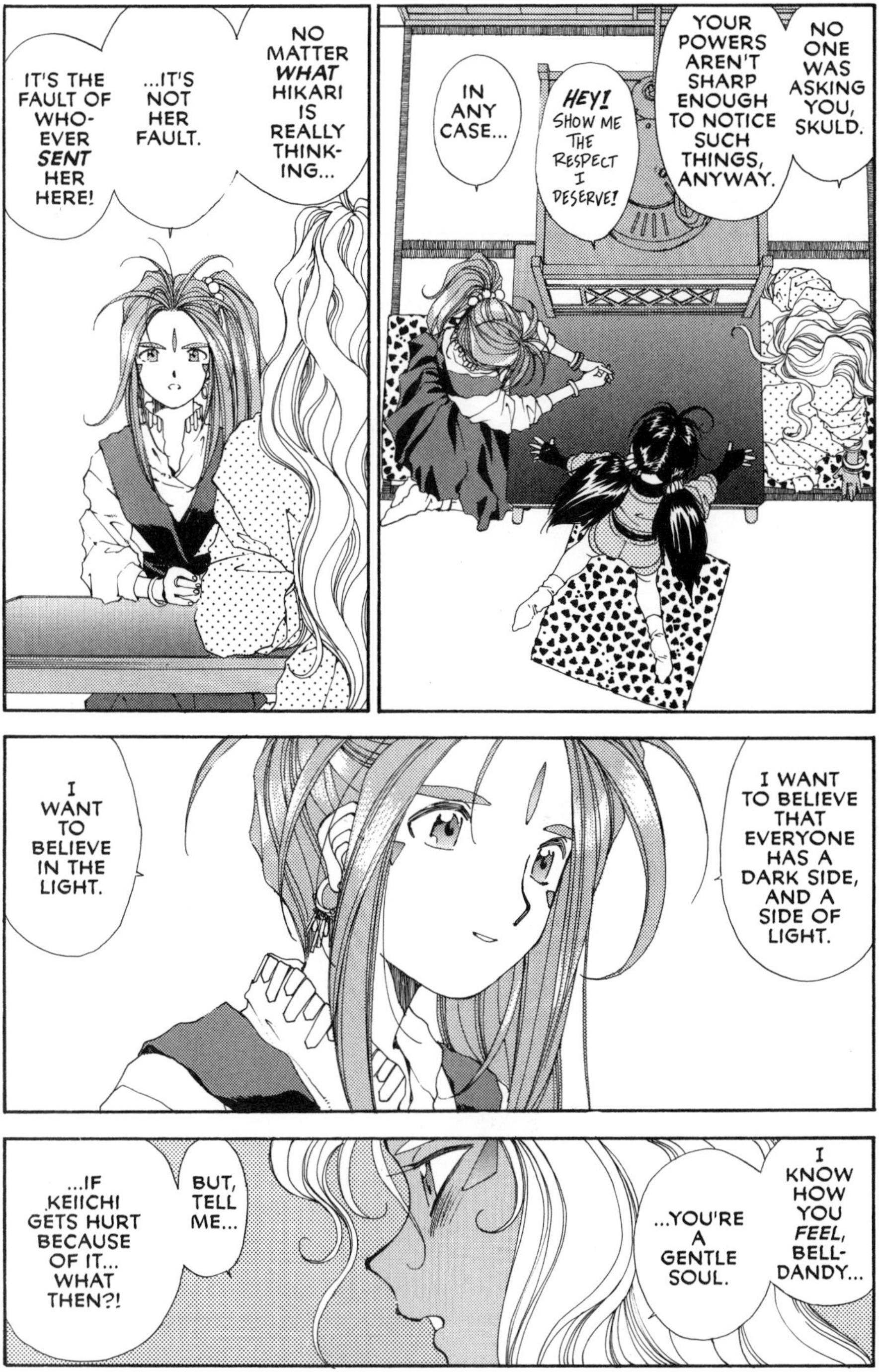
NO ONE WAS ASKING YOU, SKULD.
YOUR POWERS AREN'T SHARP ENOUGH TO NOTICE SUCH THINGS, ANYWAY.
HEY! SHOW ME THE RESPECT I DESERVE!
IN ANY CASE...
NO MATTER WHAT HIKARI IS REALLY THINKING...
...IT'S NOT HER FAULT.
IT'S THE FAULT OF WHOEVER SENT HER HERE!
I WANT TO BELIEVE THAT EVERYONE HAS A DARK SIDE, AND A SIDE OF LIGHT.
I WANT TO BELIEVE IN THE LIGHT.
I KNOW HOW YOU FEEL, BELLDANDY...
...YOU'RE A GENTLE SOUL.
BUT, TELL ME...
...IF KEIICHI GETS HURT BECAUSE OF IT... WHAT THEN?!

...WITH MY LIFE.

IF THAT DANGER APPEARS, THEN I'LL PROTECT HIM...

ZZZ

...

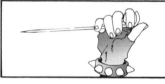

IT LOOKS LIKE THE DRUG WORKED...

IT WOULD HAVE NEVER HAD COME TO THIS.

IF *ONLY* YOU HADN'T BETRAYED OUR CLAN!

OH, KODA-MA...

ZZZ

386

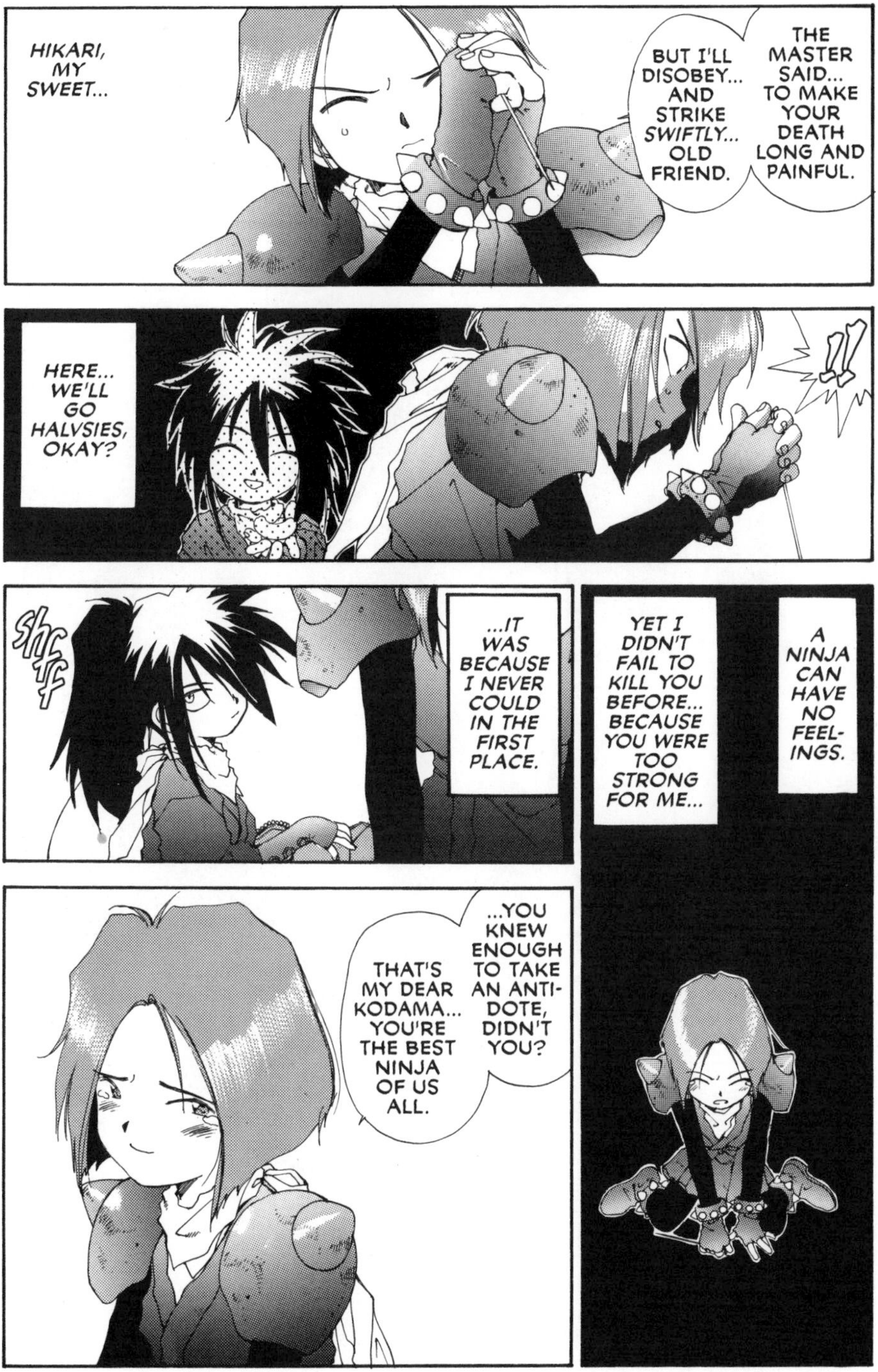
THE MASTER SAID... TO MAKE YOUR DEATH LONG AND PAINFUL.
BUT I'LL DISOBEY... AND STRIKE *SWIFTLY*... OLD FRIEND.
HIKARI, MY SWEET...
!!
HERE... WE'LL GO HALVSIES, OKAY?
A NINJA CAN HAVE NO FEEL-INGS.
YET I DIDN'T FAIL TO KILL YOU BEFORE... BECAUSE YOU WERE TOO STRONG FOR ME...
...IT WAS BECAUSE I NEVER COULD IN THE FIRST PLACE.
shff
...YOU KNEW ENOUGH TO TAKE AN ANTI-DOTE, DIDN'T YOU?
THAT'S MY DEAR KODAMA... YOU'RE THE BEST NINJA OF US ALL.

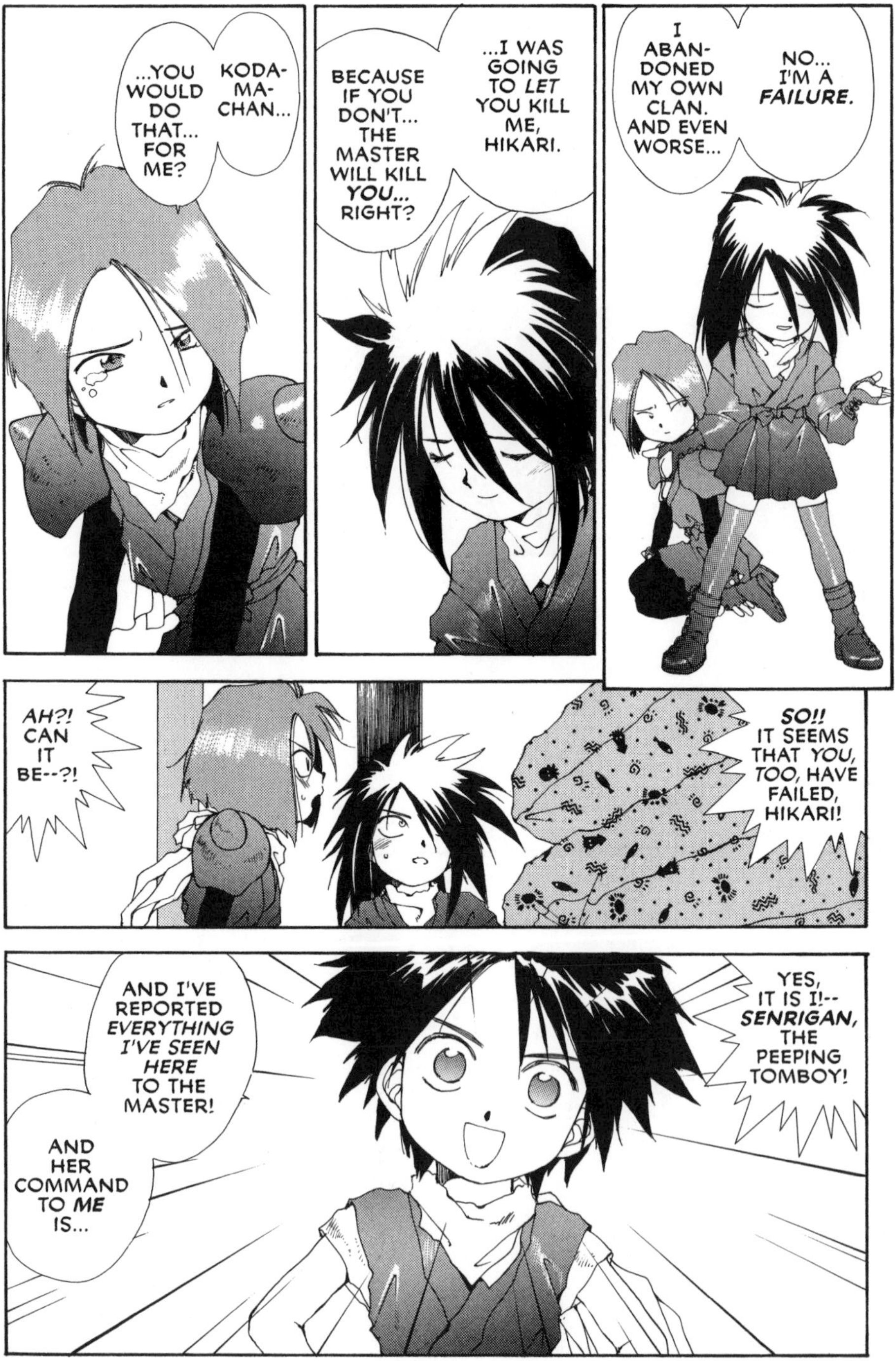
NO... I'M A *FAILURE.*
I ABANDONED MY OWN CLAN. AND EVEN WORSE...
...I WAS GOING TO *LET* YOU KILL ME, HIKARI.
BECAUSE IF YOU DON'T... THE MASTER WILL KILL *YOU...* RIGHT?
KODAMA-CHAN...
...YOU WOULD DO THAT... FOR ME?
SO!! IT SEEMS THAT *YOU, TOO,* HAVE FAILED, HIKARI!
AH?! CAN IT BE--?!
YES, IT IS I!-- *SENRIGAN,* THE PEEPING TOMBOY!
AND I'VE REPORTED *EVERYTHING I'VE SEEN HERE* TO THE MASTER!
AND HER COMMAND TO *ME* IS...

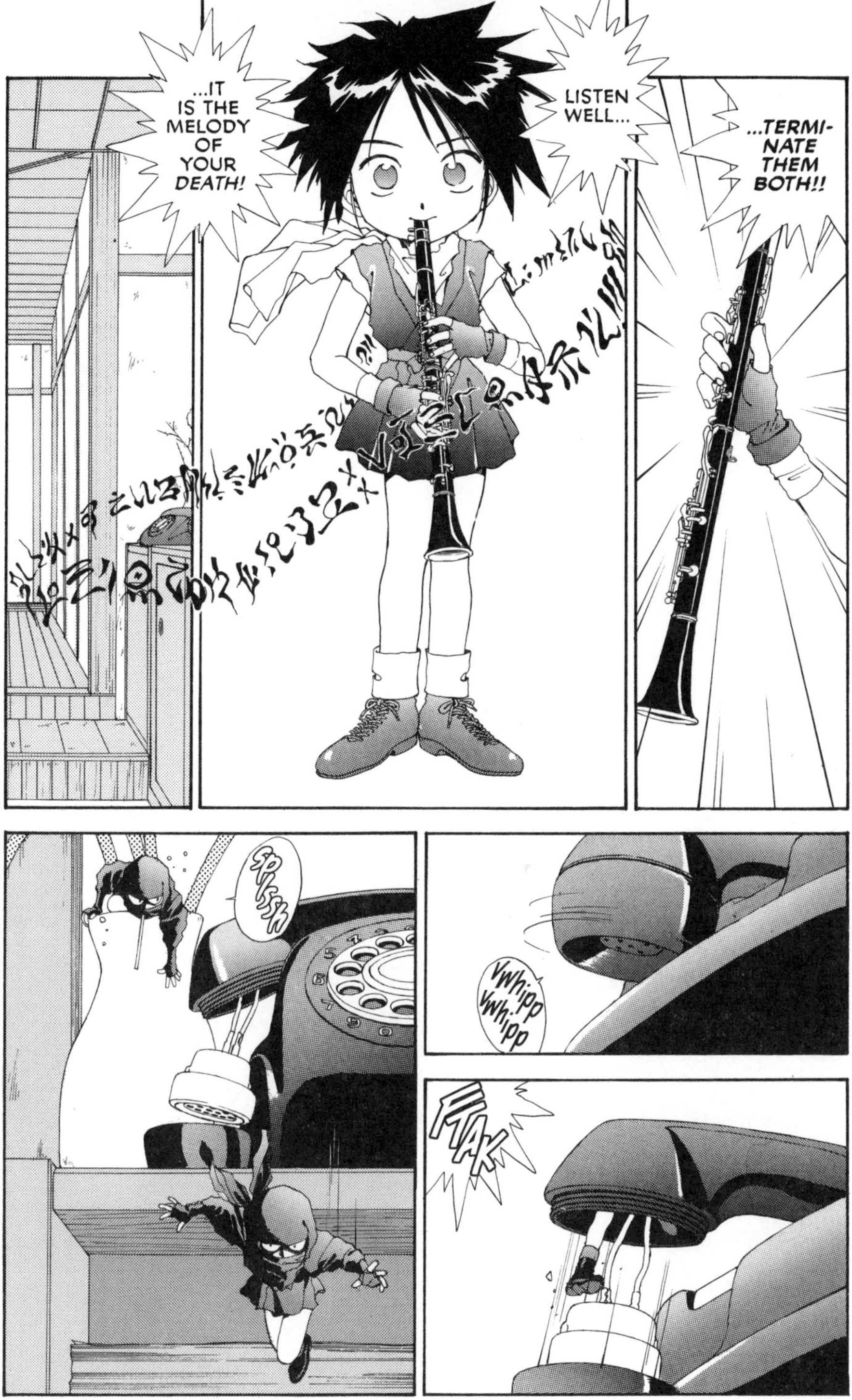
...TERMINATE THEM BOTH!!
LISTEN WELL...
...IT IS THE MELODY OF YOUR DEATH!
VWHIPP VWHIPP
FTAK
SPISSH

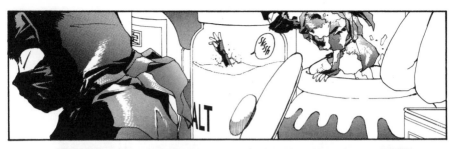

NINJA! TINY, DISGUSTING **NINJA**!!

EEEK!!

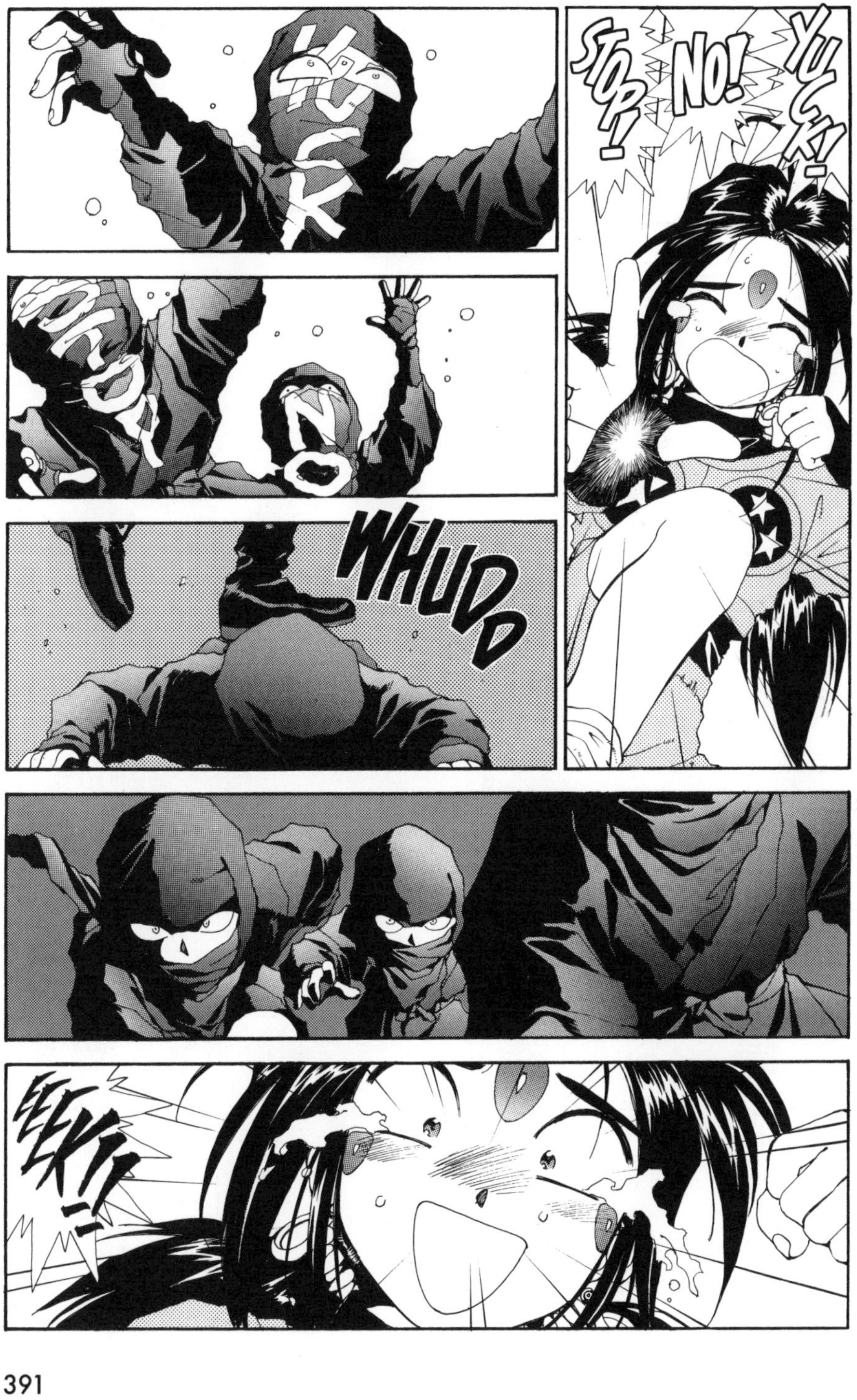
YUCK!
NO!
STOP!
HUCK
WHUDD
EEEK!!

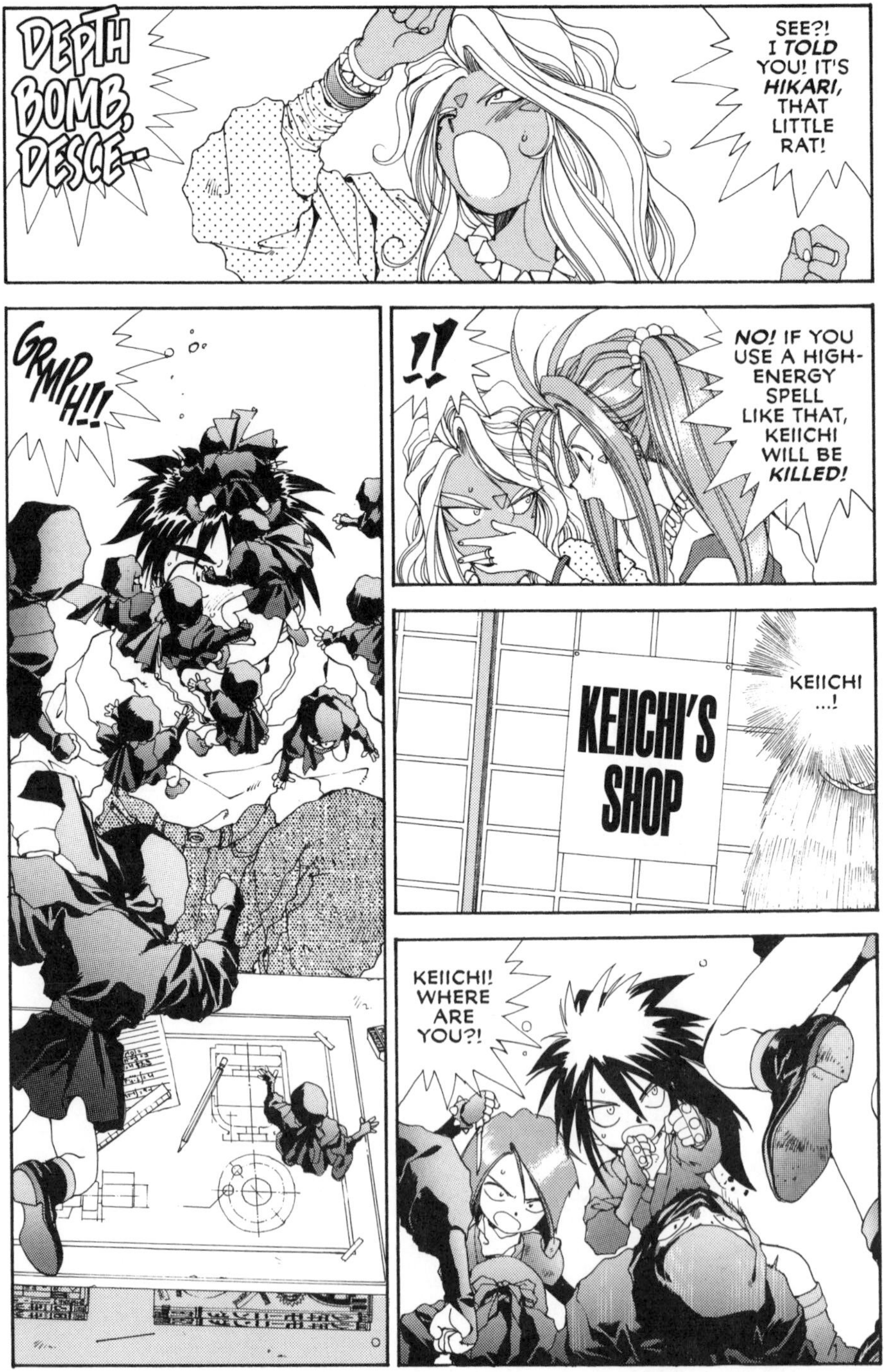
SEE?! I TOLD YOU! IT'S HIKARI, THAT LITTLE RAT!
DEPTH BOMB, DESCE--
NO! IF YOU USE A HIGH-ENERGY SPELL LIKE THAT, KEIICHI WILL BE KILLED!
!!
KEIICHI ...!
KEIICHI'S SHOP
KEIICHI! WHERE ARE YOU?!
GRMPH!!

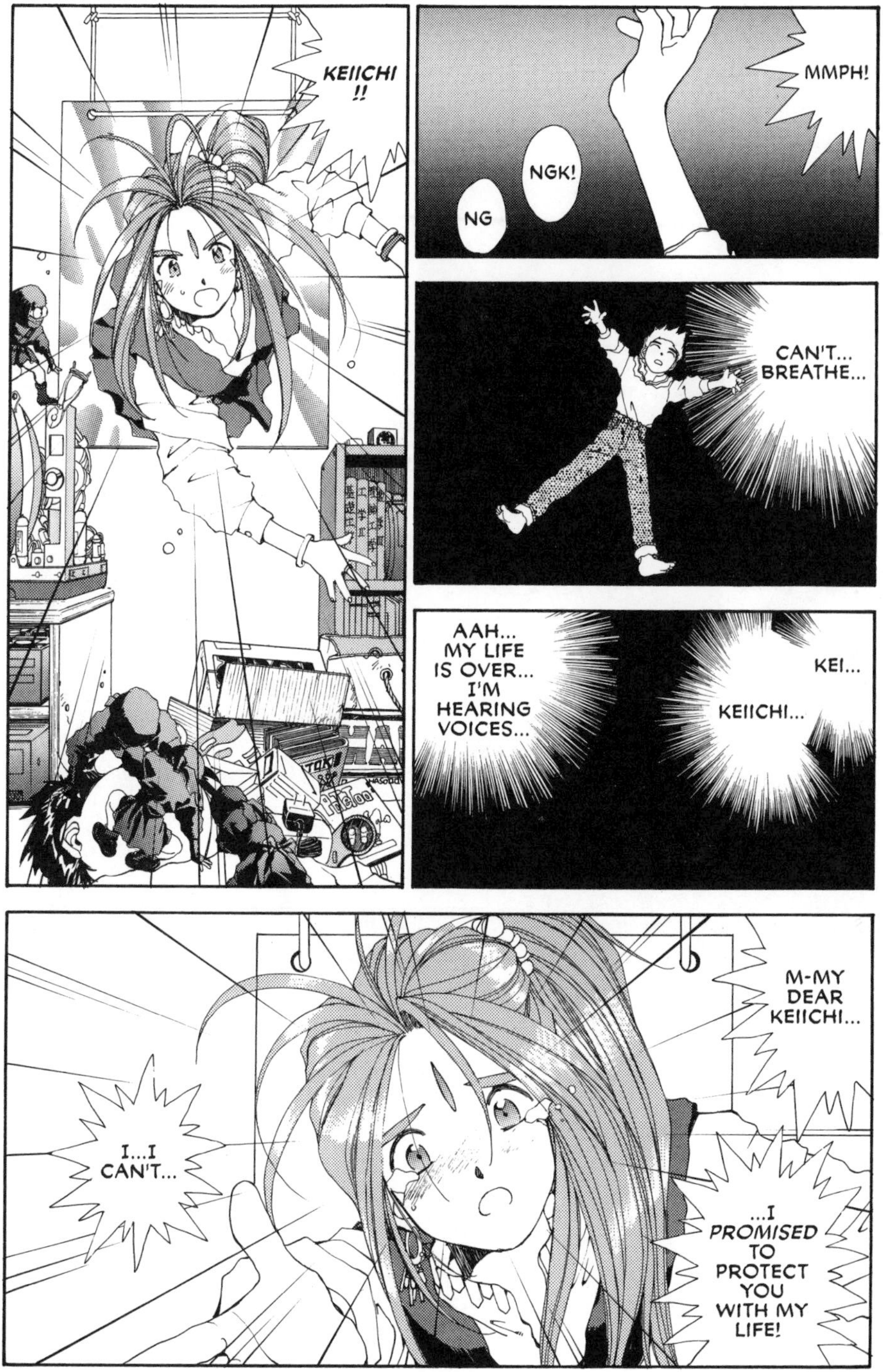
MMPH!
NGK!
NG
CAN'T... BREATHE...
KEI...
KEIICHI...
AAH... MY LIFE IS OVER... I'M HEARING VOICES...
KEIICHI !!
M-MY DEAR KEIICHI...
I...I CAN'T...
...I PROMISED TO PROTECT YOU WITH MY LIFE!

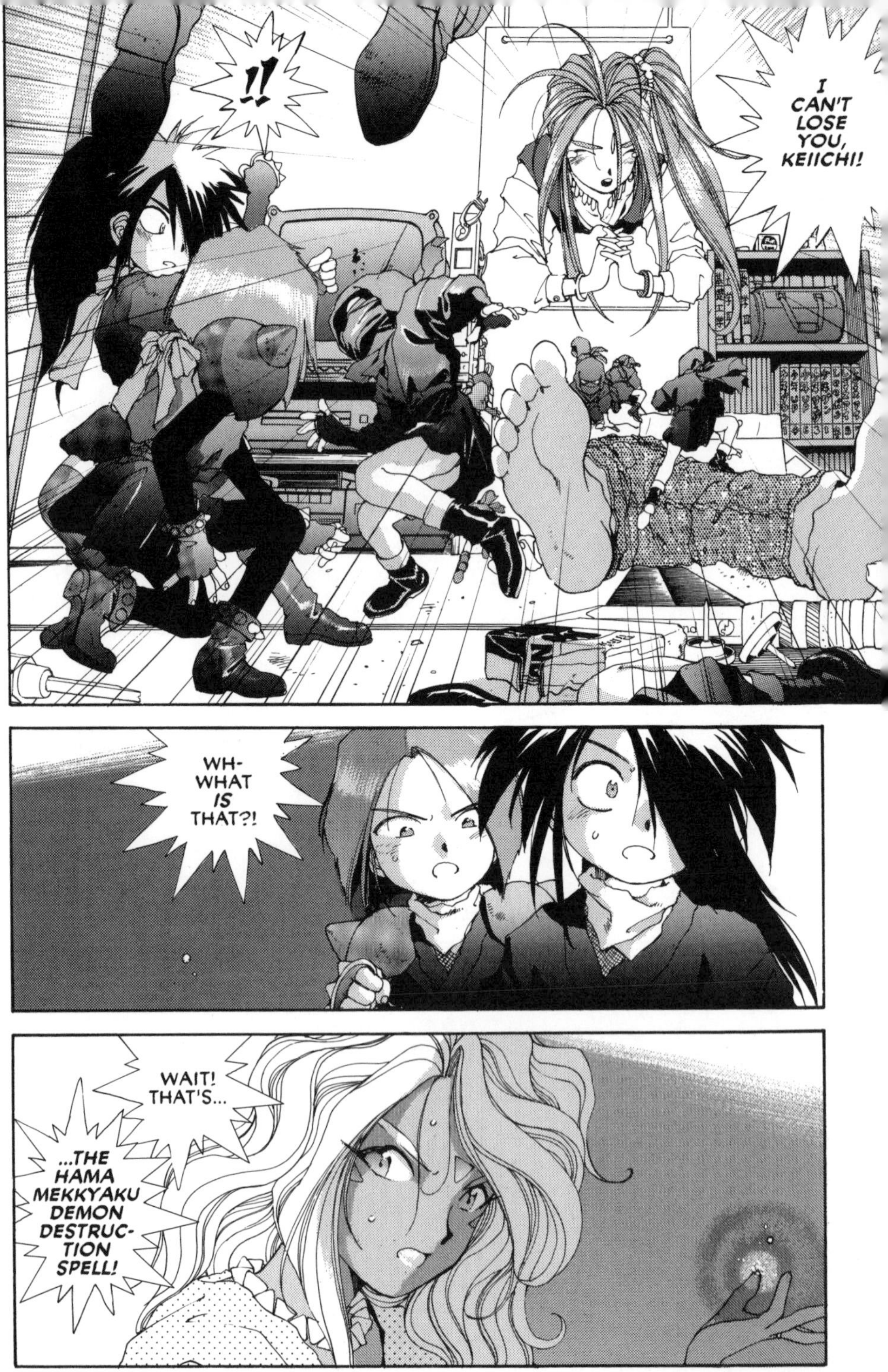
I CAN'T LOSE YOU, KEIICHI!
!!
WH-WHAT *IS* THAT?!
WAIT! THAT'S...
...THE HAMA MEKKYAKU DEMON DESTRUC-TION SPELL!

▲URD WAS ATTEMPTING *DENKO GEKISHO*: A LOWER-LEVEL SUMMONING SPELL.

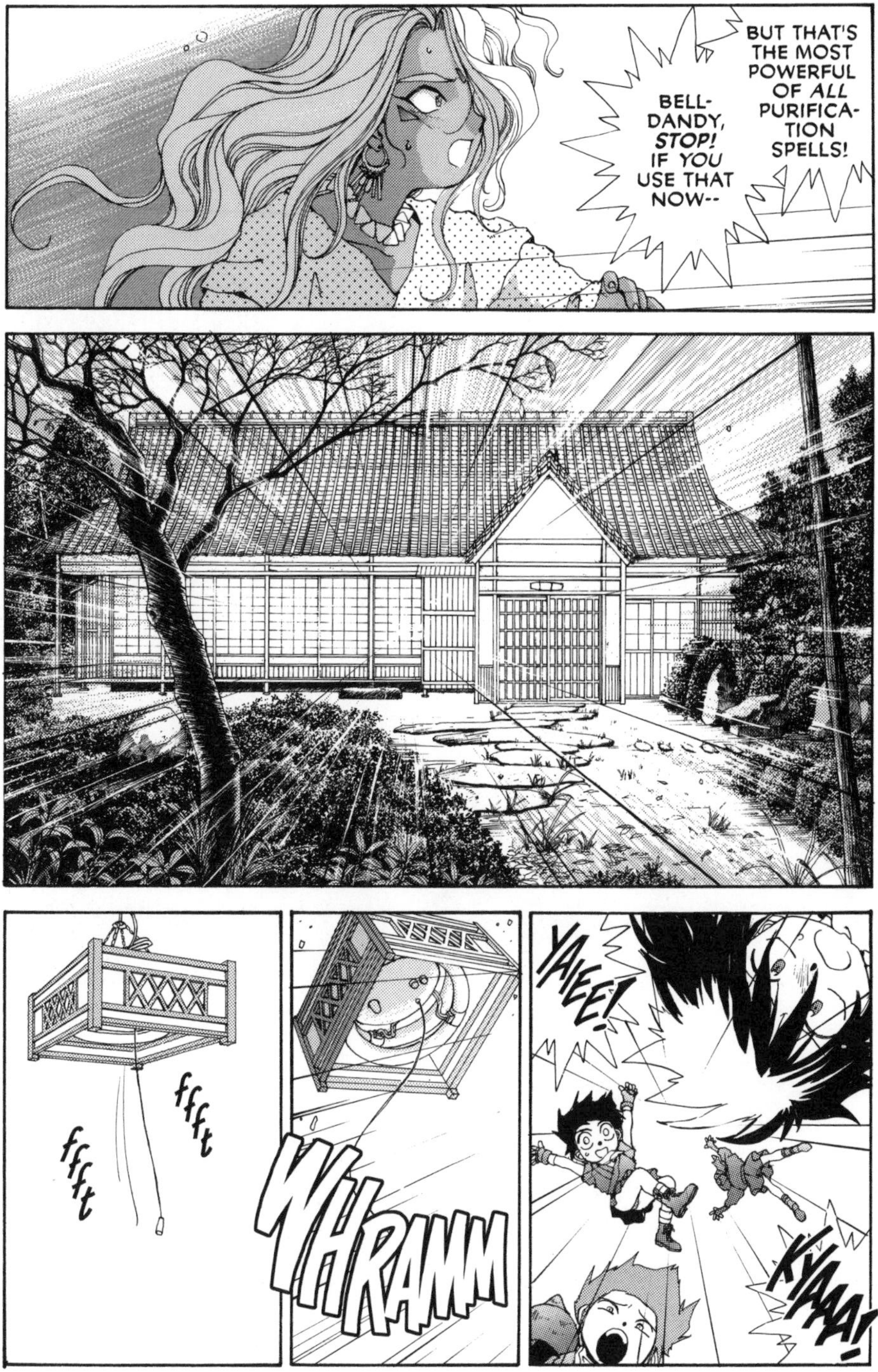
BUT THAT'S THE MOST POWERFUL OF *ALL* PURIFICATION SPELLS!
BELLDANDY, *STOP!* IF *YOU* USE THAT NOW--
YAIEE!
KYAAA!
WHRAMM
fffft
fffft

...AND AFTER YOU *PROMISED* YOU'D STOP USING HIGH-LEVEL SPELLS FOR THESE HUMANS...

YEESH...

YOU NEARLY *DID* LOSE YOUR LIFE, BELL-DANDY...

HER MOON BRACELET COULDN'T CHANNEL ALL THAT POWER... IT *BROKE* FIRST.

klak

NNNN

NNNN

DON'T SLEEP WITH SUCH A *SMILE* ON YOUR FACE, SISTER...

...YEAH, *YOU.*

uhh...

oog...

TO *ESCAPE* THOSE BONDS, EITHER WE CAN LEAVE THIS MORTAL PLANE FOREVER...

WE SHINOBI ARE BOUND ETERNALLY BY THE *LAW OF THE NINJA.*

...ARE YOU LITTLE IDIOTS PLANNING TO KEEP ON FIGHTING?

NOW, THEN...

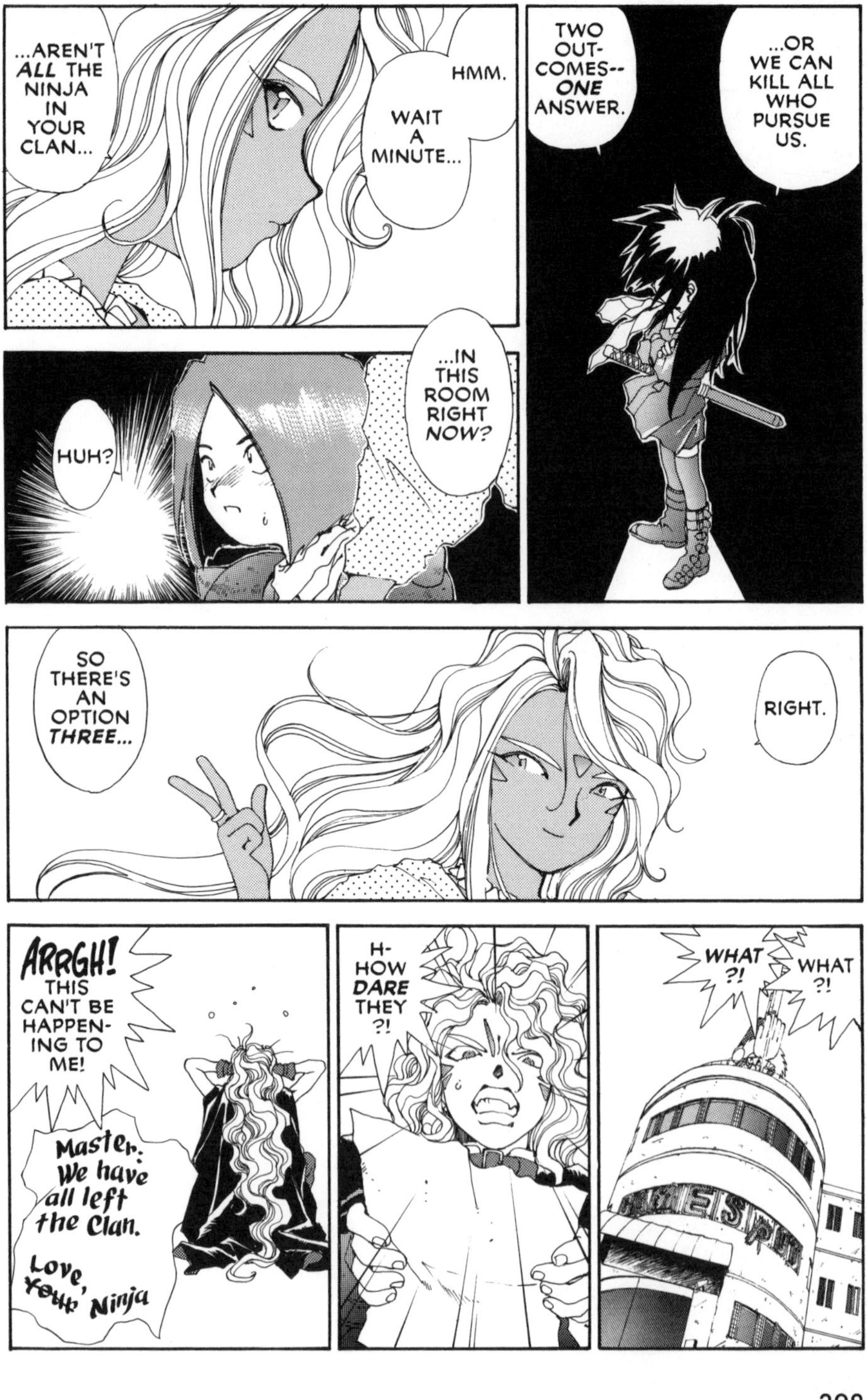

TWO OUT-COMES--ONE ANSWER.
...OR WE CAN KILL ALL WHO PURSUE US.
HMM.
WAIT A MINUTE...
...AREN'T ALL THE NINJA IN YOUR CLAN...
...IN THIS ROOM RIGHT NOW?
HUH?
SO THERE'S AN OPTION THREE...
RIGHT.
WHAT?!
WHAT?!
H-HOW DARE THEY?!
ARRGH! THIS CAN'T BE HAPPENING TO ME!
Master: We have all left the Clan.
Love, Your Ninja

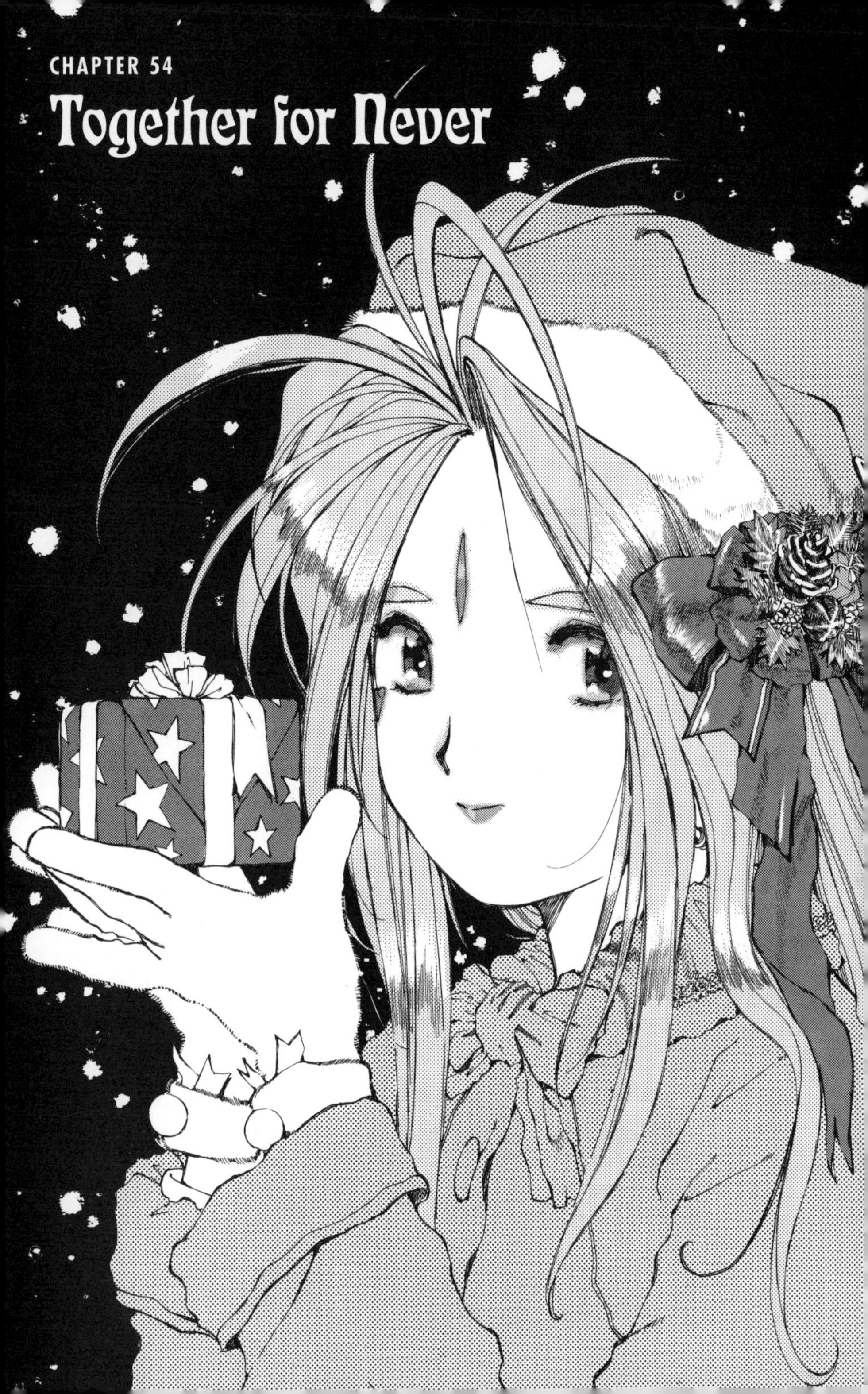
CHAPTER 54
Together for Never

THERE.

...THE SUDDEN WARMTH FROM BELLDANDY'S SCARF WHEN SHE PUT IT OVER ME...

I CERTAINLY DON'T WANT YOU TO CATCH COLD!

...IS IT REALLY JUST... THE POWER OF HER FEELINGS...?

YOU IDIOT!!

...THEY'RE AT IT AGAIN.

OR AT LEAST, THAT'S WHAT I WAS THINKING WHEN...

...I FEEL SUCH JOY THAT I MET MY LOVELY GODDESS.

WHEN I THINK THAT...

IT'S JUST THE SAME OLD MISCHIEF!

...TO BE *FOREVER* SEPARATED!

AARGH! IT MUST BE OUR DESTINY...

NOW AS FOR *ME*, I ACTUALLY *DO* HAVE A NEW POWER I'D LIKE TO SHOW YOU!

YEAH, BUT CHECK OUT HOW GREAT MY *LETTERING'S* BECOME.

POLAR ELECTRIC SHOCK WAVE--

SPPLSSHH

YOU KNOW, NOW THAT I THINK ABOUT IT, BELL AND I HAVEN'T BEEN ALONE TOGETHER FOR AGES.

YEESH...

STOP IT, *BOTH* OF YOU!

pffft! NEXT TIME MY BAKA STAMP WILL BE A MITE **TOO** STRONG!

FRESH AND **CLEAN** AS A WHISTLE!

yeahhhhh? WHO IS IT?

BRRIINGG

OR AGAIN... THAT'S WHAT I WAS THINKING...

...IT'S ...OUR LORD!

I AM THAT I AM.

twnch

WOW, LOOKS YUMMY!

REALLY...? I WONDER WHO IT WAS?

mnch THINK SHE'S ON THE PHONE WITH SOMEBODY.

DUN-NO.

HEY... WHERE'S URD?

404

KEIICHI...

!!

...MAKE SURE YOU RECORD *UGO UGO RUGO* FOR ME... OKAY...?!

glomp

YOU'LL HAVE YOUR LICENSE BACK IN *NO* TIME!

OH, THAT'S *WONDER-FUL*, URD!

SOME TEA...?

THE *BIG* BOSS HAS ORDERED ME HOME TO TAKE A REMEDIAL COURSE AT GODDESS SCHOOL.

THEY'VE GOT YGGDRASIL BACK ON-LINE.

YOU GOING SOME-WHERE?!

YAIEE! WH-WH-*WHAT?!* *WHY?!*

405

HOW WOULD YOU FEEL IF YOU WERE IN *MY* PLACE, HUH? *HUH?!*

AND I'LL BE LOCKED UP IN A *STINKY OLD SPELL SIMULATOR* FOR *HOURS!!*

...MAKE ME LISTEN TO THEIR *DULL* OLD LECTURES!

I DIDN'T SAY ANYTHING!

THEY'LL SHOW ME ALL THESE BORING OLD VIDEOS...

HA! THERE'S NOTHING *GOOD* ABOUT IT!

SO WHAT DO YOU *EXPECT?*

IT'S SUPPOSED TO BE *PUNISHMENT,* TOO, SIS.

huh?

YOU BETTER WIPE THAT SMILE OFF YOUR FACE, KID.

YOU'RE GOING BACK, TOO.

...NOW HE WANTS YOU TO DO THE PAPERWORK TO GET A *PROPER* EARTH TRAINING LICENSE.

OH, YEAH. HE SAYS HE THINKS BEING HERE IS HAVING A GOOD INFLUENCE ON YOU...

406

OUT OF THE BLUE...

IT'S JUST US TWO!!

'COURSE, YOU DON'T HAVE TO DO IT...IF YOU'RE READY TO GO BACK *PERMA-NENTLY*...

IN OTHER WORDS, YOU GOTTA LEGALIZE THE FUNKY WAY YOU GOT DOWN HERE IN THE FIRST PLACE.

GOOD GIRL!

I... I'LL DO IT...

WAIT A SEC... THAT MEANS...

HEY... YOU *ARE* A KID, REMEM-BER?!

THERE YOU GO, TREATING ME LIKE A KID AGAIN!

KEIICHI, MY LOVE...

BELL-DANDY, MY DARLING...

THANK YOU, uh, *LORD!*

Congratu-lations!!

DON'T!! JUST 'CAUSE YOU TWO ARE ALONE...

YOU *DARE* DO ANY-THING-- *GET* ME?!

HEY.

OKAY, OKAY!

GIVE *HIM* MY BEST!

...I'VE LEFT BANPEI IN SPECIAL ATTACK MODE.

AND JUST IN CASE...

urnk!

ENOUGH ALREADY, SKULD! GO, *GO!*

410

NO!
...SO WHY DON'T YOU SAY WHAT'S REALLY ON YOUR MIND?!

GET IT TOGETHER, MORISATO!! DID YOU WANT TO BE ALONE WITH HER JUST SO YOU COULD DRINK TWELVE CUPS OF TEA?!

BAM

BELL-DANDY!

Y-YES?

WE'RE, uh... YOU KNOW... FINALLY...

?

...

--!

...ALL ALONE--

WELL, OF COURSE!

DAMN... FORGOT ABOUT HIM.

SO...uh, COULD I...have some more TEA?

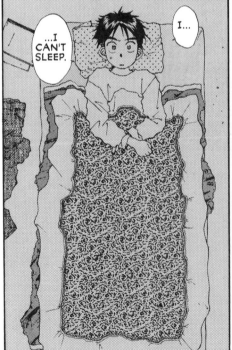

...I CAN'T SLEEP.

I...

GOOD NIGHT, KEIICHI.

GOOD NIGHT, BELLDANDY.

KEIICHI'S SHOP

...THE THOUGHT OF BEING ALONE WITH BELL-DANDY... WON'T EVEN LET ME *SLEEP?*

STARE STARE

Shiver Shiver

WHAT'S H-HAPPEN-ING? D-DON'T TELL ME...

...WAS SIMPLY CAUSED BY THE INGESTION OF TWENTY CUPS OF TEA.

GIVEN HIS CURRENT STATE OF MENTAL CONFUSION, THERE WAS NO WAY KEIICHI COULD COMPREHEND THAT HIS *INSOMNIA...*

THE NEXT DAY

HEY, MEGUMI!

IT'S BEEN HARD ENOUGH JUST STARTING A *GIRLS'* SOFT-BALL TEAM AT AN *ENGI-NEERING* SCHOOL...

NO WAY! NOT AFTER WE BOUGHT ALL THAT NEW GEAR?

...THEY'RE GONNA AX OUR FUND-ING!

HEY, IF OUR CLUB DOESN'T GET SOME MORE MEMBERS BY NEXT YEAR...

skrnch skrnch

413

LET ME STAY THERE TONIGHT.

MEGUMI. YOUR PLACE.

....AS SOON AS YOU'RE *ALONE*... YOU DON'T HAVE ANYTHING TO SAY TO HER.

IN OTHER WORDS...

RIGHT?

huh?

did you drink 20 cups of tea?

...BUT YOU'VE GOT A VERY SLIGHTLY STRANGE LOOK IN YOUR EYES, KEIICHI.

NOR-MALLY I'D SAY *YES*...

I SEE...

AND IT'S *PROBABLY* NOT MY PLACE TO BUTT IN. BUT YOU *KNOW*...

LOOK... I DON'T KNOW EXACTLY HOW THINGS ARE BE-TWEEN YOU GUYS.

AW, C'MON... YOU GOTTA BE KIDDING...

WAIT A SEC... KEIICHI... DON'T TELL ME THAT AFTER ALL THIS TIME, YOU STILL HAVEN'T... *DONE IT?!*

NO WAY !!

AFTER LIVING TOGETHER SO *LONG* ?!

YOU'RE *STILL* VIR-GINS?

HUH ?!

YEAH. SO HAVE YOU?

COME RIGHT TO THE POINT, DON'T YOU, SIS?

NO.

oh wow...

IS KEI-CHAN REALLY... A *MAN?*

OR ANY-WAY...

...THAT'S WHAT YOUR LITTLE SISTER THINKS.

...AFTER A CERTAIN POINT, IT'S OKAY TO SHOW YOUR LOVE WITH MORE THAN JUST A SHY SMILE.

SHUT UP!

...DON'T FORGET TO USE A--

AND *SINCE* YOU SEEM TO NEED A LITTLE ADVICE...

SO MAKE YOUR MOVE, BRO!

AND IF BELLDANDY'S A NORMAL GIRL, SHE'LL BE THINKING IT, TOO.

...IF BELLDANDY WAS A NORMAL GIRL...

STILL, SHE'S RIGHT...

IF SHE WAS JUST A GIRL LIKE ALL THOSE OTHER GIRLS...

416

BELL-DANDY
...?

NO, BELL-DANDY...

...BE STRONG.

YOU JUST HAVE TO HOLD OUT FOR TWO MORE NIGHTS...

URD WILL BE BACK THE DAY AFTER TOMOR-ROW.

I'M SORRY. I WAS... THINKING.

REALLY? YOUR FACE IS A LITTLE... RED...

OH...

ARE YOU OKAY? YOU DIDN'T SEEM TO HEAR ME...

WHOA!

OH ?!

Wobble

I'M SORRY. I...I STUMBLED...

THOSE EYES... SO FULL OF LONGING...

THIS FAINTLY BLUSHING FACE...

418

...BELL-DANDY!

oh...

BELL-DANDY'S FINALLY READY!

SHE *WANTS* ME!

um...

huh?

I-I'M FINE... I'M J-JUST... A LITTLE... DIZZY...

BELL-DANDY! WHAT--

AAH!

hahh

WE'RE GOING HOME RIGHT NOW!

YOU ARE *NOT* FINE!

...BUT I DON'T THINK YOUR EARTH MEDICINE WILL WORK ON ME.

THANK YOU...

HERE. TAKE THESE.

GACK! YOU'RE OFF THE SCALE!

BELL-DANDY'S USUALLY SO STRONG... SHE NEVER LETS ANYTHING SHOW.

JUST LIE DOWN...

OF COURSE... AND A DOCTOR WON'T BE ABLE TO DO ANYTHING EITHER!

I NEVER THOUGHT I'D SAY THIS... BUT-- IF ONLY URD WAS HERE!

haa

IF SHE'S LIKE THIS...IT MUST BE SOMETHING REALLY BAD...

420

SHE'S GOT A WHOLE *ROOM* FULL OF MEDICINE!

URD! OF *COURSE!*

...ANY OF THEM WOULD ACTUALLY BE... *POISON-OUS?*

BUT I DON'T SUP-POSE...

...YEAH...I GUESS SHE DOESN'T WANT ANY-ONE FOOLING AROUND WITH HER STUFF...

...ONLY *SHE* CAN UNDER-STAND THESE LABELS...

SIDE EFFECTS MAY INCLUDE (CLASSIFIED) (SECRET) AND (WOULDN'T YOU LIKE TO KNOW)!

uh...

URD'S ROOM

....

...KIND OF CODE IS *THIS?*

chirp=?

WHAT...

Shine+

groan+

423

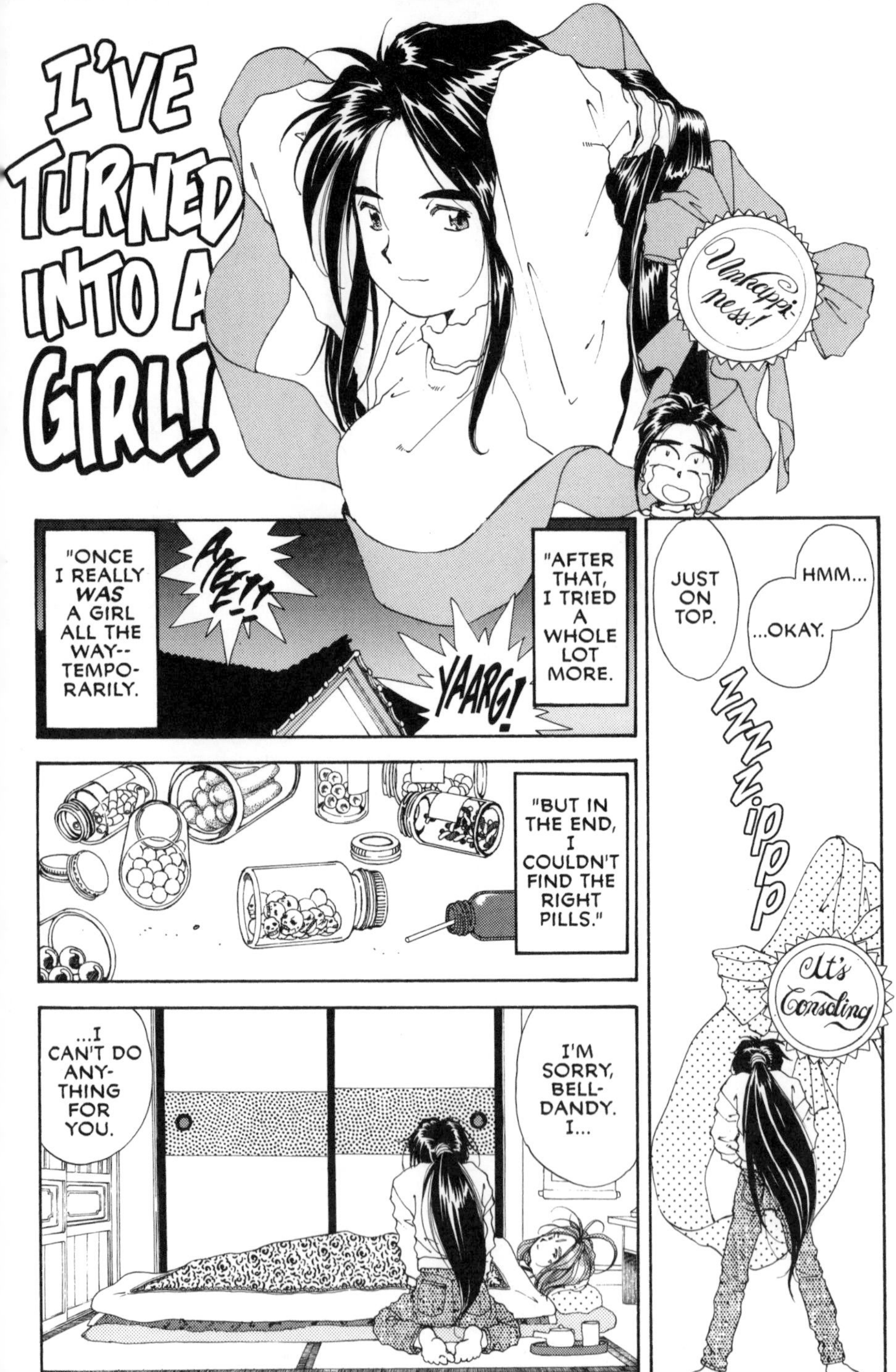
I'VE TURNED INTO A GIRL!
Unhappiness!
"ONCE I REALLY *WAS* A GIRL ALL THE WAY-- TEMPORARILY.
AIEE!!
YAARG!
"AFTER THAT, I TRIED A WHOLE LOT MORE.
"BUT IN THE END, I COULDN'T FIND THE RIGHT PILLS."
I'M SORRY, BELLDANDY. I...
...I CAN'T DO ANYTHING FOR YOU.
HMM...
...OKAY.
JUST ON TOP.
It's Consoling

426

um... KEIICHI?!

IS THAT YOU, URD?!

URD...?

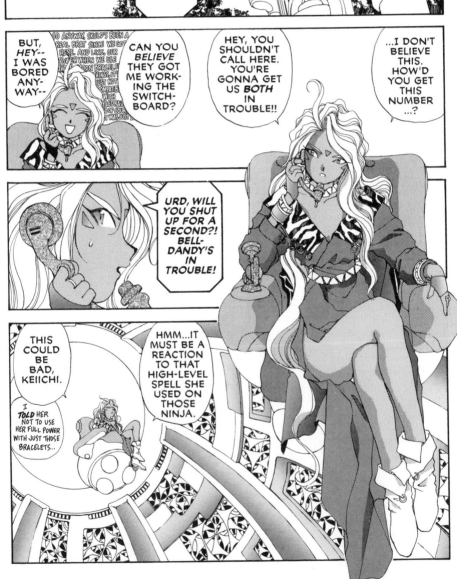

BUT, HEY-- I WAS BORED ANY-WAY--

SO ANYWAY, SKULD'S BEEN A REAL BRAT SINCE WE GOT HERE. AND LIKE, OUR POWER WHEN WE USE THE SAILOON BRACELETS... IT'S JUST NOT COMPATIBLE WITH YGGDRASIL, OF COURSE... IT WAS JUST Y...

CAN YOU *BELIEVE* THEY GOT ME WORK-ING THE SWITCH-BOARD?

HEY, YOU SHOULDN'T CALL HERE. YOU'RE GONNA GET US *BOTH* IN TROUBLE!!

...I DON'T BELIEVE THIS. HOW'D YOU GET THIS NUMBER ...?

URD, WILL YOU SHUT UP FOR A SECOND?! BELL-DANDY'S IN TROUBLE!

THIS COULD BE BAD, KEIICHI.

I *TOLD* HER NOT TO USE HER FULL POWER WITH JUST THOSE BRACELETS...

HMM...IT MUST BE A REACTION TO THAT HIGH-LEVEL SPELL SHE USED ON THOSE NINJA.

428

HEY, WAIT... GAVE ME LONG *HAIR*, AND...

WHEN IT'S ALL MELTED, POUR IT INTO A CAPSULE, AND--

THEN, USE A MATCH... IT'S GOTTA BE A SINGLE WOODEN MATCH, RIGHT, AND--

NEXT, MIX A RATIO OF 2:3:1.5 OF--

OKAY, LISTEN UP. I'LL TEACH YOU THE CURE. FIRST, ONE PART EACH OF--

YOU CAN'T JUST POP THE INGREDIENTS LIKE WASABI PEAS...

...THIS IS ALCHEMY, KEIICHI... *OCCULT KNOWLEDGE* IS REQUIRED-- *duhhh...*

YES, YES, I HAVE TWO MYSELF. YOU TOOK THEM WITHOUT *PROCESSING*, MORON?!

GAVE ME, UH, *GAVE ME...*

HEY! KEIICHI ...?!

HELLO? HELLO ...?

sigh ANYWAY, THAT SHOULD HOLD HER UNTIL I GET BACK.

AH, WELL-- I GUESS HE'LL BE OKAY.

kchak

STILL... HE *IS* AN AMAZING GUY.

HE MUST BE THE FIRST PERSON WHO EVER *TRIED* CALLING HERE AND ACTUALLY GOT THROUGH...

COOL. I DIDN'T EVEN KNOW IT WOULD DO THAT TO HUMANS.

BETTER MAKE A NOTE OF IT...

YOU'RE TRYIN' TO GET RID OF ME AGAIN! I *HATE* THAT!!

STOP IGNORING ME!

IT'S NONE OF YOUR NEVER- MIND. RUN ALONG AND GET YOUR LICENSE CHANGED, KID.

WHAT'S GOING ON? WHO WAS THAT?

430

SHE... SHE PASSED OUT...

LOOK-- I'VE GOT SOME NICE MEDICINE FOR YOU...

BELL-DANDY ...?

I'M SORRY, BELLDANDY, BUT I'VE GOT TO GIVE IT TO YOU SOME-HOW...

...PLEASE FORGIVE ME!

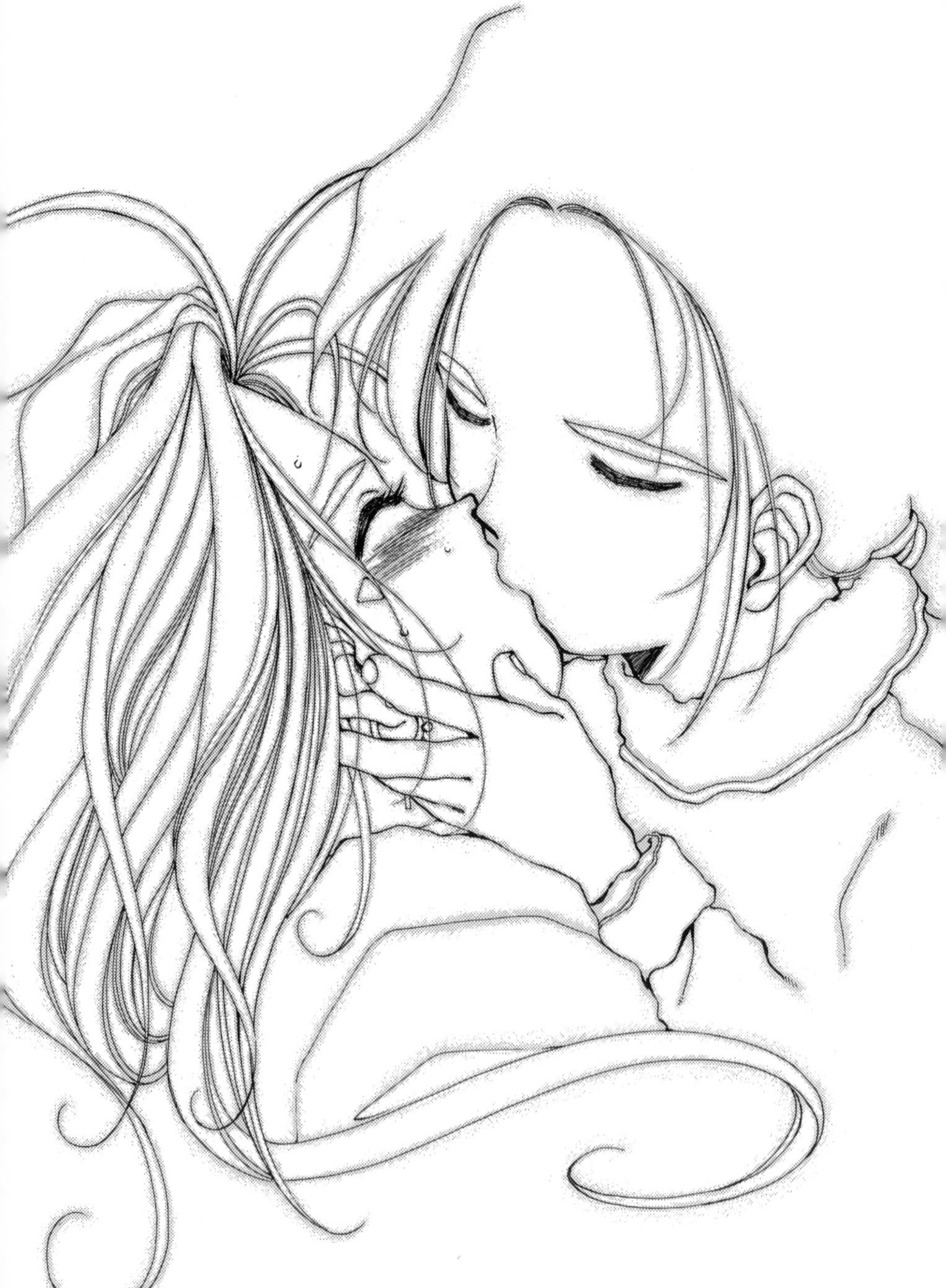

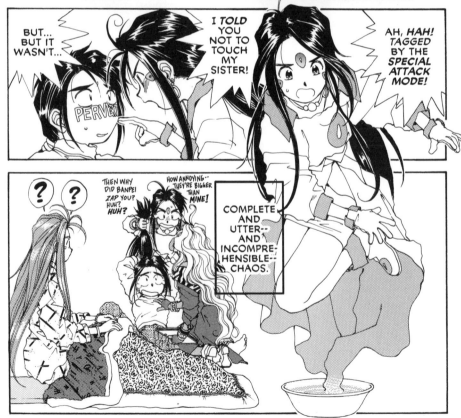

434

OH MY GODDESS!

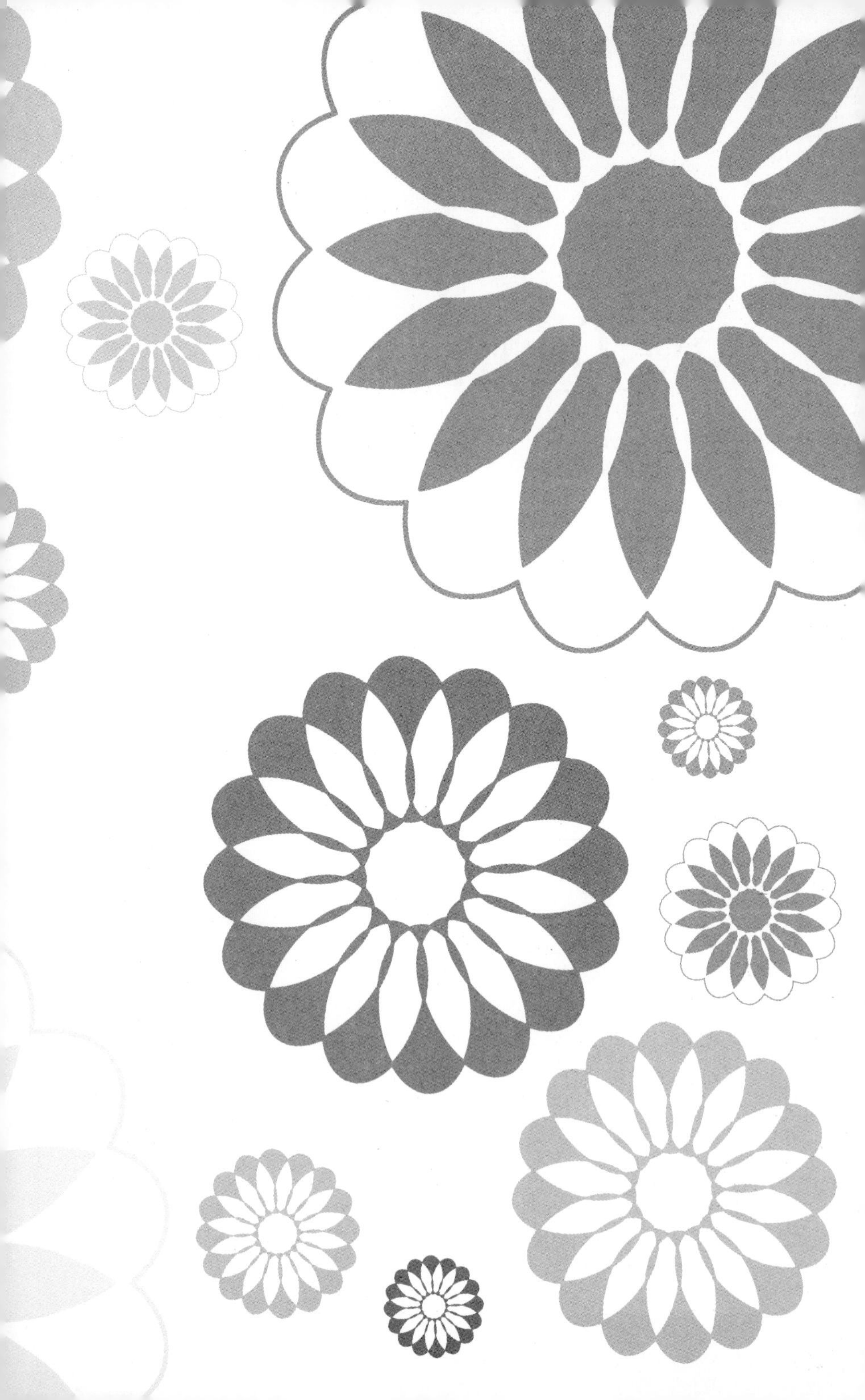

437

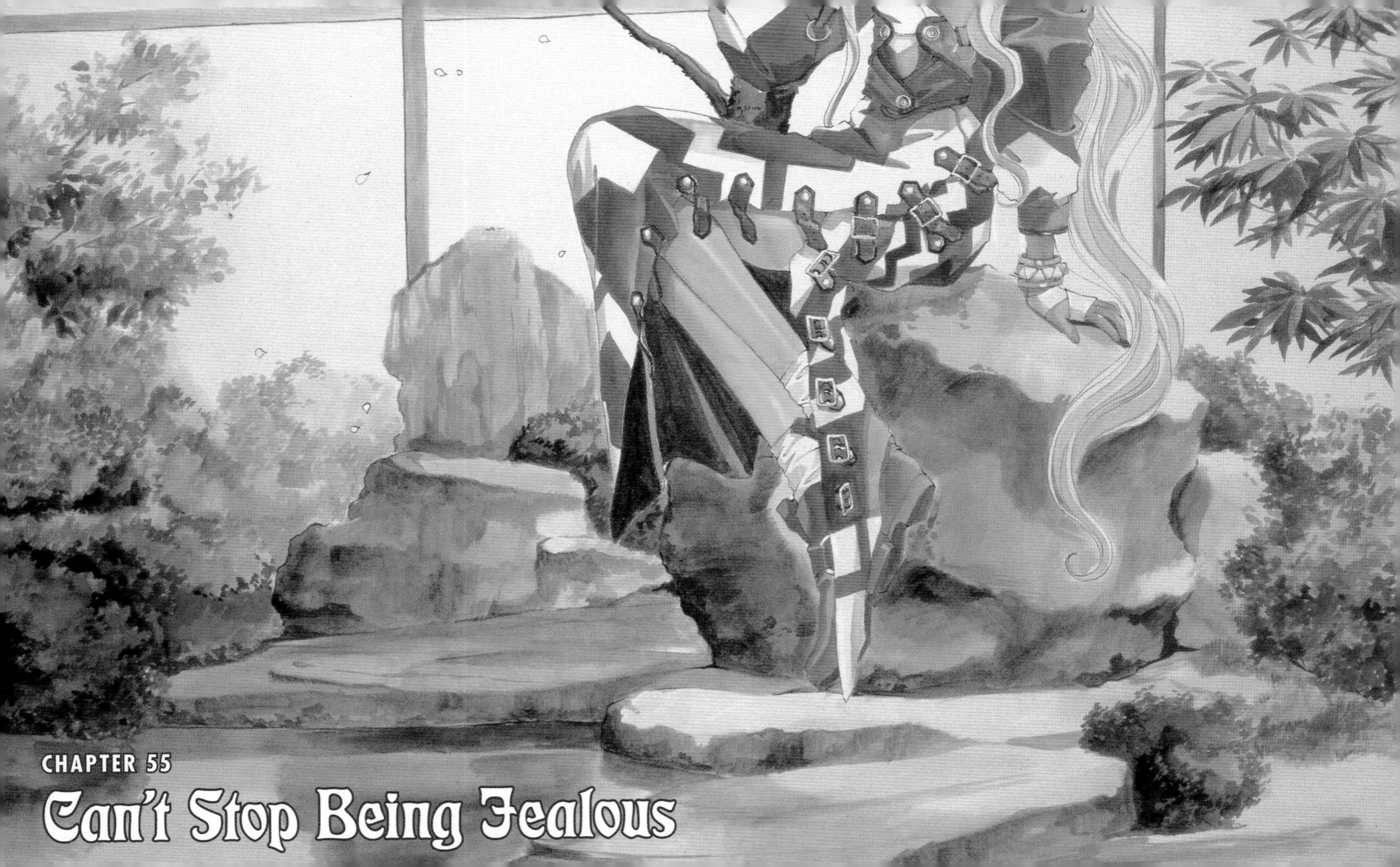
CHAPTER 55
Can't Stop Being Jealous

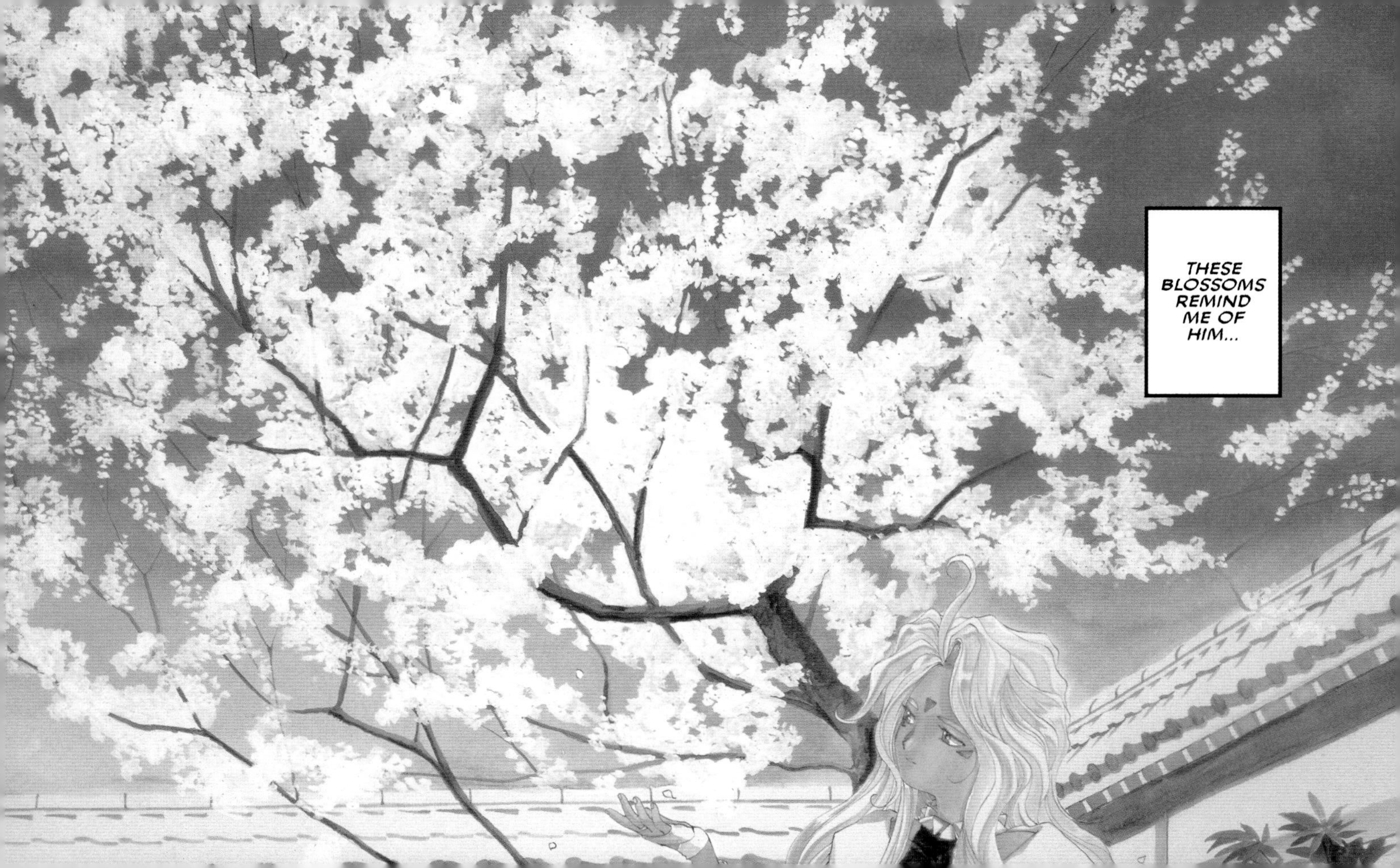
THESE BLOSSOMS REMIND ME OF HIM...

WELL, UH... YOU'VE GOT A POINT THERE...

YEAH, *SURE!* IT'S *NOT* LIKE YOU WENT INTO MY ROOM AND TOOK *MY* STUFF WITHOUT *MY* PERMISSION, RIGHT?!

C'MON-- IT WAS *YOUR* STUPID MEDICINE THAT DID THIS TO ME!

...IT'S NOT *THAT* FUNNY.

DON'T LAUGH...

OH, BUT IT IS! IT *IS* THAT FUNNY!

snort #2

SHE USES A DIFFERENT SCHOOL OF MAGIC.

I'M SORRY, KEIICHI. I CAN'T REVERSE URD'S MEDICINE.

...FOR THE REST OF MY *LIFE* ...?

M-MAYBE... I'LL BE THIS WAY...

DON'T TELL ME...

...AND SKULL DRESS-ES YOU FUNNY!!

HEY! YOU'RE UGLY...

442

443

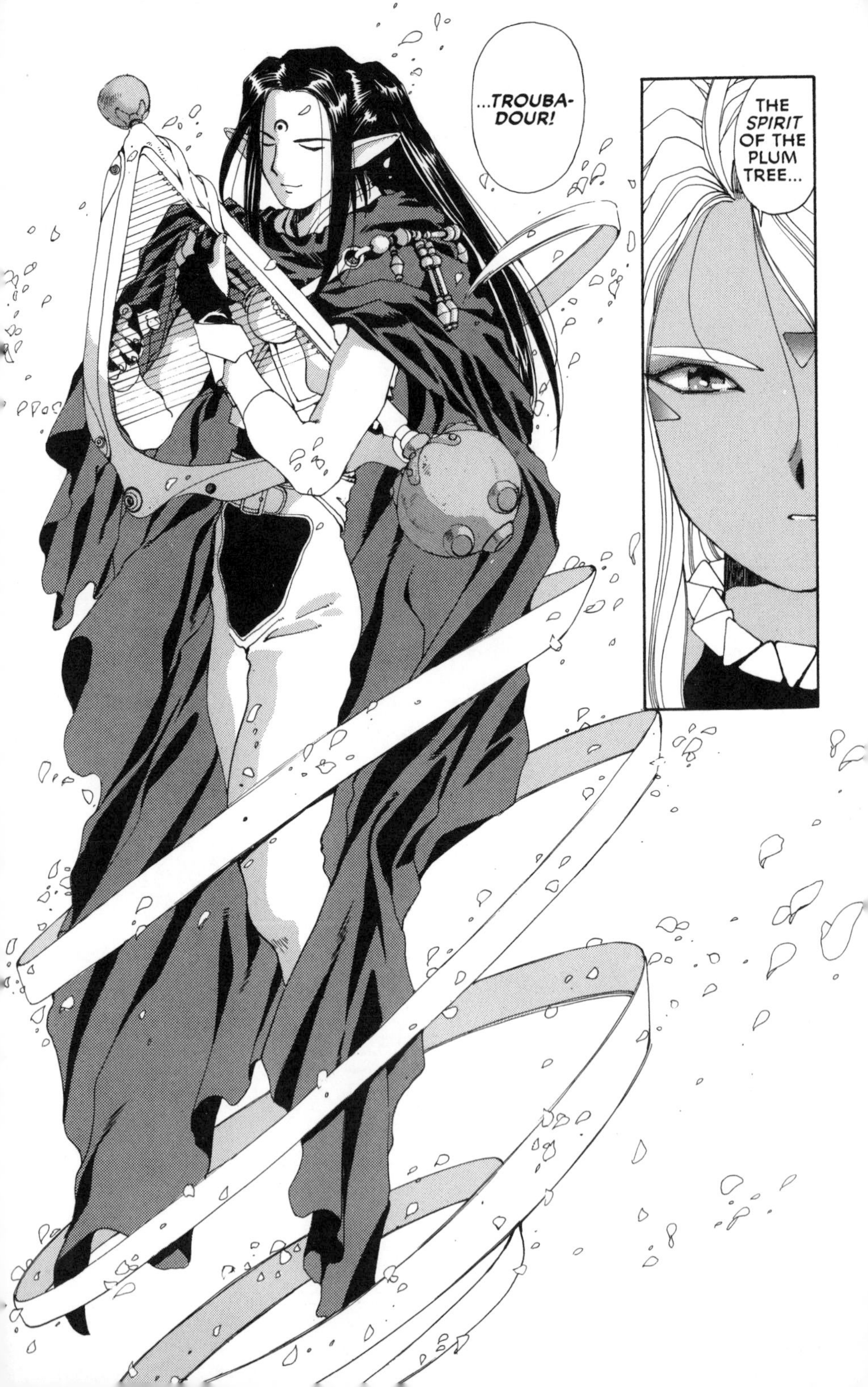
THE *SPIRIT* OF THE PLUM TREE...
...TROUBA-DOUR!

I HAVE BEEN SEARCHING FOR YOU...

...URD.

HE'S A *PLUM TREE* SPIRIT... URD'S OLD LOVE.

W-WHO IS *THAT*?!

BUT WHY WOULD HE SHOW UP *NOW*, AFTER ALL THIS TIME...?

AFTER ALL, HE WAS THE ONE WHO LEFT HER...

THAT IS WHY I HAVE COME TO THIS DISTANT AND BLEAK DIMEN-SION...

...TO ONCE AGAIN SHARE MY LOVE WITH YOU.

I AM HERE...

445

?

...THEN WHAT ABOUT MY *ANTIDOTE?!*

um... YOU DON'T SUPPOSE HE'S GOING TO TRY TO GET BACK TOGETHER... *TAKE HER AWAY...?*

I DON'T KNOW WHAT YOU THOUGHT YOU COULD ACHIEVE BY SHOWING UP HERE.

PLEASE... JUST GO AWAY.

NO WAY I'M GOING BACK TO SOMEONE WHO REJECTED ME ALREADY.

BUT, SORRY-- FORGET IT. I'M NOT THAT DESPERATE.

WELL, FOR A *START...* YOUR LOUSY *SONGS!*

TWANGG BLANGG

WHAT PART OF MY HEART DOES SHE HATE, MY HONEY BABY?!

WHY OHHH WHY?! WHY?!

...WHY DID I *RUN* TO HIM AS SOON AS HE APPEARED? AS IF HE'D *EVER* CHANGE...

WHAT AN IDIOT I AM...

...TO MAKE *INSECTS* GROW INSIDE THE GUY'S BODY UNTIL THEY *BURST OUT OF HIM.*

SO WHAT TROUBA-DOUR DID, SEE... HE USED HIS POWERS...

I'LL GET AROUND TO IT-- JUST NOT RIGHT NOW.

YEAH, YEAH, ANTI-DOTE.

HEY, URD... ABOUT THE...

♪ BUGGY BUGS ♪ ON THE MARCH...

♪ BUGS BUGS BUGGY BUGS

...

OH WHOA WHOA... URD, MY URD... WHILE I'VE BEEN GONE... YOU'VE GONE SO COLD... LIKE FIVE ZEPTOKELVINS... AND BABY THAT'S COLD...

BACK WHEN WE WERE STILL TOGETHER, THERE WAS THIS JUNIOR GOD WHO TRIED TO HIT ON ME...

BECAUSE THAT ORON-MAY IS INCREDIBLY *EALOUS-JAY...* THAT'S WHY.

B-B-BUT... WHY *NOT?!*

hmm...

COME TO THINK OF IT, URD... I HEARD A RUMOR YOU'RE LIVING WITH SOME MAN.

WELL, HE'D PROBABLY DO SOMETHING VERY CREATIVE.

IF *HE* FOUND OUT THERE WAS A *MAN* LIVING UNDER THE SAME ROOF WITH ME...

YES... *NOW* I SEE IT! THIS MAN! *HE* STOLE YOUR LOVE FROM ME!

UM...   HEY!

giggle!   *tee hee!*

AIN'T NOBODY *HERE* BUT US *GIRLS!*

AW, C'MON! ANOTHER *MAN?* WHERE ?!

THERE'S SOMETHING *FUNNY* ABOUT THAT...

IT'S BEEN BOTHERING ME SINCE I GOT HERE...

448

449

LET'S NOT GET BACK TOGETHER, AND SAY WE DID.

♪ URD'S YUMMY, YUMMY, YUMMY... I GOT LOVE IN MY SPIRITUAL, ELDRITCH TUMMY... ♪

...THEN THERE'S *NOTHING* TO STAND BETWEEN US!

WELL, ALL RIGHT. SO LONG AS THERE'S NO *MAN* IN YOUR LIFE...

YOU'VE ONLY MADE THINGS *WORSE!*

HE'S DECIDED TO *STAY!*

NOW LOOK WHAT YOU'VE DONE, URD!

KEIICHI'S SHOP

THEN I GUESS... I HAVE TO STAY LIKE THIS UNTIL HE LEAVES, HUH?

DON'T WORRY-- I WON'T LET HIM DO THAT TO YOU!

I MEAN, IT'S *THAT,* OR GIANT BUGS CRAWLING OUT OF MY BODY.

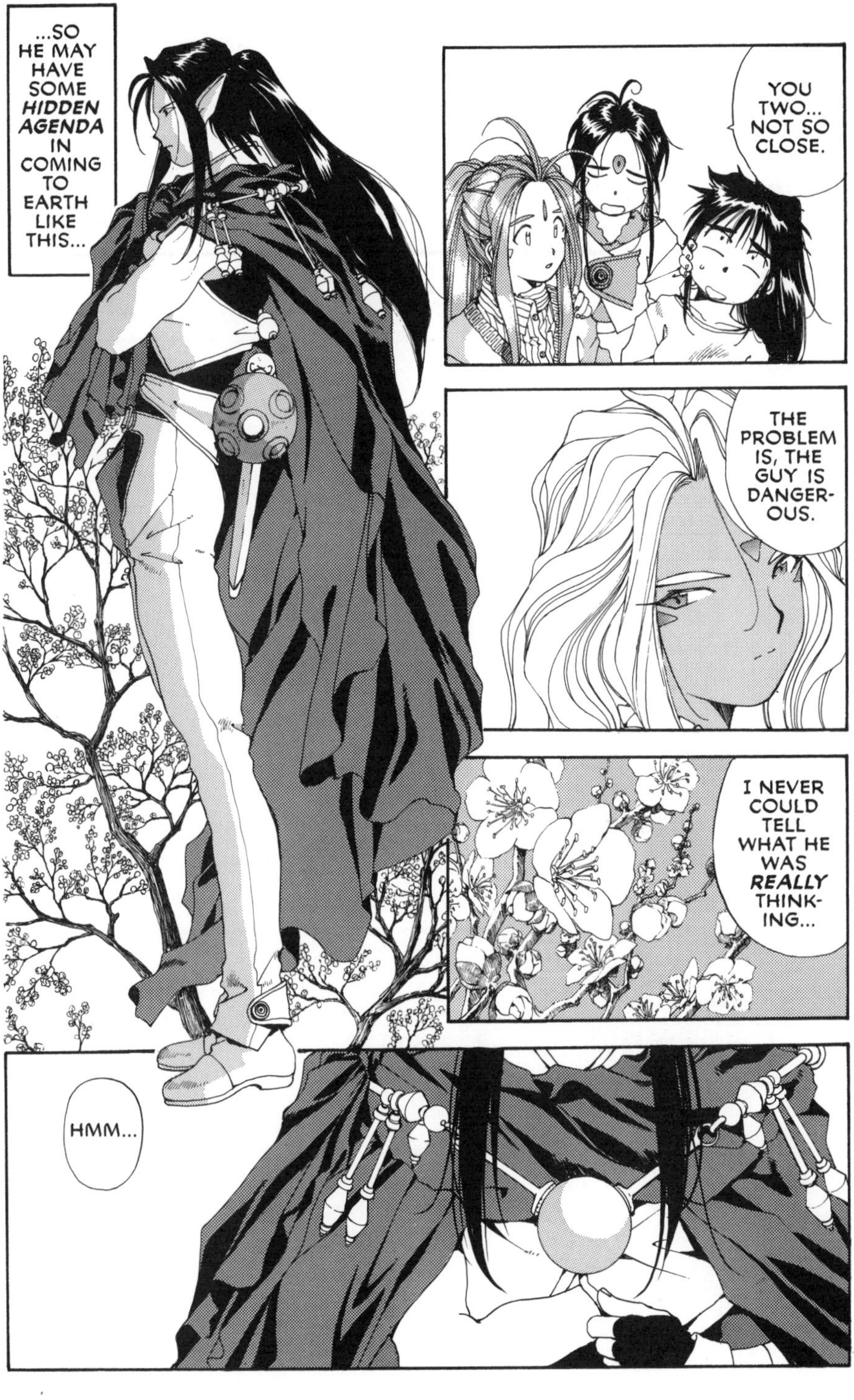
YOU TWO... NOT SO CLOSE.
THE PROBLEM IS, THE GUY IS DANGER-OUS.
I NEVER COULD TELL WHAT HE WAS *REALLY* THINK-ING...
...SO HE MAY HAVE SOME *HIDDEN AGENDA* IN COMING TO EARTH LIKE THIS...
HMM...

THE SCROLL OF GOLDEN VERSE! *THE BUSH WARBLER SUMMONING SONG!*

...IT WAITS BEYOND THIS SCROLL'S *FINAL SEAL--* AWAITS ITS MOMENT TO *SPRING TO LIFE!*

A LIFELONG DREAM RESTS NOW IN THE PALM OF MY HAND...

...WHEN TOUCHED BY *A GODDESS'S TEARS OF LOVE!*

WAITING TO *OPEN...*

452

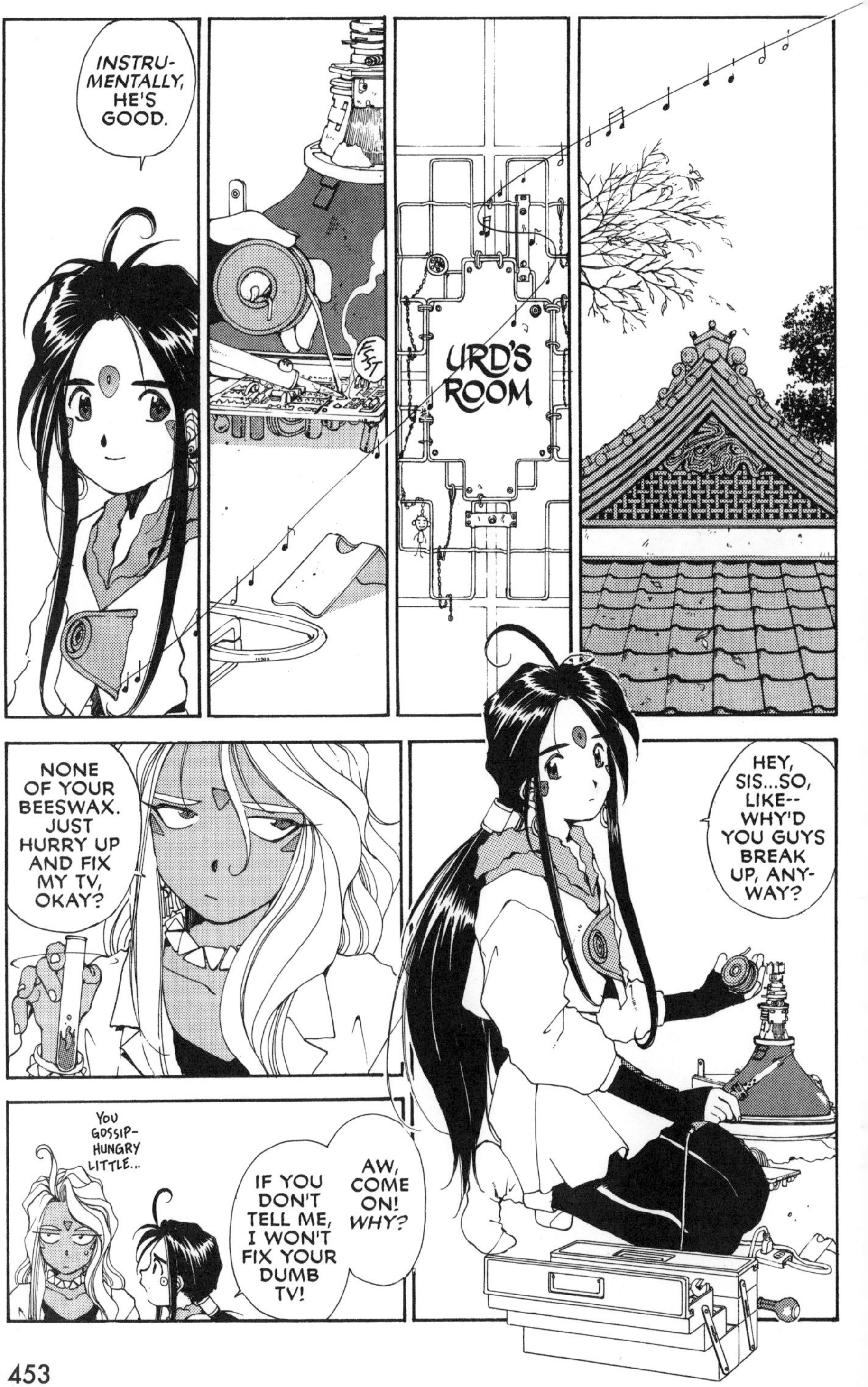
URD'S ROOM
INSTRU-MENTALLY, HE'S GOOD.
HEY, SIS...SO, LIKE-- WHY'D YOU GUYS BREAK UP, ANY-WAY?
NONE OF YOUR BEESWAX. JUST HURRY UP AND FIX MY TV, OKAY?
AW, COME ON! *WHY?*
IF YOU DON'T TELL ME, I WON'T FIX YOUR DUMB TV!
YOU GOSSIP-HUNGRY LITTLE...

ALTHOUGH... HE SEEMS A LITTLE DIFFERENT NOW...

I COULDN'T *STAND* IT. I WANTED HIM TO HAVE EYES FOR ME ALONE.

NOTHING MORE.

HE CHOSE HIS DREAMS OVER ME, THAT'S WHY.

UM...URD? ARE YOU REALLY THINKING OF GOING AWAY WITH HIM?

....

ONCE SOMEONE LEAVES ME, I COULDN'T CARE *LESS* ABOUT HIM.

DIDN'T YOU HEAR WHAT I SAID?

454

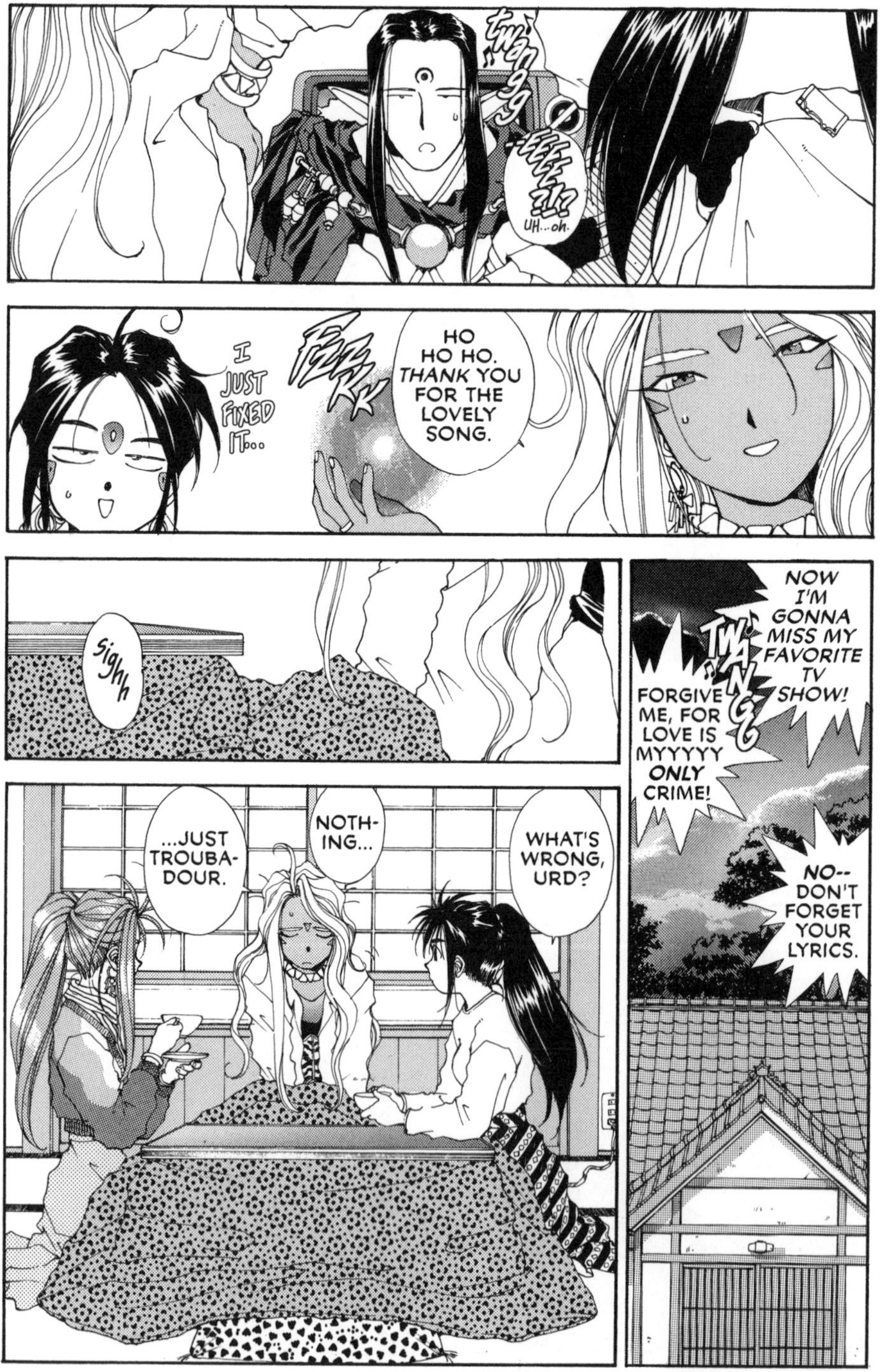
twangg
EEEEE?!!?
UH...oh.
HO HO HO. THANK YOU FOR THE LOVELY SONG.
I JUST FIXED IT...
NOW I'M GONNA MISS MY FAVORITE TV SHOW!
TWANG
FORGIVE ME, FOR LOVE IS MYYYYY ONLY CRIME!
NO-- DON'T FORGET YOUR LYRICS.
sighh
WHAT'S WRONG, URD?
NOTH-ING...
...JUST TROUBA-DOUR.

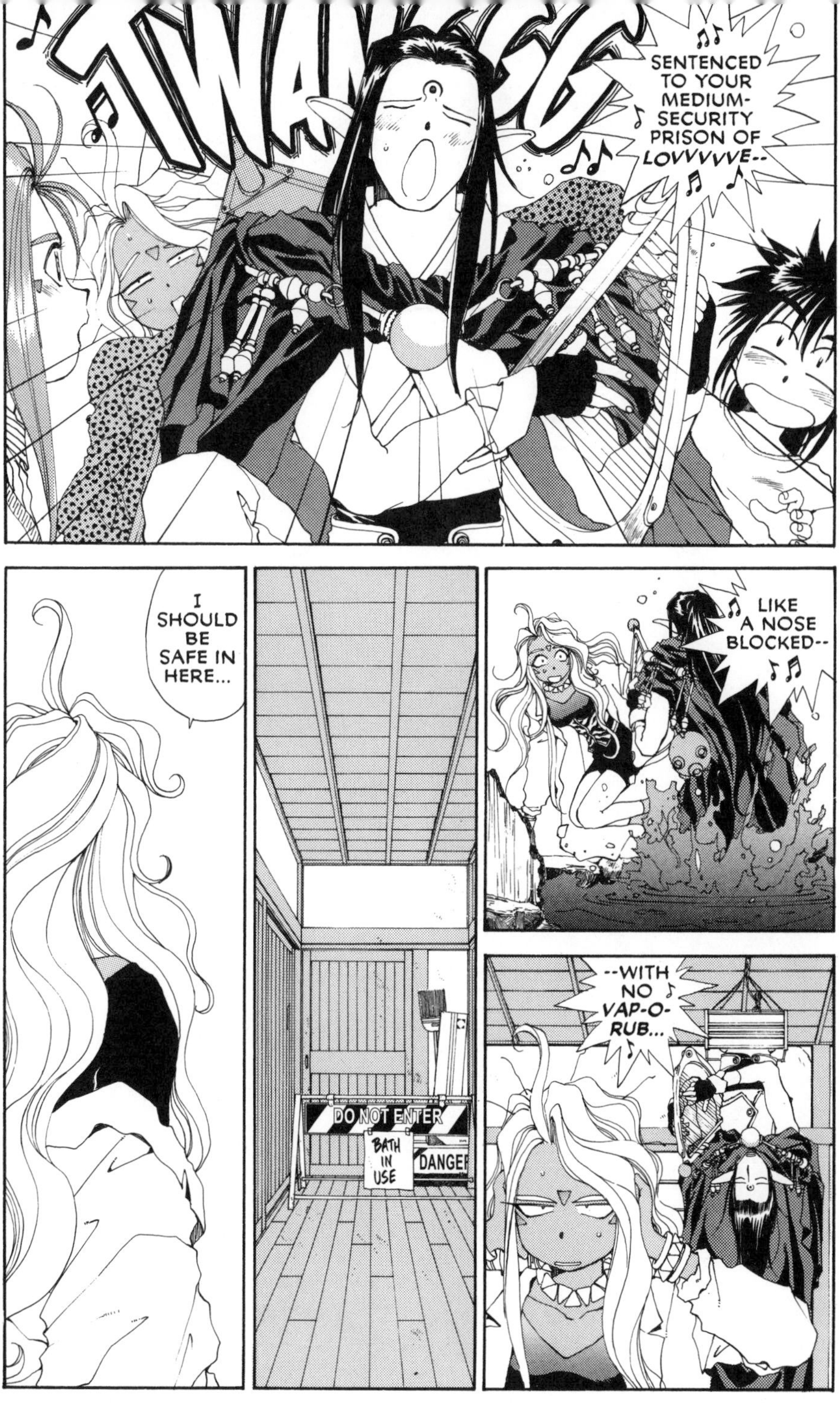
SENTENCED TO YOUR MEDIUM-SECURITY PRISON OF LOVVVVVE--
LIKE A NOSE BLOCKED--
--WITH NO VAP-O-RUB...
DO NOT ENTER
BATH IN USE
DANGER
I SHOULD BE SAFE IN HERE...

458

460

462

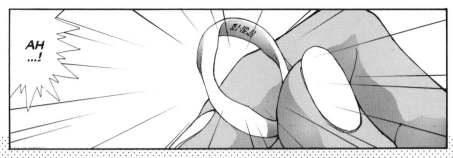

AH
...!

BACK
WHEN
WE FIRST
STARTED
GOING
OUT...

THE
TWO
OF
US...

...EX-
CHANGED
GIFTS.

463

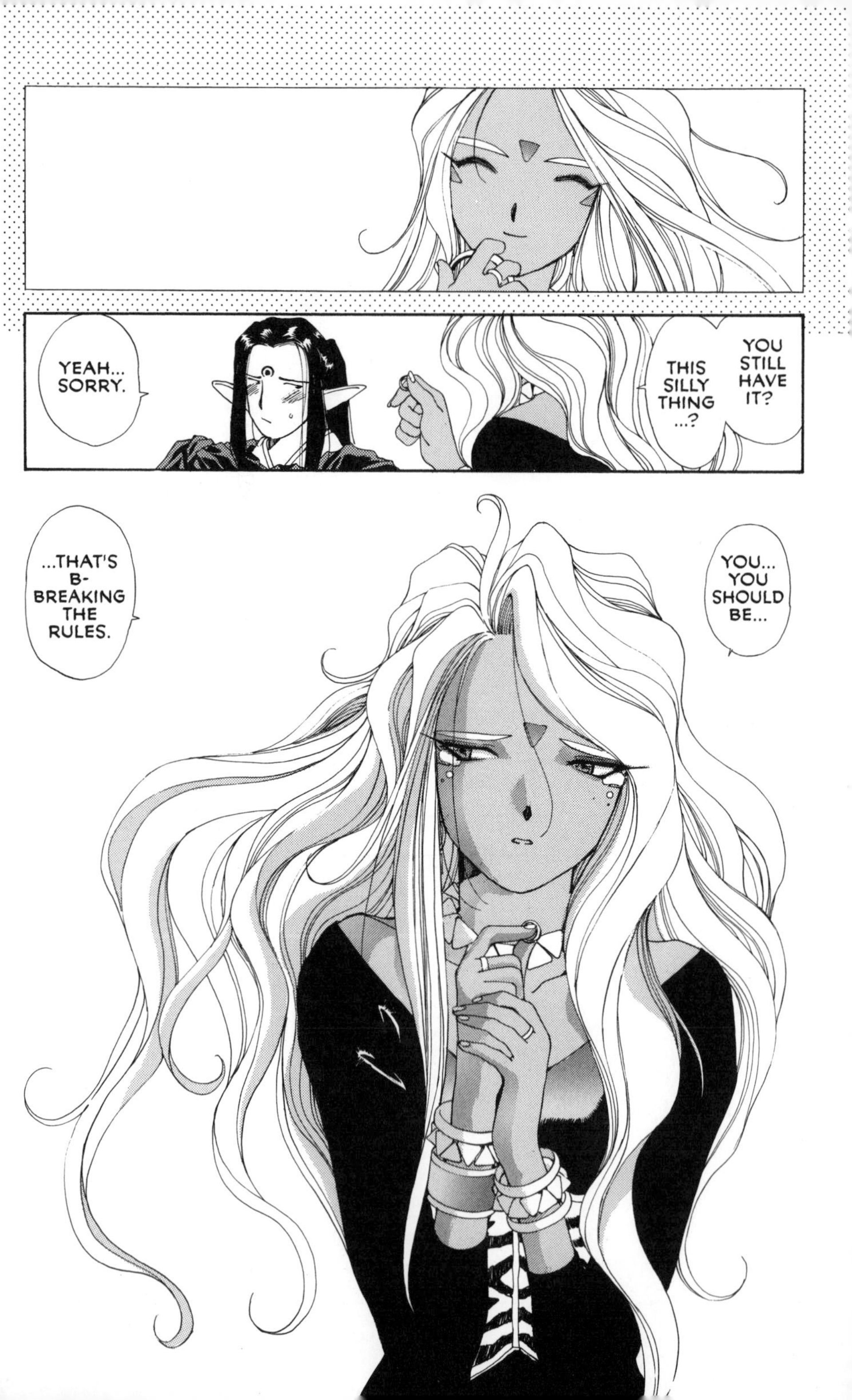
YOU STILL HAVE IT?
THIS SILLY THING ...?
YEAH... SORRY.
YOU... YOU SHOULD BE...
...THAT'S B-BREAKING THE RULES.

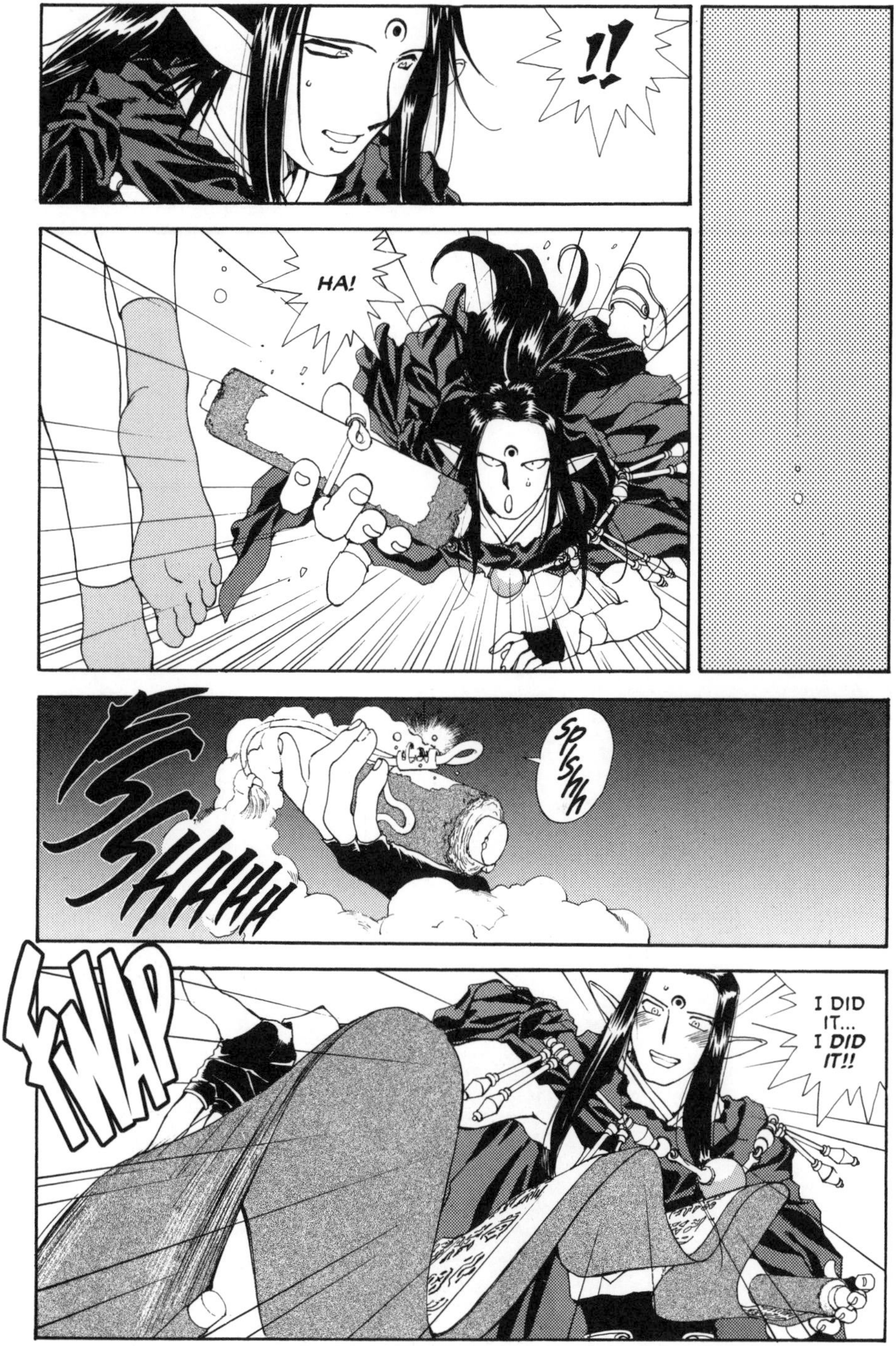
!!
HA!
SPISHH
SSSHHHH
I DID IT... I DID IT!!
FWAP

uh-oh

WH... WHAT DID YOU *DO?*

HUH ...?

...THIS *SCROLL* HERE...

UM, SEE...

I BELIEVE YOU JUST PLAYED WITH MY EMOTIONS ...?

...TO TAME IT...TO BID THAT IT SING ON MY COMMAND... IT'S MY *QUALIFYING TEST* TO *MOVE UP* AS A PLUM SPIRIT..

...TO FIND THE GOLDEN BUSH WARBLER...

AS YOU ARE AWARE, IT HAS BEEN MY *QUEST*...

ACK!!

Depth Bomb Descent!

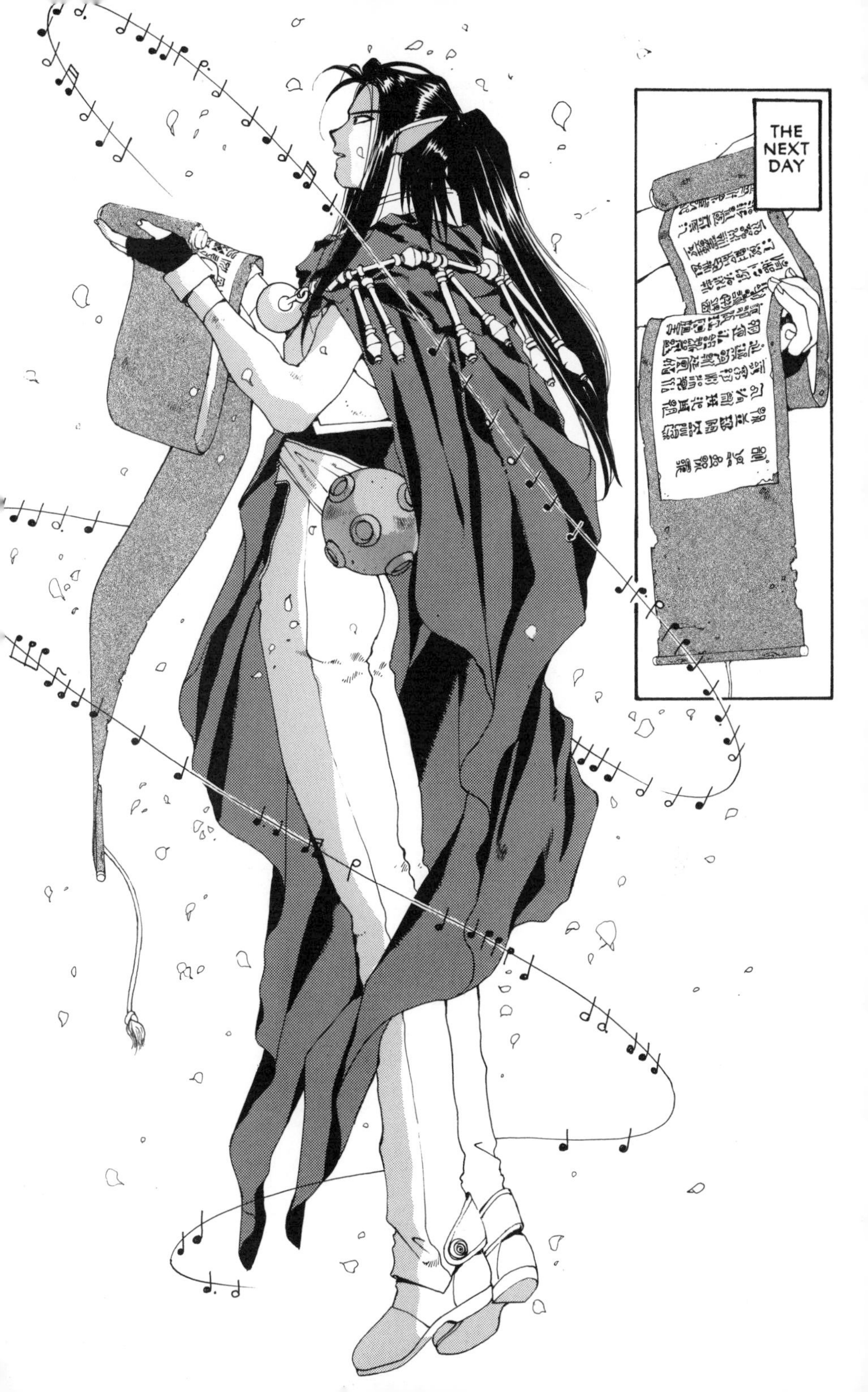
THE NEXT DAY

469

470

I SHALL PUR- SUE!

IT'S GONE-- **WITH** THE SCROLL!

CURSES!

OH... GO ON.

...

HERE... YOU FORGOT THIS.

...BUT YOU KNOW-- I WOULDN'T **WANT** A TROUBADOUR WHO'S FORGOTTEN HOW TO DREAM.

IT HURTS THAT YOU'D CHOOSE SOME SILLY BIRD OVER **ME...**

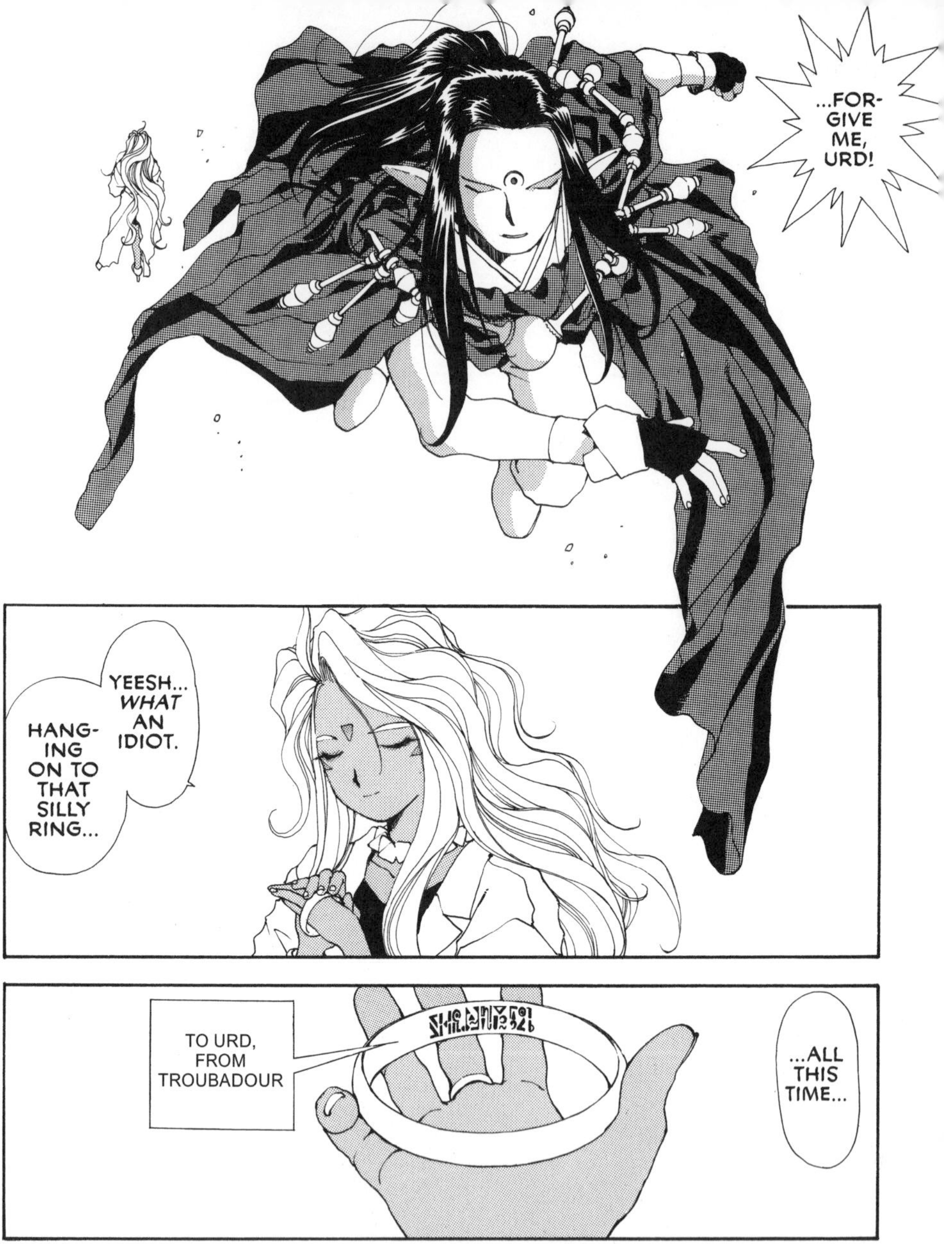
...FOR-GIVE ME, URD!
YEESH... *WHAT* AN IDIOT.
HANG-ING ON TO THAT SILLY RING...
...ALL THIS TIME...
TO URD, FROM TROUBADOUR
UH, ANTI-DOTE? PLEASE?
OOPS! I FORGOT...

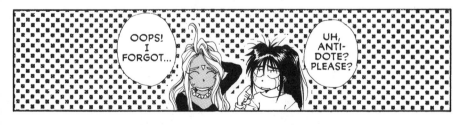

CHAPTER 56

It's Lonely at the Top

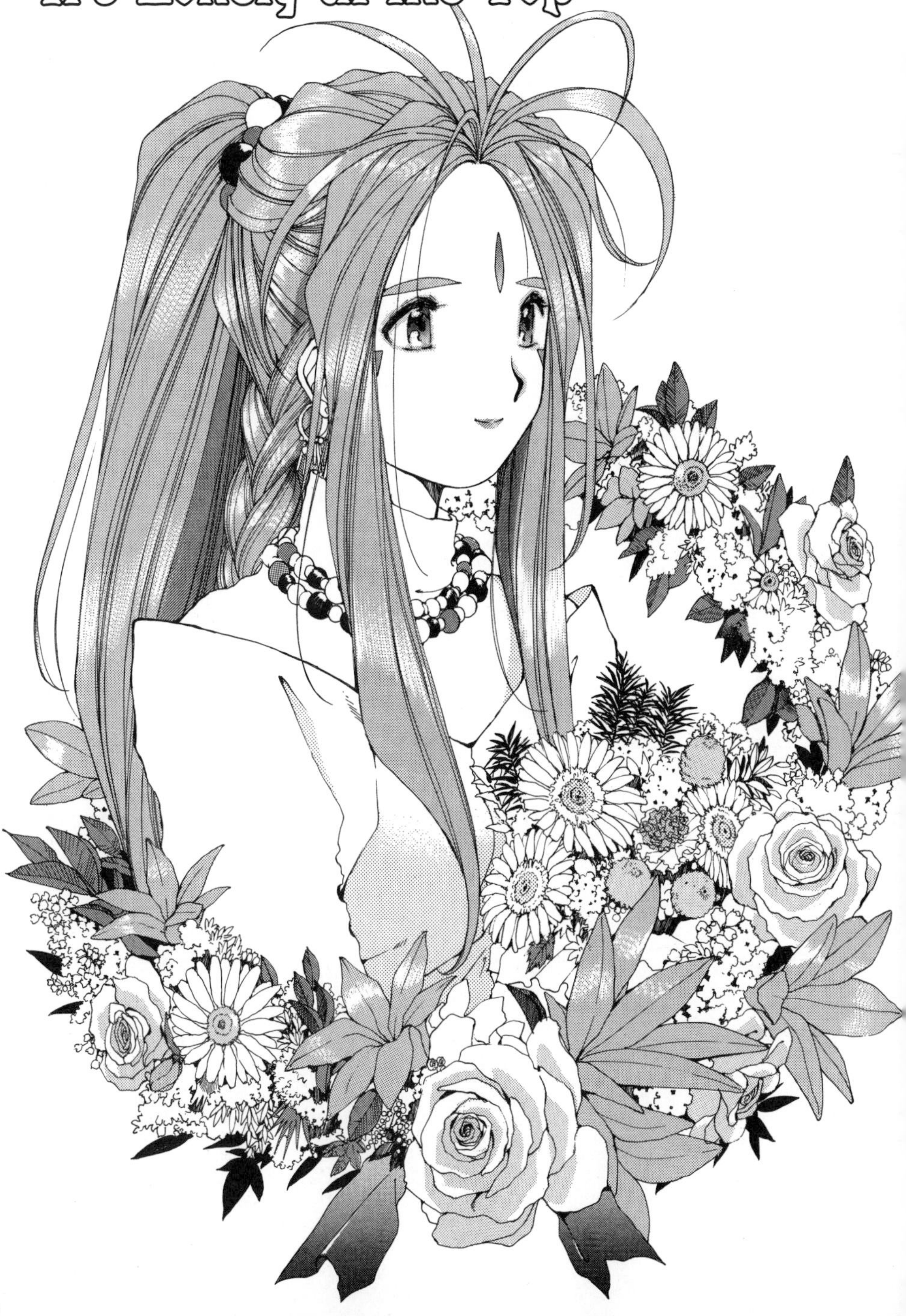

...THEY'RE **BOTH** OUT SICK?!

WHAT?! TAMIYA AND OTAKI...

...AND WHO'S GOING TO WANT TO DO **THAT?**

SO WE NEED A TEMPORARY CLUB DIRECTOR, RIGHT?

THEY SAID THERE WAS SOME KIND OF RACE COMING UP IN JUST **TWO WEEKS!**

NOW WHAT ARE WE SUP-POSED TO DO?!

HEY! **WAIT!**

HAIIIIII

...SAY "HAI!!"

ALL THOSE IN FAVOR OF **KEIICHI MORI-SATO...**

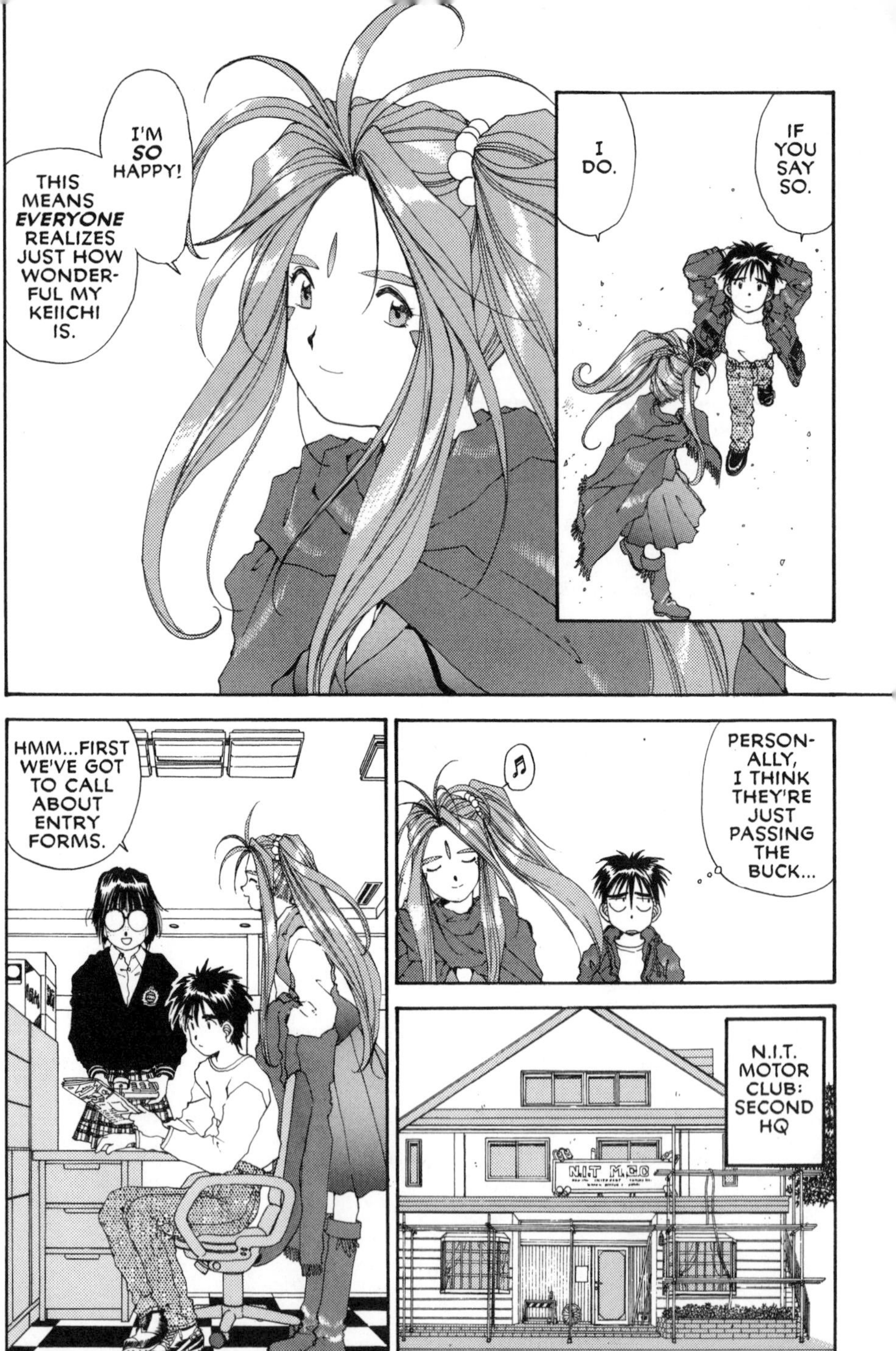
IF YOU SAY SO.
I DO.
I'M *SO* HAPPY!
THIS MEANS *EVERYONE* REALIZES JUST HOW WONDERFUL MY KEIICHI IS.
PERSONALLY, I THINK THEY'RE JUST PASSING THE BUCK...
N.I.T. MOTOR CLUB: SECOND HQ
HMM...FIRST WE'VE GOT TO CALL ABOUT ENTRY FORMS.

ACK!

Hill Climb in Japan

エントリー受付中!! ☎00-0-0000

EH?!

Designed by Haba-Kichi Co.

LET'S SEE... WHERE'S THEIR PHONE NUMBER...

Hill Climb in Japan

WHAT'S THE MATTER, SIR?

IT'S A H-HILL CLIMB ?!

Designed by Haba-Kichi Co.

WELL... NOT EXACTLY...

THEY DON'T QUITE GET IT...

PUTT PUTT

SOUNDS EASY!

WHEE!!

PICNIC ♥!

DRIVING UP A HILL... HOW PLEAS- ANT.

A HILL- CLIMBING RACE ...? WHAT FUN!

...AND YOU TRY TO MAKE IT IN *ONE WILD CHARGE!* IT'S *INSANE!*

A *HILL CLIMB* MEANS TACKLING A GRADE AS STEEP AS *SEVENTY* OR EVEN *EIGHTY* DEGREES...

...AND SPECIAL PADDLE-TREAD TIRES...

EVEN WITH A SUPER-EXTENDED SWING-ARM...

--CART-WHEELING BACKWARD DOWN AN EIGHTY-DEGREE SLOPE HUNDREDS OF FEET TO THE BOTTOM!

...LOTS OF PEOPLE NEVER MAKE IT... AND FLIP THEIR *BIKES* OVER--

IF YOU'RE WATCHING, MAYBE.

EEEK!!

WHEE!

TEA TIME!

BONK HUD

THAT SOUNDS TOTALLY *AWE-SOME!*

TAMIYA... OTAKI... WHAT A *SURPRISE*... YOU'RE *IDIOTS!!*

OH, *NO!!* THE DEADLINE WAS *YESTERDAY!!*

WELL, THEM'S THE MULTIPLE FRACTURES-- *I MEAN, BREAKS...*

UM, HI... I'D LIKE TO APPLY FOR THE RACE...

HELLO, HILL CLIMB JAPAN HEADQUARTERS!

IT'S *CLOSED* TO NEW ENTRIES?!

WHAT?!

...IT'S STILL *MY* RESPONSIBILITY TO DO SOMETHING ABOUT IT.

AS LONG AS I'M ACTING CLUB HEAD...

...CALM DOWN...!

...

DIRECTOR...? *I'LL* GO TALK WITH THEM.

...GUESS I'LL GO ASK IN PERSON. ALL I CAN DO IS TRY TO PERSUADE THEM...

IT'S OFTEN BETTER TO DELEGATE, SIR.

HUH? OH, NO, NO. I'M IN CHARGE, SO--

THE LEADER SHOULD STAY AT HQ AND MANAGE THINGS.

DON'T FORGET-- THERE'S MORE THAN *ONE* MEMBER OF THE AUTO CLUB, SIR.

...AS LONG AS THERE'S EVEN A *CHANCE* WE CAN MAKE IT, HEY?

GUESS WE BETTER GIVE IT THE OLD COLLEGE TRY...

HEH... GOOD THINK-ING, SORA.

YOU BETTER START BUILDING THE BIKE, OKAY?

OF COURSE!

WITH EVERY-ONE HELPING, IT DIDN'T TAKE LONG BEFORE...

YOU BET!

...SEE WHAT WE'VE GOT FOR USABLE PARTS.

AND YOU, OGURA...

SUZUKI! WATA-NABE!

YES, SIR!

YOU DIG UP A FRAME!

481

UM...

...WE REALIZED JUST HOW LAME WE ARE.

AND, *MIRACLE OF MIRACLES,* A *MOSTLY* COMPLETE KAWASAKI 750 TWO-STROKE *"WIDOW-MAKER"* ENGINE.

WELL, OKAY... *TWO* BOXES.

A BOX OF ASSORTED... DOO-HICKEYS?

A 50cc *MINIBIKE* WITHOUT AN *ENGINE?*

OH, YEAH?! WHAT?! *WHERE*?!

SIR! THERE *IS* ONE MORE MACHINE, SIR!

...ARE WE SUPPOSED TO DO WITH *THIS* PILE OF JUNK?!

WH... WHAT...

WE CAN'T USE *THAT*, YOU LUMMOX!

IT COST US A *FORTUNE!*

OUR *NITRO-FUELED GSX DRAG RACER*, SIR!

...WE SLAP ON AN EXTENDED BOX FRAME SWINGARM... HMM...

THEN, AS PART OF THE FRAME MODS...

WELL, OKAY... IF THIS IS WHAT WE'VE *GOT*... WE'LL MOUNT THE ENGINE INTO A HYPER-REINFORCED MINIBIKE FRAME...

...

...

...

SO...ARE YOU SURE NONE OF YOU HAVE ANY EXTRA PARTS LYING AROUND SOME-WHERE...?

NEVER SAY THAT.

THAT'S *IT*, SIR-- YOU'RE STARTING TO THINK LIKE TAMIYA AND OTAKI!

484

WHOA... LOOKS LIKE WE'VE GOT EVERY-THING WE *NEED*...!

I THINK I SAW A SET OF EXPANSION CHAMBERS AT THE SALVAGE YARD...

I GOT SOME ALUMINUM HANDLE-BARS AT HOME...

THERE WAS A SET OF CARBS, TOO...

I GOT SOME PIPE...

SIR ...?

MAYBE IT'LL BE BETTER IF WE CAN'T ENTER THE RACE AFTER ALL...

...ALTHOUGH GOD ONLY KNOWS WHAT KIND OF WEIRD BIKE WE CAN MAKE OUT OF THIS STUFF.

...OR INCREDI-BLY *UN*-SO!

...IF I'M INCREDI-BLY LUCKY...

I'M NOT SURE...

WE'RE IN THE RACE, SIR.

HOW'D YOU GET THEM TO DO IT?

WELL, ANY-WAY... THANKS, SORA!

I... I...

S-SIR...

...THEY MISTOOK ME FOR A *JUNIOR-HIGH-SCHOOL STUDENT!*

DID THOSE *SCUM* AT N.I.T. MAKE YOU RUN THEIR ERRANDS? I MEAN, HOW OLD ARE YOU? *TWELVE?* WELL, *OKAY*-- BUT YOU TELL THEM FROM ME THEY BETTER NOT EXPLOIT KIDS ANYMORE...

DID THOSE *SCUM* AT HILL CLIMB JAPAN MAKE HER...

OH, SIR, IT WAS T-TERRI-BLE...

...huh?!

Sob!

GEE, SIR! YOU ALWAYS KNOW *JUST* WHAT TO SAY!

YEAH!

JUST THINK... THAT PURE, CHILDISH FACE OF YOURS GOT US INTO THE RACE, RIGHT?

AWW... DON'T CRY, SORA.

486

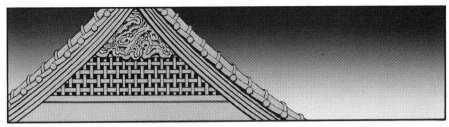

I'LL PUT THE TEA ON!

YOU KNOW... IT REALLY WEARS YOU OUT--DOING SOMETHING YOU'RE NOT USED TO.

I CAN'T WAIT TO RELAX.

K-POP!

SO THEY PUT YOU IN CHARGE OF THE NEXT RACE, EH, LOVER BOY?

ASK ME IF I CARE...

CONGRATU- LATIONS, KEI- CHAN!

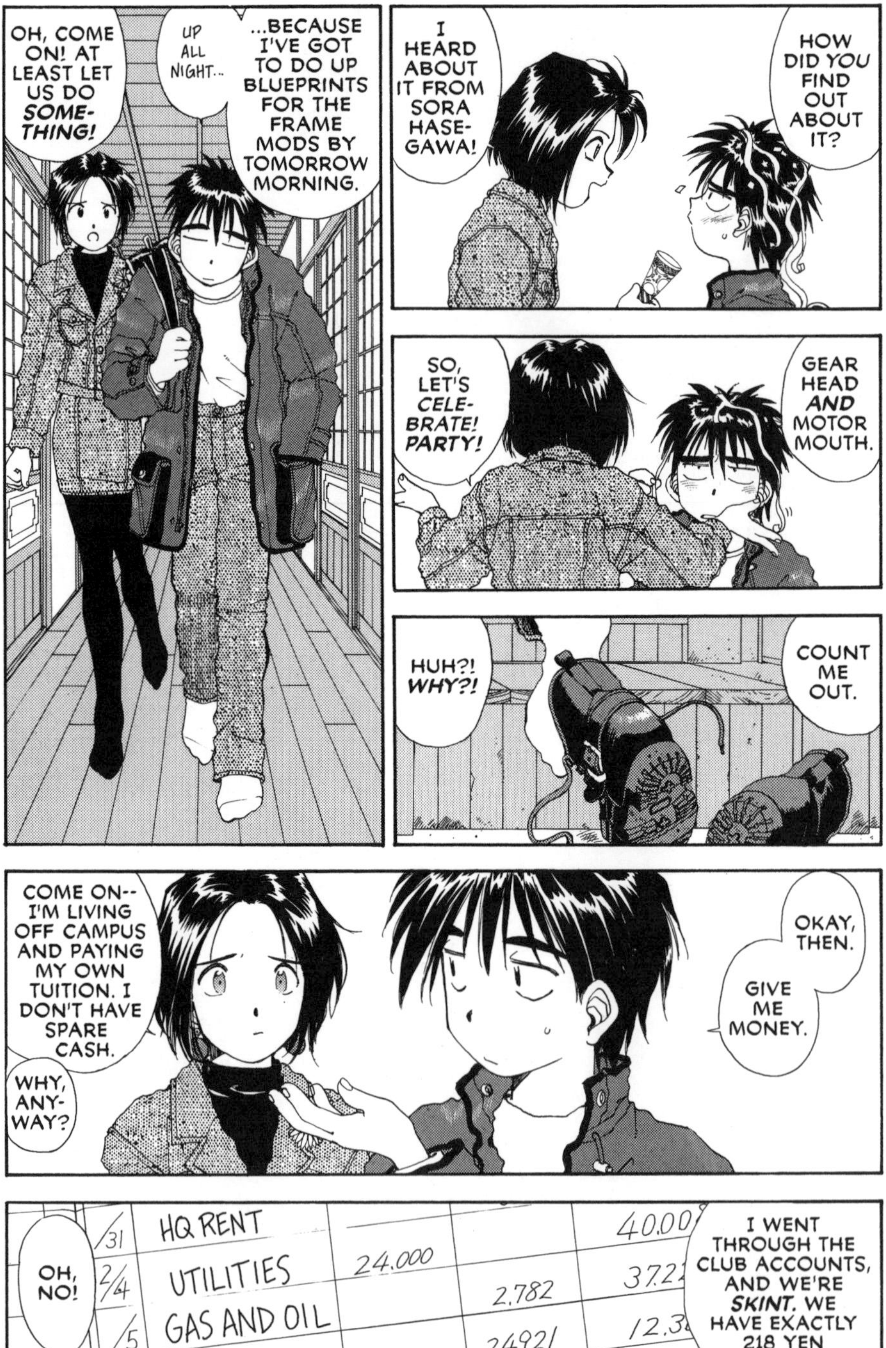
HOW DID *YOU* FIND OUT ABOUT IT?
I HEARD ABOUT IT FROM SORA HASEGAWA!
GEAR HEAD ***AND*** MOTOR MOUTH.
SO, LET'S *CELEBRATE!* ***PARTY!***
COUNT ME OUT.
HUH?! ***WHY?!***
...BECAUSE I'VE GOT TO DO UP BLUEPRINTS FOR THE FRAME MODS BY TOMORROW MORNING.
UP ALL NIGHT...
OH, COME ON! AT LEAST LET US DO ***SOMETHING!***
OKAY, THEN.
GIVE ME MONEY.
COME ON-- I'M LIVING OFF CAMPUS AND PAYING MY OWN TUITION. I DON'T HAVE SPARE CASH.
WHY, ANYWAY?
I WENT THROUGH THE CLUB ACCOUNTS, AND WE'RE ***SKINT.*** WE HAVE EXACTLY 218 YEN LEFT.
/31 HQ RENT 40,00
2/4 UTILITIES 24,000 37,2
/5 GAS AND OIL 2,782 12,3
24,921
OH, NO!

HMM...

EVEN IF WE MAKE OUR OWN PARTS, WE STILL NEED TO BUY MATERIALS AND EXPEND-ABLES...

WHAT'S *THAT* SUP-POSED TO MEAN ...?

DON'T COUNT ON IT, THOUGH, BRO.

...TO CELE-BRATE.

I *MAY* BE ABLE TO DO SOME-THING...

YOU GOING HOME ...?

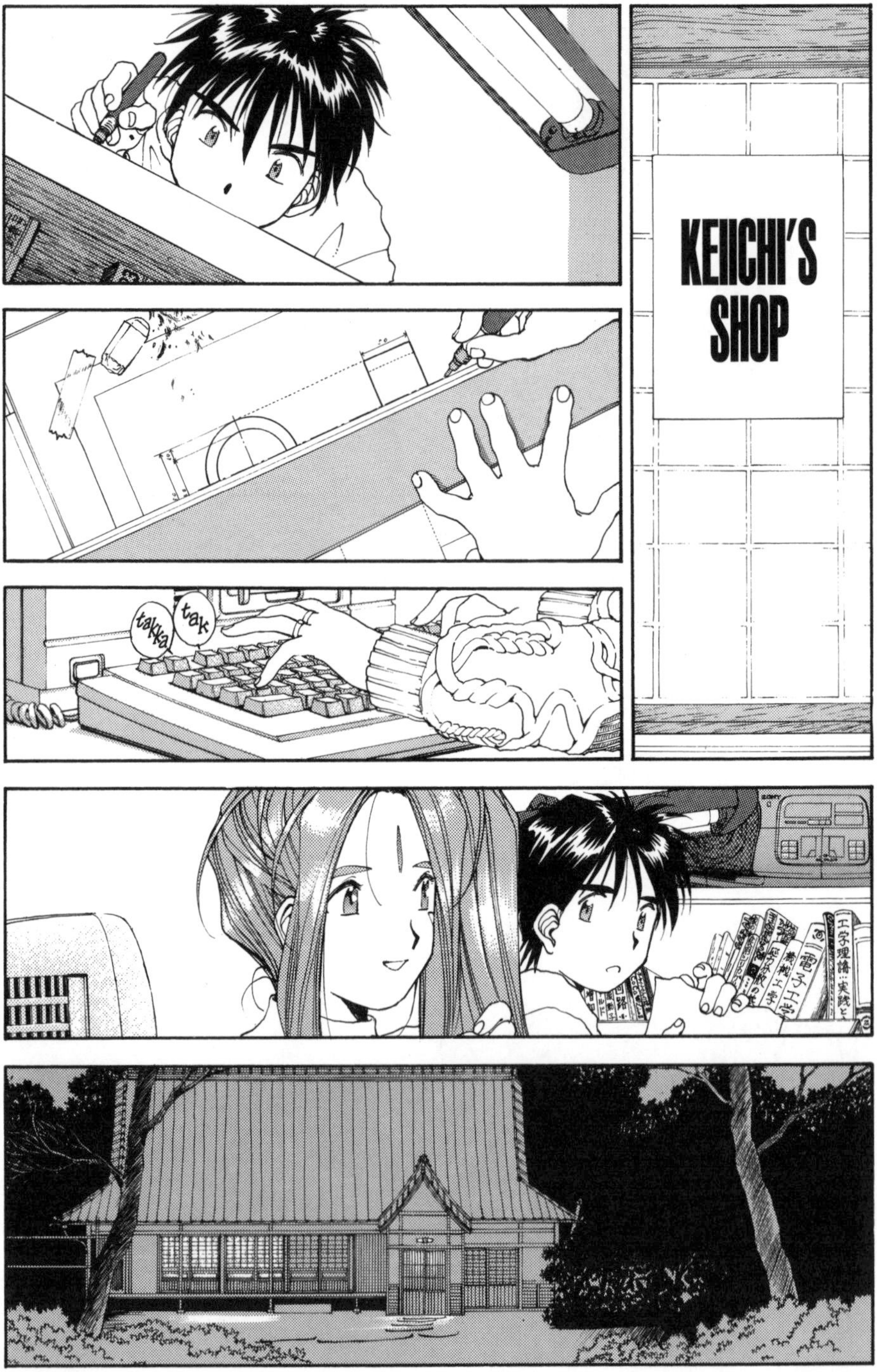
KEIICHI'S SHOP
takka
tak

...WELL, THEN... THAT'S MY JOB, TOO.

AND IF HE THINKS I'M BEING TOO PUSHY...

...YOU'RE SOMETHING ELSE, SIS.

...

I GUESS *MY* JOB IS TO ALWAYS HELP YOU OUT, EH?

WHEN YOU PUT IT LIKE THAT, YOU LEAVE ME NO CHOICE.

WHAT ABOUT *ME*?

I MEAN, I'M NOT HELPING *HIM*--I'M HELPING *BELLDANDY*, OKAY?!

YES!! I MEAN, *NO!!*

WHAT... *YOU*-- HELP KEIICHI ...?

492

HOW THE HECK ...?

...THE *WHOLE BIKE!*

THE PLANS ...? THEY'RE... *FINISHED!*

HUH ...?

AND SO, THE NEXT MORNING...

KEI-ICHI?

OH, KEIICHI!

BUT...

...AND YOU'VE GOT EVERY RIGHT TO BE ANGRY.

FORGIVE ME! I KNOW I SHOULDN'T HAVE...

494

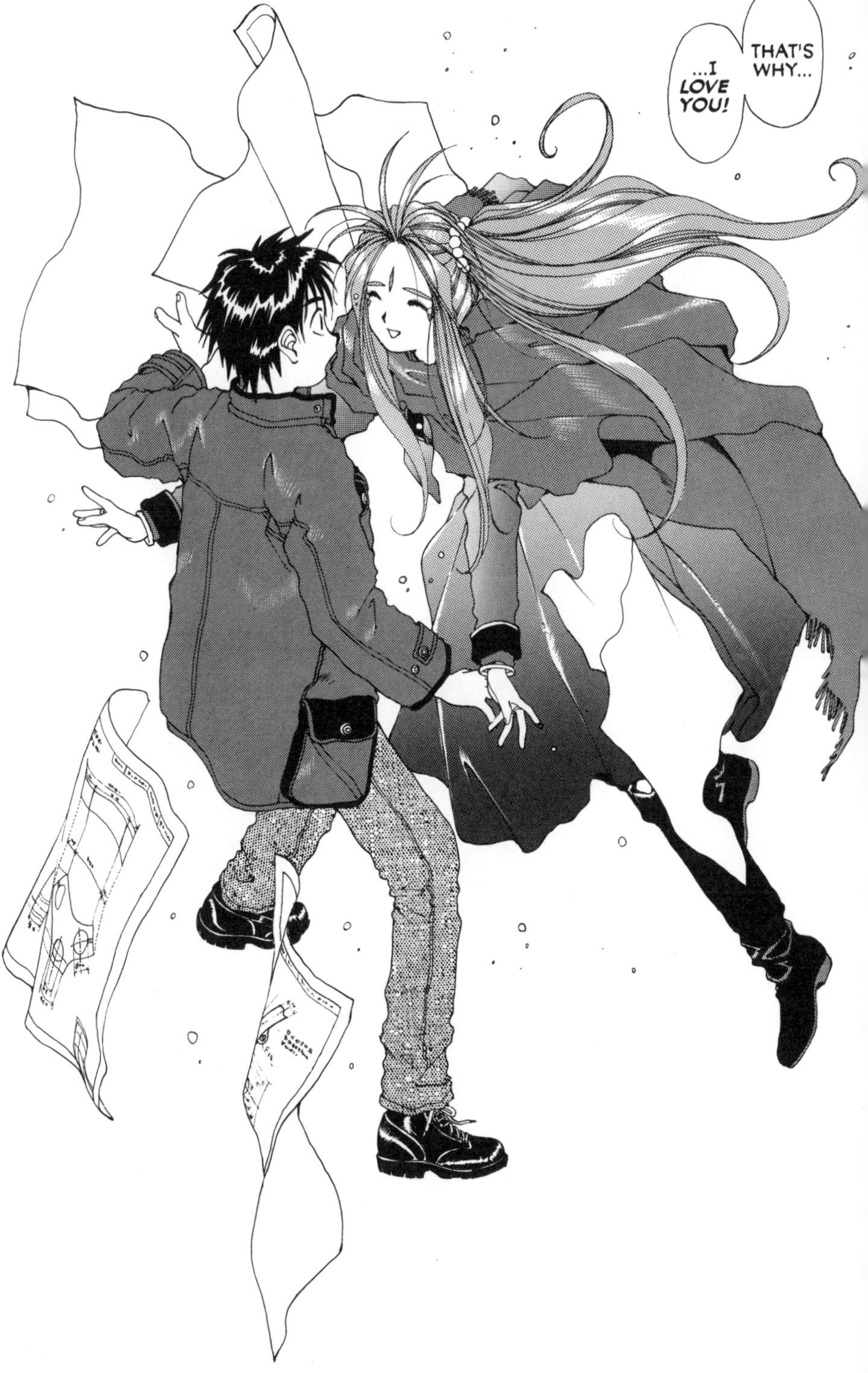
THAT'S WHY...
...I LOVE YOU!

IT FITS **PERFECTLY!** (manly tears)

...WERE BETTER THAN EVEN BRAND-NEW FACTORY COMPONENTS.

THE PARTS WE MADE USING THE GODDESSES' BLUE-PRINTS...

HUH?

KEI-CHAN! KEI-CHAN!

CHECK IT OUT!

TAA-DAA!

SO DON'T WASTE IT, KIDDO!

THINK OF IT AS YOUR LITTLE SISTER'S EXPRESSION OF SUPPORT FOR HER BIG BROTHER.

KEIICHI... YOU'RE TALKING TO YOURSELF AGAIN...

WHAT DID SHE...?

...TWO HUNDRED THOUSAND YEN!!

SO I TALKED THEM ALL INTO SPONSORING YOU.

...Y'KNOW, I'M PRETTY WELL KNOWN DOWN AT THE SHOPPING MALL.

HEH, HEH...

?

HERE YOU GO. STICK THESE ON!

HUH?

I ALMOST FORGOT THE MOST IMPORTANT THING...

OH, YEAH!

MEGUMI... YOU'RE THE BEST LITTLE SISTER--

...BUT THERE'S STILL NO SIGN OF HIM OR OTAKI.

WELL, I WAS *GOING* TO LET TAMIYA DO IT, BUT...

SO YOU WOUND UP RIDING IT *YOURSELF*, SIR...?

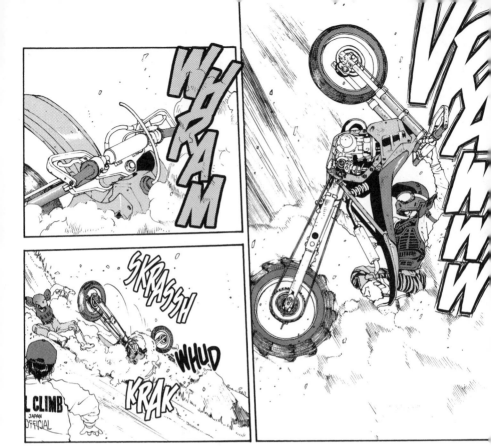

NOW DO YOU SEE WHY I WAS SO THRILLED?

YEP.

ARE YOU **SURE** YOU WANT TO DO THIS, SIR...?

BABA UNIVERSITY MOTOR- CYCLE CLUB... 52.5 METERS!

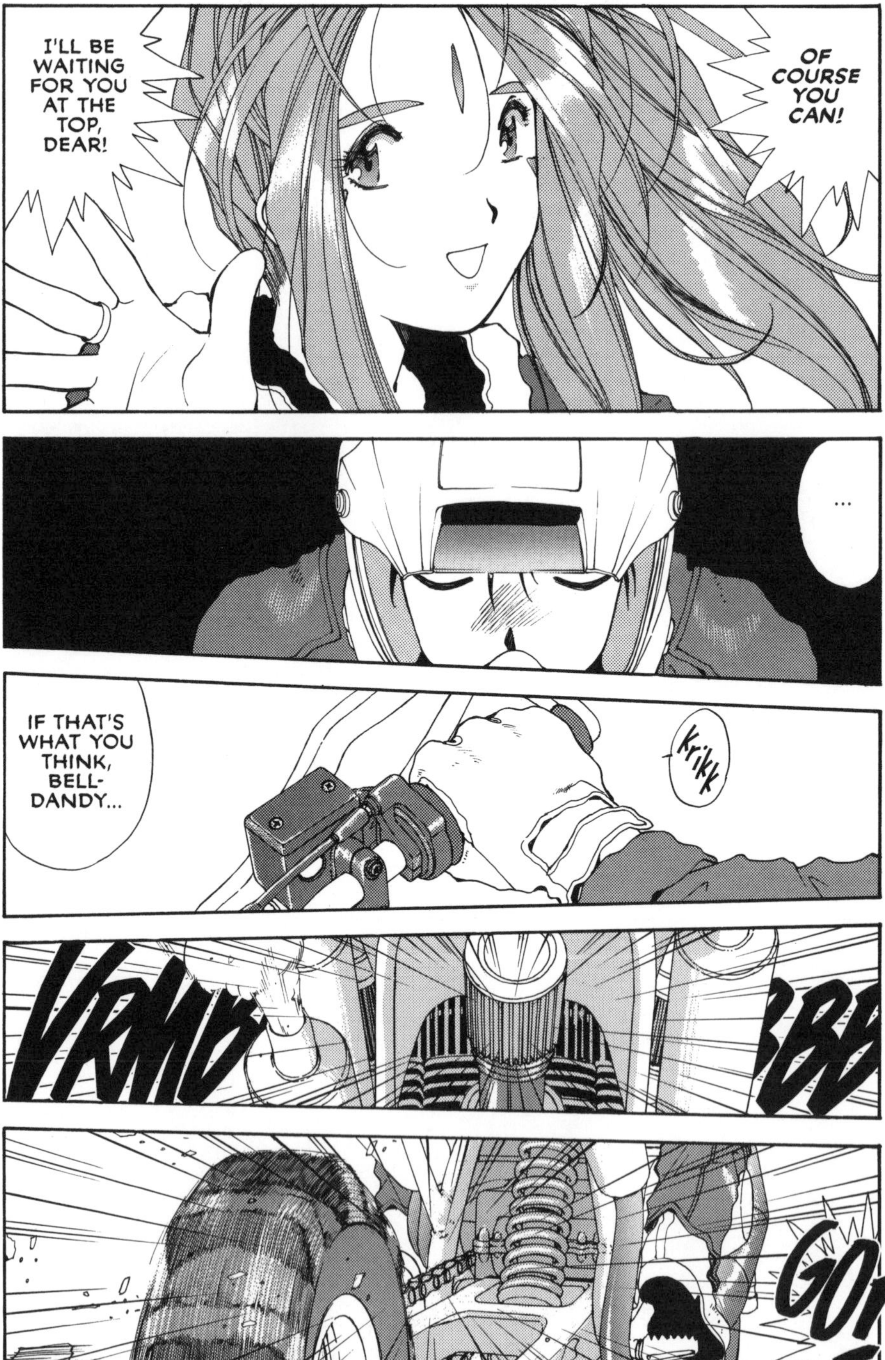
OF COURSE YOU CAN!
I'LL BE WAITING FOR YOU AT THE TOP, DEAR!
...
krikk
IF THAT'S WHAT YOU THINK, BELL-DANDY...
BBB
VRMO
GO!

YOU'VE GOT A *GODDESS* ON YOUR SIDE!

GO, MAN, *GO!!*

KEEP HER *LOW!*

...GOTTA KEEP THAT REAR TIRE *SUCKING DIRT!*

IF I CATCH TOO MUCH AIR I'LL LOSE ACCELERATION...

THE FIRST JUMP!

HUH? WHERE HAVE YOU--

YUP.

HE'S REALLY RIPPING UP THE HILL, THAT BOY.

RENTHAL

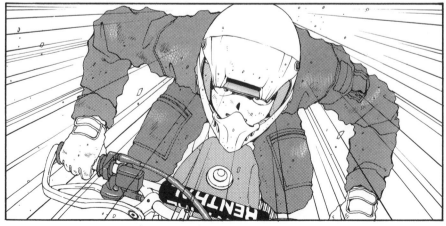

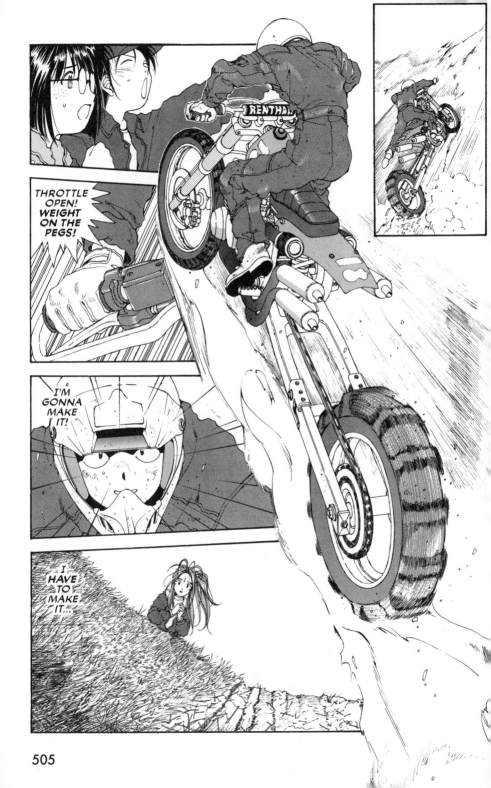

THROTTLE OPEN! WEIGHT ON THE PEGS!

I'M GONNA MAKE IT!

I HAVE TO MAKE IT...

505

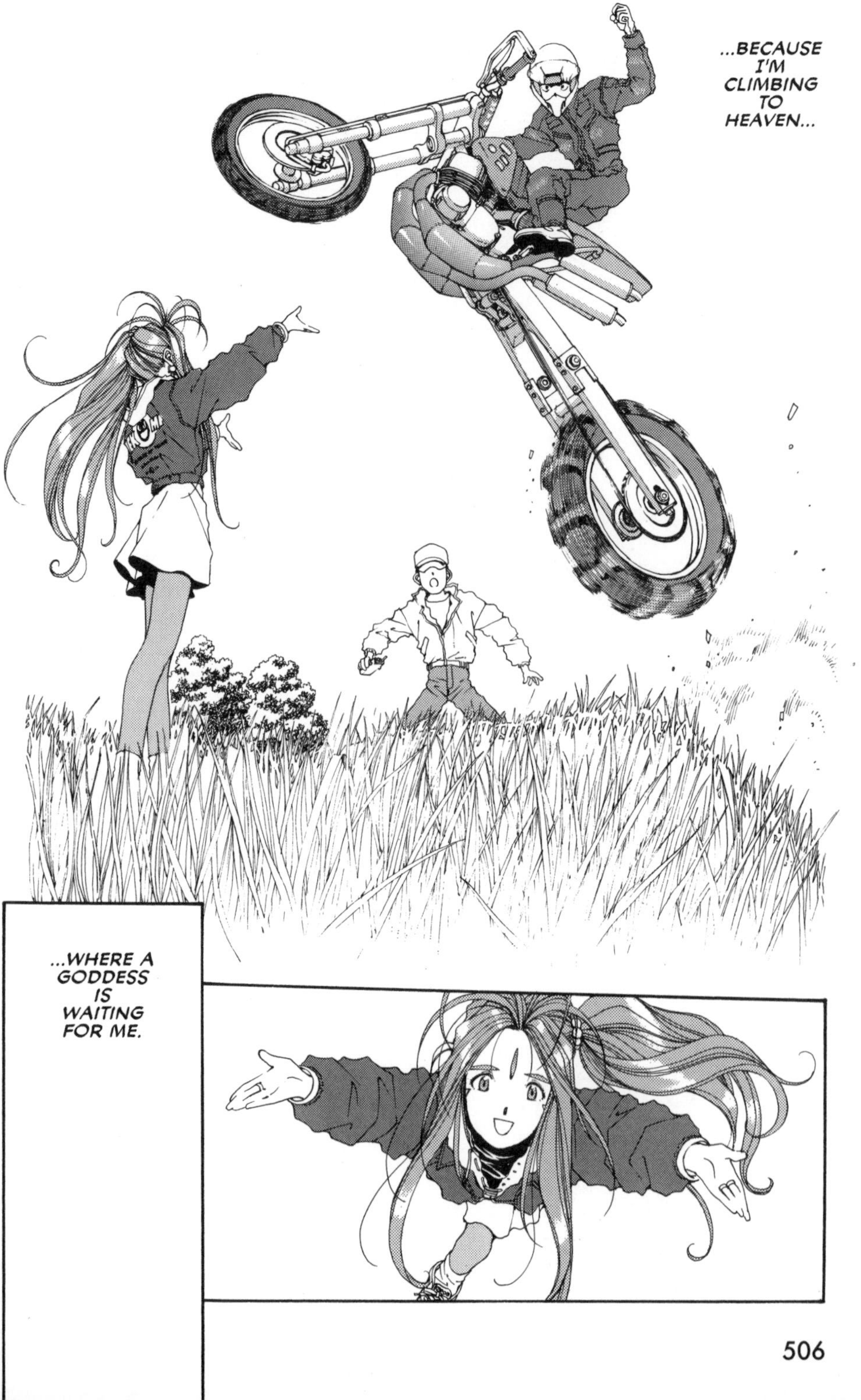
...BECAUSE I'M CLIMBING TO HEAVEN...
...WHERE A GODDESS IS WAITING FOR ME.

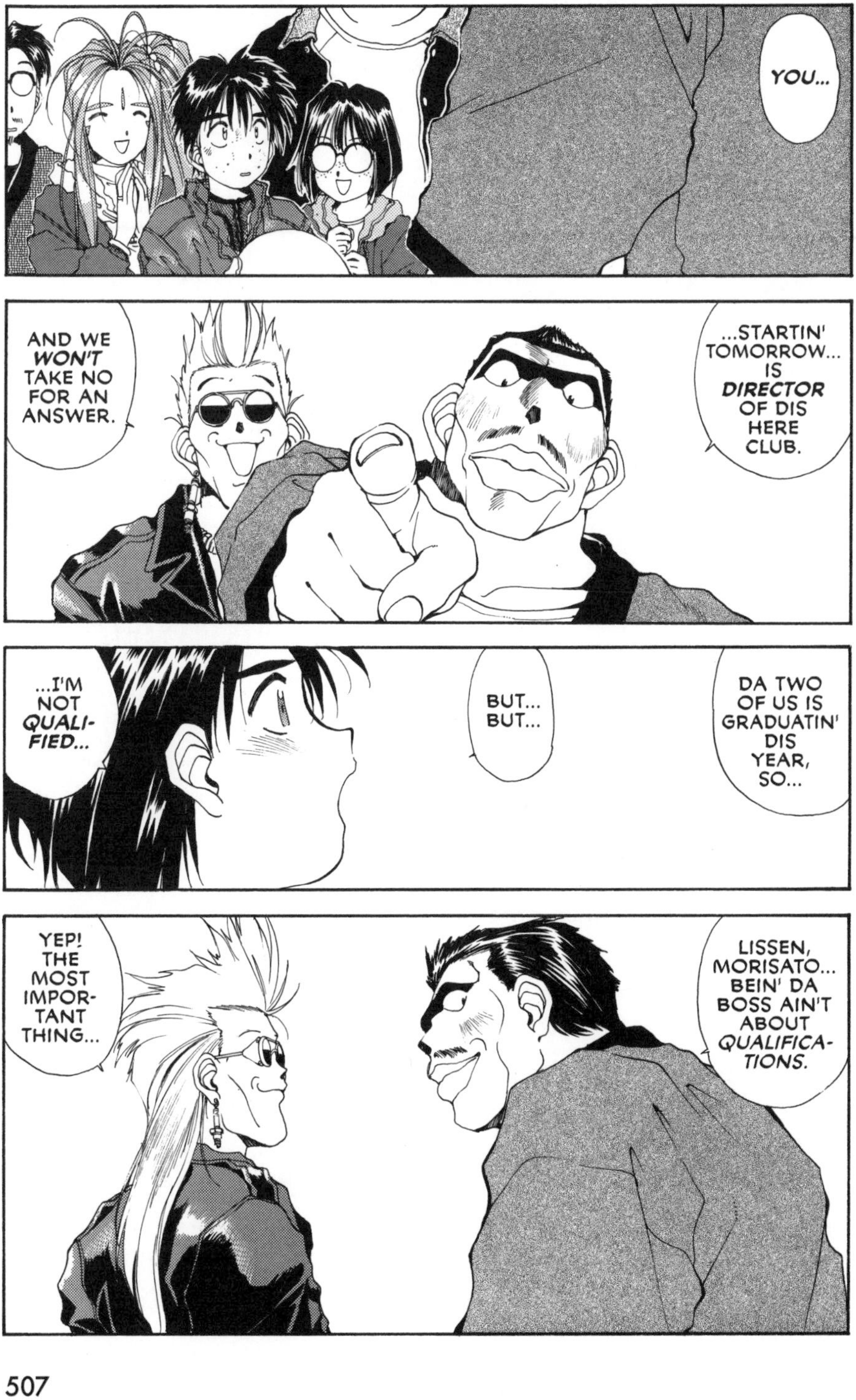
YOU...
...STARTIN' TOMORROW... IS DIRECTOR OF DIS HERE CLUB.
AND WE WON'T TAKE NO FOR AN ANSWER.
DA TWO OF US IS GRADUATIN' DIS YEAR, SO...
BUT... BUT...
...I'M NOT QUALI-FIED...
LISSEN, MORISATO... BEIN' DA BOSS AIN'T ABOUT QUALIFICA-TIONS.
YEP! THE MOST IMPOR-TANT THING...

...LEADER-SHIP!

IN OTHER WORDS...

...IS THE POWER TO MAKE PEOPLE WORK FOR, UH, *WITH* YOU!

BELL-DANDY SAYS THAT HAPPINESS IN LIFE...

TAMIYA-SEMPAI...

OTAKI-SEMPAI...

...DEPENDS ON HOW MANY TIMES YOU GET TO SAY "THANK YOU" FROM THE BOTTOM OF YOUR HEART.

THANK YOU!!

NOW I'VE GOT *ALL* THE RESPONSI-BILITY AND *NONE* OF THE POWER...

THEY DON'T MEAN BADLY...

YEAH! YOU'LL BE OUR PUPPET, KEIICHI!

OKAY. HERE'S HOW IT'S GONNA BE--ME AN' OTAKI IS STAYIN' ON FER GRADUATE SCHOOL, SO WE'S GONNA ESTABLISH A NEW SUPREME EXECUTIVE COMMITTEE OF US TWO *ABOVE* TH' DIRECTOR.

BUT LET'S JUST PRETEND *THIS* ONE DIDN'T HAPPEN.

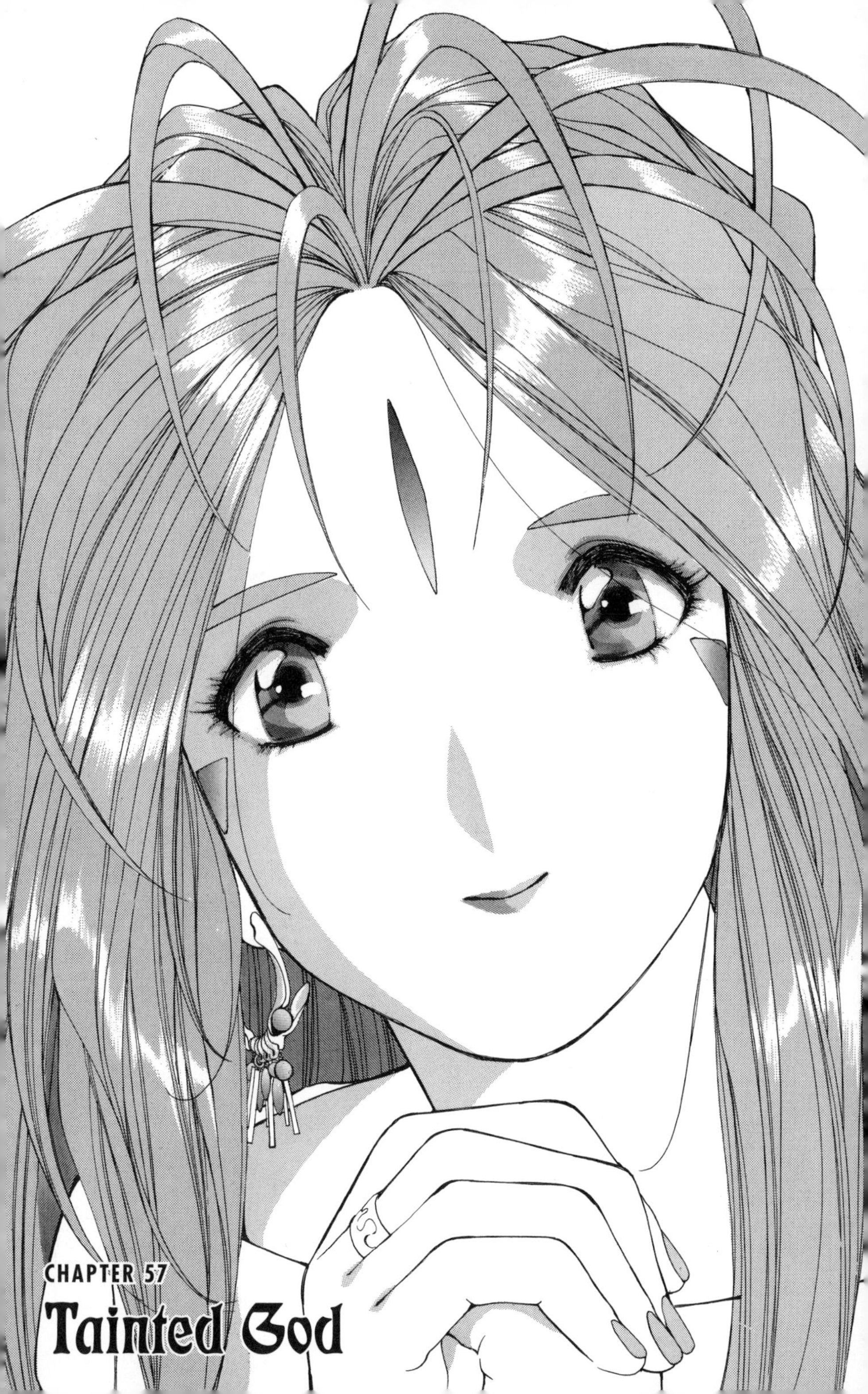

CHAPTER 57

Tainted God

角田研究室
KAKUTA LABS

DANGER HIGH VOLTAGE

TODAY'S EXPERIMENT MENU: CERAMIC SHOCK TESTING!

OKAY, WE'RE OFF TO GRAB SOME LUNCH!

IT SHOULDN'T BE COMING OUT SO BRITTLE.

...I JUST CAN'T SEEM TO STABILIZE THE TEMPERATURE IN THE FURNACE.

510

511

... ...

Dear Keiichi,
Forgive me for sending you this letter, out of the blue, but ever since I first laid eyes upon you, I have tried many times to speak to you. But

"SHIHO SAKAKI-BARA... FRESH-MAN, ELECTRON-ICS DEPART-MENT" ...?

NEVER HEARD OF HER.

WHO ...?

IT... IT'S...

But...
Alas, I could never find the right words and each of those days ended in regret. And so today, I at last find the courage.
I want to tell you my heart.
I want to tell you how I feel, in my own words.
And so...
I will be waiting in front of the fountain today until I see you. And I will wait forever...

...I RECEIVED *A LOVE LETTER!!*

...I NEVER THOUGHT I'D SEE THE DAY...

"EVER SINCE I FIRST LAID EYES UPON YOU...

IT'S N-N-N-NOTHING!

WHAT IS IT...?

I MEAN, I'VE *WRITTEN* PLENTY, BUT I NEVER DREAMED THAT SOMEDAY I'D ACTUALLY *GET ONE!*

OH, DEAR-- PERHAPS I SHOULDN'T HAVE ASKED.

FWAM

YAEET!

KEIICHI...

...IMPRESSIVE.

...A *LOVE LETTER.*

OH, WOW...

"...I HAVE TRIED MANY TIMES TO SPEAK..."

SEE? WHAT A DOPE!

Y-YES...?

urk!

I... ER... huh?

YOU *OWE* HER A PROPER ANSWER!

IT TAKES *GREAT EMOTIONAL STRENGTH* TO REVEAL ONE'S DEEPEST FEELINGS!

...THAT SHE JUST DOESN'T THINK... I'M *WORTH* GETTING JEALOUS OVER...?

OR COULD IT BE...

DOES SHE REALLY TRUST ME SO *COMPLETELY?*

...DOESN'T SHE EVEN FEEL THE *SLIGHTEST* JEALOUSY?

BUT...

okay?

THE LOOK ON HER FACE WAS *SO* SERIOUS WHEN SHE SAID IT.

IS IT *FUN* PICKING ON ME, URD?

YOU'RE GONNA TURN HER DOWN? REALLY? AH, WHAT A *WASTE!*

WELL, YEAH... A LITTLE.

WOW... THAT GIRL IS *DEVASTAT-INGLY* CUTE...

DON'T SEE ANYBODY *ELSE,* THOUGH...

NAW... *CAN'T* BE HER.

DON'T MOVE!

huh?

SORRY!

--BUT I JUST CAN'T--

I KNOW...

I'VE GOT IT...

THERE!

uh...?

wuh?

AH-HA!

I WAS RIGHT!

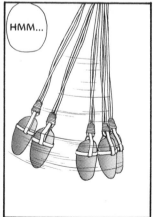

HMM...

YOU'RE EMITTING THE *PSYCHIC VIBRATIONS* OF AN *UNHUMAN BEING!*

YOU HAVE BEEN *POSSESSED!*

NO...NO WAY! HAS THE SECRET OF THE GODDESSES FINALLY *GOTTEN OUT*...?!

GASP!

FEAR NOT!

"EVIL SPIRITS" ...?

UM... EXCUSE ME?

...THOSE *EVIL SPIRITS* WITHIN YOU!

...*DRIVE OUT*...

BUT DON'T WORRY... BY MY OWN POWER, I SHALL...

WHAT ARE YOU... SOME KIND OF *EXORCIST* ...?

I SHALL *CLEANSE* YOU! HALLE-LUJAH!

"AS A HOBBY" ...?

EXACTLY! I'VE BEEN DOING IT AS A HOBBY... FOR TWO WHOLE YEARS NOW.

HOW AM I SUPPOSED TO *ENTRUST* BELLDANDY TO YOU... WHEN YOU BEHAVE LIKE *THIS?!*

IF YOU'RE *GOING* TO TELL HER NO-- THEN *TELL* HER!!

WELL, ACTUALLY, I DON'T... NEED... ANY... AT THE MOMENT...

OH, *LET* ME BE YOUR *FIRST!*

WELL, I'VE BEEN KINDA *PRACTICING* ON STUFFED ANIMALS... BUT I SWEAR...I'M *READY* FOR IT FOR *REAL!*

ARGH! I CAN'T *STAND* IT, YOU *WIMP!*

?

?

I WAS JUST *KIDDING,* OKAY?! *REALLY!*

URD, WEREN'T YOU KINDA SAYING THE OPPOSITE BEFORE...?

DOESN'T KEIICHI'S *WAFFLE-LIKE-SPINE* EVER *BOTHER* YOU...?

--YOU'RE AS BAD AS *HE* IS!

AND YOU--

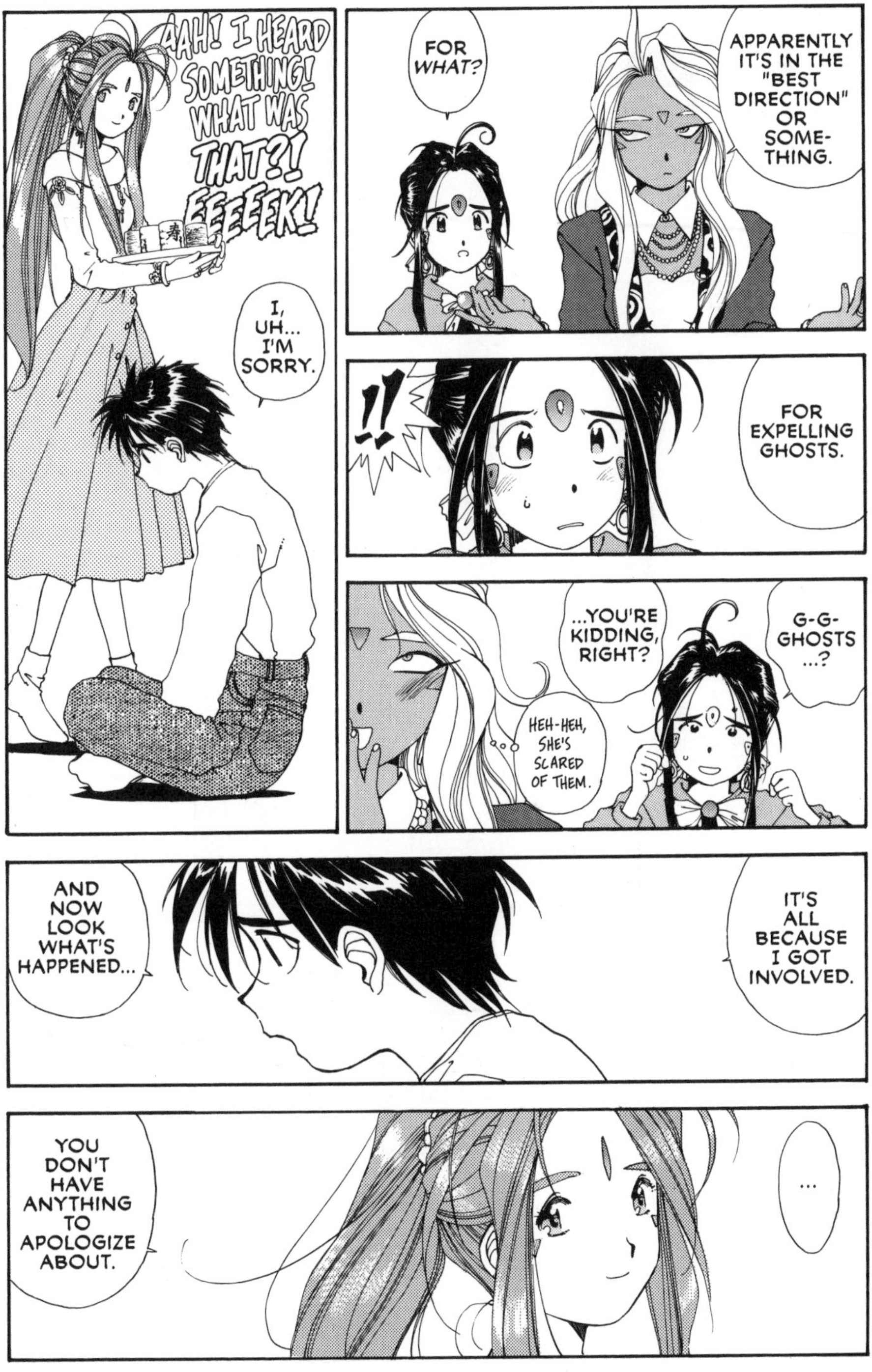
AAH! I HEARD SOMETHING! WHAT WAS THAT?!
EEEEEK!
I, UH... I'M SORRY.
FOR WHAT?
APPARENTLY IT'S IN THE "BEST DIRECTION" OR SOME-THING.
FOR EXPELLING GHOSTS.
!!
...YOU'RE KIDDING, RIGHT?
G-G-GHOSTS ...?
HEH-HEH, SHE'S SCARED OF THEM.
AND NOW LOOK WHAT'S HAPPENED...
IT'S ALL BECAUSE I GOT INVOLVED.
YOU DON'T HAVE ANYTHING TO APOLOGIZE ABOUT.
...

...I WAS AFRAID SHE WAS GOING TO GET HURT.

IF THAT GIRL REALLY *HAD* BEEN IN LOVE WITH YOU...

I *WAS* JUST A LITTLE WORRIED, THOUGH...

OR IS THAT...

...TOO ARROGANT OF ME?

THANKS FOR RUINING THE MOOD, URD.

GHOSTS LIVE UNDER MY *BED*?! WAAH! I'M SCARED!!

NOT AT ALL--

...

SORRY TO KEEP YOU WAITING.

WOW... YOU'RE EVEN DRESSED AS A SHRINE MAIDEN!

AND SO... LET US BEGIN.

AND NOW...

tee-hee DO YOU LIKE MY *MIKO* OUTFIT? I MADE IT MYSELF.

STOP. RIGHT. TH-THERE.

uh...

....

FIRST, WE MUST SYNCHRO-NIZE OUR BREATH-ING.

CALM YOUR-SELF.

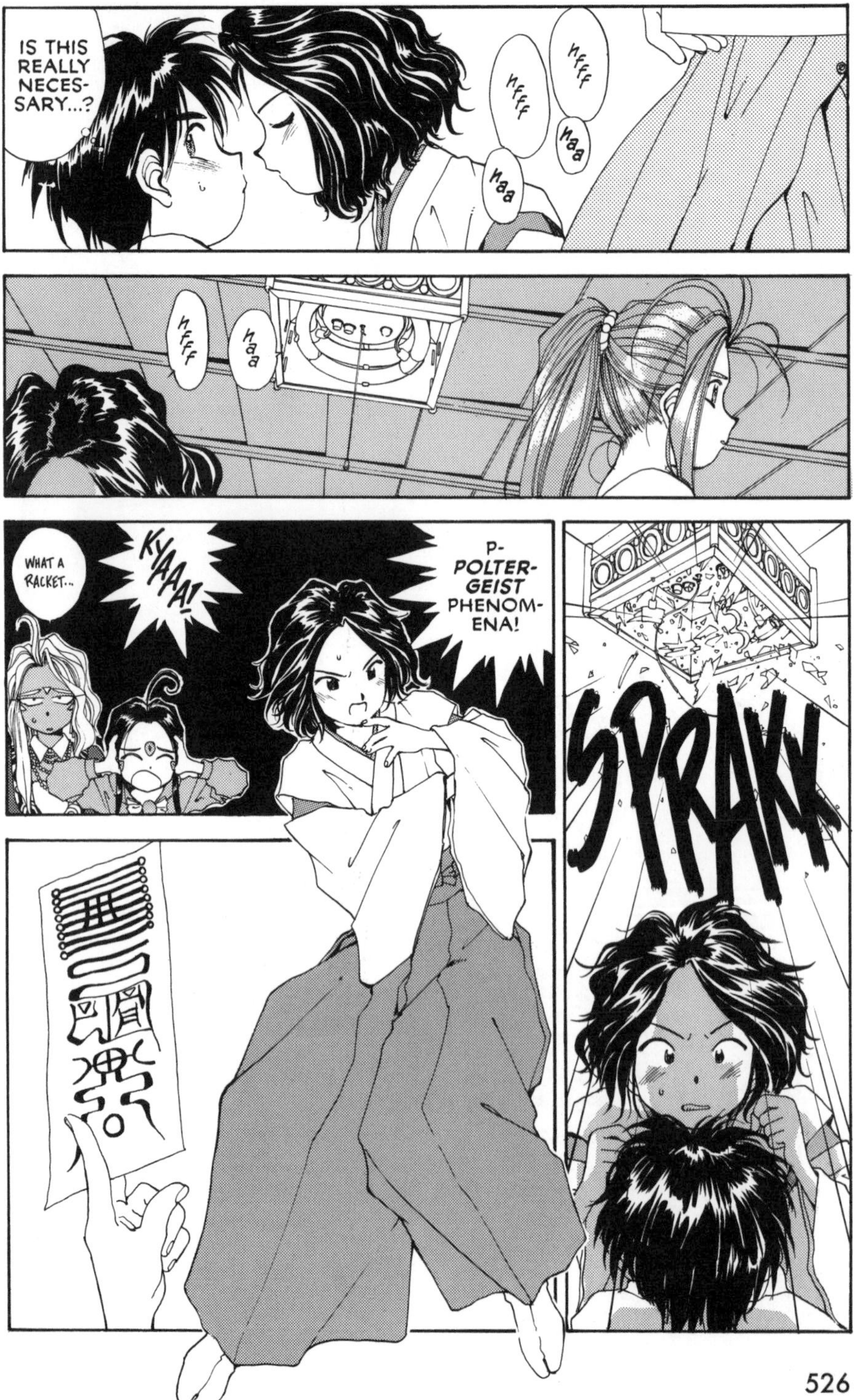

nfff
nfff
naa
naa
IS THIS REALLY NECES-SARY...?
nfff
naa
SPRAKK
P-POLTER-GEIST PHENOM-ENA!
KYAAA!
WHAT A RACKET...

527

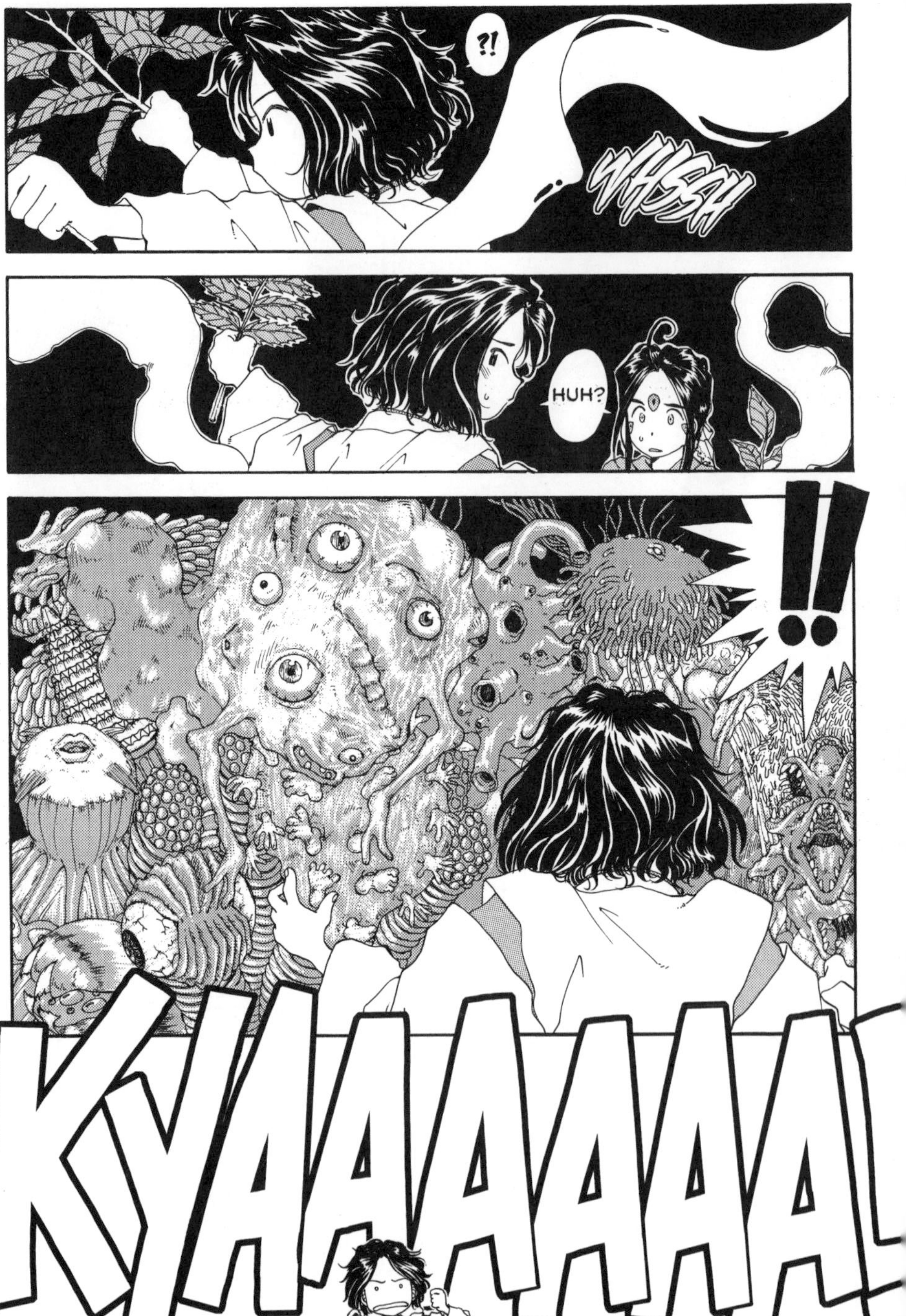
?!
WHSSH
HUH?
!!
KYAAAAAA

I KNOW.

URD, DEAR... THIS SPELL...

...

MY WARDS DIDN'T WORK! DARN!

SO D-DO SOME-THING!

Y-YOU'RE SUPPOSED TO BE AN EXORCIST, RIGHT ...?

I'M NOT VERY FAMILIAR WITH THESE SO-CALLED FORMULAS OF HERS...

BEAT IT, BUDDY.

THEY'RE *ALL* WRONG!

...BETTER TEAR THEM DOWN!

WHY DO STRANGE THINGS ALWAYS LIKE *ME* SO MUCH ...?!

IN WHICH CASE...

...BUT IT LOOKS LIKE *THIS* ONE ACTUALLY *EVOKES* LOW-LEVEL SPIRITS.

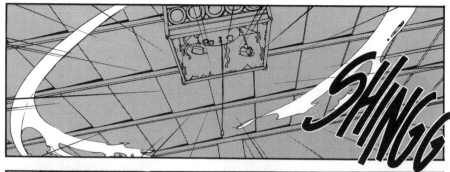

SHINGG

WHA--?

HUH?

I...

I...

OH, HEY--
THEY JUST
TOOK A
MOMENT
TO KICK
IN!

?

THEY'RE...
GONE?

I HAVE THE GIFT!!

YEAH, RIGHT!

WELL THEN. THAT'S THAT.

MORI-SATO...

NOW, SKULD!

DON'T LET THE DOOR HIT YOU ON THE WAY OUT!

...THE VERY FIRST PERSON TO EVER GO ALONG WITH MY HOBBY.

...YOU'RE THE FIRST...

THANK YOU.

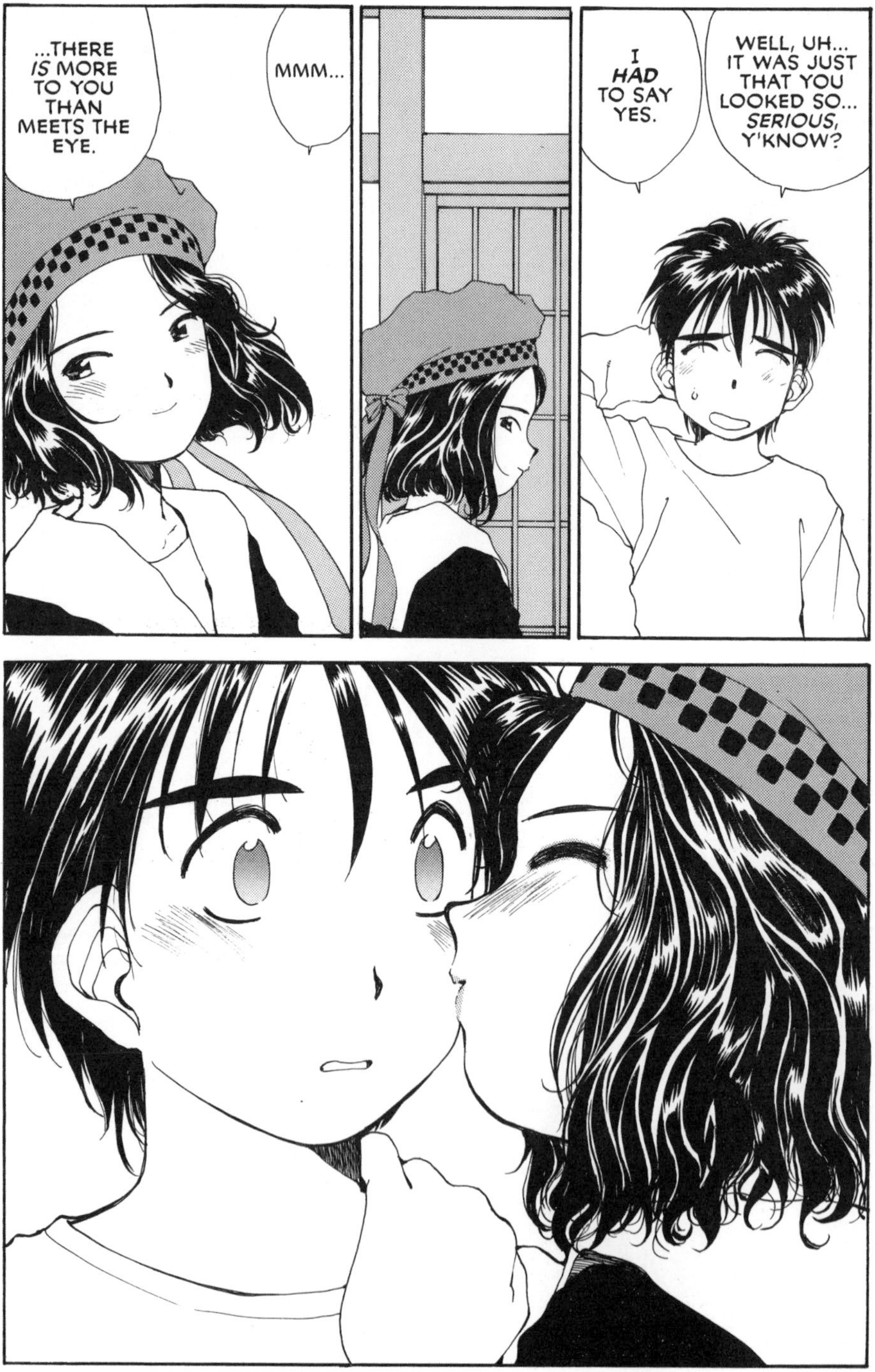
WELL, UH... IT WAS JUST THAT YOU LOOKED SO... *SERIOUS,* Y'KNOW?
I *HAD* TO SAY YES.
MMM...
...THERE *IS* MORE TO YOU THAN MEETS THE EYE.

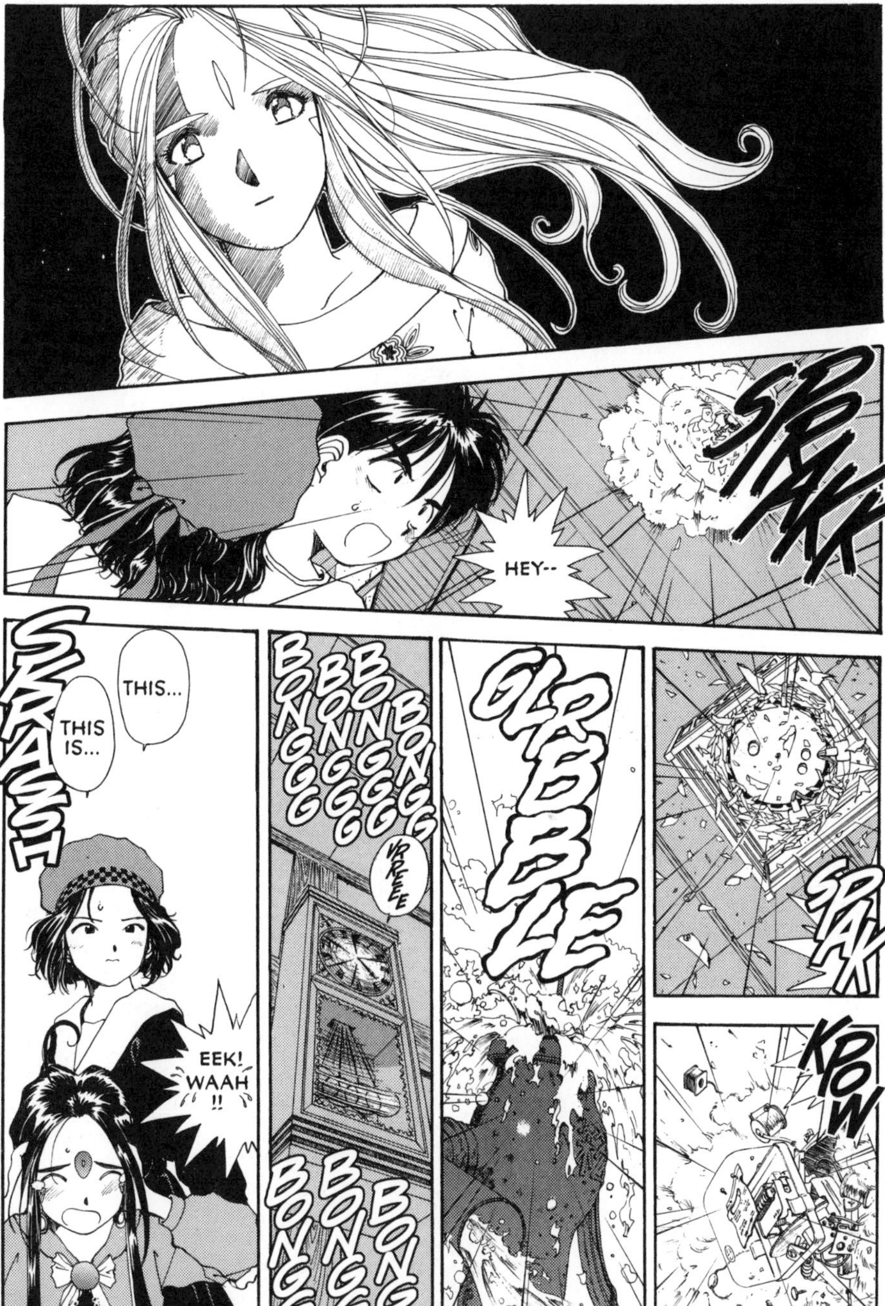
SPRAKK
HEY--
SPAK
KPOW
GLRBBLE
BONGG
BONGGG
BONGGG
BONGGG
VRREEE
BONGGG
BONGGG
BONGGG
THIS...
THIS IS...
SKRAUSH
EEK! WAAH!!

OKAY... I'M GETTING A LITTLE SCARED.

...A CHALLENGE TO ME, FROM THE SPIRITS!

NOPE.

IS THERE *REALLY*... A *GHOST* IN THE HOUSE?

WH... WHOA!

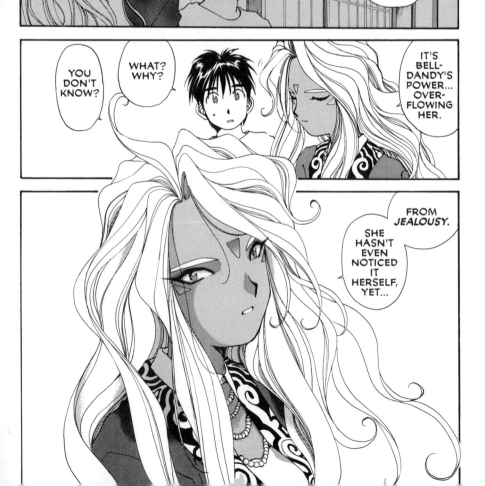

YOU DON'T KNOW?

WHAT? WHY?

IT'S BELL-DANDY'S POWER... OVER-FLOWING HER.

FROM *JEALOUSY.*

SHE HASN'T EVEN NOTICED IT HERSELF, YET...

...BUT IT ISN'T ALWAYS *PRETTY.*

FALLING IN LOVE IS *BEAUTI-FUL*...

..."NOT LIKE THAT," YOU WANT TO SAY?

KYAAA! HE'S SHORTED OUT!

BANPEI! SAVE ME!

NO WAY! BELL-DANDY'S NOT... SHE'S NOT...

MY SISTER'S NOT A *DOLL,* KEIICHI.

SHE HAS *EMOTIONS*... INCLUDING *THAT* ONE.

...SHE'S JUST TRYING TO WITH-DRAW.

WE CAN'T JUST LEAVE HER TO HERSELF NOW...

AND IF SHE DOES *THAT* MUCH LONG-ER...

...

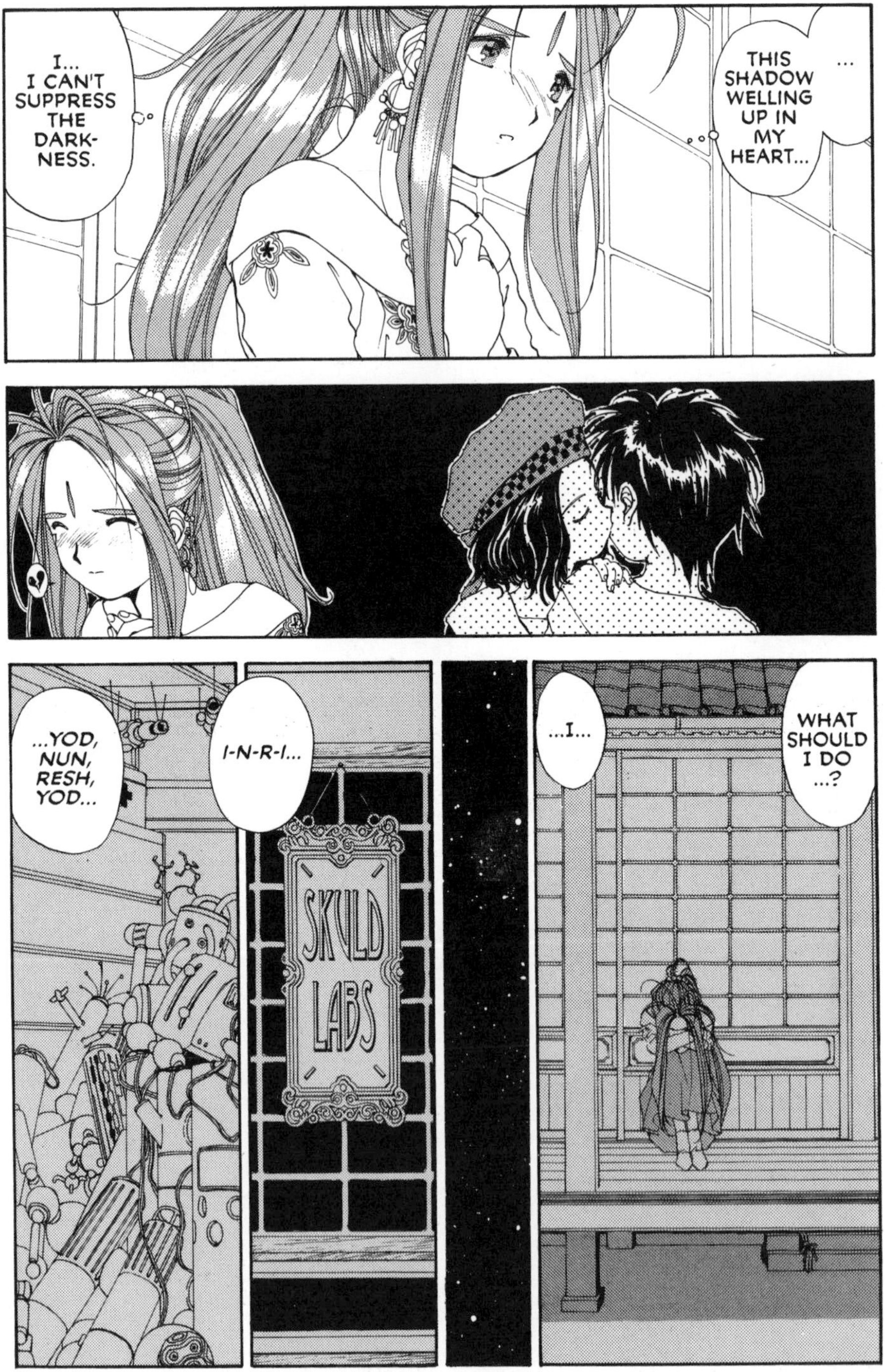
...
THIS SHADOW WELLING UP IN MY HEART...
I... I CAN'T SUPPRESS THE DARK-NESS.
WHAT SHOULD I DO ...?
...I...
I-N-R-I...
...YOD, NUN, RESH, YOD...
SKULD LABS

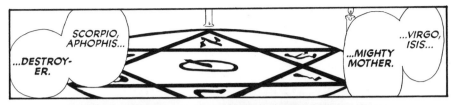

...WHAT IS IT?

...

THE *REAL* QUESTION IS...

BEATS ME... I DON'T RECOGNIZE THESE INVOCATIONS *AT ALL*.

GEE, URD... DO YOU THINK SHE'LL SUMMON SOME WEIRD CRITTERS AGAIN?

THOUGH MAYBE SHE'S A BIT PALE...? OR IS THAT JUST THE LIGHT...?

WELL, HECK... SHE LOOKS ABOUT THE SAME AS ALWAYS.

er

...IT'S NOTHING.

shingg

ARARITA!
אראריתא

538

SHWHOOMPH

--PROTECTOR OF HUMANITY AGAINST EVIL!

I DID IT! I'VE EVOKED KUNDALI--

FEAR YE THIS NAME...

SHSS

I... AM!

...DREAD WATCHDOG OF NIBELHEIM, THE LAND OF THE DEAD!

THIS NAME OF GARM...

540

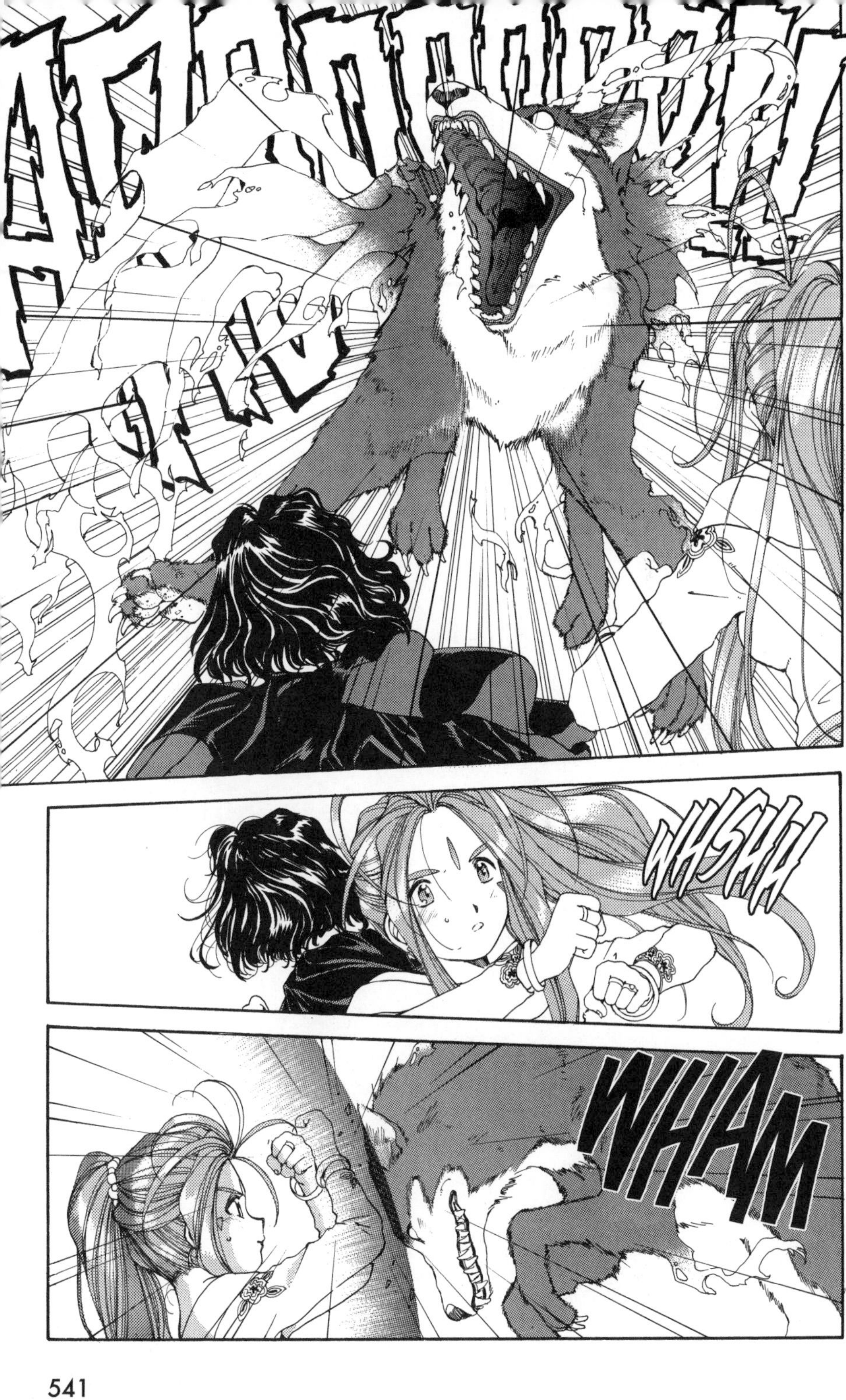
WHSHH
WHAM

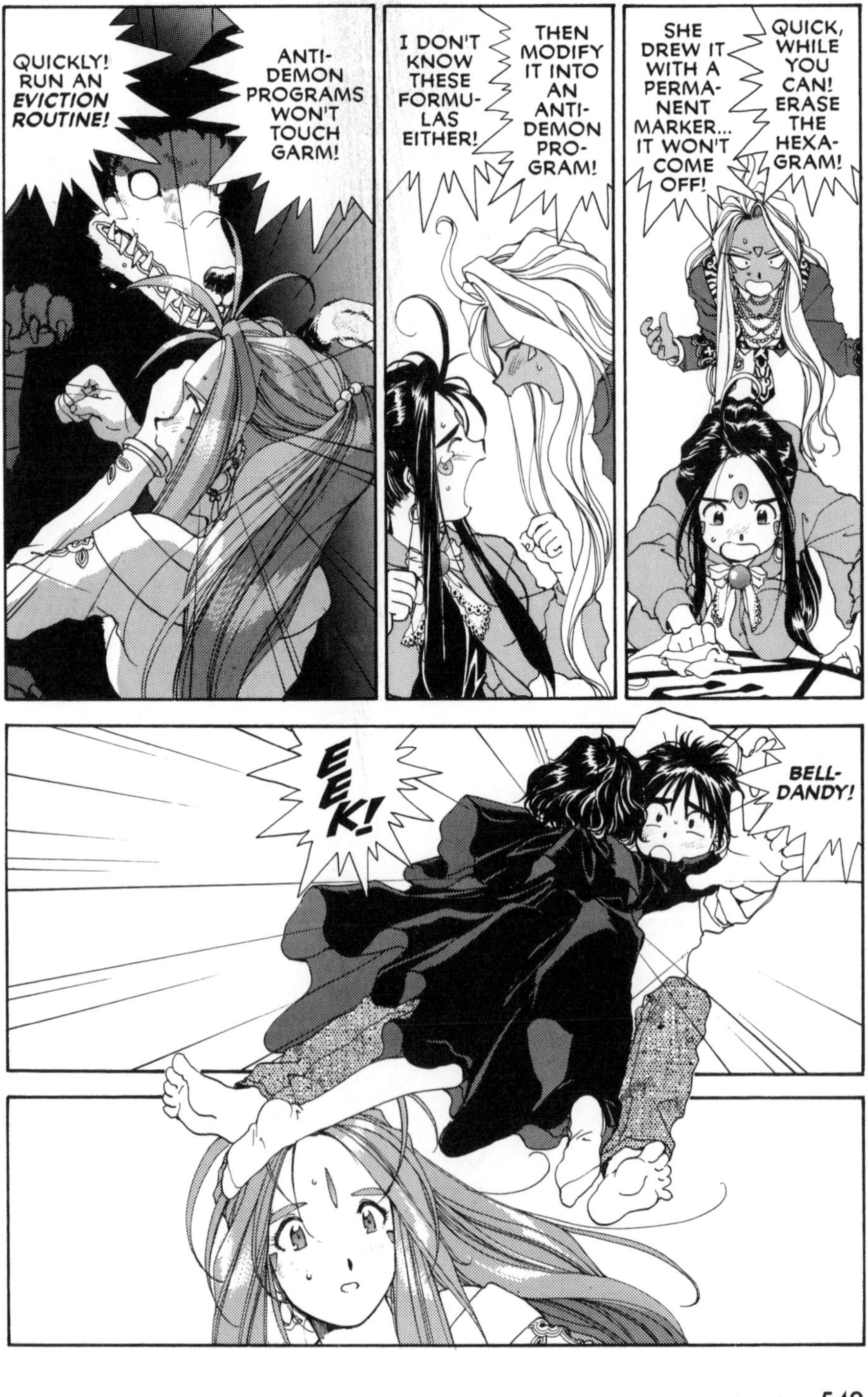

QUICK, WHILE YOU CAN! ERASE THE HEXAGRAM!
SHE DREW IT WITH A PERMANENT MARKER... IT WON'T COME OFF!
THEN MODIFY IT INTO AN ANTI-DEMON PROGRAM!
I DON'T KNOW THESE FORMULAS EITHER!
ANTI-DEMON PROGRAMS WON'T TOUCH GARM!
QUICKLY! RUN AN *EVICTION ROUTINE!*
BELLDANDY!
EEK!

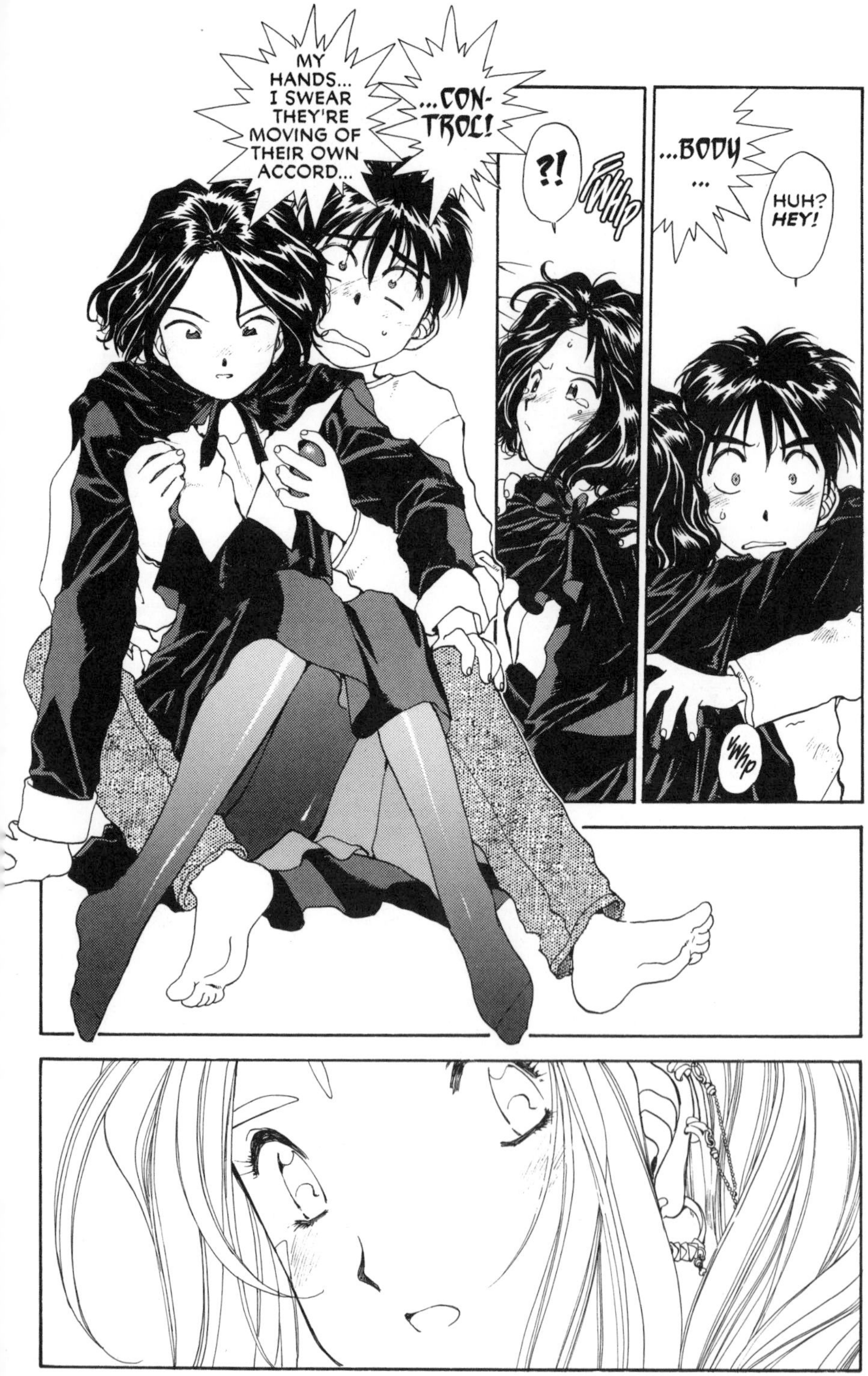
...BODY
...
HUH? HEY!
VWHP
?!
FWHIP
...CON-TROL!
MY HANDS... I SWEAR THEY'RE MOVING OF THEIR OWN ACCORD...

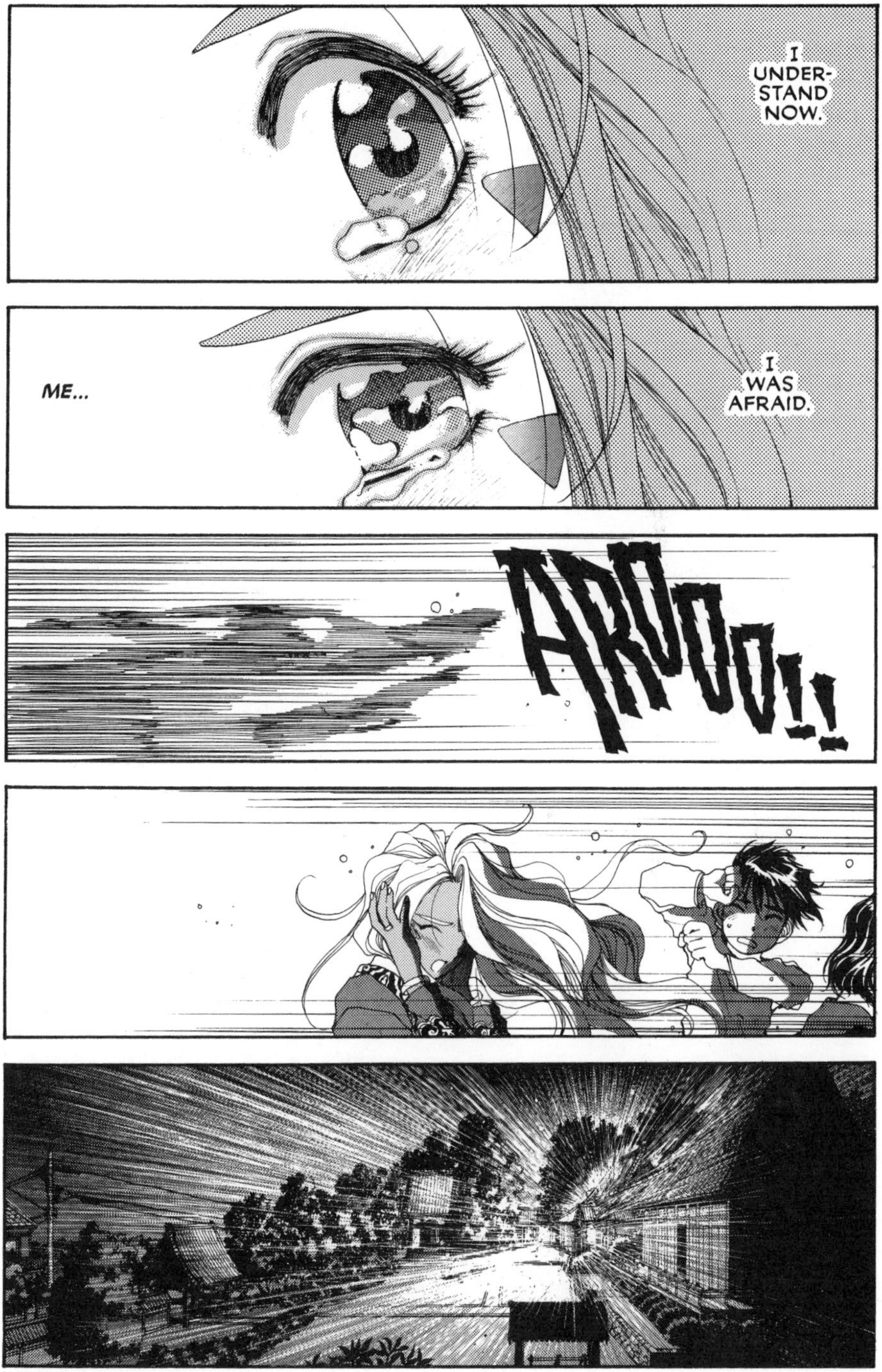
I UNDER-STAND NOW.
I WAS AFRAID.
ME...
AROOO!!

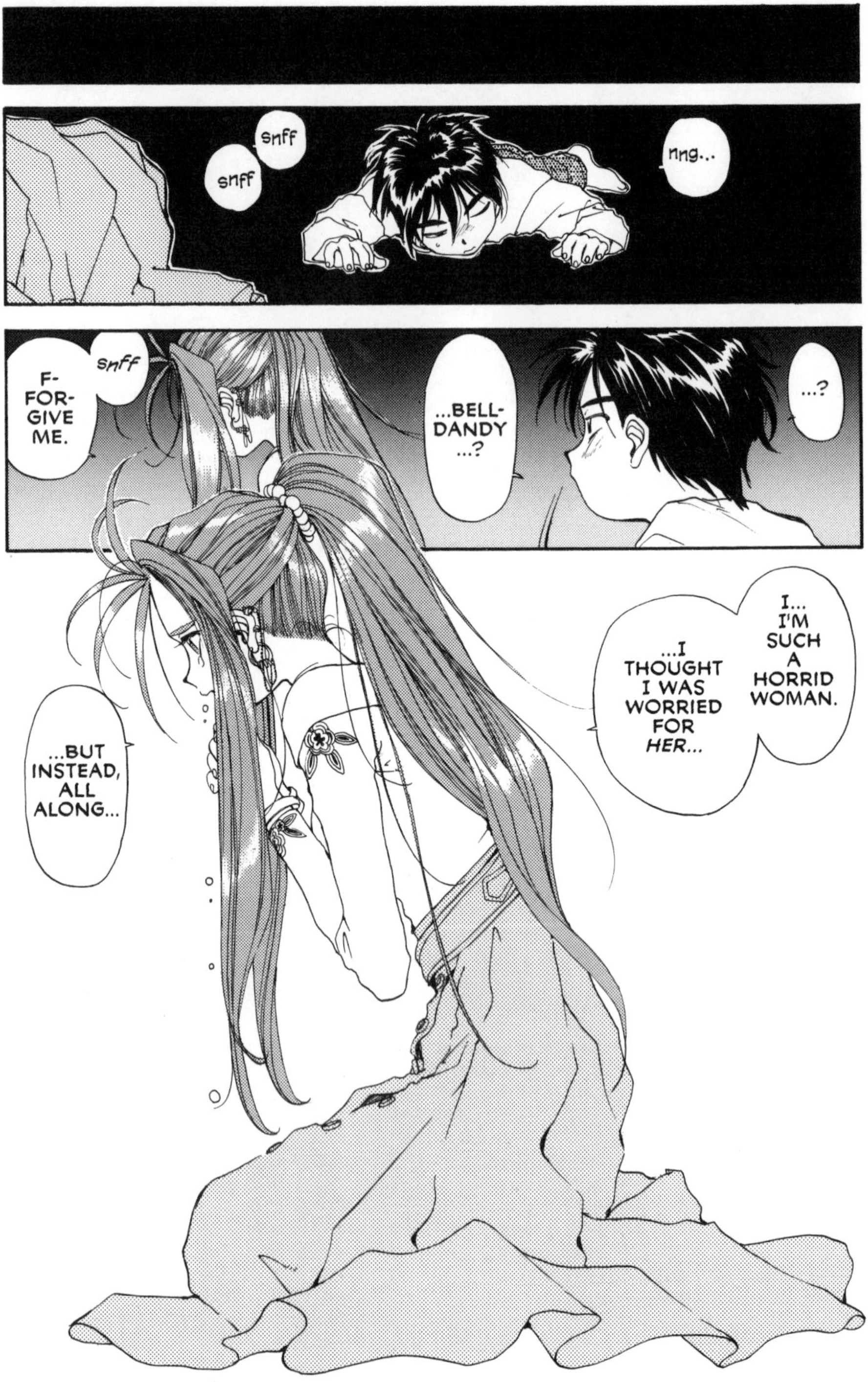
nng...
snff
snff
...?
...BELL-DANDY...?
snff
F-FORGIVE ME.
I... I'M SUCH A HORRID WOMAN.
...I THOUGHT I WAS WORRIED FOR *HER*...
...BUT INSTEAD, ALL ALONG...

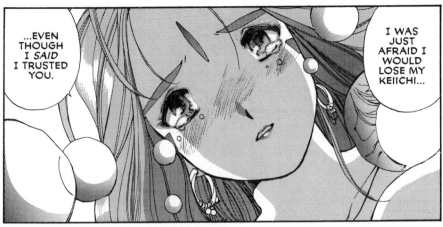

...EVEN THOUGH I *SAID* I TRUSTED YOU.

I WAS JUST AFRAID I WOULD LOSE MY KEIICHI...

N-NO.

KEIICHI, HOW YOU MUST DESPISE ME...

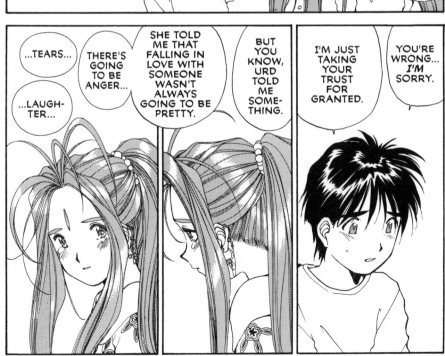

...TEARS...

...LAUGH-TER...

THERE'S GOING TO BE ANGER...

SHE TOLD ME THAT FALLING IN LOVE WITH SOMEONE WASN'T ALWAYS GOING TO BE PRETTY.

BUT YOU KNOW, URD TOLD ME SOME-THING.

I'M JUST TAKING YOUR TRUST FOR GRANTED.

YOU'RE WRONG... *I'M* SORRY.

OOH.. oog..

SHEESH... THERE THEY GO AGAIN.

THAT BIG DOGGIE... THING'S... *GONE!*

UH... HEY?!

I HAVE TH' POWER!

YET AGAIN, MY GIFTS *PREVAIL!*

I... I *DID* IT!

I KNOW. IT'S THE FLOURESCENTS.

BUT, FORTUNATELY, HER GIFT APPEARS TO HAVE BEEN A LUCKY (?) FLUKE...

WAIT! YOUR SHADOW... IT LOOKS *STRANGE!*

EXIT

SOON AFTER, SHE WENT TO WORK AS A *PROFESSIONAL* SPIRITUALIST AROUND CAMPUS.

...CALLING FORTH *GARM* TAKES... A *KIND* OF GIFT...I GUESS...

WELL, EVEN IF IT *WAS* A MISTAKE...

THE ADVENTURES OF MINI-URD

WARNING: EXCESSIVE SUBDIVISION ◆ CAN BE HAZARDOUS ◆ TO YOUR HEALTH

◆ IS THE MISO SOUP IN ◆ *YOUR HOUSE* SAFE?

TONIGHT WE'RE WATCHING *MY* FAVORITE SHOW ON TV, UNDERSTAND?

DON'T TELL ME YOU NINJA SPIRITS HAVE BEEN HIDING HERE ALL THIS TIME ...?

VERILY.

HMPH... PLANNING TO CALL A *VOTE* AGAIN, ARE YOU...?

I'M BOILING MAD!

THE GUY IN THE TEAPOT REALLY HAD IT TOUGH.

IN THE SALT.

IN THE MISO.

WE DO! WE DO!!

WHO WANTS TO WATCH *HOLMES* ...?!

HEY!

BUT ONE OF OUR COMPANIONS IS MISSING--

O-KAAY...

OKAY ?!

NEXT TIME I WON'T ARGUE-- SO *PLEASE* STOP DOING THAT!

LET ME GUESS... IS THIS HIM...?

umm...

urk!

▲ SUBDIVIDED INTO TOO MANY COPIES...

The fourth goddess, Peorth, arrives in Keiichi's life . . . to make it more complicated than ever!
Peorth, mistress of roses, is in the same business as Belldandy—granting wishes to mortals.
Keiichi thinks there must be some mistake, as he already has Belldandy in his life . . . but Peorth
is certain he can't really be satisfied, or else how was he able to contact her? Now she's de-
termined to stick around until Keiichi admits what he *really* wants . . . so she can grant it!

PRESIDENT AND PUBLISHER
Mike Richardson

EDITOR
Carl Gustav Horn

DESIGNER
Sarah Terry

DIGITAL ART TECHNICIAN
Christina McKenzie

English-language version
produced by Dark Horse Comics

OH MY GODDESS! Omnibus Book 3

Published by Dark Horse Manga
A division of Dark Horse Comics, Inc.
10956 SE Main Street
Milwaukie, OR 97222
DarkHorse.com

To find a comics shop in your area,
call the Comic Shop Locator Service
toll-free at 1-888-266-4226.

First edition: March 2016
ISBN 978-1-61655-895-6

1 3 5 7 9 10 8 6 4 2

Printed in China

NEIL HANKERSON Executive Vice President **TOM WEDDLE** Chief Financial Officer **RANDY STRADLEY** Vice President
of Publishing **MICHAEL MARTENS** Vice President of Book Trade Sales **MATT PARKINSON** Vice President of
Marketing **DAVID SCROGGY** Vice President of Product Development **DALE LaFOUNTAIN** Vice President of
Information Technology **CARA NIECE** Vice President of Production and Scheduling **KEN LIZZI** General Counsel
DAVEY ESTRADA Editorial Director **DAVE MARSHALL** Editor in Chief **SCOTT ALLIE** Executive Senior Editor **CHRIS
WARNER** Senior Books Editor **CARY GRAZZINI** Director of Print and Development **LIA RIBACCHI** Art Director
MARK BERNARDI Director of Digital Publishing

東京 TOKYO BABYLON

CLAMP

CLAMP's early epic of dangerous work
—and dangerous attraction!

It's 1991, the last days of Japan's bubble economy,
and money and elegance run through the streets. So
do the currents of darkness beneath them, nourishing
the evil spirits that only the arts of the *onmyoji*—
Japan's legendary occultists—can combat. The two most
powerful *onmyoji* are in the unlikely guises of a handsome
young veterinarian, Seishiro, and the teenage heir to the
ancient Sumeragi clan, Subaru—just a couple
of guys whom Subaru's sister Hokuto has
decided are destined to be together!

*"Tokyo Babylon is CLAMP's
first really great work."*
—Manga: The Complete Guide

Each omnibus-sized
volume features over
a dozen full-color
bonus pages!

VOLUME ONE
ISBN 978-1-61655-116-2
$19.99

VOLUME TWO
ISBN 978-1-61655-189-6
$19.99

CLAMP オキモノ キモノ
Mokona's OKIMONO KIMONO

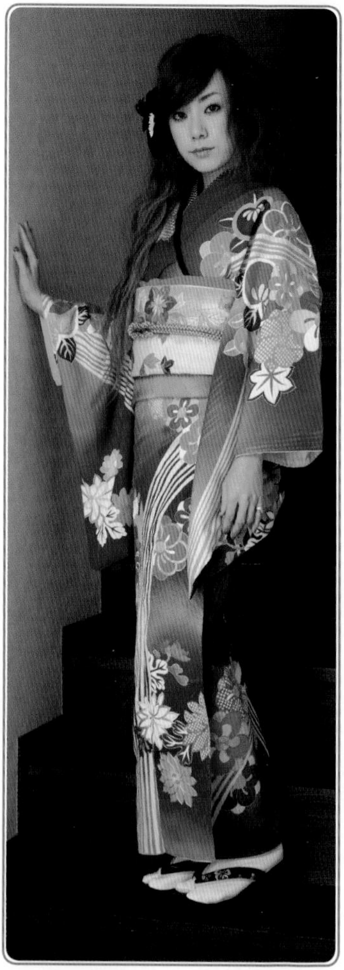

CLAMP artist Mokona loves the art of traditional Japanese kimono. In fact, she designs kimono and kimono accessories herself and shares her love in *Okimono Kimono*, a fun and lavishly illustrated book full of drawings and photographs, interviews (including an interview with Onuki Ami of the J-pop duo Puffy AmiYumi), and exclusive short manga stories from the CLAMP artists!

From the creators of such titles as *Clover, Chobits, Cardcaptor Sakura, Magic Knight Rayearth,* and *Tsubasa, Okimono Kimono* is now available in English for the first time ever!

ISBN 978-1-59582-456-1

$12.99

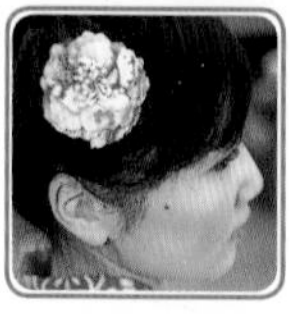

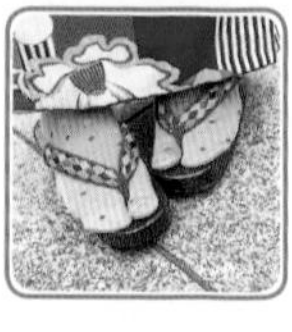

ANGELIC LAYER

Story and Art by
CLAMP

YOUNG TEEN MISAKI SUZUHARA has just arrived in Tokyo to attend the prestigious Eriol Academy. But what really excites her is Angelic Layer, the game where you control an Angel—a miniature robot fighter whose moves depend on your mind! Before she knows it, Misaki is an up-and-coming contender in Angelic Layer . . . and in way over her not-very-tall head! How far can enthusiasm take her in an arena full of much more experienced fighters . . . and a game full of secrets?

Don't miss the thrilling prequel to the acclaimed CLAMP manga *Chobits*! These omnibus-sized volumes feature not only the full story of *Angelic Layer* but also gorgeous, exclusive bonus color illustrations!

VOLUME ONE
978-1-61655-021-9

VOLUME TWO
978-1-61655-128-5

$19.99 each

From the creators of *Clover*, *Chobits*, and *Cardcaptor Sakura*!

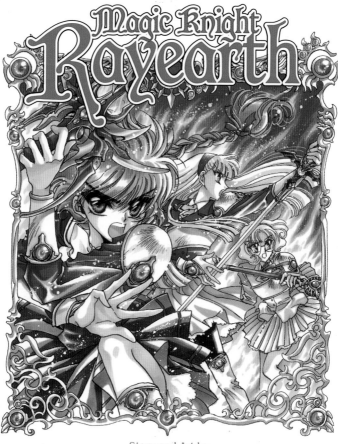

Magic Knight Rayearth

Story and Art by
CLAMP

Umi, Hikaru, and Fuu are three schoolgirls out on a field trip to Tokyo Tower, whisked suddenly away by a strange voice and light to Cefiro, a world full of spirits and sorcery. Summoned by the beautiful Princess Emeraude, could they be the trio destined to become the legendary magic knights that can save her realm?

VOLUME ONE	VOLUME TWO
ISBN 978-1-59582-588-9	ISBN 978-1-59582-669-5

$19.99 each

AVAILABLE AT YOUR LOCAL COMICS SHOP OR BOOKSTORE!
To find a comics shop in your area, call 1-888-266-4226
For more information or to order direct: • On the web: DarkHorse.com
E-mail: mailorder@darkhorse.com • Phone: 1-800-862-0052 Mon.–Fri. 9 AM to 5 PM Pacific Time
Magic Knight Rayearth © CLAMP. (BL 7090)

CLAMP

IN NEAR-FUTURE JAPAN,

the hottest style for your personal computer, or "persocom," is in the shape of an attractive android! Hideki, a poor student, finds a persocom seemingly discarded in an alley. He takes the cute, amnesiac robot home and names her "Chi."

But who is this strange new persocom in his life? Hideki finds himself having to teach Chi how to get along in the everyday world, even while he and his friends try to solve the mystery of her origins. Is she one of the urban-legendary *Chobits*—persocoms built to have the riskiest functions of all: real emotions and free will?

CLAMP's best-selling manga in America is finally available in omnibus form! Containing dozens of bonus color pages, *Chobits* is an engaging, touching, exciting story.

BOOK 1
ISBN 978-1-59582-451-6
$24.99

BOOK 2
ISBN 978-1-59582-514-8
$24.99

Cardcaptor Sakura

カードキャプターさくら

MANGA BY
CLAMP

Fourth grader Sakura Kinomoto has found a strange book in her father's library—a book made by the wizard Clow to store dangerous spirits sealed within a set of magical cards. But when Sakura opens it up, there is nothing left inside but Kero-chan, the book's cute little guardian beast...who informs Sakura that since the Clow cards seem to have escaped while he was asleep, it's now her job to capture them!

With remastered image files straight from CLAMP, Dark Horse is proud to present *Cardcaptor Sakura* in omnibus form! Each book collects three volumes of the original twelve-volume series, and features thirty bonus color pages!

OMNIBUS BOOK 1
ISBN 978-1-59582-522-3

OMNIBUS BOOK 2
ISBN 978-1-59582-591-9

OMNIBUS BOOK 3
ISBN 978-1-59582-808-8

OMNIBUS BOOK 4
ISBN 978-1-59582-889-7

$19.99 each!

DARK
HORSE
MANGA

AVAILABLE AT YOUR LOCAL COMICS SHOP OR BOOKSTORE!
To find a comics shop in your area, call 1-888-266-4226
For more information or to order direct: • On the web: DarkHorse.com
E-mail: mailorder@darkhorse.com • Phone: 1-800-862-0052 Mon.–Fri. 9 AM to 5 PM Pacific Time

STOP! This is the back of the book!

This manga collection is translated into English, but arranged in right-to-left reading format to maintain the artwork's visual orientation as originally drawn and published in Japan. If you've never read comics this way before, take a look at the diagram below to give yourself an idea of how to go about it. Basically, you'll be starting in the upper right-hand corner, and will read each word balloon and panel moving right to left. It may take a little getting used to, but you should get the hang of it very quickly. Have fun! If this is the millionth manga you've read this way, never mind. ^_^

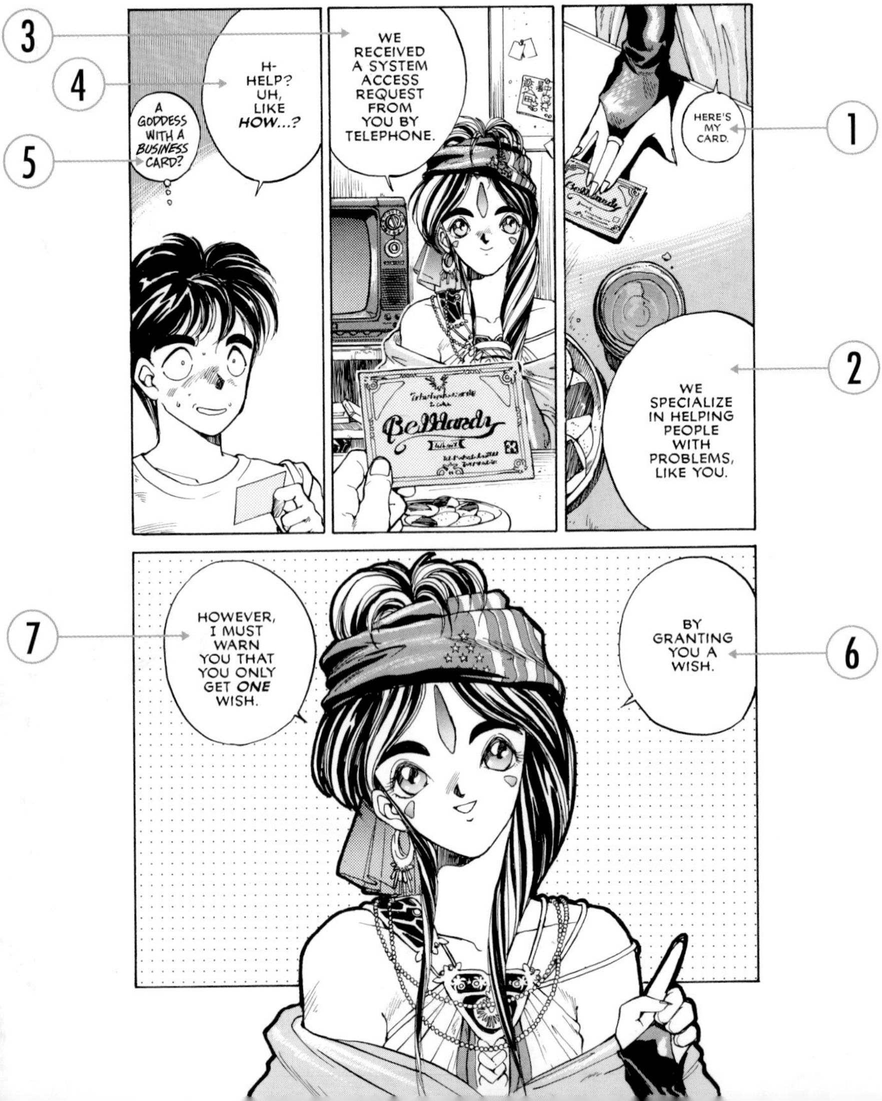
1
HERE'S MY CARD.
2
WE SPECIALIZE IN HELPING PEOPLE WITH PROBLEMS, LIKE YOU.
3
WE RECEIVED A SYSTEM ACCESS REQUEST FROM YOU BY TELEPHONE.
4
H- HELP? UH, LIKE *HOW...?*
5
A GODDESS WITH A *BUSINESS* CARD?
6
BY GRANTING YOU A WISH.
7
HOWEVER, I MUST WARN YOU THAT YOU ONLY GET *ONE* WISH.